The Western Heritage

1300–1815

VOLUME

The Western Heritage

≈ *Second Edition*

Donald Kagan YALE UNIVERSITY   1300–1815

Steven Ozment HARVARD UNIVERSITY

Frank M. Turner YALE UNIVERSITY

Macmillan Publishing Co., Inc.
NEW YORK

NOTE
The dates cited for monarchs and popes are generally the years of their reign rather than of their
births and deaths.

This book is a portion of The Western Heritage, copyright ©
1979 by Macmillan Publishing Co., Inc.

Macmillan Publishing Co., Inc.
866 Third Avenue, New York, New York 10022
Collier Macmillan Canada, Inc.

Library of Congress Cataloging in Publication Data

Kagan, Donald.
  The Western heritage.

  Includes bibliographies and indexes.
  Contents: v. A. To 1527— v. B. 1300–1815— v. C.
Since 1789.
  1. Civilization, Occidental. I. Ozment, Steven E.
II. Turner, Frank M. (Frank Miller), Date.
III. Title.
CB245.K28   1983c   909′.09821   82-20370

ISBN   0-02-362370-5

Printing: 1 2 3 4 5 6 7 8   Year: 3 4 5 6 7 8 9 0 1

Preface

IN REVISING *The Western Heritage* we have benefitted from the advice and teaching experience of fellow historians across the country. Scores of our professional colleagues sent us or our publisher suggestions for improvements. More than a dozen readers drawn from diverse institutions and areas of historical specialization formally evaluated and criticized our first edition and early drafts of the revision. We read and carefully considered all of these ideas, and we adopted many of them. Consequently, this revision has emerged from a genuinely cooperative effort between authors and readers.

The result of this cooperation is a new, substantially reshaped edition of *The Western Heritage*. Readers of our previous volume will note a condensation of materials on ancient military history and the inclusion of a new section on the culture of the early Roman Republic. We have expanded and reorganized in a major fashion the coverage of the Middle Ages, the Renaissance, and the Reformation. The sections on the medieval Catholic Church, popular religion, Islam, economic life, and social history have been enlarged. There are new or expanded treatments of virtually every aspect of the Renaissance. The previous two chapters on the Reformation have been condensed into one, and the ideas and events of the Catholic Reformation have received broader coverage. A new section on medieval Russia provides background for the reforms of Peter the Great. The discussion of the industrial revolution is more extensive as is that of Romanticism. Consideration of Europe since 1945 has been extended to cover the major events of the last few years. Further revisions in the organization, the prose style, and the section-headings appear in every chapter.

We have also included revised supplementary materials to aid the teaching and comprehension of the text itself. Most significantly, we have introduced into every chapter chronological tables of major events. More than a third of the documents and illustrations are new, and we have attempted to integrate them more closely with our general narrative. We have revised to bring up to date all the bibliographies while attempting to retain many useful older titles.

Our purpose in all of these revisions has been to produce a text that is clear, informative, interesting, and teachable. Just as the revision of a textbook is a joint effort between authors and readers, so the use of a textbook is a joint effort between teachers and students. We hope that this volume will enchance and enliven that latter relationship.

D.K.
S.O.
F.M.T.

New Haven and Cambridge

Contents

30   Political Experiments of the 1920s

31   Europe and the Depression of the 1930s

Documents

Maps

by Theodore R. Miller

Illustrations in Color

[21] *William Hogarth (1697–1764) did immensely popular paintings and etchings of scenes from the rich variety of English life in the eighteenth century. He was frequently satirical and witty, and his works make up a realistic survey of society from top to bottom. The dissolute party shown here is The Orgy, third in a series called "The Rake's Progress. It dates from approximately 1734 and is in the Sir John Soane's Museum, London. [The Granger Collection.]*

[22] *Even when past the height of its medieval commercial power, Venice in the eighteenth century was a wealthy and unusually picturesque city. One of the numerous painters of its canals, festivals, and buildings was Giovanni Antonio Canaletto (1697–1768), represented here by his Stonemason's Yard, a behind-the-scenes picture of a humbler, seamier side of the city than that usually painted. Painted near 1740, it is in the National Gallery, London. [The Granger Collection.]*

[23] With *A Pilgrimage to Cythera*, Antoine Watteau gained entry to the Paris Royal Academy of Painting and Sculpture in 1717. The painting, which is now in the Louvre, is typical of Watteau's work, which usually shows scenes of upper-class life in outdoor settings. In this painting, a group of young couples has spent the day on Cythera, the island of love (a flower-draped statue of Venus, the goddess of love, is at the far right). We see them as they are about to board the boat back to the mainland after what appears to have been a very pleasant day. [Editorial Photocolor Archives.]

[24] In a painting attributed to Pietro Longhi (1702–1785), *The Banquet at the Palazzo Nani*, we see a self-conscious party of aristocratic Venetian ladies and gentlemen posing at a large formal dinner. The picture is in the Ca' Rezzonico in Venice. [SCALA/Editorial Photocolor Archives.]

[25] *George Stubbs (1724–1806) was an artist with a special—even scientific—interest in animals, a concern that led him to dissect horses in order to get the creatures' anatomy just right. His works have been eagerly collected in this century. Lady and Gentleman in a Carriage (1787), seen here, is in the National Gallery, London. [The Granger Collection.]*

[26] *Venice may have declined as a commercial power, but as a subject for its own artists and for those of other countries it was ever fascinating. In the generation following Canaletto, Francesco Guardi (1712–1793), as in this view of the Piazza San Marco, carried on the tradition of recording the city that was itself rapidly becoming a museum. The painting hangs in the National Gallery, London. [The Granger Collection.]*

[27] *In The Death of Socrates, Jacques Louis David (1748–1825) extolls the values of discipline and idealistic self-sacrifice through his choice of subject and the austere precision with which he depicts it. The ascetic idealism of this painting anticipates David's involvement in the French Revolution. This painting is in the Metropolitan Museum of Art in New York. [Bettmann Archive.]*

[28] *The crucial naval battle of Trafalgar in 1805 between the English and the French fleets quickly caught the imagination of the English artist Joseph Mallard William Turner (1775–1851). He visited Nelson's ship immediately on its return to England with the admiral's body and in 1806 exhibited his first painting of the battle. The picture here (from the National Maritime Museum, London) is a later one (1820). Nelson's flagship,* Victory, *is in the center at the height of the battle. [The Granger Collection.]*

[29] *The work of the Spanish artist Francisco Goya (1746–1828), like David's, spanned Old Regime, Revolution, Napoleon, and Restoration. In 1814 he painted The Third of May 1808 in continuing revulsion and protest over the gunning down of Spanish hostages by French troops during the Napoleonic invasion of Spain. It remains a powerful indictment of human brutality and the horror of war. The painting is in the Prado, Madrid, [SCALA/Editorial Photocolor Archives.]*

[30]   *The painter John Constable (1776–1837) failed to find wide popularity in his lifetime. He kept his attention on the peaceful English countryside that was destined to become the victim of industry, railways, and mines, and today we find his work an important record of a different world. This is his Haywain, painted in 1821. It hangs now in the National Gallery, London. [The Granger Collection.]*

[31]   *The Funeral at Ornans (1849) by Gustave Courbet (1819–1877) shows an abandonment of the Romantic traditions of emotion and imagination in favor of a more realistic and naturalistic style. Courbet was born in the village of Ornans, and he often chose rural subjects for his work. This painting beautifully captures the somber dignity of a rural funeral. Note how the clergy and men are grouped on the left and the women on the right. This painting is in the Louvre. [The Granger Collection.]*

[32] *The hard, never-ending physical labor of the agricultural poor is the subject of The Gleaners by the Frenchman Jean François Millet (1814–1875). Millet is often thought over-sentimental, but this 1857 picture is a strong record of the necessary way of life of millions in the nineteenth century. It is in the Louvre, Paris. [The Granger Collection.]*

[33] *Although classified as a Romantic artist, Honoré Daumier (1808–1879) often depicted the realities of daily life. The Burden (1858–1860) is a sympathetic portrayal of an overworked working-class woman and her child. The painting is in the Musée des Beaux-Arts at Dijon. [The Granger Collection.]*

[34] *Nineteenth-century Romanticism reached, literally, a reckless height in the castle of Neuschwanstein, ordered by the unstable King Ludwig II of the south German state of Bavaria. When the castle was built between 1858 and 1886, art and literature had taken on a character of realism; but architecture tended to remain elaborate and ornate—although Neuschwanstein in its spectacular setting was, of course, too extreme to be typical. [The Granger Collection.]*

C-24

[35] *In The Bar at the Folies-Berberes (1882), Edouard Manet (1832–1883) has created a remarkable sense of stillness in the midst of great activity. The pensive barmaid seems completely withdrawn and remote from the festive crowd reflected in the mirror behind her. This lack of emotion typifies Manet's work; his paintings have been characterized as "pictures of pictures." This painting is in London's Courtauld Institute. [The Granger Collection.]*

[36] *The railway figures also in The Station at Penge (1871) by Camille Pissarro (1831–1903). Railroads caused a transportation revolution in the nineteenth century comparable to that of air travel in our own day, and artists were not long in creating a new kind of landscape that incorporated the new technological development. The machine, artists found, had esthetics of its own. This picture is in the Courtauld Institute, London. [The Granger Collection.]*

[37] *The Moulin de la Galette (1876) is by Pierre Auguste Renoir (1841–1919). One aspect of Parisian bourgeois leisure activity is illustrated in this painting of everyday friends of the artist enjoying the wine and the dancing at an outdoor café. The work is in the Louvre, Paris.* [*The Granger Collection.*]

[38] *This 1889 painting, The Starry Night by the Dutchman Vincent van Gogh (1853–1890), breaks out of earlier, more staid views of nature and the landscape. To van Gogh the heavens themselves are an exciting theater of colorful and continuing movement.* [*The Museum of Modern Art, New York.*]

[39] *At the age of thirty-five, Paul Gauguin (1848–1903) abandoned his family and left a successful career as a Parisian stockbroker in order to devote his life to painting. Gauguin believed that the materialism and industrialism of the West thwarted man's innate emotionalism. His search for a more natural, unspoiled way of life led him to Tahiti. He spent the rest of his life in the South Pacific, where he glorified the natives and their way of life in such works as Two Women of Tahiti (1889). [The Granger Collection.]*

[40] *Paul Cézanne (1839–1906) painted several pictures called The Card Players. Like the others, this one from about 1890 captures the personalities of its (probably) working-class subjects and is a realistic, unromanticized view of ordinary life. The painting is in the Jeu de Paume, Paris. [The Granger Collection.]*

[41]   *Although the subject is too broad for such a narrow definition, "modern art" for many means abstract, nonrepresentational painting and sculpture. This aspect of modern painting is illustrated by the colorful Panel (3) by the Russian-French artist Wassily Kandinsky (1866–1944). Note that "modern" antedates World War I, for this work was painted in 1914. [The Museum of Modern Art, New York.]*

[42]   *In contrast to Kandinsky's wild splashes of color, Dutch artist Piet Mondrian (1872–1944) used severe vertical and horizontal lines and precise blocks of primary colors, black, and white in many of his abstract paintings. Composition in Grey, Red, Yellow, and Blue (1920) is an example of a totally nonrepresentational style that Mondrian called Neo-Plasticism. [The Granger Collection.]*

C-28

[43]   *Perhaps the best known painter of recent years is the Spaniard Pablo Picasso (1881–1973). His art went through a number of phases. The picture shown here, Three Musicians, comes from 1921 when he was interested in breaking his subjects down into planes, lines, and geometric bodies. [The Museum of Modern Art. New York.]*

[44] *The dream-like world of Surrealism is seen in Painting (1949) by Joan Miró (born 1893). Surrealism borrowed many concepts from psychoanalytic theory and sought to express the pure process of thought and creativity, unhampered by convention or rationality. Miró's expressive shapes and forms show great energy and fluidity and invite the viewer to make his or her own interpretations of their meaning. [The Granger Collection.]*

[45 OPPOSITE] *Family Group by the Englishman Henry Moore (born 1898) is a large bronze statue from the 1940s by one of the leading sculptors of the last few decades, most of whose pieces are effectively planned for outdoor display. This one is more clearly representational than others. [The Museum of Modern Art, New York.]*

C-31

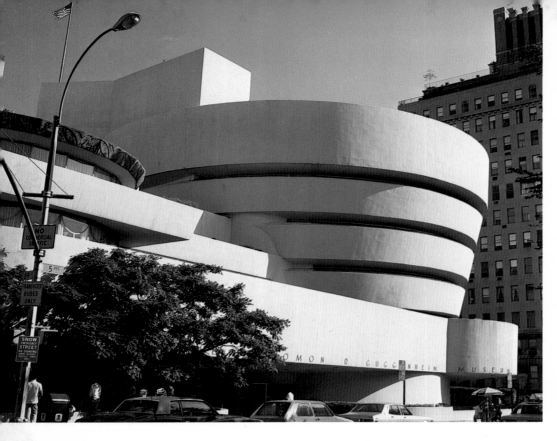

[46 LEFT] *Renowned architect Frank Lloyd Wright (1857–1959) designed the striking Solomon R. Guggenheim Museum of Art in New York City. The museum, which opened on October 21, 1959, is the home of the Solomon R. Guggenheim Foundation of Art, which supports and encourages nonobjective art.* [Photo © Ann Chwatsky, 1978. Editorial Photocolor Archives.]

[47 RIGHT] *The Georges Pompidou National Center of Art and Culture in Paris, named for a recent president of France, was built in the 1970s to designs by an Italian-English team of architects, Renzo Piano and Richard Rogers. We spoke earlier of a Gothic structure's "skeleton" being, in a sense, external and visible. Here the designers have managed to make the building appear to be almost all skeleton and in the meantime have achieved a colorful display of its engineering and functional elements.* [French Government Tourist Office, New York.]

C-32

The Western Heritage

1300–1815

338

13 The Late Middle Ages and the Renaissance: Decline and Renewal (1300-1527)

THE LATE Middle Ages and the Renaissance marked a time of unprecedented calamity and of bold new beginnings. There was the Hundred Years' War between England and France (1337–1453), an exercise in seemingly willful self-destruction, which was made even more terrible in its later stages by the invention of gunpowder and heavy artillery. There was almost universal bubonic plague, known to contemporaries as the Black Death. Between 1348 and 1350 the plague killed as much as one third of the population in many regions and transformed many pious Christians into believers in the omnipotence of death. There was a schism within the church that lasted thirty-seven years (1378–1415) and saw by 1409 the election of no fewer than three competing popes and colleges of cardinals. And there was the onslaught of the Turks, who in 1453 marched seemingly invincibly through Constantinople and toward the west. As

This Franco-Flemish painting of Joan of Arc is believed to be one of the only contemporary portraits of her. It is in the Archives Nationales in Paris. [Giraudon.]

their political and religious institutions buckled, as disease, bandits, and wolves ravaged their cities in the wake of war, and as Muslim armies gathered at their borders, Europeans beheld what seemed to be the imminent total collapse of Western civilization.

But if the late Middle Ages saw unprecedented chaos, it also witnessed a rebirth that would continue into the seventeenth century. Two modern Dutch scholars have employed the same word (*Herfsttij*, "harvesttide") with different connotations to describe the period, one interpreting the word as a "waning" or "decline" (Johan Huizinga), the other as a true "harvest" (Heiko Oberman). If something was dying away, some ripe fruit and seed grain were also being gathered in. The late Middle Ages were a creative breaking up.

It was in this period that such scholars as Marsilius of Padua, William of Ockham, and Lorenzo Valla produced lasting criticisms of medieval assumptions about the nature of God, humankind, and society. It was a period in which kings worked through parliaments and clergy through councils to place lasting limits on the pope's temporal power. The principle that a sovereign (in this case, the pope) is accountable to the body of which he is head was established. The arguments used by conciliarists (advocates of the judicial superiority of a church council over a pope) to establish papal accountability to the body of the faithful provided an example for the secular sphere, as kings, who also had an independent tradition of ruler accountability in Roman law, were reminded of their responsibility to the body politic.

The late Middle Ages also saw an unprecedented scholarly renaissance, as Italian Humanists made a full recovery of classical knowledge and languages and set in motion educational reforms and cultural changes that would spread throughout Europe in the fifteenth and sixteenth centuries. In the process the Italian Humanists invented, for all practical purposes, critical historical scholarship and exploited a new fifteenth-century invention, the "divine art" of printing with movable type. It was in this period that the vernacular, the local language, began to take its place alongside Latin, the international language, as a widely used literary and political language. The independent nation-states of Europe progressively superseded the universal church as the community of highest allegiance, as patriotism and incipient nationalism became a major force. Nations henceforth "transcended" themselves not by journeys to Rome but by competitive voyages to the Far East and the Americas, as the age of global exploration opened.

A time of both waning and harvest, constriction (in the form of nationalism) and expansion (in the sense of world exploration), the late Middle Ages saw medieval culture grudgingly give way to the age of Renaissance and Reformation.

Political and Social Breakdown

The Hundred Years' War and the Rise of National Sentiment

CAUSES OF THE WAR. From May 1337 to October 1453 England and France periodically engaged in what was for both a futile and devastating war. The conflict was initiated by the English king Edward III (1327–1377), who held a strong claim to the French throne as the grandson of Philip the Fair (1285–1314). When Charles IV (1322–1328), the last of Philip the Fair's surviving sons died, Edward, who was only fifteen at the

time, asserted his right to Capetian succession. The French barons, however, were not willing to place an English king on the French throne. They chose instead the first cousin of Charles IV, Philip VI of Valois (1328–1350), the first of a new French dynasty that was to rule into the sixteenth century.

But there was much more to the Hundred Years' War than just a defense of Edward's prestige. In the background were other equally important factors that help to explain both Edward's success in gaining popular and parliamentary support after the war started and the determination of the English and the French people to endure the war to its bitter end. For one thing, the English king held Gascony, Anjou, Guyenne, and other French territories as fiefs from the French king. Thus he was, in law, a vassal of the French king—a circumstance that stretched back to the Norman Conquest. In May 1329 Edward journeyed to Amiens and, most perfunctorily, swore fealty to Philip VI. As Philip's vassal Edward was, theoretically if not in fact, committed to support policies detrimental to England, if his French lord so commanded. If such vassalage was intolerable to Edward, the English possession of French lands was even more repugnant to the French, especially inasmuch as the English presence remained a permanent threat to the royal policy of centralization.

Still another factor that fueled the conflict was French support of the Bruces of Scotland, strong opponents of the English overlordship of Scotland who had won a victory over the English in 1314. The French and the English were also at this time quarreling over Flanders, a French fief, yet also a country whose towns were completely dependent for their livelihood on imported English wool. Edward III and his successors manipulated this situation to English advantage throughout the conflict; by controlling the export of wool to Flanders, England influenced Flanders' foreign policy. Finally, there were decades of prejudice and animosity between the French and the English people, who constantly confronted one another on the high seas and in port towns. Taken together, these various factors made the Hundred Years' War a struggle to the death for national control and identity.

FRENCH WEAKNESS. Throughout the conflict France was statistically the stronger: it had three times the population of England, was far the wealthier, and fought on its own soil. Yet for the greater part of the conflict, until after 1415, the major battles ended in often stunning English victories. France was not as strong as it appeared. It was, first of all, internally disunited by social conflict and the absence of a centralized system of taxation to fund the war. French kings raised funds by depreciating the currency, taxing the clergy, and borrowing heavily from Italian bankers—self-defeating practices that created a financial crisis by mid-century. As a tool to provide him money the king raised up a representative council of towns and noblemen that came to be known in subsequent years as the *Estates General*. It convened in 1355, and although it levied taxes at the king's request, its members also used the king's plight to enhance their own regional rights and privileges. Just how successful they were is indicated by the creation in this period of the Burgundian state, a powerful new territory that became a thorn in the sides of French kings throughout the fifteenth century. France, unlike England, was still struggling in the fourteenth century to make the transition from a fragmented feudal society to a centralized "modern" state.

Beyond this struggle, there was the clear fact of English military superiority, due to the greater discipline of its infantry and the rapid-fire and long-range capability of that ingeniously simple weapon, the English longbow, which could shoot six arrows a minute with a force sufficient to pierce an inch of wood or the armor of a knight at two hundred yards. The longbow scattered the French cavalry and crossbowmen in one engagement after the other. Only in the later stages of the war, with the introduction of heavy artillery, did the French alter their military tactics to advantage.

Finally, French weakness was related in no small degree to the comparative mediocrity of royal leadership during the Hundred Years' War. English kings were far the shrewder. Historians have found it to be a telling commentary on the leadership ability of French kings in this period that the most memorable military leader on the French side in the popular imagination is Joan of Arc.

Progress of the War

The war had three major stages of development, each ending with a seemingly decisive victory by one or the other side: (1) during the reign of Edward III (d. 1377); (2) from Edward's death to the Treaty of Troyes (1420); and (3) from the appearance of Joan of Arc (1429) to the English retreat.

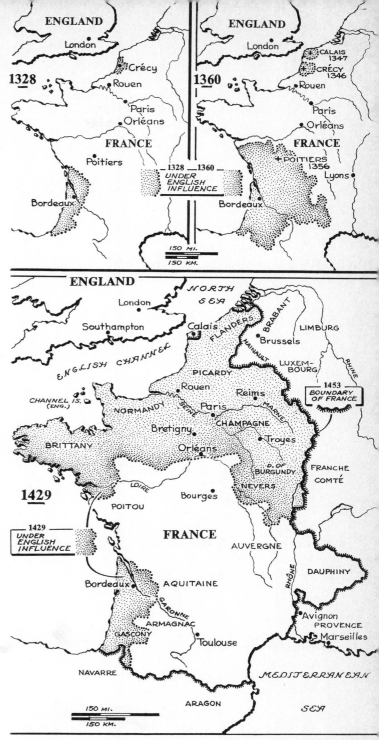

THE HUNDRED YEARS' WAR

MAP 13.1 *The Hundred Years' War went on intermittently from the late 1330s until 1453. These maps show the remarkable English territorial gains up to the sudden and decisive turning of the tide of battle in favor of the French by the forces of Joan of Arc in 1429.*

THE CONFLICT DURING THE REIGN OF ED-WARD III. Edward prepared for the first stage of the war by securing allies in the Netherlands and a personal pledge of support from the emperor Louis IV of Bavaria (1314–1347). By slapping an embargo on English wool to Flanders, Edward sparked urban rebellions by merchants and the trade guilds. Inspired by a rich merchant, Jacob van Artevelde, the Flemish cities, led by Ghent, revolted against the French. Having at first taken as neutral a stand as possible in the conflict, these cities, whose economies faced total collapse without imported English wool, signed a half-hearted alliance with England in January 1340, acknowledging Edward as king of France.

Edward defeated the French fleet in the first great battle of the war in the Bay of Sluys on June 23, 1340. But his subsequent effort to invade France by way of Flanders failed, largely because his allies proved undependable. As a stalemate developed, a truce was struck and was more-or-less observed until 1346. In that year Edward attacked Normandy and won a series of easy victories that were capped by that at Crécy in August. This was quickly followed by the seizure of Calais, which the English held thereafter for over two hundred years. Both sides employed scorched-earth tactics and completely devastated the areas of conflict.

Exhaustion and the onset of the Black Death forced a second truce in late 1347, and the war entered a lull until 1355. On September 19, 1356, the English won their greatest victory near Poitiers, routing the noble cavalry and even taking the French king, John II the Good (1350–1364), captive back to England. After Poitiers there was a complete breakdown of political order in France. Disbanded soldiers from both sides became professional bandits, roaming the land, pillaging areas untouched by the war, and bringing disaster almost as great as the war itself.

Power in France lay with the privileged classes, who expressed their will through the representative assembly of the Estates General. Convened in 1355 by the faltering king so that revenues might be provided to continue the war, the Estates General, led by powerful merchants of Paris under Étienne Marcel, had demanded and received rights similar to those granted the English privileged classes in Magna Carta. The English Parliament, too, had grown out of councils convened by kings (John, 1199–1216, and Henry III, 1216–1272), which were widely representative of the English upper classes and designed to provide the king an opportunity to discuss (and thereby to persuade those attending to adopt) the king's views on laws and taxes. During the reign of Edward I (1272–1307) these "parliaments" or "parleyings" with the king became a fixed political institution. Unlike the English Parliament, which represented the interests of a comparatively unified English nobility, the French Estates General was a many-tongued lobby, a forum for the diverse interests of the new-rich urban commercial and industrial classes, the territorial princes, and the clergy. Such a diverse body was no instrument for effective government.

The war also occasioned internal political policies that alienated and embittered the peasants. To secure their rights, the privileged classes bullied the French peasantry, who were forced to pay ever-increasing taxes and to repair without compensation the war-damaged properties of the noblemen. The pressure became more than the peasantry could bear. Burdened by the Estates General, terrified by the Black Death, and emboldened by the cowardly retreat of the French cavalry at Poitiers, the peasantry exploded in several regions in a series of bloody uprisings known as the *Jacquerie*. The revolt was, however, put down by the nobility, who matched "Jacques Bonhomme," as the peasant revolutionary was popularly known, atrocity for atrocity.

On May 9, 1360, another milestone of the war was reached when England forced the Peace of Bretigny upon the French. This agreement declared Edward's vassalage to the king of France ended and affirmed his sovereignty over English territories in France (including Gascony, Guyenne, Poitou, and Calais). France also pledged to pay a ransom of three million gold crowns to win King John's release. In return Edward renounced his claim to the French throne.

Such a partition of French territorial control was completely unrealistic, and sober observers on both sides knew it could not long continue. France became strong enough to strike back in the late 1360s, during the reign of John the Good's successor, Charles V (1364–1380). In 1369 Flanders came into the French fold when Charles's brother, Philip the Bold, who held the duchy of Burgundy as his appanage (landed inheritance), married the daughter of the Count of Flanders. Backed by the Estates General and blessed with a brilliant military commander in Bertrand du Guesclin, the French launched a successful counteroffensive. By the time of Edward's death in 1377 the English had been beaten back to coastal enclaves and the territory of Bordeaux.

FRENCH DEFEAT AND THE TREATY OF TROYES. After Edward's death the English war effort lessened considerably, partly because of domestic problems within England. During the reign of Richard II (1377–1399) England had its own version of the *Jacquerie*. To counter the economic strain of the war with France and the ravages of the Black Death, Parliament had reduced the wages of peasants and journeymen, imposed new tolls and taxes, and reasserted old domainal rights in an effort to keep the peasants bound to the land. Both the urban proletariat and the agrarian peasantry greatly resented these measures, which the king's uncle and regent, John of Gaunt, the Duke of Lancaster, enforced. In June 1381 a great revolt of the unprivileged classes exploded under the leadership of John Ball, a secular priest, and Wat Tyler, a journeyman. As in France the revolt was short-lived, brutally crushed within the year. But it left the country divided for decades.

In 1396 France and England signed still another truce, this time backed up by the marriage of Richard II to the daughter of the French king, Charles VI (1380–1422). This truce lasted through the reign of Richard's successor, Henry IV of Lancaster (1399–1413). His successor, Henry V (1413–1422), reheated the war with France by taking advantage of the internal French turmoil created by the rise to power of the duchy of Burgundy. Charles VI had gone mad in the second half of his reign, and control of the French government had devolved on his brother, the duke of Orléans. Orléans struggled manfully but in vain to contain the aggressive duke of Burgundy, John the Fearless (1404–1419). Indeed, the latter succeeded in having Orléans assassinated in 1407. Thereafter civil war enveloped France; the count of Armagnac took up the royal banner, while John the Fearless found allies in the French cities.

With France so internally divided, Henry V struck hard in Normandy. John the Fearless and the Burgundians foolishly watched from the sidelines while Henry's army routed the numerically stronger but tactically less shrewd Armagnacs at Agincourt on October 25, 1415. In the years thereafter the Burgundians closed ranks behind the royal forces as they belatedly recognized that a divided France would remain an easy prey to the English. But this inchoate French unity, which promised to bring eventual victory, shattered in September 1419. In a belated reprisal for the assassination of the duke of Orléans twelve years earlier, soldiers of Charles VI stabbed John the Fearless to death only hours after the two men had quarreled. This shocking turn of events stampeded John's son, Philip the Good (1419–1467). He determined to avenge his father's death at any price, even if it meant giving the English control of France. The result was a Burgundian alliance with England.

With Burgundian support behind the English, France became Henry V's for the taking—at least in the short run. The Treaty of Troyes in 1420 disinherited the legitimate heir to the French throne, the dauphin (a title used by the king's oldest son), the future Charles VII, and made Henry V successor to the mad Charles VI. When Henry V and Charles VI died within months of one another in 1422, the infant Henry VI of England was proclaimed in Paris to be king of both France and England under the regency of the duke of Bedford. The dream of Edward III, the pretext for continuing the great war, was now, for the moment, realized: in 1422 an English king was the proclaimed ruler of France.

The dauphin went into retreat in Bourges, where, on the death of his father, he became Charles VII to most Frenchmen, who ignored the Treaty of Troyes. Although some years were to pass before he was powerful enough to take his crown in fact, the French people would not deny the throne to a legitimate successor, regardless of the terms dictated by the Treaty of Troyes. National sentiment, spurred to unprecedented heights by Joan of Arc, soon brought the French people together as never before in a victorious coalition.

JOAN OF ARC AND THE WAR'S CONCLUSION. Joan of Arc (1412–1431), a peasant from Domrémy, presented herself to Charles VII in March 1429. When she declared that the King of Heaven had called her to deliver besieged Orléans from the English, Charles was understandably skeptical. But the dauphin and his advisers, in retreat from what seemed to be a completely hopeless war, were desperate men, willing to try anything to reverse French fortunes on the battlefield. Certainly the deliverance of Orléans, a city strategic to the control of the territory south of the Loire, would be a God-send. Charles's desperation overcame his skepticism, and he gave Joan his leave.

Circumstances worked perfectly to Joan's advantage. The English force was already exhausted by its six-month siege of Orléans and actually at the point of withdrawal when Joan arrived with fresh French troops. After the English were repulsed at Orléans, there followed a succession of French victories that were popularly attributed to Joan. Joan truly deserved much of the credit, not, however, because she was a military genius. She gave the French people and armies something military experts could not: a unique inspiration and an almost mystical confidence in themselves as a nation. Within a few months of the liberation of Orléans Charles VII received his crown in Rheims and ended the nine-year "disinheritance" prescribed by the Treaty of Troyes.

Charles forgot his liberator as quickly as he had embraced her. Joan was captured by the Burgundians in May 1430, and although he was in a position to secure her release, the French king did little to help her. She was turned over to the Inquisition in English-held Rouen. The Burgundians and the English wanted Joan publicly discredited, believing this would also discredit her patron, Charles VII, and might demoralize French resistance. The skilled inquisitors broke the courageous "Maid of Orléans" in ten weeks of merciless interrogation, and she was executed as a relapsed heretic on May 30, 1431. Charles reopened Joan's trial at a later date, and she was finally declared innocent of all the charges against her on July 7, 1456, twenty-five years after her execution. In 1920 the church declared her a saint.

Charles VII and Philip the Good made peace in

❧ Joan of Arc Refuses to Recant Her Beliefs

Joan of Arc, threatened with torture, refused to recant her beliefs and instead defended the instructions she received from the voices that spoke to her. Here is a part of her self-defense from the contemporary trial record.

On Wednesday, May 9th of the same year [1431], Joan was brought into the great tower of the castle of Rouen before us the said judges and in the presence of the reverend father, lord abbot of St. Cormeille de Compiegne, of masters Jean de Châtillon and Guillaume Erart, doctors of sacred theology, of André Marguerie and Nicolas de Venderes, archdeacons of the church of Rouen, of William Haiton, bachelor of theology, Aubert Morel, licentiate in canon law; Nicolas Loiseleur, canon of the cathedral of Rouen, and master Jean Massieu.

And Joan was required and admonished to speak the truth on many different points contained in her trial which she had denied or to which she had given false replies, whereas we possessed certain information, proofs, and vehement presumptions upon them. Many of the points were read and explained to her, and she was told that if she did not confess them truthfully she would be put to the torture, the instruments of which were shown to her all ready in the tower. There were also present by our instruction men

ready to put her to the torture in order to restore her to the way and knowledge of truth, and by this means to procure the salvation of her body and soul which by her lying inventions she exposed to such grave perils.

To which the said Joan answered in this manner: "Truly if you were to tear me limb from limb and separate my soul from my body, I would not tell you anything more: and if I did say anthing, I should afterwards declare that you had compelled me to say it by force." Then she said that on Holy Cross Day last she received comfort from St. Gabriel; she firmly believes it was St. Gabriel. She knew by her voices whether she should submit to the Church, since the clergy were pressing her hard to submit. Her voices told her that if she desired Our Lord to aid her she must wait upon Him in all her doings. She said that Our Lord has always been the master of her doings, and the Enemy never had power over them. She asked her voices if she would be burned and they answered that she must wait upon God, and He would aid her.

The Trial of Jeanne D'Arc, trans. by W. P. Barrett (New York: Gotham House, 1932), pp. 303–304.

1435, and a unified France, now at peace with Burgundy, progressively forced the English back. By 1453, the date of the war's end, the English held only the coastal enclave of Calais.

During the Hundred Years' War there were sixty-eight years of at least nominal peace and forty-four of hot war. The political and social consequences were lasting. Although the war devastated France, it also awakened the giant of French nationalism and hastened the transition in France from feudal monarchy to a centralized state. Burgundy became a major European political power. The seesawing allegiance of the Netherlands throughout the conflict encouraged the English to develop their own clothing industry and foreign markets. In both France and England the on-again, off-again war devastated the peasantry, who were forced to bear its burden in taxes and services. After the *Jacquerie* of 1358 France did not see another significant peasant uprising until the French Revolution in the eighteenth century.

The Black Death

PRECONDITIONS AND CAUSES. In the late Middle Ages nine tenths of the population were still farmers. The three-field system, in use in most areas since well before the fourteenth century, had increased the amount of arable land and thereby the food supply. The growth of cities and trade had also stimulated agricultural science and pro-

THE HUNDRED YEARS' WAR (1337–1443)

1340	English victory at Bay of Sluys
1346	English victory at Crecy and seizure of Calais
1347	Black Death strikes
1356	English victory at Poitiers
1358	*Jacquerie* disrupts France
1360	Peace of Bretigny recognizes English holdings in France
1381	English peasants revolt
1415	English victory at Agincourt
1422	Treaty of Troyes proclaims Henry VI ruler of both England and France
1429	Joan of Arc leads French to victory at Orléans
1431	Joan of Arc executed as a heretic
1453	War ends; English retain only coastal town of Calais

ductivity. But as the food supply grew, so also did the population. It is estimated that Europe's population doubled between the years 1000 and 1300. By 1300 the balance between food supply and population was decisively tipped in favor of the latter. There were now more people than food to feed them or jobs to employ them, and the average European faced the probability of extreme hunger at

More than one European in three died of the Black Death. In some localities so many people died that the traditional rites of death were abandoned in favor of hurried mass burials in communal pits. [Vincent Virga Archives.]

A flagellant procession. Flagellants paraded from city to city, chanting songs and punishing their bodies in penance for their own and mankind's sins. A typical flagellant parade lasted thirty-three days. Note their bare backs and feet, hats with crosses, and rough penitential shirts. In their hands they carry candles and whips. [Koninlijke Bibliothek, Brussels.]

least once during his or her expected thirty-five-year life span.

Famines followed the population explosion in the first half of the fourteenth century. Between 1315 and 1317 crop failures produced the greatest famine of the Middle Ages. Great suffering was inflicted on densely populated urban areas like the industrial towns of the Netherlands. Decades of overpopulation, economic depression, famine, and bad health progressively weakened Europe's population and made it highly vulnerable to a virulent bubonic plague that struck with full force in 1348. This Black Death, so called by contemporaries because of the way it discolored the body, followed the trade routes into Europe. Appearing in Sicily in late 1347, it entered Europe through the port cities of Venice, Genoa, and Pisa in 1348, and from there it swept rapidly through Spain and southern France and into northern Europe. Areas that lay outside the major trade routes, like Bohemia, appear to have remained virtually unaffected. By the end of the fourteenth century it is estimated that western Europe as a whole had lost as much as two fifths of its population, and a full recovery was not made until the sixteenth century. (See Map 13.2.)

POPULAR REMEDIES. In the Black Death people confronted a catastrophe against which they had neither understanding nor defense. Never have Western people stood so helpless against the inexplicable and the uncontrollable. Contemporary physicians did not know that the disease was transmitted by rat- or human-transported fleas,

and hence the most rudimentary prophylaxis was lacking. Popular wisdom held that a corruption in the atmosphere caused the disease. Some blamed poisonous fumes released by earthquakes and many adopted aromatic amulets as a remedy. According to the contemporary observations of Boccaccio, who recorded the varied reactions to the plague in the *Decameron* (1353), some sought a remedy in moderation and a temperate life; others gave themselves over entirely to their passions (sexual promiscuity among the stricken apparently ran high); and still others, "the most sound, perhaps, in judgment," chose flight and seclusion as the best medicine.

Among the most extreme social reactions were processions of flagellants. These were religious fanatics who beat their bodies in ritual penance until they bled, believing that such action would bring divine intervention. The Jews, who were hated by many because of centuries of Christian propaganda against them and the fact that they had become society's money lenders, a disreputable and resented profession, became scapegoats. Pogroms occurred in several cities, sometimes incited by the advent of flagellants. The terror created by the flagellants, whose dirty bodies may have actually served to transport the disease, became so socially disruptive and threatening even to established authority that the church finally outlawed such processions.

SOCIAL AND ECONOMIC CONSEQUENCES. Among the social and economic consequences of

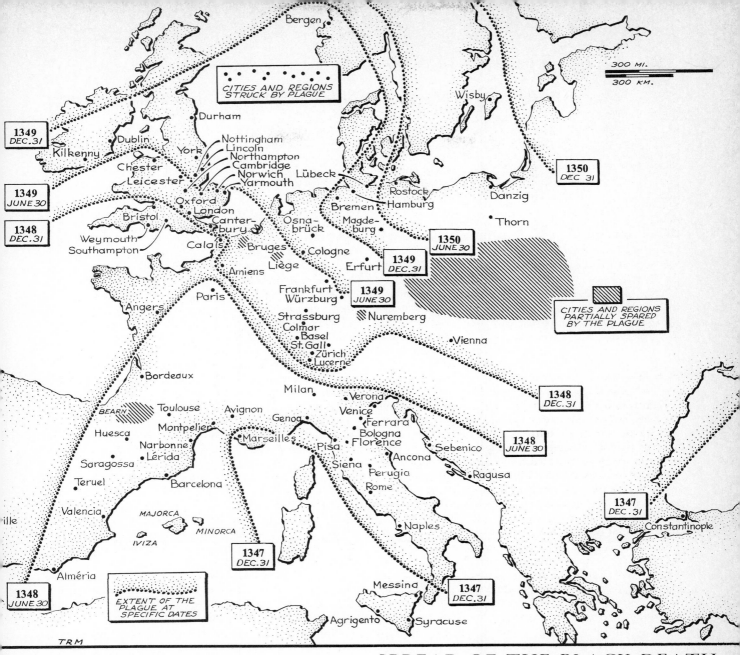

Map labels (as they appear):

Bergen · Wisby · 300 MI. · 300 KM.

CITIES AND REGIONS STRUCK BY PLAGUE

Durham · **1349 DEC. 31** · **1350 DEC 31**

Dublin · Nottingham · Lincoln · Northampton · Cambridge · Norwich · Yarmouth · Lübeck

Kilkenny · York · Chester · Leicester · Rostock · Danzig

1349 JUNE 30 · Oxford · London · Bremen · Hamburg · Thorn

Bristol · Canterbury · Osnabrück · Magdeburg

1348 DEC. 31 · Weymouth · Southampton · Calais · Bruges · Cologne · **1350 JUNE 30**

Amiens · Liège · Erfurt · **1349 DEC. 31**

CITIES AND REGIONS PARTIALLY SPARED BY THE PLAGUE

Angers · Paris · Frankfurt · Würzburg · **1349 JUNE 30**

Strassburg · Colmar · Basel · St. Gall · Zürich · Lucerne · Nuremberg · Vienna

Bordeaux · Milan · **1348 DEC. 31**

BEARN · Toulouse · Avignon · Genoa · Verona · Venice · Ferrara · Bologna · Florence · Sebenico · **1348 JUNE 30**

Huesca · Montpelier · Marseilles · Pisa · Ancona · Ragusa

Narbonne · Lérida · Siena · Perugia · Rome

Saragossa · Barcelona · Teruel

Valencia · MAJORCA · MINORCA · IVIZA · **1347 DEC. 31** · Constantinople

ille · Alméria · **1348 JUNE 30** · **1347 DEC. 31** · Naples

EXTENT OF THE PLAGUE AT SPECIFIC DATES

Messina · **1347 DEC. 31** · Agrigento · Syracuse

TRM

SPREAD OF THE BLACK DEATH

the plague were a shrunken labor supply and the devaluation of the estates of the nobility. Villages vanished in the wake of the plague. As the number of farm laborers decreased, their wages increased and those of skilled artisans soared. Many serfs now chose to commute their labor services by money payments, to abandon the farm altogether, and to pursue more interesting and rewarding jobs in skilled craft industries in the cities, an important new vocational option opened by the Black Death.

MAP 13.2 *Apparently introduced by sea-borne rats from Black Sea areas where plague-infested rodents have long been known, the Black Death brought huge human, social, and economic consequences. One of the lower estimates of Europeans dying is 25,000,000. The map charts its spread in the mid-fourteenth century. Generally following trade routes, the plague reached Scandinavia by 1350, and some believe it then went on to Iceland and even Greenland. Areas off the main trade routes were largely spared.*

347

Boccaccio Describes the Ravages of the Black Death in Florence

The Black Death provided an excuse to the poet, Humanist, and storyteller Giovanni Boccaccio (1313–1375) to assemble his great collection of tales, the *Decameron*. Ten congenial men and women flee Florence to escape the plague and while away the time telling stories. In one of the stories, Boccaccio embedded a fine clinical description of plague symptoms as seen in Florence in 1348 and of the powerlessness of physicians and the lack of remedies.

In Florence, despite all that human wisdom and forethought could devise to avert it, even as the cleansing of the city from many impurities by officials appointed for the purpose, the refusal of entrance to all sick folk, and the adoption of many precautions for the preservation of health; despite also humble supplications addressed to God, and often repeated both in public procession and otherwise, by the devout; towards the beginning of the spring of the said year (1348) the doleful effects of the pestilence began to be horribly apparent by symptoms that shewed as if miraculous.

Not such were these symptoms as in the East, where an issue of blood from the nose was a manifest sign of inevitable death; but in men and women alike it first betrayed itself by the emergence of certain tumours in the groin or the armpits, some of which grew as large as a common apple, others as an egg, some more, some less, which the common folk called gavoccioli.

From the two said parts of the body this deadly gavocciolo soon began to propagate and spread itself in all directions indifferently; after which the form of the malady began to change, black spots or livid making their appearance in many cases on the arm or the thigh or elsewhere, now few and large, now minute and numerous. And as the gavocciolo had been and still was an infallible token of approaching death, such also were these spots on whomsoever they shewed themselves. Which maladies seemed to set entirely at naught both the art of the physician and the virtues of physic; indeed, whether it was that the disorder was of a nature to defy such treatment, or that the physicians were at fault . . . and, being in ignorance of its source, failed to apply the proper remedies; in either case, not merely were those that recovered few, but almost all died within three days of the appearance of the said symptoms, sooner or later, and in most cases without any fever or other attendant malady.

The Decameron of Giovanni Boccaccio, trans. by J. M. Rigg (New York: Dutton, 1930), p. 5.

Agricultural prices fell because of lowered demand, and the price of luxury and manufactured goods—the work of skilled artisans—rose. The noble landholders suffered the greatest decline in power from this new state of affairs. They were forced to pay more for finished products and for farm labor, and they received a smaller return on their agricultural produce. Everywhere their rents were in steady decline after the plague.

To recoup their losses, some landowners converted arable land to sheep pasture, substituting more profitable wool production for labor-intensive grain crops. Others abandoned the effort to farm their land and simply leased it to the highest bidder. Most ominously, legislation was sought to force peasants to stay on their farms and to freeze their wages at low levels, that is, to close off immediately the new economic opportunities opened for the peasantry by the demographic crisis. In France the direct tax on the peasantry, the *taille*, was increased, and opposition to it was prominent among the grievances behind the *Jacquerie*. A Statute of Laborers was passed by the English Parliament in 1351 that limited wages to preplague levels and restricted the ability of peasants to leave the land of their traditional masters. Opposition to such legislation was also a prominent factor in the English Peasants' Revolt of 1381.

Although the plague hit urban populations especially hard, the cities and their skilled industries came in time to prosper from it. Cities had always been careful to protect their interests; as they grew they passed legislation to regulate competition from rural areas and to control immigration. After the plague their laws were progressively extended over the surrounding lands of nobles and feudal landlords, many of whom were peacefully integrated into urban life on terms very favorable to the cities.

The basic unit of urban industry was the master and his apprentices (usually one or two). Their numbers were purposely kept low and jealously guarded. As the craft of the skilled artisan was passed from master to apprentice only very slowly, the first wave of plague created a short supply of skilled labor almost overnight. But this short supply also raised the prices of available manufactured and luxury items to new heights. Ironically the omnipresence of death whetted the appetite for the things that only skilled urban industries could produce. Expensive cloths and jewelry, furs from the north, and silks from the south were in great demand in the second half of the fourteenth century. Faced with life at its worst, people insisted on having the very best. The townspeople profited coming and going: as wealth poured into the cities and per capita income rose, the cost to urban dwellers of agricultural products from the countryside, which were now less in demand, actually declined.

The church also profited from the plague as gifts and bequests multiplied. Although the church, as a great landholder, also suffered losses, it had offsetting revenues from the vastly increased demand for religious services for the dead and the dying.

NEW CONFLICTS AND OPPORTUNITIES. By increasing the importance of skilled artisans, the plague contributed to new conflicts within the cities. The economic and political power of local artisans and trade guilds grew steadily in the late Middle Ages along with the demand for their goods and services. The merchant and patrician classes found it increasingly difficult to maintain their traditional dominance and grudgingly gave guild masters a voice in city government. As the guilds won political power, they encouraged restrictive legislation to protect local industries. These restrictions, in turn, brought confrontations between master artisans, who wanted to keep their numbers low and expand their industries at a snail's pace, and the many journeymen, who were eager to rise to the rank of master. To the long-existing conflict between the guilds and the urban patriciate was now added a conflict within the guilds themselves.

Another indirect effect of the great plague was to assist monarchies in the development of centralized states. The plague caused the landed nobility to lose much of their economic power in the same period that the military superiority of paid professional armies over the traditional noble cavalry was being demonstrated by the Hundred Years' War. The plague also killed large numbers of clergy— perhaps one third of the German clergy fell victim to it as they heroically ministered to the sick and dying. This reduction in clerical ranks occurred in the same century in which the residence of the pope in Avignon (1309–1377) and the Schism (1378–1415) were undermining much of the church's popular support. After 1350 the two traditional "containers" of monarchy—the landed nobility and the church—were on the defensive, and to no small degree as a consequence of the plague. Kings took full advantage of the new situation, as they drew on growing national sentiment to centralize their governments and economies.

Ecclesiastical Breakdown and Revival: The Late Medieval Church

The Thirteenth-Century Papacy

At first glance the popes may appear to have been in a very favorable position in the latter half of the thirteenth century. Frederick II had been vanquished and imperial pressure on Rome had been removed. The French King Louis IX was an enthusiastic supporter of the church, as his two disastrous crusades, which won him sainthood, testify. Although it lasted only seven years, a reunion of the eastern church with Rome was proclaimed by the Council of Lyons in 1274, as the western church took advantage of the Emperor Michael Palaeologus's request for aid against the Turks. Despite these positive events, the church was not really in as favorable a position as it appeared.

As early as the reign of Pope Innocent III (1198–1216), when papal power reached its height, there were ominous developments. Innocent had elaborated the doctrine of papal plenitude of power and on that authority had declared saints, disposed of benefices, and created a centralized papal monarchy with a clearly political mission. Innocent's transformation of the papacy into a great secular power had the consequence of weakening the church religiously as he sought to strengthen it politically. Thereafter the church as a papal monarchy and the church as the "body of the faithful" came increasingly to be differentiated; it was against the "papal church" and in the name of the "true Christian church" that both reformers and heretics raised their voices in protest until the Protestant Reformation.

What Innocent began, his successors perfected. Under Urban IV (1261–1264) the papacy established its own law court, the Rota Romana, which tightened and centralized the church's legal proceedings. The latter half of the thirteenth century saw an elaboration of the system of clerical taxation; what had begun in the twelfth century as an emergency measure to raise funds for the crusades became a fixed institution. In the same period papal power to determine appointments to many major and minor church offices—the so-called reservation of benefices—was greatly broadened. The thirteenth-century papacy became a powerful political institution governed by its own law and courts, serviced by an efficient international bureaucracy, and preoccupied with secular goals.

Papal centralization of the church tended to undermine both diocesan authority and popular support. Rome's interests, not local needs, came to control church appointments, policies, and discipline. Discontented lower clergy appealed to the higher authority of Rome against the disciplinary measures of local bishops. In the second half of the thirteenth century bishops and abbots protested such undercutting of their power. To its critics the church in Rome seemed hardly more than a legalized, fiscalized, bureaucratic institution. As early as the late twelfth century heretical movements of Cathars and Waldensians had appealed to the biblical ideal of simplicity and separation from the world as opposed to a perceived materialism in official religion against which reformers loyal to the church, such as St. Francis of Assisi, would also protest.

The church of the thirteenth century was being undermined by more than internal religious disunity. The demise of imperial power meant that the papacy in Rome was no longer the leader of anti-imperial (Guelf, or propapal) sentiment in Italy. Instead of being the center of Italian resistance to the emperor, popes now found themselves on the defensive against their old allies. That was the ironic price paid by the papacy to vanquish the Hohenstaufens.

Rulers with a stake in Italian politics now directed the intrigue formerly aimed at the emperor toward dominating the College of Cardinals. Charles of Anjou, king of Sicily, for example, managed to create a French–Sicilian faction within the college. Such efforts to control the decisions of the college led Pope Gregory X (1271–1276) to establish the so-called "conclave of cardinals." This was the practice of sequestering the cardinals immediately on the death of the pope so that extraneous political influence on the election of new popes might be kept to a minimum. But the conclave proved to be of little avail, so politicized had the College of Cardinals become.

In 1294 such a college, in frustration after a deadlock of over two years, chose a saintly but inept Calabrian hermit as Pope Celestine V. Celestine abdicated under suspicious circumstances after only a few weeks in office and also died under suspicious circumstances (his successor's critics later argued that he had been murdered to ensure the unity of the papal office). His tragicomic reign shocked a majority of the college into unified affirmative action. He was quickly replaced by his very opposite, Pope Boniface VIII (1294–1303), a nobleman and a skilled politician, whose pontificate, however, saw the beginning of the end of papal pretensions to great power status.

Boniface VIII and Philip the Fair

Boniface came to rule when England and France were maturing as nation-states. In England a long tradition of consultation between the king and powerful members of English society evolved into formal "parliaments" during the reigns of Henry III (1216–1272) and Edward I (1272–1307), and these parliaments helped to create a unified kingdom. The reign of the French king Philip IV the Fair (1285–1314) saw France become an efficient, centralized monarchy. Philip was no Saint Louis, but a ruthless politician intent on ending England's continental holdings, controlling wealthy Flanders, and establishing French hegemony within the Holy Roman Empire. Boniface had the further misfortune of bringing to the papal throne memories of the way earlier popes had brought kings and emperors to their knees. Very painfully he was to discover that the papal monarchy of the early thirteenth century was no match for the new political powers of the late thirteenth century.

France and England were on the brink of all-out

war when Boniface became pope (1294). Only Edward I's preoccupation with rebellion in Scotland, which the French encouraged, prevented a full-scale English invasion of France around the turn of the century—a turn of events that would have started the Hundred Years' War a half-century earlier. As both countries mobilized for war, they used the pretext of preparing for a crusade to tax the clergy heavily. In 1215 Pope Innocent III had decreed that the clergy were to pay no taxes to rulers without prior papal consent. Viewing English and French taxation of the clergy as an assault on traditional clerical rights, Boniface took a strong stand against it. On February 5, 1296, he issued a bull, *Clericis Laicos,* which forbade lay taxation of the clergy without prior papal approval and took back all previous papal dispensations in this regard.

In England Edward I retaliated by denying the clergy the right to be heard in royal court, in effect removing from them the protection of the king. But it was Philip the Fair who struck back with a vengeance. In August 1296 he forbade the exportation of money from France to Rome, thereby denying the papacy revenues without which it could not operate. Boniface had no choice but to come quickly to terms with Philip. He conceded Philip the right to tax the French clergy "during an emergency," and, not coincidentally, he canonized Louis IX in the same year.

Boniface was at this time also under siege by powerful Italian enemies, whom Philip did not fail to patronize. A noble family (the Colonnas), rivals of Boniface's family (the Gaetani) and radical followers of Saint Francis of Assisi (the Spiritual Franciscans) were at this time seeking to invalidate Boniface's election as pope on the grounds that Celestine V had resigned the office under coercion. Charges of heresy, simony, and even the murder of Celestine, who had died shortly after his abdication, were hurled against Boniface.

In the year 1300 Boniface's fortunes appeared to revive. Tens of thousands of pilgrims flocked to Rome in that year for the Jubilee celebration. In a

A sculpture of Pope Boniface VIII (1294–1303) who opposed the taxation of clergy by the kings of France and England and issued one of the strongest declarations of papal authority, the bull Unam Sanctam. *The statue is in the Museo Civico, Bologna, Italy. [Alinari/SCALA.]*

❧ Boniface VIII Reasserts the Church's Claim to Temporal Power

Defied by the French and the English, Pope Boniface VIII (1294–1303) boldly reasserted the temporal power of the church in the bull *Unam Sanctam* (November 1302). This document claimed that both spiritual and temporal power on earth were under the pope's jurisdiction, because, in the hierarchy of the universe, spiritual power both preceded and sat in judgment on temporal power.

We are taught by the words of the Gospel that in this church and in her power there are two swords, a spiritual one and a temporal one. . . . Certainly anyone who denies that the temporal sword is in the power of Peter has not paid heed to the words of the Lord when he said, "Put up thy sword into its sheath" (Matthew 26:52). Both then are in the power of the church, the material sword and the spiritual. But the one is exercised for the church, the other by the church, the one by the hand of the priest, the other by the hand of kings and soldiers, though at the will and suffrance of the authority subject to the spiritual power. . . . For, according to the blessed Dionysius, it is the law of divinity for the lowest to be led to the highest through intermediaries. In the order of the universe all things are not kept in order in the same fashion and immediately but the lowest are ordered by the intermediate and inferiors by superiors. But that the spiritual power excels any earthly one in dignity and nobility we ought the more openly to confess in proportion as spiritual things excel temporal ones. Moreover we clearly perceive this from the giving of tithes, from benediction and sanctification, from the acceptance of this power and from the very government of things. For, the truth bearing witness, the spiritual power has to institute the earthly power and to judge it if it has not been good. So it is verified the prophecy of Jeremiah (1:10) concerning the church and the power of the church, "Lo, I have set thee this day over the nations and over kingdoms."

Brian Tierney, *The Crisis of Church and State* 1050–1300 (Englewood Cliffs, N.J.: Prentice-Hall, 1964), pp. 188–189.

Jubilee year all Catholics who visited Rome and there fulfilled certain conditions received a special indulgence, or remission of their sins. Heady with this display of popular religiosity, Boniface reinserted himself into international politics. He championed Scottish resistance to England, for which he received a firm rebuke from an outraged Edward I and from Parliament.

But once again a confrontation with the king of France proved the more costly. Philip, seemingly spoiling for another fight with the pope, arrested Boniface's Parisian legate, Bernard Saisset, the bishop of Pamiers and also a powerful secular lord, whose independence Philip had opposed. Saisset was accused of heresy and treason and was tried and convicted in the king's court. Thereafter Philip demanded that Boniface recognize the process against Saisset, something that Boniface could do only if he was prepared to surrender his jurisdiction over the French episcopate. This challenge could not be sidestepped, and Boniface acted swiftly to champion Saisset as a defender of clerical political independence within France. He demanded Saisset's unconditional release, revoked all previous agreements with Philip in the matter of clerical taxation, and ordered the French bishops to convene in Rome within a year. A bull, *Ausculta Fili* ("Listen, My Son"), was sent to Philip in December 1301, pointedly informing him that "God has set popes over kings and kingdoms."

UNAM SANCTAM (1302). Philip unleashed a ruthless antipapal campaign. Two royal apologists, Pierre Dubois and John of Paris, refuted papal claims to the right to intervene in temporal matters. Increasingly placed on the defensive, Boniface made a last-ditch stand against state control of national churches when on November 18, 1302, he issued the bull *Unam Sanctam*. This famous statement of papal power declared that temporal authority was "subject" to the spiritual power of the church. On its face a bold assertion, *Unam Sanctam* was in truth the desperate act of a besieged papacy.

After *Unam Sanctam* the French and the Colon-

Palace of the popes in Avignon, France, the papal residence from 1309 *to* 1377, *following Boniface VIII's defeat by the French king, Philip the Fair.* [*French Government Tourist Office, New York.*]

nas moved against Boniface with force. Guillaume de Nogaret, Philip's chief minister, denounced Boniface to the French clergy as a common heretic and criminal. An army, led by Nogaret and Sciarra Colonna, surprised the pope in mid-August 1303 at his retreat in Anagni. Boniface was badly beaten up and almost executed before an aroused populace liberated and returned him safely to Rome. But the ordeal proved too much for the pope, who died a few months later, in October 1303.

Boniface's immediate successor, Benedict XI (1303–1304), excommunicated Nogaret for his deed, but there was to be no lasting papal retaliation. Benedict's successor, Clement V (1305–1314), was forced into French subservience. A former archbishop of Bordeaux, Clement declared that *Unam Sanctam* should not be understood as in any way diminishing French royal authority. He released Nogaret from excommunication and pliantly condemned the Knights Templars, whose treasure Philip thereafter forcibly expropriated. Clement established the papal court at Avignon, on the southeastern border of France, in 1309. The imperial city of Avignon, situated on land that belonged to the pope, maintained its independence

from the king. In 1311 Clement made the city his permanent residence, both to escape a Rome ridden with strife after the confrontation between Boniface and Philip, and also to escape pressure from Philip. There the papacy was to remain until 1377.

After Boniface's humiliation popes never again so seriously threatened kings and emperors, despite continuing papal excommunications and political intrigue. In the future the relation between Church and State would tilt toward state control of religion within particular monarchies and the subordination of ecclesiastical to larger secular political purposes.

The Avignon Papacy (1309–1377)

The Avignon papacy was in appearance, although not always in actual fact, under strong French influence. During Clement V's pontificate the French came to dominate the College of Cardinals. Clement also expanded papal taxes, especially the practice of collecting annates, the first year's revenue of a church office or benefice bestowed by the pope—a practice that contributed much to the

Marsilius of Padua Denies Coercive Power to the Clergy

According to Marsilius, the Bible gave the pope no right to pronounce and execute sentences on any person. The clergy held a strictly moral and spiritual rule, their judgments to be executed only in the afterlife, not in the present one. Here, on earth, they should be obedient to secular authority. Marsilius argued this point by appealing to the example of Jesus.

We now wish . . . to adduce the truths of the holy Scripture . . . which explicitly command or counsel that neither the Roman bishop called pope, nor any other bishop or priest, or deacon, has or ought to have any rulership or coercive judgment or jurisdiction over any priest or non-priest, ruler, community, group, or individual of whatever condition. . . . Christ himself came into the world not to dominate men, nor to judge them [coercively] . . . not to wield temporal rule, but rather to be subject as regards the . . . present life; and moreover, he wanted to and did exclude himself, his apostles and disciples, and their successors, the bishops or priests, from all coercive authority or wordly rule, both by his example and by his word of counsel or command. . . . When he was brought before Pontius Pilate . . . and accused of having called himself king of the Jews, and [Pilate] asked him whether he had said this . . . [his] reply included these words . . . "My kingdom is not of this world," that is, I have not come to reign by temporal rule or dominion, in the way . . . worldly kings reign. . . . This, then, is the kingdom concerning which he came to teach and order, a kingdom which consists in the acts whereby the eternal kingdom is attained, that is, the acts of faith and the other theological virtues; not however, by coercing anyone thereto.

Marsilius of Padua: The Defender of Peace: The Defensor Pacis, trans. by Alan Gewirth (New York: Harper, 1967), pp. 113–116.

Petrarch Describes the Papal Residence at Avignon

Petrarch, the father of Humanism, lived in Avignon and personally observed the papacy there over a long period of time. In this letter written between 1340 and 1353, he described with deep, pious outrage the ostentation and greed of the Avignon popes.

I am now living in [Avignon], in the Babylon of the West. . . . Here reign the successors of the poor fishermen of Galilee [who] have strangely forgotten their origin. I am astounded, as I recall their predecessors, to see these men loaded with gold and clad in purple, boasting of the spoils of princes and nations; to see luxurious palaces and heights crowned with fortifications, instead of a boat turned downwards for [their] shelter. We no longer find the simple nets which were once used to gain a frugal living from the lake of Galilee. . . . One is stupefied nowadays to hear the lying tongues, and to see worthless parchments turned by a leaden seal [i.e., official bulls of the pope] into nets which are used, in Christ's name, but by the arts of Belial [i.e., the devil], to catch hordes of unwary Christians. These fish, too, are dressed and laid on the burning coals of anxiety before they fill the insatiable maw of their captors.

Instead of holy solitude we find a criminal host and crowds . . . ; instead of sobriety, licentious banquets . . . ; instead of pious pilgrimages . . . foul sloth; instead of the bare feet of the apostles . . . horses decked in gold. . . . In short, we seem to be among the kings of the Persians or Parthians, before whom we must fall down and worship, and who cannot be approached except presents be offered.

James Harvey Robinson (Ed.), Readings in European History, Vol. 1 (Boston: Athenaeum, 1904), pp. 502–530.

Renaissance justice. Depicted are the most common forms of corporal and capital punishment in Renaissance Europe. At top: burning, hanging, drowning. At center: blinding, quartering, the wheel, cutting of hair (a mark of great shame for a freeman). At bottom: thrashing, decapitation, amputation of hand (for thieves). [Herzog August Bibliothek, Wolfenbuttel.]

Avignon papacy's reputation as being materialistic and politically motivated.

POPE JOHN XXII. Pope John XXII (1316–1334), the most powerful Avignon pope, tried to restore papal independence and return to Italy. This goal led him into war with the Visconti, the most powerful ruling family of Milan, and a costly contest with Emperor Louis IV, whose election as emperor in 1314 John had challenged in favor of the rival Hapsburg candidate. The result was a minor replay of the confrontation between Philip the Fair and Boniface VIII. When John obstinately and without legal justification refused to recognize Louis's election, the emperor retaliated by declar-

ing John deposed and setting in his place an antipope. As Philip the Fair had also done, Louis enlisted the support of the Spiritual Franciscans, whose views on absolute poverty John had condemned as heretical. Two outstanding pamphleteers wrote lasting tracts for the royal cause: William of Ockham, whom John excommunicated in 1328, and Marsilius of Padua (ca. 1290–1342/43), whose teaching John declared heretical in 1327.

MARSILIUS OF PADUA. In his *Defender of Peace* (1324) Marsilius of Padua stressed the independent origins and autonomy of secular government. Clergy were subjected to the strictest apostolic ideals and confined to purely spiritual functions, and all power of coercive judgment was denied the pope. Marsilius argued that spiritual crimes must await an eternal punishment. Transgressions of divine law, over which the pope had jurisdiction, were to be punished in the next life, not in the present one, unless the secular ruler declared a divine law also a secular law. This assertion was a direct challenge of the power of the pope to excommunicate rulers and place countries under interdict. The *Defender of Peace* depicted the pope as a subordinate member of a society over which the emperor ruled supreme and in which temporal peace was the highest good.

John XXII made the papacy a sophisticated international agency and adroitly adjusted it to the growing European money economy. The more the Curia (or papal court) mastered the latter, however, the more vulnerable it became to criticism. Under John's successor, Benedict XII (1334–1342), the papacy became entrenched in Avignon. Seemingly forgetting Rome altogether, Benedict began construction of the great Palace of the Popes and attempted to reform both papal government and the religious life. His high-living French successor, Clement VI (1342–1352), placed papal policy in lockstep with the French. In this period the cardinals became barely more than lobbyists for policies favorable to their secular patrons.

NATIONAL OPPOSITION TO THE AVIGNON PAPACY. As Avignon's fiscal tentacles probed new areas, monarchies took strong action to protect their interests. The latter half of the fourteenth century saw legislation restricting papal jurisdiction and taxation in France, England, and Germany. In England, where the Avignon papacy was identified with the French enemy after the outbreak of the Hundred Years' War, statutes of *provisors* and *praemunire*, which restricted payments and appeals to Rome, were several times passed between 1351 and 1393. In France ecclesiastical appointments and taxation were regulated by the so-called Gallican liberties. These national rights over religion had long been exercised in fact and were legally acknowledged by the church in the Pragmatic Sanction of Bourges in 1438. This agreement recognized the right of the French church to elect its own clergy without papal interference, prohibited the payment of annates to Rome, and limited the right of appeals from French courts to the Curia in Rome. In German and Swiss cities in the fourteenth and fifteenth centuries local governments also took the initiative to limit and even overturn traditional clerical privileges and immunities.

John Wycliffe and John Huss

The popular lay religious movements that most successfully assailed the late medieval church were the Lollards in England and the Hussites in Bohemia. Both John Wycliffe (d. 1384) and John Huss (d. 1415) would have disclaimed the extremists who revolted in their name, yet Wycliffe's writings gave at least a theoretical justification to the demands of the Lollards and Huss' writings to the programs of both moderate and extreme Hussites.

Wycliffe's work initially served the anticlerical policies of the English government. An Oxford theologian and a philosopher of high standing, Wycliffe became within England what William of Ockham and Marsilius of Padua had been at the Bavarian court of Emperor Louis IV: a major intellectual spokesman for the rights of royalty against the secular pretensions of popes. After 1350 English kings greatly reduced the power of the Avignon papacy to make ecclesiastical appointments and collect taxes within England, a position that Wycliffe strongly supported. His views on clerical poverty followed original Franciscan ideals and, more by accident than by design, gave justification to government restriction and even confiscation of church properties within England. Wycliffe argued that the clergy "ought to be content with food and clothing." He also maintained that personal merit, not rank and office, was the only basis of religious authority—a dangerous teaching because it raised allegedly pious laypeople above allegedly corrupt ecclesiasts, regardless of the latter's official stature. There was a threat in such teaching to secular as well as ecclesiastical dominion and jurisdiction. At his posthumous condemnation by the pope, Wycliffe was accused of the ancient heresy of Donatism—the teaching that the efficacy of the church's sacraments did not lie in their sheer performance but also depended on the moral character of the clergy who administered them. Wycliffe also anticipated certain Protestant criticisms of the medieval church by challenging papal infallibility, the sale of indulgences, and the dogma of transubstantiation.

English advocates of Wycliffe's teaching were called *Lollards*. Like the Waldensians, they preached in the vernacular, disseminated translations of Holy Scripture, and championed clerical poverty. At first they came from every social class, being especially prominent among the groups who had something tangible to gain from the confiscation of clerical properties (the nobility and the gentry) or who had suffered most under the current church system (the lower clergy and the poor people). After the English Peasants' Revolt of 1381, an uprising filled with egalitarian notions that could find support in Wycliffe's teaching, Lollardy was officially viewed as subversive. Opposed by an alliance of church and crown, it became a capital offense in England by 1401.

Heresy was not so easily harnessed in Bohemia, where it coalesced with a strong national movement. The University of Prague, founded in 1348, became the center for both Czech nationalism and a native religious reform movement. The latter began within the bounds of orthodoxy and was led by local intellectuals and preachers, the most famous of whom was John Huss, the rector of the university after 1403. The reformers supported vernacular translations of the Bible and were critical of traditional ceremonies and allegedly superstitious practices, particularly those relating to the sacrament of the Eucharist. They advocated lay communion with cup as well as bread (traditionally only the priest received communion with both cup and bread, the laity with bread only, a sign of the clergy's spiritual superiority over the laity), taught that bread and wine remained bread and wine after priestly consecration, and questioned the validity of sacraments performed by priests in mortal sin. Wycliffe's teaching appears to have influenced the movement very early. Regular traffic between England and Bohemia had existed for decades, ever since the marriage in 1381 of Anne of Bohemia to King Richard II. Czech students studied at Oxford and many returned with copies of Wycliffe's writings.

Huss became the leader of the pro-Wycliffe faction at the University of Prague, and in 1410 his

A German portrayal of the burning of John Huss for heresy and the dumping of his ashes into the Rhine to prevent their becoming relics of his martyrdom. [*Vincent Virga Archives.*]

activities brought about his excommunication and the placement of Prague under papal interdict. In 1414 Huss won an audience with the newly assembled Council of Constance. He journeyed to the council eagerly, armed with a safe-conduct pass from Emperor Sigismund, and naively believing that he would convince his strongest critics of the truth of his teaching. Within weeks of his arrival in early November 1414 he was formally accused of

heresy and imprisoned. He died at the stake on July 6, 1415, and was followed there less than a year later by his colleague Jerome of Prague. The reaction in Bohemia to the execution of these national heroes was fierce revolt as militant Hussites, the Taborites, set out to transform Bohemia by force into a religious and social paradise under the military leadership of John Ziska. After a decade of belligerent protest the Hussites won significant religious reforms and control over the Bohemian church from the Council of Basel.

The Great Schism (1378–1417) and the Conciliar Movement to 1449

URBAN VI AND CLEMENT VII. Pope Gregory XI (1370–1378) reestablished the papacy in Rome in January 1377, ending what had come to be known as the "Babylonian Captivity" of the church in Avignon, the reference being to the biblical bondage of the Israelites. The return to Rome proved to be short-lived, however. Upon Gregory's death on March 27, 1378, the cardinals, in Rome, elected an Italian archbishop as Pope Urban VI (1378–1389), who immediately proclaimed his intention to reform the Curia. This announcement came as an unexpected challenge to the cardinals, most of whom were French, and made them amenable to royal pressures to return the papacy to Avignon. The French king, Charles V, not wanting to surrender the benefits of a papacy located within the sphere of French influence, lent his support to a schism. Five months after Urban's election, on September 20, 1378, thirteen cardinals, all but one of whom was French, formed their own conclave and elected a cousin of the French king as Pope Clement VII (1378–1397). They insisted, probably with some truth, that they had voted for Urban in fear of their lives, surrounded by a Roman mob that demanded the election of an Italian pope. Be that as it may, thereafter the papacy became a "two-headed thing" and a scandal to Christendom. Allegiance to the two papal courts divided along political lines: England and its allies (the Holy Roman Empire, Hungary, Bohemia, and Poland) acknowledged Urban VI, whereas France and its orbit (Naples, Scotland, Castile, and Aragon) supported Clement VII. Only the Roman line of popes, however, came to be recognized as official in subsequent church history.

Two approaches were initially taken to end the schism. One tried to win the mutual cession of both popes, thereby clearing the way for a new election of a single pope. The other sought to secure the resignation of the one in favor of the other. Both proved completely fruitless, however. Each pope considered himself fully legitimate, and too much was at stake for a magnanimous concession on the part of either. There was one way left: the forced deposition of both popes by a special council of the church.

CONCILIAR THEORY OF CHURCH GOVERNMENT. Legally a church council could be convened only by a pope, and the competing popes were not inclined to summon a council for their own deposition. Also, the deposition of a legitimate pope against his will by a council of the church was as serious a matter as the forced dethronement of a legally recognized hereditary monarch by a representative body.

The correctness of a conciliar deposition of a pope was debated a full thirty years before any direct action was taken. Conciliar theorists, chief among whom were the masters of the University of Paris, Conrad of Gelnhausen, Henry of Langenstein, Jean Gerson, and Pierre d'Ailly, challenged the popes' identification of the church's welfare with their own and developed arguments in favor of a more representative government of the church; their goal was a church in which a representative council could effectively regulate the actions of the pope. Conciliarists defined the church

as the whole body of the faithful, a body of which the elected head, the pope, was but one part, and a part whose sole purpose was to maintain the unity and well-being of the body as a whole—something that the schismatic popes were far from doing. The conciliarists further argued that a council of the church, as a Holy Spirit–inspired spokesman for a majority of the faithful, acted with greater authority than the pope alone. In the eyes of the pope(s) such a concept of the church threatened both its political and its religious unity.

THE COUNCIL OF PISA (1409–1410). On the basis of such arguments, cardinals representing both sides convened a council on their own authority in Pisa in 1409. There they deposed both the Roman and the Avignon popes and elected in their stead a new pope, Alexander V. To the council's consternation neither pope accepted its action, and after 1409 Christendom confronted the spectacle of three contending popes. Although the vast majority of Latin Christendom did at this time accept Alexander and his Pisan successor John XXIII (1410–1415), the popes of Rome and Avignon refused to step down.

THE COUNCIL OF CONSTANCE (1414–1417). This intolerable situation ended when the emperor Sigismund prevailed on John XXIII to summon a "legal" council of the church in Constance in 1414, a council also recognized by the Roman pope Greg-

---

✌ The Council of Constance Declares Conciliar Supremacy

The decree *Haec Sancta* (April 1415) asserted the supremacy of councils over popes in time of emergency in the church. This was the legal basis on which the Council of Constance proceeded to remove the contending popes from power and end the schism by electing a new pope, Martin V (1417–1431).

This holy Council of Constance . . . declares, first that is is lawfully assembled in the Holy Spirit, that it constitutes a General Council, representing the Catholic Church, and that therefore it has its authority immediately from Christ; and that all men, of every rank and condition, including the pope himself, are bound to obey it in matters concerning the Faith, the abolition of the schism, and the reformation of the Church of God in its head and its mem- *bers. Secondly, it declares that anyone, of any rank and condition, who shall contumaciously refuse to obey the orders, decrees, statutes or instructions, made or to be made by this holy Council, or by any other lawfully assembled general council . . . shall, unless he comes to a right frame of mind, be subjected to fitting penance and punished appropriately: and, if need be, recourse shall be had to the other sanctions of the law.*

From *Documents of the Christian Church*, ed. by Henry Bettenson (New York: Oxford University Press, 1961), pp. 192–193.

❧ The Chronicler Calls the Roll at the Council of Constance

The Council of Constance, in session for three years (1414–1417), not only drew many clergy and political representatives into its proceedings but also required a great variety of supporting personnel. Here is an inventory from the contemporary chronicle by Ulrich Richental.

Pope John XXIII came with 600 men.

Pope Martin, who was elected pope at Constance, came with 30 men.

5 patriarchs, with 118 men.

33 cardinals, with 3,056 men.

47 archbishops, with 4,700 men.

145 bishops, with 6,000 men.

93 suffragan bishops, with 360 men.

Some 500 spiritual lords, with 4,000 men.

24 auditors and secretaries, with 300 men.

37 scholars from the universities of all nations, with 2,000 men.

217 doctors of theology from the five nations, who walked in the processions, with 2,600 men.

361 doctors of both laws, with 1,260 men.

171 doctors of medicine, with 1,600 men.

1,400 masters of arts and licentiates, with 3,000 men.

5,300 simple priests and scholars, some by threes, some by twos, some alone.

The apothecaries who lived in huts, with 300 men. (16 of them were masters.)

72 goldsmiths, who lived in huts.

Over 1,400 merchants, shopkeepers, furriers, smiths, shoemakers, innkeepers, and handworkers, who lived in huts and rented houses and huts, with their servants.

24 rightful heralds of the King, with their squires.

1,700 trumpeters, fifers, fiddlers, and players of all kinds.

Over 700 harlots in brothels came, who hired their own houses, and some who lay in stables and wherever they could, beside the private ones whom I could not count.

In the train of the Pope were 24 secretaries with 200 men, 16 doorkeepers, 12 beadles who carried silver rods, 60 other beadles for the cardinals, auditors and auditors of the camera, and many old women who washed and mended the clothes of the Roman lords in private and public.

132 abbots, all named, with 2,000 men.

155 priors, all recorded with their names, with 1,600 men.

Our lord King, two queens, and 5 princely ladies.

39 dukes, 32 princely lords and counts, 141 counts, 71 barons, more than 1,500 knights, more than 20,000 noble squires.

Embassies from 83 kings of Asia, Africa, and Europe, with full powers; envoys from other lords without number, for they rode in and out every day. There were easily 5,000.

472 envoys from imperial cities.

352 envoys from baronial cities.

72,460 persons.

Richental's *Chronicle of the Council, Constance,* in *The Council of Constance,* ed. by J. H. Mundy and K. M. Woodey, trans. by Louise R. Roomis (New York: Columbia University Press, 1961), pp. 189–190.

ory XII. Gregory, however, soon resigned his office, raising grave doubts forevermore about whether the council was truly convened with Rome's blessing and hence valid. In a famous declaration entitled *Haec Sancta* the council fathers asserted their supremacy and proceeded to conduct the business of the church. In November 1417 the council successfully accomplished its main business when it elected a new pope, Martin V (1417–1431), after the three contending popes had either resigned (Gregory XIII) or were deposed (Benedict XIII and John XXIII). The council made provisions for regular meetings of church councils, scheduling a general council of the church for purposes of reform within five, then seven, and thereafter every ten years. Constance has remained, however, an illegitimate church council in official eyes; nor are the schismatic popes of Avignon and Pisa recognized as legitimate (for this reason another pope could take the name John XXIII in 1958).

THE COUNCIL OF BASEL (1431–1449). Conciliar government of the church both peaked and declined during the Council of Basel. In 1432 the council invited the Hussites to send a delegation to Basel to make peace. The Hussites presented a doctrinal statement known as the *Four Articles of Prague,* which served as a basis for the negotiations. This document contained requests for (1) giving the laity the Eucharist with cup as well as bread (hence their name *Utraquists,* from the Latin word meaning "both," and *Calixtines,* from the Latin word for "cup"); (2) free, itinerant preaching; (3) the exclusion of the clergy from holding secular offices and possessing property; and (4) just punishment of clergy who have committed mortal sins. In November 1433 an agreement was reached between the emperor, the council, and the Hussites. The Bohemian church received jurisdictional rights similar to those already secured by France and England. Three of the four Prague articles were conceded: communion with cup, free preaching by ordained clergy, and like punishment of clergy and laity for mortal sins. The church firmly retained the right to possess and dispose of property.

THE COUNCIL OF FERRARA–FLORENCE (1438–1439). The termination of the Hussite wars and the reform legislation curtailing the papal power of appointment and taxation were the high points of the Council of Basel. Heady with success, the Basel council seemed to its critics to assert its powers beyond the original intention of the decrees of Constance and in doing so undermined much internal and external support. Original supporters of the council, prominent among them the philosopher Nicholas of Cusa, turned their backs on the council when Pope Eugenius IV (1431–1447) ordered it to transfer to Ferrara in 1437. The pope had a golden opportunity to upstage the Council of Basel by negotiating a reunion with the eastern church, which was bargaining for western aid against new Turkish advances. A majority of Basel's members refused to transfer to Ferrara, and their defiance made Basel a schismatic council. Those in Basel watched while the reunion of the eastern and western churches was proclaimed in Florence, where the council of Ferrara had transferred because of plague, in 1439. This agreement, although short-lived, restored papal prestige

and signaled the demise of the conciliar movement.

The notion of conciliar superiority suffered a mortal blow with the collapse of the Council of Basel in 1449. A decade later the papal bull *Execrabilis* (1460) condemned appeals to councils as "erroneous and abominable" and "completely null and void."

Although many who had worked for reform now despaired of ever attaining it, the conciliar movement was not a total failure. It planted deep within the conscience of all Western peoples the conviction that the leader of an institution must be responsive to its members and that the head exists to lead and serve, not to bring disaster upon the body.

A second consequence of the conciliar movement was the devolving of religious responsibility on the laity. In the absence of papal leadership, secular control of national or territorial churches increased. Kings asserted power over the church in England and France. Magistrates and city councils reformed and regulated religious life in German, Swiss, and Italian cities. This development was not reversed by the powerful "restoration" popes of the high Renaissance. On the contrary, as the papacy became a limited territorial regime, national control of the church simply ran apace. Perceived as just one among several Italian states, the Papal States could be opposed as much on the grounds of "national" policy as for religious reasons.

Revival of Monarchy: Nation Building in the Fifteenth Century

After 1450 there was a progressive shift from divided feudal to unified national monarchies as "sovereign" rulers emerged. This is not to say that the dynastic and chivalric ideals of feudal monarchy did not continue. Territorial princes did not pass from the scene, and representative bodies persisted and in some areas even grew in influence. But in the late fifteenth and early sixteenth centuries the old problem of the one and the many was decided clearly in favor of the interests of monarchy.

The feudal monarchy of the high Middle Ages was characterized by the division of the basic powers of government between the king and his semi-autonomous vassals. The nobility and the towns acted with varying degrees of unity and success through such evolving representative assemblies as the English Parliament, the French Estates General, and the Spanish Cortes to thwart the centralization of royal power. Because of the Hundred Years' War and the schism in the church, the nobility and the clergy were in decline in the late Middle Ages. The increasingly important towns began to ally with the king. Loyal, businesswise townspeople, not the nobility and the clergy, staffed the royal offices and became the king's lawyers, bookkeepers, military tacticians, and foreign diplomats. It was this new alliance between king and town that finally broke the bonds of feudal society and made possible the rise of sovereign states.

In a sovereign state the power of taxation, war making, and law enforcement is no longer the local right of semiautonomous vassals but is concentrated in the monarch and is exercised by his chosen agents. Taxes, wars, and laws become national rather than merely regional matters. Only as monarchs were able to act independently of the nobility and the representative assemblies could they overcome the decentralization that had been the basic obstacle to nation building. Ferdinand and Isabella rarely called the Cortes into session. The French Estates General did not meet at all from 1484 to 1560. Henry VII (1485–1509) of England managed to raise revenues without going begging to Parliament after Parliament voted him customs revenues for life in 1485. Kings were also assisted by brilliant theorists, from Marsilius of Padua in the fourteenth century to Machiavelli and Jean Bodin in the sixteenth, who eloquently argued the sovereign rights of monarchy.

The many were, of course, never totally subjugated to the one, and still today the cry of "states' rights" is very distinct. But in the last half of the fifteenth century, rulers increasingly demonstrated that the law was their creature. Civil servants whose vision was no longer merely local or regional filled royal offices. In Castile they were the *corregidores,* in England the justices of the peace, in France bailiffs operating through well-drilled lieutenants. These royal ministers and agents were not immune to becoming closely attached to the localities they administered in the king's name. And regions were able to secure congenial royal appointments. Throughout England local magnates served as representatives of the

Tudor kings. Nonetheless these new executives were truly *royal* executives, bureaucrats whose outlook was "national" and whose loyalty was to the "state."

Monarchies also began to create standing national armies in the fifteenth century. As the noble cavalry receded and the infantry and the artillery became the backbone of the armies, mercenary soldiers were recruited from Switzerland and Germany to form the major part of the "king's army." Professional soldiers who fought for pay and booty proved far more efficient than feudal vassals who fought simply for honor's sake. Kings who failed to meet their payrolls, however, faced a new danger of mutiny and banditry on the part of alien troops.

The more expensive warfare of the fifteenth and sixteenth centuries increased the need to develop new national sources of royal income. The expansion of royal revenues was especially hampered by the stubborn belief among the highest classes that they were immune from government taxation. The nobility guarded their properties and traditional rights and despised taxation as an insult and a humiliation. Royal revenues accordingly grew at the expense of those least able to resist, and least able to pay. The king had several options. As a feudal lord he could collect rents from his royal domain. He could also levy national taxes on basic food and clothing, such as the *gabelle* or salt tax in France and the *alcabala* or 10 per cent sales tax on commercial transactions in Spain. The king could also levy direct taxes on the peasantry. This he did through agreeable representative assemblies of the privileged classes in which the peasantry did not sit. The French *taille,* which kings independently determined from year to year after the Estates General was suspended in 1484, was such a tax. Sale of public offices and issuance of high-interest government bonds appeared in the fifteenth century as innovative fund-raising devices. But kings did not levy taxes on the powerful nobility. They turned to rich nobles, as they did to the great bankers of Italy and Germany, for loans, bargaining with the privileged classes, who in many instances remained as much the kings' creditors and competitors as their subjects.

France

Charles VII (1422–1461) was a king made great by those who served him. His ministers created a professional army, which—thanks initially to the inspiration of Joan of Arc—drove the English out of France. And largely because of the enterprise of an independent merchant banker named Jacques Coeur, the French also developed a strong economy, diplomatic corps, and national administration during Charles VII's reign. These were the sturdy tools with which Charles' successor, the ruthless Louis XI (1461–1483), made France a great power.

There were two cornerstones of French nation-building in the fifteenth century. The first was the collapse of the English empire in France following the Hundred Years' War. The second was the defeat of Charles the Bold and the duchy of Burgundy. Perhaps Europe's strongest political power in the mid-fifteenth century, Burgundy aspired to dwarf both France and the Holy Roman Empire as the leader of a dominant middle kingdom. It might have succeeded in doing so had not the continental powers joined together in opposition. When Charles the Bold died in defeat in a battle at Nancy in 1477, the dream of Burgundian empire died with him. Louis XI and the Hapsburg Emperor Maximilian I divided the conquered Burgundian lands between them, with the treaty-wise Hapsburgs getting the better part. The dissolution of Burgundy ended its constant intrigue against the French king and left Louis XI free to secure the monarchy. The newly acquired Burgundian lands and his own Angevin inheritance permitted the king to end his reign with a kingdom almost twice the size of that with which he had started. Louis successfully harnessed the nobility, expanded the trade and industry so carefully nurtured by Jacques Coeur, created a national postal system, and even established a lucrative silk industry at Lyons (later transferred to Tours).

A strong nation is a two-edged sword. It was because Louis's successors inherited such a secure and efficient government that France was able to pursue Italian conquests in the 1490s and to fight a long series of losing wars with the Hapsburgs in the first half of the sixteenth century. By the mid-sixteenth century France was again a defeated nation and almost as divided internally as during the Hundred Years' War.

Spain

Spain, too, became a strong country in the late fifteenth century. Both Castile and Aragon had been poorly ruled and divided kingdoms in the mid-fifteenth century. The union of Isabella of Castile (1474–1504) and Ferdinand of Aragon (1479–1516) changed that situation. The two future sovereigns married in 1469, despite strong protests from neighboring Portugal and France, both of which foresaw the formidable European power such a union would create. Castile was by far the richer and more populous of the two, having an estimated five million inhabitants to Aragon's population of under one million. Castile was also distinguished by its lucrative sheep-farming industry, which was run by a government-backed organization called the *Mesta,* another example of developing centralized economic planning. Although the two kingdoms were dynastically united by the marriage of Ferdinand and Isabella in 1469, they remained constitutionally separated, as each retained its respective government agencies—separate laws, armies, coinage, and taxation—and cultural traditions.

Ferdinand and Isabella could do together what neither was able to accomplish alone: subdue their realms, secure their borders, and venture abroad militarily. Between 1482 and 1492 they conquered the Moors in Granada. Naples became a Spanish possession in 1504. By 1512 Ferdinand had secured his northern borders by conquering the kingdom of Navarre. Internally Ferdinand and Isabella won the allegiance of the Hermandad, a powerful league of cities and towns, which served them against stubborn landowners. Townspeople allied themselves with the crown and progressively replaced the nobility within the royal administration. The crown also extended its authority over the wealthy chivalric orders, a further circumscription of the power of the nobility.

Spain had long been remarkable among European lands as a place where three religions—Islam, Judaism, and Christianity—coexisted with a certain degree of toleration. This toleration was to end dramatically under Ferdinand and Isabella, who made Spain the prime example of state-controlled religion. Ferdinand and Isabella exercised almost total control over the Spanish church as they placed religion in the service of national unity. They appointed the higher clergy and the officers of the Inquisition. The Inquisition, run by Tomás de Torquemada (d. 1498), Isabella's confessor, was a key national agency established in 1479 to monitor the activity of converted Jews (*conversos*) and Muslims (*Moriscos*) in Spain. In 1492 the Jews were exiled and their properties were confiscated. In 1502 nonconverting Moors in Granada were driven into exile by Cardinal Francisco Jiménez de

Cisneros (1437–1517), the great spiritual reformer and educator. Spanish spiritual life remained largely uniform and successfully controlled—a major reason for Spain's remaining a loyal Catholic country throughout the sixteenth century and providing a base of operation for the European Counter-Reformation.

Despite a certain internal narrowness, Ferdinand and Isabella were rulers with wide horizons. They contracted anti-French marriage alliances that came to determine a large part of European history in the sixteenth century. In 1496 their eldest daughter, Joanna, later known as "the Mad," married Archduke Philip, the son of Emperor Maximilian I. The fruit of this union, Charles I of Spain, the first ruler over a united Spain, came by his inheritance and election as emperor in 1519 to rule over a European kingdom almost equal in size to that of Charlemagne. A second daughter, Catherine of Aragon, wed Arthur, the son of the English King Henry VII, and after Arthur's premature death, she married his brother, the future King Henry VIII. The failure of this latter marriage became the key factor in the emergence of the Anglican church and the English Reformation.

The new Spanish power was also revealed in Ferdinand and Isabella's promotion of overseas exploration. Their patronage of the Genoese adventurer Christopher Columbus (1451–1506), who discovered the islands of the Caribbean while sailing west in search of a shorter route to the spice markets of the Far East, led to the creation of the Spanish empire in Mexico and Peru, whose gold and silver mines helped to make Spain Europe's dominant power in the sixteenth century.

England

The last half of the fifteenth century was a period of especially difficult political trial for the English. Following the Hundred Years' War, a defeated England was subjected to internal warfare between two rival branches of the royal family, the House of York and the House of Lancaster. This conflict, known to us today as the War of the Roses (as York's symbol, according to legend, was a white rose, and Lancaster's a red rose), kept England in turmoil from 1455 to 1485.

The Lancastrian monarchy of Henry VI (1422–1461) was consistently challenged by the duke of York and his supporters in the prosperous southern towns. In 1461 Edward IV (1461–1483), son of the duke of York, successfully seized power and instituted a strong-arm rule that lasted over twenty years, being only briefly interrupted in 1470–1471 by Henry VI's short-lived restoration. Edward, assisted by loyal and able ministers, effectively bent Parliament to his will. His brother and successor was Richard III (1483–1485). During the reign of the Tudors a tradition arose that painted Richard III as an unprincipled villain who murdered Edward's sons in the Tower of London to secure the throne. The best-known version of this characterization—perhaps unjust according to some—is found in Shakespeare's *Richard III*. Be that as it may, Richard's reign saw the growth of support for the exiled Lancastrian Henry Tudor. Henry returned to England to defeat Richard on Bosworth Field in August 1485.

Henry Tudor ruled as Henry VII (1485–1509), the first of the new Tudor dynasty that would dominate England throughout the sixteenth century. In order to bring the rival royal families together and to make the hereditary claim of his offspring to the throne uncontestable, Henry married Edward IV's daughter, Elizabeth of York. He succeeded in disciplining the English nobility through a special instrument of the royal will known as the *Court of Star Chamber*. Created in 1487 with the sanction of Parliament, this court enabled the king to act quickly and decisively against his opponents. Henry shrewdly construed legal precedents to the advantage of the crown, using English law to further his own ends. He managed to confiscate noble lands and fortunes with such success that he governed without dependence on Parliament for royal funds, always a cornerstone of strong monarchy. In these ways Henry began to shape a monarchy that would develop into one of early modern Europe's most exemplary governments during the reign of his granddaughter, Elizabeth I.

The Holy Roman Empire

Germany and Italy are the striking exceptions to the steady development of centralized nation-states in the last half of the fifteenth century. Unlike France, Spain, and England, the empire saw the many thoroughly repulse the one. In Germany territorial rulers and cities resisted every effort at national consolidation and unity. As in Carolingian times rulers continued to partition their kingdoms, however small, among their sons, and by the late fifteenth century Germany was hopelessly divided into some three hundred autonomous political entities.

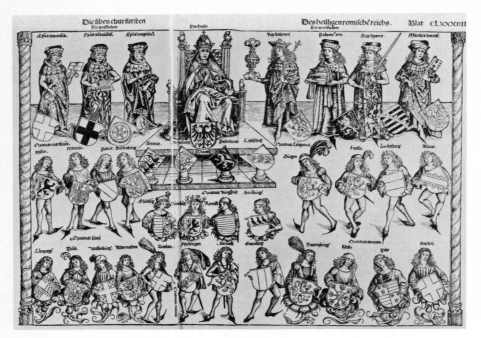

The Holy Roman Emperor is shown here with the seven electors. The three ecclesiastical are to his right and the four secular to his left. Also represented here are the territorial kingdoms or principalities (dukedoms, margraviates, landgraviates, and burgraviates) and the imperial cities. [Konrad Kolbl Reprint Verlag, Grunwald bei Munchen.]

The princes and the cities did work together to create the machinery of law and order, if not of union, within the divided empire. An agreement reached between the emperor and the major German territorial rulers in 1356, known as the *Golden Bull,* established a seven-member electoral college consisting of the archbishops of Mainz, Trier, and Cologne; the duke of Saxony; the margrave of Brandenburg; the count Palatine; and the king of Bohemia. This group also functioned as an administrative body. They elected the emperor and, in cooperation with him, provided what transregional unity and administration existed. The figure of the emperor gave the empire a single ruler in law, if not in actual fact. As the conditions of his rule and the extent of his powers over his subjects, especially the seven electors, were renegotiated with every imperial election, the rights of the many (the princes) were always balanced against the power of the one (the emperor). In the fifteenth century an effort was made to control incessant feuding by the creation of an imperial diet (*Reichstag*). This was a national assembly of the seven electors, the non-electoral princes, and the sixty-five imperial free cities. The cities were the weakest of the three bodies represented at the diet. During such an assembly in Worms in 1495 the members won from the emperor, Maximilian I (1493–1519), concessions

Emperor Maximilian (1493–1519) and his family, painted in 1515 by Bernard Strigel. Note the prominent Hapsburg chin of the middle child. [Kunsthistorisches Museum, Vienna.]

that had been successfully resisted by his predecessor, Frederick III (1440–1493). Led by Berthold of Henneberg, the archbishop of Mainz, the Diet of Worms secured an imperial ban on private warfare, a court of justice (the *Reichskammergericht*) to enforce internal peace, and an imperial Council of Regency (the *Reichsregiment*) to coordinate imperial and internal German policy. The latter was very grudgingly conceded by the emperor because it gave the princes a share in executive power.

Although important, these reforms were still a poor substitute for true national unity. In the sixteenth and seventeenth centuries the territorial princes became virtually sovereign rulers in their various domains. Such disunity aided religious dissent and conflict. It was in the cities and territories of still-feudal, fractionalized, backward Germany that the Protestant Reformation broke out in the sixteenth century.

The Renaissance in Italy (1375–1527)

In his famous study, *Civilization of the Renaissance in Italy* (1860), Jacob Burckhardt described the Renaissance as the prototype of the modern world. He believed that it was in fourteenth- and fifteenth-century Italy, through the revival of ancient learning, that new secular and scientific values first began to supplant traditional religious beliefs. This was the period in which people began to adopt a rational, objective, and statistical approach to reality and to rediscover the importance of the individual and his or her artistic creativity. The result, in Burckhardt's words, was a release of the "full, whole nature of man."

Other scholars have found Burckhardt's description far too modernizing an interpretation of the Renaissance and have accused him of overlooking the continuity between the Middle Ages and the Renaissance. His critics especially stress the still strongly Christian character of Humanism and the fact that earlier "renaissances," especially that of the twelfth century, also revived the ancient classics, professed interest in Latin language and Greek science, and appreciated the worth and creativity of individuals.

Despite the exaggeration and bias of Burckhardt's portrayal of the Renaissance, most scholars agree that the Renaissance was a time of transition from the medieval to the modern world. Medieval Europe, especially before the twelfth century, had been a fragmented feudal society with an agriculturally based economy, and its thought and culture were largely dominated by the church. Renaissance Europe, especially after the fourteenth century, was characterized by growing national consciousness and political centralization, an urban economy based on organized commerce and capitalism, and ever greater lay and secular control of thought and culture, including religion.

It was especially in Italy between the late fourteenth and the early sixteenth centuries, from roughly 1375 to 1527, the year of the infamous sack of Rome by imperial soldiers, that the distinctive features and achievements of the Renaissance, which also deeply influenced northern Europe (see p. 397), are most strikingly revealed.

The home in Bourges of the brilliant French merchant and finance minister, Jacques Coeur (1395–1456), who helped transform France into a strong nation state. Built between 1443 and 1451, it has two false windows above and flanking the entrance that seem to frame insiders looking out. [French Cultural Services, New York.]

The courtyard of the so-called Casa de Pilatos in Seville, Spain, the home of the duke of Medinaceli. It dates from about 1500. [AHM.]

The Italian City-State: Social Conflict and Despotism

Renaissance society was no simple cultural transformation. It first took distinctive shape within the cities of late medieval Italy. Italy had always had a cultural advantage over the rest of Europe because its geography made it the natural gateway between east and west. Venice, Genoa, and Pisa traded uninterruptedly with the Near East throughout the Middle Ages and maintained vibrant urban societies. When commerce revived on a large scale in the eleventh century, Italian merchants quickly mastered the business skills of organization, bookkeeping, scouting new markets, and securing monopolies. During the thirteenth and fourteenth centuries trade-rich cities expanded to become powerful city-states, dominating the political and economic life of the surrounding countryside. By the fifteenth century the great Italian cities had become the bankers of much of Europe.

The growth of Italian cities and urban culture was assisted by the endemic warfare between the emperor and the pope and the Guelf (propapal) and Ghibelline (proimperial) factions that this warfare had created. Either of these might have successfully challenged the cities had they permitted the other to concentrate on it. They chose instead to weaken one another and thus strengthened the

merchant oligarchies of the cities. Unlike northern Europe, where the cities tended to be dominated by kings and territorial princes, the great Italian cities were left free to expand into states. They became independent states, absorbing the surrounding countryside and assimilating area nobility in a unique urban meld of old and new rich. There were five such major, competitive states in Italy: the duchy of Milan; the republics of Florence and

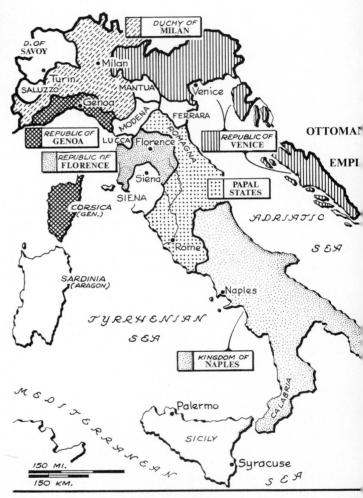

RENAISSANCE ITALY

MAP 13.3   *The city-states of Renaissance Italy were self-contained principalities whose internal strife was monitored by their despots and whose external aggression was long successfully controlled by treaty.*

Venice; the Papal States; and the kingdom of Naples (see Map 13.3).

Social strife and competition for political power were so intense within the cities that, for sheer survival's sake, most evolved into despotisms by the fifteenth century. Venice was the notable exception to this rule. It was ruled by a successful merchant oligarchy with power located in a patrician senate of three hundred members and a ruthless judicial body, the Council of Ten, that anticipated and suppressed rival groups. Elsewhere the new social classes and divisions within society produced by rapid urban growth fueled chronic, near-anarchic conflict.

Florence was the most striking example. There were four distinguishable social groups within the city. The first was the old rich, or *grandi,* the nobles and merchants who traditionally ruled the city. The second group was the emergent new-rich merchant class, capitalists and bankers known as the *popolo grasso,* or "fat people." They began to challenge the old rich for political power in the late thirteenth and early fourteenth centuries. Then there were the middle-burgher ranks of guildmasters, shopkeepers, and professionals, those small businessmen who, in Florence as elsewhere, tended to take the side of the new rich against the conservative policies of the old rich. Finally, there was the omnipresent *popolo minuto,* the poor masses who lived literally from hand to mouth. In 1457 one third of the population of Florence, about thirty thousand people, were officially listed as paupers.

These social divisions produced conflict at every level of society, to which was added the ever-present fear of foreign intrigue. In 1378 feuding between the old and the new rich combined with the social pressures of the Black Death, which cut the city's population almost in half, and with the collapse of the banking houses of Bardi and Peruzzi, to ignite a great revolt by the poor. It was known as the Ciompi Revolt and established a chaotic four-year reign of power by the lower Florentine classes. True stability did not return to Florence until the ascent to power in 1434 of Cosimo de' Medici (1389–1464).

Cosimo de' Medici, the wealthiest Florentine and an astute statesman, controlled the city internally from behind the scenes, skillfully manipulating the constitution and influencing elections. Florence was governed by a council of six (later eight) members known as the *Signoria.* These men were cho-

A terra cotta bust of Lorenzo de' Medici by the sculptor Andrea del Verrocchio (ca. 1435–1488). [National Gallery of Art, Washington; Samuel H. Kress Collection.]

sen from the most powerful guilds—those representing the major clothing industries (cloth, wool, fur, and silk) and such other groups as bankers, judges, and doctors. Through his informal, cordial relations with the electoral committee, Cosimo was able to keep councillors loyal to him in the *Signoria.* As head of the Office of Public Debt, he was able to favor congenial factions. His grandson, Lorenzo the Magnificent (1449–1492), ruled Florence in almost totalitarian fashion during the last quarter of the fifteenth century, having been made cautious by the assassination of his brother in 1478 by a rival Florentine family, the Pazzi, who plotted with the pope against Medici rule.

Despotism was less subtle elsewhere. In order to prevent internal social conflict and foreign intrigue from paralyzing their cities, the dominant groups cooperated to install a hired strongman, known as a *podestá,* for the purpose of maintaining law and order. He was given executive, military, and judicial authority, and his mandate was direct and simple: to permit, by whatever means required, the normal flow of business activity without which not the old rich, the new rich, or the poor of a city could long survive. Because these despots could not depend on the divided populace, they operated through mercenary armies, which they obtained through military brokers known as *condottieri.* It was a hazardous job. Despots were not only subject to dismissal by the oligarchies that hired them, but they were also popular objects of assassination attempts. However, the spoils of success were very great. In Milan it was as despots that the Visconti family came to power in 1278 and the Sforza family in 1450, both ruling without constitutional restraints or serious political competition. The latter produced one of Machiavelli's heroes, Ludovico il Moro.

Political turbulence and warfare gave birth to diplomacy, by which the various city-states were able to stay abreast of foreign military developments and, if shrewd enough, to gain power and advantage short of actually going to war. Most city-states established resident embassies in the fifteenth century, and their ambassadors not only represented them in ceremonies and as negotiators but also became their watchful eyes and ears at rival courts.

Whether within the comparatively tranquil republic of Venice, the strong-arm democracy of Florence, or the undisguised despotism of Milan, the disciplined Italian city proved a most congenial climate for an unprecedented flowering of thought and culture. Italian Renaissance culture was promoted as vigorously by despots as by republicans and by secularized popes as enthusiastically as by the more spiritually minded. This support was related to the fact that the main requirement for patronage of the arts and letters was the one thing that Italian cities of the high Renaissance had in abundance: great wealth.

Humanism

There are several schools of thought on the essence of Humanism. Those who follow the nineteenth-century historian Jacob Burckhardt, who saw the Italian Renaissance as the birth of modernity, view it as an unchristian philosophy that stressed the dignity of humankind and championed individualism and secular values. Others argue that Humanists were the very champions of authentic Catholic Christianity, who opposed the pagan teaching of Aristotle and the ineloquent Scholasticism his writings nurtured. Still others see Humanism as a form of scholarship consciously designed to promote a sense of civic responsibility and political liberty. One of the most authoritative modern commentators, Paul O. Kristeller, has accused all these views of dealing more with the secondary effects than with the essence of Humanism. Humanism, he believes, was no particular philosophy or value system but simply an educational program concentrated on rhetoric and sound scholarship for their own sake.

There is truth in each of these definitions. Humanism was the scholarly study of the Latin and Greek classics and the ancient Church Fathers both for their own sake and in the hope of a rebirth of ancient norms and values. Humanists were advocates of the *studia humanitatis*, a liberal arts program of study that embraced grammar, rhetoric, poetry, history, politics, and moral philosophy. Not only were these subjects considered a joy in themselves, they were also seen as celebrating the dignity of humankind and preparing people for a life of virtuous action. The Florentine Leonardo Bruni (1374–1444) first gave the name *humanitas* ("humanity") to the learning that resulted from such scholarly pursuits. Bruni was a student of Manuel Chrysoloras, a Byzantine scholar who opened the world of Greek scholarship to a generation of young Italian Humanists when he taught at Florence between 1397 and 1403.

The first Humanists were orators and poets. They wrote original literature, in both the classical and the vernacular languages, inspired by and modeled on the newly discovered works of the ancients, and they taught rhetoric within the universities. When Humanists were not employed as teachers of rhetoric, their talents were sought as secretaries, speech writers, and diplomats in princely and papal courts.

The study of classical and Christian antiquity existed before the Italian Renaissance. There were recoveries of ancient civilization during the Carolingian renaissance of the ninth century, within the cathedral school of Chartres in the twelfth century, during the great Aristotelian revival in Paris in the thirteenth century, and among the Augustinians in the early fourteenth century. However, these precedents only partially compare with the grand achievements of the Italian Renaissance of the late Middle Ages. The latter was far more secular and lay-dominated, possessed much broader interests, was blessed with far more recovered manuscripts, and was endowed with far superior technical skills than had been the case in the earlier "rebirths" of antiquity. Unlike their Scholastic rivals, Humanists were less bound to recent tradition; their method was not to summarize and compare the views of recognized authorities on a text or question, but to go directly to the original source itself and draw their own conclusions. Avidly searching out manuscript collections, Italian Humanists made the full sources of Greek and Latin antiquity available to scholars during the fourteenth and fifteenth centuries. Mastery of Latin and Greek was the surgeon's tool of the Humanist. There is a kernel of truth—but only a kernel—in the arrogant boast of the Humanists that the period between themselves and classical civilization was a "dark middle age."

PETRARCH, DANTE, AND BOCCACIO. Francesco Petrarch (1304–1374) was the father of Humanism. He left the legal profession to pursue his love of letters and poetry. Although most of his life was spent in and around Avignon, he became caught up in Cola di Rienzo's popular revolt and two-year reign (1347–1349) in Rome as "tribune" of the Roman people. He also served the Visconti family in Milan in his later years. Petrarch celebrated ancient Rome in his *Letters to the Ancient Dead,* fancied personal letters to Cicero, Livy, Vergil, and Horace. He also wrote a Latin epic poem (*Africa,* a poetic historical tribute to the Roman general Scipio Africanus) and a set of biographies of famous Romans (*Lives of Illustrious Men*). His critical textual studies, elitism, and contempt for the allegedly useless learning of the Scholastics were features many later Humanists also shared. Petrarch's most famous contemporary work was a collection of highly introspective love sonnets to a certain Laura, a married woman whom he romantically admired from a safe distance. Classical and Christian values coexist, not always harmoniously, in his work, and this uneasy coexistence is true, too, of many later Humanists. Medieval Christian values can be seen in Petrarch's imagined dialogues with Saint Augustine and in tracts written to defend the personal immortality of the soul against the Aristotelians. Petrarch was, however, far more secular in orientation than his famous near contemporary Dante Alighieri (1265–1321), whose *Vita Nuova* and *Divine Comedy* form with Petrarch's sonnets the cornerstones of Italian vernacular literature. Petrarch's student and friend Giovanni Boccaccio (1313–1375), author of the *Decameron,* one hundred bawdy tales told by three men and seven women in a country retreat from the plague that ravaged Florence in 1348, was also a pioneer of

❧ Petrarch's Letter to Posterity

In old age Petrarch wrote a highly personal letter to posterity in which he summarized the lessons he had learned during his lifetime. The letter also summarizes the original values of Renaissance Humanists: their suspicion of purely materialistic pleasure, the importance they attached to friendship, and their utter devotion to and love of antiquity.

I have always possessed extreme contempt for wealth; not that riches are not desirable in themselves, but because I hate the anxiety and care which are invariably associated with them . . . I have, on the contrary, led a happier existence with plain living and ordinary fare. . . .

The pleasure of dining with one's friends is so great that nothing has ever given me more delight than their unexpected arrival, nor have I ever willingly sat down to table without a companion. . . .

The greatest kings of this age have loved and courted me. . . . I have fled, however, from many . . . to whom I was greatly attached; and such was my innate longing for liberty that I studiously avoided those whose very name seemed incompatible with the freedom I loved.

I possess a well-balanced rather than a keen intellect—one prone to all kinds of good and wholesome study, but especially to moral philosophy and the art of poetry. The latter I neglected as time went on, and took delight in sacred literature. . . . Among the many subjects that interested me, I dwelt especially upon antiquity, for our own age has always repelled me, so that, had it not been for the love of those dear to me, I should have preferred to have been born in any other period than our own. In order to forget my own time, I have constantly striven to place myself in spirit in other ages, and consequently I delighted in history. . . .

If only I have lived well, it matters little to me how I have talked. Mere elegance of language can produce at best but an empty fame.

Frederic A. Ogg (Ed.), *A Source Book of Mediaeval History* (New York: American Book Company, 1908), pp. 470–473.

Dante Aligheri as seen by his contemporary, Giotto. [*The Granger Collection.*]

The ideal of a useful education and well-rounded people inspired far-reaching reforms in traditional education. Quintilian's *Education of the Orator,* the full text of which was discovered by Poggio Bracciolini (d. 1459) in 1416, became the basic classical guide for the Humanist revision of the traditional curriculum. The most influential Renaissance tract on education, Vergerio's *On the Morals That Befit a Free Man,* was written directly from classical models. Vittorino da Feltre (d. 1446) was a teacher who not only directed his students to a highly disciplined reading of Pliny, Ptolemy, Terence, Plautus, Livy, and Plutarch but also combined vigorous physical exercise and games with intellectual pursuits. Another educator, Guarino da Verona (d. 1460), rector of the new University of Ferrara and a student of the Greek scholar Manuel Chrysoloras, streamlined the study of classical languages and gave it systematic form. Baldassare Castiglione's famous *Book of the Courtier,* written for the cultured nobility at the court of Urbino, also embodied the highest ideals of Italian Humanism. It stressed the importance of integrating knowledge of language and history with athletic, military, and musical skills, as well as good manners and moral character.

Humanists were not bashful scholars. They delighted in going directly to primary sources. They

Humanist studies. An avid collector of manuscripts, Boccaccio also assembled an encyclopedia of Greek and Roman mythology.

EDUCATIONAL REFORMS AND GOALS. The goal of Humanist studies was to be wise and to speak eloquently, both to know what is good and to practice virtue. Learning was not to remain abstract and unpracticed. "It is better to will the good than to know the truth," Petrarch had taught, and this became a motto of many later Humanists. Pietro Paolo Vergerio (1349–1420) left a classic summary of the Humanist concept of a liberal education:

We call those studies liberal which are worthy of a free man; those studies by which we attain and practice virtue and wisdom; that education which calls forth, trains, and develops those highest gifts of body and mind which ennoble men and which are rightly judged to rank next in dignity to virtue only, for to a vulgar temper, gain and pleasure are the one aim of existence, to a lofty nature, moral worth and fame.[1]

[1] Cited by De Lamar Jensen, *Renaissance Europe: Age of Recovery and Reconciliation* (Lexington, Mass.; D. C. Heath, 1981), p. 111.

OPPOSITE: *The developing knowledge of human anatomy and physiology.*

A: *Medieval conception of the human body, from a manuscript of about 1292, depicting the venous system and what purport to be a few internal organs. Since post-mortems were forbidden, medieval renderings of the human body were based on a combination of speculation and animal dissection.* [*The Bodleian Library, Oxford.*]

B: *A chart showing the points of blood-letting, long an accepted medical practice. From the* Guidebook of the Barber Surgeons of York *(fifteenth century), now in the British Museum.* [*Egerton MS. 2572, f. 50. Reproduced by permission of the British Library Board.*]

C: *Leonardo da Vinci's drawings of the human fetus. Renaissance artists and scientists, in contrast to medieval artists, began to base their portrayal of the human body on the actual study of it.* [*Bettmann Archive.*]

D: *A woodcut illustration by John of Carcar from* De Humanis corporis fabrica (Structure of the Human body) *(Basel, 1543), by the great Flemish anatomist, Andreas Vesalius (1514–1564), the foundation work of modern knowledge of human anatomy.* [*Bettmann Archive.*]

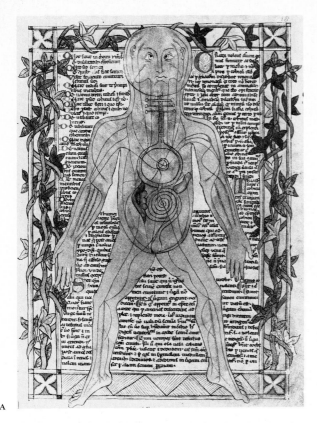

A

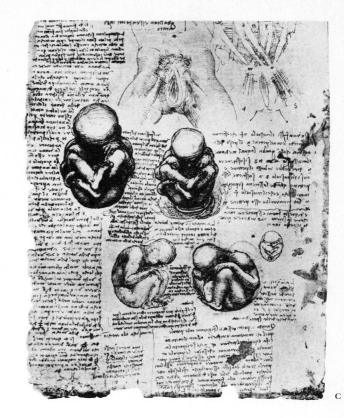

C

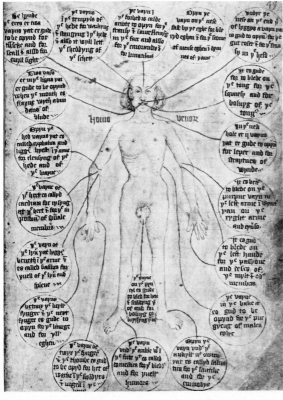

B

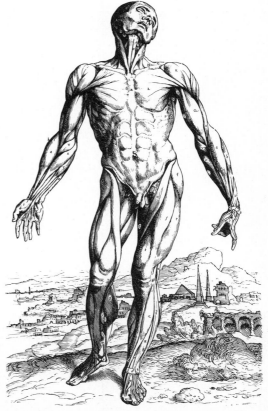

D

refused to be slaves of tradition, satisfied, as they felt their Scholastic rivals to be, with the commentaries of the accepted masters. Such an attitude made Humanists not only innovative educators but also restless manuscript hunters, ever in search of new sources of information. Poggio Bracciolini and Francesco Filelfo (d. 1481) assembled magnificent manuscript collections.

THE FLORENTINE ACADEMY AND THE REVIVAL OF PLATONISM. Of all the important recoveries of the past made during the Italian Renaissance none stands out more than the revival of Greek studies, especially the works of Plato, in fifteenth-century Florence. Many factors combined to bring this revival about. An important foundation was laid in 1397 when the city invited Manuel Chrysoloras to come from Constantinople and promote Greek learning. A half-century later (1439) the ecumenical Council of Ferrara–Florence, having convened to negotiate the reunion of the eastern and western churches, opened the door for many Greek schol-

ars and manuscripts to enter the west. After the fall of Constantinople to the Turks in 1453, Greek scholars fled to Florence for refuge. This was the background against which the Florentine Platonic Academy evolved under the patronage of Cosimo de' Medici and the supervision of Marsilio Ficino (1433–1499) and Pico della Mirandola (1463–1494).

Although the thinkers of the Renaissance were interested in every variety of ancient wisdom, they seemed to be especially attracted to the Platonic tradition and those Church Fathers who tried to synthesize Platonic philosophy and Christian teaching. The Florentine Academy, a small villa designed for comfortable discussion, became both a cultic and a scholarly center for the revival of Plato and the Neoplatonists: Plotinus, Proclus, Porphyry, and Dionysius the Areopagite. There Ficino edited and saw to the publication of the complete works of Plato.

The appeal of Platonism lay in its flattering view

❧ Pico della Mirandola States the Renaissance Image of Man

One of the most eloquent descriptions of the Renaissance image of mankind comes from the Italian Humanist Pico della Mirandola (1463–1494). In his famed *Oration on the Dignity of Man* (ca. 1486) Pico described humans as free to become whatever they choose.

The best of artisans [God] ordained that that creature (man) to whom He had been able to give nothing proper to himself should have joint possession of whatever had been peculiar to each of the different kinds of being. He therefore took man as a creature of indeterminate nature and, assigning him a place in the middle of the world, addressed him thus: "Neither a fixed abode nor a form that is thine alone nor any function peculiar to thyself have we given thee, Adam, to the end that according to thy longing and according to thy judgment thou mayest have and possess what abode, what form, and what functions thou thyself shalt desire. The nature of all other beings is limited and constrained within the bounds of laws prescribed by Us. Thou, constrained by no limits, in accordance with thine own free will,

in whose hand We have placed thee, shall ordain for thyself the limits of thy nature. We have set thee at the world's center that thou mayest from thence more easily observe whatever is in the world. We have made thee neither of heaven nor of earth, neither mortal nor immortal, so that with freedom of choice and with honor, as though the maker and molder of thyself, thou mayest fashion thyself in whatever shape thou shalt prefer. Thou shalt have the power to degenerate into the lower forms of life, which are brutish. Thou shalt have the power, out of thy soul's judgment, to be reborn into the higher forms, which are divine." O supreme generosity of God the Father, O highest and most marvelous felicity of man! To him it is granted to have whatever he chooses, to be whatever he wills.

Giovanni Pico della Mirandola, *Oration on the Dignity of Man*, in *The Renaissance Philosophy of Man*, ed. by E. Cassirer et al. (Chicago: Phoenix Books, 1961), pp. 224–225.

of human nature. Platonism distinguished between an eternal sphere of being and the perishable world in which humans actually lived. Human reason was believed to belong to the former, indeed, to have preexisted in this pristine world and to continue to commune with it, as the present knowledge of mathematical and moral truth bore witness. Strong Platonic influence can be seen in Pico's *Oration on the Dignity of Man,* perhaps the most famous Renaissance statement on the nature of humankind. Pico wrote the *Oration* as an introduction to a pretentious collection of nine hundred theses, which were published in Rome in December 1486 and were intended to serve as the basis for a public debate on all of life's important topics. The *Oration* drew on Platonic teaching to depict man as the one creature in the world who possessed the freedom to be whatever he chose, able at will to rise to the height of angels or to descend to the level of pigs.

CRITICAL WORK OF THE HUMANISTS: LORENZO VALLA. Because they were guided by a scholarly ideal of philological accuracy and historical truthfulness, the Humanists could become critics of tradition even when that was not their intention. Dispassionate critical scholarship shook long-standing foundations, not the least of which were those of the medieval church.

The work of Lorenzo Valla (1406–1457), author of the standard Renaissance text on Latin philology, the *Elegances of the Latin Language* (1444), reveals the explosive character of the new learning. Although a good Catholic, Valla became a hero to later Protestants. His popularity among Protestants stemmed from his defense of predestination against the advocates of free will and especially from his exposé of the Donation of Constantine, a fraudulent document written in the eighth century alleging that the Emperor Constantine had given vast territories to the pope. The exposé of the Donation was not intended by Valla to have the devastating force that Protestants attributed to it. He only demonstrated in a careful, scholarly way what others had long suspected. Using the most rudimentary textual analysis and historical logic, Valla proved that the document was filled with such anachronistic terms as *fief* and made references that were meaningless in the fourth century. In the same dispassionate way Valla also pointed out errors in the Latin Vulgate, still the authorized version of the Bible for the Roman Catholic church.

Such discoveries did not make Valla any less loyal to the church, nor did they prevent his faithful fulfillment of the office of Apostolic Secretary in Rome under Pope Nicholas V. Nonetheless, historical criticism of this type served those less loyal to the medieval church, and it was no accident that young Humanists formed the first identifiable group of Martin Luther's supporters.

CIVIC HUMANISM. Italian Humanists were exponents of applied knowledge; their basic criticism of traditional education was that much of its learning was useless. Education, they believed, should promote individual virtue and public service. This ideal inspired what has been called *civic Humanism,* by which is meant examples of Humanist leadership of the political and cultural life, the most striking instance of which was to be found in the city of Florence. There three Humanists served as chancellors: Colluccio Salutati (1331–1406), Leonardo Bruni (ca. 1370–1444), and Poggio Braccolini (1380–1459). Each used his rhetorical skills to rally the Florentines against the aggression of Naples and Milan. Bruni and Poggio also wrote adulatory histories of the city. Another accomplished Humanist scholar, Leon Battista Alberti (1402–1472), was a noted architect and builder in the city.

On the other hand, many Humanists became clubbish and snobbish, an intellectual elite concerned only with pursuing narrow, antiquarian interests and writing pure, classical Latin in the quiet of their studies. It was in reaction against this elitist trend that the Humanist historians Niccolò Machiavelli and Francesco Guicciardini adopted the vernacular and made contemporary history their primary source and subject matter.

Renaissance Art

In Renaissance Italy, as in Reformation Europe, the values and interests of the laity were no longer subordinated to those of the clergy. In education, culture, and religion the laity assumed a leading role and established models for the clergy to imitate. This was a development due in part to the church's loss of its international power during the great crises of the late Middle Ages. But it was also encouraged by the rise of national sentiment, the creation of competent national bureaucracies staffed by laymen rather than clerics, and the rapid growth of lay education during the fourteenth and fifteenth centuries. Medieval Christian values were

The town hall of Antwerp, Belgium, built between 1561 and 1565. Here, Gothic has given way to Renaissance styling, with high belfries and elaborate carvings. On the right are guild halls. [Belgian National Tourist Office, New York.]

Madonna and Child, by Giotto. Giotto was the first artist to bring naturalism and realism to the depiction of religious and spiritual subjects. [National Gallery of Art, Washington, D.C., Samuel H. Kress Collection.]

adjusting to a more this-worldly spirit. Men and women began again to appreciate and even glorify the secular world, secular learning, and purely human pursuits as ends in themselves.

This new perspective on life is very prominent in the painting and sculpture of the high Renaissance, the late fifteenth and early sixteenth centuries, when Renaissance art reached its full maturity. In imitation of Greek and Roman art, painters and sculptors attempted to create harmonious, symmetrical, and properly proportioned figures and to portray the human form with a glorified realism. Whereas Byzantine and Gothic art had been religious and idealized in the extreme, Renaissance art, especially in the fifteenth century, became a realistic reproduction of nature. The new direction was signaled by Giotto (1266–1336), the father of Renaissance painting. An admirer of Saint Francis of Assisi, whose love of nature he shared, Giotto painted a more natural world than his Byzantine and Gothic predecessors. Though still filled with religious seriousness, his work was no longer quite so abstract and unnatural a depiction of the world.

Renaissance artists had the considerable advantage of new technical skills developed during the fifteenth century. In addition to the availability of oil paints, the techniques of using shading to enhance realism (*chiaroscuro*) and adjusting the size of figures so as to give the viewer a feeling of continuity with the painting (linear perspective) were per-

374

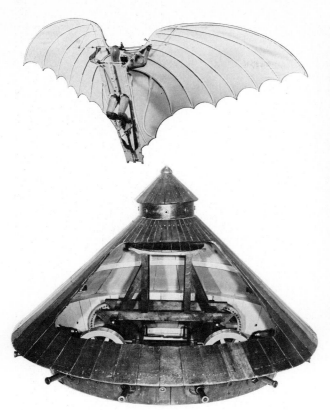

Leonardo da Vinci's portrait of Ginevra de' Benci, an Italian noblewoman. The psychological acuity of Leonardo's portraits results in part from his technique. Leonardo was the first Italian to paint in oils, a medium that had been developed earlier in Northern Europe. Oils allow the artist to take more time and care and to produce colors that are more permanent and translucent. Leonardo was also the first to use light and shade effectively to bring a figure into the foreground of a painting. [National Gallery of Art, Washington, D.C., Alisa Mellon Bruce Fund.]

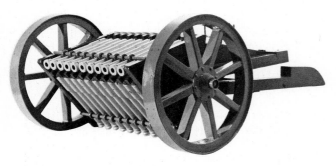

Models of some of Leonardo da Vinci's military inventions, which were creative but sometimes beyond the capacity of late fifteenth century technology. [International Business Machines.]

TOP: *A flying machine based on the principle of flight by birdlike flapping of flexible wings. The aviator worked the wings by pulleys connected with stirrups moved by his feet.*

MIDDLE: *An armored tank, equipped with breech-loading cannons and maneuverable from the inside.*

BELOW: *A triple-tier machine gun, with eleven barrels in each tier. While one is being fired, the tier just fired is cooling, and the third one is being loaded.*

fected. Compared with their flat Byzantine and Gothic counterparts, Renaissance paintings were filled with energy and life and stood out from the canvas in three dimensions.

Masaccio (1401–1428) carried Giotto's naturalism to a new maturity. His painting was almost a direct slice of life. What Masaccio was to painting, Donatello (1386–1466) was to sculpture. His famous equestrian statue of the Venetian *condottiere* Gattamelata seems to pulsate with life. The realism of Masaccio and Donatello was the point of departure for the greatest masters of the high Renaissance: Leonardo da Vinci (1452–1519), Raphael (1483–1520), and Michelangelo Buonarroti (1475–1564).

LEONARDO DA VINCI. More than any other person in the period Leonardo exhibited the Ren-

❧ A Contemporary Description of Leonardo

Giorgio Vasari (1512–1574), friend and biographer of the great Renaissance painters, sculptors, and architects, described Leonardo's versatility as actually a handicap, as it prevented him from dwelling on one pursuit sufficiently.

The richest gifts are occasionally seen to be showered, as by celestial influence, upon certain human beings; nay, they sometimes supernaturally and marvelously gather in a single person—beauty, grace, and talent united in such a manner that to whatever the man thus favored may turn himself, his every action is so divine as to leave all other men far behind. . . . This was . . . the case of Leonardo da Vinci . . . who had . . . so rare a gift of talent and ability that to whatever subject he turned his attention . . . he presently made himself absolute master of it. . . .

He would without doubt have made great progress in the learning and knowledge of the sciences had he not been so versatile and changeful. The instability of his character led him to undertake many things, which, having commenced, he afterwards abandoned. In arithmetic, for example, he made such rapid progress in the short time he gave his attention to it, that he often confounded the master who was teaching him. . . . He also commenced the study of music and resolved to acquire the art of playing the lute . . . singing to the instrument most divinely. . . .

Being also an excellent geometrician, Leonardo not only worked in sculpture but also in architecture; likewise he prepared . . . designs for . . . entire buildings. . . . While only a youth, he first suggested the formation of a canal from Pisa to Florence by means of certain changes . . . in the river Arno. He made designs for mills, fulling machines, and other engines run by water. But as he had resolved to make painting his profession, he gave the greater part of his time to drawing from nature.

James Harvey Robinson (Ed.), *Readings in European History,* Vol. 1 (Boston: Athenaeum, 1904), pp. 535–536.

aissance ideal of the universal person, one who is not only a jack-of-all-trades but also a true master of many. One of the greatest painters of all time, Leonardo was also a military engineer for Ludovico il Moro in Milan, Cesare Borgia in Romagna, and the French king Francis I. Leonardo advocated scientific experimentation, dissected corpses to learn anatomy, and was an accomplished, self-taught botanist. His inventive mind foresaw such modern machines as airplanes and submarines. Indeed, the

❧ Vasari Describes the Magic of Raphael's Personality

There was among his many extraordinary gifts one of such value and importance that I can never sufficiently admire it and always think thereof with astonishment. This was the power accorded him by heaven of bringing all who approached his presence into harmony, an effect . . . contrary to the nature of our artists. Yet all . . . became as of one mind once they began to labor in the society of Raphael, and they continued in such unity and concord that all harsh feelings and evil dispositions became subdued and disappeared at the sight of him. . . . This happened because all were surpassed by him in friendly courtesy as well as in art. All confessed the influence of his sweet and gracious nature. . . . Not only was he honored by men, but even by the very animals who would constantly follow his steps and always loved him.

James Harvey Robinson (Ed.), *Readings in European History,* Vol. 1 (Boston: Athenaeum, 1904), pp. 536–537.

The School of Athens, fresco by Raphael in the Vatican in Rome, painted ca. 1510–1511. The symmetry and organic unity of the painting, as well as its theme of antiquity, make it one of the most telling examples of Renaissance classicism. [Bettmann Archive.]

variety of his interests was so great that it tended to shorten his attention span, so that he was constantly moving from one activity to another. His great skill in conveying inner moods through complex facial features can be seen in the most famous of his his paintings, the *Mona Lisa,* as well as in his self-portrait.

RAPHAEL. Raphael, an unusually sensitive man whose artistic career was cut short by his premature death at thirty-seven, was apparently loved by contemporaries as much for his person as for his work. He is famous for his tender madonnas, the best known of which graces the monastery of San Sisto in Piacenza. Art historians praise his fresco, *The School of Athens,* an involved portrayal of the

St. George and the Dragon, by Raphael. Although painted when the arist was only twenty-two or twenty-three, the painting clearly reveals his serenity and his seemingly effortless mastery of his art. [National Gallery of Art, Washington, D.C., Andrew W. Mellon Collection.]

❧ Michelangelo's Inability Ever to Be Satisfied with His Work

According to Vasari, Michelangelo was such an extreme perfectionist that he found fault in everything he did and frequently abandoned his sculptures and paintings before they were completed.

Michelangelo worked . . . almost every day at a group of four figures [in St. Peter's in Rome], but he broke up the block at last, either because it was found to have numerous veins, or was excessively hard and caused the chisel to strike fire, or because his judgment was so severe that he could never content himself with anything that he did. . . . Few of the works undertaken in his manhood were ever entirely completed, those finished being the productions of his youth. . . . He would himself often remark that if he were really permitted to satisfy himself in the works [he was commissioned] to produce, he would give lit-tle or nothing of it to public view. And the reason for this is obvious. He had advanced to such an extent of knowledge in art that the very slightest error could not exist in any figure without his immediate discovery; and having found such after the work had been given to view, he would never attempt to correct it, but would commence some other production, believing that a like failure would not happen again. This was, as he often declared, the reason why the number of pictures and statues finished by his hand was so small.

James Harvey Robinson (Ed.), *Readings in European History*, Vol. 1 (Boston: Athenaeum, 1904), pp. 540–541.

great masters of Western philosophy, as one of the most perfect examples of Renaissance artistic theory and technique. It depicts Plato and Aristotle surrounded by the great philosophers and scientists of antiquity, who are portrayed with features of Raphael's famous contemporaries, including Leonardo and Michelangelo.

MICHELANGELO. The melancholy genius Michelangelo also excelled in a variety of arts and crafts. His eighteen-foot godlike sculpture *David*, which long stood majestically in the great square of Florence, is a perfect example of the Renaissance artist's devotion to harmony, symmetry, and proportion, as well as his extreme glorification of the human form. Four different popes commissioned works by Michelangelo, the most famous of which are the frescoes for the Sistine Chapel, painted during the pontificate of Pope Julius II (1503–1513), who also set Michelangelo to work on his own magnificent tomb. The Sistine frescoes originally covered 10,000 square feet and involved 343 figures, over half of which exceeded 10 feet in height. This labor of love and piety, painted while Michelangelo was lying on his back or stooping, took four years to complete and left Michelangelo partially crippled. A man of incredible energy and endurance who lived to be ninety, Michelangelo insisted on doing almost everything himself and permitted his assistants only a few of the many chores involved.

His later works are more complex and suggest deep personal changes within the artist himself. They mark, artistically and philosophically, the passing of high Renaissance painting and the advent of a new, experimental style known as *mannerism*, which reached its peak in the late sixteenth and early seventeenth centuries. A reaction against the simplicity and symmetry of high Renaissance art, which also found expression in music and literature, mannerism made room for the strange and even the abnormal and gave freer reign to the subjectivity of the artist. It derived its name from the fact that it permitted the artist to express his own individual perceptions and feelings, to paint, compose, or write in a "mannered" or "affected" way. Tintoretto (d. 1594) and especially El Greco (d. 1614) became its supreme representatives.

David, by Michelangelo. One of the most famous—and popular—of all the world's sculptures, it was made in the period 1501–1504 and now stands in the Galleria dell' Accademia in Florence. [Alinari/SCALA.]

Moses, by Michelangelo. This statue was planned as part of the tomb of Pope Julius II (1503–1513) but is now in the church of S. Pietro in Vincoli, Rome. [Bettmann Archive.]

The Feast of the Gods, by the Venetian painter Giovanni Bellini (1430–1516). The classical gods are portrayed in the guise of ordinary people. The scene is taken from a tale of the Roman poet Ovid about the annual sacrifice that the Romans offered to Priapus, the male god of fertility. A remarkable feature of this painting is that the landscape in the background was repainted by another Venetian painter, Titian, to make the picture harmonize with others in the collection of the Duke of Ferrara. [National Gallery of Art, Washington, D.C., Widener Collection.]

Portrait of a Venetian Gentleman, by Giovanni Bellini. Both Bellini's father, Jacobo, and his brother, Gentile, were also famous painters. Although the Renaissance came later to Venice than to other Italian cities, there were a number of great Venetian Renaissance painters. Venetian Renaissance painting is noted for its remarkable use of color which seems to reflect the city's centuries-long connection with the Byzantine East. [National Gallery of Art, Washington, D.C., Samuel H. Kress Collection.]

The Adoration of the Magi, by Sandro Botticelli (1444–1510). Botticelli was one of the favorite artists of the Medici rulers of Florence. His paintings, which combined Christian and pagan themes, reflect the glittering elegance on display in Renaissance Florence. [National Gallery of Art, Washington, D.C., Andrew W. Mellon Collection.]

Venus with a Mirror, by Titian (1477–1576). Titian's paintings convey the richness, flamboyance, and sensuality of life in Venice at the height of the city's power. [National Gallery of Art, Washington, D.C., Andrew W. Mellon Collection.]

St. John in the Desert, by Domenico Veneziano (1420–1461). Venetian by birth, Veneziano moved to Florence in 1439, where he was much influenced by the sculptor Donatello. His depiction of St. John as a nude youth may reflect the influence of Donatello's similar treatment of David in a famous bronze cast in 1432. [National Gallery of Art, Washington, D.C., Samuel H. Kress Collection.]

Christ at the Sea of Galilee, by Tintoretto (1518–1594), Venetian school. An example of Mannerist painting, which broke with classical symmetry and subordinated form to need and imagination. [National Gallery of Art, Washington; Samuel H. Kress Collection.]

Self-portrait (1498), by Albrecht Dürer (1471–1528). Renaissance appreciation of individuality and subjectivity is openly revealed in the self-portraits of the period. [Museo del Prado, Madrid.]

The Baptism of Christ, by El Greco (ca. 1541–1614). Elongated figures and somber religious mood mark his work. [Museo del Prado, Madrid.]

Italy's Political Decline: The French Invasions (1494-1527)

The Treaty of Lodi

As a land of autonomous city-states, Italy's peace and safety from foreign invasion, especially from invasion by the Turks, had always depended on internal cooperation. Such cooperation had been maintained during the last half of the fifteenth century, thanks to a carefully constructed political alliance known as the Treaty of Lodi (1454–1455). The terms of the treaty brought Milan and Naples, long traditional enemies, into alliance with Florence. These three stood together for decades against Venice, which was frequently joined by the Papal States to create an internal balance of power that also made possible a unified front against external enemies.

Around 1490, following the rise to power of the Milanese despot Ludovico il Moro, hostilities between Milan and Naples resumed. The peace made possible by the Treaty of Lodi ended in 1494 when Naples, supported by Florence and the Borgia Pope Alexander VI (1492–1503), prepared to attack Milan. Ludovico made what proved to be a fatal response to these new political alignments: he appealed for aid to the French. French kings had ruled Naples from 1266 to 1435, before they were driven out by Duke Alfonso of Sicily. Breaking a wise Italian rule, Ludovico invited the French to reenter Italy and revive their dynastic claim to Naples. In his haste to check his rival, Naples, Ludovico did not recognize sufficiently that France also had dynastic claims to Milan, nor did he foresee how insatiable the French appetite for Italian territory would become once French armies had crossed the Alps.

Charles VIII's March Through Italy

The French king, Louis XI, had resisted the temptation to invade Italy, while nonetheless keeping French dynastic claims in Italy alive. His successor, Charles VIII (1483–1498), an eager youth in his twenties, responded to Ludovico's call with lightning speed. Within five months he had crossed the Alps (August 1495) and raced as conqueror through Florence and the Papal States into Naples.

As Charles approached Florence, the Florentine ruler, Piero de' Medici, who had allied with Naples against Milan, tried to placate the French king by handing over Pisa and other Florentine possessions. Such appeasement only brought about Piero's forced exile by a population that was revolutionized at this time by the radical preacher Girolamo Savonarola (1452–1498). Savonarola convinced a majority of the fearful Florentines that the French king's advent was a long-delayed and fully justified divine vengeance on their immorality.

Charles entered Florence without resistance and, thanks to Savonarola's flattery and the payment of a large ransom, spared the city a threatened destruction. Savonarola continued to rule Florence for four years after Charles's departure. The Florentines proved, however, not to be the stuff theocracies are made of. Savonarola's puritanism and antipapal policies made it impossible for him to survive indefinitely. This was especially true after the Italian cities reunited and the ouster of the French invader, whom Savonarola had praised as a godsend, became national policy. Savonarola was imprisoned and executed in May 1498.

Charles's lightning march through Italy also struck terror in non-Italian hearts. Ferdinand of Aragon, whose native land and self-interests as king of Sicily now became vulnerable to a French–Italian axis, took the initiative to create a counteralliance: the League of Venice, formed in March 1495, with Venice, the Papal States, and the Emperor Maximilian I joining Ferdinand against the French. The stage was set for a conflict between France and Spain that would not end until 1559.

Ludovico il Moro meanwhile recognized that he had sown the wind; having desired a French invasion only so long as it weakened his enemies, he now saw Milan threatened by the whirlwind of events he had himself created. In reaction he joined the League of Venice, and this alliance was able to send Charles into retreat by May. Charles remained thereafter on the defensive until his death in April 1498.

Pope Alexander VI and the Borgia Family

The French returned to Italy under Charles's successor, Louis XII (1498–1515), this time assisted by a new Italian ally, the Borgia pope, Alexander VI (1492–1503). Alexander, probably the most corrupt pope who ever sat on the papal throne, openly promoted the political careers of the children he had had before he became pope, Cesare and Lucrezia, as he placed the efforts of the powerful Borgia family to secure a political base in Romagna in tandem with papal policy there.

In Romagna several principalities had fallen away from the church during the Avignon papacy, and Venice, the pope's ally within the League of Venice, continued to contest the Papal States for their loyalty. Seeing that a French alliance could give him the opportunity to reestablish control over the region, Alexander took steps to secure French favor. He annulled Louis XII's marriage to Charles VIII's sister so that Louis could marry Charles's widow, Anne of Brittany—a popular political move designed to keep Brittany French. The pope also bestowed a cardinal's hat on the archbishop of Rouen, Louis's favorite cleric. But most importantly, Alexander agreed to abandon the League of Venice, a withdrawal of support that made the league too weak to resist a French reconquest of Milan. In exchange, Cesare Borgia received the sister of the king of Navarre, Charlotte d'Albret, in marriage, a union that greatly enhanced Borgia military strength. Cesare also received land grants from Louis XII and the promise of French military aid in Romagna.

All in all it was a scandalous tradeoff, but one that made it possible for both the French king and the pope to realize their ambitions within Italy. Louis successfully invaded Milan in August 1499. Ludovico il Moro, who had originally opened the Pandora's box of French invasion, spent his last years languishing in a French prison. In 1500 Louis and Ferdinand of Aragon divided Naples between them, while the pope and Cesare Borgia conquered the cities of Romagna without opposition. Alexander awarded his victorious son the title "duke of Romagna."

Pope Julius II

Cardinal Giuliano della Rovere, a strong opponent of the Borgia family, became Pope Julius II (1503–1513). He suppressed the Borgias and placed their newly conquered lands in Romagna under papal jurisdiction. Julius came to be known as the "warrior pope" because he brought the Renaissance papacy to a peak of military prowess and diplomatic intrigue. Shocked as were other contemporaries by this thoroughly secular papacy, the Humanist Erasmus (1466?–1536), who had witnessed in disbelief a bullfight in the papal palace during a visit to Rome, wrote a popular anony-

mous satire entitled *Julius Excluded from Heaven.* This humorous account purported to describe the pope's unsuccessful efforts to convince Saint Peter that he was worthy of admission to heaven.

Assisted by his powerful allies, Pope Julius succeeded in driving the Venetians out of Romagna in 1509, thereby ending Venetian claims in the region and fully securing the Papal States. Having realized this longsought papal goal, Julius turned to the second major undertaking of his pontificate: ridding Italy of his former ally, the French invader. Julius, Ferdinand of Aragon, and Venice formed a second Holy League in October 1511, and within a short period Emperor Maximilian I and the Swiss joined them. By 1512 the league had the French in full retreat, and they were soundly defeated by the Swiss in 1513 at Novara.

The French were nothing if not persistent. They invaded Italy still a third time under Louis's successor, Francis I (1515–1547). French armies massacred Swiss soldiers of the Holy League at Marignano in September 1515, revenging the earlier defeat at Novara. The victory won from the pope the Concordat of Bologna in August 1516, an agreement that gave the French king control over the French clergy in exchange for French recognition of the pope's superiority over church councils and his right to collect annates in France. This was an important compromise that helped keep France Catholic after the outbreak of the Protestant Reformation. But the new French entry into Italy also led to the first of four major wars with Spain in the first half of the sixteenth century: the Hapsburg–Valois wars, none of which France won.

Niccolò Machiavelli

The period of foreign invasions made a shambles of Italy. The same period that saw Italy's cultural peak in the work of Leonardo, Raphael, and Michelangelo also witnessed Italy's political tragedy. One who watched as French, Spanish, and German armies wreaked havoc on his country was Niccolò Machiavelli (1469–1527). The more he saw, the more convinced he became that Italian political unity and independence were ends that justified any means. A Humanist and a careful student of ancient Rome, Machiavelli was impressed by the deliberate and heroic acts of ancient Roman rulers, what Renaissance people called *Virtù.* Stories of the unbounded patriotism and self-sacrifice of the old Roman citizenry were his favorites, and he lamented the absence of such traits among

A bust of Niccolò Machiavelli (1469–1527), who advised Renaissance princes to practice artful deception if necessary and to inspire fear in their subjects if they wished to be successful. [Bettmann Archive.]

MAJOR POLITICAL EVENTS OF THE ITALIAN RENAISSANCE (1375–1527)	
1378–1382	The Ciompi Revolt in Florence
1434	Medici rule in Florence established by Cosimo de Medici
1454–1455	Treaty of Lodi allies Milan, Naples, and Florence (in effect until 1494)
1494	Charles VIII of France invades Italy.
1494–1498	Savonarola controls Florence
1495	League of Venice unites Venice, Milan, the Papal States, the Holy Roman Empire, and Spain against France.
1499	Louis XII invades Milan (the second French invasion of Italy)
1500	The Borgias conquer Romagna
1512–1513	The Holy League (Pope Julius II, Ferdinand of Aragon, Emperor Maximilian, and Venice) defeat the French
1513	Machiavelli writes *The Prince*
1515	Francis I leads the third French invasion of Italy
1516	Concordat of Bologna between France and the papacy
1527	Sack of Rome by imperial soldiers

his compatriots. Machiavelli's romanticization of the ancient Romans caused his interpretation of both ancient and contemporary history to be somewhat exaggerated. His Florentine contemporary, Guicciardini, who was a more sober historian and was less given to idealizing antiquity, wrote truer chronicles of Florentine and Italian history.

❧ Machiavelli Discusses the Most Important Trait for a Ruler

Machiavelli believed that the most important personality trait of a successful ruler was the ability to instill fear in his subjects.

Here the question arises; whether it is better to be loved than feared or feared than loved. The answer is that it would be desirable to be both but, since that is difficult, it is much safer to be feared than to be loved, if one must choose. For on men in general this observation may be made: they are ungrateful, fickle, and deceitful, eager to avoid dangers, and avid for gain, and while you are useful to them they are all with you, offering you their blood, their property, their lives, and their sons so long as danger is remote, as we noted above, but when it approaches they turn on you. Any prince, trusting only in their words and having no other preparations made, will fall to his ruin, for friendships that are bought at a price and not by greatness and nobility of soul are paid for indeed, but they are not owned and cannot be called upon in time of need. Men have less hesitation in offending a man who is loved than one who is feared, for love is held by a bond of obligation which, as men are wicked, is broken whenever personal advantage suggests it, but fear is accompanied by the dread of punishment which never relaxes.

Niccolò Machiavelli, *The Prince* (1513), trans. and ed. by Thomas G. Bergin (New York: Appleton-Century-Crofts, 1947), p. 48.

Scenes from Northern Urban Life.

Children's Games, by Pieter Brueghel, painted in 1560. Seventy-eight different games are here depicted. [Kunsthistorisches Museum, Vienna.]

A Family at Table by Georg Pencz. Detailed instructions in table manners accompanied this drawing. Some examples: wash hands and cut nails before eating; don't forget to say the blessing; don't cut your bread on your chest; take small bites and close your mouth when chewing; avoid eating like a pig; don't lick your lips like a dog; don't poke the person next to you with your elbows. [From Max Geisberg, The German Single-Leaf Woodcut, 1500–1550, *edited by Walter L. Strauss. Hacker Art Books, 1974. Used by permission of Hacker Art Books.]*

Junckfraw jr folt euch wol gehaben
Gott hat euch reichlich thun begaben
Mit eim solchen erlichen gfellen
Als jr in wünschen möcht vnd wellen
Darumb halt in werdt freundtlich vnd schon
So gündt euch Gott des himels thron.

Ja Praut ich mag mit warhait jehen
Seins gleichen hab ich nye gesehen
Zu schimpff vnd scherz ist er ein man
Darumb seit jm recht vnterthan
Wie dann Gott selbe gebotten hat
So erlange jr glück vnd Gottes gnat.

A Wedding Procession, by Georg Pencz. Here a bride is led by two escorts to the altar. As they walk they instruct her to be friendly and obedient to her future husband, whom they describe as an exceptionally good catch. [From Max Geisberg, The German Single-Leaf Woodcut, 1500–1550, *edited by Walter L. Strauss. Hacker Art Books, 1974. Used by permission of Hacker Art Books.]*

The Legend of Saint Eligius and Godeberta, by the Flemish painter Petrus Christus (ca. 1420–1473), painted 1449. Eligius, the patron saint of goldsmiths, sells a ring to a bridal couple. [Metropolitan Museum of Art, New York, 1975.]

A Banker and His Wife, by Quentin Massys (ca. 1466–1530) painted 1514. While the wife thumbs an illustrated Bible, her husband counts his money. Note also the pearls on the table. [Musée du Louvre, Paris. Cliché des Musées Nationaux.]

Members of a Gun Club, by Kirck Barends, painted 1562. The note held by the man in the far left corner reads, "In wine, truth"—an informal touch in this very sober group. Also note the member holding an arrow. [Stedelijk Museum, Amsterdam.]

Loose Company, by Jan Sanders von Hemessen. Here a man is about to be robbed in the parlor of a bawdy house, another in the background receives services, and a third is enticed to enter. [Staatliche Kunsthalle, Karlsruhe, West Germany.]

The Butcher's Stall, by Pieter Aertsen (ca. 1508–ca. 1575), painted 1551. Everything from fish to fowl could be purchased from the butcher. [Universitetets Konstmuseum, Uppsala, Sweden.]

This street scene in fifteenth-century Flanders is a detail from a painting by Rogier van der Weyden, entitled St. Luke Painting the Virgin. [Museum of Fine Arts, Boston. Gift of Mr. and Mrs. Henry Lee Higginson.]

The juxtaposition of what Machiavelli believed the ancient Romans had been with the failure of contemporary Romans to realize such high ideals made him the famous cynic we know in the popular epithet *Machiavellian*. Only an unscrupulous strongman, he concluded, using duplicity and terror, could impose order on so divided and selfish a people; the moral revival of the Italians required an unprincipled dictator.

It has been argued that Machiavelli wrote *The Prince* in 1513 as a cynical satire on the way rulers actually did behave and not as a serious recommendation of unprincipled despotic rule. To take his advocacy of tyranny literally, it is argued, contradicts both his earlier works and his own strong family tradition of republican service. But Machiavelli seems to have been in earnest when he advised rulers to discover the advantages of fraud and brutality. He apparently hoped to see a strong ruler emerge from the Medici family, which had captured the papacy in 1513 with the pontificate of Leo X (1513–1521). At the same time, the Medici family retained control over the powerful territorial state of Florence—a situation similar to that of Machiavelli's hero Cesare Borgia and his father Pope Alexander VI, who had earlier brought factious Romagna to heel by placing secular family goals and religious policy in tandem. *The Prince* was pointedly dedicated to Lorenzo de' Medici, duke of Urbino and grandson of Lorenzo the Magnificent.

Whatever Machiavelli's hopes may have been, the Medicis were not destined to be Italy's deliverers. The second Medici pope, Clement VII (1523–1534), watched helplessly as Rome was sacked by the army of Emperor Charles V in 1527, also the year of Machiavelli's death.

Suggested Readings

MARGARET ASTON, *The Fifteenth Century: The Prospect of Europe* (1968). Crisp social history, with pictures.

HANS BARON, *The Crisis of the Early Italian Renaissance*, Vols. 1 and 2 (1966). A major work, setting forth the civic dimension of Italian Humanism.

BERNARD BERENSON, *Italian Painters of the Renaissance* (1901).

JACOB BURCKHARDT, *The Civilization of the Renaissance in Italy* (1867). The old classic that still has as many defenders as detractors.

WALLACE K. FERGUSON, *The Renaissance* (1940). A brief, stimulating summary of the Renaissance in both Italy and northern Europe.

WALLACE K. FERGUSON, *Europe in Transition* 1300–1520 (1962). A major survey that deals with the transition from medieval to Renaissance society.

MYRON GILMORE, *The World of Humanism* 1453–1517 (1952). A comprehensive survey, especially strong in intellectual and cultural history.

J. R. HALE, *Renaissance Europe: The Individual and Society,* 1480–1520 (1971). Many-sided treatment of social history.

DENYS HAY, *Europe in the Fourteenth and Fifteenth Centuries* (1966). Many-sided treatment of political history.

JOHAN HUIZINGA, *The Waning of the Middle Ages: A Study of the Forms of Life, Thought, and Art in France and the Netherlands in the Dawn of the Renaissance* (1924). A classic study of "mentality" at the end of the Middle Ages.

DE LAMAR JENSEN, *Renaissance Europe: Age of Recovery and Reconciliation* (1981).

PAUL O. KRISTELLER, *Renaissance Thought: The Classic, Scholastic, and Humanist Strains* (1961). A master shows the many sides of Renaissance thought.

ROBERT E. LERNER, *The Age of Adversity: The Fourteenth Century* (1968). Brief, comprehensive survey.

HARRY A. MISKIMIN, *The Economy of Early Renaissance Europe* 1300–1460 (1969). Shows interaction of social, political, and economic change.

HEIKO A. OBERMAN, *The Harvest of Medieval Theology* (1963). A demanding synthesis and revision.

EDOUARD PERROY, *The Hundred Years War*, trans. by W. B. Wells (1965). The most comprehensive one-volume account.

YVES RENOUARD, *The Avignon Papacy* 1305–1403, trans. by D. Bethell (1970). Standard narrative.

MATTHEW SPINKA, *John Hus's Concept of the Church* (1966).

QUENTIN SKINNER, *The Foundations of Modern Political Thought I: The Renaissance* (1978). Broad survey, very comprehensive.

J. W. THOMPSON, *Economic and Social History of Europe in the Later Middle Ages* 1300–1530 (1958). A bread-and-butter account.

BRIAN TIERNEY, *Foundations of the Conciliar Theory* (1955). Important study showing the origins of conciliar theory in canon law.

BRIAN TIERNEY, *The Crisis of Church and State* 1050–1300 (1964). Part IV provides the major documents in the clash between Boniface VIII and Philip the Fair.

WALTER ULLMANN, *Origins of the Great Schism* (1948). A basic study by a controversial interpreter of medieval political thought.

CHARLES T. WOOD, *Philip the Fair and Boniface VIII* (1967). Excerpts from the scholarly debate over the significance of this confrontation.

H. B. WORKMAN, *John Wyclif*, Vols. 1 and 2 (1926). Dated but still standard.

PHILIP ZIEGLER, *The Black Death* (1969). Highly readable journalistic account.

IMAGO · ERASMI · ROTERODA
MI · AB · ALBERTO · DVRERO · AD
VIVAM · EFFIGIEM · DELINIATA ·

ΤΗΝ · ΚΡΕΙΤΤΩ · ΤΑ · ΣΥΓΓΡΑΜ
ΜΑΤΑ · ΔΙΞΕΙ

· MDXXVI ·

390

14 The Age of Reformation

I N THE second decade of the sixteenth century there began in Saxony in Germany a powerful religious movement that rapidly spread throughout northern Europe, deeply affecting society and politics as well as the spiritual lives of men and women. Attacking what they believed to be burdensome superstitions that robbed people of both their money and their peace of mind, Protestant reformers led a broad revolt against the medieval church. In a relatively short span of time hundreds of thousands of people from all social classes set aside the beliefs of centuries and adopted a more simplified religious practice.

The Protestant Reformation challenged aspects of the Renaissance, especially its tendency to follow classical sources in glorifying human nature and its loyalty to traditional religion. Protestants were more impressed by the human potential for evil

Erasmus of Rotterdam in a 1526 engraving by Albrecht Dürer. Erasmus influenced all of the reform movements of the sixteenth century. He was popularly said to have "laid the egg that Luther hatched." [National Gallery of Art, Washington, D.C.]

than by the inclination to do good and encouraged parents, teachers, and magistrates to be firm disciplinarians. On the other hand, Protestants also embraced many Renaissance values, especially in the sphere of educational reform and particularly with regard to training in ancient languages. Like the Italian Humanists, the Protestant reformers studied ancient languages and went directly to the original sources; only for them this meant the study of the Hebrew and Greek Scriptures and the consequent challenge of traditional institutions on the authority of the Bible.

We are, however, getting well ahead of our story. The road to the Reformation was long in preparation. As the Protestant ethic influenced an entire age, it was also itself born out of changes in European society beyond those within the purely religious and ecclesiastical spheres.

For Europe the late fifteenth and the sixteenth centuries were a period of unprecedented territorial expansion and ideological experimentation. Permanent colonies were established within the Americas, and the exploitation of the New World's human and seemingly endless mineral resources was begun. The American gold and silver imported into Europe spurred scientific invention and a weapons industry and touched off an inflationary spiral that produced a revolution in prices by century's end. The new bullion also helped create international traffic in African slaves, who were needed in ever-increasing numbers to work the mines and the plantations of the New World as replacements for faltering natives. This period further saw social engineering and political planning on a large scale as newly centralized governments were forced as never before to develop long-range economic policies, a practice that came to be known as *mercantilism.*

The late fifteenth and the sixteenth centuries also marked the first wide-scale use of the printing press, an invention greatly assisted by the development of a process of cheap paper manufacture and publishers eager to exploit a fascinating new technology. Printing with movable type was invented by Johann Gutenberg (d. 1468) in the mid-fifteenth century in the German city of Mainz. Residential colleges and universities had greatly expanded in northern Europe during the fourteenth and fifteenth centuries, and there was a growing literate public in the cities eager to possess and read books. The new technology also made propaganda possible on a massive scale, as thousands of inexpensive pamphlets could now be rapidly produced and disseminated.

Voyages of Discovery and Changes in Society

Spices, Gold, and Silver

On the eve of the Reformation the geographical as well as the intellectual horizons of Western people were broadening. The fifteenth century saw the beginning of western Europe's global expansion and the transference of commercial supremacy from the Mediterranean and the Baltic to the Atlantic seaboard. Mercenary motives, reinforced by traditional missionary ideals, inspired Prince Henry the Navigator (1394–1460) to sponsor the Portuguese exploration of the African coast. His main object was the gold trade, which for centuries had been an Arab monopoly. By the last decades of the fifteenth century gold from Guinea was entering Europe by way of Portuguese ships calling at

Model of the Portuguese caravel, a light, fast ship used extensively in trade and exploration. [National Maritime Museum, London.]

the port cities of Lisbon and Antwerp, rather than by Arab land routes. Antwerp became the financial center of Europe, a commercial crossroads where the enterprise and derring-do of the Portuguese and the Spanish met the capital funds of the German banking houses of Fugger and Welser.

The rush for gold quickly expanded into a rush for the spice markets of India. In the fifteenth century the diet of most Europeans was a dull combination of bread and gruel, cabbage, turnips, peas, lentils, and onions, together with what meat became available during seasonal periods of slaughter. Spices, especially pepper and cloves, were in great demand both to preserve and to enhance the taste of food. Bartholomew Dias (d. 1500) opened the Portuguese empire in the East when he rounded the Cape of Good Hope at the tip of Africa in 1487. A decade later, in 1498, Vasco da Gama (d. 1524) reached the coast of India. When he returned to Portugal, he brought with him a cargo worth sixty times the cost of the voyage. In subsequent years the Portuguese established themselves firmly on the Malabar Coast with colonies in Goa and Calicut and successfully challenged the Arabs and the Venetians for control of the European spice trade.

While the Portuguese concentrated on the Indian Ocean, the Spanish set sail across the Atlantic. They did so in the hope of establishing a shorter route to the rich spice markets of the East Indies. Rather than beating the Portuguese at their own game, however, Christopher Columbus (1451–1506) discovered the Americas instead.

Amerigo Vespucci (1451–1512) and Ferdinand Magellan (1480–1521) demonstrated that these new lands were not the outermost territory of the Far East, as Columbus died believing, but an entirely new continent that opened on the still greater Pacific Ocean. Magellan died in the Philippines.

The discovery of gold and silver in vast quantities more than compensated for the disappointment of failing to find a shorter route to the Indies. Still greater mines were opened in the 1520s and the 1530s when Hernando Cortes (1485–1547) conquered the Aztecs of Mexico and Francisco Pizarro (ca. 1470–1541) conquered the Incas of Peru, enslaving the native Indian populations and forcing them to work the new mines. As the forced labor and the new European diseases killed American natives in large numbers, a boom in still another item of trade was created: African slaves. In the sixteenth century they came in great numbers to replace native populations in the mines and on the sugar cane plantations of the New World.

Rise in Prices and the Development of Capitalism

The influx of spices and precious metals into Europe was not an unmixed blessing. It contributed to a steady rise in prices during the sixteenth century that created an inflation rate estimated at 2 per cent a year. The new supply of bullion from the Americas joined with enlarged European production to increase greatly the amount of coinage in circulation, and this increase in turn fed infla-

❧ Columbus Reports His Discovery of the Entrance to Paradise

During his third voyage, Columbus reached the mouth of the Orinoco River in Venezuela. He believed he was in the East Indies, where, according to tradition, Adam and Eve had first trod the earth. Columbus believed that he had now come upon the very entrance into Paradise. In October 1498 he wrote of this discovery to his patrons, Ferdinand and Isabella, monarchs of Spain.

I have already described my ideas concerning this hemisphere and its form [he believed it to be pear-shaped]. I have no doubt that if I could pass below the equinoctial line, after reaching the highest point . . . I should find a much milder temperature and a variation in the stars and in the water. Not that I suppose that elevated point to be navigable, nor even that there is water there; indeed, I believe it is impossible to ascend to it, because I am convinced that it is the spot of the earthly paradise, whither none can go but by God's permission. . . .

I do not suppose that the early paradise is in the form of a rugged mountain, as the descriptions of it have made it appear, but that it is on the summit of the spot, which I have described as being in the form of the stalk of a pear. The approach to it . . . must be by constant and gradual ascent, but I believe that . . . no one could ever reach the top. I think also that the water I have described may proceed from it, though it be far off, and that stopping at the place which I have just left, it forms this lake. There are great indications of this being the terrestrial paradise, for its site coincides with the opinion of the holy and wise theologians whom I have mentioned. Moreover, the other evidences agree . . . for I have never read or heard of fresh water coming in so large a quantity in close conjunction with the water of the sea. The idea is also corroborated by the blandness of the temperature. If the water of which I speak does not proceed from the earthly paradise, it seems to be a still greater wonder, for I do not believe that there is any river in the world so large or so deep.

The Renaissance and the Reformation 1300–1600, ed. by Donald Weinstein (New York: The Free Press, 1965), pp. 138–139.

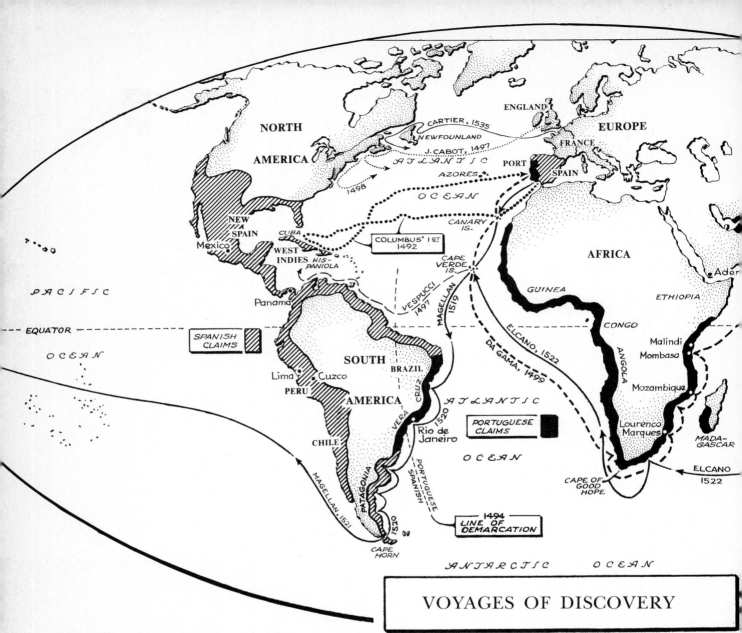

VOYAGES OF DISCOVERY

MAP 14.1 *The map dramatizes the expansion of the area of European interest in the fifteenth and sixteenth centuries. Not until today's "space age" has a comparable widening of horizons been possible.*

tion. Fortunately the increase in prices was by and large spread over a long period of time and was not sudden. Prices doubled in Spain by mid-century, quadrupled by 1600. In Luther's Wittenberg the cost of basic food and clothing increased almost 100 per cent between 1519 and 1540. Generally wages and rents remained well behind the rise in prices.

The new wealth enabled governments and private entrepreneurs to sponsor basic research and expansion in the printing, shipping, mining, textile, and weapons industries—the growth industries of the Age of Reformation. There is also evi-

dence of mercantilism or large-scale government planning in such ventures as the French silk industry and the Hapsburg–Fugger development of mines in Austria and Hungary.

In the thirteenth and fourteenth centuries capitalist institutions and practices had already begun to develop in the rich Italian cities (one may point

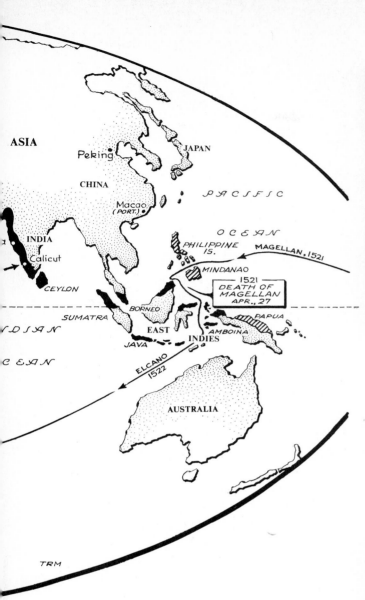

A sixteenth-century print by Stradanus of a nautical engineer surrounded by the tools and symbols of his craft: globes, maps and charts, a model of an ocean-going vessel, a compass and angles, and an elaborate tub for measuring the displacement of objects in water. Advances in ship design in the fifteenth and sixteenth centuries helped facilitate the European voyages of exploration. [Courtesy of the Trustees of the National Maritime Museum, London.]

Detail of a portrait of Christopher Columbus by Sebastiano del Piombo (1485–1547). It shows Columbus, who died in 1506, late in life. [Metropolitan Museum of Art, New York; gift of J. Pierpont Morgan, 1900.]

to the Florentine banking houses of Bardi and Peruzzi). Those who owned the means of production, either privately or corporately, were clearly distinguished from the workers who operated them. Wherever possible, monopolies were created in basic goods. High interest was charged on loans—actual, if not legal, usury. And the "capitalist" virtues of thrift, industry, and orderly planning were everywhere in evidence—all intended to permit the free and efficient accumulation of wealth.

The late fifteenth and the sixteenth centuries saw the maturation of such capitalism together with its peculiar social problems. The new wealth

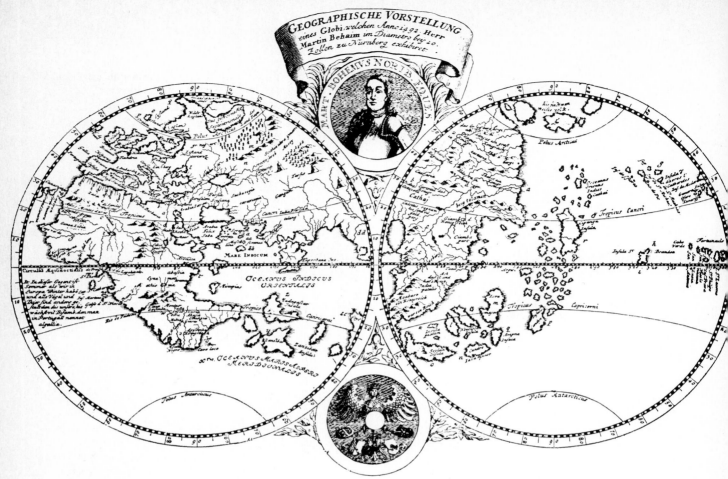

The world as shown on Martin Behaim's globe of 1492, the first such representation that we know of, clearly reflecting awareness that the earth was round and not flat. This two-dimensional adaptation of the globe's surface was made by J. G. Doppelmayer in the eighteenth century. Note the absence of the North and South American continents—a gap on the map leaving Columbus free to assume that he could go west from Spain (in the upper left) to reach the Indies. The original of Behaim's "earth-apple," as he called his globe, is in a museum in Nuremberg, West Germany.

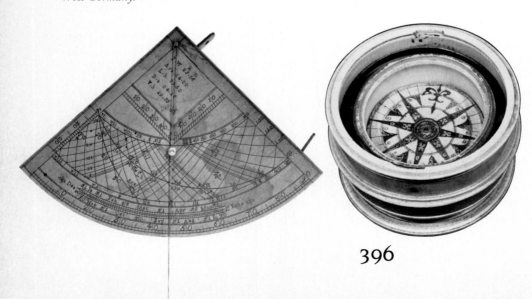

A quadrant (seventeenth century) and early compass (sixteenth century) of the types that made possible the long voyages of discovery. [National Maritime Museum, London.]

and industrial expansion raised the expectations of the poor and the ambitious and heightened the reactionary tendencies within the established and wealthy classes. This effect, in turn, greatly aggravated the traditional social divisions between the clergy and the laity, the higher and the lower clergy, the urban patriciate and the guilds, masters and journeymen, and the landed nobility and the agrarian peasantry.

Such social divisions may indirectly have prepared the way for the Reformation by making many people critical of traditional institutions and open to new ideas—especially those that seemed to promise a greater degree of freedom and equality.

The far-flung transactions created by the new commerce increased the demand for lawyers and bankers. The Medicis of Florence grew very rich as bankers of the pope, as did the Fuggers of Augsburg as bankers of the Hapsburg rulers. The Fuggers lent Charles I of Spain over 500,000 florins to buy his election as Holy Roman Emperor in 1519, and they later boasted that they had created the emperor. But those who paid out their money also took their chances. Both the Fuggers and the Medicis were later bankrupted by popes and kings who defaulted on their heavy debts.

The Northern Renaissance

The scholarly works of northern Humanists created a climate favorable to religious and educational reforms on the eve of the Reformation. Northern Humanism was initially stimulated by the importation of Italian learning through such varied intermediaries as students who had studied in Italy, merchants, and the Brothers of the Common Life (an influential lay religious movement that began in the Netherlands and permitted men and women to live a shared religious life without making formal vows of poverty, chastity, and obedience). The northern Humanists, however, developed their own distinctive culture. They tended to come from more diverse social backgrounds and to be more devoted to religious reforms than their Italian counterparts. They were also more willing to write for lay audiences as well as for a narrow intelligentsia.

Erasmus

The most famous of the northern Humanists was Desiderius Erasmus (1466–1536), the reputed

"prince of the Humanists." Erasmus gained fame as both an educational and a religious reformer. Earning his living by tutoring when patrons were in short supply, Erasmus prepared short Latin dialogues for his students that were intended to teach them how to speak and live well, inculcating good manners and language by encouraging them to imitate what they read. These dialogues were published under the title *Colloquies* and grew in number and length in consecutive editions, coming also to embrace anticlerical dialogues and satires on popular religious superstition. Erasmus collected ancient and contemporary proverbs, as well, which he published under the title *Adages,* beginning with about eight hundred examples and increasing his collection to over five thousand in the final edition of the work. Among the sayings the *Adages* popularized are such common modern expressions as "to leave no stone unturned" and "where there is smoke, there is fire."

Erasmus aspired to unite the classical ideals of humanity and civic virtue with the Christian ideals of love and piety. He believed that disciplined study of the classics and the Bible, if begun early enough, was the best way to reform both individuals and society. He summarized his own beliefs with the phrase *philosophia Christi,* a simple, ethical piety in imitation of Christ. He set this ideal in starkest contrast to what he believed to be the dogmatic, ceremonial, and factious religious practice of the later Middle Ages. What most offended him about the Scholastics, both those of the late Middle Ages and, increasingly, the new Lutheran ones, was their letting doctrine and disputation overshadow humble piety and Christian practice.

To promote his own religious beliefs, Erasmus labored to make the ancient Christian sources available in their original versions, for, he believed, only as people drank from the pure, unadulterated sources could moral and religious health result. He edited the works of the Church Fathers and made a Greek edition of the New Testament (1516), which became the basis for his new, more accurate Latin translation (1519).

These various enterprises did not please church authorities, who were unhappy with both Erasmus's "improvements" on the Vulgate, Christendom's Bible for over a thousand years, and his popular anticlerical satires. At one point in the mid-sixteenth century all of Erasmus's works were placed on the *Index of Forbidden Books.* Erasmus also received Luther's unqualified condemnation for his views on the freedom of human will. Still,

❧ Erasmus Describes the "Philosophy of Christ"

Although Erasmus called his ideal of how people should live the "philosophy of Christ," he found it taught by classical authors as well. In this selection he commented on its main features, with obvious polemic against the philosophy of the Scholastics.

This kind of philosophy [the philosophy of Christ] is. located more truly in the disposition of the mind than in syllogisms. Here life means more than debate, inspiration is preferable to erudition, transformation [of life] a more important matter than intellectual comprehension. Only a very few can be learned, but all can be Christian, all can be devout, and—I shall boldly add—all can be theologians. Indeed, this philosophy easily penetrates into the minds of all; it is an action in special accord with human nature. What else is the philosophy of Christ, which he himself calls a rebirth, than the restoration of human nature. . . ? Although no one has taught this more perfectly . . . than Christ, nevertheless one may find in the books of the pagans very much which does agree with it. There was never so coarse a school of philosophy that taught that money rendered a man happy. Nor has there ever been one so shameless that fixed the chief good in vulgar honors and pleasures. The Stoics understood that no one was wise unless he was good. . . . According to Plato, Socrates teaches . . . that a wrong must not be repaid with a wrong, and also that since the soul is immortal, those should not be lamented who depart this life for a happier one with the assurance of having led an upright life. . . . And Aristotle has written in the Politics *that nothing can be a delight to us . . . except virtue alone. . . . If there are things that belong particularly to Christianity in these ancient writers, let us follow them.*

The *Paraclesis* in *Christian Humanism and the Reformation: Desiderius Erasmus,* ed. and trans. by John C. Olin (New York: Harper, 1965), pp. 100–101.

Erasmus's didactic and scholarly works became basic tools of reform in the hands of both Protestant and Catholic reformers.

Humanism in Germany

Peter Luder (d. 1474) and Rudolf Agricola (1443–1485) brought Italian learning to Germany. Agricola, the father of German Humanism, spent ten years in Italy. Like later German Humanists, he aspired to outdo the Italians in classical learning, thereby adding a nationalist motivation to German scholarship. Conrad Celtis (d. 1508), the first German poet laureate, and Ulrich von Hutten (1488–1523), a fiery knight, were exponents of romantic cultural nationalism. The life and work of Von Hutten especially illustrates the union of Humanism, German nationalism, and Luther's religious reform. A poet who admired Erasmus and attacked Scholasticism and bad Latin, Von Hutten was also a member of the fading landed nobility who aspired to a revival of ancient German virtue—he died in 1523 in a hopeless knights' revolt against the princes. He was also an advocate of religious reform who attacked indulgences and published an edition of Valla's exposé of the Donation of Constantine.

THE REUCHLIN AFFAIR. The *cause célèbre* that brought Von Hutten onto the historical stage and unified many reform-minded German Humanists was the Reuchlin affair. Johann Reuchlin (1455–1522) was Europe's foremost Christian authority on Hebrew and Jewish learning. He had written the first reliable Hebrew grammar by a Christian scholar and was personally attracted to Jewish mysticism. Around 1506 a converted Jew named Pfefferkorn, supported by the Dominican Order in Cologne (the city that was known as "the German Rome"), began a movement to suppress Jewish writings. When Pfefferkorn attacked Reuchlin, many German Humanists, in the name of academic freedom and good scholarship, not for any pro-Jewish sentiment, rushed to Reuchlin's defense. The controversy, which lasted several years, produced one of the great satires of the period, the *Letters of Obscure Men* (1515), a merciless satire on the narrowness and irrelevance of monks and Scholastics, particularly those in Cologne, written by Crotus Rubeanus and Ulrich von Hutten. When Luther came under attack after his famous ninety-five theses against indulgences in 1517, many German Humanists tended to see in his plight a repetition of the Scholastic attack on Reuchlin; religious reform and academic freedom were again at stake. Although, following Erasmus's lead, many of these same men ceased to support Luther when the revolutionary direction of his theology became clear, German Humanists formed the first identifiable group of Luther's supporters, and many young Humanists became Lutheran pastors.

Humanism in England

Humanists also promoted basic educational and religious reforms in England and France. English scholars and merchants and visiting Italian prelates brought Italian learning to England. The Oxford lectures of William Grocyn (d. 1519) and Thomas Linacre (d. 1524) and the Cambridge lectures of the visiting Erasmus (1510–1513), who worked on his Greek edition of the New Testament while in England, marked the scholarly maturation of English Humanism. John Colet (1467–1519), after 1505 dean of St. Paul's Cathedral, became renowned for his sermons and commentaries on the New Testament and his patronage of Humanist studies for the young. Like the other English Humanists, only more so, he stressed the relevance of Scripture to the problems of religious reform.

The best known of early English Humanists was Thomas More (1478–1535), a close friend of Erasmus. It was while visiting More that Erasmus wrote his most famous work, *The Praise of Folly,* an amusing and profound exposé of human self-deception. More's *Utopia* (1516), a criticism of contemporary society, still rivals the plays of Shakespeare as the most-read sixteenth-century English work. *Utopia* depicted an imaginary society based on reason and tolerance that had overcome social and political injustice by holding all property and goods in common and by requiring all to earn their bread by the sweat of their own brow.

A bureaucrat under Henry VII, More became one of Henry VIII's most trusted diplomats, succeeding Cardinal Wolsey as lord chancellor in 1529. More resigned that position in May 1532

Thomas More by Hans Holbein the Younger, painted in 1527. The English statesman and author was beheaded by Henry VIII for his refusal to recognize the king's sovereignty over the English church. [The Frick Collection.]

because he could not in good conscience support the king's break with the papacy and his pretension to being head of the English church "so far as the law of Christ allows." More's repudiation of the Act of Supremacy (1534) and his refusal to recognize the king's marriage to Anne Boleyn led to his execution in July 1535.

Although More remained staunchly Catholic, Humanism in England, as in Germany, played an important role in preparing the way for the English Reformation. A circle of English Humanists, under the direction of Henry VIII's minister Thomas Cromwell, translated and disseminated, to the king's advantage, such pertinent works as Marsilius of Padua's *Defender of Peace,* a work that exalted the sovereignty of rulers over popes and therefore had been condemned by the church, and writings of Erasmus that urged church reform.

Humanism in France

It was through the French invasions of Italy that Italian learning penetrated France, traffic in books and ideas going hand in hand with the transport of men and matériel to and fro. Guillaume Budé (1468–1540), an accomplished Greek scholar, and Jacques Lefèvre d'Etaples (1454–1536) were the leaders of French Humanism. Lefèvre's two main works—the *Quincuplex Psalterium,* five Latin versions of the psalms arranged in parallel columns, and a translation and commentary on Saint Paul's Epistle to the Romans—not only exemplified the new critical scholarship but also influenced the theology of Martin Luther. French Humanism had two powerful political patrons: Guillaume Briçonnet (1470–1533), after 1516 the bishop of Meaux, and Marguerite d'Angoulême (1492–1549), sister of Francis I and the future queen of Navarre, who made her own reputation as a writer. The future Protestant reformer John Calvin was a product of this native reform circle. Calvin was the first of three major vernacular writers with Humanist backgrounds who created the modern French language. The others were the physician François Rabelais (1494–1553), an ex-Franciscan and Benedictine monk whose *Gargantua* and *Pantagruel* satirized his age, and the skeptical essayist Michel de Montaigne (1533–1592), who ridiculed the authoritarian Scholastic mind.

Humanism in Spain

Whereas in Germany, England, and France Humanism prepared the way for Protestant reforms, in Spain it entered the service of the Catholic church. Here the key figure was Francisco Jiménez de Cisneros (1437–1517), a confessor to Queen Isabella, and after 1508 Grand Inquisitor—a position from which he was able to enforce the strictest religious orthodoxy. Jiménez was a conduit for Humanist scholarship and learning. He founded the University of Alcalá near Madrid in 1509, printed a Greek edition of the New Testament, and translated many religious tracts that aided clerical reform and control of lay religious life. His greatest achievement, taking fifteen years to complete, was the *Complutensian Polyglot Bible,* a six-volume work that placed the Hebrew, Greek, and Latin versions of the Bible in parallel columns. Such scholarly projects and internal church reforms joined with the repressive measures of Ferdinand and Isabella to keep Spain strictly Catholic throughout the Age of Reformation.

Religious Life

Popular Religious Movements and Criticism of the Church

The Protestant Reformation could not have occurred without the monumental crises of the medieval church during the "exile" in Avignon, the Great Schism, the conciliar period, and the Renaissance papacy. For increasing numbers of people the medieval church had ceased also to provide a viable religious piety. There was a crisis in the traditional teaching and spiritual practice of the church among many of its intellectuals and laity. Between the secular pretensions of the papacy and the dry teaching of Scholastic theologians, laity and clerics alike began to seek a more heartfelt, idealistic, and—often in the eyes of the pope—increasingly heretical religious piety. The late Middle Ages were marked by independent lay and clerical efforts to reform local religious practice and by widespread experimentation with new religious forms.

A variety of factors contributed to the growth of lay criticism of the church. In the cities the laity were far more knowledgeable about the world and those who controlled their lives. The laity traveled widely—as soldiers, pilgrims, explorers, and traders. New postal systems and the printing press increased the information at their disposal. The new age of books and libraries raised literacy and heightened curiosity. Lay people were increasingly in a position to take the initiative in shaping the cultural life of their communities.

From the Albigensians, Waldensians, Beguines, and Beghards in the thirteenth century to the Lollards and Hussites in the fifteenth, lay religious movements shared a common goal of religious simplicity in imitation of Jesus. Practically without exception they were inspired by an ideal of apostolic poverty in religion; that is, all wanted a religion of true self-sacrifice like that of Jesus and the first disciples. The laity sought a more egalitarian church, one that gave the members as well as the head of the church a voice, and a more spiritual church, one that lived manifestly according to its New Testament model.

THE MODERN DEVOTION. One of the most constructive lay religious movements in northern Europe on the eve of the Reformation was that of the Brothers of the Common Life, or what came to be known as the *Modern Devotion.* The brothers fostered the religious life outside formal ecclesiastical offices and apart from formal religious vows. Established by Gerard Groote (1340–1384) and centered at Zwolle and Deventer in the Netherlands, the brother and less numerous sister houses of the Modern Devotion spread rapidly throughout northern Europe and influenced parts of southern Europe as well. In these houses clerics and laity came together to share a common life, stressing individual piety and practical religion. Lay members were not expected to take special religious vows or to wear special religious dress, not did they abandon their ordinary secular vocations.

The brothers were also active in education. They worked as copyists, sponsored many religious and a few classical publications, ran hospices for poor students, and conducted schools for the young, especially for boys preparing for the priesthood or a monastic vocation. As youths, Nicholas of Cusa, Johannes Reuchlin, and Desiderius Erasmus were looked after by the brothers. Thomas à Kempis (d. 1471) summarized the philosophy of the brothers in what became the most popular religious book of the period, the *Imitation of Christ,* a semimystical guide to the inner life intended primarily for monks and nuns, but widely appropriated by laity who also wanted to pursue the ascetic life.

The Modern Devotion has been seen as the source of Humanist, Protestant, and Catholic reform movements in the sixteenth century, although some scholars believe that it represented an individualistic approach to religion, indifferent and even harmful to the sacramental piety of the church. It was actually a very conservative movement. The brothers retained the old clerical doctrines and values, while placing them within the new framework of an active common life. They clearly met a need for a more personal piety and a better-informed religious life. Their movement appeared at a time when the laity were demanding good preaching in the vernacular and were even taking the initiative to endow special preacherships to ensure it. The Modern Devotion permitted laity to practice the religious life to the fullest, yet without having to surrender their life in the world.

LAY CONTROL OVER RELIGIOUS LIFE. On the eve of the Reformation, Rome's international network of church offices, which had unified Europe religiously during the Middle Ages, began to fall apart in many areas, hurried along by a growing sense of regional identity—incipient nationalism—and local secular administrative competence. A widespread attitude of "Mother Church, we would rather do it ourselves" was evident. The long-entrenched benefice system of the medieval church, which had permitted important ecclesiastical posts to be sold to the highest bidders and had left residency requirements in parishes unenforced, did not result in a vibrant local religious life. The substitutes hired by nonresident holders of benefices, who lived elsewhere (mostly in Rome) and milked the revenues of their offices, performed their chores mechanically and had neither firsthand knowledge of nor much sympathy with local needs and problems. Rare was the late medieval German town that did not have complaints about the maladministration, concubinage, and/or fiscalism of their clergy, especially the higher clergy (i.e., bishops, abbots, and prelates).

Communities loudly protested the financial abuses of the medieval church long before Luther published his famous summary of economic grievances in the *Address to the Christian Nobility of the German Nation.* The sale of indulgences, a practice that was greatly expanded on the eve of the Reformation and seemed now to permit people to buy release from religious punishment in purgatory both for their own and their deceased loved ones' sins, had also been repeatedly attacked before Luther came on the scene. Rulers and magistrates had little objection to and could even encourage the sale of indulgences as long as a generous portion of the income remained within the local coffers. But when an indulgence was preached primarily for the benefit of distant interests, as was the case with the Saint Peter's indulgence protested by Luther, resistance arose for strictly financial reasons, because their sale drained away local revenues.

Indulgences could not pass from the scene until rulers found new ways to profit from religion and a more effective popular remedy for religious anxiety was at hand. The Reformation provided the former by sanctioning the secular dissolution of monasteries and the confiscation of ecclesiastical properties. It held out the latter in its new theology of justification by faith.

City governments also undertook to improve local religious life on the eve of the Reformation by endowing preacherships. These were beneficed positions that provided for well-trained and dedicated pastors and regular preaching and pastoral care, which went beyond the routine performance of the Mass and traditional religious functions. In many instances these preacherships became platforms for Protestant preachers.

Magistrates also carefully restricted the growth of ecclesiastical properties and clerical privileges. During the Middle Ages special clerical rights in both property and person had come to be recognized by canon and civil law. Because they were holy places, churches and monasteries had been exempted from the taxes and laws that affected others. They were treated as special places of "sacral peace" and asylum. It was considered inappropriate for holy persons (clergy) to be burdened with such "dirty jobs" as military service, compulsory labor, standing watch at city gates, and other obligations of citizenship. Nor was it thought right that the laity, of whatever rank, should sit in judgment on those who were their shepherds and intermediaries with God. The clergy, accordingly, came to enjoy an immunity of place (which exempted ecclesiastical properties from taxes and recognized their right of asylum) and an immunity of person (which exempted the clergy from the jurisdiction of civil courts).

On the eve of the Reformation measures were passed to restrict these privileges and to end their abuses—efforts to regulate ecclesiastical acquisition of new property, to circumvent the right of asylum in churches and monasteries (a practice that posed a threat to the normal administration of justice), and to bring the clergy under the local tax code. Governments had understandably tired of ecclesiastical interference in what seemed to them to be strictly political spheres of competence and authority.

Martin Luther and German Reformation to 1525

Unlike France and England, late medieval Germany lacked the political unity to enforce "national" religious reforms during the late Middle Ages. There were no lasting Statutes of Provisors and *praemunire*, as in England, nor a Pragmatic Sanction of Bourges, as in France, limiting papal jurisdiction and taxation on a national scale. What happened on a unified national level in England and France occurred only locally and piecemeal within German territories and towns. As popular

Martin Luther in 1521, near the beginning of his career as a reformer. The portrait is by Lucas Cranach the Elder (1472–1553). [Metropolitan Museum of Art, New York; gift of Robert Lehman, 1955.]

resentment of clerical immunities and ecclesiastical abuses, especially the selling of indulgences, spread among German cities and towns, an unorganized "national" opposition to Rome formed. German Humanists had long given voice to such criticism, and by 1517 it was pervasive enough to provide a solid foundation for Martin Luther's reform.

Luther (1483–1546) was the son of a successful Thüringian miner. He was educated in Mansfeld, Magdeburg, where the Brothers of the Common Life were his teachers, and Eisenach. Between 1501 and 1505 he attended the University of Erfurt, where the nominalist teachings of William of Ockham and Gabriel Biel (d. 1495) prevailed within the Philosophical Faculty. After receiving his master of arts degree in 1505, Luther registered with the Law Faculty in accordance with his parents' wishes. But he never began the study of law. To the shock and disappointment of his family, he instead entered the Order of the Hermits of Saint Augustine in Erfurt on July 17, 1505. This decision had apparently been building for some time and was resolved during a lightning storm in which a terrified Luther, crying out to Saint Anne for assistance (Saint Anne was the patron saint of travelers in distress), promised to enter a monastery if he escaped death.

Ordained in 1507, Luther pursued a traditional course of study, becoming in 1509 a *baccalaureus biblicus* and *sententiarius,* that is, thoroughly trained in the Bible and the *Sentences* of Peter Lombard. In 1510 he journeyed to Rome on the business of his order, finding there justification for the many criticisms of the church he had heard in Germany. In

1511 he was transferred to the Augustinian monastery in Wittenberg, where he earned his doctorate in theology in 1512, thereafter becoming a leader within the monastery, the new university, and the spiritual life of the city.

JUSTIFICATION BY FAITH ALONE. Reformation theology grew out of a problem common to many of the clergy and the laity at this time: the failure of traditional medieval religion to provide either full personal or intellectual satisfaction. Luther was especially plagued by the disproportion between his own sense of sinfulness and the perfect righteousness that medieval theology taught that God required for salvation. Traditional church teaching and the sacrament of penance proved to be of no consolation. Luther wrote that he came to despise the phrase "righteousness of God," for it seemed to demand of him a perfection he knew neither he nor any other human being could ever achieve. His insight into the meaning of "justification by faith alone" was a gradual process that extended over several years, between 1513 and 1518. The righteousness God demands, he concluded, was not one that came from many religious works and ceremonies but was present in full measure in those who simply believed and trusted in the work of Jesus Christ, who alone was the perfect righteousness satisfying to God. To believe in Christ was to stand before God clothed in Christ's sure righteousness.

THE ATTACK ON INDULGENCES. An indulgence was a remission of the temporal penalty imposed by the priest on penitents as a "work of satisfaction" for their committed mortal sins. According to medieval theology, after the priest had absolved penitents of guilt for their sins, they still remained under an eternal penalty, a punishment God justly imposed on them for their sins. After absolution, however, this eternal penalty was said to be transformed into a temporal penalty, a manageable "work of satisfaction" that the penitent could perform here and now (for example, prayers, fasting, almsgiving, retreats, and pilgrimages). Penitents who defaulted on such prescribed works of satisfaction could expect to suffer for them in purgatory.

At this point indulgences came into play as an aid to a laity made genuinely anxious by the belief in a future suffering in purgatory for neglected penances or unrepented sins. In 1343 Pope Clement VI (1342–1352) had proclaimed the existence of a "treasury of merit," an infinite reservoir of good works in the church's possession that could be dis-

Luther and the Wittenberg reformers with Elector John Frederick of Saxony (1532–1547), painted about 1543 by Lucas Cranach the Younger (1515–1586). Luther is on the far left, Philip Melanchthon in the front row on the far right. [Toledo Museum of Art, Toledo, Ohio; gift of Edward Drummond Libbey.]

pensed at the pope's discretion. It was on the basis of this declared treasury that the church sold "letters of indulgence," which covered the works of satisfaction owed by penitents. In 1476 Pope Sixtus IV (1471–1484) extended indulgences also to purgatory. Originally indulgences had been given only for the true self-sacrifice of going on a crusade to the Holy Land. By Luther's time they were regu-

❧ Martin Luther Discovers Justification by Faith Alone

Many years after the fact, Martin Luther described his discovery that God's righteousness was not an active, punishing righteousness but a passive, transforming righteousness, which made those who believed in him righteous as God himself is righteous.

Though I lived as a monk without reproach, I felt that I was a sinner before God with an extremely disturbed conscience. I could not believe that he was placated by my satisfaction. I did not love, yes, I hated the righteous God who punishes sinners, and secretly, if not blasphemously, certainly murmuring greatly, I was angry with God, and said, "As if, indeed, it is not enough, that miserable sinners, eternally lost through original sin, are crushed by every kind of calamity by the law of the decalogue, without having God add pain to pain by the gospel and also by the gospel threatening us with his righteousness and wrath!" Thus I raged with a fierce and troubled conscience. Nevertheless, I beat importunately upon Paul at that place, most ardently desiring to know what St. Paul wanted.

*At last, by the mercy of God, meditating day and night, I gave heed to the context of the words, namely, "In it the righteousness of God is revealed, as it is written, 'He who through faith is righteous shall live'" [Romans 1:17]. There I began to understand that the righteousness of God is that by which the righteous lives by a gift of God, namely by faith. And this is the meaning: the righteousness of God is revealed by the gospel, namely, the passive righteousness with which **merciful** God justifies us by faith, as it is written, "He who through faith is righteous shall live." Here I felt that I was altogether born again and had entered paradise itself through open gates. There a totally other face of the entire Scripture showed itself to me. Thereupon I ran through the Scriptures from memory. I also found in other terms an analogy, as, the work of God, that is, what God does in us, the power of God, with which he makes us strong, the wisdom of God, with which he makes us wise, the strength of God, the salvation of God, the glory of God.*

And I extolled my sweetest word with a love as great as the hatred with which I had before hated the word "righteousness of God." Thus that place in Paul was for me truly the gate to paradise.

Preface to the Complete Edition of Luther's Latin Writings (1545), in *Luther's Works*, Vol. 34, ed. by Lewis W. Spitz (Philadelphia: Muhlenberg Press, 1960), pp. 336–337.

larly dispensed for small cash payments (very modest sums that were regarded as a good work of almsgiving) and were presented to the laity as remitting not only their own future punishments, but also those of their dead relatives presumed to be suffering in purgatory.

In 1517 a Jubilee indulgence, proclaimed during the pontificate of Pope Julius II (1503–1513) to raise funds for the rebuilding of Saint Peter's in Rome, was revived and preached on the borders of Saxony in the territories of Archbishop Albrecht of Mainz. Albrecht was much in need of revenues because of the large debts he had incurred in order to hold, contrary to church law, three ecclesiastical appointments: the archbishoprics of Mainz and Magdeburg in addition to the bishopric of Halberstadt. The selling of the indulgence was a joint venture by Albrecht, the Augsburg banking-house of Fugger, and Pope Leo X, half the proceeds going to the pope and half to Albrecht and his creditors. The famous indulgence preacher John Tetzel (d. 1519) was enlisted to preach the indulgence in Albrecht's territories because he was a seasoned professional who knew how to stir ordinary people to action. As he exhorted on one occasion:

Don't you hear the voices of your dead parents and other relatives crying out, "Have mercy on us, for we suffer great punishment and pain. From this you could release us with a few alms. . . . We have created you, fed you, cared for you, and left you our temporal goods. Why do you treat us so cruelly and leave us to suffer in the flames, when it takes only a little to save us?"[1]

[1]*Die Reformation in Augenzeugen berichtet*, ed. by Helmar Junghaus (Düsseldorf: Karl Rauch Verlag, 1967), p. 44.

Pope Leo X (1513–1521), of the Medici family, with two cardinals, as painted about 1517–18 by Raphael. Leo was pope when the Reformation began and condemned Luther for heresy in 1520. [Alinari/SCALA.]

When on October 31, 1517, Luther posted his ninety-five theses against indulgences, according to tradition, on the door of Castle Church in Wittenberg, he protested especially against the impression created by Tetzel that indulgences actually remitted sins and released the dead from punishment in purgatory—claims he believed went far beyond the traditional practice and seemed to make salvation something that could be bought and sold.

ELECTION OF CHARLES V. The ninety-five theses were embraced by Humanists and other proponents of reform. They made Luther famous overnight and prompted official proceedings against him. In April 1518 he was summoned to appear before the general chapter of his order in Heidelberg, and the following October he was called before the papal legate and general of the Dominican Order, Cardinal Cajetan, in Augsburg. As sanctions were being prepared against Luther, Emperor Maximilian I died (January 12, 1519), and

this event, fortunate for the Reformation, turned all attention from heresy in Saxony to the contest for a new emperor.

The pope backed the French king, Francis I. However, Charles I of Spain, a youth of nineteen, succeeded his grandfather and became Emperor Charles V. Charles was assisted by both a long tradition of Hapsburg imperial rule and a massive Fugger campaign chest, which secured the votes of the seven electors. The electors, who traditionally enhanced their power at every opportunity, wrung new concessions from Charles for their votes. The emperor agreed to a revival of the Imperial Supreme Court and the Council of Regency and promised to consult with a diet of the empire on all major domestic and foreign affairs that affected the empire. These measures also helped the development of the Reformation by preventing unilateral imperial action against the Germans, something Luther could be thankful for in the early years of the Reformation.

LUTHER'S EXCOMMUNICATION AND THE DIET OF WORMS. In the same month in which Charles was elected emperor, Luther entered a debate in Leipzig (June 27, 1519) with the Ingolstadt professor John Eck. During this contest Luther challenged the infallibility of the pope and the iner-

The young Charles I of Spain about 1517. Charles was elected emperor as Charles V two years later at age 19 and reigned until 1556 when, weary and disillusioned by the success of Protestantism, he retired to a monastery. The wooden bust shown here is attributed to Conrad Meit. [Stedelijke Musea, Bruges, Belgium. Copyright A.C.L., Brussels.]

rancy of church councils, appealing, for the first time, to the sovereign authority of Scripture alone. All his bridges to the old church were burned when he further defended certain teachings of John Huss condemned by the Council of Constance. In 1520 Luther signaled his new direction with three famous pamphlets: the *Address to the Christian Nobility of the German Nation,* which urged the German princes to force reforms on the Roman church, especially to curtail its political and economic power in Germany; the *Babylonian Captivity of the Church,* which attacked the traditional seven sacraments, arguing that only two were proper, and exalted the authority of Scripture, church councils, and secular princes over that of the pope; and the eloquent *Freedom of a Christian,* which summarized the new teaching of salvation by faith alone. On June 15, 1520, the papal bull *Exsurge Domine* condemned Luther for heresy and gave him sixty days to retract. The final bull of excommunication, *Decet Pontificem Romanum,* was issued on January 3, 1521.

In April 1521 Luther presented his views before a diet of the empire in Worms, over which the newly elected Emperor Charles V presided. Or-dered to recant, Luther declared that to do so would be to act against Scripture, reason, and his own conscience. On May 26, 1521, he was placed under the imperial ban and thereafter became an "outlaw" to secular as well as to religious authority. For his own protection friends hid him in Wartburg Castle, where he spent almost a year in seclusion, from April 1521 to March 1522. During his stay, he translated the New Testament into German, using Erasmus's new Greek text, and he attempted by correspondence to oversee the first stages of the Reformation in Wittenberg.

IMPERIAL DISTRACTIONS: FRANCE AND THE TURKS. The Reformation was greatly assisted in these early years by the emperor's war with France and the advance of the Ottoman Turks into eastern Europe. Against both adversaries Charles V, who also remained a Spanish king with dynastic responsibilities outside the empire, needed German troops, and to that end he promoted friendly relations with the German princes. Between 1521 and 1559 Spain (the Hapsburg dynasty) and France (the Valois dynasty) fought four major wars over disputed territories in Italy and along their borders. In 1526 the Turks overran Hungary at

❧ Luther Calls on the German Nobility to Reform the Church

In his *Address to the Christian Nobility of the German Nation* (1520) Luther protested against the three "walls" of Rome that had prevented reform in the church by making the pope immune to corrective action on the basis of secular, biblical, and conciliar authority. In the following Luther urged the nobility to tear down these walls.

The Romanists have with great dexterity built around themselves three walls, which hitherto have protected them against reform; and thereby is Christianity fearfully fallen.

In the first place, when the temporal power has pressed them hard [to reform], they have . . . maintained that the temporal power has no jurisdiction over them, that, on the contrary, the spiritual [power] is above the temporal.

Secondly, when it was proposed to admonish them from the Holy Scriptures they said, "It befits no one but the pope to interpret the Scriptures."

And, thirdly, when they were threatened with a *council, they invented the idea that no one but the pope can call a council.*

Thus have they secretly stolen our three rods so that they may go unpunished, and entrenched themselves safely behind these three walls in order to carry on all the knavery and wickedness that we now see. . . .

Now may God help us, and give us one of those trumpets that overthrew the walls of Jerico, so that we may also blow down these walls of straw and paper and . . . regain possession of our Christian rods for the chastisement of sin and expose the craft and deceit of the Devil.

James Harvey Robinson (Ed.), *Readings in European History,* Vol. 2 (Boston: Ginn and Co., 1906), p. 75.

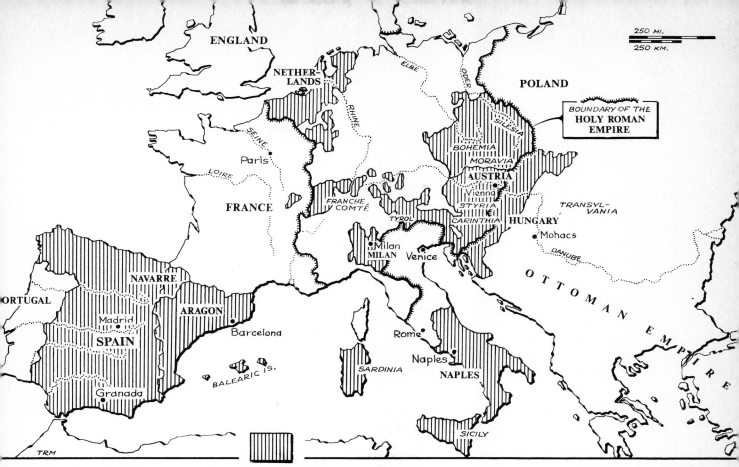

MAP 14.2 showing the Empire of Charles V, with the BOUNDARY OF THE HOLY ROMAN EMPIRE. Labeled regions: ENGLAND, NETHERLANDS, POLAND, FRANCE, SPAIN, PORTUGAL, NAVARRE, ARAGON, SILESIA, BOHEMIA, MORAVIA, AUSTRIA, STYRIA, CARINTHIA, HUNGARY, TRANSYLVANIA, TYROL, FRANCHE COMTÉ, MILAN, NAPLES, SARDINIA, SICILY, OTTOMAN EMPIRE. Cities: Paris, Madrid, Barcelona, Granada, Milan, Venice, Rome, Naples, Vienna, Mohacs. Rivers: SEINE, LOIRE, RHINE, ELBE, ODER, DANUBE. Islands: BALEARIC IS. Scale: 250 MI. / 250 KM. TRM.

THE EMPIRE OF CHARLES V

MAP 14.2 *Dynastic marriages and simple chance concentrated into Charles's hands rule over the lands shown here, plus Spain's overseas possessions. Crowns and titles rained in on him; election in 1519 as emperor gave him new burdens and responsibilities.*

the Battle of Mohacs, while in western Europe the French-led League of Cognac formed against Charles for the second Hapsburg–Valois war. Thus preoccupied, the emperor agreed through his representatives at the German Diet of Speyer in 1526 that each German territory was free to enforce the Edict of Worms (1521) against Luther "so as to be able to answer in good conscience to God and the emperor." That concession in effect gave the German princes territorial sovereignty in religious matters and the Reformation time to put down deep roots. Later (in 1555) such local princely control over religion would be enshrined in imperial law by the Peace of Augsburg.

THE PEASANTS' REVOLT. In its first decade the Protestant movement suffered more from internal division than from imperial interference. By 1525

Luther had become as much an object of protest within Germany as was the pope. Original allies, sympathizers, and fellow travelers declared their independence from him.

Thomas Müntzer (died 1525), Luther's fiercest opponent and a leader of the Peasants' Revolt of 1525. His name became synonymous with rebellion and anarchy. He is seen here in a woodcut portrait of about 1600 by Christoffel van Sichem the Elder. [Bildarchiv Preussischer Kulturbesitz.]

❧ German Peasants Protest Rising Feudal Exactions

In the late fifteenth and early sixteenth centuries German feudal lords, both secular and ecclesiastical, tried to increase the earnings from their lands by raising demands on their peasant tenants. As the personal freedoms of peasants were restricted, their properties confiscated, and their traditional laws and customs overridden, massive revolts occurred in southern Germany in 1525. Not a few historians, especially those of Marxist persuasion, see this uprising and the social and economic conditions that gave rise to it, as the major historical force in early modern history. The following, from Memmingen, in modern West Germany, is the most representative and well-known statement of peasant grievances.

1. *It is our humble petition and desire . . . that in the future . . . each community should choose and appoint a pastor, and that we should have the right to depose him should he conduct himself improperly. . . .*

2. *We are ready and willing to pay the fair tithe of grain. . . . The small tithes [of cattle], whether [to] ecclesiastical or lay lords, we will not pay at all, for the Lord God created cattle for the free use of man. . . .*

3. *We . . . take it for granted that you will release us from serfdom as true Christians, unless it should be shown us from the Gospel that we are serfs.*

4. *It has been the custom heretofore that no poor man should be allowed to catch venison or wildfowl or fish in flowing water, which seems to us quite unseemly and unbrotherly as well as selfish and not agreeable to the Word of God. . . .*

5. *We are aggrieved in the matter of woodcutting, for the noblemen have appropriated all the woods to themselves. . . .*

6. *In regard to the excessive services demanded of us which are increased from day to day, we ask that this matter be properly looked into so that we shall not continue to be oppressed in this way. . . .*

7. *We will not hereafter allow ourselves to be further oppressed by our lords, but will let them demand only what is just and proper according to the word of* the agreement between the lord and the peasant. The lord should no longer try to force more services or other dues from the peasant without payment. . . .

8. *We are greatly burdened because our holdings cannot support the rent exacted from them. . . . We ask that the lords may appoint persons of honor to inspect these holdings and fix a rent in accordance with justice. . . .*

9. *We are burdened with a great evil in the constant making of new laws. . . . In our opinion we should be judged according to the old written law. . . .*

10. *We are aggrieved by the appropriation . . . of meadows and fields which at one time belonged to a community as a whole. These we will take again into our own hands. . . .*

11. *We will entirely abolish the due called* Todfall *[that is, heriot or death tax, by which the lord received the best horse, cow, or garment of a family upon the death of a serf] and will no longer endure it, nor allow widows and orphans to be thus shamefully robbed against God's will, and in violation of justice and right. . . .*

12. *It is our conclusion and final resolution, that if any one or more of the articles here set forth should not be in agreement with the Word of God, as we think they are, such article we will willingly retract.*

Translations and Reprints from the Original Sources of European History, Vol. 2 (Philadelphia: Department of History, University of Pennsylvania, 1897).

Like the German Humanists, the German peasantry also had at first believed Luther to be an ally. The peasantry had been organized since the late fifteenth century against efforts by territorial princes to override their traditional laws and customs and to subject them to new regulations and taxes. Peasant leaders, several of whom were convinced Lutherans, saw in Luther's teaching about Christian freedom and his criticism of monastic landowners a point of view close to their own, and

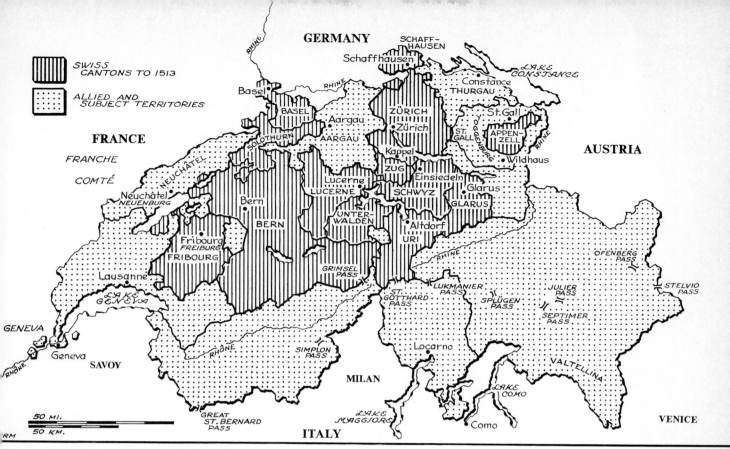

THE SWISS CONFEDERATION

MAP 14.3   *While nominally still a part of the Holy Roman Empire, Switzerland grew from a loose defensive union of the central "forest cantons" in the thirteenth century to a fiercely independent association of regions with different languages, histories, and, finally, religions.*

they openly solicited Luther's support of their political and economic rights, including their revolutionary request for release from serfdom. Luther and his followers sympathized with the peasants; indeed, for several years Lutheran pamphleteers made *Karsthans* ("crude Hans"), the burly, honest peasant who earned his bread by the sweat of his brow and sacrificed his own comfort and well-being for others, a symbol of the simple life that God desired all people to live. The Lutherans, however, were not social revolutionaries, and when the peasants revolted against their masters in 1524–1525, Luther not surprisingly condemned them in the strongest possible terms as "unchristian" and urged the princes to crush their revolt without mercy. Tens of thousands of peasants (estimates run between 70,000 and 100,000) had died by the time the revolt was put down.

For Luther, the freedom of the Christian was an inner release from guilt and anxiety, not a right to restructure society by violent revolution. Had Luther supported the Peasants' Revolt, he would not only have contradicted his own teaching and belief but also ended any chance of the survival of his reform beyond the 1520s.

Zwingli and the Swiss Reformation

Switzerland was a loose confederacy of thirteen autonomous cantons or states and allied areas (see Map 14.3). Some cantons (e.g., Zurich, Bern, Basel, and Schaffhausen) became Protestant, some (especially around the Lucerne heartland) remained Catholic, and a few other cantons and regions managed to effect a compromise. Among the preconditions of the Swiss Reformation were the growth of national sentiment occasioned by opposition to foreign mercenary service (providing mercenaries for Europe's warring nations was a major source of Switzerland's livelihood) and a desire for church reform that had persisted in Switzerland since the councils of Constance (1414–1417) and Basel (1431–1449).

The Reformation in Zurich

Ulrich Zwingli (1484–1531), the leader of the Swiss Reformation, had been humanistically educated in Bern, Vienna, and Basel. He was strongly influenced by Erasmus, whom he credited with having set him on the path to reform. He served as a chaplain with Swiss mercenaries during the disastrous Battle of Marignano in 1515 and thereafter became an eloquent critic of mercenary service. Zwingli believed that this service threatened both the political sovereignty and the moral well-being of the Swiss confederacy. By 1518 Zwingli was also widely known for opposition to the sale of indulgences and to religious superstition. In 1519 he entered the competition for the post of people's priest in the main church of Zurich. His candidacy was contested because of his acknowledged fornication with a barber's daughter, an affair he successfully minimized in a forcefully written self-defense. Actually his conduct was less scandalous to his contemporaries, who sympathized with the plight of celibate clergy, than it may be to the modern reader. One of Zwingli's first acts as a reformer was to petition for an end to clerical celibacy and for the right of all clergy to marry, a practice that quickly became accepted in all Protestant lands.

From his new position as people's priest in Zurich, Zwingli engineered the Swiss Reformation. In March 1522 he was party to the breaking of the Lenten fast—an act of protest analogous to burning one's national flag today. Zwingli's reform guideline was very simple and very effective: whatever lacked literal support in Scripture was to be neither believed nor practiced. As had also happened with Luther, that test soon raised questions about such honored traditional teachings and practices as fasting, transubstantiation, the worship of saints, pilgrimages, purgatory, clerical celibacy, and certain sacraments. A disputation held on January 29, 1523, concluded with the city government's sanction of Zwingli's Scripture test. Thereafter Zurich became, to all intents and purposes, a Protestant city and the center of the Swiss Reformation. A harsh discipline was imposed by the new Protestant regime, making Zurich one of the first examples of a puritanical Protestant city.

The Marburg Colloquy

Landgrave Philip of Hesse (1504–1567) sought to unite Swiss and German Protestants in a mutual defense pact, a potentially significant political alliance. His efforts were spoiled, however, by theological disagreements between Luther and Zwingli over the nature of Christ's presence in the Eucharist. Zwingli maintained a symbolic interpretation of Christ's words, "This is my body"; Christ he argued, was only spiritually, not bodily, present in the bread and wine of the Eucharist. Luther, to the contrary, insisted that Christ's human nature could share the properties of his divine nature; hence, where Christ was spiritually present, he could also be bodily present, for his was a special nature. Luther wanted no part of an abstract, spiritualized Christ. Zwingli, on the other hand, feared that Luther had not broken sufficiently with medieval sacramental theology.

Philip of Hesse brought the two Protestant leaders together in his castle in Marburg in early October 1529, but they were unable to work out their differences on this issue. Luther left thinking Zwingli a dangerous fanatic. Although cooperation between the two sides did not cease, the disagreement splintered the Protestant movement theologically and politically. Separate defense leagues formed, and semi-Zwinglian theological views came to be embodied in the *Confessio Tetrapolitana,* a confession of faith prepared by the Strasbourg reformers Martin Bucer and Caspar Hedio for presentation to the Diet of Augsburg (1530) as an alternative to the Lutheran *Augsburg Confession.*

Swiss Civil Wars

As the Swiss cantons divided between Protestantism and Catholicism, civil wars began. There were two major battles, both at Kappel, one in June 1529 and a second in October 1531. The first ended in a Protestant victory, which forced the Catholic cantons to break their foreign alliances and to recognize the rights of Swiss Protestants. During the second battle Zwingli was found wounded on the battlefield and unceremoniously executed, his remains scattered to the four winds so that his followers would have no relics to console and inspire them. The subsequent treaty confirmed the right of each canton to determine its own religion. Heinrich Bullinger (1504–1575), who was Zwingli's protégé and later married his daughter, became the new leader of the Swiss Reformation and guided its development into an established religion.

Anabaptists and Radical Protestants

The moderate pace and seemingly low ethical results of the Lutheran and Zwinglian reformations discontented many people, among them some of the original co-workers of Luther and Zwingli. Many desired a more rapid and thorough implementation of primitive Christianity—that is, a more visible moral transformation—and accused the major reformers of going only halfway. The most important of these radical groups were the Anabaptists, the sixteenth-century ancestors of the modern Mennonites and Amish. The Anabaptists were especially distinguished by their rejection of infant baptism and their insistence on only adult baptism (*anabaptism* derives from the Greek word meaning "to rebaptize"), believing that baptism as a consenting adult conformed to Scripture and was more respectful of human freedom.

~ Zwingli Lists the Errors of the Roman Church

Religious argument can become confusing. A clear summary of issues is often helpful—both to the disputants and to interested bystanders. Prior to the first Zurich Disputation (1523), which effectually introduced the Protestant Reformation in Zurich, the reformer Zwingli prepared such a summary of the new Evangelical truths and the errors of the Roman church, known as the *Sixty-Seven Articles*. Here are some of them.

All who consider other teachings equal to or higher than the Gospel err, and they do not know what the Gospel is.

In the faith rests our salvation, and in unbelief our damnation; for all truth is clear in Christ.

In the Gospel one learns that human doctrines and decrees do not aid in salvation.

That Christ, having sacrificed himself once, is to eternity a certain and valid sacrifice for the sins of all faithful, wherefrom it follows that the Mass is not a sacrifice, but is a remembrance of the sacrifice and assurance of the salvation which Christ has given us.

That God desires to give us all things in his name, whence it follows that outside of this life we need no [intercession of the saints or any] mediator except himself.

That no Christian is bound to do those things which God has not decreed, therefore one may eat at all times all food, wherefrom one learns that the decree about cheese and butter [i.e., fasting from such foods at certain times of the year] is a Roman swindle.

That no special person can impose the ban upon [i.e., excommunicate] anyone, but the Church, that is, the congregation of those among whom the one to be banned dwells, together with their watchman, i.e., the pastor.

All that the so-called spiritual [i.e., the papal church] claims to have of power and protection belongs to the lay [i.e., the secular magistracy], if they wish to be Christians.

Greater offence I know not than that one does not allow priests to have wives, but permits them to hire prostitutes.

Christ has borne all our pains and labor. Hence whoever assigns to works of penance what belongs to Christ errs and slanders God.

The true divine Scriptures know naught about purgatory after this life.

The Scriptures know no priests except those who proclaim the word of God.

Ulrich Zwingli (1484–1531): *Selected Works*, ed. by Samuel M. Jackson (Philadelphia: University of Pennsylvania Press, 1972), pp. 111–117.

Conrad Grebel and the Swiss Brethren

Conrad Grebel (1498–1526), with whom Anabaptism originated, performed the first adult rebaptism in Zurich in January 1525. Initially a coworker with Zwingli and an even greater biblical literalist, Grebel broke openly with Zwingli after a religious disputation in October 1523 in which Zwingli supported the city government's plea for a gradual removal of traditional religious practices. The alternative of the Swiss Brethren, as Grebel's group came to be called, was set forth in the *Schleitheim Confession* of 1527. This document distinguished Anabaptists not only by their practice of adult baptism but also by their refusal to go to war, swear oaths, and participate in the offices of secular government. Anabaptists physically separated from society to form a more perfect community in imitation of what they believed to be the example of the first Christians. Because of the close connection between religious and civic life in this period, such separatism was viewed by the political authorities as a threat to basic social bonds.

The Anabaptist Reign in Münster

At first, Anabaptism drew its adherents from all social classes. But as Lutherans and Zwinglians joined with Catholics in opposition to the Anabaptists and persecuted them within the cities, a more rural, agrarian class came to make up the great majority. In 1529 rebaptism became a capital offense throughout the Holy Roman Empire. It has been estimated that between 1525 and 1618 at least one thousand and perhaps as many as five thousand men and women were executed for rebaptising themselves as adults. Brutal measures were universally applied against nonconformists after Anabaptist extremists came to power in the German city of Münster in 1534–1535. Led by two Dutch emigrants, a baker, Jan Matthys of Haarlem, and a tailor, Jan Beukelsz of Leiden, the Anabaptist majority in this city forced Lutherans and Catholics either to convert or to emigrate. As the Lutherans and Catholics left, Münster transformed itself into an Old Testament theocracy, replete with charismatic leaders and the practice of polygamy. The outside world was deeply shocked. Protestant and Catholic armies united to crush the radicals, and the skeletons of their leaders long hung in public view as a warning to all who would so offend traditional Christian sensitivities. After this episode, moderate, pacifistic Anabaptism became the norm among most nonconformists. The moderate Anabaptist leader Menno Simons (1496–1561), the founder of the Mennonites, set the example for the future.

Spiritualists

In addition to the Anabaptists there were radicals known as *Spiritualists*. These were mostly isolated individuals distinguished by their disdain of all traditions and institutions. They believed that the only religious authority was God's spirit, which spoke here and now to every individual. Among them were several former Lutherans: Thomas Müntzer (d. 1525), who had close contacts with Anabaptist leaders in Germany and Switzerland and died as a leader of a peasants' revolt; Sebastian Franck (d. 1541), a free-lance critic of all dogmatic religion who proclaimed the religious autonomy of every individual soul; and Caspar Schwenckfeld (d. 1561), a prolific writer and wanderer after whom the Schwenckfeldian Church is named.

Antitrinitarians

A final group of radical Protestants was the Antitrinitarians, exponents of a commonsense, rational, and ethical religion. Chief among this group were the Spaniard Michael Servetus (1511–1553), executed in 1553 in Geneva for "blasphemies against the Holy Trinity," and the Italians Lelio (d. 1562) and Faustus Sozzini (d. 1604), the founders of Socinianism. These thinkers were the strongest opponents of Calvinism (to be discussed later), especially its belief in original sin and predestination, and have a deserved reputation as defenders of religious toleration.

Political Consolidation of the Lutheran Reformation

The Diet of Augsburg

Charles V, who spent most of his time on politics and military maneuvers outside the empire, especially in Spain and Italy, returned to the empire in 1530 to direct the Diet of Augsburg, a meeting of Protestant and Catholic representatives assembled

The siege of Münster in 1534–1535. A joint Catholic-Protestant army recaptured the city from the Anabaptists led by Jan of Leiden. [Bilderchiv Foto Marburg.]

for the purpose of imposing a settlement of the religious divisions. With its terms dictated by the Catholic emperor, the diet adjourned with a blunt order to all Lutherans to revert to Catholicism. The Reformation was by this time too firmly established for that to occur, and in February 1531 the Lutherans responded with the formation of their own defensive alliance, the Schmalkaldic League. The league took as its banner the *Augsburg Confession,* a moderate statement of Protestant beliefs that had been spurned by the emperor at the Diet of Augsburg. In 1538 Luther drew up a more strongly worded Protestant confession known as the *Schmalkaldic Articles.* Under the leadership of Landgrave Philip of Hesse and Elector John Frederick of Saxony, the league achieved a stalemate with the emperor, who was again distracted by renewed war with France and the ever-resilient Turks.

The Expansion of the Reformation

In the 1530s German Lutherans formed regional consistories, judicial bodies composed of theologians and lawyers, which oversaw and administered the new Protestant churches. These consistories replaced the old Catholic episcopates. Under the leadership of Philip Melanchthon, the "praeceptor of Germany," educational reforms were enacted that provided for compulsory primary education, schools for girls, a Humanist revision of the traditional curriculum, and catechetical instruction of the laity in the new religion.

The Reformation also dug in elsewhere. Introduced into Denmark by Christian II (ruled 1513–1523), Danish Lutheranism throve under Frederick I (1523–1533), who joined the Schmalkaldic League. Under Christian III (1536–1559) Lutheranism became the state religion, and the Wittenberg preacher Johannes Bugenhagen arrived to organize the Danish Lutheran church.

In Sweden Gustavus Vasa (1523–1560), supported by a Swedish nobility greedy for church lands, confiscated church property and subjected the clergy to royal authority at the Diet of Vesteras (1527).

In politically splintered Poland, Lutherans, Anabaptists, Calvinists, and even Antitrinitarians found room to practice their beliefs, as Poland, primarily because of the absence of a central political author-

A Catholic caricature of Martin Luther as a seven-headed monster. This picture served as the title page of a pamphlet by one of Luther's strongest Catholic critics, Johannes Cochlaeus.

ity, became a model of religious pluralism and toleration in the second half of the sixteenth century.

REACTION AGAINST PROTESTANTS: THE INTERIM. Charles V made abortive efforts in 1540–1541 to enforce a compromise agreement between Protestants and Catholics. As these and other conciliar efforts failed, he turned to a military solution. In 1547 imperial armies crushed the Protestant Schmalkaldic League. John Frederick of Saxony was defeated in April 1547, and Philip of Hesse was taken captive shortly thereafter.

The emperor established puppet rulers in Saxony and Hesse and issued as imperial law the *Augsburg Interim,* a new order that Protestants everywhere must readopt old Catholic beliefs and practices. There were a few cosmetic Protestant concessions, for example, clerical marriage (with papal approval of individual cases) and communion in both kinds (that is, bread *and* wine). Although the *Interim* met only surface acceptance

within Germany, it forced many Protestant leaders into exile. The Strasbourg reformer Martin Bucer, for example, departed to England, where he played an important role in the drafting of the religious documents of the English Reformation during the reign of Edward VI. In Germany, Magdeburg became a refuge for persecuted Protestants and the center of Lutheran resistance.

The Peace of Augsburg

The Reformation was too entrenched by 1547 to be ended even by brute force. Maurice of Saxony, hand-picked by Charles V to rule Saxony, recognized the inevitability of Protestantism and shifted his allegiance to the Protestants. Confronted by fierce Protestant resistance and weary from three decades of war, the emperor was forced to relent. After a defeat by Protestant armies in 1552 Charles

A Protestant caricature of the pope as a monster with the characteristics of several beasts. Note in the background the flag with the pope's "keys" to heaven and hell.

reinstated John Frederick and Philip of Hesse and guaranteed Lutheran religious freedoms in the Peace of Passau (August 1552), a declaration that effectively surrendered his lifelong quest for European religious unity.

The division of Christendom was made permanent by the Peace of Augsburg in September 1555. This agreement recognized in law what had already been well established in practice: *cuius regio, eius religio,* meaning that the ruler of a land would determine the religion of the land. Lutherans were permitted to retain all church lands forcibly seized before 1552. An "ecclesiastical reservation" was added, however, that was intended to prevent high Catholic prelates who converted to Protestantism from retaining their lands, titles, and privileges. Those discontent with the religion of their region were permitted to migrate to another.

Calvinism and Anabaptism were not recognized as legal forms of Christian belief and practice by the Peace of Augsburg. Anabaptists had long adjusted to such exclusion by forming their own separatist communities. Calvinists, however, were not separatists and could not choose this route; they remained determined not only to secure the right to worship publicly as they pleased but also to shape society according to their own religious convictions. While Anabaptists retreated and Lutherans enjoyed the security of an established religion, Calvinists organized to lead national revolutions throughout northern Europe in the second half of the sixteenth century.

John Calvin and the Genevan Reformation

In the second half of the sixteenth century Calvinism replaced Lutheranism as the dominant Protestant force in Europe. Calvinism was the religious ideology that inspired or accompanied massive political resistance in France, the Netherlands, and Scotland. It established itself within the Palatinate during the reign of Elector Frederick III (1559–1576). Believing strongly in both divine predestination and the individual's responsibility to reorder society according to God's plan, Calvinists became zealous reformers determined to transform and order society in such a way that men and women would act externally as they believed, or should believe, internally and were destined to live eternally. In a famous study, *The Protestant Ethic*

The Genevan reformer and Protestant theologian, John Calvin (1509–1564). [Musée Historique de la Réformation et Bibliothèque Calvinienne, Geneva. H. Pattusch.]

and the Spirit of Capitalism (1904), the German sociologist Max Weber argued that this peculiar combination of confidence and self-disciplined activism produced an ethic that stimulated and reinforced the spirit of emergent capitalism, bringing Calvinism and later Puritanism into close association with the development of modern capitalist societies.

The founder of Calvinism, John Calvin (1509–1564), was born into a well-to-do family, the son of the secretary to the bishop of Noyon in Picardy. He received church benefices at age twelve, which financed the best possible education at Parisian colleges and a law degree at Orléans. Calvin associated with members of the indigenous French reform party, a group of Catholic Humanists led by Jacques Lefèvre d'Étaples and Marguerite d'Angoulême, the queen of Navarre after 1527. Although Calvin finally rejected this group as ineffectual, its members contributed to his preparation as a religious reformer. Their sincere but largely hortatory approach to reform was portrayed in Calvin's first published work, a commentary on Seneca's *De Clementia* in 1533.

It was probably in the spring of 1534 that Calvin experienced that conversion to Protestantism by which he says his "long stubborn heart" was "made teachable" by God—a personal model of reform he would later apply to the recalcitrant citizenry of Geneva. In May 1534 he dramatically surrendered the benefices he had held for so long and at such profit and joined the Reformation.

Political Revolt and Religious Reform in Geneva

Whereas in Saxony religious reform paved the way for a political revolution against the emperor, in Geneva a political revolution against the local prince-bishop laid the foundation for the religious change. Genevans successfully revolted against the House of Savoy and their resident prince-bishop in the late 1520s. Assisted by the Swiss city-states of Fribourg and Bern, the Genevans drove out the prince-bishop in August 1527, and the city councils assumed his legal and political powers. In late 1533 Bern dispatched the Protestant reformers Guillaume Farel (1489–1565) and Antoine Froment (1508–1581) to Geneva. In the summer of 1535, after much internal turmoil, the Protestants triumphed, and the traditional Mass and other religious practices were removed. On May 21, 1536, the city voted officially to adopt the Reformation: "to live according to the Gospel and the Word of God . . . without . . . any more masses, statues, idols, or other papal abuses."

CALVIN AND FAREL. Calvin arrived in Geneva after these events, in July 1536. He might not have come to Geneva at all had the third Hapsburg–Valois war not forced him to detour there. Calvin was actually en route to a scholarly refuge in Strasbourg, in flight from Protestant persecution in France, when the war forced him to turn sharply south to Geneva. Farel successfully pleaded with him to stay and assist the Reformation, threatening Calvin with divine vengeance if he turned away from this task.

Before a year had passed, Calvin had drawn up articles for the governance of the new church as well as a catechism to guide and discipline the people, both of which were presented for approval to the city councils in early 1537. Because of the strong measures proposed to govern Geneva's moral life, the reformers were suspected by many of desiring to create a "new papacy." Their orthodoxy was attacked, and Geneva's powerful Protestant ally, Bern, which had adopted a more moderate Protestant reform, pressured Geneva's magistrates to restore the traditional religious ceremonies and holidays abolished by Calvin and Farel. Both within and outside Geneva Calvin and Farel

were perceived as going too far too fast. In February 1538 the four syndics (the chief magistrates of the city) chosen in the annual election turned against Calvin and Farel. Two months later the defiant reformers were exiled from the city.

Calvin went to Strasbourg, a model Protestant city, where he became pastor to the French exiles there. During his long stay in Strasbourg Calvin wrote biblical commentaries and a second edition of his masterful *Institutes of the Christian Religion,* which many consider the definitive theological statement of the Protestant faith. Calvin also married and participated in the ecumenical discussions urged on Protestants and Catholics by Charles V. Most importantly, he learned from the Strasbourg reformer Martin Bucer how to implement the Protestant Reformation successfully.

CALVIN'S GENEVA. In 1540 Geneva elected syndics who were both favorable to Calvin and determined to establish full Genevan political and religious independence from Bern. They knew Calvin would be a valuable ally in the latter project and invited him to return. This he did in September 1540, never to leave the city again. Within months of his arrival new ecclesiastical ordinances were implemented that provided for cooperation between the magistrates and the clergy in matters of internal discipline. Following the Strasbourg model, the Genevan church was organized into four offices: (1) pastors, of whom there were five; (2) teachers or doctors to instruct the populace in and to defend true doctrine; (3) elders, a group of twelve laymen chosen by and from the Genevan councils and empowered to "oversee the life of everybody"; and (4) deacons to dispense church goods and services to the poor and the sick.

Calvin and his followers were motivated above all by a desire to transform society morally. Faith, Calvin taught, did not sit idly in the mind but conformed one's every action to God's law. The "elect" should live in a manifestly god-pleasing way, if they were truly God's elect. In the attempted realization of this goal Calvin spared no effort. The consistory became Calvin's instrument of power. This body was composed of the elders and the pastors and was presided over by one of the four syndics. It enforced the strictest moral discipline, meting out punishments for a broad range of moral and religious transgressions—from missing church services (a fine of 3 sous) to fornication (six days on bread and water and a fine of 60 sous)—and, as time passed, increasingly for criticism of Calvin and

❧ Theodore Beza Describes John Calvin's Final Days

Calvin's ceaseless labor to make Geneva a bulwark of Protestantism left him an ill and worn-out man at fifty-five. He remained nonetheless a model of discipline to the end. The following description comes from an admiring biography by Calvin's successor, Theodore Beza.

On the 6th of February, 1564, . . . he delivered his last sermon. . . . From this period he taught no more in public, except that he was carried at different times, until the last day of March, to the meeting of the congregation, and addressed them in a few words. His diseases, contracted by incredible labours of mind and body, were various and complicated. . . . He was naturally of a spare and feeble frame, tending to consumption. During sleep he seemed almost awake, and spent a great part of the year in preaching, teaching, and dictating. For at least ten years . . . the only food he [had taken] was at supper, so that it is astonishing how he could so long escape consumption. He frequently suffered from migraine, which he cured only by fasting, so as occasionally to refrain from food for thirty-six hours. But by overstraining his voice and . . . by an immoderate use of aloes, he suffered from hemorrhoids, which degenerated into ulcers, and five years before

his death he was occasionally attacked by a spitting of blood. [He also suffered from] gout in the right leg, frequently returning pains of colic, and stone, which he had only felt a few months before his death. . . . The physicians neglected no remedies, and he observed the directions of his medical attendants with a strictness which none could surpass. . . . Though tormented by so many diseases, no one ever heard him utter a word unbecoming a man of bravery, much less a Christian. Only lifting up his eyes to heaven, he used to say, "How long, O Lord!" for even in health he often had this sentence on his lips, when he spoke of the calamities of his brethren, with whose sufferings he was both day and night more afflicted than with any of his own. When admonished and entreated by us to forbear, at least in his sickness, from the labour of dictating, or at least of writing, "What, then," he said, "would you have my Lord find me idle when he cometh?"

Theodore Beza, *The Life of John Calvin*, trans. by Francis Gibson (Philadelphia: Westminster, 1836), pp. 78–79.

the consistory. Calvin ridiculed his opponents as undisciplined "Libertines."

Among the many personal conflicts in Geneva that gave Calvin his reputation as a stern moralist, none proved more damaging than his active role in the capture and execution of the Spanish physician and amateur theologian Michael Servetus in 1553. After 1555 the city's syndics were all devout Calvinists, and Geneva became home to thousands of exiled Protestants who had been driven out of France, England, and Scotland. Refugees (more than five thousand), most of them utterly loyal to Calvin, came to make up over one third of the population of Geneva. From this time until his death in 1564, Calvin's position in the city was greatly strengthened and the syndics were very cooperative.

Catholic Reform and Counter-Reformation

Sources of Catholic Reform

The Protestant Reformation did not take the medieval church completely by surprise. There were much internal criticism and many efforts at internal reform before there was a Counter-Reformation in reaction to Protestant successes. Before the Reformation ambitious proposals had been set forth to bring about the long-demanded reform of the church in head and members. One of the boldest attempts came on the eve of the Fifth Lateran Council (1513–1517), the last reform council before the Reformation, and was drafted by two Venetian monks, Tommaso Giustiniani and Vincenzo Quirini. Their program went so far as to call for a revision of the *Corpus Juris Canonici,* the massive body of church law that authorized papal practices and ensured papal prerogatives. Sixteenth-century popes, ever mindful of the way the councils of Constance and Basel had stripped the pope of his traditional powers, quickly squelched such efforts to bring about basic changes in the laws and institutions of the church. High Renaissance popes preferred the charge given to the Fifth Lateran Council in the keynote address by Giles of Viterbo, the superior general of the Hermits of Saint Augustine: "Men are to be changed by, not to change, religion." The Fifth Lateran Council remained a regional council completely within the pope's control and brought about no significant reforms. The very month after its adjournment Martin Luther posted his ninety-five theses.

As the Fifth Lateran Council suggests, the most important reform initiatives did not always issue from the papal court. Catholic reformers were found within a variety of self-motivated lay and clerical movements. Two important organizations that brought reform-minded clergy and laity together were the Modern Devotion (already discussed) and the Oratory of Divine Love. The latter, founded in Rome in 1517, was an exclusive informal organization of earnest laity and clergy who were both learned and deeply committed to traditional religious devotion. Like that of Erasmus, whose religious writings the members admired, their basic belief was that inner piety and good Christian living, not theological arguments and disputations, were the surest way to reform the church.

Many new religious orders also sprang up in the sixteenth century to lead a broad revival of piety within the church. The first of these was the Theatines, an elitist order, founded in 1524 to groom devout and reform-minded leaders at the higher levels of the church hierarchy. One of the cofounders was Bishop Gian Pietro Carafa, the future Pope Paul IV. Another new order, whose mission pointed in the opposite direction, was the Capuchins. Authorized by the pope in 1528, they sought to return to the original ascetic and charitable ideals of Saint Francis and became very popular among the ordinary people, to whom they directed their ministry. The Somaschi, who became active in the mid-1520s, and the Barnabites, founded in 1530, endeavored to repair the moral, spiritual,

and physical damage done to people in war-torn areas of Italy. The members of the new order of Ursulines, founded in 1535, established convents in Italy and France for the religious education of girls from all social classes and became very influential. Another new religious order, the Oratorians, officially recognized in 1575, was an elite group of secular clerics, who devoted themselves to the promotion of religious literature and church music. Among their members was the great Catholic hymnist and musician Giovanni Palestrina (1526–1594).

In addition to these lay and clerical movements the Spanish mystics Saint Teresa of Avila (1515–1528) and Saint John of the Cross (1542–1591) revived and popularized the mystical piety of medieval monasticism.

Ignatius of Loyola and the Jesuits

Of the various reform groups none was more instrumental in the success of the Counter-Reformation than the Society of Jesus, the new order of Jesuits, organized by Ignatius of Loyola in the 1530s and officially recognized by the church in 1540. The Society grew within the space of a century from its original ten members to more than fifteen thousand members scattered throughout

Ignatius of Loyola, founder of the Society of Jesus. After a painting by Peter Paul Rubens (1577–1640). [Bettman Archive.]

❧ Ignatius of Loyola's "Rules for Thinking With the Church"

As leaders of the Counter-Reformation, the Jesuits attempted to live by and instill in others the strictest obedience to church authority. The following are some of the eighteen rules included by Ignatius in his *Spiritual Exercises* to give pious Catholics positive direction. These rules also indicate the Catholic reformers' refusal to compromise with Protestants.

In order to have the proper attitude of mind in the Church Militant we should observe the following rules:

1. Putting aside all private judgment, we should keep our minds prepared and ready to obey promptly and in all things the true spouse of Christ our Lord, our Holy Mother, the hierarchical Church.

2. To praise sacramental confession and the reception of the Most Holy Sacrament once a year, and much better once a month, and better still every week. . . .

3. To praise the frequent hearing of Mass. . . .

4. To praise highly the religious life, virginity, and continence; and also matrimony, but not as highly. . . .

5. To praise the vows of religion, obedience, poverty, chastity, and other works of perfection and supererogation. . . .

6. To praise the relics of the saints . . . [and] the stations, pilgrimages, indulgences, jubilees, Crusade indulgences, and the lighting of candles in the churches.

7. To praise the precepts concerning fasts and abstinences . . . and acts of penance. . . .

8. To praise the adornments and buildings of churches as well as sacred images. . . .

9. To praise all the precepts of the church. . . .

10. To approve and praise the directions and recommendations of our superiors as well as their personal behaviour. . . .

11. To praise both positive and scholastic theology. . . .

12. We must be on our guard against making comparisons between the living and those who have already gone to their reward, for it is no small error to say, for example: 'This man knows more than St. Augustine'; 'He is another Saint Francis, or even greater'. . . .

13. If we wish to be sure that we are right in all things, we should always be ready to accept this principle: I will believe that the white that I see is black, if the hierarchical Church so defines it. For I believe that between . . . Christ our Lord and . . . His Church, there is but one spirit, which governs and directs us for the salvation of our souls.

The Spiritual Exercises of St. Ignatius, trans. by Anthony Mottola (Garden City, N.Y.: Doubleday, 1964), pp. 139–141.

the world, with thriving missions in India, Japan, and the Americas.

The founder of the Jesuits, Ignatius of Loyola (1491–1556), was a truly heroic figure. A dashing courtier and caballero in his youth, he began his spiritual pilgrimage in 1521 after he had been seriously wounded in the legs during a battle with the French. During a lengthy and painful convalescence, he passed the time by reading Christian classics. So impressed was he with the heroic self-sacrifice of the church's saints and their methods of overcoming mental anguish and pain that he underwent a profound religious conversion; henceforth he, too, would serve the church as a soldier of Christ.

After recuperating, Ignatius applied the lessons he had learned during his convalescence to a program of religious and moral self-discipline that came to be embodied in the *Spiritual Exercises*. This psychologically perceptive devotional guide contained mental and emotional exercises designed to teach one absolute spiritual self-mastery over one's feelings. It taught that a person could shape his or her own behavior, even create a new religious self, through disciplined study and regular practice.

Whereas in Jesuit eyes Protestants had distin-

The Council of Trent in session. The Council met in three separate sessions over an eighteen-year period beginning in 1545 and formed the Catholic response to the theological divisions of the later Middle Ages and to the Protestant Reformation. This painting is possibly by the Venetian painter Titian (1477–1576). [Musée du Louvre, Paris. Cliché des Musées Nationaux.]

guished themselves by disobedience to church authority and religious innovation, the exercises of Ignatius were intended to teach good Catholics to deny themselves and submit without question to higher church authority and spiritual direction. Perfect discipline and self-control were the essential conditions of such obedience. To these was added the enthusiasm of traditional spirituality and mysticism—a potent combination that helped counter the Reformation and win many Protestants back to the Catholic fold, especially in Austria and Bavaria and along the Rhine.

The Council of Trent (1545–1563)

The broad success of the Reformation and the insistence of the Emperor Charles V forced Pope Paul to call a general council of the church to define religious doctrine. In anticipation Pope Paul appointed a reform commission, chaired by Caspar Contarini (1483–1542). Contarini, a member of the Oratory of Divine Love, was open to many reforms (his critics even described him as "semi-Lutheran"), and his committee consisted of some very liberal Catholic clergy. Their report, presented to the pope in February 1537, bluntly criticized the fiscality and simony of the papal Curia as the primary source of the church's loss of esteem. This report was so critical, in fact, that Pope Paul attempted unsuccessfully to suppress its publication. Protestants reprinted and circulated it as justification of their criticism.

The long-delayed council of the church met in 1545 in the imperial city of Trent in northern Italy.

There were three sessions, spread over eighteen years, with long interruptions due to war, plague, and imperial and papal politics. The council met from 1545 to 1547, from 1551 to 1552, and from 1562 to 1563, a period that spanned the careers of four different popes.

Unlike the general councils of the fifteenth century, Trent was strictly under the pope's control, with high Italian prelates very prominent in the proceedings. Initially four of the five attending archbishops and twenty-one of the twenty-three attending bishops were Italians. Even at its final session in 1562 over three quarters of the council fathers were Italians. Voting was limited to high churchmen; university theologians, the lower clergy, and the laity were not permitted to share in the council's decisions.

The council's most important reforms concerned internal church discipline. Steps were taken to curtail the selling of church offices and other religious goods. Many bishops who resided in Rome rather than within their dioceses were forced to move to their appointed seats of authority. Trent strengthened the authority of local bishops so that they could effectively discipline popular religious practice. The bishops were also subjected to new rules that required them not only to reside in their dioceses, but also to be highly visible by preaching regularly and conducting annual visitations. Trent also sought to give the parish priest a brighter image by requiring him to be neatly dressed, better educated, strictly celibate, and active among his parishioners. To this end Trent also called for the construction of a seminary in every diocese.

Not a single doctrinal concession was made to the Protestants, however. In the face of Protestant criticism the Council of Trent gave a ringing reaffirmation to the traditional Scholastic education of the clergy; the role of good works in salvation; the authority of tradition; the seven sacraments; transubstantiation; the withholding of the Eucharistic cup from the laity; clerical celibacy; the reality of purgatory; the veneration of saints, relics, and sacred images; and the granting of letters of indulgence. The council resolved medieval Scholastic quarrels in favor of the theology of Saint Thomas Aquinas, further enhancing his authority within the church. The strongest resistance was thereafter offered by the church to groups like the Jansenists, who strongly endorsed the medieval Augustinian tradition, a source of alternative Catholic as well as many Protestant doctrines.

PROGRESS OF PROTESTANT REFORMATION ON THE CONTINENT

1513–1517	Fifth Lateran Council fails to bring about reform in the church
1517	Luther posts 95 theses against indulgences
1519	Charles I of Spain elected Holy Roman Emperor (as Charles V)
1519	Luther challenges infallibility of pope and inerrancy of church councils at Leipzig Debate
1521	Papal bull excommunicates Luther for heresy
1521	Diet of Worms condemns Luther
1521–1522	Luther translates the New Testament into German
1524–1525	The Peasants' Revolt in Germany
1527	The *Schleitheim Confession* of the Anabaptists
1529	The Marburg Colloquy between Luther and Zwingli
1530	The Diet of Augsburg fails to settle religious differences
1531	Formation of Protestant Schmalkaldic League
1534–1535	Anabaptists assume political power in city of Münster
1536	Calvin arrives in Geneva
1540	Jesuits, founded by Ignatius of Loyola, recognized as order by pope
1546	Luther dies
1547	Armies of Charles V crush Schmalkaldic League
1548	Augsburg *Interim* outlaws Protestant practices
1555	Peace of Augsburg recognizes rights of Lutherans to worship as they please
1545–1563	Council of Trent institutes reforms and responds to the Reformation

Rulers initially resisted Trent's reform decrees, fearing a revival of papal political power within their lands. But with the passage of time and the pope's assurances that religious reforms were his sole intent, the new legislation took hold and parish life revived under the guidance of a devout and better-trained clergy.

The English Reformation to 1553

The Preconditions of Reform

Late medieval England had a reputation for maintaining the rights of the crown against the pope. Edward I (d. 1307) had rejected efforts by Pope Boniface VIII to prevent secular taxation of the clergy. Parliament passed the first Statutes of Provisors and *Praemunire* in the mid-fourteenth century curtailing payments and judicial appeals to Rome. The English Franciscan William of Ockham had defended the rights of royalty against Pope John XXII, and John Wycliffe even sanctioned secular confiscation of clerical property in support of the principle of apostolic poverty. Lollardy, Humanism, and widespread anticlerical sentiment prepared the way religiously and intellectually for Protestant ideas, which began to enter England in the early 1520s.

In the early 1520s future English reformers met at the White Horse Inn in Cambridge to discuss Lutheran writings smuggled into England by merchants and scholars. One of these future reformers was William Tyndale (ca. 1492–1536), who translated the New Testament into English in 1524–1525, while in Germany. Published in Cologne and Worms, Tyndale's New Testament began to circulate in England in 1526, and thereafter the vernacular Bible became the centerpiece of the English Reformation. Cardinal Thomas Wolsey (ca. 1475–1530), the chief minister of King Henry VIII, and Sir Thomas More (1478–1535), Wolsey's successor, guided royal opposition to incipient Protestantism. The king himself defended the seven sacraments against Luther, receiving as a reward the title "Defender of the Faith" from Pope Leo X. Following Luther's intemperate reply to Henry's amateur theological attack, More wrote a lengthy *Response to Luther* in 1523.

THE KING'S AFFAIR. While Lollardy and Humanism may be said to have prepared the soil for the seeds of Protestant reform, it was King Henry's unhappy marriage that furnished the plough that truly broke it. Henry had married Catherine of Aragon (d. 1536), daughter of Ferdinand and Isabella of Spain, and the aunt of Emperor Charles V. By 1527 the union had produced no male heir to the throne and only one surviving child, a daughter, Mary. Henry was justifiably concerned about the political consequences of leaving only a female heir. People in this period believed it unnatural for women to rule over men: at best, a woman ruler meant a contested reign; at worst, turmoil and revolution. Henry even came to believe that his union with Catherine, who had numerous miscarriages and stillbirths, had been cursed by God, because prior to their marriage Catherine had been the wife of his brother, Arthur. Henry's father, King Henry VII, had betrothed Catherine to Henry after Arthur's untimely death in order to keep the English alliance with Spain intact. They were officially married in 1509, a few days before Henry VIII received his crown. Marriage to the wife of one's brother was prohibited by both canon and biblical law (see Leviticus 18:16, 20:21), and a special dispensation had been required from Pope Julius II before Henry married Catherine.

By 1527 Henry was thoroughly enamoured of Anne Boleyn, one of Catherine's ladies in waiting, and determined to put Catherine aside and take Anne to wife. This he could not do in Catholic England without papal annulment of the marriage to Catherine. And therein lay a special problem. The year 1527 was also the year when soldiers of the Holy Roman Empire mutinied and sacked Rome, and the reigning pope, Clement VII, was at the time a prisoner of Charles V, Catherine's nephew. Even if this had not been the case, it would have been virtually impossible for the pope to grant an annulment of a marriage that had not only survived for eighteen years but had been made possible in the first place by a special papal dispensation, the king's denial of the latter's validity notwithstanding.

Cardinal Wolsey, who aspired to become pope, was placed in charge of securing the royal annulment. Lord Chancellor since 1515 and papal legate-at-large since 1518, Wolsey had long been Henry's "heavy" and the object of much popular resentment. When he failed to secure the annulment, through no fault of his own, he was dismissed in disgrace in 1529. Thomas Cranmer (1489–1556) and Thomas Cromwell (1485–1540), both of whom harbored Lutheran sympathies, thereafter became the king's closest advisers. Finding the way to a papal annulment closed, Henry's new advisers struck a different course: Why not simply declare the king supreme in English spiritual affairs as he was in English temporal affairs? Then the king himself could settle the king's affair.

Hampton Court Palace, a major home to the English kings after it was taken over by Henry VIII from Cardinal Wolsey, its builder, early in the sixteenth century. In the seventeenth century, Sir Christopher Wren, the great architect of the Restoration period, made additions not shown here. [British Tourist Authority, New York.]

The Reformation Parliament

In 1529 Parliament convened for what would be a seven-year session that earned it the title the "Reformation Parliament." During this period, it passed a flood of legislation that harassed and finally placed royal reins on the clergy. In January 1531 the clergy in Convocation (a legislative assembly representing the English clergy) publicly recognized Henry as head of the church in England "as far as the law of Christ allows." In 1532 the Act of Supplication of the Commons Against the Ordinaries was passed, a list of grievances against the church ranging from alleged indifference to the needs of the laity to an excessive number of religious holidays. In the same year Parliament passed the Submission of the Clergy, effectively placing canon law under royal control and thereby the clergy under royal jurisdiction. The Act in Conditional Restraint of Annates further gave the English king the power to withhold from Rome these lucrative "first fruits" of new ecclesiastical appointments.

In January 1533 Henry wed the pregnant Anne Boleyn, with Thomas Cranmer officiating. In February 1533 the Act for the Restraint of Appeals made the king the highest court of appeal for all English subjects. In March 1533 Cranmer became archbishop of Canterbury and led the convocation in invalidating the king's marriage to Catherine. In 1534 Parliament ended all payments by the English clergy and laity to Rome and gave Henry sole juris-

diction over high ecclesiastical appointments. The Act of Succession in the same year made Anne Boleyn's children legitimate heirs to the throne, and the Act of Supremacy declared Henry "the only supreme head in earth of the church of England." Refusal to recognize these two acts brought the execution of Thomas More and John Fisher, bishop of Rochester—events that made clear the king's determination to have his way regardless of the cost. In 1536 came the first Act for Dissolution of Monasteries, which affected only the smaller

Catherine of Aragon, the first wife of Henry VIII, in a portrait by an unknown artist. [National Portrait Gallery, London.]

❧ Thomas More Stands By His Conscience

More, loyal Catholic to the end, repudiated the Act of Supremacy as unlawful; he believed that it contradicted both the laws of England and the king's own coronation oath. More importantly, he believed that the act transgressed centuries of European tradition, by which he felt bound by conscience to stand, even if it meant certain death. In the following excerpt, More defended himself in a final interrogation, as reported by his prosecutors.

"Seeing that . . . ye are determined to condemn me [More said] . . . I will now in discharge of my conscience speak my mind plainly and freely. . . . Forasmuch as this indictment is grounded upon an Act of Parliament directly repugnant to the laws of God and his holy Church, the supreme government of which . . . may no temporal prince presume by any law to take upon him . . . it is . . . insufficient to charge any Christian man [who refuses to recognize this Act]."

For proof thereof, he [More] declared that this realm, being but one member and small part of the Church, might not make a particular law disagreeable with the general law of Christ's universal Catholic Church, no more than the city of London, being but one poor member in respect of the whole realm, might make a law against an Act of Parliament to bind the whole realm. So further showed he that it was contrary both to the laws and statutes of our own land . . . and also contrary to the sacred oath which the King's Highness himself and every Christian

prince always with great solemnity received at their coronations. . . .

Then . . . the Lord Chancellor . . . answered that seeing that all the bishops, universities, and best learned men of the realm had to this Act agreed, it was much marvel that he [More] alone against them all would so stiffly stick thereat. . . .

To this Sir Thomas replied . . . : "Neither as yet have I chanced upon any ancient writer or doctor that so advanceth, as your Statute doth, the supremacy of any secular and temporal prince. . . . and therefore am I not bounden, my Lord, to conform my conscience to the Council of one realm against the general Council of [the whole of] Christendom. For of the foresaid holy bishops I have, for every bishop of yours, above one hundred. And for one Council or Parliament of yours (God knoweth what manner of one), I have all the Councils made these thousand years. And for this one Kingdom [of England], I have all other Christian realms."

The Reformation in England: To the Accession of Elizabeth I, ed. by A. G. Dickens and Dorothy Carr (New York: St. Martin's Press, 1968), pp. 71–72.

---

ones; three years later a second act dissolved all English monasteries and turned their endowments over to the king.

WIVES OF HENRY VIII. Henry's domestic life proved to lack the consistency of his political life. In 1536 Anne Boleyn was executed for adultery and her daughter, Elizabeth, was declared illegitimate. Henry had four further marriages. His third wife, Jane Seymour, died in 1537 shortly after giving birth to the future Edward VI. Henry wed Anne of Cleves sight unseen on the advice of Cromwell, the purpose being to create by the marriage an alliance with the Protestant princes. Neither the alliance nor Anne—whom Henry found to have a remarkable resemblance to a horse— proved worth the trouble; the marriage was an-

nulled by Parliament and Cromwell dismissed and eventually executed. Catherine Howard, Henry's fifth wife, was beheaded for adultery in 1542. His last wife, Catherine Parr, a patron of Humanists and reformers, for whom Henry was the third husband, survived him to marry still a fourth time— obviously she was a match for the English king.

THE KING'S RELIGIOUS CONSERVATISM. Henry's political and domestic boldness was not carried over to the religious front, although the pope did cease to be the head of the English church and English Bibles were placed in English churches. Despite his political break with Rome, the king remained decidedly conservative in his religious beliefs, and Catholic doctrine remained prominent in a country seething with Protestant sentiment.

Despite his many wives and amorous adventures, Henry absolutely forbade the English clergy to marry and threatened any clergy who were twice caught in concubinage with execution. The Ten Articles of 1536 prescribed Catholic doctrine with only mild Protestant concessions. Angered by the growing popularity of Protestant views, even among his chief advisers, Henry struck directly at them in the Six Articles of 1539. These reaffirmed transubstantiation, denied the Eucharistic cup to the laity, declared celibate vows inviolable, provided for private masses, and ordered the continuation of auricular confession. Protestants referred to the articles as the "whip with six stings." Although William Tyndale's English New Testament grew into the Coverdale Bible (1535) and the Great Bible (1539) and the latter was mandated for every English parish during Henry's reign, England had to await Henry's death before it could become a genuinely Protestant country.

The Protestant Reformation Under Edward VI

When Henry died, his son and successor, Edward VI (1547–1553), was only ten years old. Edward reigned under the successive regencies of Edward Seymour, who became the duke of Somerset (1547–1550), and the earl of Warwick, who became known as the duke of Northumberland (1550–1553), during which time England fully enacted the Protestant Reformation. The new king and Somerset corresponded directly with John Calvin. During Somerset's regency, Henry's Six Articles and laws against heresy were repealed, and clerical marriage and communion with cup were sanctioned.

In 1547 the chantries, places where endowed masses had traditionally been said for the dead, were dissolved. In 1549, the Act of Uniformity imposed Thomas Cranmer's *Book of Common Prayer* on all English churches. Images and altars were removed from the churches in 1550. Still more radical Protestant reforms were carried out by the duke of Northumberland. After Charles V's victory over the German princes in 1547, German Protestant leaders had fled to England for refuge, and several directly assisted the completion of the English Reformation, Martin Bucer prominent among them. The Second Act of Uniformity, passed in 1552, imposed a revised edition of the *Book of Common Prayer* on all English churches. A forty-two-article confession of faith, also written by Thomas Cranmer, was adopted, setting forth a moderate Protestant doctrine. It taught justification by faith and the supremacy of Holy Scripture, denied transubstantiation (although not real presence), and recognized only two sacraments.

All these changes were short-lived, however. In 1553 Catherine of Aragon's daughter, Mary, succeeded Edward (who had died in his teens) to the English throne and proceeded to restore Catholic doctrine and practice with a singlemindedness that rivaled that of her father. It was not until the reign of Anne Boleyn's daughter, Elizabeth (1558–1603), that a lasting religious settlement was worked out in England (to be discussed in Chapter 15).

MAIN EVENTS OF THE ENGLISH REFORMATION

1529	Reformation Parliament convenes
1532	Parliament passes the Submission of the Clergy, an act placing Canon law and the English clergy under royal jurisdiction
1533	Henry VIII weds Anne Boleyn; Convocation proclaims marriage to Catherine of Aragon invalid
1534	Act of Succession makes Anne Boleyn's children legitimate heirs to the English throne
1534	Act of Supremacy declares Henry VIII "the only supreme head of the church of England"
1535	Thomas Moore executed for opposition to Acts of Succession and Supremacy
1535	Publication of Coverdale Bible
1539	Henry VIII imposes the Six Articles, condemning Protestantism and reasserting traditional doctrine.
1547	Edward VI succeeds to the throne under protectorships of Somerset and Northumberland
1549	First Act of Uniformity imposes *Book of Common Prayer* on English churches
1553–1558	Mary Tudor restores Catholic doctrine
1558–1603	Elizabeth I fashions an Anglican religious settlement

Moral and Social Problems in the Age of Reformation

The Injustice of the Law. This woodcut by an unknown artist is entitled the Spider Web. In it the law is compared to a spider web, which easily catches the weak and the poor, who are seen hanging on the gallows and the wheel on the left, while permitting the rich and powerful to escape punishment for their crimes. Note the hole in the spider web made by the large bee, while the smaller bugs become hopelessly trapped. [From Max Geisberg. The German Single-Leaf Woodcut, 1500–1550, edited by Walter L. Strauss. Hacker Art Books, 1974. Use by permission of Hacker Art Books.]

Tyranny. The Rabbits Catching the Hunters, by Georg Pencz. The rabbits, long brutalized by the hunters and their dogs, organize and then subject the hunters to the treatment the rabbits have long received from them. This woodcut is a warning to all tyrants that tyranny brings rebellion. [From Max Geisberg, The German Single-Leaf Woodcut, 1500–1550, edited by Walter L. Strauss. Hacker Art Books, 1974. Used by permission of Hacker Art Books.]

Drunkenness. The Winebag and His Wheelbarrow, by Hans Weidt. Alcoholism was a very serious problem in the sixteenth century. It was caricatured by artists and railed against by Catholic and Protestant clergymen. [From Max Geisberg, The German Single-Leaf Woodcut, 1500–1550, edited by Walter L. Strauss. Hacker Art Books, 1974. Used by permission of Hacker Art Books.]

Greed. The Power of Money, by Peter Spitzer. The caption reads: "Were my mother a whore (she can be seen in bed with a man in the upper left corner) and my father a thief (he can be seen hanging on the gallows in the upper right corner), still, if I had a lot of money I would have no grief." [From Max Geisberg, The German Single-Leaf Woodcut, 1500–1550, edited by Walter L. Strauss. Hacker Art Books, 1974. Used by permission of Hacker Art Books.]

Adultery. The Chastity Belt, by H. Vogtherr gives one view—that of the wronged husband—of this age-old marital problem. Here a husband departing on a business trip has placed his wife, who does not love him, in a chastity belt. She takes his money, which he gladly gives her in exchange for promises of fidelity, to buy a key that will set her free to do as she pleases during his absence. [From Max Geisburg, The German Single-Leaf Woodcut, 1500–1550, *edited by Walter L. Strauss. Hacker Art Books, 1974. Used by permission of Hacker Art Books.]*

Old Age. A Peasant Couple by Christoph Amberger. The man is saying that he is now too old to hunt birds and must therefore depend on an owl to do his hunting. [From Max Geisburg, The German Single-Leaf Woodcut, 1500–1550, *edited by Walter L. Strauss. Hacker Art Books, 1974. Used by permission of Hacker Art Books.]*

Failed Marriages. The Subservient Husband, by Hans Schaufelein. In the sixteenth century the husband who failed to rule his wife properly was thought to risk creating a shrew who would assume authority in the marriage. Note that in this woodcut the woman has the pocketbook and keys around her waist, for she has become master of the house. Her husband has been forced to do "woman's work," which was considered a sure sign of a house no longer in order. [From Max Geisburg, The German Single-Leaf Woodcut, 1500–1550, *edited by Walter L. Strauss. Hacker Art Books, 1974. Used by permission of Hacker Art Books.]*

Witches. In this woodcut by Lucas Cranach the Younger, four witches who were burned at the stake in Wittenberg in 1540 are shown. The four were accused of commerce with the Devil and harmful magic against their neighbor's persons and property. [From Max Geisburg, The German Single-Leaf Woodcut, 1500–1550, *edited by Walter L. Strauss. Hacker Art Books, 1974. Used by permission of Hacker Art Books.]*

The Social Significance of the Reformation in Western Europe

It was a common feature of the Lutheran, Zwinglian, and Calvinist reforms to work within the framework of reigning political power. Luther, Zwingli, and Calvin saw themselves and their followers as citizens of the world, subject to definite civic responsibilities and obligations. Their adjustments in this regard have led scholars to characterize them as "magisterial reformers," meaning not only that they were the leaders of the major Protestant movements but also that they succeeded by the force of the magistrate's sword. It was probably not a matter of compromising the principles of the Gospels and choosing the way of brute force, as some have argued. The reformers never contemplated a reform outside or against the societies of which they were members. They wanted a reform that took shape within the laws and institutions of the sixteenth century, and to that end they remained highly sensitive to what was politically and socially possible in their age.

Some scholars believe that these reformers were too conscious of the historically possible, that their reforms went forward with such caution that they not only changed late medieval society very little but actually encouraged acceptance of the sociopolitical status quo.

There *is* a very conservative side to the Reformation. On the other hand, by the end of the sixteenth century the Reformation also brought about radical changes in the religious beliefs and practices of many people. As it developed, the Reformation eliminated or put severe restrictions on such traditional practices as mandatory fasting; auricular confession; the veneration of saints, relics, and images; indulgences; pilgrimages and shrines; vigils; weekly, monthly, and annual Masses for the dead; the belief in purgatory; Latin worship services; the sacrifice of the Mass; numerous religious ceremonies, festivals, and holidays; the canonical hours; monasteries and mendicant orders; the sacramental status of marriage, extreme unction, confirmation, holy orders, and penance; clerical celibacy; clerical immunity from civil taxation and criminal jurisdiction; nonresident benefices; excommunication and interdict; canon law; episcopal and papal authority; and the traditional Scholastic education of the clergy. Some Protestant lands (Switzerland, for example) enacted more of these reforms, and more radically, than others (England, for example).

It may be argued that by the second half of the sixteenth century Protestant religion had become just as burdensome as medieval religion had ever been. As Protestants won power in cities and towns, they tended to use their new position to erect what critics called "new papacies." In its first decades, however, the Reformation was presented and perceived by those who embraced it as a profound simplification of religious life. It was freeing precisely because it required less rather than more from those who wanted to be pious Christians and because it gave clearer focus to their ethical obligations.

The Reformation and Education

Another important cultural achievement of the Reformation was its implementation of many of the educational reforms of Humanism in the new Protestant schools and universities. Many Protestant reformers in Germany, France, and England were Humanists. Even when their views on church doctrine and humankind separated them from the Humanist movement, the Protestant reformers continued to share with the Humanists a common opposition to Scholasticism and a belief in the unity of wisdom, eloquence, and action. The Humanist program of studies, which provided the language skills to deal authoritatively with original sources, proved to be a more appropriate tool for the elaboration of Protestant doctrine than did Scholastic dialectic.

The connections between Humanism and the Reformation were recognized by the Catholic counterreformers. Ignatius of Loyola observed the way in which the new learning had been embraced by and served the Protestant cause. In his *Spiritual Exercises* he insisted that when the Bible and the Church Fathers were read directly, they be read under the guidance of the authoritative Scholastic theologians: Peter Lombard, Bonaventura, and Thomas Aquinas. The latter, Ignatius argued, being "of more recent date," had the clearer understanding of what Scripture and the Fathers meant and therefore should guide the study of the past.

When in August 1518 Philip Melanchthon, a young Humanist and professor of Greek, arrived at the University of Wittenberg, his first act was to implement curricular reforms on the Humanist model. In his inaugural address, entitled *On Improving the Studies of the Young,* Melanchthon presented himself as a defender of good letters and classical studies against "barbarians who practice barbarous arts." By the latter he meant the Scholastic theologians of the later Middle Ages, whose methods of juxtaposing the views of conflicting authorities and seeking to reconcile them by disputation had, he believed, undermined both good letters and sound biblical doctrine. Scholastic dominance in the universities was seen by Melanchthon as having bred contempt for the Greek language and learning and as having encouraged neglect of the study of mathematics, sacred studies, and the art of oratory. Melanchthon urged the careful study of history, poetry, and other Humanist disciplines.

Together Luther and Melanchthon completely restructured the University of Wittenberg's curriculum. Commentaries on Lombard's *Sentences* were dropped, as was canon law, and old Scholastic lectures on Aristotle were replaced by straightforward historical study. Students read primary sources directly, not by way of accepted Scholastic commentators. Candidates for theological degrees defended the new doctrine on the basis of their own exegesis of the Bible. New chairs of Greek and Hebrew were created. Luther and Melanchthon also pressed for universal compulsory education so that both boys and girls could reach vernacular literacy in the Bible.

In Geneva John Calvin and his successor, Theodore Beza, founded the Genevan Academy, which later evolved into the University of Geneva. This institution, created primarily for the purpose of training Calvinist ministers, pursued ideals similar to those set forth by Luther and Melanchthon. Calvinist refugees trained in the academy carried Protestant educational reforms to France, Scotland, England, and the New World. Through such efforts a working knowledge of Greek and Hebrew became commonplace in educated circles in the sixteenth and seventeenth centuries.

Some contemporaries decried what they saw as a narrowing of the original Humanist program as Protestants took it over. Erasmus, for example, came to fear the Reformation as a threat to the liberal arts and good learning, and Sebastian Franck pointed to parallels between Luther's and Zwingli's debates over Christ's presence in the Eucharist and such old Scholastic disputations as that over the Immaculate Conception of the Virgin.

Humanist culture and learning nonetheless re-

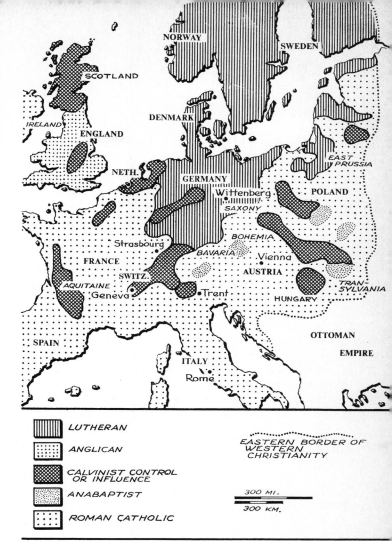

Legend:
- LUTHERAN
- ANGLICAN
- CALVINIST CONTROL OR INFLUENCE
- ANABAPTIST
- ROMAN CATHOLIC

EASTERN BORDER OF WESTERN CHRISTIANITY

300 MI.
300 KM.

THE RELIGIOUS SITUATION ABOUT 1560

MAP 14.4 *By 1560 Luther, Zwingli, and Loyola were dead, Calvin near the end of his life, the English break from Rome fully accomplished, and the last session of the Council of Trent about to assemble. Here is the religious geography of Western Europe at this time.*

mained indebted to the Reformation. The Protestant endorsement of the Humanist program of studies remained as significant for the Humanist movement as the latter had been for the Reformation. Protestant schools and universities consolidated and preserved for the modern world many of the basic pedagogical achievements of Humanism. There the *studia humanitatis,* albeit often as little more than a handmaiden to theological doctrine, found a permanent home, one that remained hospitable even in the heyday of Protestant Scholasticism.

The Reformation and the Changing Role of Women

The Protestant reformers took a positive stand on clerical marriage and strongly opposed monasticism and the celibate life. From this position they challenged the medieval tendency alternately to degrade women as temptresses (following the model of Eve) and to exalt them as virgins (following the model of Mary). Protestants opposed the popular antiwoman and antimarriage literature of the Middle Ages. They praised woman in her own right but especially in her biblical vocation as mother and housewife. Although relief of sexual frustration and a remedy of fornication were motives behind Protestant promarriage arguments, and although motherhood and housewifery were considered woman's basic vocation, the reformers also viewed their wives as indispensable companions in their work, and this not solely because they took domestic cares off their husbands' minds. Luther, who married in 1525 at the age of forty-one, wrote of women:

Imagine what it would be like without women. The home, cities, economic life, and government would virtually disappear. Men cannot do without women. Even if it were possible for men to beget and bear children, they still could not do without women.[2]

John Calvin wrote at the death of his wife:

I have been bereaved of the best companion of my life, of one who, had it been so ordered, would not only have been the willing sharer of my indigence, but even of my death. During her life she was the faithful helper of my ministry.[3]

Such tributes were intended in part to overcome Catholic criticism of clerical marriage as a distraction from one's ministry. They were primarily the expression of a new value placed on the estate of marriage and family life. In opposition to the celibate ideal of the Middle Ages Protestants stressed as no religious movement before them the

sacredness of home and family and this contributed to a more respectful and sharing relationship between husbands and wives and between parents and children. The ideal of the companionate marriage—that is, of husband and wife as co-workers in a special God-ordained community of the family—led to an important expansion of the grounds for divorce in Protestant cities as early as the 1520s and ensured women an equal right to leave husbands who flagrantly violated the marriage contract. The new stress on companionship in marriage also worked indirectly to make contraception and planned parenthood a respectable choice for married couples, as it made husbands sensitive to the suffering and unhappiness that many pregnancies brought on their wives.

Protestant doctrines were as attractive to women as they were to men. Women who had been maligned as the concubines of priests came to know a new dignity as the "honorable wives" of Protestant ministers. Renegade nuns wrote exposés of the nunnery in the name of Christian freedom and justification by faith. Women in the higher classes, who were enjoying new social and political freedoms during the Renaissance, found in Protestant theology a religious complement to their greater independence in other walks of life.

Because of their desire to have women become pious housewives, Protestants also encouraged the education of girls to vernacular literacy, expecting them thereafter to model their lives on the Bible. Women came in the course of such study, however, to find in the Bible passages that made them the equals to men in the presence of God. Such education further gave them a role in the Reformation as independent authors. These may seem like small advances from a modern perspective, but they were significant, if indirect, steps in the direction of the emancipation of women.

Suggested Readings

ROLAND H. BAINTON, *Erasmus of Christendom* (1960). Charming presentation.

S. T. BINDHOFF, *Tudor England* (1950). Basic political narrative.

CHARLES BOXER, *Four Centuries of Portuguese Expansion 1415–1825* (1961). Comprehensive survey by a leading authority.

OWEN CHADWICK, *The Reformation* (1964). Among the best short histories and especially strong on theological and ecclesiastical issues.

---

[2] *Luther's Works*, Vol. 54: Table Talk, ed. and trans. by Theodore G. Tappert (Philadelphia: Fortress Press, 1967), p. 161.
[3] *Letters of John Calvin*, Vol. 2, trans. by J. Bonnet (Edinburgh: T. Constable and Co., 1858), p. 216.

Norman Cohn, *The Pursuit of the Millennium* (1957). Traces millennial speculation and activity from the Old Testament to the sixteenth century.

A. G. Dickens, *The Counter Reformation* (1969). Brief narrative with pictures.

A. G. Dickens, *The English Reformation* (1974). The best one-volume account.

G. Donaldson, *The Scottish Reformation* (1960). Dependable, comprehensive narrative.

G. R. Elton, *Reformation Europe 1517–1559* (1966). Among the best short treatments and especially strong on political issues.

Erik Erikson, *Young Man Luther: A Study in Psychoanalysis and History* (1962). Controversial study that has opened a new field of historiography.

H. Outram Evennett, *The Spirit of the Counter Reformation* (1968). Essay on the continuity of Catholic reform and its independence from the Protestant Reformation.

Rene Fülop-Miller, *The Jesuits: A History of the Society of Jesus,* trans. by F. S. Flint and D. F. Tait (1963). A critical survey, given to psychological analysis.

Harold Grimm, *The Reformation Era: 1500–1650* (1973). Very good on later Lutheran developments.

Werner L. Gundersheimer (Ed.), *French Humanism 1470–1600* (1969). Collection of essays that both summarize and provoke.

Hubert Jedin, *A History of the Council of Trent,* Vols. 1 and 2 (1957–1961). Comprehensive, detailed, authoritative.

De Lamar Jensen, *Reformation Europe, Age of Reform and Revolution* (1981). Excellent, up-to-date survey.

Wilbur K. Jordan, *Edward VI: The Young King* (1968). The basic biography.

Robert M. Kingdon, *Transition and Revolution: Problems and Issues of European Renaissance and Reformation History* (1974). Covers politics, printing, theology, and witchcraft.

John H. Leith, *The Reformed Tradition* (1979). Beliefs and confessions of the Zwinglian–Calvinist tradition.

John F. McNeill, *The History and Character of Calvinism* (1954). The most comprehensive account and very readable.

E. W. Monter, *Calvin's Geneva* (1967). Dependable sketch derived from authoritative studies.

Donald Nugent, *Ecumenism in the Age of Reformation: The Colloquy of Poissy* (1974). Study of the last ecumenical council of the sixteenth century.

Steven Ozment, *Mysticism and Dissent* (1973). Treats dissenters from Lutheranism and Calvinism.

Steven Ozment, *The Reformation in the Cities* (1975). An essay on why people thought they wanted to be Protestants.

Steven Ozment, *The Age of Reform 1250–1550: An Intellectual and Religious History of Late Medieval and Reformation Europe* (1980).

J. H. Parry, *The Age of Reconnaissance* (1964). A comprehensive account of explorations from 1450 to 1650.

R. R. Post, *The Modern Devotion* (1968). Currently the authoritative interpretation.

Eugene F. Rice, Jr., *The Foundations of Early Modern Europe 1460–1559* (1970). Broad, succinct narrative.

Jaspar G. Ridley, *Thomas Cranmer* (1962). The basic biography.

E. Gordon Rupp, *Patterns of Reformation: Oecolampadius, Karlstadt, Muntzer* (1969). Effort to demonstrate the variety within early Protestantism.

J. J. Scarisbrick, *Henry VIII* (1968). The best account of Henry's reign.

Quentin Skinner, *The Foundations of Modern Political Thought II: The Age of Reformation* (1978). A comprehensive survey that treats *every* political thinker and tract.

Lewis Spitz, *The Religious Renaissance of the German Humanists* (1963). Comprehensive and entertaining.

James Stayer, *Anabaptists and the Sword* (1972).

Gerald Strauss (Ed. and trans.), *Manifestations of Discontent in Germany on the Eve of the Reformation* (1971). Rich collection of sources for both rural and urban scenes.

R. H. Tawney, *Religion and the Rise of Capitalism* (1947). Advances beyond Weber's arguments relating Protestantism and capitalist economic behavior.

Ernst Troeltsch, *The Social Teaching of the Christian Churches,* Vols 1 and 2, trans. by Olive Wyon (1960).

Robert C. Walton, *Zwingli's Theocracy* (1968). Deals with origins and nature of Zwingli's reforms in Zurich.

Max Weber, *The Protestant Ethic and the Spirit of Capitalism,* trans. by Talcott Parsons (1958). First appeared in 1904–1905 and has continued to stimulate debate over the relationship between religion and society.

François Wendel, *Calvin: The Origins and Development of His Religious Thought,* trans. by Philip Mairet (1963). The best treatment of Calvin's theology.

George H. Williams, *The Radical Reformation* (1962). Broad survey of the varieties of dissent within Protestantism.

432

15 The Age of Religious Wars

HE LATE sixteenth century and the first half of the seventeenth century are described as an "age of religious wars" because of the bloody opposition of Protestants and Catholics across the length and breadth of Europe. In France, the Netherlands, England, and Scotland in the second half of the sixteenth century Calvinists fought Catholic rulers for the right to form their own communities and to practice their chosen religion openly. In the first half of the seventeenth century Lutherans, Calvinists, and Catholics marched against one another in central and northern Europe during the Thirty Years' War. And by the middle of the seventeenth century English Puritans had successfully revolted against the Stuart monarchy and the Anglican church.

The Fall of the Angels, by Pieter Brueghel, (ca. 1520–1569), painted in 1562. With Dürer and Hans Holbein the Younger (ca. 1497–1543), Brueghel was a leader among northern Renaissance painters and was one of the most imaginative ones ever. This picture looks like modern surrealism or perhaps a scene from Star Wars. *[Musées Royaux des Beaux-Arts, Brussels. Copyright A.C.L., Brussels.]*

In the second half of the sixteenth century the political conflict, which had previously been confined to central Europe and a struggle for Lutheran rights and freedoms, shifted to western Europe—to France, the Netherlands, England, and Scotland—and became a struggle for Calvinist recognition. War-weary German Lutherans and Catholics agreed to live and let live in the Peace of Augsburg (1555): *cuius regio, eius religio,* which means that he who controls the land may determine its religion. Lutheranism thereafter became a legal religion within the Holy Roman Empire. Non-Lutheran Protestants, however, were not recognized by the Peace of Augsburg: both sides scorned Anabaptists and other sectarians as anarchists, and Calvinists were not yet strong enough to demand legal standing.

If German Lutherans had reason to take quiet satisfaction, Protestants elsewhere obviously did not. The struggle for Protestant religious rights had intensified in most countries outside the empire by the mid-sixteenth century. The Council of Trent adjourned in 1563 committed to an international Catholic counteroffensive against Protes-

433

tants to be led by the Jesuits. At the time of John Calvin's death in 1564, Geneva had become both a refuge for Europe's persecuted Protestants and an international school for Protestant resistance, producing leaders fully equal to the new Catholic challenge.

Genevan Calvinism and Catholicism as revived by the Council of Trent were two equally dogmatic, aggressive, and irreconcilable church systems. Although Calvinists looked like "new papists" to critics when they dominated cities like Geneva, they were firebrands and revolutionaries when, as minorities, they found their civil and religious rights denied. Calvinism adopted a presbyterian organization that magnified regional and local religious authority; boards of presbyters, or elders, representing the many individual congregations of Calvinists, directly shaped the policy of the church at large. By contrast, the Counter-Reformation spon-

The Ecstasy of Saint Teresa, by Gianlorenzo Bernini (1598–1680). This depiction of the saint in mystical rapture is one of the most famous Baroque sculptures. It is in the church of Santa Maria della Vittoria in Rome. [Bettmann Archive.]

Self-portrait by Rembrandt van Rijn (1606–1669). Note the contemplative eyes and Rembrandt's characteristic use of strong light contrasted with deep shadow. This portrait is in the Frick Collection, New York. [Bettmann Archive.]

sored a centralized episcopal church system, hierarchically arranged from pope to parish priest, which stressed absolute obedience to the person at the top. The high clergy—the pope and his bishops—not the synods of local churches, ruled supreme. Calvinism proved attractive to proponents of political decentralization in contest with totalitarian rulers, whereas Catholicism remained congenial to the proponents of absolute monarchy determined to maintain "one king, one church, one law" throughout the land.

The opposition between the two religions can be

OPPOSITE: *The Crucifixion of Saint Peter by Rubens. The latter, based on the tradition that Peter was crucified head-downwards, is an example of the intense energy of much Baroque painting. [Municipal Museums, Cologne.]*

seen even in the art and architecture each came to embrace. The Catholic Counter-Reformation found the Baroque style congenial. A successor to Mannerism, Baroque art is a grandiose, three-dimensional display of life and energy. Great Baroque artists like Peter Paul Rubens (1571–1640) and Gianlorenzo Bernini (1598–1680) were Catholics. Protestants by contrast seemed to opt for a simpler, restrained, almost self-effacing art and architecture, as can be seen in the English churches of Christopher Wren (1632–1723) and the gentle, searching portraits of the Dutch Mennonite Rembrandt van Rijn (1606–1669).

As religious wars engulfed Europe, the intellectuals perceived the wisdom of religious pluralism and toleration more quickly than did the politicians. A new skepticism, relativism, and individualism in religion became respectable in the sixteenth and seventeenth centuries. Sebastian Castellio's (1515–1563) pithy censure of John Calvin for his role in the execution of the Antitrinitarian Michael Servetus summarized a sentiment that was to grow in early modern Europe: "To kill a man is not to defend a doctrine, but to kill a man."[1] As a new skepticism greeted the failure of the great reform movements, the French essayist Michel de Montaigne (1533–1592) asked in scorn of the dogmatic mind: "What do I know?" The Lutheran Valentin Weigel (1533–1588), surveying a half-century of religious strife in Germany, advised people to look within themselves for religious truth and no longer to churches and creeds.

Such views gained currency in larger political circles only by the most painful experiences. Where religious strife and its attendant civil war were best held in check, rulers tended to subordinate theological doctrine to political unity, urging tolerance, moderation, and compromise—even indifference—in religious matters. Such rulers came to be known as *politiques,* and the most successful among them was Elizabeth I of England. By contrast, rulers like Mary I of England, Philip II of Spain, and Oliver Cromwell, who tended to take their religion with the utmost seriousness and refused every compromise, did not in the long run achieve their political goals.

As we shall see, the wars of religion were both internal national conflicts and truly international wars. While Catholic and Protestant subjects strug-gled against one another for control of the crown of France, the Netherlands, and England, the Catholic governments of France and Spain conspired and finally sent armies against Protestant regimes in England and the Netherlands. The outbreak of the Thirty Years' War in 1618 made the international dimension of the religious conflict especially clear; before it ended in 1648, the war drew every major European nation directly or indirectly into its deadly net.

The French Wars of Religion (1562-1598)

Anti-Protestant Measures and the Struggle for Political Power

French Protestants came to be known as *Huguenots,* a term derived from Besançon Hugues, the leader of Geneva's political revolt against the House of Savoy in the 1520s, a prelude to that city's Calvinist Reformation in the 1530s. As early as the 1520s, however, the Sorbonne was vigilant against the Lutheran writings and doctrines that were circulating in Paris.

The capture of the French king Francis I by the forces of Charles V at the Battle of Pavia in 1525 provided a motive for the first wave of Protestant persecution in France. Hoping to pacify their Spanish conqueror, a fierce opponent of German Protestants, and to win their king's swift release, the French government took repressive measures against the native reform movement, led by Jacques Lefèvre d'Étaples and Bishop Briçonnet of Meaux, that had proved a seedbed of Protestant sentiment.

A second major crackdown came a decade later. When Protestants plastered Paris and other cities with anti-Catholic placards on October 18, 1534, mass arrests of suspected Protestants occurred. Government retaliation for this action drove John Calvin and other members of the French reform party into exile. In 1540 the Edict of Fontainebleau subjected French Protestants to the Inquisition. Henry II (1547–1559) established legal procedures against Protestants in the Edict of Chateaubriand in 1551. Save for a few brief interludes, the French monarchy remained a staunch Catholic foe of the Protestants until the ascension to the throne of Henry of Navarre in 1589.

[1]*Contra libellum Calvini* (N.P., 1562), p. E 2 a.

ABOVE: *The splendor of a Baroque church. This is the interior of the eighteenth-century cloister church at Ottobeuren in Bavaria, West Germany. The architect was Johann Michael Fischer. Note how the atmosphere is charged with energy and action. [Bettmann Archive.]*

The Hapsburg–Valois wars (see Chapter 14) ended with the Treaty of Cateau-Cambrésis in 1559, and Europe experienced a moment of peace. But only a moment. The same year marked the beginning of internal French conflict and the shift of the European balance of power in favor of Spain. It began with an accident. During a tournament held to celebrate the marriage of his thirteen-year-old daughter, Elizabeth, to Philip II, the son of Charles V and heir to the Spanish Hapsburg lands, the French king, Henry II, was mortally wounded (a lance pierced his visor). This unfore-

RIGHT: *The interior of St. Paul's Cathedral in London, by Sir Christopher Wren (1632–1723). Although elaborately decorated, the interior is subdued in effect. [Bettmann Archive.]*

seen event brought to the throne Henry's sickly fifteen-year-old son, Francis II, under the regency of the queen mother, Catherine de Medicis. With the monarchy so weakened by Henry's death, three powerful families saw their chance to control France and began to compete for the young king's ear. They were the Bourbons, whose power lay in the south and west; the Montmorency-Chatillons, who controlled the center of France; and the Guises, who were dominant in eastern France.

The Guises were far the strongest and had little trouble establishing firm control over the young king. Francis, duke of Guise, had been Henry II's general, and his brothers, Charles and Louis, were cardinals of the church. Mary Stuart, Queen of Scots and wife of Francis II, was their niece. Throughout the latter half of the sixteenth century the name of Guise remained interchangeable with militant, reactionary Catholicism. The Bourbon and Montmorency-Chatillon families, in contrast, developed strong Huguenot sympathies, largely for political reasons. The Bourbon Louis I, prince of Condé (d. 1569), and the Montmorency-Chatillon Admiral Gaspard de Coligny (1519–1572) became the political leaders of the French Protestant resistance. They collaborated early in an abortive plot to kidnap Francis II from his Guise advisers in the Conspiracy of Amboise in 1560. This conspiracy was strongly condemned by John Calvin, who considered such tactics a disgrace to the Reformation.

Appeal of Calvinism

Often for quite different reasons ambitious aristocrats and discontented townspeople joined Calvinist churches in opposition to the Guise-dominated French monarchy. In 1561 over two thousand Huguenot congregations existed throughout France, although Huguenots were a majority of the population in only two regions, Dauphiné and Languedoc. Although they made up only about one fifteenth of the population, Huguenots were in important geographic areas and were heavily represented among the more powerful segments of French society. Over two fifths of the French aristocracy became Huguenots. Many apparently hoped to establish within France a principle of territorial sovereignty akin to that secured within the Holy Roman Empire by the Peace of Augsburg (1555). In this way Calvinism indirectly served the forces of political decentralization.

John Calvin and Theodore Beza consciously sought to advance their cause by currying the favor of powerful aristocrats. Beza converted Jeanne d'Albret, the mother of the future Henry IV. The Prince of Condé was apparently converted in 1558 under the influence of his Calvinist wife. For many aristocrats—Condé seems clearly to have been among them—Calvinist religious convictions were attractive primarily as aids to long-sought political goals. The military organization of Condé and Coligny progressively merged with the religious organization of the French Huguenot churches, creating a potent combination that benefited both political and religious dissidents. Calvinism gave political resistance justification and inspiration, and the forces of political resistance made Calvinism a viable religious alternative in Catholic France. Each side had much to gain from the other. The confluence of secular and religious motives, although beneficial to aristocratic resistance and Calvinist religion alike, tended to cast suspicion on the religious appeal of Calvinism. Clearly religious conviction was neither the only nor always the main reason for becoming a Calvinist in France in the second half of the sixteenth century.

Catherine de Medicis and the Guises

Following Francis II's death in 1560, Catherine de Medicis continued as regent for her minor son, Charles IX (1560–1574). At a colloquy in Poissy she tried unsuccessfully to reconcile the Protestant and Catholic factions. Fearing the power and guile of the Guises, Catherine, whose first concern was always to preserve the monarchy, sought allies among the Protestants. In 1562, after conversations with Beza and Coligny, she issued the January Edict, a measure that granted Protestants freedom to worship publicly outside towns—although only privately within them—and to hold synods. In March this royal toleration came to an abrupt end when the duke of Guise surprised a Protestant congregation at Vassy in Champagne and proceeded to massacre several score—an event that marked the beginning of the French wars of religion (March 1562).

Had Condé and the Huguenot armies rushed immediately to the queen's side after this attack, Protestants might well have secured an alliance with the crown, so great was the queen mother's fear of Guise power at this time. But the hesitation of the Protestant leaders, due primarily to indeci-

Catherine de' Medicis (1519–1589). Following the death of her husband, King Henry II of France, in 1559, Catherine, as Queen Mother, exercized much power during the reigns of her three sons, Francis II (1559–1560), Charles IX (1560–1574), and Henry III (1574–1589). She is most remembered for her role in the Saint Bartholomew's Day Massacre in 1572. [Bettmann Archive.]

August 1570. In this period Condé was killed and Huguenot leadership passed to Coligny—actually a blessing in disguise for the Protestants because Coligny was far the better military strategist. In the Peace of Saint Germain-en-Laye (1570), which ended the third war, the crown, acknowledging the power of the Protestant nobility, granted the Huguenots religious freedoms within their territories and the right to fortify their cities.

Perpetually caught between fanatical Huguenot and Guise extremes, Queen Catherine had always sought to balance the one side against the other. Like the Guises, she wanted a Catholic France; she did not, however, desire a Guise-dominated monarchy. After the Peace of Saint Germain-en-Laye the crown tilted manifestly toward the Bourbon faction and the Huguenots, and Coligny became Charles IX's most trusted adviser. Unknown to the king, Catherine began at this time to plot with the Guises against the ascendant Protestants. As she had earlier sought Protestant support when Guise power threatened to subdue the monarchy, so she now sought Guise support as Protestant influence grew.

There was reason for Catherine to fear Coligny's hold on the king. Louis of Nassau, the leader of Protestant resistance to Philip II in the Netherlands, had gained Coligny's ear, and Coligny used his position of influence to win the king of France over to a planned French invasion of the Netherlands in support of the Dutch Protestants. Such a course of action would have placed France squarely on a collision course with mighty Spain. Catherine recognized far better than her son that France stood little chance in such a contest. She and her advisers had been much sobered in this regard by news of the stunning Spanish victory over the Turks at Lepanto in October 1571 (to be discussed later).

THE SAINT BARTHOLOMEW'S DAY MASSACRE. When Catherine lent her support to the infamous Saint Bartholomew's Day Massacre of Protestants, she did so out of a far less reasoned judgment. Her decision appears to have been made in a state of near panic. On August 22, 1572, four days after the Huguenot Henry of Navarre had married the king's sister, Marguerite of Valois—still another sign of growing Protestant power—Coligny was struck down, although not killed, by an assassin's bullet. Catherine had apparently been party to this Guise plot to eliminate Coligny. After its failure she feared both the king's reaction to her complicity

sive leadership on the part of Condé, placed the young king and the queen mother, against their deepest wishes, in firm Guise control, as cooperation with the Guises became the only alternative to capitulation to the Protestants.

During the first French war of religion, fought between April 1562 and March 1563, the duke of Guise was assassinated. It is a measure of the international character of the struggle in France that troops from Hesse and the Palatinate fought alongside the Huguenots. A brief resumption of hostilities in 1567–1568 was followed by the bloodiest of all the conflicts between September 1568 and

❧ Coligny's Death on Saint Bartholomew's Day

The following description of Coligny's murder by henchmen of the duke of Guise
was written by an eyewitness to the Saint Bartholomew's Day Massacre, the statesman and historian Jacques-Aguste De Thou.

*It was determined to exterminate all the Protestants,
and the plan was approved by the queen. . . . The
duke of Guise . . . was put in full command of the
enterprise. . . . The signal to commence the massacre
would be given by the bell of the palace, and the
marks by which they [the Catholic Swiss mercenaries
and the French soldiers who were to carry it out]
should recognize each other in the darkness were a bit
of white linen tied around the left arm and a white
cross on the hat.*

*[As the massacre began] Coligny awoke and rec-
ognized from the noise that a riot was taking
place. . . . When he perceived that the noise increased and that someone had fired an arquebus in
the courtyard of his dwelling . . . , conjecturing
what it might be, but too late, he arose from his bed
and having put on his dressing gown said his prayers. . . . [Then] he said: "I see clearly that which
they seek, and I am ready steadfastly to suffer that
death which I have never feared. . . ."*

*Meanwhile the conspirators, having burst through
the door of the chamber, entered, and [one named]
Besme, sword in hand, demanded of Coligny, who*

*stood near the door, "Are you Coligny?" Coligny re-
plied, "Yes, I am he. . . ." As he spoke, Besme gave
him a sword thrust through the body, and having
withdrawn his sword, another thrust in the mouth, by
which his face was disfigured. So Coligny fell, killed
with many thrusts. Others have written that Coligny
in dying pronounced . . . these words: "Would that I
might at least die at the hands of a soldier and not [at
those] of a valet. . . ."*

*Then the duke of Guise inquired of Besme from the
courtyard if the thing were done, and when Besme
answered him that it was, the duke replied that the
Chevalier d'Angoulême was unable to believe it unless he saw it. . . . [So] they threw the body through
the window into the courtyard, disfigured as it was
with blood. When the Chevalier d'Angoulême, who
could scarcely believe his eyes, had wiped away with a
cloth the blood which overran the face and finally
recognized him, some say he spurned the body with his
foot . . . [and] said: "Cheer up my friends! Let us do
thoroughly that which we have begun. The king commands it."*

James Harvey Robinson (Ed.), *Readings in European History,* Vol. 2 (Boston: Ginn and Co.,
1906), pp. 180–182.

with the Guises and the Huguenot response under
a recovered Coligny. Summoning all her motherly
charm and fury, Catherine convinced Charles that
a Huguenot coup was afoot, inspired by Coligny,
and that only the swift execution of Protestant
leaders could save the crown from a Protestant
attack on Paris. On Saint Bartholomew's Day,
1572, Coligny and three thousand fellow Huguenots were butchered in Paris. Within three days an
estimated twenty thousand Huguenots were executed in coordinated attacks throughout France. It
is a date that has ever since lived in infamy for Protestants.

Pope Gregory XIII and Philip II of Spain reportedly greeted the news of the Protestant mas-

sacre with special religious celebrations. Philip especially had good reason to rejoice, for the
massacre ended for the moment any planned
French opposition to his efforts to subdue his rebellious subjects in the Netherlands since France
was now thrown into civil war. But the massacre of
thousands of Protestants also gave the discerning
Catholic world cause for new alarm. The event
changed the nature of the struggle between Protestants and Catholics both within and beyond the
borders of France. It was thereafter no longer an
internal contest between Guise and Bourbon factions for French political influence, nor was it simply a Huguenot campaign to win basic religious
freedoms. Henceforth, in Protestant eyes, it be-

The Catholic massacre of Huguenots in Paris on Saint Batholomew's Day, August 24, 1572, as remembered by François Dubois, a Huguenot eyewitness. [The Granger Collection.]

came an international struggle to the death for sheer survival against an adversary whose cruelty now justified any means of resistance.

PROTESTANT RESISTANCE THEORY. Only as Protestants faced suppression and sure defeat did they begin to sanction active political resistance. At first they tried to practice the biblical precept of obedient subjection to worldly authority (Romans 13:1). Luther had only grudgingly approved resistance to the emperor after the Diet of Augsburg in 1530. In 1550 Lutherans in the city of Magdeburg had published a highly influential defense of the right of lower authorities to oppose the emperor's order that all Lutherans return to the Catholic fold.

Calvin, who never faced the specter of total political defeat after his return to Geneva in 1541, had always condemned willful disobedience and rebellion against lawfully constituted governments as unchristian. But he also taught that lower magis-

trates, as part of the lawfully constituted government, had the right and duty to oppose tyrannical higher authority.

The exiled Scottish reformer John Knox, who had seen his cause crushed by Mary, Queen of Scots, and Mary I of England, had pointed the way for later Calvinists in his famous *Blast of the Trumpet Against the Terrible Regiment of Women* (1558). Knox declared that the removal of a heathen tyrant was not only permissible, but a Christian duty. He had the Catholic queen of England in mind.

After the great massacre of French Protestants on Saint Bartholomew's Day, 1572, Calvinists everywhere came to appreciate the need for an active defense of their religious rights. Classical Huguenot theories of resistance appeared in three major works of the 1570s. The first was the *Franco-Gallia* of François Hotman (1573), a Humanist argument that the representative Estates General of France historically held higher authority than the French king. The second was Theodore Beza's *On the Right of Magistrates over Their Subjects* (1574), which, going beyond Calvin's views, justified the correction and even the overthrow of tyrannical rulers by lower authorities. Finally, there was Philippe du Plessis Mornay's *Defense of Liberty Against Tyrants* (1579), an admonition to princes, nobles, and magistrates beneath the king, as guardians of the rights of the body politic, to take up arms against tyranny in other lands.

The Rise to Power of Henry of Navarre

Henry III (1574–1589), who was Henry II's third son and the last to wear the French crown,

found the monarchy wedged between a radical Catholic League, formed in 1576 by Henry of Guise, and vengeful Huguenots. Neither group would have been reluctant to assassinate a ruler whom they considered heretical and a tyrant. Like the queen mother, Henry sought to steer a middle course, and in this effort he received support from a growing body of neutral Catholics and Huguenots, who put the political survival of France above its religious unity. Such *politiques* were prepared to compromise religious creeds as might be required to save the nation.

The Peace of Beaulieu in May 1576 granted the Huguenots almost complete religious and civil freedom. At this time, however, France was not

❧ Theodore Beza Defends the Right to Resist Tyranny

One of the oldest problems in political and social theory has been that of knowing when resistance to repression in matters of conscience is justified. Since Luther's day Protestant reformers, although accused by their Catholic critics of fomenting social division and revolution, had urged their followers to strict obedience to established political authority. After the 1572 Massacre of Saint Bartholomew's Day, however, Protestant pamphleteers urged Protestants to resist tyrants and persecutors with armed force. In 1574, Theodore Beza pointed out the obligation of rulers to their subjects and the latter's right to resist rulers who failed to meet the conditions of their office.

It is apparent that there is a mutual obligation between the king and the officers of a kingdom; that the government of the kingdom is not in the hands of the king in its entirety, but only the sovereign degree; that each of the officers has a share in accord with his degree; and that there are definite conditions on either side. If these conditions are not observed by the inferior officers, it is the part of the sovereign to dismiss and punish them. . . . If the king, hereditary or elective, clearly goes back on the conditions without which he would not have been recognized and acknowledged, can there be any doubt that the lesser magistrates of the kingdom, of the cities, and of the provinces, the administration of which they have received from the sovereignty itself, are free of their oath, at least to the extent that they are entitled to resist flagrant oppression of the realm which they *swore to defend and protect according to their office and their particular jurisdiction? . . .*

We must now speak of the third class of subjects, which though admittedly subject to the sovereign in a certain respect, is, in another respect, and in cases of necessity the protector of the rights of the sovereignty itself, and is established to hold the sovereign to his duty, and even, if need be, to constrain and punish him. . . . The people is prior to all the magistrates, and does not exist for them, but they for it. . . . Whenever law and equity prevailed, nations neither created nor accepted kings except upon definite conditions. From this it follows that when kings flagrantly violate these terms, those who have the power to give them their authority have no less power to deprive them of it.

Constitutionalism and Resistance in the Sixteenth Century: Three Treatises by Hotman, Beza, and Mornay, trans. and ed. by Julian H. Franklin (New York: Pegasus, 1969), pp. 111–114.

Henry of Navarre (king of France as Henry IV). Henry brought religious peace to France when he promulgated the Edict of Nantes in 1598. This gave French Protestants freedom of worship in selected places and permitted them to maintain garrisons for their own protection. The seventeenth-century painter is not known. [Château de Versailles. Giraudon.]

ready for such sweeping toleration. Within seven months of the Peace of Beaulieu, the Catholic League forced Henry to return again to the illusory quest for absolute religious unity in France. In October 1577 the king issued the Edict of Poitiers, which truncated the Peace of Beaulieu, and once again circumscribed areas of permitted Huguenot worship. Thereafter Huguenot and Catholic factions quickly returned to their accustomed anarchical military solutions, the Protestants under the leadership of Henry of Navarre, now heir to the French throne.

In the mid-1580s the Catholic League, supported by the Spanish, became completely dominant in Paris. In what came to be known as the Day of the Barricades, Henry III attempted to rout the league with a surprise attack in 1588. The effort failed badly and the king had to flee Paris. Forced by his weakened position into unkingly guerrilla

tactics, and also emboldened by news of the English victory over the Spanish Armada in 1588, Henry successfully plotted the assassination of both the duke and the cardinal of Guise. These assassinations sent France reeling once again. Led by still another Guise brother, Charles, duke of Mayenne, the Catholic League reacted with a fury that matched the earlier Huguenot response to the Massacre of Saint Bartholomew's Day. The king now had only one course of action: he struck an alliance with the Protestant Henry of Navarre in April 1589.

As the two Henrys prepared to attack the Guise stronghold of Paris, however, a fanatical Jacobin friar stabbed Henry III to death. Thereupon the Bourbon Huguenot Henry of Navarre succeeded the childless Valois king to the French throne as Henry IV (1589–1610). Pope Sixtus V and Philip II stood aghast at the sudden prospect of a Protestant France. They had always wanted France to be religiously Catholic and politically weak, and they now acted to achieve that end. Spain rushed troops to support the besieged Catholic League. Philip II apparently even harbored hopes of placing his eldest daughter, Isabella, the granddaughter of Henry II and Catherine de Medicis, on the French throne.

Direct Spanish intervention in the affairs of France seemed only to strengthen Henry IV's grasp on the crown. The French people viewed his right to hereditary succession more seriously than his espoused Protestant confession. Henry was also widely liked. Notoriously informal in dress and manner—a factor that made him especially popular with the soldiers—Henry also had the wit and charm to neutralize the strongest enemy in a face-to-face confrontation. He came to the throne as a *politique*, long weary with religious strife and fully prepared to place political peace above absolute religious unity. He believed that a royal policy of tolerant Catholicism would be the best way to achieve such peace. On July 25, 1593, he publically abjured the Protestant faith and embraced the traditional and majority religion of his country. "Paris is worth a mass," he is reported to have said.

It was, in fact, a decision he had made only after a long period of personal agonizing. The Huguenots were understandably horrified by this turnabout and Pope Clement VIII remained skeptical of Henry's sincerity. But the majority of the French church and people, having known internal strife too long, rallied to the king's side. By 1596 the Catholic League was dispersed, its ties with Spain were broken, and the wars of religion in France, to all intents and purposes, had ground to a close.

The Edict of Nantes

On April 13, 1598, a formal religious settlement was proclaimed in Henry IV's famous Edict of Nantes, and the following month, on May 2, 1598, the Treaty of Vervins ended hostilities between France and Spain. The Edict of Nantes recognized and sanctioned minority religious rights within what was to remain an officially Catholic country. In the earlier Edict of Mantes (not to be confused with Nantes) (1591) Henry IV had already assured the Huguenots of at least qualified religious freedoms. The Edict of Nantes made good that promise. This religious truce—and it was never more than that—granted the Huguenots, who by this time numbered well over one million, freedom of public worship, the right of assembly, admission to

❧ Henry IV Recognizes Huguenot Religious Freedom

By the Edict of Nantes (April 13, 1598) Henry IV recognized Huguenot religious freedoms and the rights of Protestants to participate in French public institutions. Here are some of its provisions.

We have by this perpetual and irrevocable Edict pronounced, declared, and ordained and we pronounce, declare and ordain:

Art. I. Firstly, that the memory of everything done on both sides from the beginning of the month of March, 1585, until our accession to the Crown and during the other previous troubles, and at the outbreak of them, shall remain extinct and suppressed, as if it were something which had never occurred. . . .

Art. II. We forbid all our subjects, of whatever rank and quality they may be, to renew the memory of these matters, to attack, be hostile to, injure or provoke each other in revenge for the past, whatever may be the reason and pretext . . . but let them restrain themselves and live peaceably together as brothers, friends, and fellow-citizens. . . .

Art. III. We ordain that the Catholic, Apostolic, and Roman religion shall be restored and re-established in all places and districts of this our kingdom and the countries under our rule, where its practice has been interrupted. . . .

Art. VI. And we permit those of the so-called Reformed religion to live and dwell in all the towns and districts of this our kingdom and the countries under our rule, without being annoyed, disturbed, molested or constrained to do anything against their conscience, or for this cause to be sought out in their houses and districts where they wish to live, provided that they conduct themselves in other respects to the provisions of our present Edict. . . .

Art. XXI. Books dealing with the matters of the aforesaid so-called Reformed religion shall not be printed and sold publicly, except in the towns and districts where the public exercise of the said religion is allowed. . . .

Art. XXII. We ordain that there shall be no difference or distinction, because of the aforesaid religion, in the reception of students to be instructed in Universities, Colleges, and schools, or of the sick and poor into hospitals, infirmaries, and public charitable institutions.

Art. XXVII. In order to reunite more effectively the wills of our subjects, as is our intention, and to remove all future complaints, we declare that all those who profess or shall profess the aforesaid so-called Reformed religion are capable of holding and exercising all public positions, honours, offices, and duties whatsoever . . . in the towns of our kingdom . . . notwithstanding all contrary oaths.

Church and State Through the Centuries: A Collection of Historic Documents, trans. and ed. by S. Z. Ehler and John B. Morrall (New York: Biblo and Tannen, 1967), pp. 185–187.

MAIN EVENTS OF FRENCH WARS OF RELIGION (1562–1598)

1559	Treaty of Cateau-Cambrésis ends Hapsburg-Valois wars
1559	Francis II succeeds to French throne under regency of his mother, Catherine de' Medicis
1560	Conspiracy of Amboise fails
1562	Protestant worshipers massacred at Vassy in Champagne by the Duke of Guise
1572	The St. Bartholomew's Day Massacre leaves thousands of Protestants dead
1589	Assassination of Henry III brings Huguenot Henry of Navarre to throne as Henry IV
1593	Henry IV embraces Catholicism
1598	Henry IV grants Huguenots religious and civil freedoms in the Edict of Nantes
1610	Henry IV assassinated

public offices and universities, and permission to maintain fortified towns. Most of the new freedoms, however, were to be exercised within their own towns and territories. Concession of the right to fortify their towns reveals the continuing distrust between French Protestants and Catholics. As significant as it was, the edict only transformed a long hot war between irreconcilable enemies into a long cold war. To its critics it had only created a state within a state.

A Catholic fanatic assassinated Henry IV in May 1610. Although Henry is remembered most for the religious settlement of the Edict of Nantes, it was he and his finance minister, the duke of Sully, who laid the foundations for the later transformation of France into the absolute state of Cardinal Richelieu and Louis XIV. It would be in pursuit of the political and religious unity that had escaped Henry IV that Louis XIV, calling for "one king, one church, one law," would revoke the Edict of Nantes in 1685 and force France and Europe to learn again by bitter experience the hard lessons of the wars of religion. Rare is the politician who has preferred to learn from the lessons of history rather than repeating its mistakes.

Imperial Spain and the Reign of Philip II (1556-1598)

Pillars of Spanish Power

Until the English defeated his mighty Armada in 1588, no one person stood larger in the second half of the sixteenth century than Philip II of Spain. Philip was heir to the intensely Catholic and militarily supreme western Hapsburg kingdom. The eastern Hapsburg lands of Austria, Bohemia, and Hungary had been given over by his father, Charles V, to Philip's uncle, the Emperor Ferdinand I, and they remained, together with the imperial title, in the possession of the Austrian branch of the family. Populous and wealthy Castile gave Philip a solid home base. Additional wealth was provided by the regular arrival in Seville of bullion from the Spanish colonies in the New World. In the 1540s great silver mines had been opened in Potosí in present-day Bolivia and in Zacatecas in Mexico. These gave Philip the great sums needed to pay his bankers and mercenaries. He nonetheless never managed to erase the debts left by his father nor to finance his own foreign adventures fully. He later contributed to the bankruptcy of the Fuggers when, at the end of his life, he defaulted on his enormous debts.

The new American wealth brought dramatic social change to the peoples of Europe during the second half of the sixteenth century. As Europe became richer, it was also becoming more populous, especially in the economically and politically active towns of France, England, and the Netherlands, where populations had tripled and quadrupled by the early seventeenth century. Europe's population approached an estimated 100 million by 1600.

The combination of increased wealth and population triggered a serious inflation, a steady 2 per cent a year in much of Europe, with serious cumulative effects by mid-century. As there were more people and greater coinage in circulation, but less food and fewer jobs, wages stagnated while prices doubled and tripled in much of Europe. This was especially the case in Spain. Because the new wealth was concentrated in the hands of a few, the traditional gap between the "haves"—the propertied, privileged, and educated classes—and the "have-nots" greatly widened. Nowhere did the unprivileged suffer more than in Spain, where the

Philip II of Spain (1556–1598) at age 24, by Titian. Philip controlled the dominant political power of the second half of the sixteenth century. However, he was finally denied victory over the two areas in which he most sought to impose his will, the Netherlands and England. [Museo del Prado, Madrid.]

The Escorial, Philip II's massive palace-monastery-mausoleum northwest of Madrid. Built between 1563 and 1584, the Escorial is a monument to the piety of the king. Philip had vowed to build the complex after the Spanish victory at Saint-Quentin over the French in 1557, which was won on St. Lawrence's day. Because the symbol of St. Lawrence is a grill—legend has it that he was martyred by being roasted alive—the Escorial's floor plan was designed to resemble a grill. [Editorial Photocolor Archives.]

The great naval battle of Lepanto (in the Gulf of Corinth in Greece), October 7, 1571, the largest pitched sea fight of the sixteenth century, in which the Spanish and their allies defeated the Ottoman Turkish fleet. It ended the threat of Ottoman sea power in the Mediterranean Sea. [National Maritime Museum, London.]

Castilian peasantry, the backbone of Philip II's great empire, became the most heavily taxed people of Europe. Those who contributed most to making possible Spanish hegemony in Europe in the second half of the sixteenth century prospered least from it.

A subjugated peasantry and wealth from the New World were not the only pillars of Spanish strength. Philip II shrewdly organized the lesser nobility into a loyal and efficient national bureaucracy. A reclusive man, he managed his kingdom by pen and paper rather than by personal presence. He was also a learned and pious Catholic, although some popes suspected that he used religion as much for political as for devotional purposes. That he was a generous patron of the arts and culture can be seen in his unique retreat outside Madrid, the Escorial, a combination palace, church, tomb, and monastery. Philip also knew personal sorrows. His mad and treacherous son, Don Carlos, died under suspicious circumstances in 1568—some contemporaries suspected that Philip had him quietly executed—only three months before the death of the queen.

During the first half of Philip's reign, attention focused almost exclusively on the Mediterranean and the Turkish threat, a constant European preoccupation. By history, geography, and choice, Spain had traditionally been Catholic Europe's champion against Islam. During the 1560s the Turks advanced deep into Austria, while their fleets dominated the Mediterranean. Between 1568 and 1570 armies under Philip's half-brother, Don John of Austria, the illegitimate son of Charles V, suppressed and dispersed the Moors in Granada. In May 1571 a Holy League of Spain, Venice, and the pope, again under Don John's command, formed to check Turkish belligerence in the Mediterranean. In what became the largest naval battle of the sixteenth century, Don John's fleet engaged the Ottoman navy under Ali Pasha off Lepanto in the Gulf of Corinth on October 7, 1571. Before the engagement ended, thirty thousand Turks had died and over one third of the Turkish fleet was sunk or captured. The Mediterranean for the moment belonged to Spain, and the Europeans had only themselves to fear. Philip's armies also succeeded in putting down resistance in neighbor-

447

The mosque of Ottoman Sultan Suleiman the Magnificent (1520–1566) in Constantinople (modern Istanbul). It was built by Suleiman's architect Sinan at the height of the Ottoman Empire's glory. Like many Ottoman mosques, it was clearly inspired by neighboring Hagia Sophia built by Byzantine Emperor Justinian a thousand years earlier. [Turkish Government Tourism and Information Office, New York.]

ing Portugal, which Spain annexed in 1580. The conquest of Portugal not only added to Spanish seapower but also brought the magnificent Portuguese overseas empire in Africa, India, and the Americas into the Spanish orbit.

The Revolt in the Netherlands

The spectacular Spanish military success in southern Europe was not repeated in northern Europe. When Philip attempted to impose his will within the Netherlands and upon England and France, he learned the lessons of defeat. The resistance of the Netherlands especially proved the undoing of Spanish dreams of world empire.

St. Peter's in Rome was built in the sixteenth and seventeenth centuries replacing Emperor Constantine's early Christian Basilica of the fourth century on the probable site of the saint's tomb. The great church had many architects, among them Michelangelo, who designed the great dome. The vast piazza in front was designed by Bernini; note how the thrown-open arms extend to embrace pilgrims and draw them into the church. A portion of the pope's residence, the Vatican palace, is at the right center. [Fotocielo.]

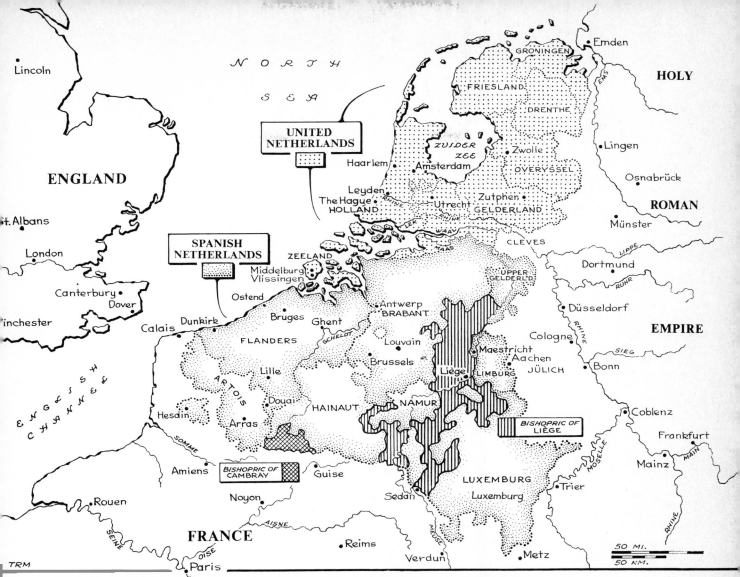

THE NETHERLANDS DURING THE REFORMATION

MAP 15.1 *The northern and southern provinces of the Netherlands. The former, the United Provinces, were mostly Protestant in the second half of the sixteenth century, while the southern, the Spanish Netherlands, made peace with Spain and remained largely Catholic.*

CARDINAL GRANVELLE. The Netherlands were not only the richest area of Philip's Hapsburg kingdom, but of Europe as well. In 1559 Philip had departed the Netherlands for Spain, never again to return. His half-sister, Margaret of Parma, assisted by a special council of state, became regent in his absence. The council was headed by Philip's hand-picked lieutenant, the extremely able Antoine Perrenot (1517–1586), after 1561 Cardinal Granvelle. Granvelle hoped to check Protestant gains by internal church reforms, and he planned to break down the traditional local autonomy of the seventeen Netherlands provinces by stages and establish in its place a centralized royal government directed from Madrid. A politically docile and religiously uniform country was the objective.

The merchant towns of the Netherlands were, however, Europe's most independent; many, like magnificent Antwerp, were also Calvinist strongholds. By tradition and temperament the people of the Netherlands inclined far more toward variety and toleration than toward obeisant conformity and hierarchical order. Two members of the council of state formed a stubborn opposition to the Spanish overlords, who now sought to reimpose their traditional rule with a vengeance. They were the Count of Egmont (1522–1568) and William of Nassau, the Prince of Orange (1533–1584), known as "the Silent" because of his extremely small circle of confidants.

Like other successful rulers in this period, William of Orange was a *politique* who placed the Netherlands' political autonomy and well-being above religious creeds. He personally passed through successive Catholic, Lutheran, and Calvinist stages. In 1561 he married Anne of Saxony, the daughter of the Lutheran Elector Maurice and the granddaughter of the late Landgrave Philip of Hesse. He maintained his Catholic practices until 1567, at which time he turned Lutheran. After the Saint Bartholomew's Day Massacre (1572), Orange became an avowed Calvinist.

In 1561 Cardinal Granvelle proceeded with a planned ecclesiastical reorganization of the Netherlands that was intended to tighten the control of the Catholic hierarchy over the country and to accelerate its consolidation as a Spanish ward. Orange and Egmont, organizing the Dutch nobility in opposition, succeeded in gaining Granvelle's removal from office in 1564, with Regent Margaret's blessing. But aristocratic control of the country after Granvelle's departure proved woefully inefficient, and popular unrest continued to grow, especially among urban artisans, who joined the congregations of radical Calvinist preachers in increasing numbers.

THE COMPROMISE. The year 1564 also saw the first fusion of political and religious opposition to Margaret's government. This opposition resulted from Philip II's unwise insistence that the decrees of the Council of Trent be enforced throughout the Netherlands. William of Orange's younger brother, Louis of Nassau, who had been raised a Lutheran, led the opposition, and it received support from the Calvinist-inclined lesser nobility and townspeople. A national covenant was drawn up called the *Compromise,* a solemn pledge to resist the decrees of Trent and the Inquisition. Grievances were loudly and persistently voiced, and when Margaret's government spurned the protesters as "beggars" in 1566, Calvinists rioted through the country. Louis called on French Huguenots and German Lutherans to send aid to the Netherlands, and a full-scale rebellion against the Spanish regency appeared imminent.

THE DUKE OF ALBA. The rebellion failed to materialize, however, because the Netherlands' higher nobility would not support it. Their shock at Calvinist iconoclasm and anarchy was as great as their resentment of Granvelle's more subtle repression. Philip, determined to make an example of the Protestant rebels, dispatched the duke of Alba to suppress the revolt. His army of ten thousand men journeyed northward from Milan in 1567 in a show of combined Spanish and papal might. A special tribunal, known to the Spanish as the Council of Troubles and among the Netherlanders as the Council of Blood, reigned over the land. The counts of Egmont and Horn and several thousand suspected heretics were publicly executed before Alba's reign of terror ended.

The Spanish levied new taxes, forcing the Netherlands to pay for the suppression of its own revolt. One of these taxes, the "tenth penny," a 10 percent sales tax, met such resistance from merchants and artisans that it remained uncollectable in some

The Duke of Alba (ca. 1508–1583), who was sent into the Netherlands by Philip II to crush the Dutch civil and religious revolt against Spanish rule. Engraving from the sixteenth century. [The Granger Collection.]

areas even after a reduction to 3 percent. Combined persecution and taxation sent tens of thousands fleeing from the Netherlands during Alba's cruel six-year rule. Alba came to be more hated than Granvelle or the radical Calvinists had ever been.

RESISTANCE AND UNIFICATION. William of Orange was an exile in Germany during these turbulent years. He now emerged as the leader of a broad movement for the Netherlands' independence from Spain. The northern, Calvinist-inclined provinces of Holland, Zeeland, and Utrecht, of which Orange was the *stadholder*, or governor, became his base. As in France, political resistance in the Netherlands gained both organization and inspiration by merging with Calvinism.

The early victories of the resistance attest to the popular character of the revolt. A case in point is the capture of the port city of Brill by the "Sea Beggars." These men were an international group of anti-Spanish exiles and criminals, among them many Englishmen. William of Orange did not hesitate to enlist their services. Their brazen piracy, however, had forced Queen Elizabeth to disassociate herself from them and to bar their ships from English ports. In 1572 the Beggars captured Brill and other seaports in Zeeland and Holland. Mixing with the native population, they quickly sparked rebellions against Alba in town after town and spread the resistance southward. In 1574 the people of Leiden heroically resisted a long Spanish siege. The Dutch opened the dikes and flooded their own country to repulse the hated Spanish.

The faltering Alba had by that time ceded power to Don Luis de Requesens, who replaced him as commander of Spanish forces in the Netherlands in November 1573.

THE PACIFICATION OF GHENT. The greatest atrocity of the war came after Requesens's death in 1576. Spanish mercenaries, leaderless and unpaid, ran amok in Antwerp on November 4, 1576, and they left seven thousand people dead in the streets. The event came to be known as the Spanish Fury.

These atrocities accomplished in four short days what neither religion nor patriotism had previously been able to do. The ten largely Catholic southern provinces (what is roughly modern Belgium) now came together with the seven largely Protestant northern provinces (what is roughly the modern Netherlands) in unified opposition to Spain. This union, known as the Pacification of Ghent, was accomplished on November 8, 1576. It declared internal regional sovereignty in matters of religion, a key clause that permitted political cooperation among the signatories, who were not agreed over religion. It was a Netherlands version of the territorial settlement of religious differences brought about in the Holy Roman Empire in 1555 by the Peace of Augsburg. Four provinces initially held out, but they soon made the resistance unanimous two months later by joining the all-embracing Union of Brussels in January 1577. For the next two years the Spanish faced a unified and determined Netherlands.

Don John, the victor over the Turks at Lepanto in 1571, had taken command of Spanish land

The Milch Cow, a sixteenth-century satirical painting depicting the Netherlands as a milk cow in whom all the powers are interested. Elizabeth of England is feeding the cow— England had long-standing commercial ties with Flanders; Philip II of Spain is attempting to ride her— Spain was trying to reassert its control over the country; William of Orange is trying to milk the animal—he had placed himself at the head of the anti-Spanish rebellion; and the King of France holds the cow's tail—France sought to profit from the rebellion at Spain's expense. [Rijksmuseum, Amsterdam.]

forces in November 1576. He now experienced his first defeat. Confronted by unified Netherlands resistance, he signed the Perpetual Edict in February 1577, a humiliating treaty that provided for the removal of all Spanish troops from the Netherlands within twenty days. This withdrawal of troops not only gave the country to William of Orange but also effectively ended for the present whatever plans Philip may have had for using the Netherlands as a staging area for an invasion of England.

THE UNION OF ARRAS AND THE UNION OF UTRECHT. The Spanish, however, were nothing if not persistent. Don John and Alessandro Farnese of Parma, the regent Margaret's son, revived Spanish power in the southern provinces, where constant fear of Calvinist extremism had moved the leaders to break the Union of Brussels. In January 1579 the southern provinces formed the Union of Arras, and within five months they made peace with Spain. These provinces later served the cause of the Counter-Reformation. The northern provinces responded with the formation of the Union of Utrecht.

NETHERLANDS INDEPENDENCE. Seizing what now appeared to be a last opportunity to break the back of Netherlands resistance, Philip II declared William of Orange an outlaw and placed a bounty of 25,000 crowns on his head. The act predictably stiffened the resistance of the northern provinces. In a famous defiant speech to the Estates General of Holland in December 1580, known as the

❧ Philip II Declares William of Orange an Outlaw (1580)

In the following proclamation the king of Spain accused William of Orange of being the "chief disturber of the public peace" and offered his captors, or assassins, generous rewards.

Philip, by the grace of God king of Castile, etc. to all to whom these presents may come, greeting:

It is well known to all how favorably the late emperor, Charles V, . . . treated William of Nassau. . . . Nevertheless, as everyone knows, we had scarcely turned our back on the Netherlands before the said William . . . (who had become . . . prince of Orange) began . . . by sinister arts, plots, and intrigues . . . to gain [control] over those whom he believed to be malcontents, or haters of justice, or anxious for innovations, and . . . above all, those who were suspected in the matter of religion. . . . With the knowledge, advice, and encouragement of the said Orange, the heretics commenced to destroy the images, altars, and churches. . . . So soon as the said Nassau was received into the government of the provinces, he began, through his agents and satellites, to introduce heretical preaching. . . . Then he introduced liberty of conscience . . . which soon brought it about that the Catholics were openly persecuted and driven out. . . . Moreover he obtained such a hold upon our poor subjects of Holland and Zeeland . . . that nearly all the towns, one after the other, have been besieged. . . .

Therefore, for all these just reasons, for his evil doings as chief disturber of the public peace . . . we outlaw him forever and forbid our subjects to associate with him . . . in public or in secret. We declare him an enemy of the human race, and in order the sooner to remove our people from his tyranny and oppression, we promise, on the word of a king and as God's servant, that if one of our subjects be found so generous of heart and so desirous of doing us a service and advantaging the public that he shall find the means of executing this decree and of ridding us of the said pest, either by delivering him to us dead or alive, or by depriving him at once of life, we will give him and his heirs landed estates or money, as he will, to the amount of twenty-five thousand gold crowns. If he has committed any crime, of any kind whatsoever, we will pardon him. If he be not noble, we will ennoble him for his valor; and should he require other persons to assist him, we will reward them according to the service rendered, pardon their crimes, and ennoble them too.

James Harvey Robinson (Ed.), *Readings in European History,* Vol. 2 (Boston: Ginn and Co., 1906), pp. 174–177.

Apology, Orange publicly denounced Philip as a heathen tyrant whom the Netherlands need no longer obey. On July 22, 1581, the member provinces of the Union of Utrecht met in The Hague and formally declared Philip no longer their ruler. They turned in his stead to the French duke of Alençon, Catherine de Medicis' youngest and least satisfactory son, a man to whom the southern provinces had also earlier looked as a possible middle way between Spanish and Calvinist overlordship. All the northern provinces save Holland and Zeeland accepted Alençon as their "sovereign" (Holland and Zeeland distrusted him almost as much as they did Philip II), but with the understanding that he would be only a titular ruler. But Alençon, an ambitious failure, saw this as his one chance at greatness. When he rashly attempted to take actual control of the provinces in 1583, he was deposed and returned to France.

Spanish efforts to reconquer the Netherlands continued into the 1580s. William of Orange was assassinated in July 1584, to be succeeded by his seventeen-year-old son, Maurice (1567–1625), who, with the assistance of England and France, continued Dutch resistance. Fortunately for the Netherlands Philip II began at this time to meddle directly in French and English affairs. He signed a secret treaty with the Guises (the Treaty of Joinville in December 1584) and sent armies under Farnese into France in 1590. Hostilities with the English, who had openly aided the Dutch rebels, also increased, gradually building toward the climax of 1588, when Philip's great Armada was defeated in the English Channel. These new Spanish fronts strengthened the Netherlands as Spain became badly overextended. Spanish preoccupation with France and England permitted the northern provinces to drive out all Spanish soldiers by 1593. In 1596 France and England formally recognized the independence of these provinces. Peace was not, however, concluded with Spain until 1609, when the Twelve Years' Truce gave the northern provinces their virtual independence. Full recognition came finally in the Peace of Westphalia in 1648.

England and Spain (1553-1603)

Mary I

Before Edward VI died in 1553, he agreed to a device to make Lady Jane Grey, the teen-age daughter of a powerful Protestant nobleman and,

Mary I. During her five-year reign as queen of England, she reversed Protestant gains and reimposed the Catholic religion on England. Her execution of Protestant leaders won her the title "Bloody Mary" among Protestants. [Bettmann Archive.]

more importantly, the granddaughter on her mother's side of Henry VIII's younger sister Mary, his successor in place of the Catholic Mary Tudor (1553–1558). But popular support for the principle of hereditary monarchy was too strong to deprive Mary of her rightful rule. Popular uprisings in London and elsewhere led to Jane Grey's removal from the throne within days of her crowning, and she was eventually beheaded.

Once enthroned, Mary proceeded to act even beyond the worst fears of the Protestants. In 1554 she entered a highly unpopular political marriage with Prince Philip (later Philip II) of Spain, a symbol of militant Catholicism to English Protestants, and pursued at his direction a foreign policy that in 1558 cost England its last enclave on the Continent, Calais.

Mary's domestic measures were equally shocking and even more divisive. During her reign Parliament repealed the Protestant statutes of Edward and reverted to the strict Catholic religious practice of her father, Henry VIII. The great Protestant leaders of the Edwardian age—John Hooper, Hugh Latimer, Miles Coverdale, and Thomas Cranmer—were executed for heresy. Hundreds of Protestants either joined them in martyrdom (282 persons were burned at the stake during Mary's reign) or took flight to the Continent. These "Marian exiles," prominent among whom was the future leader of the Reformation in Scotland, John Knox, settled in Germany and Switzerland, forming especially large communities in Frankfurt, Strasbourg, and Geneva. There they worshiped in their own congregations, wrote tracts justifying armed resistance, and waited for the time when a Protestant counteroffensive could be launched in their homelands.

Elizabeth I

Mary's successor was her half-sister, Elizabeth I (1558–1603), the daughter of Henry VIII and Anne Boleyn, and perhaps the most astute politician of the sixteenth century in both domestic and foreign policy. Assisted by a shrewd adviser, Sir William Cecil (1520–1598, Lord Burghley after 1571), Elizabeth built a true kingdom on the ruins of Mary's reign. Between 1559 and 1563 she and Cecil guided a religious settlement through Parlia-

ment that prevented England from being torn asunder by religious differences in the sixteenth century, as the Continent was. A *politique* who subordinated religious to political unity, Elizabeth merged a centralized episcopal system, which she firmly controlled, with broadly defined Protestant doctrine and traditional Catholic ritual. In the resulting Anglican church inflexible extremes were not permitted in religion.

In 1559 an Act of Supremacy passed Parliament repealing all the anti-Protestant legislation of Mary Tudor and asserting Elizabeth's right as "supreme governor" over both spiritual and temporal affairs. An Act of Uniformity in the same year mandated a revised version of the second *Book of Common Prayer* (1552) for every English parish. The issuance of the Thirty-Nine Articles on Religion in 1563—

❧ An Unknown Contemporary Describes Queen Elizabeth

No sixteenth-century ruler governed more effectively than Elizabeth of England (1558–1603), who was both loved and feared by her subjects. An unknown contemporary has left the following description, revealing not only her intelligence and shrewdness but also something of her tremendous vanity.

I will proceed with the description of the queen's disposition and natural gifts of mind and body, wherein she either matched or exceeded all the princes of her time, as being of a great spirit yet tempered with moderation, in adversity never dejected, in prosperity rather joyful than proud; affable to her subjects, but always with due regard to the greatness of her estate, by reason whereof she was both loved and feared.

In her later time, when she showed herself in public, she was always magnificent in apparel; supposing haply thereby that the eyes of her people (being dazzled by the glittering aspect of her outward ornaments) would not so easily discern the marks of age and decay of natural beauty; and she came abroad the more seldom, to make her presence the more grateful and applauded by the multitude, to whom things rarely seen are in manner as new.

She suffered not, at any time, any suitor to depart discontented from her, and though ofttimes he obtained not that he desired, yet he held himself satisfied

with her manner of speech, which gave hope of success in the second attempt. . . .

Latin, French, and Italian she could speak very elegantly, and she was able in all those languages to answer ambassadors on the sudden. . . . Of the Greek tongue she was also not altogether ignorant. She took pleasure in reading of the best and wisest histories, and some part of Tacitus' Annals *she herself turned into English for her private exercise. She also translated Boethius'* On the Consolation of Philosophy *and a treatise of Plutarch,* On Curiosity, *with divers others. . . .*

It is credibly reported that not long before her death she had a great apprehension of her own age and declination by seeing her face (then lean and full of wrinkles) truly represented to her in a glass, which she a good while very earnestly beheld; perceiving thereby how often she had been abused by flatterers (whom she held in too great estimation) that had informed her the contrary.

James Harvey Robinson (Ed.), *Readings in European History,* Vol. 2 (Boston: Ginn and Co., 1906), pp. 191–193.

which were a revision of Thomas Cranmer's original forty-two—made a moderate Protestantism the official religion within the Church of England.

CATHOLIC AND PROTESTANT EXTREMISTS. Elizabeth hoped to avoid both Catholic and Protestant extremism at the official level by pursuing a middle way. Her first archbishop of Canterbury, Matthew Parker (d. 1575), represented this ideal. But Elizabeth could not prevent the emergence of subversive Catholic and Protestant zealots. When she ascended the throne, Catholics were in the majority in England, and the extremists among them, encouraged by the Jesuits, plotted against her. They were also encouraged and later directly assisted by the Spanish, who were piqued both by Elizabeth's Protestant sympathies and by her refusal to follow the example of her half-sister Mary and take Philip II's hand in marriage. Elizabeth remained unmarried throughout her reign, using the possibility of a marriage alliance very much to her diplomatic advantage.

Catholic extremists hoped eventually to replace Elizabeth with Mary Stuart, Queen of Scots. Unlike Elizabeth, who had been declared illegitimate during the reign of her father, Mary Stuart had an unblemished claim to the throne by way of her grandmother Margaret, who was the sister of Henry VIII. Elizabeth acted swiftly against Catholic assassination plots and rarely let emotion override her political instincts. Despite proven cases of Catholic treason and even attempted regicide, however, she executed fewer Catholics during her forty-five years on the throne than Mary Tudor had executed Protestants during her brief five-year reign.

Elizabeth dealt cautiously with the Puritans, who were Protestants working within the national church to "purify" it of every vestige of "popery" and to make its Protestant doctrine more precise. The Puritans had two special grievances: (1) the retention of Catholic ceremony and vestments within the Church of England, which made it appear to the casual observer that no Reformation had occurred, and (2) the continuation of the episcopal system of church governance, which conceived of the English church theologically as the true successor to Rome, while placing it politically under the firm hand of the queen and her compliant archbishop.

Sixteenth-century Puritans were not separatists. Enjoying wide popular support and led by widely respected men like Thomas Cartwright (d. 1603),

Elizabeth I of England painted in 1592 by Marcus Gheeraerts. Note that she is standing on a map of her kingdom. Elizabeth is considered by many to be the most successful ruler of the sixteenth century. [National Portrait Gallery, London.]

they worked through Parliament to create an alternative national church of semiautonomous congregations governed by representative presbyteries (hence, Presbyterians), following the model of Calvin and Geneva. Elizabeth dealt firmly but subtly with this group, conceding absolutely nothing that lessened the hierarchical unity of the Church of England and her control over it.

The more extreme Puritans wanted every congregation to be autonomous, a law unto itself, with neither higher episcopal nor presbyterian control. They came to be known as *Congregationalists*. Elizabeth and her second archbishop of Canterbury, John Whitgift (d. 1604), refused to tolerate this group, whose views on independence seemed to them to be patently subversive. The Conventicle Act of 1593 gave such separatists the option of either conforming to the practices of the Church of England or facing exile or death.

DETERIORATION OF RELATIONS WITH SPAIN. A series of events led inexorably to war between England and Spain, despite the sincerest desires on the part of both Philip II and Elizabeth to avoid a direct confrontation. In 1567 the Spanish duke of Alba marched his mighty army into the Netherlands, which was, from the English point of view, simply a convenient staging area for a Spanish invasion of England. Pope Pius V (1566–1572), who favored a military conquest of Protestant England, "excommunicated" Elizabeth for heresy in 1570—a mischievous act that only encouraged both internal resistance and international intrigue against the queen. Two years later the piratical Sea Beggars, many of whom were Englishmen, occupied the port city of Brill in the Netherlands and aroused the surrounding countryside against the Spanish.

Following Don John's demonstration of Spain's awesome seapower at the famous naval battle of Lepanto in 1571, England signed a mutual defense pact with France. Also in the 1570s, Elizabeth's famous seamen, John Hawkins (1532–1595) and Sir Francis Drake (1545?–1596), began to prey regularly on Spanish shipping in the Americas. Drake's circumnavigation of the globe between 1577 and 1580 was one in a series of dramatic demonstrations of English ascendancy on the high seas.

After the Saint Bartholomew's Day Massacre, Elizabeth's was the only bosom to which Protestants in France and the Netherlands could cleave. In 1585 she signed the Treaty of Nonsuch, which provided English soldiers and cavalry to the Netherlands. Funds that had previously been funneled covertly to support Henry of Navarre's army in France now flowed openly.

MARY, QUEEN OF SCOTS. These events made a tinderbox of English–Spanish relations. The spark that finally touched it off was Elizabeth's reluctant but necessary execution of Mary, Queen of Scots (1542–1587).

Mary was the daughter of King James V of Scotland and Mary of Guise and had resided in France from the time she was six years old. This thor-

Mary, Queen of Scots. This portrait, done in about 1610, is by N. Hilliard. [National Portrait Gallery, London.]

oughly French and Catholic queen had returned to Scotland after the death of her husband, the French king Francis II, in 1561, there to find a successful, fervent Protestant Reformation that had won legal sanction the year before in the Treaty of Edinburgh (1560). As hereditary heir to the throne of Scotland, Mary remained queen by divine and human right. She was not intimidated by the Protestants who controlled her realm. She established an international French court culture, the gaiety and sophistication of which impressed many Protestant noblemen, whose religion tended to make their lives exceedingly dour.

Mary was closely watched by the ever-vigilant eye of the Scottish reformer John Knox, who fumed publicly and always with effect against the queen's private Mass and Catholic practices, which Scottish law made a capital offense for everyone else. Knox won support in his role of watchdog from Elizabeth and Cecil. Elizabeth personally despised Knox and never forgave him for writing the *First Blast of the Trumpet Against the Terrible Regiment of Women,* a work aimed at provoking a revolt against Mary Tudor but published in the year of Elizabeth's ascent to the throne. Elizabeth and Cecil tolerated Knox because he served their foreign policy, never permitting Scotland to succumb to the young Mary and her French and Catholic ways.

In 1568 a public scandal forced Mary's abdication and flight to her cousin Elizabeth in England. Mary's reputed lover, the earl of Bothwell, was, with cause, suspected of having killed her legal husband, Lord Darnley. When a packed court acquitted Bothwell and he subsequently abducted Mary and married her, the outraged reaction from Protestant nobles forced Mary to surrender the throne to her one-year-old son, who became James VI of Scotland (and, later, Elizabeth's successor as King James I of England). Because of Mary's clear claim to the English throne, she remained an international symbol of a possible Catholic England. Her presence in England, where she resided under mild house arrest for nineteen years, was of constant discomfort to Elizabeth.

In 1583 Elizabeth's vigilant secretary, Sir Francis Walsingham, uncovered a plot against Elizabeth involving the Spanish ambassador Mendoza, a frequent companion of Mary Stuart. After Mendoza's deportation in January 1584, popular antipathy toward Spain and support for Protestant resistance in France and the Netherlands became massive throughout England.

In 1586 Walsingham uncovered still another plot against Elizabeth, the so-called Babington plot, and this time he had uncontestable proof of Mary's complicity. Elizabeth believed that the execution of a sovereign, even a dethroned sovereign, weakened royalty everywhere. She was also aware of the outcry that Mary's execution would create throughout the Catholic world, and Elizabeth sincerely wanted peace with English Catholics. But she really had no choice in the matter and consented to Mary's execution on February 18, 1587. This event dashed all Catholic hopes for a bloodless reconversion of Protestant England. After the execution of the Catholic queen of Scotland, Pope Sixtus V (1585–1590), who feared Spanish domination almost as much as he abhorred English Protestantism, could no longer withhold public support for a Spanish invasion of England. Philip II ordered his Armada to make ready.

THE ARMADA. Spain's war preparations were interrupted in the spring of 1587 by Sir Francis Drake's successful shelling of the port city of Cadiz, an attack that inflicted heavy damage on Spanish ships and stores. After "singeing the beard of Spain's king," Drake raided the coast of Portugal, further incapacitating the Spanish. The success of these strikes forced the Spanish to postpone their planned invasion of England until the spring of 1588. On May 30 of that year, a mighty fleet of 130 ships bearing twenty-five thousand sailors and soldiers under the command of the duke of Medina-Sidonia set sail for England. But the day belonged completely to the English. The invasion barges that were to transport Spanish soldiers from the galleons onto English shores were prevented from leaving Calais and Dunkirk. The swifter English and Netherlands ships, assisted by what came to be known as an "English wind," dispersed the waiting Spanish fleet, over one third of which never returned to Spain.

The news of the Armada's defeat gave heart to Protestant resistance everywhere. Although Spain continued to win impressive victories in the 1590s, it never fully recovered from this defeat. Spanish soldiers faced unified and inspired French, English, and Dutch armies. By the time of Philip's death on September 13, 1598, his forces had been successfully rebuffed on all fronts. His seventeenth-century successors—Philip III (1598–1621), Philip IV (1621–1665), and Charles II (1665–1700)—were all inferior leaders who never knew responsibilities equal to Philip's. Nor did

Engravings based on tapestries that hung in the British House of Lords try to show two phases of the running battle of the Spanish Armada with the English fleet in the summer of 1588.

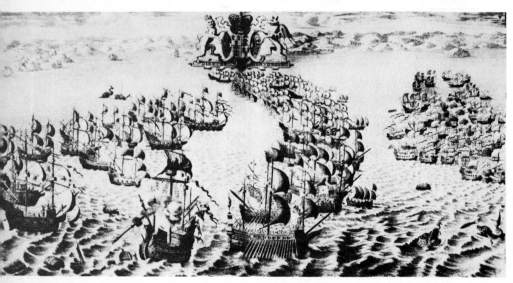

The Spanish tried to keep their half-moon formation but were finally overcome by English fire ships, lack of supplies, unwieldy vessels, and bad weather. England was not invaded; almost half the Spanish were lost. [Granger Collection.]

Spain ever again know such imperial grandeur. The French soon dominated the Continent, while in the New World the Dutch and the English progressively whittled away Spain's once glorious overseas empire.

Elizabeth died on March 23, 1603, knowing comparatively few national wounds and leaving behind her a strong nation, destined to become an empire on which the sun would not set.

The Thirty Years' War (1618-1648)

Preconditions for War

FRAGMENTED GERMANY. In the second half of the sixteenth century Germany was an almost ungovernable land of around 360 autonomous politi-

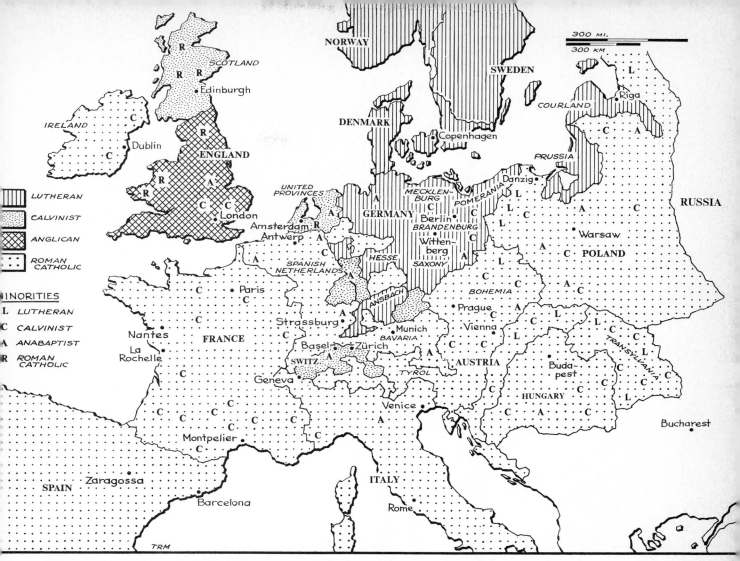

RELIGIOUS DIVISIONS ABOUT 1600

MAP 15.2 *By 1600 few could seriously expect Christians to return to a uniform religious allegiance. In Spain and southern Italy Catholicism remained relatively unchallenged, but note the existence of large religious minorities, both Catholic and Protestant, elsewhere.*

cal entities. There were independent secular principalities (duchies, landgravates, and marches); ecclesiastical principalities (archbishoprics, bishoprics, and abbeys); numerous free cities; and castle regions dominated by knights. The Peace of Augsburg (1555) had given each a significant degree of sovereignty within its own borders. Each levied its own tolls and tariffs and coined its own money, practices that made land travel and trade between

the various regions difficult, where not impossible. In addition, many of these little "states" were filled with great power pretensions. Political decentralization and fragmentation characterized Germany as the seventeenth century opened; it was not a unified nation like Spain, England, or even strife-filled France.

Germany had always been Europe's highway; during the Thirty Years' War it became its stomping ground. Europe's rulers pressed in on Germany both for reasons of trade and because some of them held lands or legal privileges within certain German principalities. German princes, in their turn, looked to import and export markets beyond German borders. They opposed any efforts to con-

N O R T H
S E A

B A L T I C
S E A

DENMARK

HOLSTEIN

Königsberg

P R U S S I

POLAND

MECKLEN-
BURG

Hamburg
Bremen

BRANDEN-
BURG
Berlin

UNITED
PROVINCES

Amsterdam

MARCHE
OF
MAGDEB'G

SILESIA

SPANISH
NETHERLANDS

BISH.
OF
LIÈGE

Cologne

Leipzig
SAXONY

LUXEM-
BURG

PALATINATE

Mainz

Prague

BOHEMIA

MORAVIA

FRANCE

Paris

Trier

Heidelberg

UPPER
PALATINATE

LORRAINE

WÜRTT-
EMBERG

BAVARIA

Vienna
AUSTRIA

Augsburg

Munich

FRANCH-
COMTE

Basel

Zürich

ARCHB.
OF
SALZBURG

STYRIA

HAPSBURG HUNGARY

OTTOMAN

SWISS CONFEDERATION

TYROL

CARINTHIA

EMPIRE

Geneva

B. OF
TRENT

CARNIOLA

BOUNDARY OF THE
HOLY ROMAN EMPIRE

VENICE

CATHOLIC
GOVERNMENT

LUTHERAN
GOVERNMENT

Milan

CALVINIST
GOVERNMENT

Genoa

PAPAL

150 MI.

STATES

150 KM.

M E D I T E R R A N E A N
S E A

TUSCANY

TRM

ITALY

MAP 15.3 *On the eve of the Thirty Years' War
the Empire was politically and religiously
fragmented, as revealed by the somewhat simplified
map. Lutherans dominated the north and Catholics
the south, while Calvinists controlled the United
Provinces and the Palatinate and were important
in Switzerland and Brandenburg.*

THE HOLY ROMAN
EMPIRE ABOUT 1618

solidate the Holy Roman Empire, lest their territorial rights, confirmed by the Peace of Augsburg in the principle *cuius regio, eius religio,* be overturned. German princes were not loath to turn to Catholic France or to the kings of Denmark and Sweden for allies against the Hapsburg emperor. The latter's dynastic connections with Spain generated policies that were perceived to be against the best interests of the territorial states of the empire. Even the pope found political reasons for supporting Bourbon France against the menacing international Hapsburg kingdom.

After the Council of Trent, Protestants in the empire gravely suspected the operation of an imperial and papal conspiracy to re-create the Catholic Europe of pre-Reformation times. The imperial diet, which was controlled by the German princes, demanded that the constitutional rights of Germans, as set forth in electoral agreements with the emperor since the mid-fourteenth century, be strictly observed, and it effectively countered every move by the emperor to impose his will in the empire. In the late sixteenth century the emperor ruled in the empire only to the degree to which he was prepared to use force of arms against his subjects.

RELIGIOUS DIVISION. Religious conflict accentuated the international and internal political divisions (see Map 15.3). During this period the population within the Holy Roman Empire was about equally divided between Catholics and Protestants, the latter having perhaps a slight numerical edge by 1600. The terms of the Peace of Augsburg (1555) had attempted to freeze the territorial holdings of the Lutherans and the Catholics. In the intervening years, however, the Lutherans had gained political control in some Catholic areas, as had the Catholics in a few previously Lutheran areas. Such territorial reversals, or the threat of them, only increased the suspicion and antipathy between the two sides.

The Lutherans had been far more successful in securing their rights to worship in Catholic lands than the Catholics had been in securing such rights in Lutheran lands, because the Catholic rulers, who were in a weakened position after the Reformation, had no choice but to make concessions to Protestant communities within their territories. Such communities remained a sore point. Also the Catholics wanted a strict enforcement of the "Ecclesiastical Reservation" of the Peace of Augsburg which Protestants had made little effort to recognize; the Catholics demanded that all ecclesiastical princes, electors, archbishops, bishops, and abbots who had deserted the Catholic for the Protestant side be immediately deprived of their religious offices and positions and that their ecclesiastical principalities be promptly returned to Catholic control. The Lutherans, and especially the Calvinists in the Palatinate, ignored this stipulation at every opportunity.

There was religious strife in the empire not only between Protestants and Catholics but also between liberal and conservative Lutherans and between Lutherans and the growing numbers of Calvinists. The last half of the sixteenth century was a time of warring Protestant factions within German universities. In addition to the heightened religious strife, the anxiety of religious people of all persuasions was increased by the challenge of the new scientific and material culture that was becoming ascendant in important intellectual and political circles. The age of religious wars was also an age of growing preoccupation with magic, mysticism, witchcraft, and the occult, as fears, doubts, and suspicions stampeded religious feeling.

CALVINISM AND THE PALATINATE. As elsewhere in Europe, Calvinism was the political and religious leaven within the Holy Roman Empire on the eve of the Thirty Years' War. Unrecognized as a legal religion by the Peace of Augsburg, Calvinism had established a strong foothold within the empire when Frederick III (1559–1576), a devout convert to Calvinism, had made it the official religion of his land on becoming Elector Palatine (ruler within the Palatinate) in 1559. Heidelberg became a German Geneva in the 1560s: both a great intellectual center of Calvinism and a staging area for Calvinist penetration into the empire. By 1609 Palatine Calvinists headed a Protestant defensive alliance that received outside support from Spain's sixteenth-century enemies: England, France, and the Netherlands. The Lutherans came to fear the Calvinists almost as much as they did the Catholics. Palatine Calvinists seemed to the Lutherans directly to threaten the Peace of Augsburg—and hence the legal foundation of the Lutheran states—by their bold missionary forays into the empire. The more religiously conservative Lutherans were also shocked by outspoken Calvinist criticism of the doctrine of Christ's real presence in the Eucharist. The Elector Palatine once expressed his disbelief in transubstantiation by publicly shredding the host and mocking it as a "fine God." To

Lutherans, such religious disrespect and aggressiveness disgraced the Reformation.

MAXIMILIAN OF BAVARIA AND THE CATHOLIC LEAGUE. If the Calvinists were active within the Holy Roman Empire, so also were their Catholic counterparts, the Jesuits. Staunchly Catholic Bavaria, supported by Spain, became militarily and ideologically for the Counter-Reformation what the Palatinate was for Protestantism. From there the Jesuits launched successful missions throughout the empire, winning such major cities as Strasbourg and Osnabrück back to the Catholic fold by 1600. In 1609 Maximilian, duke of Bavaria, organized a Catholic League to counter a new Protestant alliance that had been formed in the same year under the leadership of the Calvinist Elector Palatine, Frederick IV (1583–1610). When the league fielded a great army under the command of Count Johann von Tilly, the stage was set, both internally and internationally, for the worst of the religious wars, the Thirty Years' War.

Four Periods of War

The war went through four distinguishable periods, and during its course it drew in every major western European nation—at least diplomatically and financially if not in terms of direct military involvement. The four periods were the Bohemian (1618–1625); the Danish (1625–1629); the Swedish (1630–1635); and the Swedish–French (1635–1648).

THE BOHEMIAN PERIOD. The war broke out in Bohemia after the ascent to the Bohemian throne in 1618 of the Hapsburg Ferdinand, the archduke of Styria, who was also in the line of succession to the imperial throne. Educated by the Jesuits and a fervent Catholic, Ferdinand was determined to restore the traditional faith throughout Austria, Bohemia, and Poland—the eastern Hapsburg lands.

No sooner had Ferdinand become king of Bohemia than he revoked the religious freedoms of

Marauding armies during the Thirty Years' War, by Jan Brueghel (1568–1625) and Sebastien Vrancx (1573–1647), both Flemish artists. During breaks in the fighting, mercenary armies pillaged local villages and towns. [Kunsthistorisches Museum, Vienna.]

Bohemian Protestants. These freedoms had been in force since 1575 and had even been recently broadened by Emperor Rudolf II (1576–1612) in his Letter of Majesty in 1609. The Protestant nobility in Prague responded to Ferdinand's act in May 1618 by literally throwing his regents out the window. The event has ever since been known as the "defenestration of Prague." The three officials fell fifty feet into a dry moat that, fortunately, was padded with manure, which cushioned their fall and spared their lives. When in the following year Ferdinand became Holy Roman Emperor as Ferdinand II, by the unanimous vote of the seven electors, the Bohemians defiantly deposed him in Prague and declared the Calvinist Elector Palatine, Frederick V. (1616–1623), their overlord.

What had begun as a revolt of the Protestant nobility against an unpopular king of Bohemia thereafter escalated into an international war. Spain sent troops to Ferdinand, who found more immediate allies in Maximilian of Bavaria and the opportunistic Lutheran Elector John George I of Saxony (1611–1656). John George saw a sure route to territorial gain by joining in an easy victory over the weaker Elector Palatine. This was not the only time politics and greed would overshadow religion during this long conflict, although Lutheran–Calvinist religious animosity also overrode a common Protestantism. We shall find other instances of such conflicts.

Ferdinand's army under Tilly routed Frederick V's troops at the Battle of White Mountain in 1620. By 1622 Ferdinand had managed not only to subdue and re-Catholicize Bohemia but to conquer the Palatinate as well. While he and his allies enjoyed the spoils of these victories, the fighting extended into northwestern Germany as the duke of Bavaria pressed the conflict. Laying claim to land as he went, he continued to pursue Ernst von Mansfeld, one of Frederick's surviving mercenary generals, into the north.

THE DANISH PERIOD. The emperor's subjugation of Bohemia and the Palatinate and Maximilian's forays into northwestern Germany raised new fears that a reconquest and re-Catholicization of the whole empire now loomed. This was in fact precisely Ferdinand II's design. Encouraged by the English, the French, and the Dutch, the Lutheran King Christian IV (1588–1648) of Denmark, who already held territory within the empire as the duke of Holstein and was eager to extend Danish influence over the coastal towns of the North Sea, picked up the Protestant banner of resistance, opening the Danish period of the conflict (1625–1629). Christian's forces were not, however, up to the challenge. Entering Germany with his army in 1626, he was quickly humiliated by Maximilian and forced to retreat back into Denmark.

As military success made Maximilian stronger and more difficult to control, Ferdinand II sought a more pliant tool for his policies by hiring a powerful, complex mercenary, Albrecht of Wallenstein (1583–1634). Wallenstein was another opportunistic Protestant who had gained a great deal of territory by joining Ferdinand during the conquest of Bohemia. A brilliant and ruthless military strategist, Wallenstein not only completed Maximilian's work by bringing the career of the elusive Ernst von Mansfeld to an end but also penetrated into Denmark with an occupying army. By 1628 Wallenstein commanded a crack army of over 100,000 men. Running afoul of Ferdinand's best-laid plans, he became a law unto himself within the empire, completely outside the emperor's control. Pandora's box had now been fully opened.

Wallenstein broke Protestant resistance so successfully that Ferdinand issued the Edict of Restitution in 1629. This proclamation dramatically reasserted the Catholic safeguards of the Peace of Augsburg (1555). It reaffirmed the illegality of Calvinism—a completely unrealistic move in 1629—and it ordered the return of all church lands acquired by the Lutherans since 1552, an equally unrealistic mandate. Compliance with the latter demand would have involved the return of no less than sixteen bishoprics and twenty-eight cities and towns to Catholic allegiance. Although based on legal precedent and certainly within Ferdinand's power to command, the expectations of the edict were not adjusted to the political realities of 1629. It struck panic into the hearts of Protestants and Hapsburg opponents everywhere, who now saw clearly the emperor's plan to re-create a Catholic Europe. Resistance quickly refueled.

THE SWEDISH PERIOD. Gustavus Adolphus of Sweden (1611–1632), a deeply pious king of a unified Lutheran nation, became the new leader of Protestant forces within the empire, opening the Swedish period of the war (1630–1635). He was handsomely bankrolled by two very interested bystanders: the French minister Cardinal Richelieu, whose foreign policy was to protect French interests by keeping Hapsburg armies tied down in Germany, and the Dutch, who had not forgotten Spanish Hapsburg domination in the sixteenth century. The Swedish king found ready allies in the electors of Brandenburg and Saxony and soon won a smashing victory at Breitenfeld in 1630. The Protestant victory at Breitenfeld so dramatically reversed the course of the war that it has been regarded as the most decisive, although far from the final, engagement of the long conflict.

One of the reasons for the overwhelming Swedish victory at Breitenfeld was the military genius of Gustavus Adolphus. The Swedish king brought a new mobility to warfare by having both his infantry and his cavalry master fire and charge tactics. At six deep his infantry squares were smaller than the traditional ones, and he filled them with equal numbers of musketeers and pikesmen. His cavalrymen also alternated pistol shot with sword charges. His artillery was lighter and more mobile in battle. Each unit of his army—infantry, cavalry, and artillery—had *both* defensive and offensive capability and could quickly change from one to the other.

Gustavus Adolphus died at the hands of Wallenstein's forces during the Battle of Lützen (November 1632)—a very costly engagement for both sides that created a brief standstill. Ferdinand had long been resentful of Wallenstein's independence, although he was the major factor in imperial success. In 1634 Ferdinand had Wallenstein assassinated. By that time Wallenstein had not only served his purpose for the emperor, but, ever opportunistic, he was even trying openly to strike bargains with the Protestants for his services. The Wallenstein episode is a telling commentary on this war without honor. Despite the deep religious motivations, greed and political gain were the real forces at work in the Thirty Years' War, and even allies who owed one another their success were not above treating each other as mortal enemies.

In the Peace of Prague in 1635 the German Protestant states, led by Saxony, reached a compromise agreement with Ferdinand. The Swedes, however, received continued support from France and the Netherlands. Desiring to maximize their investment in the war, they refused to join the agreement. Their resistance to settlement plunged the war into its fourth and most devastating phase, the Swedish–French period (1635–1648).

THE SWEDISH–FRENCH PERIOD. The French openly entered the war in 1635, sending men and munitions as well as financial subsidies. After their entrance the war dragged on for thirteen years,

with French, Swedish, and Spanish soldiers looting the length and breadth of Germany—warring, it seemed, simply for the sake of warfare itself. The Germans, long weary of the devastation, were too disunited to repulse the foreign armies; they simply watched and suffered. By the time peace talks began in the Westphalian cities of Münster and Osnabrück in 1644, an estimated one third of the German population had died as a direct result of the war. It was the worst European catastrophe since the Black Death of the fourteenth century.

The Treaty of Westphalia

The Treaty of Westphalia in 1648 brought all hostilities within the Holy Roman Empire to an end. It rescinded Ferdinand's Edict of Restitution and firmly reasserted the major feature of the religious settlement of the Peace of Augsburg (1555), as the ruler of each land was again permitted to determine the religion of his land. The treaty also gave the Calvinists their long-sought legal recognition. The independence of the Swiss Confederacy and the United Provinces of Holland, long recognized in fact, was now proclaimed in law. And the treaty elevated Bavaria to the rank of an elector state. The provisions of the treaty made the German princes supreme over their principalities. Yet, as guarantors of the treaty, Sweden and France found many occasions to meddle in German affairs until the century's end, France to considerable territorial gain. Brandenburg–Prussia emerged as the most powerful north German state.

France and Spain remained at war outside the empire until 1659, when French victories forced on the Spanish the humiliating Treaty of the Pyrenees. Thereafter France became Europe's dominant power, and the once vast Hapsburg kingdom waned.

By confirming the territorial sovereignty of Germany's many political entities, the Treaty of Westphalia perpetuated German division and political weakness into the modern period. Only two German states attained any international significance during the seventeenth century: Austria and Brandenburg–Prussia. The petty regionalism within the empire also reflected on a small scale the drift of larger European politics. In the seventeenth century distinctive nation-states, each with its own political, cultural, and religious identity, reached maturity and firmly established the competitive nationalism of the modern world.

C. V. Wedgwood has described the outcome of the Thirty Years' War:

After the expenditure of so much human life to so little purpose, men might have grasped the essential futility of putting the beliefs of the mind to the judgment of the sword. Instead, they rejected religion as an object to fight for and found others. . . . The war solved no problem. Its effects, both immediate and indirect, were either negative or disastrous. Morally subversive, economically destructive, socially degrading, confused in its causes, devious in its course, futile in its result, it is the outstanding example in European history of meaningless conflict.[2]

Suggested Readings

FERNAND BRAUDEL, *The Mediterranean and the Mediterranean World in the Age of Philip the Second,* Vols. 1 and 2 (1976). Widely acclaimed work of a French master historian.

RICHARD DUNN, *The Age of Religious Wars 1559–1689* (1979). Excellent brief survey of every major conflict.

J. H. ELLIOTT, *Europe Divided 1559–1598* (1968). Direct, lucid narrative account.

G. R. ELTON, *England Under the Tudors* (1955). Masterly account.

[2] In T. K. Rabb, *The Thirty Years' War: Problems of Motive, Extent and Effect* (Boston: D. C. Heath, 1964), pp. 18–19.

JULIAN H. FRANKLIN (Ed. and Trans.), *Constitutionalism and Resistance in the Sixteenth Century: Three Treatises by Hotman, Beza, and Mornay* (1969). Three defenders of the right of people to resist tyranny.

PIETER GEYL, *The Revolt of the Netherlands, 1555–1609* (1958). The authoritative survey.

JOHN LYNCH, *Spain Under the Hapsburg I: 1516–1598* (1964). Political narrative.

J. RUSSELL MAJOR, *Representative Institutions in Renaissance France* (1960). An essay in French constitutional history.

GARRETT MATTINGLY, *The Armada* (1959). A masterpiece and novel-like in style.

J. E. NEALE, *The Age of Catherine de Medici* (1962). Short, concise summary.

JOHN NEALE, *Queen Elizabeth I* (1934). Superb biography.

THEODORE K. RABB (Ed.), *The Thirty Years' War* (1972). Excerpts from the scholarly debate over the war's significance.

JASPER G. RIDLEY, *John Knox* (1968). Large, detailed biography.

J. H. M. SALMON (Ed.), *The French Wars of Religion: How Important Were the Religious Factors?* (1967). Scholarly debate over the relation between politics and religion.

J. H. M. SALMON, *Society in Crisis: France in the Sixteenth Century* (1976).

ALFRED SOMAN (Ed.), *The Massacre of St. Bartholomew's Day: Reappraisals and Documents* (1974). Results of an international symposium on the anniversary of the massacre.

C. V. WEDGWOOD, *The Thirty Years' War* (1939). The authoritative account.

C. V. WEDGWOOD, *William the Silent* (1944). Excellent political biography.

466

16 England and France in the Seventeenth Century

Constitutional Crisis and Settlement in Stuart England

Between 1603 and 1715 England experienced the most tumultuous years of its long history. In this period Puritan resistance to the Elizabethan religious settlement merged with fierce parliamentary opposition to the aspirations to absolute monarchy of the Stuart kings. During these years no fewer than three foreigners occupied the English throne, and between 1649 and 1660 England was without a king altogether. Yet by the end of this century of crisis England provided a model to Europe of limited monarchy, parliamentary government, and measured religious toleration.

Louis the XIV of France, the dominant political figure in Europe in the second half of the seventeenth century. Known as the Sun King, Louis built his spectacular palace at Versailles as a testament to his glorification of the monarchy. [New York Public Library Picture Collection.]

James I

The first of England's foreign monarchs was James VI of Scotland (the son of Mary Stuart, Queen of Scots), who in 1603 succeeded the childless Elizabeth as James I of England. This first Stuart king inherited not only the crown but also a royal debt of almost one-half million pounds, a fiercely divided church, and a Parliament already restive over the extent of his predecessor's claims to royal authority. Under James each of these problems worsened. The new king utterly lacked tact, was ignorant of English institutions, and strongly advocated the divine right of kings, a subject on which he had written a book in 1598 entitled *A Trew Law of Free Monarchies*. He rapidly alienated both Parliament and the politically powerful Puritans.

The breach with Parliament was opened by James's seeming usurpation of the power of the purse. Royal debts, his own extravagance, and an inflation he could not control made it necessary for the king to be constantly in quest of additional revenues. These he sought largely by levying—solely

467

on the authority of ill-defined privileges claimed to be attached to the office of king—new custom duties known as "impositions." These were a version of the older such duties known as tonnage and poundage. Parliament resented such independent efforts to raise revenues as an affront to its power, and the result was a long and divisive court struggle between the king and Parliament.

As the distance between king and Parliament widened, the religious problems also worsened. The Puritans, who were prominent among the lesser landed gentry and within Parliament, had hoped that James's experience with the Scottish Presbyterian church and his own Protestant upbringing would incline him to favor their efforts to "purify" the Anglican church. Since the days of Elizabeth the Puritans had sought to eliminate elaborate religious ceremonies and to replace the hierarchical episcopal system of church governance with a more representative presbyterian form like that of the Calvinist churches on the Continent. In January 1604 they had their first direct dealing with the new king. James responded in that month to a statement of Puritan grievances, the so-called Millenary Petition, at a special religious conference at Hampton Court. To the dismay of the Puritans the king firmly declared his intention to maintain and even enhance the Anglican episcopacy. "A Scottish presbytery," he snorted, "agreeth as well with monarchy as God and the devil. No bishops, no king." Nonconformists were clearly forewarned.

Both sides departed the conference with their worst suspicions of one another largely confirmed, and as the years passed, the distrust between them only deepened. It was during James's reign in 1620 that Puritan separatists founded Plymouth Colony in Cape Cod Bay in North America, preferring flight from England to Anglican conformity. The Hampton Court conference did, however, sow one fruitful seed. A commission was appointed to render a new translation of the Bible, a mission fulfilled in 1611 when the eloquent Authorized or King James Version of the Bible was published.

Though he inherited major political and religious difficulties, James also created special problems for himself. His court became a center of scandal and corruption. He governed by favorites, the most influential of whom was the duke of Buckingham, whom rumor made the king's homosexual lover. Buckingham controlled royal patronage and openly sold peerages and titles to the highest bidders—a practice that angered the nobility

because it cheapened their rank. James's pro-Spanish foreign policy also displeased the English. In 1604 he concluded a much needed peace with Spain, England's chief adversary during the second half of the sixteenth century. His subjects viewed is as a sign of pro-Catholic sentiment. James further increased suspicions when he attempted unsuccessfully to relax the penal laws against Catholics. The English had not forgotten the brutal reign of Mary Tudor and the acts of treason by Catholics during Elizabeth's reign. In 1618 James hesitated, not unwisely, to rush English troops to the aid of Protestants in Germany at the outbreak of the Thirty Years' War. This hesitation caused his loyalty to the Anglican church to be openly questioned by some. In the king's last years, as his health failed and the reins of government were increasingly given over to his son Charles and Buckingham, parliamentary power and Protestant sentiment combined to undo his pro-Spanish foreign policy, which had also failed to meet the king's own expectations. In 1624 England entered a continental war against Spain.

James I feasting with the Spanish ambassadors, 1624. James's policy of peace with Spain was unpopular with many of his subjects, but the king persevered with it for most of his reign, even negotiating unsuccessfully in 1623 for a marriage between his heir, the future Charles I, and a Spanish princess. [BBC Hulton Picture Library.]

Charles I

Charles I (1625–1649) flew even more brazenly in the face of Parliament and the Puritans than did his father. Unable to gain adequate funds from Parliament for the Spanish war, Charles, like his father, resorted to extraparliamentary measures. He levied new tariffs and duties, attempted to collect discontinued taxes, and even subjected the English people to a so-called forced loan (a tax theoretically to be repaid), imprisoning those who refused to pay. Troops in transit to war zones were quartered in private English homes.

When Parliament met in 1628, its members were furious. Taxes were being illegally collected for a war that was going badly for England and that now, through royal blundering, involved France as well as Spain. Parliament expressed its displeasure by making the king's request for new funds conditional on his recognition of the Petition of Right. This major document of constitutional freedom declared that henceforth there should be no forced loans or taxation without the consent of Parliament, that no freeman should be imprisoned without due cause, and that troops should not be billeted in private homes. Though Charles agreed to the petition, there was little confidence that he would keep his word.

In August 1628 Charles's chief minister, Buckingham, with whom Parliament had been in open dispute since 1626, was assassinated. His death, while sweet to many, did not resolve the hostility between king and Parliament. In January 1629 Parliament further underscored its resolve to limit royal prerogative. It declared that religious innovations leading to "popery"—Charles's high-church policies were meant—and the levying of taxes without parliamentary consent were acts of treason. Perceiving that things were getting out of hand, Charles promptly dissolved Parliament and did not recall it again until 1640, when war with Scotland forced him to do so.

To conserve his limited resources, Charles made peace with France and Spain in 1629 and 1630, respectively. His chief minister, Thomas Wentworth (after 1640 earl of Stafford), instituted a policy known as "thorough," that is, strict efficiency and administrative centralization in government. This policy aimed at absolute royal control of England and required for its success the king's ability to operate independently of Parliament. Every legal fund-raising device was exploited to the full. Neglected laws suddenly were enforced, and existing

Portrait of King Charles I of England hunting, by Anthony van Dyck (1599–1641). Charles was executed by order of Parliament in 1649 following the rise to power of Oliver Cromwell who, among other things, then sold the royal picture collection, so that this portrait is now in France. [Musée du Louvre, Paris. Cliché des Musées Nationaux.]

taxes were extended into new areas. An example of the latter tactic was the inland collection of "ship money." This tax normally was levied only on coastal areas to pay for naval protection, but after 1634 it was gradually applied to the whole of England, interior and coastal towns alike. A great landowner named John Hampden unsuccessfully challenged its extension in a close legal contest. Although the king prevailed, it was a costly victory, for it deepened the animosity toward him among the powerful landowners, who both elected and sat in Parliament.

Charles had neither the royal bureaucracy nor the standing army to rule as an absolute monarch. This became abundantly clear when he and his re-

❧ Parliament Attacks Charles I's Royal Abuses of His Subjects

The tension between King Charles I (1625–1649) and Parliament had very few causes that did not go back to earlier reigns. The Petition of Right can, therefore, be seen as a general catalog of reasons for opposing arbitrary royal power. Specifically, angered by Charles and his levying of new taxes and other revenue-gathering devices, his coercion of freemen, and his quartering of troops in transit in private homes, Parliament refused to grant the king any funds until he rescinded such practices by recognizing the Petition of Right (June 7, 1628). Here is the Petition and the king's reply.

[The Lords Spiritual and Temporal, and Commons in Parliament assembled] do humbly pray your Most Excellent Majesty, that no man hereafter be compelled to make or yield any gift, loan, benevolence, tax, or such like charge, without common consent by Act of Parliament; and that none be called to make answer, or take such oath, or to give attendance, or be confined, or otherwise molested or disquieted concerning the same, or for refusal thereof; and that no freeman, in any such manner as is before-mentioned, be imprisoned or detained; and that your Majesty will be pleased to remove the said soldiers and mariners [who have been quartered in private homes], and that your people may not be so burdened in time to come; and that the foresaid commissions for proceeding by martial law, may be revoked and annulled; and that hereafter no commissions of like

nature may issue forth to any person or persons whatsoever, to be executed as aforesaid, lest by colour of them any of your Majesty's subjects be destroyed or put to death, contrary to the laws and franchise of the land.

All which they most humbly pray of your Most Excellent Majesty, as their rights and liberties according to the laws and statutes of this realm.

[The King's reply: The King willeth that right be done according to the laws and customs of the realm; and that the statutes be put in due execution, that his subjects may have no cause to complain of any wrong or oppressions, contrary to their just rights and liberties, to the preservation whereof he holds himself as well obliged as of his prerogative.]

The Constitutional Documents of the Puritan Revolution, ed. by Samuel R. Gardiner (Oxford, England: Clarendon Press, 1889), pp. 4–5.

ligious minister, William Laud (1573–1645; after 1633 the archbishop of Canterbury), provoked a war with Scotland. They tried to impose the English episcopal system and a prayer book almost identical to the Anglican *Book of Common Prayer* on the Scots as they had done throughout England. From his position within the Court of High Commission, Laud had already radicalized the Puritans by denying them the right to publish and preach.

Facing resistance from the Scots, Charles was forced to seek financial assistance from a Parliament that opposed his policies almost as much as the foreign invaders. Led by John Pym (1584–1643), Parliament refused even to consider funds for war until the king agreed to redress a long list of political and religious grievances. The result was the king's immediate dissolution of

Parliament—hence its name, the Short Parliament (April–May 1640). When the Presbyterian Scots invaded England and defeated an English army at the battle of Newburn in the summer of 1640, Charles found himself forced to reconvene Parliament. This time it was on the latter's terms and for what would be a long and most fateful duration.

THE LONG PARLIAMENT. The landowners and the merchant classes represented by Parliament had resented the king's financial measures and paternalistic rule for some time. To this resentment was added fervent Puritan opposition. Hence the Long Parliament (1640–1660) acted with widespread support and general unanimity when it convened in November 1640. Both the earl of Stafford and Archbishop Laud were impeached by the House of Commons. Disgraced and convicted by a

The House of Commons in session in 1648 *toward the end of the Civil War, as seen in a contemporary engraving.* [*The Granger Collection.*]

Parliamentary bill of attainder (a judgment of treason entailing loss of civil rights), Stafford was executed in 1641. Laud was imprisoned and later executed (1645). The Court of Star Chamber and the Court of High Commission, royal instruments of political and religious "thorough," respectively, were abolished. The levying of new taxes without consent of Parliament and the inland extension of ship money now became illegal. Finally, it was resolved that no more than three years should elapse between meetings of Parliament and that Parliament could not be dissolved without its own consent.

Marxist historians have seen in these measures a major triumph of the "bourgeoisie" over the aristocracy. But lesser aristocratic groups (the gentry) were actually divided between the parliamentary and royal camps, so more was obviously at issue than simple class warfare. The accomplishment of the Long Parliament was to issue a firm and lasting declaration of the political and religious rights of the many English people represented in Parliament, both high and low, against autocratic royal government.

There remained division within Parliament over the precise direction of religious reform. Both moderate Puritans (the Presbyterians) and extreme Puritans (the Independents) wanted the complete abolition of the episcopal system and the *Book of Common Prayer*. The majority Presbyterians sought to reshape England religiously along Calvinist lines, with local congregations subject to higher representative governing bodies (presbyteries). Independents wanted every congregation to be its own final authority. There were also a considerable number of conservatives in both houses who were determined to preserve the English church in its current form, although their numbers fell dramatically after 1642, when those who sympathized with the present Anglican church departed the House of Commons.

The division within Parliament was further intensified in October 1641, when a rebellion erupted in Ireland requiring an army to suppress it. Pym and his followers, loudly reminding the House of Commons of the king's past misdeeds, argued that Charles could not be trusted with an army and that Parliament should become the com-

EUROPE IN 1648

Legend:
- SWEDISH DOMINIONS
- BRANDENBURG-PRUSSIA
- SPANISH MONARCHY
- AUSTRIA HAPSBURGS
- CHURCH LANDS

NORWAY
Bergen
Christiana
Stavanger

S W E D E
Stockholm
FINLAND
Reva
ESTON
LIVO
Ri
COURLAND
Meme

KINGDOM OF DENMARK AND NORWAY
DENMARK
Copenhagen
Danzig
E.
PRUS
SCHLESWIG
HOLSTEIN

SCOTLAND
Edinburgh
Belfast
York
IRELAND
Dublin
ENGLAND
Cork
WALES
London
Bristol
Plymouth

N O R T H   S E A

BOUNDARY OF THE EMPIRE

UNITED PROVINCES
SPANISH NETH.
Brussels

BRANDEN-BURG
Posen
P
Warsaw
Breslau
SILESIA
Cracow
G
SAXONY
MINOR HESSE GERMAN STATES
Prague
BOHEMIA
MORAVIA
HUNGARY
Pressburg
Budap
AUSTRIA HAPSBURG
Vienna
HUNGA

A T L A N T I C

O C E A N

Rouen
Paris
Reims
Orleans
Tours
BAVARIA
FRANCHE COMTÉ

FRANCE
Nantes
Lyons
SWITZ.
SAVOY
PIED-MONT
AVIGNON

VENICE
Venice
MILAN
PAR.
MOD. Bologna
Genoa
LUCCA

CROATIA
SLAVONIA
SAVA
Belgr
BOSNIA
SER
Spalato
VEN.
MONT NEGR
REP.
RAGUSA
Cattaro (VEN.)
ALBA

Bordeaux
Toulouse
LANGUEDOC
Marseilles

TUSCANY
CORSICA (GEN.)
ITALY
Rome
PAPAL STATES
Capua
Bari
Naples

Oporto
León
NAVARRE
Burgos
Salamanca
Saragossa
CASTILE
ARAGON
Barcelona
Madrid
Toledo
SPAIN
PORTUGAL
Lisbon
Cordova
Seville
Granada
Cadiz
BALEARIC IS.
SARDINIA (SP.)
KINGDOM OF THE TWO SICILIES
SICILY

Tangier (PORT.)
Ceuta (SP.)
FEZ & MOROCCO
Algiers
ALGERIA
Tunis (OTT.)

M E D I T E R R A N E A N   S E A

B A L T I C   S E A

A D R I A T I C   S E A

mander-in-chief of English armed forces. Parliamentary conservatives, who had winced once at Puritan religious reforms, winced thrice at this bold departure from English practice. On December 1, 1641, Parliament presented Charles with the "Grand Remonstrance," a more-than-200-article summary of popular and parliamentary grievances against the crown.

Charles saw the division within Parliament as a last chance to regain power. In January 1642 he invaded Parliament with his soldiers. He intended to arrest Pym and the other leaders, but they had been forewarned and managed to escape. Shocked by the king's action, a majority of the House of Commons thereafter passed the Militia Ordinance, a measure that gave Parliament control of the army. The die was now cast. For the next four years (1642–1646) civil war engulfed England.

Charles assembled his forces at Nottingham, and in August the civil war began. The main issues were whether England would be ruled by an absolute monarchy or by a parliamentary government and whether English religion would be conformist high Anglican and controlled by the king's bishops or cast into a more decentralized, presbyterian system of church governance. Charles's supporters, known as *Cavaliers*, were located in the northwestern half of England. The parliamentary opposition, known as *Roundheads* because of their close-cropped hair, had its stronghold in the southeastern half of the country. The nobility, identifying the power of their peerage with the preservation of the current form of the monarchy and the church, became prominent supporters of the king, whereas the townspeople supported the Parliamentary army.

Oliver Cromwell and the Puritan Republic

Two factors led finally to Parliament's victory. The first was an alliance with Scotland in 1643 consummated when John Pym persuaded Parliament to accept the terms of the Solemn League and Covenant, an agreement committing Parliament, with the Scots, to a presbyterian system of church government. The second was the reorganization of the parliamentary army under Oliver

MAP 16.1 *At the end of the Thirty Years' War Spain still had extensive possessions, Austria and Brandenburg-Prussia were prominent, the independence of the United Provinces and Switzerland was recognized, and Sweden held important river mouths in north Germany.*

ꙮ A Portrait of Oliver Cromwell

Statesman and historian Edward Hyde, the earl of Clarendon (1609–1674), was an enemy of Oliver Cromwell. However, his portrait of Cromwell, which follows, mixes criticism with grudging admiration for the Puritan leader.

He was one of those men whom his enemies cannot condemn without at the same time also praising. For he could never have done half that mischief without great parts of courage and industry and judgment. And he must have had a wonderful understanding of the natures and humours of men and a great dexterity in applying them . . . [to] raise himself to such a height. . . .

When he first appeared in the Parliament, he seemed to have a person in no degree gracious, no ornament of discourse, none of those talents which reconcile the affections of the standers-by; yet as he grew into his place and authority, his parts seemed to be renewed, as if he concealed faculties til he had occasion to use them. . . .

After he was confirmed and invested Protector . . . he consulted with very few . . . nor communicated any enterprise he resolved upon with more than those who were to have principal parts in the execution of it; nor to them sooner than was absolutely necessary. What he once resolved . . . he would not be dissuaded

from, nor endure any contradiction. . . .

In all other matters which did not concern . . . his jurisdiction, he seemed to have great reverence for the law. . . . And as he proceeded with . . . indignation and haughtiness with those who were refractory and dared to contend with his greatness, so towards those who complied with his good pleasure, and courted his protection, he used a wonderful civility, generosity, and bounty.

To reduce three nations [England, Ireland, and Scotland], which perfectly hated him, to an entire obedience to all his dictates; to awe and govern those nations by an army that was not devoted to him and wished his ruin; this was an instance of a very prodigious address. But his greatness at home was but a shadow of the glory he had abroad. It was hard to discover which feared him most, France, Spain, or the Netherlands. . . . As they did all sacrifice their honour and their interest to his pleasure, so there is nothing he could have demanded that any of them would have denied him.

James Harvey Robinson (Ed.), *Readings in European History,* Vol. 2 (Boston: Ginn and Co., 1906), pp. 248–250.

Cromwell (1599–1658), a middle-aged country squire of iron discipline and strong Independent religious sentiment. Cromwell and his "godly men" favored neither the episcopal system of the king nor the pure presbyterian system of the Solemn League and Covenant. They were willing to tolerate an established majority church, but only if it also permitted Protestant dissenters to worship outside it. The allies won the Battle of Marston Moor in 1644, the largest engagement of the war, and in June 1645 Cromwell's New Model Army, which fought with a disciplined fanaticism, decisively defeated the king at Naseby.

Though defeated militarily, Charles again took advantage of the deep divisions within Parliament, this time seeking to win the Presbyterians and the Scots over to the royalist side. But Cromwell's army firmly imposed its will. In December 1648 Colonel

Thomas Pride physically barred the Presbyterians, who made up a majority of Parliament, from taking their seats. After "Pride's Purge," only a "rump" of less than fifty members remained. Though small in numbers, this Independent Rump Parliament had supreme military power within England. It did not hesitate to use this power. On January 30, 1649, after trial by a special court, it executed Charles as a public criminal and thereafter abolished the monarchy, the House of Lords, and the Anglican church. The revolution was consummated by events hardly contemplated at its outset.

From 1649 to 1660 England became officially a Puritan republic. During this period Cromwell's army conquered Ireland and Scotland, creating the single political entity of Great Britain. Cromwell, however, was a military man and no politician.

Oliver Cromwell. Cromwell's New Model Army defeated the royalists in the English Civil War. After the execution of Charles I in 1649, Cromwell dominated the short-lived English republic, conquered Ireland and Scotland and ruled as Lord Protector from 1653 until his death in 1658. This bust was made in 1766 by Joseph Wilton. [Victoria and Albert Museum.]

He was increasingly frustrated by what seemed to him to be pettiness and dawdling on the part of Parliament. When in 1653 the House of Commons entertained a motion to disband the expensive army of fifty thousand men, Cromwell responded by marching in and disbanding Parliament. He ruled thereafter as Lord Protector.

But his military dictatorship proved no more effective than Charles's rule had been and became just as harsh and hated. Cromwell's great army and

The bleeding head of Charles I is exhibited to the crowd after his execution on a cold day in January 1649. The contemporary Dutch artist also professed to see the immediate ascension of Charles's soul to heaven. In fact, to many the king was seen as a martyr. [The Granger Collection.]

✌ An Account of the Execution of Charles I

Convicted of "high treason and other high crimes," Charles I was beheaded on January 30, 1649. In his last minutes he conversed calmly with the attending bishop and executioner, anxious only that the executioner not strike before he gave the signal.

To the executioner he said, "I shall say but very short prayers, and when I thrust out my hands—"

Then he called to the bishop for his cap, and having put it on, asked the executioner, "Does my hair trouble you?" and the executioner desired him to put it under his cap, which as he was doing by the help of the bishop and the executioner, he turned to the bishop and said, "I have a good cause, and a gracious God on my side."

The bishop said, "There is but one stage more, which, though turbulent and troublesome, yet is a very short one. . . . It will carry you from earth to heaven . . . to a crown of glory. . . ."

Then the king asked the executioner, "Is my hair well?"

And taking off his cloak and George [the Order of the Garter, bearing a figure of Saint George], he delivered his George to the bishop. . . .

Then putting off his doublet and being in his waistcoat, he put on his cloak again, and looking upon the block, said to the executioner, "You must set it fast."

The executioner. "It is fast, sir."

King. "It might have been a little higher."

Executioner. "It can be no higher, sir."

King. "When I put out my hands this way, then—"

Then having said a few words to himself, as he stood with hands and eyes lifted up, immediately stooping down he laid his neck upon the block; and the executioner, again putting his hair under his cap, his Majesty, thinking he had been going to strike, bade him, "Stay for the sign."

Executioner. "Yes, I will, as it please your Majesty."

After a very short pause, his Majesty stretching forth his hands, the executioner at one blow severed his head from his body; which being held up and showed to the people, was with his body put into a coffin covered with black velvet and carried into his lodging.

His blood was taken up by divers persons for different ends: by some as trophies of the villainy; by others as relics of a martyr.

James Harvey Robinson (Ed.), *Readings in European History*, Vol. 2 (Boston: Ginn and Co., 1906), pp. 244–245.

---

foreign adventures inflated his budget to three times that of Charles's. Trade and commerce suffered throughout England, as near chaos reigned in many places. Puritan prohibitions of such pastimes as theaters, dancing, and drunkenness were widely resented. Cromwell's treatment of Anglicans came to be just as intolerant as Charles's treatment of Puritans had been. In the name of religious liberty, political liberty had been lost. And Cromwell was unable to get along even with the new Parliaments that were elected under the auspices of his army. By the time of his death in 1658, a majority of the English were ready to end the Puritan experiment and return to the traditional institutions of government.

Charles II and the Restoration of the Monarchy

The Stuart monarchy was restored in 1660 when Charles II (1660–1685), son of Charles I, returned to England amid great rejoicing. A man of considerable charm and political skill, Charles set a refreshing new tone after eleven years of somber Puritanism. His restoration returned England to the status quo of 1642, as once again a hereditary monarch sat on the throne and the Anglican church was religiously supreme.

Because of his secret Catholic sympathies the king favored a policy of religious toleration. He wanted to allow all persons outside the Church of

England, Catholics as well as Puritans, to worship freely so long as they remained loyal to the throne. But the ultraroyalist Anglicans in Parliament decided otherwise. They did not believe patriotism and religion could be so disjointed. Between 1661 and 1665, through a series of laws known as the Clarendon Code, Parliament excluded Roman Catholics, Presbyterians, and Independents from the religious and political life of the nation. Penalties were imposed for attending non-Anglican worship services, strict adherence to the *Book of Common Prayer* and the Thirty-Nine Articles was required, and all who desired to serve in local government were made to swear oaths of allegiance to the Church of England. This trampling of Puritan sentiments did not go unopposed in Parliament, but the opposition was not strong enough to override the majority.

Under Charles II England stepped up its challenge of the Dutch to become Europe's commercial and business center. Navigation Acts were passed that required all imports into England to be carried either in English ships or in ships registered to the same country as the imports they carried. Because the Dutch were the original suppliers of hardly more than tulips and cheese, these laws struck directly at their lucrative role as Europe's commercial middlemen. A series of naval wars between England and Holland ensued. Charles also undertook at this time to tighten his grasp on the rich English colonies in North America and the Caribbean, many of which had been settled and developed by separatists who desired independence from English rule.

Although Parliament strongly supported the monarchy, Charles, following the habit of his predecessors, required greater revenues than Parliament appropriated. These Charles managed to get in part by increased customs. He also received French aid. In 1670 England and France formally allied against the Dutch in the Treaty of Dover. A secret portion of this treaty pledged Charles to announce his conversion to Catholicism as soon as conditions in England permitted, a declaration for which Louis XIV of France promised to pay 167,000 pounds. (Such a declaration never came to pass.) Charles also received a French war chest of 250,000 pounds per annum.

In an attempt to unite the English people behind the war with Holland, and as a sign of good faith to Louis XIV, Charles issued a Declaration of Indulgence in 1672 suspending all laws against Roman

Charles II of England in a portrait from an unknown hand. [*The Granger Collection.*]

Catholics and Protestant nonconformists. But again the conservative Tory Parliament proved less generous than the king and refused to grant money for the war until Charles rescinded the measure. After Charles withdrew the declaration, Parliament passed the Test Act, which required all officials of the crown, civil and military, to swear an oath against the doctrine of transubstantiation—a requirement that no loyal Roman Catholic could honestly meet.

The Test Act was aimed in large measure at the king's brother, James, duke of York, heir to the throne and a recent, devout convert to Catholicism. In 1678 a notorious liar named Titus Oates swore before a magistrate that Charles's Catholic wife, through her physician, was plotting with Jesuits and Irishmen to kill the king so that James could assume the throne. The matter was taken before Parliament, where it was believed. In the ensuing hysteria, known as the "Popish Plot," several people were tried and executed. In 1680–1681, riding the crest of anti-Catholic sentiment, opposition Whig members of Parliament, led by the earl of

Shaftsbury (1621–1683), made an impressive but unsuccessful effort to enact a bill excluding James from succession to the throne.

More suspicious than ever of Parliament, Charles II turned again to increased customs revenue and the assistance of Louis XIV for extra income and was able to rule from 1681–1685 without recalling Parliament. In these years Charles suppressed much of his opposition, driving the earl of Shaftsbury into exile, executing several Whig leaders for treason, and bullying local corporations into electing members of Parliament submissive to the royal will. When Charles died in 1685 (after a deathbed conversion to Catholicism), he left James the prospect of a Parliament filled with royal friends.

James II and Renewed Fears of a Catholic England

James II (1685–1688) did not know how to make the most of a good thing. He alienated Parliament by insisting upon the repeal of the Test Act. When Parliament balked, he dissolved it and proceeded openly to appoint known Catholics to high positions in both his court and the army. In 1687 James issued a Declaration of Indulgence, which suspended all religious tests and permitted free worship. Local candidates for Parliament who opposed the declaration were removed from their offices by the king's soldiers and were replaced by Catholics. In June 1688 James went so far as to imprison seven Anglican bishops who had refused to publicize his suspension of laws against Catholics.

Under the guise of a policy of enlightened toleration James was actually seeking to subject all English institutions to the power of the monarchy. His goal was absolutism, and even conservative, loyalist Tories could not abide this. The English had reason to fear that James planned to imitate the policy of Louis XIV, who in 1685 had revoked the Edict of Nantes (which had protected French Protestants for almost a century) and had returned France to Catholicism, where necessary, with the aid of dragoons. A national consensus very quickly formed against the monarchy of James II.

The direct stimulus for parliamentary action came when on June 20, 1688, James's second wife, a Catholic, gave birth to a son, a male Catholic heir to the English throne. The English had hoped that James would die without a male heir and that the throne would revert to his Protestant eldest daughter, Mary. Mary was the wife of William III of Orange, *stadholder* of the Netherlands, great-grandson of William the Silent, and the leader of European opposition to Louis XIV's imperial designs. Within days of the birth of a Catholic male heir, Whig and Tory members of Parliament formed a coalition and invited Orange to invade England to preserve "traditional liberties," that is, the Anglican church and parliamentary government.

The "Glorious Revolution."

William of Orange arrived with his army in November 1688 and was received without opposition by the English people. In the face of sure defeat James fled to France and the protection of Louis XIV. With James gone, Parliament declared the throne vacant and on its own authority proclaimed William and Mary the new monarchs in 1689, completing a successful bloodless revolution. William and Mary in turn recognized a Bill of Rights that limited the powers of the monarchy and guaranteed the civil liberties of the English privileged classes. Henceforth, England's monarchs would rule by the consent of Parliament and be subject to law. The Bill of Rights also pointedly prohibited Roman Catholics from occupying the English throne. The Toleration Act of 1689 permitted worship by all Protestants and outlawed Roman Catholics and antitrinitarians (those who denied the Christian doctrine of the Trinity).

The final measure closing the century of strife was the Act of Settlement in 1701. This bill provided for the English crown to go to the Protestant House of Hanover in Germany if Queen Anne (1702–1714), the second daughter of James II and the last of the Stuart monarchs, was not survived by her children. Consequently in 1714 the Elector of Hanover became King George I of England, the third foreign monarch to occupy the English throne in just over a century.

The "Glorious Revolution" of 1688 established a framework of government by and for the governed. It received classic philosophical justification in John Locke's *Second Treatise of Government* (1690), wherein Locke described the relationship of a king and his people in terms of a bilateral contract. If the king broke that contract, the people, by whom Locke meant the privileged and powerful, had the right to depose him. Although it was, neither in fact nor in theory, a "popular" revolution such as would occur in France and America a hundred years later, the Glorious Revolution did estab-

With her husband already in exile and William and Mary about to be proclaimed sovereigns, the ex-queen, wife of James II, is pictured fleeing London in December 1688. [The Granger Collection.]

William of Orange landing at Exmouth Bay in England in 1688. William accepted the English throne primarily to bring England into the continental struggle against the aggression of Louis XIV. [The Mansell Collection.]

The coronation of William III and Mary II, April 11, 1689. This is a detail of a large engraving commemorating the coronation ceremonies. Mary was the daughter of James II. Although closely allied to the Stuarts by birth and marriage—his mother was the daughter of Charles I— William's rule was based on the consent of Parliament, and his powers were limited by law. [The Mansell Collection.]

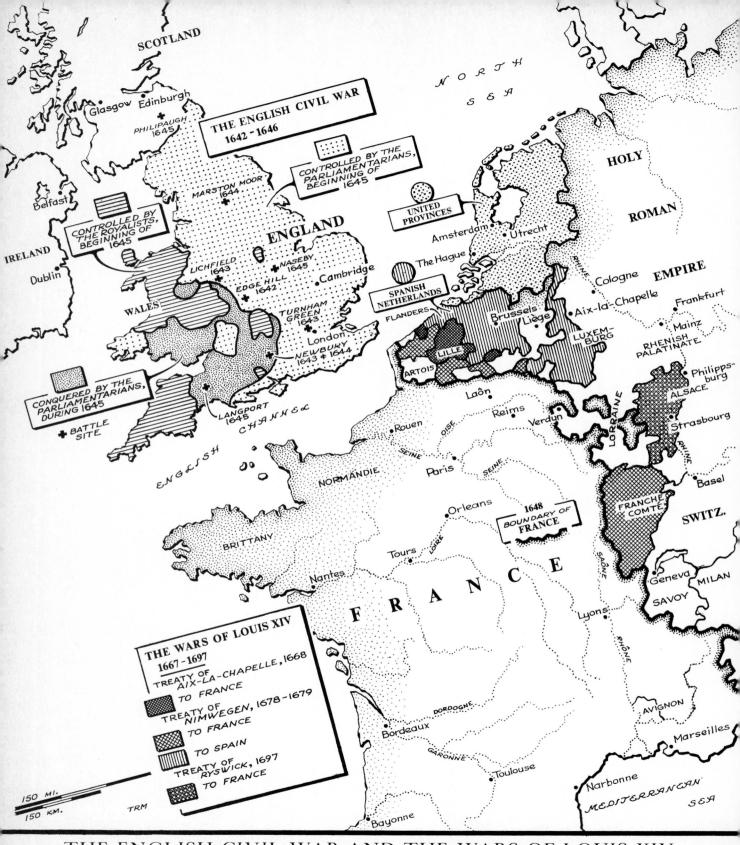

SCOTLAND

Glasgow • Edinburgh

PHILIPAUGH
1645

IRELAND

Belfast •

Dublin •

THE ENGLISH CIVIL WAR
1642 - 1646

CONTROLLED BY THE
PARLIAMENTARIANS,
BEGINNING OF
1645

CONTROLLED BY
THE ROYALISTS,
BEGINNING OF 1645

MARSTON MOOR
1644

ENGLAND

LICHFIELD
1643   ✚ NASEBY
              1645

✚ EDGE HILL
     1642   • Cambridge

WALES

TURNHAM
GREEN
1643 •

London •

NEWBURY
1643 ✚ 1644

CONQUERED BY THE
PARLIAMENTARIANS,
DURING 1645

✚ BATTLE
     SITE

LANGPORT
1645

ENGLISH CHANNEL

N O R T H

S E A

UNITED
PROVINCES

Amsterdam • • Utrecht

The Hague •

SPANISH
NETHERLANDS

FLANDERS

ARTOIS

LILLE

Brussels •
• Liège

HOLY

ROMAN

Cologne •

Aix-la-Chapelle •

LUXEM-
BURG

EMPIRE

• Frankfurt

• Mainz

RHENISH
PALATINATE

Laôn •

Rouen •

OISE

SEINE

Reims •

Verdun •

LORRAINE

Philipps-
burg •

ALSACE

Strasbourg •

RHINE

• Basel

NORMANDIE

Paris •

SEINE

1648
BOUNDARY OF
FRANCE

SAÔNE

FRANCHE
COMTÉ

SWITZ.

Orleans •

BRITTANY

Tours •

LOIRE

F R A N C E

Geneva •

MILAN

SAVOY

Nantes •

Lyons •

RHÔNE

THE WARS OF LOUIS XIV
1667 - 1697
TREATY OF
AIX-LA-CHAPELLE, 1668
     TO FRANCE
TREATY OF
NIMWEGEN, 1678-1679
     TO FRANCE
     TO SPAIN
TREATY OF
RYSWICK, 1697
     TO FRANCE

DORDOGNE

AVIGNON

Bordeaux •

GARONNE

Marseilles •

Toulouse •

150 MI.

150 KM.   TRM

Bayonne •

Narbonne •

MEDITERRANEAN   SEA

THE ENGLISH CIVIL WAR AND THE WARS OF LOUIS XIV

MAP 16.2   *In the English Civil War, 1645 was a crucial year; here the rapidly deteriorating Royalist position is shown. A bit later in France we see the territorial changes resulting from Louis XIV's first three major wars. The War of the Spainsh Succession was yet to come.*

ENGLAND IN THE SEVENTEENTH CENTURY

1603	James VI of Scotland becomes James I of England
1604	Hampton Court Conference
1611	Publication of the Authorized or King James Version of the English Bible
1625	Charles I becomes English Monarch
1628	Petition of Right
1629	Charles I dissolves Parliament and embarks on eleven years of personal rule
1640	April–May Short Parliament November Long Parliament convenes
1641	Great Remonstrance
1642	Outbreak of the Civil War
1645	Charles I defeated at Naseby
1648	Pride's Purge
1649	Charles I executed
1649–1660	Various attempts at a Puritan Commonwealth
1660	Charles II restored to the English throne
1670	Secret Treaty of Dover between France and England
1672	Parliament passes the Test Act
1678	Popish Plot
1685	James II becomes king of England
1688	Glorious Revolution
1689	William and Mary come to the throne of England
1701	Act of Settlement provides for Hanoverian Succession
1702–1715	Reign of Queen Anne the last of the Stuarts

---

lish in England a permanent check on monarchical power by the classes represented in Parliament.

Rise of Absolutism in France

Regional rights and a degree of religious diversity were recognized within the Holy Roman Empire, England, and the Netherlands during the seventeenth century. The assertion of local autonomy by the numerous member states and cities of the Holy Roman Empire made a strong central government there unthinkable. In England and the Netherlands centuries of parliamentary practice permitted regional freedoms to coexist with a strong central government.

Following the devastation of the Thirty Years' War, the Peace of Westphalia (1648) reaffirmed religious pluralism within the Holy Roman Empire. A degree of religious diversity, long a Netherlands tradition, received final confirmation also in England after decades of dogged Puritan resistance, when the Toleration Act of 1689 granted rights of worship to Protestant nonconformists.

Seventeenth-century France, in contrast, saw both representative government and religious pluralism crushed by the absolute monarchy and the closed Catholic state of Louis XIV (1643–1715). An aggressive ruler who sought glory ("*la gloire*") in foreign wars, Louis subjected his subjects at home to "one king, one law, one faith."

Henry IV and Sully

The foundation was well laid for Louis's grand reign by his predecessors and their exceptional ministers. It was Henry IV (1589–1610) (see Chapter 15) who began in earnest the curtailment of the privileges of the French nobility necessary for the creation of a strong centralized state. His targets were the provincial governors and the regional *parlements*, especially the powerful *Parlement* of Paris, where a divisive spirit lived on. Here were to be found the old privileged groups, tax-exempt magnates whose sole preoccupation was to prevent royal laws from infringing on their self-interests. During Louis XIV's reign their activities came under the strict supervision of royal civil servants known as *intendants*, who implemented the king's will with remarkable success in the provinces.

Also during Henry IV's reign an economy more amenable to governmental regulation emerged as part of the task of reconstruction after the long decades of religious and civil war. Henry and his finance minister, the duke of Sully (1560–1641), prepared the way for the later mercantilist policies of Louis XIV and his minister Colbert by establishing government monopolies on gunpowder, mines, and salt. A canal system was begun to link the Atlantic and the Mediterranean by joining the Saône, the Loire, the Seine, and the Meuse rivers. An involuntary national labor force was created by the introduction of a royal *corvée*, and this drafting of workers provided the labor to improve roads and the conditions of internal travel. Sully even dreamed of the political and commercial organization of the whole of Europe in a kind of common market.

Louis XIII and Richelieu

Henry IV was assassinated in 1610, and the following year Sully retired. Because Henry's successor, Louis XIII (1610–1643), was only nine years old when his father was assassinated, the task of governing fell to the queen mother, Marie de Medicis (d. 1642). Finding herself in a vulnerable position, she sought security abroad by signing a ten-year mutual defense pact with arch-rival Spain in the Treaty of Fontainebleau (1611), an alliance that also arranged for the later marriage of Louis XIII to the Spanish infanta as well as for the marriage of the queen's daughter Elizabeth to the heir to the Spanish throne. The queen sought internal security against the French nobility by promoting the career of Cardinal Richelieu (1585–1642) both as cardinal and as the king's chief adviser, although Richelieu never became her pawn. Richelieu, loyal and shrewd, aspired to make France a supreme European power and he, more than any one person, was the secret of French success in the first half of the seventeenth century.

An apparently devout Catholic who also believed that the church best served both his own ambition and the welfare of France, Richelieu was strongly anti-Hapsburg in politics. On the one hand, he supported the Spanish alliance of the queen and Catholic religious unity within France; on the other, he was determined to contain Spanish power and influence, even when that meant aiding and abetting Protestant Europe. It is an indication both of Richelieu's awkward political situation and of his diplomatic agility that he could pledge funds to the Protestant army of Gustavus Adolphus in the Treaty of Bär Walde, in 1631, while at the same time insisting that Catholic Bavaria be spared from attack and that Catholics in conquered countries be permitted to practice their religion.

At home Richelieu pursued his policies utterly without sentiment. Supported by the king, whose best decision was to let his chief minister make all the decisions of state, Richelieu stepped up the campaign against the separatist provincial governors and *parlements*. He made it clear to all that there was but one law, that of the king, and that none could stand above it. When disobedient noblemen defied his edicts, they were imprisoned and

Cardinal Richelieu, the shrewd mastermind behind French political power in the seventeenth century, in the striking triple portrait by the Flemish-French painter Philippe de Champaigne (1602–1674). [Reproduced by courtesy of the Trustees, The National Gallery, London.]

even executed. Louis XIV had Richelieu to thank for the fact that many of the French nobility became docile beggars at his court. Such treatment of the nobility won Richelieu much enmity, even from the queen mother, who was not always prepared to place the larger interests of the state above the pleasure of favorite princes. But the king let no criticism weaken his chief minister, not even that of his mother. The queen mother had largely ignored Louis during his youth—he was educated mostly at the hands of his falconer—and they remained estranged and ill at ease in each other's presence. This was doubtless a factor in the king's firm support of Richelieu when his mother became Richelieu's accuser.

Richelieu inspired the campaign against the Huguenots that would end in 1685 with Louis XIV's revocation of the Edict of Nantes. Royal armies conquered major Huguenot cities in 1629, and the subsequent Peace of Alais (1629) truncated the Edict of Nantes by denying Protestants the right to maintain garrisoned cities, separate political organizations, and independent law courts. Only Richelieu's foreign policy prevented the earlier implementation of the extreme intolerance of Louis XIV. In the same year that the independent political status of the Huguenots was rescinded,

Richelieu also entered negotiations to make Gustavus Adolphus his counterweight to the expansion of Hapsburg power within the Holy Roman Empire. By 1635 the Catholic soldiers of France fought openly with Swedish Lutherans against the emperor's army in the final phase of the Thirty Years' War.

In the best Machiavellian tradition Richelieu employed the arts and the printing press to defend his actions and to indoctrinate the French in the meaning of *raison d'état* ("reason of state")—again setting a precedent for Louis XIV's elaborate use of royal propaganda and spectacle. It is one measure of Richelieu's success that France made substantial gains in land and political influence when the Treaty of Westphalia (1648) ended hostilities in the Holy Roman Empire and the Treaty of the Pyrenees (1659) sealed peace with Spain.

Young Louis XIV and Mazarin

Richelieu's immediate legacy, however, was strong resentment of the monarchy on the part of the French aristocracy and the privileged bourgeoisie. During the minority of Louis XIV, who was only five years old when Louis XIII died in 1643, the queen mother, Anne of Austria (d. 1666), placed the reins of government in the hands of Cardinal Mazarin (1602–1661), who happened also to be her lover and, some report, her secret husband. Mazarin continued Richelieu's determined policy of centralization. During his regency the long-building backlash occurred when France was shaken to its foundations by the Fronde (1649–1652). Named after the slingshot used by street boys, the Fronde was a series of widespread

Cardinal Mazarin, in whose hands lay the real power in France during the minority of Louis XIV. [The Granger Collection.]

rebellions by segments of the French nobility and townspeople aimed at reversing the drift toward absolute monarchy—a last-ditch effort to preserve their local autonomy. These privileged groups saw their traditional position in French society thoroughly undermined by the crown's steady multipli-

Anne of Austria, the queen mother, surrounded by her court shortly after the death of Louis XIII. On the left are Cardinal Mazarin, in whose hands Anne placed control of the government during Louis XIV's minority, and the five-year-old Louis XIV. This sixteenth-century French engraving was done by Nicolas Picart. [The Granger Collection.]

Jacques-Benigne Bossuet, Bishop of Meaux. Called the "Eagle of Meaux," Bossuet was an eloquent advocate of the "divine right of kings" and a strong defender of the autonomy of the French church against the claims to direct rule by the Pope. This portrait by Hyacinthe Rigaud is in the Louvre. [Giraudon.]

anarchy of government by the nobility made them very welcome. The period of the Fronde convinced a majority of the French that being left to the mercy of a strong king was preferable to being subjected to the competing and irreconcilable claims of many regional magnates. After 1652 the French were ready to experiment in earnest with absolute rule.

The World of Louis XIV

Unity at Home

Thanks to the forethought of Mazarin, Louis XIV was well prepared to rule France. The turbulent periods of his youth seem also to have made an indelible impression. Louis wrote in his memoirs that the Fronde caused him to loathe "kings of straw" and made him determined never to become one. Indoctrinated with a strong sense of the grandeur of his crown, he never missed an opportunity to impress it on the French people. When the dauphin (the heir to the French throne) was born in 1662, for example, Louis appeared for the celebration dressed as a Roman emperor. Although his rule became the prototype of the modern centralized state, its inspiration remained a very narrow ideal of personal glory.

King by Divine Right

Reverence for the king and the personification of government in him had been nurtured in France since Capetian times. It was a maxim of French law and popular opinion, evolved during the later Middle Ages through royal efforts to secure the king's domain, that "the king of France is emperor in his realm," that the king's wish is the law of the land.

An important theorist for Louis's even grander concept of royal authority was the Jesuit tutor of the dauphin, Bishop Jacques-Bénigne Bossuet (1627–1704). An ardent champion of the Gallican Liberties—the traditional rights of the French king and church in matters of ecclesiastical appointments and taxation—Bossuet defended what he called the "divine right of kings." He cited the Old Testament example of rulers divinely appointed by and answerable only to God. As medieval popes had insisted that only God could judge a pope, so Bossuet argued that none save God could sit in

cation of royal offices, the replacement of local with "state" agents, and a reduction of the patronage they received.

The *Parlement* of Paris initiated the revolt in 1649, and the nobility at large soon followed. The latter were urged on by the influential wives of princes who had been imprisoned by Mazarin for treason. The many briefly triumphed over the one when Mazarin released the imprisoned princes in February 1651. He and Louis XIV thereafter entered a short exile (Mazarin leaving France, Louis fleeing Paris) and were unable to return to Paris until October 1652, when the inefficiency and near

❧ Bishop Bossuet Defends the Divine Right of Kings

The revolutions of the seventeenth century caused many to fear anarchy far more than tyranny, among them the influential French bishop Jacques Bénigne Bossuet (1627–1704), the leader of French Catholicism in the second half of the seventeenth century. Louis XIV made him court preacher and tutor to his son, for whom Bossuet wrote a celebrated *Universal History*. In the following excerpt Bossuet defended the divine right and absolute power of kings, whom he depicted as embracing in their person the whole body of the state and the will of the people they governed and, as such, as being immune from judgment by any mere mortal.

The royal power is absolute. . . . The prince need render account of his acts to no one. "I counsel thee to keep the king's commandment, and that in regard of the oath of God. Be not hasty to go out of his sight; stand not on an evil thing for he doeth whatsoever pleaseth him. Where the word of a king is, there is power: and who may say unto him, What doest thou? Whoso keepeth the commandment shall feel no evil thing" [Eccles. 8:2–5]. Without this absolute authority the king could neither do good nor repress evil. It is necessary that his power be such that no one can hope to escape him, and finally, the only protection of individuals against the public authority should be their innocence. This confirms the teaching of St. Paul: "Wilt thou then not be afraid of the power? Do that which is good" [Rom. 13–3].

God is infinite, God is all. The prince, as prince, is not regarded as a private person: he is a public personage, all the state is in him; the will of all the people is included in his. As all perfection and all strength are united in God, so all the power of individuals is united in the person of the prince. What grandeur that a single man should embody so much! . . .

Behold an immense people united in a single person; behold this holy power, paternal and absolute; behold the secret cause which governs the whole body of the state, contained in a single head: you see the image of God in the king, and you have the idea of royal majesty. God is holiness itself, goodness itself, and power itself. In these things lies the majesty of God. In the image of these things lies the majesty of the prince.

From *Politics Drawn from the Very Words of Holy Scripture*, in James Harvey Robinson (Ed.), *Readings in European History*, Vol. 2 (Boston: Ginn and Co., 1906), pp. 275–276.

judgment on the king. Although kings remained duty-bound to reflect God's will in their rule—and in this sense Bossuet considered them always subject to a higher authority—as God's regents on earth they could not be bound to the dictates of mere princes and parliaments. Such were among the assumptions that lay behind Louis XIV's alleged declaration: "L'état, c'est moi" ("I am the state").

Versailles

The palace court at Versailles on the outskirts of Paris became Louis's permanent residence after 1682 and was a true temple to royalty, architecturally designed and artistically decorated to proclaim the glory of the Sun King, as Louis was known. A spectacular estate with magnificent fountains and acres of orange groves, it became home to thousands of aristocrats, royal officials, and servants. Although its physical maintenance and new additions, which continued throughout Louis's lifetime, consumed over half his annual revenues—around five million livres a year—Versailles paid political dividends well worth the investment.

Life at court was organized around the king's daily routine.

His rising and dressing were a time of rare intimacy, when nobles, who entered their names on waiting lists to be in attendance, whispered their special requests in Louis's ear.

After the morning Mass, which Louis always observed, there followed long hours in council with the chief ministers, assemblies from which the no-

Versailles as it appeared in 1668 in a painting by Pierre Patel the Elder (1605–1676). The central building is the hunting lodge built for Louis XIII earlier in the century, and some of the first expansion undertaken by Louis XIV appears as wings. The painting is in the Versailles museum. [Cliché des Musées Nationaux, Paris.]

The sumptuous Salon de la Guerre in the Palace of Versailles. It was begun in 1678. Several rooms of the palace were badly damaged by a terrorist's bomb in June 1978. [French Embassy Press and Information Division, New York.]

bility was carefully excluded. Louis's ministers and councilors were hand-picked townsmen, servants who owed everything they had to the king's favor and were for that reason inclined to serve faithfully and without question. There were three main councils: the Council of State, a small group of four or five who met thrice weekly to rule on all matters of state, but especially on foreign affairs and war policy; the Council of Dispatches, which regularly assessed the reports from the *intendants* in the towns and provinces, a boring business that the king often left to his ministers; and finally, the Council of Finances, which handled matters of taxation and commerce.

The afternoons were spent hunting, riding, or strolling about the lush gardens. Evenings were given over to planned entertainment in the large salons (plays, concerts, gambling, and the like), followed by supper at 10:00 P.M.

Even the king's retirement was a part of the day's

A full view of Versailles as it appears today. Louis XIV vastly enlarged his father's hunting lodge into a palace estate beginning in 1661. It became not only the royal residence but the seat of the French government, a symbol of royal and national power, and the frequently imitated model for other seventeenth- and eighteenth-century monarchs. This photograph is from the opposite direction to Patel's painting; the coaches in his picture are arriving on the diagonal road at the top left of the photograph. [French Government Tourist Office, New York.]

Bishop Cornelis Jansen (1585–1638) was the author of the intellectual and theological foundations of what came to be called Jansenism. Several of his key beliefs were eventually declared heretical by the Catholic Church. [The Granger Collection.]

spectacle. Fortunate nobles were permitted briefly to hold his night candle as they accompanied him to his bed.

Although only five feet, four inches in height, the king had presence and was always engaging in conversation. An unabashed ladies' man, he encouraged the belief at court that it was an honor to lie with the king. Married to the Spanish Infanta Marie Thérèse for political reasons in 1660, he kept many mistresses. After Marie's death in 1683 he settled down in secret marriage with one, Madame de Maintenon, and apparently became much less the philanderer.

All this ritual and play served the political purpose of keeping an impoverished nobility, barred by law from high government positions, busy and dependent so that they had little time to plot revolt. The dress codes and the high-stakes gaming at court contributed to the indebtedness and dependency of nobility on the king. Court life was a carefully planned and successfully executed domestication of the nobility.

Suppression of the Jansenists

Like Richelieu before him, Louis believed that political unity required religious conformity. To that end he suppressed two groups of religious dissenters: the Catholic Jansenists, who were opponents of the Jesuits, and the Protestant Huguenots.

Although the king and the French church had always jealously guarded their traditional independence from Rome (the Gallican Liberties), the years following the conversion of Henry IV to Catholicism saw a great influx of Catholic religious orders into France, prominent among which were the Jesuits. Because of their leadership at the Council of Trent and their close Spanish connections, Catherine de Medicis had earlier banned the Jesuits from France. Henry IV lifted the ban in

The abbey of Port Royal near Paris in the seventeenth century, the main center of Jansenist theological activity. Its picture gives a good impression of the layout of a religious community of the time. [The Granger Collection.]

1603, with certain conditions: there was to be a limitation on the number of new colleges they could open; special licenses were required for activities outside their own buildings; and each member of the order was subjected to an oath of allegiance to the king. The Jesuits were not, however, easily harnessed. They rapidly monopolized the education of the upper classes, and their devout students promoted the religious reforms and doctrine of the Council of Trent throughout France. It is a measure of their success that Jesuits served as confessors to Henry IV, Louis XIII, and Louis XIV.

In the 1630s a group that came to be known as *Jansenists* formed an intra-Catholic opposition to both the theology and the political influence of the Jesuits. They were Catholics who adhered to the Augustinian tradition, out of which many Protestant teachings had also come. Serious and uncompromising in their religious doctrine and practice, the Jansenists opposed Jesuit teachings about free will. They believed with Saint Augustine that original sin dominated humankind so completely that individuals could do absolutely nothing good or contributing to their salvation unless they were first specially assisted by the grace of God. The namesake of the Jansenists, Cornelis Jansen (d. 1638), a Flemish theologian and the bishop of Ypres, was the author of a posthumously published book entitled *Augustinus* (1640), which assailed mainly Jesuit teaching on grace and salvation.

Jean du Vergier de Hauranne (1581–1643), the abbot of Saint-Cyran and Jansen's close friend, was instrumental in bringing into the Jansenist fold a Parisian family, the Arnaulds, who were prominent opponents of the Jesuits. The Arnauld family, like many other French people, believed that the Jesuits had been behind the assassination of Henry IV in 1610. Arnauld support added a strong political element to the Jansenists' theological opposition to the Jesuits. Jansenist communities at Port-Royal and Paris were dominated by the Arnaulds during the 1640s. In 1643 Antoine Arnauld published a work entitled *On Frequent Communion* in which he criticized the Jesuits for confessional practices that permitted the easy redress of almost any sin. The Jesuits, in turn, condemned the Jansenists as "crypto-Calvinists" in their theology.

On May 31, 1653, Jansenism was declared a heresy. On that day Pope Innocent X deemed heretical five Jansenist theological propositions on grace and salvation, earlier condemned by the Sorbonne. In 1656 the Pope banned Jansen's *Augustinus*, and

the Sorbonne censured Antoine Arnauld. In this same year Antoine's friend, Blaise Pascal (d. 1662), the most famous of Jansen's followers, published the first of his *Provincial Letters* in defense of Jansenism. A deeply religious man, Pascal tried to reconcile the "reasons of the heart" with growing seventeenth-century reverence for the clear and distinct ideas of the mind. He found Jesuit moral theology to be not only lax and shallow, but also a rationalized approach to religion that did injustice to religious experience.

In 1660 Louis permitted the enforcement of the papal bull *Ad Sacram Sedem* (1656), which banned Jansenism, and he closed down the Port-Royal community. Thereafter Jansenists either capitulated by signing retractions or went underground. At a later date (1710) the French king lent his support to a still more thorough Jesuit purge of Jansenist sentiment. With the fall of the Jansenists went any hope of a Catholicism broad enough to attract the Huguenots.

Revocation of the Edict of Nantes

Since 1598, when the Edict of Nantes was proclaimed, a cold war had existed between the great Catholic majority (nine tenths of the French population remained Catholic) and the Protestant minority. Despite their respectable numbers, about 1.75 million by the 1660s, the Huguenots were in decline in the second half of the seventeenth century. Government harassment had forced the more influential members to withdraw their support. Officially the French Catholic church had long denounced Calvinists as heretical and treasonous and had supported their persecution as both a pious and a patriotic act. Following the Peace of Nijmegen in 1678–1679, which halted for the moment Louis's aggression in Europe, Louis launched a methodical government campaign against the French Huguenots in a determined effort to unify France religiously. He hounded the Huguenots out of public life, banned them from government office, and excluded them from such professions as printing and medicine. Subsidies and selective taxation also became weapons to encourage their conversion to Catholicism. In 1681 Louis further bullied Huguenots by quartering his troops in their towns. The final stage of the persecution came in October 1685, when Louis revoked the Edict of Nantes. In practical terms the revocation meant the closing of Protestant churches and

❧ Louis XIV Revokes the Edict of Nantes

Believing that a country could not be under one king and one law unless it was also under one religious system, Louis XIV stunned much of Europe in October 1685 by revoking the Edict of Nantes, which had protected the religious freedoms and civil rights of French Protestants since 1598.

Art. 1. Know that we . . . with our certain knowledge, full power and royal authority, have by this present, perpetual and irrevocable edict, suppressed and revoked the edict of the aforesaid king our grandfather, given at Nantes in the month of April, 1598, in all its extent . . . together with all the concessions made by [this] and other edicts, declarations, and decrees, to the people of the so-called Reformed religion, of whatever nature they be . . . and in consequence we desire . . . that all the temples of the people of the aforesaid so-called Reformed religion situated in our kingdom . . . should be demolished forthwith.

Art. 2. We forbid our subjects of the so-called Reformed religion to assemble any more for public worship of the above-mentioned religion. . . .

Art. 3. We likewise forbid all lords, of whatever rank they may be, to carry out heretical services in houses and fiefs . . . the penalty for . . . the said worship being confiscation of their body and possessions.

Art. 4. We order all ministers of the aforesaid so-called Reformed religion who do not wish to be converted and to embrace the Catholic, Apostolic, and Roman religion, to depart from our kingdom and the lands subject to us within fifteen days from the publication of our present edict . . . on pain of the galleys.

Art. 5. We desire that those among the said [Reformed] ministers who shall be converted [to the Catholic religion] shall continue to enjoy during their life, and their wives shall enjoy after their death as long as they remain widows, the same exemptions from taxation and billeting of soldiers, which they enjoyed while they fulfilled the function of ministers. . . .

Art. 8. With regard to children who shall be born to those of the aforesaid so-called Reformed religion, we desire that they be baptized by their parish priests. We command the fathers and mothers to send them to the churches for that purpose, on penalty of a fine of 500 livres or more if they fail to do so; and afterwards, the children shall be brought up in the Catholic, Apostolic, and Roman religion. . . .

Art. 10. All our subjects of the so-called Reformed religion, with their wives and children, are to be strongly and repeatedly prohibited from leaving our aforesaid kingdom . . . or of taking out . . . their possessions and effects. . . .

The members of the so-called Reformed religion, while awaiting God's pleasure to enlighten them like the others, can live in the towns and districts of our kingdom . . . and continue their occupation there, and enjoy their possessions . . . on condition . . . that they do not make public profession of [their religion].

Church and State Through the Centuries: A Collection of Historic Documents, trans. and ed. by S. Z. Ehler and John B. Morrall (New York: Biblo and Tannen, 1967), pp. 209–213.

schools, the exile of Protestant ministers, the placement of nonconverting members of the laity in galleys as slaves, and the ceremonial baptism of Protestant children by Catholic priests.

The revocation of the Edict of Nantes became the major blunder of Louis's reign. Thereafter he was viewed throughout Protestant Europe as a new Philip II, intent on a Catholic reconquest of the whole of Europe, who must be resisted at all costs. Internally the revocation of the Edict of Nantes led

to the voluntary emigration of over a quarter million French, who formed new communities and joined the French resistance movement in England, Germany, Holland, and the New World. Thousands of French Huguenots served in the army of Louis's arch foe, William III of the Netherlands, later King William III of England. Those who remained in France became an uncompromising guerrilla force. But despite the many domestic and foreign liabilities created for France by the rev-

Ever since 1525 the Huguenots suffered harrassment and persecution by the French government. This occurred despite measures of toleration granted temporarily by such documents as the January Edict of 1562, shown here, and the Edict of Nantes. [*The Granger Collection.*]

A drawing depicting the announcement of the revocation of the Edict of Nantes in 1685. Louis XIV considered the revocation of the policy of religious toleration one of the most important acts of his reign. [*The Granger Collection.*]

ocation of the Edict of Nantes, Louis to his death, like many other devout Catholics, considered it his most pious act, one that placed God in his debt.

War Abroad

War was the normal state for seventeenth-century rulers and for none more so than for Louis XIV, who would confess on his deathbed that he had "loved war too much." Periods of peace became opportunities for the discontented in town and countryside to plot against the king; war served national unity as well as "glory." By the 1660s France was superior to any other nation in administrative bureaucracy, armed forces, and national unity. It had a population of nineteen million, prosperous farms, vigorous trade, and much taxable wealth. By every external measure Louis was in a position to dominate Europe.

LOUVOIS, VAUBAN, COLBERT. The great French war machine became the work of three ministers: Louvois, Vauban, and Colbert. The army, which maintained a strength of about a quarter of a million men, was the creation of Michel le Tellier and his more famous son, the marquis of Louvois (1641–1691). The latter, who served as Louis's war minister from 1677 to 1691, was a superior military tactician.

Before Louvois the French army had been an amalgam of local recruits and mercenaries, uncoordinated groups whose loyalty could not always be counted on. Louvois disciplined the French army and made it a respectable profession. He placed a limit on military commissions and intro-

duced a system of promotion by merit, policies that brought dedicated fighting men into the ranks. Enlistment was for four years and was restricted to single men. The pay was good and regular. *Intendants,* those ubiquitous civil servants, carried out regular inspections, monitoring conduct at all levels and reporting to the king.

What Louvois was to military organization Sebastien Vauban (1633–1707) was to military engineering. He perfected the arts of fortifying and besieging towns. He also devised the system of trench warfare and developed the concept of defensive frontiers that remained basic military tactics through World War I.

War cannot be successful without financing, and here Louis had the guidance of his most brilliant minister, Jean-Baptiste Colbert (1619–1683). Colbert worked to centralize the French economy with the same rigor that Louis had worked to centralize the French government. He put the nation to work under state supervision and carefully regulated the flow of imports and exports through tariffs. He created new national industries and organized factories around a tight regimen of work and ideology. Administrative bureaucracy was simplified, unnecessary positions were abolished, and the number of tax-exempt nobles was reduced. Colbert also increased the *taille* on the peasantry, the chief source of royal wealth. Although the French economy continued to be a puppet controlled by many different strings, more of these strings were now in the hand of the king than had been the case in centuries past. This close government control of the economy came to be known as *mercantilism.* Its aim was to maximize foreign exports and the internal reserves of bullion, the gold and silver necessary for making war. Modern scholars argue that Colbert overcontrolled the French economy and cite his "paternalism" as a major reason for French failures in the New World. Be that as it may, Colbert's policies unquestionably transformed France into a major industrial and commercial power, with foreign bases in Africa, India, and the Americas from Canada to the Caribbean.

THE WAR OF DEVOLUTION. Louis's first great foreign adventure was the War of Devolution (1667–1668). It was fought, as still a later and greater war would be, over Louis's claim to a Spanish inheritance through his wife, Marie Thérèse (1638–1683). According to the terms of the Treaty of the Pyrenees (1659), Marie had renounced her claim to the Spanish succession on condition that a 500,000-crown dowry be paid to Louis within eighteen months of the marriage, a condition that was not met. When Philip IV of Spain died in September 1665, he left all his lands to his sickly four-year-old son by a second marriage, Charles II (1665–1700), and explicitly excluded his daughter Marie from any share. Louis had always harbored the hope of turning the marriage to territorial gain and argued even before Philip's death that Marie was entitled to a portion of the inheritance.

Louis had a legal argument on his side, which gave the war its name. He maintained that because in certain regions of Brabant and Flanders, which were part of the Spanish inheritance, property "devolved" to the children of a first marriage rather than to those of a second, Marie had a higher claim than Charles II to these regions. The argument was not accepted—such regional laws could hardly bind the king of Spain—but Louis was not deterred from moving his armies, under the vicomte de Turenne, into Flanders and the Franche-Comté in 1667. In response to this aggression England, Sweden, and the United Provinces of Holland formed the Triple Alliance, a force sufficient to bring Louis to peace terms in the Treaty of Aix-la-Chapelle (1668).

INVASION OF THE NETHERLANDS. In 1670 England and France became allies against the Dutch by signing the Treaty of Dover, a move that set the Stuart monarchy of Charles II on a new international course. With the departure of the English from its membership, the Triple Alliance crumbled. This left Louis in a stronger position to invade the Netherlands for a second time, which he did in 1672. This second invasion was aimed directly at Holland, the organizer of the Triple Alliance in 1667 and the country held accountable by Louis for foiling French designs in Flanders. Louis had been mightily offended by Dutch boasting after the Treaty of Aix-la-Chapelle; cartoons like one depicting the sun (Louis was the "Sun King") eclipsed by a great moon of Dutch cheese cut the French king to the quick. It was also clear that there could be no French acquisition of land in the Spanish Netherlands, nor European hegemony beyond that, until Holland was neutralized.

Louis's successful invasion of the United Provinces in 1672 brought the downfall of Jan and Cornelius De Witt, Dutch statesmen who were blamed for the French success. In their place came the twenty-seven-year-old Prince of Orange, after 1689 King William III of England. Orange was the great-grandson of William the Silent, who had repulsed Philip II and dashed Spanish hopes of dominating the Netherlands in the sixteenth century.

Orange proved to be Louis's undoing. This unpretentious Calvinist, who was in almost every way Louis's opposite, galvanized the seven provinces into a fierce fighting unit that did not shrink from opening the dikes on French armies. In 1673 he united the Holy Roman Emperor, Spain, Lorraine, and Brandenburg in an alliance against Louis, who was now seen by his enemies to be "the Christian Turk," a menace to the whole of western Europe, Catholic and Protestant alike. Subsequent battles saw Louis lose his ablest generals, Turenne and Condé, in 1675, while the defeat of the Dutch fleet by Admiral Duquesne established French control of the Mediterranean in 1676. The Peace of Nimwegen, signed with different parties in successive years (1678, 1679), ended the hostilities of this second war. In 1678 France entered agreements with Holland and Spain and in 1679 with the Holy Roman Emperor, Brandenburg, and Denmark.

The settlements were not unfavorable to France—Spain, for example, surrendered the Franche-Comté—but France still fell far short of the European empire to which Louis aspired.

THE LEAGUE OF AUGSBURG. Between the Treaty of Nimwegen and the renewal of full-scale war in 1689, Louis restlessly probed his perimeters. The army was maintained at full strength. In 1681 it conquered the free city of Strasbourg, setting off the formation of new defensive coalitions against Louis. The League of Augsburg, created in 1686 to resist French expansion into Germany, grew by 1689 to include the Emperor Leopold, Spain, Sweden, the United Provinces, the electorates of Bavaria, Saxony, and the Palatinate, and the England of William and Mary. That year saw the beginning of the Nine Years' War (1689–1697) between France and the League of Augsburg. For the third time stalemate and exhaustion forced the combatants into an interim settlement. The Peace of Ryswick in September 1697 became a personal triumph for William, now William III of England,

The siege of Tournai in 1709 *during the War of the Spanish Succession. Tournai, a fortress city on the border between France and the Spanish Netherlands, had been captured by the French in* 1667. *Here it is beseiged by the English and Imperial forces under Marlborough and Prince Eugene. Under the terms of the Treaty of Utrecht (*1713*), France ceded Tournai to Austria. This* 1709 *engraving is by P. Mortier.* [*BBC Hulton Picture Library.*]

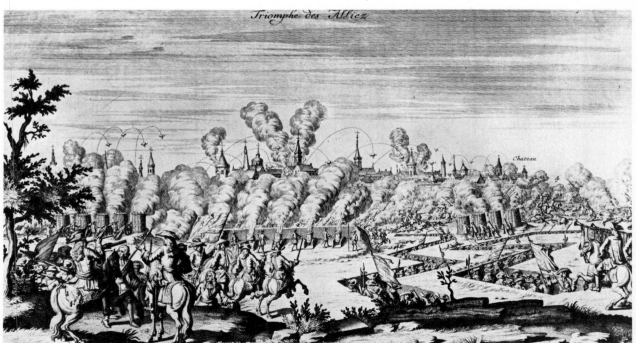

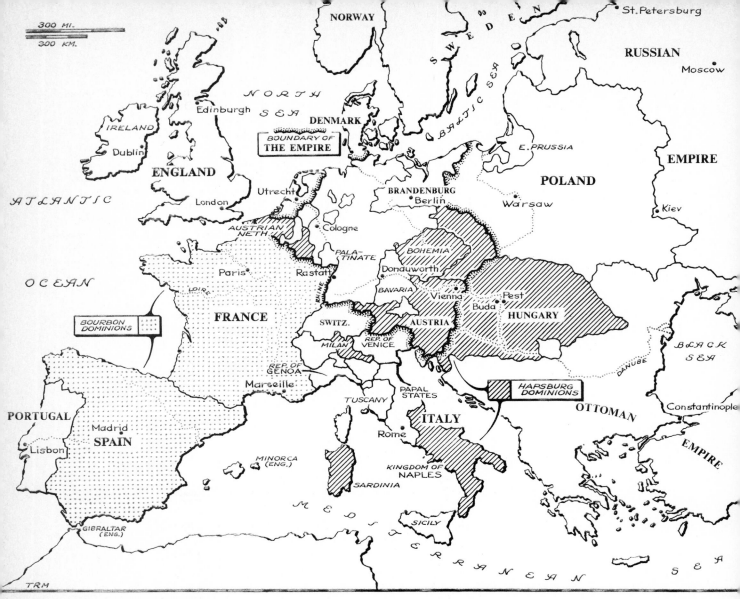

NORWAY

St.Petersburg

RUSSIAN

Moscow

N O R T H
S E A

Edinburgh

DENMARK

IRELAND

Dublin

ENGLAND

London

A T L A N T I C

O C E A N

BOUNDARY OF
THE EMPIRE

Utrecht

AUSTRIAN
NETH.

Cologne

PALA-
TINATE

Rastatt

RHINE

BRANDENBURG
Berlin

BOHEMIA

Donauworth

BAVARIA

Vienna

AUSTRIA

Buda

Pest

HUNGARY

DANUBE

E. PRUSSIA

EMPIRE

POLAND

Warsaw

Kiev

B A L T I C S E A

S W E D E N

BOURBON
DOMINIONS

FRANCE

Paris

LOIRE

SWITZ.

REP. OF
MILAN

REP. OF
VENICE

REP. OF
GENOA

Marseille

BLACK
SEA

HAPSBURG
DOMINIONS

OTTOMAN

Constantinople

EMPIRE

PORTUGAL

Madrid

SPAIN

Lisbon

MINORCA
(ENG.)

TUSCANY

PAPAL
STATES

ITALY

Rome

KINGDOM OF
NAPLES

SARDINIA

GIBRALTAR
(ENG.)

SICILY

M E D I T E R R A N E A N   S E A

300 MI.

300 KM.

TRM

EUROPE IN 1714

MAP 16.3   *The War of the Spanish Succession ended in the year before the death of the aged Louis XIV. By then France and Spain, although not united, were ruled by members of the Bourbon family, and Spain had lost her non-Iberian possessions. Austria had continued to grow.*

and the Emperor Leopold, as it secured Holland's borders and thwarted Louis's expansion into Germany. During this same period England and France fought for control of North America in what came to be known as King William's War (1689–1697).

WAR OF THE SPANISH SUCCESSION: TREATIES OF UTRECHT — RASTADT. After Ryswick, Louis, who seemed to thrive on partial success, made still a fourth attempt to realize his grand design of French European domination, this time assisted by an unforeseen turn of events. On November 1, 1700, Charles II of Spain, known as "the Sufferer" because of his genetic deformities and lingering illnesses, died. Both Louis and the Austrian Emperor Leopold had claims to the Spanish inheritance through their grandsons: Louis by way of his marriage to Marie Thérèse and Leopold through his marriage to her younger sister, Margaret Thérèse.

Although the dauphin had the higher blood claim, it was assumed that the inheritance would go to the grandson of the emperor. The French raised the specter of a belligerent Hapsburg kingdom like that of Charles V in the sixteenth century should Spain come under the imperial crown. Maria Thérèse, however, had renounced any right to the Spanish inheritance in the Treaty of the Pyrenees (1659).

The nations of Europe were far more fearful of a union of the French and Spanish crowns than they were of a union of the imperial and Spanish crowns. Indeed, they were determined that the former alliance should not occur. Hence before Charles's death negotiations began to partition the inheritance in such a way that the current balance of power would be maintained.

Charles II upset all plans by leaving the entire Spanish inheritance to Philip of Anjou, Louis's grandson. At a stroke the Spanish inheritance had fallen to France. Although Louis had been party to the partition agreements in advance of Charles's death, he now saw God's hand in Charles's will and chose to enforce its terms fully rather than abide by those of the partition treaty. Philip of Anjou moved to Madrid and became Philip V of Spain, and Louis, in what was interpreted as naked French

aggression, sent his troops once again into Flanders, this time to remove Dutch soldiers from Spanish territory in the name of the new French king of Spain. He also declared Spanish America open to French ships.

In September 1701 the Grand Alliance of England, Holland, and the Holy Roman Emperor formed against Louis in The Hague. Its intent was to preserve the balance of power by once-and-for-all securing Flanders as a neutral barrier between Holland and France and by gaining for the emperor his fair share of the Spanish inheritance. After the formation of the alliance Louis increased the stakes of battle by recognizing the son of James II of England as James III, king of England.

Once again total war enveloped western Europe as the twelve-year War of the Spanish Succession (1702–1714) began. France, for the first time, went to war with inadequate finances, a poorly equipped army, and mediocre military leadership. The English had advanced weaponry (flintlock rifles, paper cartridges, and ring bayonets) and superior tactics (thin, maneuverable troop columns rather than the traditional deep ones). John Churchill, the duke of Marlborough, who succeeded William of Orange as leader of the alliance, bested Louis's soldiers in every major engagement. Marlborough routed

❧ An Appraisal of Louis XIV

In his history of the reigns of the first three Bourbon kings, written in 1746, the Duc de Saint Simon (1675–1755), an army officer and public official during Louis XIV's reign, left the following highly critical portrait of Louis as a king smitten by vanity.

Louis XIV's vanity was without limit or restraint; it colored everything and convinced him that no one even approached him in military talents, in plans and enterprises, and in government. Hence, those pictures and inscriptions in the gallery at Versailles which disgust every foreigner; those opera prologues that he himself tried to sing; that flood of prose and verse in his praise for which his appetite was insatiable; those dedications of statues copied from pagan sculpture, and the insipid and sickening compliments that were continually offered to him in person and

which he swallowed with unfailing relish; hence, his distaste for all merit, intelligence, education, and, most of all, independence of character and sentiment in others; his mistakes of judgment in matters of importance; his familiarity and favor reserved entirely for those to whom he felt himself superior in acquirements and ability; and, above everything else, a jealousy of his own authority which determined and took precedence over every other sort of justice, reason, and consideration whatever.

James Harvey Robinson (Ed.), *Readings in European History*, Vol. 2 (Boston: Ginn and Co., 1906), pp. 286—287.

THE REIGN OF LOUIS XIV (1643–1715)

1648	Peace of Westphalia reaffirms religious pluralism in Holy Roman Empire
1649–1652	The Fronde, a revolt of nobility and townsmen against confiscatory policies of the crown
1653	Jansenism declared a heresy by the pope
1659	Treaty of Pyrenees ends hostilities between France and Spain
1660	Louis XIV enforces papal ban on Jansenists
1667–1668	War of Devolution fought over Louis' claims to lands in Brabant and Flanders by virtue of his Spanish inheritance through his wife
1668	The Triple Alliance (England, Sweden, and the United Provinces) repels Louis' army from Flanders and forces the Treaty of Aix-la-Chapelle
1670	Treaty of Dover brings French and English together against the Netherlands
1672	France invades the United Provinces
1678–1679	Peace of Nimwegen ends French wars in United Provinces
1685	Louis XIV revokes Edict of Nantes
1689–1697	Nine Years' War between France and League of Augsburg, a Europe-wide alliance against Louis XIV
1697	Peace of Ryswick ends French expansion into Holland and Germany
1702–1714	England, Holland, and Holy Roman Emperor resist Louis' claim to the Spanish throne in the war of Spanish Succession
1712	Treaty of Utrecht between England and France
1714	Treaty of Rastadt between Spain and France

French armies at Blenheim in August 1704 and on the plain of Ramillies in 1706—two decisive battles of the war. In 1708–1709 famine, revolts, and uncollectable taxes tore France apart internally. Despair pervaded the French court, and Louis wondered aloud how God could forsake one who had done so much for Him.

Though ready to make peace in 1709, Louis could not bring himself to accept the stiff terms of the alliance, which included the demand that he transfer all Spanish possessions to the emperor's grandson Charles and remove Philip V from Madrid. An immediate result of this failure to come to terms was a clash of forces at Malplaquet (September 1709), which left carnage on the battlefield unsurpassed until modern times.

Under the English minister Bolingbroke the allies renewed peace talks in 1711. France signed an armistice with England at Utrecht in July 1712, and hostilities were concluded with Holland and the emperor in the Treaty of Rastadt in March 1714. These agreements confirmed Philip V as king of Spain. They gave England Gibraltar, which made England thereafter a Mediterranean power, and won Louis's recognition of the House of Hanover's right of accession to the English throne.

Politically the eighteenth century would belong to England as the sixteenth had belonged to Spain and the seventeenth to France. The emperor received control of the Spanish Netherlands, which were established as a barrier between France and Holland, with Dutch troops stationed in key towns. France kept the cities of Strasbourg and Lille. Although France remained intact and quite strong, the realization of Louis XIV's ambition had to await the rise of Napoleon Bonaparte. On his deathbed on September 1, 1715, a dying Louis fittingly warned the dauphin not to imitate his love of buildings and his liking for war.

When one looks back on Louis's reign, the grandeur and power of it still remain undimmed by his presumptuous glory-seeking and military ambitions. One remembers not only a king who loved war too much, but also one who built the palace of Versailles and brought a new majesty to France; a king who managed with consummate skill the French aristocracy and bourgeoisie at court and controlled a French peasantry that had all too many just grievances; a king who shrewdly raised up skilled and trustworthy ministers, councillors, and *intendants* from the middle classes; and a king who created a new French empire by the successful expansion of trade into Asia and the colonization of North America.

Suggested Readings

MAURICE ASHLEY, *The Greatness of Oliver Cromwell* (1966). Detailed biography.

TREVOR ASTON (Ed.), *Crisis in Europe 1560–1660* (1965). Essays by major scholars focused on social and economic forces.

WILLIAM F. CHURCH (Ed.), *The Greatness of Louis XIV: Myth or Reality?* (1959). Excerpts from the scholarly debate over Louis's reign.

C. H. FIRTH, *Oliver Cromwell and the Rule of the Puritans in England* (1900). Old but still very authoritative work.

WILLIAM HALLER, *The Rise of Puritanism* (1957). Interesting study based largely on Puritan sermons.

CHRISTOPHER HILL, *The Century of Revolution 1603–1714* (1961). Bold, imaginative synthesis by a controversial master.

W. H. LEWIS, *The Splendid Century* (1953). Focuses on society, especially in the age of Louis XIV.

DAVID OGG, *Europe in the Seventeenth Century* (1925). Among the most authoritative syntheses.

STUART E. PRALL, *The Puritan Revolution: A Documentary History* (1968). Comprehensive document collection.

LAWRENCE STONE, *The Causes of the English Revolution 1529–1642* (1972). Brief survey stressing social history and ruminating over historians and historical method.

G. R. R. TREASURE, *Seventeenth Century France* (1966). Broad, detailed survey of entire century.

MICHAEL WALZER, *The Revolution of the Saints: A Study in the Origins of Radical Politics* (1965). Effort to relate ideas and politics that depicts Puritans as true revolutionaries.

C. V. WEDGWOOD, *Richelieu and the French Monarchy* (1950). Fine biography.

JOHN B. WOLF, *Louis XIV* (1968). Very detailed political biography.

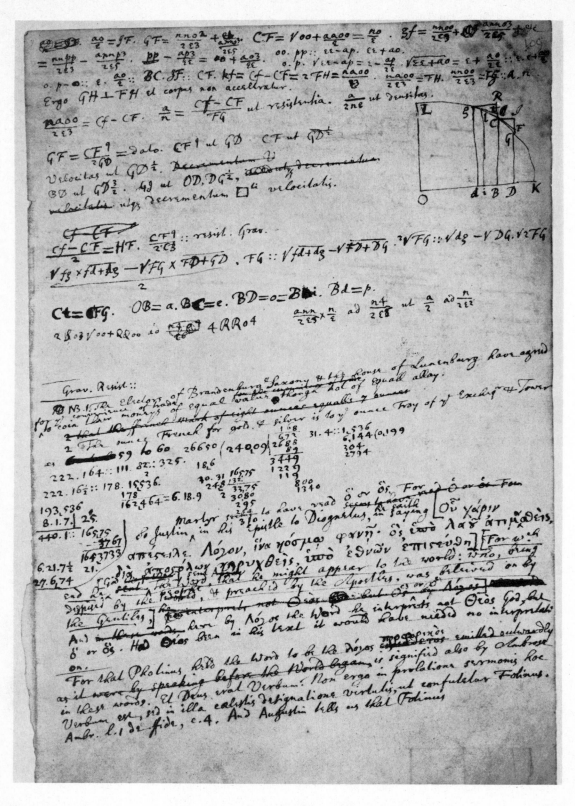

17 New Directions in Science and Thought in the Sixteenth and Seventeenth Centuries

The Scientific Revolution

New Departures

The sixteenth and seventeenth centuries witnessed a sweeping change in the scientific view of the universe. An earth-centered picture of the universe gave way to one in which the earth was only another planet orbiting about the sun. The sun itself became one of millions of stars. This transformation of humankind's perception of its place in the larger scheme of things led to a vast rethinking of moral and religious matters as well as of scientific theory. At the same time the new scientific concepts and the methods of their construction became so impressive that subsequent knowledge in the Western world has been deemed correct

Sir Isaac Newton (1642–1727) was the most illustrious figure of the scientific revolution. This page from his manuscripts shows the variety of his interests: calculations of motion at the top, comparisons of foreign currency in the middle, notes on theology at the bottom. [The University Library, Cambridge.]

only as it has approximated knowledge as defined by science. Perhaps no single intellectual development proved to be more significant for the future of European and Western civilization.

The process by which this new view of the universe and of scientific knowledge came to be established is normally termed the *Scientific Revolution*. However, care must be taken in the use of this metaphor. The word *revolution* normally denotes fairly rapid changes in the political world, involving large numbers of people. The Scientific Revolution was not rapid, nor did it involve more than a few hundred human beings. It was a complex movement with many false starts and many brilliant people with wrong as well as useful ideas. It took place in the studies and the crude laboratories of thinkers in Poland, Italy, Bohemia, France, and Great Britain. It stemmed from two major tendencies. The first, as illustrated by Nicolaus Copernicus, was the imposition of important small changes on existing models of thought. The second, as embodied by Francis Bacon, was the desire to pose new kinds of questions and to use new methods of investigation. In both cases, scientific thought changed the current and traditional opinions in other fields.

Nicolaus Copernicus

Copernicus (1473–1543) was a Polish astronomer who enjoyed a very high reputation throughout his life. He had been educated in Italy and corresponded with other astronomers throughout Europe. However, he had not been known for strikingly original or unorthodox thought. In 1543, the year of his death, Copernicus published *On the Revolutions of the Heavenly Spheres*. Because he died near the time of publication, the fortunes of his work are not the story of one person's crusade for progressive science. Copernicus's book was "a revolution-making rather than a revolutionary text."[1] What Copernicus did was to provide an intellectual springboard for a complete criticism of the then-dominant view of the position of the earth in the universe.

At the time of Copernicus the standard explanation of the earth and the heavens was that associated with Ptolemy and his work entitled the *Almagest* (A.D. 150). There was not just one Ptolemaic system; rather, several versions had been de-

[1] Thomas S. Kuhn, *The Copernican Revolution: Planetary Astronomy in the Development of Western Thought* (New York: Vintage, 1959), p. 135.

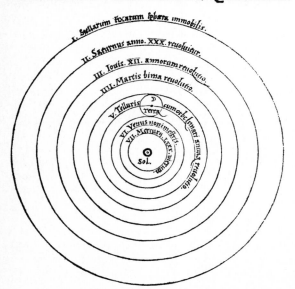

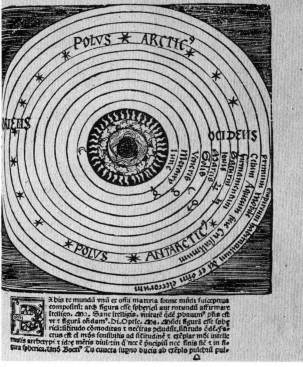

View of the universe as described by Claudius Ptolemy, an astronomer of Alexandria, Egypt, in the second century. Ptolemy's view, which put the earth unmoving in the center with the other heavenly objects circling it (the sun being in the fourth circle), dominated astronomy until the sixteenth century. The illustration is from a book by Gregor Reisch, Margarita Philosophica *(1515). [The British Library, London.]*

veloped over the centuries by commentators on the original book. Most of these systems assumed that the earth was the center of the universe. Above the earth lay a series of crystalline spheres, one of which contained the moon, another the sun, and still others the planets and the stars. This was the astronomy found in such works as Dante's *Divine Comedy*. At the outer regions of these spheres lay the realm of God and the angels. Aristotelian physics provided the intellectual underpinnings of the Ptolemaic systems. The earth had to be the center

Nicolaus Copernicus's view of the universe with the sun in the center. The basis of the scientific and intellectual revolution initiated by the Polish astronomer (1473–1543) is summarized in this diagram printed in his De Revolutionibus Orbium Coelestium (On the Revolutions of Heavenly Bodies) *of 1543. [The British Library, London.]*

because of its heaviness. The stars and the other heavenly bodies had to be enclosed in the crystalline spheres so that they could move. Nothing could move unless something was actually moving it. The state of rest was natural; motion was the condition that required explanation.

Numerous problems were associated with this system, and these had long been recognized. The most important was the observed motions of the planets. Planets could be seen moving in noncircular patterns around the earth. At certain times the planets actually appeared to be going backward. The Ptolemaic systems explained these strange motions primarily through *epicycles*. The planets were said to make a second revolution in an orbit tangent to their primary orbit around the earth. The epicycle was compared with a jewel on a ring. Other intellectual but nonobservational difficulties

❧ Copernicus Ascribes Movement to the Earth

Copernicus published *De Revolutionibus Orbium Caelestium (On the Revolutions of the Heavenly Spheres)* in 1543. In his preface, which was addressed to Pope Paul III, he explained what had led him to think that the earth moved around the sun and what he thought were some of the scientific consequences of the new theory. The reader should note how important Copernicus considered the opinions of ancient writers who had also ascribed motion to the earth. This is a good example of the manner in which familiarity with the ancients gave many Renaissance writers the self-confidence to criticize medieval ideas.

I may well presume, most Holy Father, that certain people, as soon as they hear that in this book about the Revolutions of the Spheres of the Universe I ascribe movement to the earthly globe, will cry out that, holding such views, I should at once be hissed off the stage. . . .

So I should like your Holiness to know that I was induced to think of a method of computing the motions of the spheres by nothing else than the knowledge that the Mathematicians [who had previously considered the problem] are inconsistent in these investigations.

For, first, the mathematicians are so unsure of the movements of the Sun and Moon that they cannot even explain or observe the constant length of the seasonal year. Secondly, in determining the motions of these and of the other five planets, they use neither the same principles and hypotheses nor the same demonstrations of the apparent motions and revolutions. . . . Nor have they been able thereby to discern or deduce the principal thing—namely the shape of the Universe and the unchangeable symmetry of its parts. . . .

I pondered long upon this uncertainty of mathematical tradition in establishing the motions of the

system of the spheres. At last I began to chafe that philosophers could by no means agree on any one certain theory of the mechanism of the Universe, wrought for us by a supremely good and orderly Creator. . . . I therefore took pains to read again the works of all the philosophers on whom I could lay hand to seek out whether any of them had ever supposed that the motions of the spheres were other than those demanded by the [Ptolemaic] mathematical schools. I found first in Cicero that Hicetas [of Syracuse, fifth century B.C.] had realized that the Earth moved. Afterwards I found in Plutarch that certain others had held the like opinion. . . .

Thus assuming motions, which in my work I ascribe to the Earth, by long and frequent observations I have at last discovered that, if the motions of the rest of the planets be brought into relation with the circulation of the Earth and be reckoned in proportion to the circles of each planet, not only do their phenomena presently ensue, but the orders and magnitudes of all stars and spheres, nay the heavens themselves, become so bound together that nothing in any part thereof could be moved from its place without producing confusion of all the other parts of the Universe as a whole.

As quoted in Thomas S. Kuhn, *The Copernican Revolution: Planetary Astronomy in the Development of Western Thought* (New York: Vintage Books, 1959), pp. 137–139, 141–142.

related to the immense speed at which the spheres had to move around the earth. To say the least, the Ptolemaic systems were cluttered. However, they were effective explanations as long as one assumed Aristotelian physics and the Christian belief that the earth rested at the center of the created universe.

Copernicus's *On the Revolutions of the Heavenly Spheres* challenged this picture in the most conservative manner possible. It suggested that if the earth were assumed to move about the sun in a circle, many of the difficulties with the Ptolemaic systems would disappear or become simpler. Although not wholly eliminated, the number of epicycles would be somewhat fewer. The motive behind this shift away from an earth-centered universe was to find a solution to the problems of planetary motion. By allowing the earth to move around the sun, Copernicus was able to construct a more mathematically elegant basis for astronomy. He had been discontented with the traditional system because it was mathematically clumsy and inconsistent. The primary appeal of his new system was its mathematical aesthetics: with the sun at the center of the universe, mathematical astronomy would make more sense. A change in the conception of the position of the earth meant that the planets were actually moving in circular orbits and only seemed to be doing otherwise because of the position of the observers on earth.

Except for the modification in the position of the earth, most of the other parts of Copernicus's book were Ptolemaic. The path of the planets remained circular. Genuine epicycles still existed in the heavens. His system was no more accurate than the existing ones for predicting the location of the planets. He had employed no new evidence. The major impact of his work was to provide another way of confronting some of the difficulties inherent in Ptolemaic astronomy. This work did not immediately replace the old astronomy, but it did allow other people who were also discontented with the Ptolemaic systems to think in new directions.

Copernicus's concern about mathematics provided an example of the single most important factor in the developing new science. The key to the future development of the Copernican revolution lay in the fusion of mathematical astronomy with further empirical data and observation, and mathematics became the model to which the new scientific thought would conform. The new empirical evidence helped to persuade the learned public.

Hypothetical reconstruction of the printing press of Johannes Gutenberg of Mainz (in what is not West Germany). Between about 1435 and 1455, Gutenberg worked out the complete technology of making individual rectangular metal types, composing the type into pages held together by pressure, and printing from those on an adaptation of the wooden standing press with ink of lampblack mixed with oil varnish. This new technology for the first time made it possible to manufacture numerous identical copies of written works and was basic to the intellectual development of the West. [Gutenberg-Museum, Mainz.]

Tycho Brahe and Johannes Kepler

The next major step toward the conception of a sun-centered system was taken by Tycho Brahe (1546–1601). He actually spent most of his life opposing Copernicus and advocating a different kind of earth-centered system. He suggested that the moon and the sun revolved around the earth and that the other planets revolved around the sun. However, in attacking Copernicus, he gave the latter's ideas more publicity. More importantly, this Danish astronomer's major weapon against Copernican astronomy was a series of new naked-eye astronomical observations. Brahe constructed the most accurate tables of observations that had been drawn up for centuries.

When Brahe died, these tables came into the possession of Johannes Kepler (1571–1630), a German astronomer. Kepler was a convinced Copernican, but his reasons for taking that position were not scientific. Kepler was deeply influenced by Renaissance Neoplatonism and its honoring of the sun. These Neoplatonists were also determined to discover mathematical harmonies in those numbers that would support a sun-centered universe. After much work Kepler discovered that to keep the sun at the center of things, he must abandon the Copernican concept of circular orbits. The mathematical relationships that emerged from a consideration of Brahe's observations suggested that the orbits of the planets were elliptical. Kepler published his findings in 1609 in a book entitled *On the Motion of Mars*. He had solved the problem of planetary orbits by using Copernicus's sun-centered universe and Brahe's empirical data.

Kepler had, however, also defined a new problem. None of the available theories could explain why the planetary orbits were elliptical. That solution awaited the work of Sir Isaac Newton.

Galileo Galilei

From Copernicus to Brahe to Kepler there had been little new information about the heavens that might not have been known to Ptolemy. However, in the same year that Kepler published his volume on Mars, an Italian scientist named Galileo Galilei (1564–1642) first turned a telescope on the heavens. Through that recently invented instrument he saw stars where none had been known to exist, mountains on the moon, spots moving across the sun, and moons orbiting Jupiter. The heavens were far more complex than anyone had formerly suspected. None of these discoveries proved that the earth orbited the sun, but they did suggest the complete inadequacy of the Ptolemaic system. It simply could not accommodate itself to all of these new phenomena. Some of Galileo's colleagues at the university of Padua were so unnerved that they refused to look through the telescope. Galileo publicized his findings and arguments for the Copernican system in numerous works, the most famous of

which was his *Dialogues on the Two Chief Systems of the World* (1632). This book brought down on him the condemnation of the Roman Catholic church. He was compelled to recant his opinions. However, he is reputed to have muttered after the recantation, "E pur si muove" ("It [the earth] still moves").

Galileo's discoveries and his popularization of the Copernican system were of secondary importance in his life work. His most important achievement was to articulate the concept of a universe totally subject to mathematical laws. More than any other writer of the century he argued that nature in its most minute details displayed mathematical regularity. He once wrote:

Galileo Galilei, the Florentine whose observations through a telescope helped confirm Copernicus' theories. Galileo's revolutionary findings showed the inaccuracy of the Ptolemaic assumption that the earth was the center of the universe and laid the foundations of modern astronomy. [New York Public Library Picture Collection.]

❧ Galileo Discusses the Relationship of Science and the Bible

The religious authorities were often critical of the discoveries and theories of six-teenth- and seventeenth-century science. For many years religious and scientific writers debated the implications of the Copernican theory in the reading of the Bible. For years before his condemnation by the Roman Catholic Church in 1633, Galileo had contended that scientific theory and religious piety were compatible. In his *Letter to the Grand Duchess Christiana* (of Tuscany) written in 1615, Galileo argued that God had revealed truth in both the Bible and physical nature and that the truth of physical nature did not contradict the Bible if the latter were properly under-stood.

The reason produced for condemning the opinion that the earth moves and the sun stands still is that in many places in the Bible one may read that the sun moves and the earth stands still. . . .

With regard to this argument, I think in the first place that it is very pious to say and prudent to affirm that the holy Bible can never speak untruth—whenever its true meaning is understood. But I be-lieve nobody will deny that it is often very abstruse, and may say things which are quite different from what its bare words signify. . . .

*This being granted, I think that in discussions of physical problems we ought to begin not from the au-thority of scriptural passages, but from sense-experi-ences and necessary demonstrations; for the holy Bible and the phenomena of nature proceed alike from the divine Word, the former as the dictate of the Holy Ghost and the latter as the observant executrix of God's commands. It is necessary for the Bible, in order to be accommodated to the understanding of every man, to speak many things which appear to differ from the absolute truth so far as the bare mean-ing of the words is concerned. But Nature, on the other hand, is inexorable and immutable; she never transgresses the laws imposed upon her, or cares a whit whether her abstruse reasons and methods of operation are understandable to men. For that rea-son it appears that nothing physical which sense-*experience sets before our eyes, or which necessary demonstrations prove to us, ought to be called in question (much less condemned) upon the testimony of biblical passages which may have some different meaning beneath their words. For the Bible is not chained in every expression to conditions as strict as those which govern all physical effects; nor is God any less excellently revealed in Nature's actions than in the sacred statements of the Bible. . . .*

From this I do not mean to infer that we need not have an extraordinary esteem for the passages of holy Scripture. On the contrary, having arrived at any certainties in physics, we ought to utilize these as the most appropriate aids in the true exposition of the Bible and in the investigation of those meanings which are necessarily contained therein for these must be concordant with demonstrated truths. I should judge the authority of the Bible was designed to per-suade men of those articles and propositions which, surpassing all human reasoning, could not be made credible by science, or by any other means than through the very mouth of the Holy Spirit. . . .

But I do not feel obliged to believe that the same God who has endowed us with senses, reason, and intellect has intended to forgo their use and by some other means to give us knowledge which we can at-tain by them.

Discoveries and Opinions of Galileo, trans. and ed. by Stillman Drake (Garden City, N.Y.: Double-day Anchor Books, 1957), pp. 181–183.

Philosophy is written in that great book which ever lies before our eyes—I mean the universe—but we cannot understand it if we do not first learn the language and grasp the symbols in which it is written. This book is writ-ten in the mathematical language, and the symbols are triangles, circles, and other geometrical figures, without whose help it is impossible to comprehend a single word of it; without which one wanders through a dark laby-rinth.[2]

[2] Quoted in E. A. Burtt, *The Metaphysical Foundations of Modern Physical Science* (Garden City, N.Y.: Anchor-Doubleday, 1954), p. 75.

ABOVE: *Galileo, working at first from others' suggestion, effectively invented the telescope. This is his 1609 instrument. His observations of the physical features on earth's moon and of the cyclical phases of the planet Venus and his discovery of the most prominent moons of the planet Jupiter were the first major astronomical observations since antiquity and had revolutionary intellectual and theological implications. [Istituto e Museo de Storia della Scienza, Florence.]*

BELOW: *A page from Galileo's notebook showing his notations about his observations of Jupiter and its satellites. [Dr. G.B. Pineider, Florence.]*

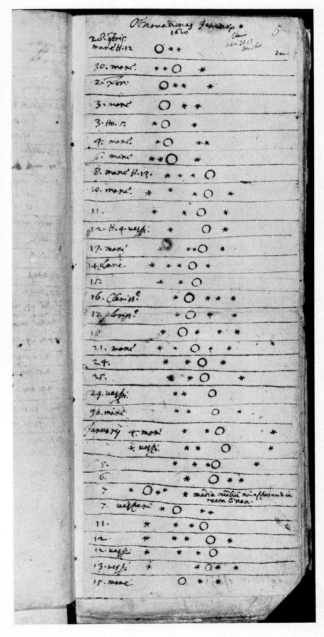

The microscope was the telescope's companion as a major optical invention of the seventeenth century. Several people, including Galileo, had a hand in its development, but the greatest progress—and the most amazing results—came from the Hollander Anton van Leeuwenhoek (1632–1723) who, using only primitive simple instruments made by himself, was the first person actually to see protozoa and bacteria, and from the Englishman Robert Hooke (1635–1703). Hooke's fairly elaborate microscope is shown here. [Courtesy Bausch and Lomb, Inc.]

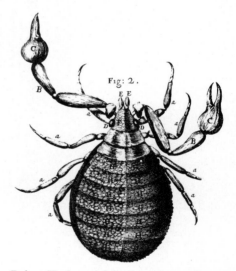

ABOVE: Robert Hooke carefully drew the startling results of his microscopic explorations. From his book Micrographia (1665) comes this rendering of the body louse; even such familiar small creatures had not been seen before in this detail.

AT LEFT: Spectacles were an earlier optical aid. They were known at least as early as the fourteenth century, and by the sixteenth they appear fairly frequently in portraits. Here the sixteenth-century German painter Hermann Tom Ring imagines the classical Roman author Vergil reading with spectacles. [Bettmann Archive.]

The universe was rational; however, its rationality was not that of Scholastic logic but of mathematics. Copernicus had thought that the heavens conformed to mathematical regularity; Galileo saw this regularity throughout all physical nature. He believed that the smallest atom behaved with the same mathematical precision as the largest heavenly sphere.

Galileo's thought meant that a world of quantity was replacing one of qualities. Mathematical quantities and relationships would henceforth increasingly be used to describe nature. Color, beauty, taste, and the like would be reduced to numerical relationships. And eventually social relationships would be envisioned in a mathematical model. Nature was cold, rational, mathematical, and mechanistic. What was real and lasting in the world was what was mathematically measurable. Few intellectual shifts have wrought such momentous changes for Western civilization.

René Descartes

No writer of the seventeenth century more fully adopted the geometric spirit of contemporary mathematics than René Descartes (1596–1650). He was a gifted mathematician who invented analytic geometry, and he was the author of major works on numerous scientific topics. However, his most important contribution was to scientific method. He wanted to proceed by deduction rather than by empirical observation and induction.

In 1637 Descartes published a *Discourse on Method* in which he attempted to provide a basis for all thinking founded on a mathematical model. He published the work in French rather than in Latin because he wanted it to have wide circulation and application. He began by saying that he would doubt everything except those propositions about which he could have clear and distinct ideas. This approach rejected all forms of intellectual authority except the conviction of his own reason. He concluded that he could not doubt his own act of thinking and his own existence. From this base he proceeded to deduce the existence of God. The presence of God was important to Descartes because God was the guarantor of the correctness of clear and distinct ideas. Because God was not a deceiver, the ideas of God-given reason could not be false.

Descartes believed that this powerful human rea-

Rene Descartes, the reputed father of modern philosophy. He was famed for his declaration "Cogito, ergo sum" ("I think, therefore I am"). This engraving was made from a picture by Francis Hals in the Louvre. [New York Public Library Picture Collection.]

son could fully comprehend the world. He divided existing things into mind and body. Thinking was the characteristic of the mind, extension of the body. Within the material world, mathematical laws reigned supreme. These could be grasped by the human reason. Because the laws were mathematical, they could be deduced from each other and constituted a complete system. The world of extension was the world of the scientist, whereas the mind was related to theology and philosophy. In the material world there was no room for spirits, divinity, or anything nonmaterial. Descartes had separated mind from body in order to banish the former from the realm of scientific speculation. He wanted to resurrect the speculative use of reason, but in a limited manner. It was to be applied only to the mechanical and mathematical realm of matter.

Descartes's emphasis on deduction and rational speculation exercised broad influence. Well into the eighteenth century European thinkers ap-

MAJOR WORKS OF THE SCIENTIFIC REVOLUTION

1543   *On the Revolutions of the Heavenly Spheres* (Copernicus)
1605   *The Advancement of Learning* (Bacon)
1609   *On the Motion of Mars* (Kepler)
1620   *Novum Organum* (Bacon)
1632   *Dialogues on the Two Chief Systems of the World* (Galileo)
1637   *Discourse on Method* (Descartes)
1687   *Principia Mathematica* (Newton)

An 1827 engraving of Sir Francis Bacon by J. Thompson. Bacon's beliefs that knowledge should produce useful results and that one must observe phenomena before trying to explain them challenged Scholastic modes of thinking and learning. [New York Public Library Picture Collection.]

pealed to Descartes's method, which moved from broad intellectual generalizations to specific phenomena. The method then attempted to see how the phenomena could be interpreted so as to mesh with the generalization. However, that method was eventually overcome by the force of scientific induction, whereby the observer or scientist began with observations of empirical data and then attempted to draw generalizations from those observations. The major champion of the inductive method during the early seventeenth century had been Francis Bacon.

Francis Bacon

Bacon (1561–1626) was an Englishman of almost universal accomplishment. He was a lawyer, a high royal official, and the author of histories, moral essays, and philosophical discourses. Traditionally he has been regarded as the father of empiricism and of experimentation in science. Much of this reputation is unearned. Bacon was not a scientist except in the most amateur fashion. His accomplishment was setting a tone and helping to create a climate in which other scientists worked. In books such as *The Advancement of Learning* (1605), the *Novum Organum* (1620), and the *New Atlantis* (1627), Bacon attacked the Scholastic belief that most truth had already been discovered and only required explanation, as well as the Scholastic reverence for intellectual authority in general. He believed that Scholastic thinkers paid too much attention to tradition and to knowledge achieved by the ancients. He urged contemporaries to strike out on their own in search of a new understanding of nature. He wanted seventeenth-century Europeans

to have confidence in themselves and their own abilities rather than in the people and methods of the past. Bacon was one of the first major European writers to champion the desirability of innovation and change.

Bacon believed that human knowledge should produce useful results. In particular, knowledge of nature should be brought to the aid of the human condition. Those goals required the modification or abandonment of Scholastic modes of learning and thinking. Bacon contended, "The [Scholastic] logic now in use serves more to fix and give stability to the errors which have their foundation in commonly received notions than to help the search after truth."[3] Scholastic philosophers could not escape from their syllogisms to examine the foundations of their thought and intellectual presuppositions. Bacon urged that philosophers and investi-

[3] Quoted in Franklin Baumer, *Main Currents of Western Thought,* 4th ed. (New Haven, Conn.: Yale, 1978), p. 281.

gators of nature examine the evidence of their senses before constructing logical speculations. In a famous passage he divided all philosophers into "men of experiment and men of dogmas." He observed:

The men of experiment are like the ant, they only collect and use; the reasoners resemble spiders, who make cobwebs out of their own substance. But the bee takes a middle course: it gathers its material from the flowers of the garden and of the field, but transforms and digests it by a power of its own. Not unlike this is the true business of philosophy.[4]

By directing scientists toward an examination of empirical evidence, Bacon hoped that they would achieve new knowledge and thus new capabilities for humankind.

[4]Quoted in ibid., p. 288.

Bacon Attacks the Idols That Harm Human Understanding

Francis Bacon wanted the men and women of his era to have the courage to change the way in which they thought about physical nature. In this famous passage from the *Novum Organum* (1620) Bacon attempted to explain why people had such difficulty in asking new questions and seeking new answers. His observations may still be relevant to the manner in which people form and hold their opinions in our own day.

The idols and false notions which are now in possession of the human understanding, and have taken deep root therein, not only so beset men's minds that truth can hardly find entrance, but even after entrance is obtained, they will again in the very instauration of the sciences meet and trouble us, unless men being forewarned of the danger fortify themselves as far as may be against their assaults.

There are four classes of Idols which beset men's minds. To these for distinction's sake I have assigned names,—calling the first class Idols of the Tribe; the second, Idols of the Cave; the third, Idols of the Marketplace; the fourth, Idols of the Theatre.

. . . .

The Idols of the Tribe have their foundation in human nature itself; and in the tribe or race of men. For it is a false assertion that the sense of man is the measure of things. On the contrary, all perceptions as well as the sense as of the mind are according to the measure of the individual and not according to the measure of the universe. And the human understanding is like a false mirror, which, receiving rays irregularly, distorts and discolours the nature of things by mingling its own nature with it.

The Idols of the Cave are the idols of the individual man. For every one (besides the errors common to human nature in general) has a cave or den of his own, which refracts and discolours the light of nature; owing either to his own proper and peculiar nature; or to his education and conversation with others; or to the reading of books, and the authority of those whom he esteems and admires. . . .

There are also Idols formed by the intercourse and association of men with each other, which I call Idols of the Marketplace, on account of the commerce and consort of men there. For it is by discourse that men associate; and words are imposed according to the apprehension of the vulgar. And therefore the ill and unfit choice of words wonderfully obstructs the understanding. . . .

Lastly, there are Idols which have immigrated into men's minds from the various dogmas of philosophies, and also from wrong laws of demonstration. These I call Idols of the Theatre; because in my judgment all the received systems are but so many stage-plays, representing worlds of their own creation after an unreal and scenic fashion.

Francis Bacon, *Essays, Advancement of Learning, New Atlantis, and Other Pieces,* ed. by Richard Foster Jones (New York: Odyssey, 1937), pp. 278–280.

Bacon compared himself with Columbus plotting a new route to intellectual discovery. The comparison is significant, because it displays the consciousness of a changing world that appears so often in writers of the late sixteenth and early seventeenth centuries. They were rejecting the past not from simple hatred but rather from a firm understanding that the world was much more complicated than their medieval forebears had thought.

Neither Europe nor European thought could remain self-contained. There were not only new worlds on the globe but also new worlds of the mind. Most of the people in Bacon's day, including the intellectuals, thought that the best era of human history lay in antiquity. Bacon dissented vigorously from that point of view. He looked to a future of material improvement achieved through the empirical examination of nature. His own theory of induction from empirical evidence was quite unsystematic, but his insistence on appeal to experience influenced others whose methods were more productive. His great achievement was persuading increasing numbers of thinkers that scientific thought must conform to empirical experience.

Bacon gave science a progressionist bias. Science was to have a practical purpose and the goal of human improvement. Some scientific investigation does possess this character. Much pure research does not. However, Bacon linked in the public mind the concepts of science and material progress. This was a powerful idea and has continued to influence Western civilization to the present day. It has made science and those who can appeal to the authority of science major forces for change and innovation. Thus, though not making any major scientific contribution himself, Bacon directed investigators of nature to a new method and a new purpose.

Isaac Newton

Isaac Newton (1642–1727) drew on the work of his predecessors and his own brilliance to solve the major remaining problem of planetary motion and to establish a basis for physics that endured more than two centuries. The question that continued to perplex seventeenth-century scientists who accepted the theories of Copernicus, Kepler, and Galileo was how the planets and other heavenly bodies moved in an orderly fashion. The Ptolemaic

and Aristotelian answer had been the crystalline spheres and a universe arranged in the order of the heaviness of its parts. Numerous unsatisfactory theories had been set forth to deal with the question.

In 1687 Newton published *The Mathematical Principles of Natural Philosophy,* better known by its Latin title of *Principia Mathematica.* Much of the research and thinking for this great work had taken place more than fifteen years earlier. Newton was heavily indebted to the work of Galileo and particularly to the latter's view that inertia could exist in either a state of motion or a state of rest. Galileo's mathematical bias permeated Newton's thought. Newton reasoned that the planets and all other physical objects in the universe moved through mutual attraction. Every object in the uni-

Sir Isaac Newton, discoverer of the mathematical and physical laws governing the force of gravity. Newton believed that religion and science were compatible and mutually supportive. To study nature was to gain a better understanding of the Creator. [New York Public Library Picture Collection.]

William Blake's Newton is, of course, not a portrait of an individual. Instead, it dramatizes and glorifies the detached, almost God-like scientist who can solve the mysteries of the universe and display the results with mathematical precision. [The Tate Gallery, London.]

verse affected every other object through gravity. The attraction of gravity explained why the planets moved in an orderly rather than a chaotic manner. He had found that "the force of gravity towards the whole planet did arise from and was compounded of the forces of gravity towards all its parts, and towards every one part was in the inverse proportion of the squares of the distances from the part."[5] Newton demonstrated this relationship mathematically. He made no attempt to explain the nature of gravity itself.

[5] Quoted in A. Rupert Hall, *From Galileo to Newton, 1630–1720* (London: Fontana, 1970), p. 300.

Newton was a great mathematical genius, but he also upheld the importance of empirical data and observation. He believed, in good Baconian fashion, that one must observe phenomena before attempting to explain them. The final test of any theory or hypothesis for him was whether it described what could actually be observed. He was a great opponent of Descartes's rationalism, which he believed included insufficient guards against error. As Newton's own theory of universal gravitation became increasingly accepted, the Baconian bias also became more fully popularized.

With the work of Newton the natural universe became a realm of law and regularity. Spirits and

Newton Sets Forth Rules of Reasoning in Philosophy

Philosophy was the term that seventeenth-century writers used to describe the new science. In this passage from his *Principia Mathematica* (1687) Isaac Newton laid down what he regarded as the fundamental rules for scientific reasoning. The reader should notice the importance he placed on experimental evidence and his desire to find rules or regularities that exist throughout the natural order.

Rule I. We are to admit no more causes of natural things than such as are both true and sufficient to explain their appearances.

To this purpose the philosophers say that Nature does nothing in vain, and more is in vain when less will serve; for Nature is pleased with simplicity, and affects not the pomp of superfluous causes.

Rule II. Therefore to the same natural effects we must, as far as possible, assign the same causes.

As to respiration in a man and in a beast; the descent of stones in Europe and in America; the light of our culinary fire and of the sun; the reflection of light in the earth, and in the planets.

Rule III. The qualities of bodies, which admit neither intension nor remission of degrees, and which are found to belong to all bodies within the reach of our experiments, are to be esteemed the universal qualities of all bodies whatsoever.

For since the qualities of bodies are only known to us by experiments, we are to hold for universal all such as universally agree with experiments and such as are not liable to diminution can never be quite taken away. We are certainly not to relinquish the evidence of experiments for the sake of dreams and vain fictions of our own devising. . . . We no other way know the extension of bodies than by our senses,

nor do these reach it in all bodies; but because we perceive extension in all that are sensible, therefore we ascribe it universally to all others also. That abundance of bodies are hard, we learn by experience; and because the hardness of the whole arises from the hardness of the parts, we therefore justly infer the hardness of the undivided particles not only of the bodies we feel but of all others. That bodies are impenetrable, we gather not from reason, but from sensation. . . .

Lastly, if it universally appears, by experiments and astronomical observations, that all bodies about the earth gravitate towards the earth, and that in proportion to the quantity of matter which they severally contain; . . . we must, in consequence of this rule, universally allow that all bodies whatsoever are endowed with a principle of universal gravitation. . . .

Rule IV. In experimental philosophy we are to look upon propositions collected by general induction from phaenomena as accurately or very nearly true, notwithstanding any contrary hypotheses that may be imagined, till such time as other phaenomena occur, by which they may either be made more accurate, or liable to exceptions.

This rule must follow, that the argument of induction may not be evaded by hypotheses.

Introduction to Contemporary Civilization in the West, 3rd ed., Vol. 1 (New York: Columbia University Press, 1960), pp. 850–852.

---

divinities were no longer necessary to explain its operation. Thus the Scientific Revolution liberated human beings from the fear of a chaotic or haphazard universe. Most of the scientists were very devout people. They saw the new picture of physical nature as suggesting a new picture of God. The Creator of this rational, lawful nature must also be rational. To study nature was to come to a better understanding of that Creator. Science and religious faith were not only compatible but mutually supporting. As Newton wrote, "The main Business of Natural Philosophy is to argue from Phaenomena without feigning Hypothesis, and to deduce Causes from Effects, till we come to the very first Cause, which certainly is not mechanical."[6]

This reconciliation of faith and science allowed

[6]Quoted in Baumer, p. 323.

the new physics and astronomy to spread rapidly. At the very time when Europeans were finally tiring of the wars of religion, the new science provided the basis for a view of God that might lead away from irrational disputes and wars over religious doctrine. Faith in a rational God encouraged faith in the rationality of human beings and in their capacity to improve their lot once liberated from the traditions of the past. The Scientific Revolution provided the great model for the desirability of change and of criticism of inherited views. Yet at the same time the new science caused some people to feel that the mystery had been driven from the universe and that the rational Creator was less loving and less near to humankind than the God of earlier ages.

Writers and Philosophers

The end of the sixteenth century saw weariness with religious strife and incipient unbelief as many could no longer embrace either old Catholic or new Protestant absolutes. Intellectually as well as politically the seventeenth century was a period of transition, one already well prepared for by the thinkers of the Renaissance, who had reacted strongly against medieval intellectual traditions, especially those informed by Aristotle and Scholasticism.

Even as they sought to find a purer culture before the Middle Ages in pagan and Christian antiquity, however, Humanists and Protestants continued to share much of the medieval vision of a unified Christendom. Few were prepared to embrace the secular values and preoccupations of the growing scientific movement, which found its models in mathematics and the natural sciences, rather than in the example and authority of antiquity. Some strongly condemned the work of Copernicus, Kepler, and Galileo, whose theories seemed to fly in the face of commonsense experience as well as to question hallowed tradition.

The thinkers of the Renaissance and the Reformation nonetheless paved the way for the new science and philosophy, both by their attacks on tradition and by their own failure to implement radical reforms. The Humanist revival of interest in ancient skepticism proved an effective foundation for attacks on traditional views of authority and rationality in both religion and science. Already such thinkers as the Italian Pico della Mirandola (1463–1494), the German Agrippa of Nettisheim (1486–1535), and the Frenchman François Rabelais (1494–1553) had questioned the ability of reason to obtain certitude. Sebastian Castellio (1515–1563), Michel de Montaigne (1533–1592), and Pierre Charron (1541–1603) had been as much repulsed by the new Calvinist religion as John Calvin had been by medieval religion. It was in the wake of such criticism that René Descartes developed a more modest, yet surer, definition of rationality as the tool of the new scientific philosophy.

The writers and philosophers of the seventeenth century were aware that they lived in a period of transition. Some embraced the new science wholeheartedly (Hobbes and Locke), some tried to straddle the two ages (Cervantes, Shakespeare, and Milton), and still others ignored or opposed the new developments that seemed mortally to threaten traditional values (Pascal and Bunyan).

Miguel de Cervantes Saavedra (1547–1616)

Spanish literature of the sixteenth and seventeenth centuries was influenced by the peculiar religious and political history of Spain in this period. Spain was dominated by the Catholic church. Since the joint reign of Ferdinand and Isabella (1479–1504) the church had received the unqualified support of reigning political power. Although there was religious reform in Spain, a Protestant Reformation never occurred, thanks largely to the abiding power of the church and the Inquisition.

The second influence was the aggressive piety of the Spanish rulers Charles I—who became the Holy Roman Emperor as Charles V (1516–1556)—and his son, Philip II (1556–1598). The intertwining of Catholic piety and Spanish political power underlay the third major influence on Spanish literature: preoccupation with medieval chivalric virtues—in particular, questions of honor and loyalty. The novels and plays of the period almost invariably focus on a special decision involving a character's reputation as his honor or loyalty is tested. In this regard Spanish literature may be said to have remained more Catholic and medieval than that of England and France, where major Protestant movements had occurred. Two of the most important Spanish writers in this period became priests (Lope de Vega and Pedro Calderón de la Barca), and the one generally acknowledged to be the greatest Spanish writer of all time, Cervantes, was preoccupied in his work with the strengths and weaknesses of religious idealism.

Cervantes was born in Alcalá, the son of a nomadic physician. Having received only a smattering of formal education, he educated himself by insatiable reading in vernacular literature and immersion in the "school of life." As a young man he worked in Rome for a Spanish cardinal. In 1570 he became a soldier and was even decorated for gallantry in the Battle of Lepanto (1571), an engagement that maimed his left hand. While he was returning to Spain in 1575, his ship was captured by pirates, and Cervantes spent five years as a slave in Algiers. On his release and return to Spain he held many odd jobs, among them that of a tax collector. He was several times imprisoned for padding his accounts. He conceived and began to write his most famous work, *Don Quixote,* in 1603, while languishing in prison.

Don Quixote and Sancho Panza, from a nineteenth-century French edition of Cervantes's Don Quixote *illustrated by the French artist Doré.* Don Quixote *is perhaps the supreme literary work of its age.* [*New York Public Library Picture Collection.*]

The first part of *Don Quixote* appeared in 1605 and a second part followed in 1615. If, as many argue, the intent of this work was to satirize the chivalric romances so popular in Spain, Cervantes nonetheless failed to conceal his deep affection for the character he created as an object of ridicule, Don Quixote. The work is satire only on the surface and has remained as much an object of study by philosophers and theologians as by students of Spanish literature. Don Quixote, a none-too-stable middle-aged man, is presented by Cervantes as one driven mad by reading too many chivalric romances. He finally comes to believe that he is an aspirant to knighthood and must prove by brave deeds his worthiness of knightly rank. To this end he acquires a rusty suit of armor, mounts an aged steed (named Rozinante), and chooses for his inspiration a quite unworthy peasant girl, Dulcinea, whom he fancies to be a noble lady to whom he can, with honor, dedicate his life.

Don Quixote's foil in the story—Sancho Panza, a clever, worldly wise peasant who serves as Don Quixote's squire—is an equally fascinating character. Sancho Panza watches with bemused skepticism, but also with genuine sympathy, as his lord does battle with a windmill (which he mistakes for a dragon) and repeatedly makes a fool of himself as he gallops across the countryside. The story ends tragically with Don Quixote's humiliating defeat by a well-meaning friend, who, disguised as a knight, bests Don Quixote in combat and forces him to renounce his quest for knighthood. The humiliated Don Quixote does not, however, come to his senses as a result. He returns sadly to his village to die a shamed and broken-hearted old man.

Throughout *Don Quixote* Cervantes juxtaposed the down-to-earth realism of Sancho Panza with the old-fashioned religious idealism of Don Quixote. The reader perceives that Cervantes really admired the one as much as the other and meant to portray both as representing attitudes necessary for a happy life. Like his English counterpart, William Shakespeare, Cervantes understood the complexity of human nature. He wanted his readers to remember that if they are to be truly happy, men and women need dreams, even impossible ones, just as much as they need a sense of reality.

The other major Spanish writers of the period had a far less universal vision than Cervantes. Lope Felix de Vega Carpio (1562–1635), the author of an incredible number of epics, romances, novels, lyrics, and plays, pandered to popular Spanish tastes and remained content to meet the contemporary demand for entertainment rather than venturing on profound and lasting works. He never wanted for variety in his work, however, and almost singlehandedly created the Spanish national theater. Pedro Calderón de la Barca (1600–1681) wrote court dramas, comedies, and highly sentimental "point of honor" plays that spoke to current national interests and became favorites among later Romantic writers.

William Shakespeare (1564–1616)

Shakespeare, the greatest playwright in the English language, was born in Stratford-on-Avon, where he lived almost all of his life except for the years when he wrote in London. There is much less factual knowledge about him than one would expect of such an important figure. Shakespeare married in 1582 at the early age of eighteen, and he and his wife, Anne Hathaway, had three children (two were twins) by 1585. He apparently worked as a schoolteacher for a time and in this capacity acquired his broad knowledge of Renaissance learning and literature. The argument of some scholars that he was an untutored natural genius is highly questionable. His own learning and his enthusiasm for the education of his day are manifest in the many learned allusions that appear in his plays.

Shakespeare was a man of the country as well as of the town and manifestly enjoyed the life of a country gentleman. There is none of the Puritan distress over worldliness in his work. He took the new commercialism and the bawdy pleasures of the Elizabethan Age in stride and with amusement. The few allusions to the Puritans that exist in his works appear to be more critical than complimentary. In matters of politics, as in those of religion, he was very much a man of his time and not inclined to offend his queen.

That Shakespeare was interested in politics is apparent from his history plays and the references to contemporary political events that fill all his plays. He seems to have viewed government simply, however, through the character of the individual ruler, whether Richard III or Elizabeth Tudor, not in terms of ideal systems or social goals. By modern standards he was a political conservative, accepting the social rankings and the power structure of his day and demonstrating unquestioned patriotism.

The English dramatist and poet, William Shakespeare. This engraving by Martin Droeshout appears on the title page of the collected edition of his plays published in 1623 and is probably as close as we shall come to knowing what he looked like.

Shakespeare knew the theatre as one who participated in every phase of its life—as a playwright, an actor, and a part owner of a theater. He was a member and principal dramatist of a famous company of actors known as the King's Men. During the tenure of Edmund Tilney, who was Queen Elizabeth's Master of Revels during the greater part of Shakespeare's active period (1590–1610), many of Shakespeare's plays were performed at court. The queen was herself a most enthusiastic patron of plays and pageants.

Elizabethan drama was already a distinctive form when Shakespeare began writing. Unlike French drama of the seventeenth century, which was dominated by the court and classical models, English drama developed in the sixteenth and seventeenth centuries as a blending of many extant forms, ranging from classical comedies and tragedies to the medieval morality play and contemporary Italian short stories. In Shakespeare's own library were

planctes siue arena.

Ex obseruationibus Londinensibus·
Johannis de witt

This 1596 sketch of the interior of the Swan Theater in
London by Johannis de Witt, a Dutch visitor, is the only
known contemporary view of an Elizabethan playhouse. In
this kind of setting the plays of Marlowe, Shakespeare,
Jonson, and their fellows were first seen. [The Granger
Collection.]

to be found Holinshed's and other English chronicles; the works of Plutarch, Ovid, and Vergil,
among other Latin authors; Arthurian romances
and popular songs and fables; the writings of Montaigne and Rabelais; and the major English poets
and prose writers.

Shakespeare's tragedies were especially influenced by the work of two of his contemporaries:
Thomas Kyd and Christopher Marlowe. Kyd
(1558–1594) was the author of the first dramatic
version of *Hamlet* and a master at weaving together
motive, plot, and tragic intensity. The tragedies of
Marlowe (1564–1593) set a model for character,
poetry, and style that only Shakespeare among the
English playwrights of the period surpassed.

Shakespeare's work was an original synthesis of the
best past and current achievements.

Shakespeare mastered the psychology of human
motivation and passion. He had a unique talent
for psychological penetration, one rivaled only by
the French Jansenist dramatist Jean Racine (1639–
1699), who, however, remained confined to classical forms and rules. Later Romantic writers
claimed Shakespeare as one of their own and contrasted his work sharply with the neoclassicism of
Pierre Corneille and Racine, whom they found by
comparison to be narrow and mechanical.

Shakespeare wrote histories, comedies, and tragedies. *Richard III* (1593), a very early play, stands
out among the examples of the first genre, although some historians have criticized as histori-
cally inaccurate his patriotic depiction of Richard,
the foe of Henry Tudor, as an unprincipled villain.
Shakespeare's comedies, while not attaining the
heights of his tragedies, surpass in originality his
history plays. Save for *The Tempest* (1611), his last
play, the comedies most familiar to modern readers were written between 1598–1602: *Much Ado
About Nothing* (1598–1599), *As You Like It* (1598–
1600), and *Twelfth Night* (1602).

The tragedies are considered his unique achievement. Four of these were written within a three-
year period: *Hamlet* (1603), *Othello* (1604), *King
Lear* (1605), and *Macbeth* (1606). The most original
of the tragedies, *Romeo and Juliet* (1597), transformed an old popular story into a moving drama
of "star-cross'd lovers." Both Romeo and Juliet,
denied a marriage by their factious families, die
tragic deaths. Romeo, finding Juliet and thinking
her dead after she has taken a sleeping potion, poi-
sons himself. Juliet, awakening to find Romeo
dead, stabs herself to death with his dagger.

Throughout his lifetime and ever since, Shakespeare has been immensely popular with both the
playgoer and the play reader. As Ben Jonson, a
contemporary classical dramatist who created his
own school of poets, aptly put it in a tribute affixed
to the First Folio edition of Shakespeare's plays
(1623): "He was not of an age, but for all time."

John Milton (1608–1674)

John Milton was the son of a devout Puritan father. Educated at Saint Paul's School and then at
Christ's College of Cambridge University, he became a careful student of Christian and pagan classics. In 1638 he traveled to Italy, where he found in

the lingering Renaissance a very congenial intellectual atmosphere. The Phlegraean Fields near Naples, a volcanic region, later became the model for hell in *Paradise Lost,* and it is suspected by some scholars that the Villa d'Este provided the model for paradise in *Paradise Regained.* Milton remained throughout his life a man more at home in the Italian Renaissance, with its high ideals and universal vision, than in the strife-torn England of the seventeenth century.

A man of deep inner conviction and principle, Milton believed that standing a test of character was the most important thing in an individual's life. This belief informed his own personal life and is the subject of much of his literary work. An early poem, *Lycidas,* was a pastoral elegy dealing with one who lived well but not long, Edward King, a close college friend who tragically drowned. In

The English writer and poet John Milton in an engraving by William Faithorne—one of the few authentic contemporary likenesses of him. [The Granger Collection.]

1639 Milton joined the Puritan struggle against Charles I and Archbishop Laud. Employing his literary talents as a pamphleteer, he defended the presbyterian form of church government against the episcopacy and supported other Puritan reforms. After a month-long unsuccessful marriage in 1642 (a marriage later reconciled), he wrote several tracts in defense of the right to divorce. These writings became a factor in Parliament's passage of a censorship law in 1643, against which Milton wrote an eloquent defense of the freedom of the press, *Areopagitica* (1644).

Until the upheavals of the civil war moderated his views, Milton believed that government should have the least possible control over the private lives of individuals. When Parliament divided into Presbyterians and Independents, he took the side of the latter, who wanted to dissolve the national church altogether in favor of the local autonomy of individual congregations. He also defended the execution of Charles I in a tract on the *Tenure of Kings and Magistrates* and later served as secretary to the executive committee of Parliament during Cromwell's protectorate. It was after his intense labor on this tract that his eyesight failed. Milton was totally blind when he wrote his acclaimed masterpieces.

Paradise Lost, Milton's masterpiece of English blank verse, was completed in 1665 and published in 1667. A study of the destructive qualities of pride and the redeeming possibilities of humility, it elaborates in traditional Christian language and concept the revolt of Satan in heaven and the fall of Adam on earth. Milton was throughout preoccupied with the motives of Satan and all who rebel against God. His proud but tragic Satan, one of the great figures of all literature, represents the absolute corruption of potential greatness.

In *Paradise Lost* Milton aspired to give England a lasting epic like that given Greece in Homer's *Iliad* and ancient Rome in Vergil's *Aeneid.* In choosing biblical subject matter, he revealed the influence of contemporary theology on his work. Milton tended to agree with the Arminians, who, unlike the extreme Calvinists, did not believe that all worldly events, including the Fall of Man, were immutably fixed in the eternal decree of God. Milton shared the Arminian belief that human beings must take responsibility for their fate and that human efforts to improve character could, with God's grace, bring salvation.

Perhaps his own blindness, joined with the hope

of making the best of a failed religious revolution, inclined Milton to sympathize with those who urged people to make the most of what they had, even in the face of seemingly sure defeat. That is a manifest concern of his last works, *Samson Agonistes,* which recounts the biblical story of Samson, and *Paradise Regained,* the story of Christ's temptation in the wilderness, both published in 1671.

John Bunyan (1628–1688)

Bunyan was the English author of two classics of sectarian Puritan spirituality: *Grace Abounding* (1666) and *The Pilgrim's Progress* (1678). A Bedford tinker, his works speak especially for the seventeenth-century working people and popular religious culture. Bunyan received only the most basic education before taking up his father's craft. He was drafted into Oliver Cromwell's revolutionary army in 1644 and served for two years, although without seeing actual combat. The visionary fervor of the New Model Army and the imagery of warfare abound in Bunyan's work.

After the restoration of the monarchy in 1660 Bunyan was arrested for his fiery preaching and remained in prison for twelve years. Had he been willing to agree to give up preaching, he might have been released much sooner. But Puritans considered the compromise of one's beliefs a tragic flaw, and Bunyan steadfastly refused all such suggestions.

It was during this period of imprisonment that Bunyan wrote his famous autobiography, *Grace Abounding.* It is both a very personal statement and a model for the faithful. Like *The Pilgrim's Progress,* Bunyan's later masterpiece, *Grace Abounding* expresses Puritan piety at its most fervent. Puritans believed that individuals could do absolutely nothing to save themselves, and this made them extremely restless and introspective. The individual believer could only trust that God had placed her or him among the elect and try each day to live a life that reflected such a favored status. So long as men and women struggled successfully against the flesh and the world, they had presumptive evidence that they were among God's elect. To falter or to become complacent in the face of temptation was to cast doubt on one's faith and salvation and even to raise the specter of eternal damnation.

This anxious questing for salvation came to classic expression in *The Pilgrim's Progress,* a work unique in its contribution to Western religious sym-

A seventeenth-Century illustration from The Pilgrim's Progress. *Bunyan's chief purpose in writing the work was to illustrate the manner in which a Christian could, with faith, successfully confront the temptations of life.* [*The Fotomas Index, London.*]

bolism and imagery. The story of the journey of Christian and his friends Hopeful and Faithful to the Celestial City, it teaches that one must deny spouse, children, and all earthly security and go in search of "Life, life, eternal life." During the long journey, the travelers must resist the temptations of Worldly-Wiseman and Vanity Fair, pass through the Slough of Despond, and endure a long dark night in Doubting Castle, their faith being tested at every turn. Bunyan later wrote a work tracing the progress of Christian's opposite, entitled *The Life*

Major Works of Seventeenth-Century Literature and Philosophy

1605	*King Lear* (Shakespeare)
	Don Quixote, Part I (Cervantes)
1651	*Leviathan* (Hobbes)
1656–1657	*Provincial Letters* (Pascal)
1667	*Paradise Lost* (Milton)
1677	*Ethics* (Spinoza)
1678	*Pilgrim's Progress* (Bunyan)
1690	*Two Treatises of Government* (Locke)
	An Essay Concerning Human Understanding (Locke)

and Death of Mr. Badman (1680), the story of a man so addicted to the bad habits of Restoration society, of which Bunyan strongly disapproved, that he journeyed steadfastly not to heaven but to hell.

The loss of national unity during the Puritan struggle against the Stuart monarchy and the Anglican church took its toll on English literature and drama during the seventeenth century. In 1642 the Puritans had closed the theaters of London. They were reopened after the Restoration of Charles II in 1660, and drama revived following the long Puritan interregnum.

Literary thought thereafter became less experimental and adopted proven classical forms, as a new movement to subject reality to the strict rules of reason began. During the so-called Augustan Age, from John Dryden (1631–1700) to Alexander Pope (1688–1744), classicism was the literary rule.

There was a preoccupation with the world of mundane facts, rather than with universal ideals, and a waning of the transcendental concerns of the Elizabethans and the Puritan divines. As in France, where the French comedy writer Molière (1622–1673) is the outstanding example, English writers tried to please the royal court and aristocracy by turning to more earthy and entertaining popular topics.

Blaise Pascal (1623–1662)

Pascal was a French mathematician and a physical scientist widely acclaimed by his contemporaries. He was also a most devout man, who surrendered all his wealth so that he might more easily pursue an austere, self-disciplined life. Torn between the continuing dogmatism and the new skepticism of the seventeenth century, he aspired to write a work that would refute both the Jesuits, whose casuistry (i.e., confessional tactics designed to minimize and even excuse sinful acts) he considered a distortion of Christian teaching, and the skeptics of his age, who either denied religion altogether (atheists) or accepted it only as it conformed to reason (deists). Such a definitive work was never realized, and his views on these matters exist only in piecemeal form. He wrote against the Jesuits in his *Provincial Letters* (1656–1657), and he left behind a provocative collection of reflections on humankind and religion that was published posthumously under the title *Pensées*.

Pascal was early influenced by the Jansenists, seventeenth-century Catholic opponents of the Jesuits. His sister was a member of the Jansenist

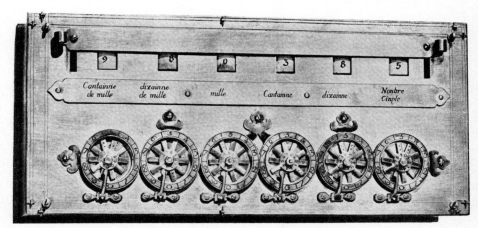

The arithmetical machine invented in 1642 by Blaise Pascal, the French philosopher and mathematician. Its main feature was the automatic carry-forward. The wheels, each divided into nine sections, were connected in such a way that the complete rotation of one of them caused the wheel on the left of it to move forward by one digit. The foundations of adding machines and other mechanical calculators were thus laid by this device. [Culver Pictures.]

∾ Pascal Meditates on Human Beings As Thinking Creatures

Pascal was both a great religious and a great scientific writer. Unlike other scientific thinkers of the seventeenth century, he was not overly optimistic about the ability of science to improve the human condition. Pascal believed that science and philosophy would instead help human beings to understand their situation better. In these passages from his *Pensées (Thoughts)*, he discussed the uniqueness of human beings as the creatures who alone in all the universe are capable of thinking.

339

I can well conceive a man without hands, feet, head (for it is only experience which teaches us that the head is more necessary than feet). But I cannot conceive man without thought; he would be a stone or a brute.

344

Reason commands us far more imperiously than a master; for in disobeying the one we are unfortunate, and in disobeying the other we are fools.

346

Thought constitutes the greatness of man.

347

Man is but a reed, the most feeble thing in nature; but he is a thinking reed. The entire universe need not arm itself to crush him. A vapour, a drop of water suffices to kill him. But, if the universe were to crush him, man would still be more noble than that which killed him, because he knows that he dies and the advantage which the universe has over him; the universe knows nothing of this.

All our dignity consists, then, in thought. By it we must elevate ourselves, and not by space and time which we cannot fill. Let us endeavour, then, to think well; this is the principle of morality.

348

A thinking reed—It is not from space that I must seek my dignity, but from the government of my thought. I shall have no more if I possess worlds. By space the universe encompasses and swallows me up like an atom; by thought I comprehend the world.

Blaise Pascal, *Pensées and The Provincial Letters* (New York: Modern Library, 1941), pp. 115–116.

community of Port Royal near Paris, and after 1654 Pascal himself closely identified with this community. The Jansenists shared with the Calvinists St. Augustine's belief in man's total sinfulness, his eternal predestination by God, and his complete dependence on faith and grace for knowledge of God and salvation.

Pascal believed that reason and science, although attesting to human dignity, remained of no avail in matters of religion. Here only the reasons of the heart and a "leap of faith" could prevail. Pascal saw two essential truths in the Christian religion: that a loving God, worthy of human attainment, exists, and that human beings, because they are corrupted in nature, are utterly unworthy of God. Pascal believed that the atheists and the deists of the age had spurned the lesson of reason. For him rational analysis of the human condition attested humankind's utter mortality and corruption and exposed the weakness of reason itself in resolving the problems of human nature and destiny. Reason should rather drive those who truly heed it to faith and dependence on divine grace.

Pascal made a famous wager with the skeptics. It

is a better bet, he argued, to believe that God exists and to stake everything on his promised mercy than not to do so, because if God does exist, everything will be gained by the believer, whereas the loss incurred by having believed in him should he prove not to exist is by comparison very slight.

Pascal was convinced that belief in God measurably improved earthly life psychologically and disciplined it morally, regardless of whether or not God proved in the end to exist. He thought that great danger lay in the surrender of traditional religious belief. Pascal urged his contemporaries to seek self-understanding by "learned ignorance" and to discover humankind's greatness by recognizing its misery. Thereby Pascal hoped to counter what he believed to be the false optimism of the new rationalism and science.

Even before Pascal's day, of course, there was a tradition of elaborate mechanical devices throughout Europe. For example, by 1500 there were public clocks in practically every town. One of the most famous is the astronomical clock of Strasbourg's cathedral in France, which presents a parade of allegorical figures every day at noon. [French Government Tourist Office, New York.]

The Glockenspiel, or clock performance, occurring hourly at the Munich city hall, is another ingenious time-keeping device. [German Information Center, New York.]

Baruch Spinoza (1632–1677)

The most controversial thinker of the seventeenth century was Baruch Spinoza, the son of a Jewish merchant of Amsterdam. Spinoza's philosophy caused his excommunication by his own synagogue in 1656. In 1670 he published his *Treatise on Religious and Political Philosophy*, a work that criticized the dogmatism of Dutch Calvinists and championed freedom of thought. During his lifetime both Jews and Protestants attacked him as an atheist.

Spinoza's most influential writing, the *Ethics*, was published after his death in 1677. Religious leaders universally condemned it for its apparent espousal of pantheism. God and nature were so closely identified by Spinoza that little room seemed left either for divine revelation in scripture or for the personal immortality of the soul, denials equally repugnant to Jews and to Christians. The *Ethics* was a very complicated work, written in the spirit of the new science as a geometrical system of definitions, axioms, and propositions. It was divided into five parts, which dealt with God, the mind, emotions, human bondage, and human freedom.

The most controversial part of the *Ethics* deals with the nature of substance and of God. According to Spinoza, there is but one substance, which is self-caused, free, and infinite, and God is that substance. From this definition it follows that everything that exists is in God and cannot even be conceived of apart from him. Such a doctrine is not literally pantheistic because God is still seen to be more than the created world that he, as primal substance, embraces. It may perhaps best be described as *panentheism:* the teaching that all that is is within God, yet God remains more than and beyond the natural world. Nonetheless, in Spinoza's view, statements about the natural world are also statements about divine nature. Mind and matter are seen to be extensions of the infinite substance of God; what transpires in the world of humankind and nature is a necessary outpouring of the divine.

Such teaching clearly ran the danger of portraying the world as eternal and human actions as unfree and inevitable, the expression of a divine fatalism. Such points of view have been considered heresies by Jews and Christians because they deny the creation of the world by God in time and destroy any voluntary basis for personal reward and punishment.

Spinoza found enthusiastic supporters in the nineteenth-century German philosopher Georg Wilhelm Friedrich Hegel and in romantic writers of the same century, especially Johann Wolfgang von Goethe and Percy Bysshe Shelley. Modern thinkers who are unable to accept traditional religious language and doctrines have continued to find in Spinoza a congenial rational religion.

Thomas Hobbes (1588–1679)

Thomas Hobbes was incontestably the most original political philosopher of the seventeenth century. The son of a clergyman, he was educated at Magdalen College of Oxford University during a period when Puritanism was dominant there. Although he never broke with the Church of England, he came to share basic Calvinist beliefs, especially the low view of human nature and the ideal of a commonwealth based on a covenant, both of which find eloquent expression in Hobbes's political philosophy.

Hobbes was an urbane and much-traveled man and one of the most enthusiastic supporters of the new scientific movement. He worked as tutor and secretary to three earls of Devonshire over a fifty-year period. During the 1630s he visited Paris, where he came to know Descartes, and after the outbreak of the Puritan Revolution in 1640, he lived as an exile in Paris until 1651. In 1646 Hobbes became the tutor of the Prince of Wales, the future Charles II, and remained on good terms with him after the restoration of the Stuart monarchy. Hobbes also spent time with Galileo in Italy and took a special interest in the works of William Harvey (1578–1657). Harvey was a physiologist famed for the discovery of how blood circulated through the body; his scientific writings influenced Hobbes's own tracts on bodily motions. Hobbes became an expert in geometry and optics. Also highly trained in classical languages, his first published work was a translation of Thucydides' *History of the Peloponnesian War,* the first English translation of this work and one that is still reprinted today.

Hobbes was driven to the vocation of political philosophy by the English Civil War. In 1651 his *Leviathan* appeared. Written as the concluding part of a broad philosophical system that analyzed physical bodies and human nature, the work established Hobbes as a major European thinker. Its subject was the political consequences of human passions and its originality lay in (1) its making natural law, rather than common law (i.e., custom or precedent), the basis of all positive law, and (2) its defense of a representative theory of absolute authority against the theory of the divine right of kings. Hobbes maintained that statute law found its justification only as an expression of the law of nature and that political authority came to rulers by way of the consent of the people.

Hobbes viewed humankind and society in a thoroughly materialistic and mechanical way. Human beings are defined as a collection of material particles in motion. All their psychological processes begin with and are derived from bare sensation, and all their motivations are egoistical, intended to increase pleasure and minimize pain. The human power of reasoning, which Hobbes defined unspectacularly as a process of adding and subtracting the consequences of agreed-upon general names of things, develops only after years of concentrated industry. Human will Hobbes defined as simply "the last appetite before choice."

Despite this seemingly low estimate of human beings, Hobbes believed much could be accomplished by the reasoned use of science. All was contingent, however, on the correct use of that

Non est potestas Super Terram quæ Comparetur ei Iob. 41. 24.

The famous title-page illustration for Hobbes's Leviathan. *The ruler is pictured as absolute lord of his lands, but note that the ruler incorporates the mass of individuals whose self-interests are best served by their willing consent to accept him and cooperate with him.*

greatest of all human powers, one compounded of the powers of most people: the commonwealth, in which people are united by their consent in one all-powerful person.

The key to Hobbes's political philosophy is a brilliant myth of the original state of humankind. According to this myth, human beings in the natural state are generally inclined to a "perpetual and restless desire of power after power that ceases only in death."[7] As all people desire and in the state of nature have a natural right to everything, their equality breeds enmity, competition, diffidence, and the desire for glory beget perpetual quarreling—"a war of every man against every man."[8] As Hobbes put it in a famous summary:

In such condition there is no place for industry, because the fruit thereof is uncertain; and consequently no culture of the earth; no navigation nor use of the commodities that may be imported by sea; no commodious building; no instruments of moving and removing such things

[7] *Leviathan Parts I and II,* ed. by H. W. Schneider (Indianapolis: Bobbs-Merrill, 1958), p. 86.

[8] Ibid., p. 106.

as require much force; no knowledge of the face of the earth; no account of time; no arts; no letters; no society; and, which is worst of all, continual fear and danger of violent death; and the life of man solitary, poor, nasty, brutish, and short.[9]

Whereas earlier and later philosophers saw the original human state as a paradise from which humankind had fallen, Hobbes saw it as a corruption from which only society had delivered people. Contrary to the views of Aristotle and Christian thinkers like Thomas Aquinas, in the view of Hobbes human beings are not by nature sociable, political animals; they are self-centered beasts, law unto themselves, utterly without a master unless one is imposed by force.

According to Hobbes, people escape the impossible state of nature only by entering a social contract that creates a commonwealth tightly ruled by law and order. They are driven to this solution by their fear of death and their desire for "commodious living." The social contract obliges every person, for the sake of peace and self-defense, to agree to set aside personal rights to all things and to be content with as much liberty against others as he or she would allow others against himself or herself. All agree to live according to a secularized version of the golden rule: "Do not that to another which you would not have done to yourself."[10]

Because words and promises are insufficient to guarantee this state, the social contract also establishes the coercive force necessary to compel compliance with the covenant. Hobbes believed that the dangers of anarchy were far greater than those of tyranny and conceived of the ruler as absolute and unlimited in power, once established in office. There is no room in Hobbes's political philosophy for political protest in the name of individual conscience, nor for resistance to legitimate authority by private individuals—features of the *Leviathan* criticized by contemporary Catholics and Puritans alike. To his critics, who lamented the loss of their individual liberty in such a government, Hobbes pointed out the alternative:

The greatest that in any form of government can possibly happen to the people in general is scarce sensible in respect of the miseries and horrible calamities that accompany a civil war or that dissolute condition of master-

less men, without subjection to laws and a coercive power to tie their hands from rapine and revenge.[11]

It is puzzling why Hobbes believed that absolute rulers would be more benevolent and less egoistic than all other people. He simply placed the highest possible value on a strong, efficient ruler who could save human beings from the chaos attendant on the state of nature. In the end it mattered little to Hobbes whether this ruler was Charles I, Oliver Cromwell, or Charles II, each of whom received Hobbes's enthusiastic support, once he was established in power.

John Locke (1632–1704)

Locke has proved to be the most influential political thinker of the seventeenth century. His political philosophy came to be embodied in the Glorious Revolution of 1688–1689. Although he was not as original as Hobbes, his political writings were a major source of the later Enlightenment criticism of absolutism, and they gave inspiration to both the American and the French revolutions.

Locke was reared in a family whose sympathies lay with the Puritans and the Parliamentary forces that challenged the Stuart monarchy. His father fought with the Parliamentary army during the English Civil War. Locke read deeply in the works of Francis Bacon, René Descartes, and Isaac Newton and was a close friend of the English physicist and chemist Robert Boyle (1627–1691). Some argue that Locke was the first philosopher to be successful in synthesizing the rationalism of Descartes and the experimental science of Bacon, Newton, and Boyle.

Locke was for a brief period strongly influenced by the conservative political views of Hobbes. This influence changed, however, after his association with Anthony Ashley Cooper, the earl of Shaftesbury. In 1667 Locke moved into Shaftesbury's London home, where he served as physician, secretary, and traveling companion. A zealous Protestant, Shaftesbury was considered by his contemporaries a radical in both religion and politics. He organized an unsuccessful rebellion against Charles II in 1682 in the hope of excluding Charles's Catholic brother, James, from the English throne and putting the king's bastard son, the earl

[9] Ibid., p. 107.
[10] Ibid., p. 130.

[11] Ibid., p. 152.

of Monmouth, in James's place. Although Locke had no part in the plot, both he and Shaftesbury were forced to flee to Holland after its failure.

Locke's two most famous works are the *Essay Concerning Human Understanding* (1690), completed during his exile in Holland, and the *Two Treatises of Government* (1690). In the *Essay Concerning Human Understanding* Locke stressed the creative function of the human mind. He believed that the mind at birth was a blank tablet. In Locke's view, contrary to that of much medieval philosophy, there are no innate ideas; all knowledge is derived from actual sensual experience. Human ideas are either simple (that is, passive receptions from daily experience) or complex (that is, products of sustained mental exercise). What people know is not the external world in itself but the results of the interaction of the mind with the outside world. Locke also denied the existence of innate moral norms. Moral ideals are the product of humankind's subjection of their

❧ John Locke Explains the Sources of Human Knowledge

An Essay Concerning Human Understanding (1690) was probably the most influential philosophical work ever written in English. Locke's most fundamental idea, which is explicated in the passage below, was that human knowledge is grounded in the experiences of the senses and in the reflection of the mind on those experiences. He rejected any belief in innate ideas. His emphasis on experience led to the wider belief that human beings are creatures of their environment. After Locke, numerous writers argued that human beings could be improved if the environment in which they lived were reformed.

Let us then suppose the mind to be, as we say, white paper void of all characters, without any ideas. How comes it to be furnished? Whence comes it by that vast store which the busy and boundless fancy of man has painted on it with an almost endless variety? Whence has it all the materials of reason and knowledge? To this I answer, in one word, from experience; *in that all our knowledge is founded, and from that it ultimately derives itself. Our observation, employed either about* external sensible objects, *or about the internal operations of our minds perceived and reflected on by ourselves, is that which supplies our understanding with all the materials of thinking. These two are the fountains of knowledge, from whence all the ideas we have, or can naturally have, do spring.*

First, our senses, *conversant about particular sensible objects, do* convey into the mind *several distinct* perceptions *of things, according to those various ways wherein those objects do affect them. And thus we come by those* ideas *we have of* yellow, white, heat, cold, soft, hard, bitter, sweet, *and all those which we call sensible qualities. . . . This great source of most of the* ideas *we have, depending wholly upon our senses, and derived by them to the understanding, I call SENSATION.*

Secondly, the other fountain from which experience furnisheth the understanding with ideas *is the perception of the operations of our own minds within us, as it is employed about the* ideas *it has got. . . . And such are* perception, thinking, doubting, believing, reasoning, knowing, willing, *and all the different actings of our own minds. . . . I call this REFLECTION, the* ideas *it affords being such only as the mind gets by reflecting on its own operations within itself. . . . These two, I say, viz. external material things as the objects of SENSATION, and the operations of our own minds within as the objects of REFLECTION, are to me the only originals from whence all our* ideas *take their beginnings. . . .*

The understanding seems to me not to have the least glimmering of any ideas *which it doth not receive from one of these two.*

John Locke, *An Essay Concerning Human Understanding*, Vol. 1 (London: Everyman's Library, 1961), pp. 77–78.

self-love to their reason—a freely chosen self-disciplining of natural desires so that conflict in conscience may be avoided and happiness attained. Locke also believed that the teachings of Christianity were identical to what uncorrupted reason taught about the good life. A rational person would therefore always live according to simple Christian precepts. Although Locke firmly denied toleration to Catholics and atheists—both were considered subversive in England—he otherwise sanctioned a variety of Protestant religious practice.

Locke wrote *Two Treatises of Government* during the reign of Charles II. They are directed against the argument that rulers were absolute in their power. According to the preface of the published edition, which appeared after the Glorious Revolution, the treatises were written "to justify to the world the people of England, whose love of their just and natural rights, with their resolution to preserve them, saved the nation when it was on the brink of slavery and ruin."[12] Locke opposed particularly the views of Sir Robert Filmer and Thomas Hobbes.

Filmer had written a work entitled *Patriarcha, or the Natural Power of Kings* (published in 1680), in which the rights of kings over their subjects were compared with the rights of fathers over their children. Locke devoted the entire first treatise to a refutation of Filmer's argument, maintaining not only that the analogy was inappropriate, but that even the right of a father over his children could not be construed as absolute and was subject to a higher natural law. Both fathers and rulers, Locke argued, remain bound to the law of nature, which is the voice of reason, teaching that "all mankind [are] equal and independent, [and] no one ought to harm another in his life, health, liberty, or possessions,"[13] inasmuch as all human beings are the images and property of God. According to Locke, people enter into social contracts, empowering legislatures and monarchs to "umpire" their disputes, precisely in order to preserve their natural rights, and not to give rulers an absolute power over them. Rulers are rather "entrusted" with the preservation of the law of nature and transgress it at their peril:

Whenever that end [namely, the preservation of life, liberty, and property for which power is given to rulers by a commonwealth] is manifestly neglected or opposed, the trust must necessarily be forfeited and the power devolve into the hands of those that gave it, who may place it anew where they think best for their safety and security.[14]

From Locke's point of view absolute monarchy was "inconsistent" with civil society and could be "no form of civil government at all."

Locke's main differences with Hobbes stemmed from the latter's well-known views on the state of nature. Locke believed that the natural human state was one of perfect freedom and equality. Here the natural rights of life, liberty, and property were enjoyed, in unregulated fashion, by all. The only thing lacking in the state of nature was a single authority to give judgment when disputes inevitably arose because of the natural freedom and equality possessed by all. Contrary to the view of Hobbes, human beings in their natural state were not creatures of monomaniacal passion but were possessed of extreme goodwill and rationality. They did not surrender their natural rights unconditionally when they entered the social contract; rather, they established a means whereby these rights could be better preserved. The state of warfare that Hobbes believed characterized the state of nature emerged for Locke only when rulers failed in their responsibility to preserve the freedoms of the state of nature and attempted to enslave people by absolute rule, that is, to remove them from their "natural" condition. Only then were the peace, goodwill, mutual assistance, and preservation in which human beings naturally live and socially ought to live undermined, and a state of war was created.

Suggested Readings

V. M. Brittain, *Valiant Pilgrim: The Story of John Bunyan and Puritan England* (1950). Illustrated historical biography.

K. C. Brown, *Hobbes Studies* (1965). A collection of important essays.

Herbert Butterfield, *The Origins of Modern Science 1300–1800* (1949). An authoritative survey.

---

[12] *The Second Treatise of Government*, ed. by T. P. Peardon (Indianapolis: Bobbs-Merrill, 1952), Preface.

[13] Ibid., Ch. 2, sects. 4–6, pp. 4–6.

[14] Ibid., Ch. 13, sect. 149, p. 84.

JOHN CAIRD, *Spinoza* (1971). Intellectual biography by a philosopher.

NORMAN F. CANTOR, (Ed.), *Seventeenth Century Rationalism: Bacon and Descartes* (1969).

CERVANTES, *The Portable Cervantes*, ed. and trans. by Samuel Putnam (1969).

HARDIN CRAIG, *Shakespeare: A Historical and Critical Study with Annotated Texts of Twenty-one Plays* (1958).

MAURICE CRANSTON, *Locke* (1961). Brief biographical sketch.

J. DUNN, *The Political Thought of John Locke; An Historical Account of the "Two Treatises of Government"* (1969). An excellent introduction.

MANUEL DURAN, *Cervantes* (1974). Detailed biography.

GALILEO GALILEI, *Discoveries and Opinions of Galileo*, ed. and trans. by Stillman Drake (1957).

A. R. HALL, *The Scientific Revolution 1500–1800: The Formation of the Modern Scientific Attitude* (1966). Traces undermining of traditional science and rise of new sciences.

THOMAS HOBBES, *Leviathan. Parts I and II*, ed. by H. W. Schneider (1958).

MARGARET JACOB, *The Newtonians and The English Revolution* (1976). A controversial book that attempts to relate science and politics.

T. E. JESSOP, *Thomas Hobbes* (1960). Brief biographical sketch.

H. KEARNEY, *Science and Change 1500–1700* (1971). Broad survey.

ALEXANDER KOYRE, *From the Closed World to the Infinite Universe* (1957). Treated from perspective of the historian of ideas.

THOMAS S. KUHN, *The Copernican Revolution* (1957). A scholarly treatment.

PETER LASLETT, *Locke's Two Treatises of Government*, 2nd ed. (1970). Definitive texts with very important introductions.

JOHN D. NORTH, *Isaac Newton* (1967). Brief biography.

ALAN G. R. SMITH, *Science and Society* (1973). A readable, well-illustrated history of the Scientific Revolution.

E. M. W. TILLYARD, *Milton* (1952). Brief biographical sketch.

RICHARD S. WESTFALL, *Never at Rest: A Biography of Isaac Newton* (1981). A new and very important major study.

528

18 The Waxing and Waning of States (1686-1740)

The late seventeenth and early eighteenth centuries witnessed significant shifts of power and influence among the states of Europe. Nations that had been strong lost their status as significant military and economic units. Other countries, which had in some cases figured only marginally in international relations, came to the fore. Great Britain, France, Austria, Russia, and Prussia emerged during this period as the powers that would dominate Europe until at least World War I. The establishment of their political and economic dominance occurred at the expense of Spain, the United Netherlands, Poland, Sweden, and the Ottoman Empire. Equally essential to their rise was the weakness of the Holy Roman Empire after the Treaty of Westphalia (1648).

Peter the Great, who epitomized the state-building monarchs of the late seventeenth and early eighteenth centuries. This portrait, which was done by Kneller in 1698, is in Kensington Palace in London. [New York Public Library Picture Collection.]

The successful competitors for international power were those states that in differing fashions created strong central political authorities. Far-sighted observers in the late seventeenth century already understood that in the future those domains that would become or remain great powers must imitate the political and military organization of Louis XIV. Monarchy alone could impose unity of purpose on the state. The turmoil of seventeenth-century civil wars and aristocratic revolts had impressed people with the value of the monarch as a guarantor of minimum domestic tranquillity. Imitation of French absolutism involved other factors besides belief in a strong monarchy. It usually required building a standing army, organizing an efficient tax structure to support the army, and establishing a bureaucracy to collect the taxes. Moreover the political classes of the country, especially the nobles, had to be converted to a sense of duty and loyalty to the central government that was more intense than their loyalty to other competing political and social institutions.

The waning powers of Europe were those whose leaders failed to achieve such effective organization. They were unable to employ their political, economic, and human resources to resist external aggression or to overcome the forces of domestic dissolution. The internal and external failures were closely related. If a state failed to maintain or establish a central political authority with sufficient power over the nobility, the cities, the guilds, and the church, it could not raise a strong army to defend its borders or its economic interests. More often than not the key element leading to success or failure was the character, personality, and energy of the monarch.

The Maritime Powers

In western Europe, Britain and France emerged as the dominant powers. This development represented a shift of influence away from Spain and the United Netherlands. Both the latter countries had been quite strong and important during the sixteenth and seventeenth centuries, but they became negligible during the course of the eighteenth century. However, neither disappeared from the map. Both retained considerable economic vitality and influence. The difference was that France and Britain attained so much more power and economic strength.

Spain

Spanish power had depended on the influx of wealth from the Americas and on the capacity of the Spanish monarchs to rule the still largely autonomous provinces of the Iberian peninsula. The economic life of the nation was never healthy. Except for wool Spain had virtually no exports with which to pay for its imports. Instead of promoting domestic industries, the Spanish government financed imports by using the gold and silver mined in its New World empire. This external source of wealth was not certain because the treasure fleets from the New World could be and sometimes were captured by pirates or the navies of other nations. The political life of Spain was also weak. Within Castile, Aragon, Navarre, the Basque provinces, and other districts, the royal government could not operate without the close cooperation of strong local nobles and the church. From the defeat of the Spanish Armada in 1588 to the Treaty of the Pyrenees in 1659, Spain experienced a series of foreign policy reverses that harmed the domestic

The reign of Charles II of Spain (1665–1700) saw the power of the crown greatly weaken. He was the last Hapsburg king of the country, for in him the line at last failed; deformed (the Hapsburg jaw carried to parody made it almost impossible for him to eat), dull, and impotent, he left no heir. Louis XIV's successful determination to have his grandson succeed Charles led to the War of the Spanish Succession. [The Granger Collection.]

prestige of the monarchy. Furthermore, between 1665 and 1700 the physically malformed, dull-witted, and sexually impotent Charles II was monarch. Throughout his reign the local provincial estates and the nobility increased their power. On his death the War of the Spanish Succession saw the other powers of Europe contesting the issue of the next ruler of Spain.

The Treaty of Utrecht (1713) gave the Spanish crown to Philip V (1770–1746), who was a Bourbon and the grandson of Louis XIV. The new king should have attempted to consolidate his internal power and to protect Spanish overseas trade. However, his second wife, Elizabeth Farnese, wanted to use Spanish power to carve out interests for her sons on the Italian peninsula. Such machinations diverted government resources and allowed the nobility and the provinces to continue to assert their privileges against the authority of the monarchy. Not until the reign of Charles III (1759–1788) did Spain possess a monarch concerned with efficient administration and internal improvement. By the third quarter of the century the country was better governed, but it could no longer compete effectively in power politics.

The Netherlands

The demise of the United Netherlands occurred wholly within the eighteenth century. After the death of William III in 1702, the various local provinces successfully prevented the emergence of another strong *stadtholder*. Unified political leadership therefore vanished. During the earlier long wars of the Netherlands with Louis XIV and England, naval supremacy slowly but steadily had passed to the British. The fishing industry declined, and the Dutch lost their technological superiority in shipbuilding. Countries between which Dutch ships had once carried goods now came to trade directly with each other. For example, the British began to use more and more of their own vessels in the Baltic traffic with Russia. Similar stag-

Dutch shipbuilding remained important throughout the seventeenth and eighteenth centuries, although not as prosperous as in the sixteenth. Ships, such as this one being constructed at Amsterdam in 1694, were the sinews of trade during the period. The building in the background is the headquarters of the Dutch West Indies Company, which settled New Amsterdam (subsequently New York). [The Granger Collection.]

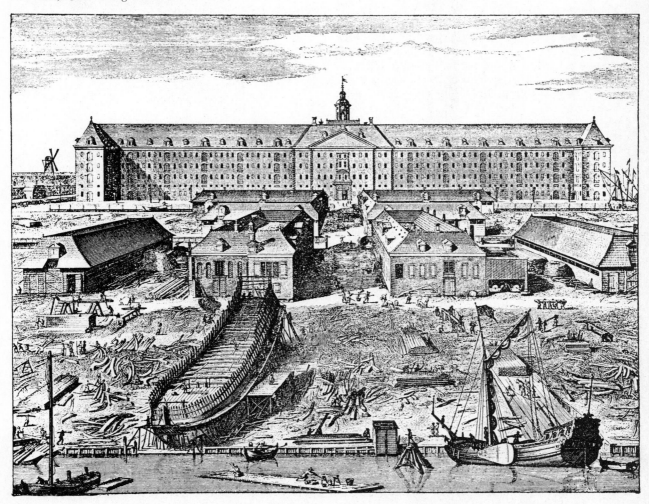

nation overtook the Dutch domestic industries, such as textile finishing, paper making, and glass blowing. The disunity of the provinces and the absence of vigorous leadership hastened this economic decline and prevented action that might have slowed or halted it. What saved the United Netherlands from becoming completely insignificant in European matters was their continued dominance of the financial community. Well past the middle of the century their banks continued to provide loans and financing for European trade.

France After Louis XIV

Despite its military losses in the War of the Spanish Succession, France remained a great power. It was less strong in 1715 than in 1680, but it still possessed a large population, an advanced if troubled economy, and the administrative structure bequeathed it by Louis XIV. Moreover, even if France and its resources had been badly drained by the last of Louis's wars, the other major states of Europe emerged from the conflict similarly debilitated. What the country required was a period of economic recovery and consolidation, wiser political leadership, and a less ambitious foreign policy. It did enjoy a period of recovery, but the quality of its leadership was at best indifferent. Louis XIV was succeeded by his five-year-old great-grandson Louis XV (1715–1774). The young boy's uncle, the duke of Orléans, became regent and remained so until 1720. The regency further undermined the already faltering prestige of the monarchy.

The duke of Orléans was a gambler, and for a time he turned over the financial management of the kingdom to John Law (1671–1729), a Scottish mathematician and fellow gambler. Law believed that an increase in the paper money supply would stimulate the postwar economic recovery of the country. With the permission of the regent he established a bank in Paris that issued paper money. Law then organized the Mississippi Company, which was to possess a monopoly on trading privileges with the French colony of Louisiana in North America.

The Mississippi Company also assumed the management of the French national debt. The company issued shares of its own stock in exchange for government bonds, which had fallen sharply in value. In order to redeem large quantities of bonds, Law encouraged speculation in Mississippi Company stock. In 1719 the price of the stock rose handsomely. However, smart investors took their profits by selling their stock in exchange for money from Law's bank. Then they sought to exchange the currency for gold. To make the second transaction, they went to Law's bank, but that institution lacked sufficient gold to redeem all the money brought to it.

In February 1720 all gold payments were halted in France. Soon thereafter Law himself fled the country. The Mississippi Bubble, as the affair was called, had burst. The fiasco brought disgrace on the government that had made Law its controller general. The Mississippi Company was later reorganized and functioned quite profitably, but fear of paper money and speculation marked French economic life for the rest of the century.

The duke of Orléans made a second departure that also lessened the power of the monarchy. He attempted to draw the French nobility once again

The Duke of Orleans was regent of France during the minority of Louis XV, years marked by financial scandal and weak administration. [The Granger Collection.]

❦ Saint-Simon Shows the French Nobility's Incapacity to Govern

The regent under the young Louis XV hoped that France's nobility might assume an active role in government in place of the passive role assigned to them by Louis XIV. This plan involved displacing many nonnoble bureaucrats and others who were regarded as noble by virtue of holding office rather than by virtue of noble birth ("nobles of the robe"). As described by the duke of Saint-Simon (1675–1755), the plan failed because the real nobles proved unequal to their new duties.

The design was to begin to put the nobility into the ministry, with the dignity and authority befitting them, at the expense of the high civil servants and nobles of the robe, and by degree and according to events to guide affairs wisely so that little by little those commoners would lose all those administrative duties that are not purely judicial . . . in order to submit to the nobility all modes of administration. The difficulty was the ignorance, the frivolity, and the lack of diligence of the nobility who were accus-tomed to being good for nothing except getting killed, succeeding at war only by seniority, and romping around for the rest of the time in the most mortal uselessness. As a result they were devoted to idleness and disgusted with all knowledge outside war by their conditioned incapacity for being able to provide themselves with anything useful to do. It was impossi-ble to make the first step in this direction without overturning the monster that had devoured the nobil-ity, the controller general and the secretaries of state.

Duc de Saint-Simon, *Memoires,* trans. by Frank M. Turner, cited in John Lough, *An Introduction to Eighteenth Century France* (New York: David MacKay, 1964), pp. 135–136.

---

into the decision-making processes of the government. Louis XIV had downgraded the nobility and had filled his ministries and bureaucracies with persons of nonnoble families. The regent was seeking to restore a balance. He adopted a system of councils on which the nobles were to serve along with the bureaucrats. However, the years of noble domestication at Versailles had worked too well, and the nobility seemed to lack both the talent and the desire to govern. The experiment failed.

The failure of the great French nobles to function as satisfactory councilors did not mean that they had surrendered their ancient ambition to assert their rights, privileges, and local influence over those of the monarchy. The chief feature of the French political life from this time until the French Revolution was the attempt of the nobility to impose its power on the monarchy. The most effective instrument in this process was the *parlements,* or courts dominated by the nobility. The French *parlements* were very different institutions from the English Parliament. These French courts, the most important of which was the *Parlement* of Paris, did not have the power to legislate. Rather, they had the power to recognize or not to recognize the legality of an act or law promulgated by the monarch. By long tradition their formal approval had been required to make a royal law valid. Louis XIV had often overridden stubborn, uncooperative *parlements.* However, in another of his many major political blunders, the duke of Orléans had formally approved the reinstitution of the *parlements'* power to allow or disallow laws. Thereafter the growing financial and moral weakness of the eighteenth-century monarchy allowed these aristocratic judicial institutions to reassert their authority. This situation meant that for the rest of the century until the revolution the *parlements* became natural centers for aristocratic resistance to royal authority.

By 1726 the chief minister of the French court was Cardinal Fleury (1653–1743). He was the last of those great churchmen who had so loyally and effectively served the French monarchy. Like his seventeenth-century predecessors, the cardinals Richelieu and Mazarin, Fleury was a realist. He understood the political ambition and incapacity of the nobility and worked quietly to block their undue influence. Fleury was also aware of the pre-

In 1722 the young great-grandson of Louis XIV was crowned the new King of France as
Louis XV in the Cathedral of Rheims. He was then twelve years old and had already been king
for seven years. This painting by J. B. Martin shows the moment in the darkened cathedral
when the young king was anointed. It is now in the museum at Versailles. [Cliché des Musées
Nationaux.]

carious financial situation in which the wars of
Louis XIV had left the royal treasury.

The cardinal, who was seventy-three years old
when he came to office, was determined to give the
country a period of peace. He surrounded himself
with generally able assistants who attempted to
solve the financial problems. Part of the national
debt was repudiated. New industries enjoying special privileges were established, and new roads and
bridges were built. On the whole the nation pros-

534

pered, but Fleury was never able to draw from the nobles or the church sufficient tax revenues to put the state on a stable financial footing.

Fleury died in 1743, having unsuccessfully attempted to prevent France from intervening in the war then raging between Austria and Prussia. All of his financial pruning and planning had come to nought. Another failure must also be credited to this elderly churchman. Despite his best efforts he had not trained Louis XV to become an effective monarch. Louis XV possessed most of the vices and almost none of the virtues of his great-grandfather. He wanted to hold on to absolute power but was unwilling to work the long hours required. He did not choose many wise advisers after Fleury. He was tossed about by the gossip and intrigues of the court nobles. His personal life was scandalous. His reign became more famous for his mistress, Madame de Pompadour, than for anything else. Louis

Cardinal Fleury, tutor and chief minister of Louis XV from 1726 until 1743. He strove to bring peace and financial stability to France but was finally unsuccessful on both counts. This portrait by Hyacinthe Rigaud is at Versailles. [Photographie Bulloz, Paris.]

Louis XV in coronation robes, painted by Hyacinthe Rigaud in 1730. Although by no means unintelligent, Louis was lazy and pleasure-loving. His scandalous private life lessened respect for the French monarchy. [Photographie Bulloz, Paris.]

XV was not an evil person but a mediocre one. And in a monarch mediocrity was unfortunately often a greater fault than vice.

Despite this political drift France remained a great power. Its army at mid-century was still the largest and strongest military force on the Continent. Its commerce and production expanded. Its colonies produced wealth and spurred domestic industries. Its cities grew and prospered. The wealth of the nation waxed as the absolutism of the monarchy waned. France did not lack sources of power and strength, but it did lack the political leadership that could organize, direct, and inspire its people.

Madame de Pompadour (1721–1764) was the first official mistress of Louis XV and a person of beauty, cultivation, and ambition. After her death the king had an increasing number of mistresses, both unofficial and official, but none were as cultured as she, and inevitably, the increasingly low moral tone of the French court did much to undermine the loyalty of the general public for the throne. This lovely portrait of his patroness is by one of the eighteenth century's masters, François Boucher (1703–1770). It is now in the National Gallery of Scotland in Edinburgh. [The Granger Collection.]

Great Britain: The Age of Walpole

In 1713 Britain had emerged as a victor over Louis XIV, but the nation required a period of recovery. As an institution the British monarchy was not in the degraded state of the French monarchy, but its stability was not certain. In 1714 the Hanoverian dynasty, designated by the Act of Settlement (1701), came to the throne. Almost immediately George I (1714–1727) confronted a challenge to his new title. The Stuart pretender James Edward (1688–1766), the son of James II, landed in Scotland in December 1715. His forces marched southward but met defeat less than two months later.

Although militarily successful against the pretender, the new dynasty and its supporters saw the need for consolidation. During the seventeenth

FRANCE AND GREAT BRITAIN IN THE EARLY EIGHTEENTH CENTURY

1713	Treaty of Utrecht ends the War of the Spanish Succession
1714	George I becomes king of Great Britain and thus establishes the Hanoverian dynasty
1715	Louis XV becomes King of France
1715–1720	Regency of the duke of Orléans in France
1720	Mississippi Bubble bursts in France and South Sea Bubble bursts in Great Britain
1720–1742	Robert Walpole dominates British politics
1726–1743	Cardinal Fleury serves as Louis XV's chief minister
1727	George II becomes king of Great Britain
1733	Excise bill crisis in Britain
1739	War of Jenkins's Ear commences between England and Spain

George I of Great Britain was originally the Elector of Hanover in Germany. He succeeded to the British throne in 1714. This painting is from Godfrey Kneller's studio. [The Granger Collection.]

century England had been one of the most politically restive countries in Europe. The closing years of Queen Anne's reign (1702–1714) had seen sharp clashes between the political factions of Whigs and Tories over the coming Treaty of Utrecht. The Tories had urged a rapid peace settlement and after 1710 had opened negotiations with France. During the same period the Whigs were seeking favor from the Elector of Hanover, who would soon be their monarch. His concern for his domains in Hanover made him unsympathetic to the Tory peace policy. In the final months of Anne's reign some Tories, fearing loss of power under the waiting Hanoverian dynasty, opened channels of communication with the Stuart pretender; and a few even rallied to his losing cause.

Under these circumstances it was little wonder that George I, on his arrival in Britain, clearly favored the Whigs and proceeded with caution. Previously the differences between the Whigs and the Tories had been vaguely related to principle. The Tories emphasized a strong monarchy, low taxes for landowners, and firm support of the Anglican church. The Whigs supported monarchy but wanted Parliament to retain final sovereignty.

They tended to favor urban commercial interests as well as the prosperity of the landowners. They encouraged a policy of religious toleration toward the Protestant nonconformists in England. Socially both groups supported the status quo. Neither was organized like a modern political party. Organizationally, outside of Parliament, each party consisted of political networks based on local political connections and local economic influence. Each group acknowledged a few spokesmen on the national level who articulated positions and principles. However, after the Hanoverian accession and the eventual Whig success in achieving the firm confidence of George I, the chief difference for almost forty years between the Whigs and the Tories was that one group did have access to public office and patronage and the other did not. This early Hanoverian proscription of Tories from public life was one of the most prominent features of the age.

The political situation after 1715 had at first remained in a state of flux until Robert Walpole (1676–1745) took over the helm of government. This Norfolk squire had been active in the House of Commons since the reign of Queen Anne, and he had served as a cabinet minister. What gave him special prominence under the new dynasty was a British financial scandal similar to the French Mississippi Bubble.

Management of the British national debt had been assigned to the South Sea Company, which

A series of four Hogarth etchings satirizing an English parliamentary election. In a savage indictment of the notoriously corrupt English electoral system, Hogarth shows the voters going to the polls after having been bribed and intoxicated with free gin. (Note that voting was in public. The secret ballot was not introduced in England until 1872.) The fourth etching, *Chairing the Member*, shows the triumphal procession of the victorious candidate, which is clearly turning into a brawl. [Metropolitan Museum of Art.]

Sir Robert Walpole (1676–1745) dominated the British government under George I and George II from 1721 to 1742. He brought political stability to eighteenth-century Britain by winning the king's trust and by his skillful, if sometimes ruthless, use of government patronage. [National Portrait Gallery, London.]

exchanged government bonds for company stock. As in the French case, the price of the stock flew high, only to crash in 1720 when prudent investors sold their holdings and took their speculative profits. Parliament intervened and under Walpole's leadership adopted measures to honor the national debt. To most contemporaries Walpole had saved the financial integrity of the country and, in so doing, had proved himself a person of immense administrative capacity and political ability.

George I gave Walpole his full confidence. For this reason Walpole has often been regarded as the first prime minister of Great Britain and the originator of the cabinet system of government. However, unlike a modern prime minister he was not chosen by the majority of the House of Commons.

His power largely depended on the good will of George I and later of George II (1727–1760). Walpole generally demanded that all of the ministers in the cabinet agree on policy, but he could not prevent frequent public differences on policy. The real source of Walpole's power was the combination of the personal support of the king, his ability to handle the House of Commons, and his iron-fisted control of government patronage. To oppose Walpole on either minor or more substantial matters was to risk the almost certain loss of government patronage for oneself, one's family, or one's friends. Through the skillful use of patronage Walpole bought support for himself and his policies from people who wanted to receive jobs, appointments, favors, and government contracts. Such corruption supplied the glue of political loyalty.

Walpole's favorite slogan was *quieta non movere* (roughly, "let sleeping dogs lie"). To that end he pursued a policy of peace abroad and promotion of the status quo at home. In this regard he and Cardinal Fleury were much alike. The structure of the eighteenth-century British House of Commons aided Walpole in his pacific policies. It was neither a democratic nor a representative body. Each of the counties elected two members. But if the more powerful landed families in a county agreed on the candidates, there was no contest. Other members were elected from units called *boroughs*, of which there were a considerable variety. There were many more borough seats than county seats. A few were large enough for elections to be relatively democratic. However, most boroughs had a very small number of electors. For example, a local municipal corporation or council of only a dozen members might have the legal right to elect a member of Parliament. In Old Sarum, one of the most famous corrupt or "rotten" boroughs, the Pitt family for many years simply bought up those pieces of property to which a vote was attached and thus in effect owned a seat in the House of Commons. Through proper electoral management, which involved favors to the electors, the House of Commons could be controlled.

The structure of Parliament and the manner in which it was elected meant that the government of England was dominated by the owners of property and by especially wealthy nobles. They did not pretend to represent people and districts or to be responsive to what would later be called public opinion. They regarded themselves as representing various economic and social interests, such as the West Indian interest, the merchant interest, or the landed interest. These owners of property were suspicious of an administrative bureaucracy controlled by the crown or its ministers. For this reason they or their agents served as local government administrators, judges, militia commanders, and tax collectors. In this sense the British nobility and other substantial landowners actually did govern the nation. And because they regarded the Parliament as the political sovereign, there was no absence of central political authority and direction. Consequently the supremacy of Parliament provided Britain with the kind of unity that elsewhere in Europe was sought through the institutions of absolutism.

British political life was genuinely more free than that on the Continent. There were real limits to the power of Robert Walpole. Parliament could not be wholly unresponsive to popular political pressure. Even with the extensive use of patronage many members of Parliament maintained independent views. Newspapers and public debate flourished. Free speech could be exercised, as could freedom of association. There was no large standing army. Tories barred from political office and Whig enemies of Walpole could and did voice their opposition to his policies, as would not have been possible on the Continent.

For example, in 1733 Walpole presented to the House of Commons a scheme for an excise tax that would have raised revenue somewhat in the fash-

❧ Lady Mary Wortley Montagu Gives Advice on Election to Parliament

In this letter of 1714 Lady Mary Wortley Montagu discussed with her husband the various paths that he might follow to gain election to the British House of Commons. Note the emphasis she placed on knowing the right people and on having large amounts of money to spend on voters. Eventually her husband was elected to Parliament in a borough that was controlled through government patronage.

You seem not to have received my letters, or not to have understood them: you had been chose undoubtedly at York, if you had declared in time; but there is not any gentleman or tradesman disengaged at this time; they are treating every night. Lord Carlisle and the Thompsons have given their interest to Mr Jenkins. I agree with you of the necessity of your standing this Parliament, which, perhaps, may be more considerable than any that are to follow it; but, as you proceed, 'tis my opinion, you will spend your money and not be chose. I believe there is hardly a borough unengaged. I expect every letter should tell me you are sure of some place; and, as far as I can perceive you are sure of none. As it has been managed, perhaps it will be the best way to deposit a certain sum in some friend's hands, and buy some little Cornish borough: it would, undoubtedly, look better to be chose for a considerable town; but I take it to be now too late. If you have any thoughts of Newark, it

will be absolutely necessary for you to enquire after Lord Lexington's interest; and your best way to apply yourself to Lord Holdernesse, who is both a Whig and an honest man. He is now in town, and you may enquire of him if Brigadier Sutton stands there; and if not, try to engage him for you. Lord Lexington is so ill at the Bath, that it is a doubt if he will live 'till the elections; and if he dies, one of his heiresses, and the whole interest of his estate, will probably fall on Lord Holdernesse.

'Tis a surprize to me, that you cannot make sure of some borough, when a number of your friends bring in so many Parliament-men without trouble or expense. 'Tis too late to mention it now, but you might have applied to Lady Winchester, as Sir Joseph Jekyl did last year, and by her interest the Duke of Bolton brought him in, for nothing; I am sure she would be more zealous to serve me, than Lady Jekyl.

Lord Wharncliffe (ed.), *Letters and Works of Lady Mary Wortley Montagu*, 3rd ed., Vol. 1 (London, 1861), p. 211.

ion of a modern sales tax. The public outcry in the press, on the public platform, and in the streets was so great that he eventually withdrew the measure. What the English regarded as their traditional political rights raised a real and potent barrier to the power of the government. Again in 1739, the public outcry over the Spanish treatment of British merchants in the Caribbean pushed Britain into the War of Jenkins's Ear, which Walpole opposed and deplored.

Walpole's ascendancy, which lasted until 1742, did little to raise the level of British political morality, but it brought the nation a kind of stability that it had not enjoyed for well over a century. Its foreign trade grew steadily and spread from New England to India. Agriculture improved its productivity. All forms of economic enterprise seemed to prosper. The navy became stronger. As a result of this political stability and economic growth, Great Britain became a European power of the first order and stood at the beginning of its era as a world power. Its government and economy during the next generation became a model for all progressive Europeans.

Central and Eastern Europe

The major factors in the shift of political influence among the maritime nations were naval strength, economic progress, foreign trade, and sound domestic administration. The conflicts among them occurred less in Europe than on the high seas and in their empires. These nations already existed in well-defined geographical areas with established borders. Their populations generally accepted the authority of the central government.

The situation in central and eastern Europe was rather different. Except for the cities on the Baltic, the economy was agrarian. There were fewer cities and many more large estates populated by serfs. The states in this region did not possess overseas empires. Changes in the power structure normally involved changes in borders, or at least in the prince who ruled a particular area. Military conflicts took place at home rather than overseas. The political structure of this region, which lay largely east of the Elbe River, was very "soft." The almost constant warfare of the seventeenth century had led to a habit of temporary and shifting political loyalties. The princes and aristocracies of small

states and principalities were unwilling to subordinate themselves voluntarily to a central monarchical authority. Consequently the political life of the region and the kind of state that emerged there were different from those of western Europe.

Beginning in the last half of the seventeenth century, eastern and central Europe began to assume the political and social contours that would characterize it for the next two hundred years. After the Peace of Westphalia the Austrian Hapsburgs recognized the basic weakness of the position of Holy Roman Emperor and began a new consolidation of their power. At the same time the state of Prussia began to emerge as a factor in north German politics and as a major challenger to Hapsburg domination of Germany. Most importantly, Russia at the opening of the eighteenth century rose to the status of a military power of the first order. These three states (Austria, Prussia, and Russia) achieved their new status largely as a result of the political decay or military defeat of Sweden, Poland, and the Ottoman Empire.

Sweden: The Ambitions of Charles XII

Under Gustavus Adolphus II (1611–1632) Sweden had played an important role as a Protestant combatant in the Thirty Years' War. During the rest of the seventeenth century Sweden had consolidated its control of the Baltic, preventing Russian possession of a Baltic port and permitting Polish and German access to the sea only on Swedish terms. The Swedes also possessed one of the better armies in Europe. However, Sweden's economy, based primarily on the export of iron, was not strong enough to ensure continued political success.

In 1697 Charles XII (1697–1718) came to the throne. He was headstrong, to say the least, and perhaps insane. In 1700 Russia began a drive to the west against Swedish territory. The Russian goal was a foothold on the Baltic. In the resulting Great Northern War (1700–1721) Charles XII led a vigorous and often brilliant campaign, but one that eventually resulted in the defeat of Sweden. In 1700 he defeated the Russians at the battle of Narva, but then he turned south to invade Poland. The conflict dragged on, and the Russians were able to strengthen their forces. In 1708 the Swedish monarch began a major invasion of Russia but became bogged down in the harsh Russian winter. The next year his army was decisively defeated at

Charles XII of Sweden (1697–1718). Although a brave and sometimes brilliant general, Charles overreached himself. After his death, Sweden was never again the dominant Northern Power. [Svenska Portrattarkivet, National-museum, Stockholm.]

the battle of Poltava. Thereafter the Swedes could maintain only a holding action. Charles himself sought refuge with the Ottoman army and then eventually returned to Sweden in 1714. He was shot four years later while fighting the Norwegians.

The Great Northern War came to a close in 1721. Sweden had exhausted its military and economic resources and had lost its monopoly on the Baltic coast. Russia had conquered a large section of the eastern Baltic, and Prussia had gained a portion of Pomerania. Internally, after the death of Charles XII, the Swedish nobles were determined to reassert their power over that of the monarchy. They did so but then fell into quarrels among themselves. Sweden played a very minor role in European affairs thereafter.

The Ottoman Empire

At the southeastern extreme of Europe the Ottoman Empire lay as a barrier to the territorial ambitions of the Austrian Hapsburgs and of Poland and Russia. The empire in the late seventeenth century still controlled most of the Balkan peninsula and the entire coastline of the Black Sea. It was an aggressive power that had for two centuries attempted to press its control further westward in Europe. The Ottoman Empire had probably made its greatest military impression on Europe in 1683, when it laid siege to the city of Vienna.

However, the Ottomans had overextended themselves politically, economically, and militarily. The major domestic political groups resisted any substantial strengthening of the central government in Constantinople. Rivalries for power among army leaders and nobles weakened the effectiveness of the government. In the outer provinces, such as Transylvania, Wallachia, and Moldavia (all parts of modern Romania), the empire depended on the goodwill of local rulers, who never submitted themselves fully to the imperial power. The empire's economy was weak, and its exports were primarily raw materials. Moreover the actual conduct of most of its trade had been turned over to representatives of other nations.

By the early eighteenth century the weakness of the Ottoman Empire meant that on the southeastern perimeter of Europe there existed an immense political vacuum. In 1699 the Turks concluded a treaty with their longtime Hapsburg enemy and surrendered all pretensions of control over Hungary, Transylvania, Croatia, and Slavonia. From this time onward Russia also attempted to extend its territory and influence at the expense of the empire. For almost two hundred years the decay of the Ottoman Empire constituted a major factor in European international relations. The area always proved tempting to the major powers, but their distrust of each other and their conflicting rivalries, as well as a considerable residual strength on the part of the Turks, prevented the dismemberment of the empire.

Poland

In no other part of Europe was the failure to maintain a competitive political position so complete as in Poland. In 1683 King John III Sobieski (1673–1696) had led a Polish army to rescue Vi-

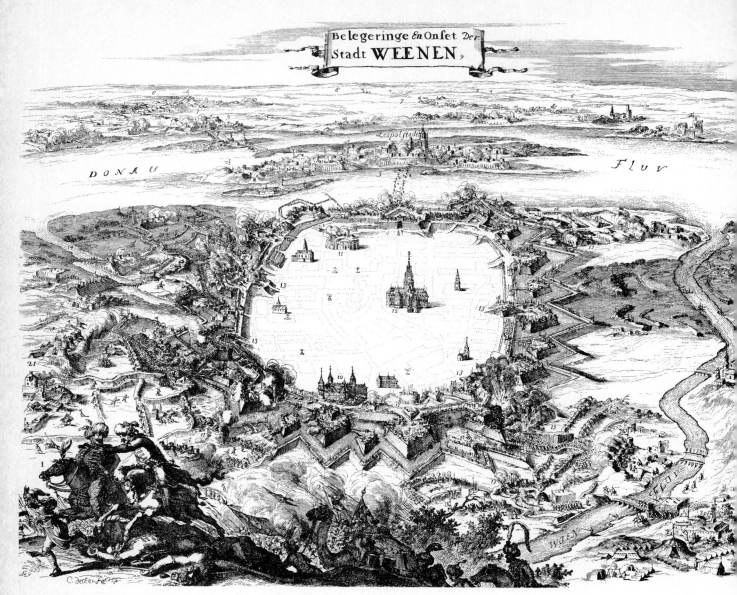

A contemporary Dutch print views the 1683 Turkish siege of Vienna from a remarkably revealing position in the hills west of the city. We are fortunate to capture the scene on the point of
the Turkish forces deciding to give up the summer-long attack; their commanders, the Ottoman
Grand Vizier and the Pasha of Adrianople, lower left, are just beginning their flight back
toward the Ottoman homelands. Polish and other Christian aid for the beleaguered Hapsburg
forces had arrived, and the battle was clearly going against the Turks. Vienna was not captured, and never again did the progressively weakening Muslim Ottoman Empire penetrate so
far west.

In the picture, note the Danube River toward the top, the elaborate zig-zag fortifications outside the walls, and bursts of artillery fire at several points. Most details inside the walled city
are omitted, but the central cathedral and the imperial palace, toward the bottom, are shown.
The walls themselves, when later torn down, made space for the Ring, the famous boulevard still
encircling central Vienna.

One unforeseen lasting social result of the siege was the further boost given to coffee drinking
by the Viennese discovery of the beverage in the deserted Turkish camps around the city. [The
Granger Collection.]

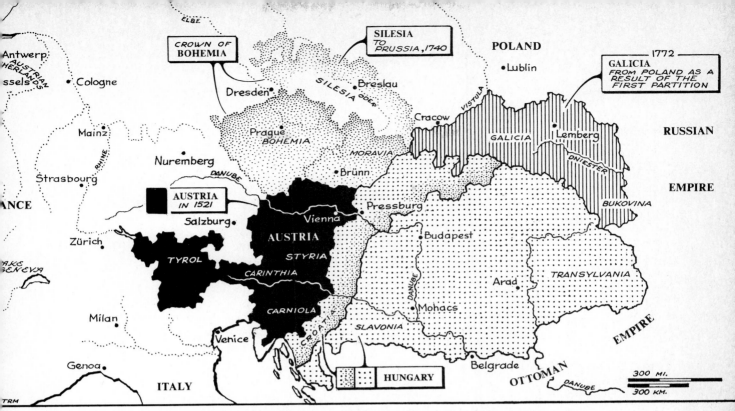

THE AUSTRIAN HAPSBURG EMPIRE, 1521–1772

MAP 18.1   *The Empire had three main units—Austria,
Bohemia, Hungary. Expansion was mainly eastward: east
Hungary from the Ottomans (17th century) and Galicia
from Poland (1772). Meantime, Silesia was lost, but Hapsburgs retained German influence as Holy Roman Emperors.*

enna from the Turkish siege. But following that
spectacular effort, Poland became little more than
a byword for the dangers of aristocratic independence. In Poland as nowhere else on the Continent
the nobility became the single most powerful political factor in the country. Unlike the British nobility
and landowners, the Polish nobility would not even
submit to a central authority of their own making.
There was no effective central authority in the
form of either a king or a parliament.

The Polish monarchy was elective, but the deep
distrust and divisions among the nobility prevented
their electing a king from among their own numbers. Sobieski was a notable exception. Most of the
Polish monarchs came from outside the borders of
the kingdom and were the tools of foreign powers.
The Polish nobles did have a central legislative
body called the *Diet*. It included only the nobles
and specifically excluded representatives from corporate bodies, such as the towns. In the Diet, however, there existed a practice known as the *liberum*

veto, whereby the staunch opposition of any single
member could require the body to disband. Such
opposition was termed *exploding the Diet*.

Government as it was developing elsewhere in
Europe simply was not tolerated in Poland.
Localism reminiscent of the Middle Ages continued to hold sway as the nobles used all their energy
to maintain their traditional "Polish liberties."
There was no way to collect sufficient taxes to build
up an army. The price of this noble liberty was
eventually the disappearance of Poland from the
map of Europe during the last half of the eighteenth century.

The Hapsburg Empire and
the Pragmatic Sanction

The close of the Thirty Years' War marked a fundamental turning point in the history of the Austrian Hapsburgs. Previously, in alliance with the
Spanish branch of the family, they had hoped to
dominate all of Germany politically and to bring it
back to the Catholic fold. They had failed to achieve
either goal, and the decline of Spanish power meant
that in future diplomatic relations the Austrian

Hapsburgs were very much on their own. The Treaty of Westphalia permitted Protestantism within the Holy Roman Empire, and the treaty also recognized the political autonomy of more than three hundred corporate German political entities within the empire. These included large units (such as Saxony, Hanover, Bavaria, and Brandenburg) and also scores of small cities, bishoprics, principalities, and territories of independent knights.

After 1648 the Hapsburg family retained firm hold on the title of Holy Roman Emperor, but the effectiveness of the title depended less on force of arms than on the cooperation that the emperor could elicit from the various political bodies in the empire. The Diet of the empire sat at Regensburg from 1663 until its dissolution in 1806. The Diet and the emperor generally regulated the daily economic and political life of Germany. The post-Westphalian

Holy Roman Empire in many ways resembled Poland with its lack of central authority. However, unlike its Polish neighbor, the Holy Roman Empire was reorganized from within as the Hapsburgs attempted to regain their authority and, as will be seen shortly, as Prussia set out on its course toward European power.

While establishing a new kind of position among the German states, the Hapsburgs began to consolidate their power and influence within their hereditary possessions. These included, first, the kingdom of Bohemia (in modern Czechoslovakia), which encompassed Silesia and Moravia, and second, the Crown of Saint Stephen, which ruled Hungary, Croatia, and Transylvania. The Hapsburgs also possessed stretches of northern Italy, as well as the Austrian Netherlands, which is present-day Belgium. In the next two centuries Haps-

Schönbrunn Palace of the Austrian Hapsburgs stands outside Vienna. Like many royal palaces of the eighteenth century, it was modeled after Louis XIV's palace of Versailles. [Austrian Information Service, New York.]

burg power and influence in Europe would be based primarily on these territories rather than on their position in Germany.

In the second half of the seventeenth century and later the Hapsburgs confronted immense problems in these hereditary territories. In each they ruled by virtue of a different title and had to gain the cooperation of the local nobility. The most difficult province was Hungary, where the Magyar nobility seemed ever ready to rebel. There was almost no common basis for political unity among peoples of such diverse languages, customs, and geography. Even the Hapsburg zeal for Roman Catholicism no longer proved a bond for unity as they continued to confront the equally zealous Calvinism of the Magyar nobles. The Hapsburgs established various central councils to chart common policies for their far-flung domains. None of these proved effective because the dynasty repeatedly had to bargain with nobles in one part of Europe in order to maintain their position in another. Consequently, for all practical purposes, not until well into the nineteenth century did the Vienna government directly affect the lives of any social group below the nobility.

Despite all these internal difficulties Leopold I (1657–1705) rallied his domains to resist the advances of the Turks and to resist the aggression of Louis XIV. He achieved Ottoman recognition of his sovereignty over Hungary in 1699 and suppressed the long rebellion of his new Magyar subjects between 1703 and 1711. He also extended his territorial holdings over much of what is today Yugoslavia and western Romania. These southeastward extensions allowed the Hapsburgs to hope to develop Mediterranean trade through the port of Trieste. The expansion at the cost of the Ottoman Empire also helped the Hapsburgs to compensate for their loss of domination over the Holy Roman Empire. Strength in the east gave them greater political leverage in Germany. Leopold was succeeded by Joseph I (1705–1711), who continued his policies.

When Charles VI (1711–1740) succeeded Joseph, he added a new problem to the old chronic one of territorial diversity. He had no male heir, and there was only the weakest of precedents for a female ruler of the Hapsburg domains. Charles feared that on his death the Austrian Hapsburg lands might fall prey to the surrounding powers, as had those of the Spanish Hapsburgs in 1700. He was determined to prevent that disaster and to provide his domains with the semblance of legal unity. To those ends, he devoted most of his reign to seeking the approval of his family, the estates of his realms, and the major foreign powers for a curious document called the *Pragmatic Sanction*.

This instrument provided the legal basis for a single line of inheritance within the Hapsburg dynasty through Charles VI's daughter Maria Theresa (1740–1780). Other members of the Hapsburg family recognized her as the rightful heir. The nobles of the various Hapsburg domains did likewise after extracting various concessions from Charles. The major states of Europe followed a similar course. Consequently, when Charles VI died in October 1740, he believed that he had secured legal unity for the Hapsburg Empire and a safe succession for his daughter. Less than two months after his death the fragility of such a paper agreement became all too apparent. In December 1740 Frederick II of Prussia invaded the Hapsburg province of Silesia. Maria Theresa would have to fight to defend her inheritance.

Prussia and the Hohenzollerns

The Hapsburg achievement was to draw together into an uncertain legal unity a collection of domains possessed by dint of separate feudal titles. The achievement of the Hohenzollerns of Brandenburg–Prussia was to acquire a similar collection of titular holdings and then to forge them into a cen-

---

AUSTRIA AND PRUSSIA IN THE LATE
SEVENTEENTH AND EARLY
EIGHTEENTH CENTURIES

1640–1688	Reign of Frederick William, the Great Elector
1657–1705	Leopold I rules Austria and resists the Turkish invasions
1683	Turkish siege of Vienna
1688–1713	Reign of Frederick I of Prussia
1699	Peace Treaty between Turks and Hapsburgs
1711–1740	Charles VI rules Austria and secures agreement to the Pragmatic Sanction
1713–1740	Frederick William I builds up the military power of Prussia
1740	Maria Theresa succeeds to the Hapsburg throne
	Frederick II violates the Pragmatic Sanction by invading Silesia

❧ Maria Theresa Discusses One Weakness of Her Throne

Scattered subjects of the multilanguage Austrian Empire (Germans, Hungarians, Czechs, Slovaks, Slovenes, Croatians, Poles, and Romanians, for example) made impossible the unifying of the empire into a strong centralized monarchy. Maria Theresa, writing in 1745, explained how previous Hapsburg rulers had impoverished themselves by attempting with little success to purchase the political and military support of the nobles in different provinces. The more privileges they gave the nobles, the more they were expected to give.

To return once again to my ancestors, these individuals not only gave away most of the crown estates, but absorbed also the debts of those properties confiscated in time of rebellion, and these debts are still in arrears. Emperor Leopold [1658–1705] found little left to give away, but the terrible wars he fought no doubt forced him to mortgage or pawn additional crown estates. His successors did not relieve these burdens, and when I became sovereign, the crown revenues barely reached eighty thousand gulden. Also in the time of my forebears, the ministers received enormous payments from the crown and from the local Estates because they knew not only how to exploit selfishly the good will, grace, and munificence of the Austrian house by convincing each ruler that his predecessor had won fame by giving freely but also how to win the ears of the provincial lords and

clergy so that these ministers acquired all that they wished. In fact they spread their influence so wide that in the provinces they were more feared and respected than the ruler himself. And when they had finally taken everything from the sovereign, these same ministers turned for additional compensation to their provinces, where their great authority continuously increased. Even though complaints reached the monarch, out of grace and forebearance toward the ministers, he simply allowed the exploitations to continue. . . .

This system gave the ministers such authority that the sovereign himself found it convenient for his own interests to support them because he learned by experience that the more prestige enjoyed by the heads of the provinces, the more of the sovereign's demands these heads could extract from their Estates.

Maria Theresa, *Political Testament*, cited in Karl A. Roider (ed. and trans.), *Maria Theresa* (Englewood Cliffs, N.J.: Prentice-Hall, 1973), pp. 32–33.

trally administered unit. In spite of the geographical separation of their territories and the paucity of their natural economic resources, they transformed feudal ties and structures into bureaucratic ones. They subordinated every social class and most economic pursuits to the strengthening of the one institution that united their far-flung realms: the army. In so doing they made the term *Prussian* synonymous with administrative rigor and military discipline.

The rise of Prussia occurred within the German power vacuum created by the Peace of Westphalia. It is the story of the extraordinary Hohenzollern family, which had ruled the German territory of Brandenburg since 1417. Through inheritance the family had acquired the Duchy of Cleves and the counties of Mark and Ravensburg in 1609, the Duchy of East Prussia in 1618, and the Duchy of

Pomerania in 1637. Except for Pomerania, none of these lands was contiguous with Brandenburg. East Prussia lay inside Poland and outside the authority of the Holy Roman Emperor. All of the territories lacked good natural resources, and many of them were devastated during the Thirty Years' War. At Westphalia the Hohenzollerns lost part of Pomerania to Sweden but were compensated by receiving three more bishoprics and the promise of the archbishopric of Magdeburg when it became vacant, as it did in 1680. By the late seventeenth century the scattered Hohenzollern holdings represented a block of territory within the Holy Roman Empire second in size only to that of the Hapsburgs.

Despite its size the Hohenzollern conglomerate was weak. The areas were geographically separate, and there was no mutual sympathy or common con-

The Brandenburg Gate in Berlin, 1764. Berlin had become the principal seat of the Hohenzollerns in the fifteenth century. In the 1760s it had about 70,000 inhabitants. [Landesbildstelle Berlin.]

cern among them. In each there existed some form of local noble estates that limited the power of the Hohenzollern prince. The various areas were exposed to foreign aggression.

The person who began to forge these areas and nobles into a modern state was Frederick William (1640–1688), who became known as the Great Elector. He established himself and his successors as the central uniting power by breaking the estates, organizing a royal bureaucracy, and establishing a strong army.

Between 1655 and 1660 Sweden and Poland engaged in a war that endangered the Great Elector's holdings in Pomerania and East Prussia. Frederick William had neither an adequate army nor the tax revenues to confront this foreign threat. In 1655 the Brandenburg estates refused to grant him new taxes; however, he proceeded to collect the required taxes by military force. In 1659 a different grant of taxes, originally made in 1653, elapsed; Frederick William continued to collect them as well as those he had imposed by his own authority. He used the money to build up an army, which allowed him to continue to enforce his will without the approval of the nobility. Similar processes of threats and coercion took place against the nobles in his other territories.

However, there was a political and social trade-off between the elector and his various nobles. These *Junkers*, or German noble landlords, were allowed almost complete control over the serfs on their estates. In exchange for their obedience to the Hohenzollerns the *Junkers* received the right to demand obedience from their serfs. Frederick William also tended to choose as the local administrators of the tax structure men who would normally have been members of the noble estates. In this fashion, he coopted potential opponents into his service. The taxes fell most heavily on the backs of the peasants and the urban classes. As the years passed, sons

of *Junkers* increasingly dominated the army officer corps, and this practice became even more pronounced during the eighteenth century. All officials and army officers took an oath of loyalty directly to the elector. The army and the elector thus came to embody the otherwise absent unity of the state. The existence of the army made Prussia a valuable potential ally and a state with which other powers needed to curry favor.

Yet even with the considerable accomplishments of the Great Elector, the house of Hohenzollern did not possess a crown. The achievement of a royal title was one of the few state-building accomplishments of Frederick I (1688–1713). This son of the Great Elector was the least "Prussian" of his family during these crucial years. He built palaces, founded Halle University (1694), patronized the arts, and lived luxuriously. However, in 1700, at the outbreak of the War of the Spanish Succession, he put his army at

Frederick William I of Prussia ruthlessly forged the Prussian army into a major instrument of state. But he also attempted to avoid committing his valuable troops to warfare. [The Granger Collection.]

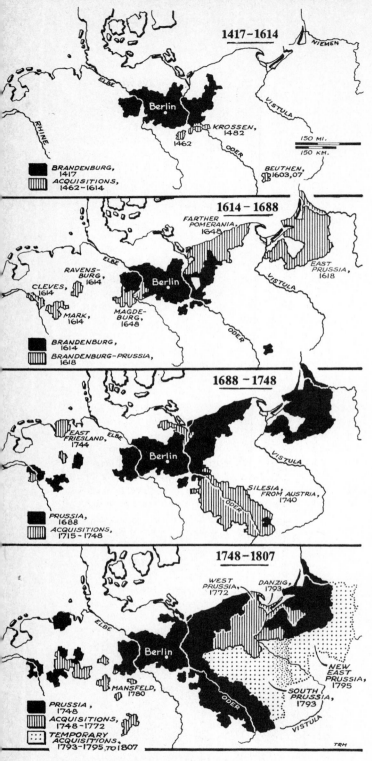

1417–1614

BRANDENBURG, 1417
ACQUISITIONS, 1462–1614

1614–1688

FARTHER POMERANIA, 1648
EAST PRUSSIA, 1618
RAVENS-BURG, 1614
CLEVES, 1614
MARK, 1614
MAGDE-BURG, 1648
BRANDENBURG, 1614
BRANDENBURG-PRUSSIA, 1618

1688–1748

EAST FRIESLAND, 1744
SILESIA FROM AUSTRIA, 1740
PRUSSIA, 1688
ACQUISITIONS, 1715–1748

1748–1807

WEST PRUSSIA, 1772
DANZIG, 1793
NEW EAST PRUSSIA, 1795
SOUTH PRUSSIA, 1793
MANSFELD, 1780
PRUSSIA, 1748
ACQUISITIONS, 1748–1772
TEMPORARY ACQUISITIONS, 1793–1795, TO 1807

EXPANSION OF BRANDENBURG–PRUSSIA

the disposal of the Hapsburg Holy Roman Emperor. In exchange for this loyal service the emperor permitted Frederick to assume the title of "King in Prussia." Thereafter Frederick became Frederick I, and he passed the much-desired royal title to his son Frederick William I in 1713.

Frederick William I (1713–1740) was both the most eccentric personality to rule the Hohenzollern domains and one of its most effective monarchs. After giving his father a funeral that matched the luxury of his life, Frederick William I immediately imposed policies of strict austerity. In some cases jobs were abolished, and in others salaries were lowered. His political aims seem to have been nothing else than the consolidation of an obedient, compliant bureaucracy and the expansion of the army. He initiated a policy of *Kabinett* government, which meant that lower officials submitted all relevant documents to him in his office or *Kabinett*. Then he alone examined the papers, made his decision, and issued his orders. Frederick William I thus skirted the influence of ministers and ruled alone.

Frederick William organized the bureaucracy along the lines of military discipline. He united all departments under the *General-Ober-Finanz-Kriegs-und-Domänen-Direktorium*, which is more happily known to us as the *General Directory*. He imposed taxes on the nobility and changed most remaining feudal dues into money payments. He sought to transform feudal and administrative loyalties into a sense of duty to the monarch as a political institution rather than as a person. He once described the perfect royal servant as

an intelligent, assiduous, and alert person who after God values nothing higher than his king's pleasure and serves him out of love and for the sake of honor rather than money and who in his conduct solely seeks and constantly bears in mind his king's service and interests, who, moreover, abhors all intrigues and emotional deterrents.[1]

Service to the state and the monarch was to become

[1] Quoted in Hans Rosenberg, *Bureaucracy, Aristocracy, and Autocracy* (Boston: Beacon Press 1958), p. 93.

MAP 18.2 *Seventeenth-century Brandenburg-Prussia expanded mainly by acquiring dynastic titles in geographically separated lands. Eighteenth-century expansion occurred through aggression to the east: Silesia seized in 1740 and various parts of Poland in 1772, 1793, and 1795.*

impersonal, mechanical, and, in effect, unquestioning.

The discipline that Frederick William applied to the army was little less than fanatical. During his reign the size of the military force grew from about thirty-nine thousand in 1713 to over eighty thousand in 1740. It was the third or fourth largest army in Europe, whereas Prussia ranked thirteenth in size of population. Rather than using recruiters, the king made each canton or local district responsible for supplying a certain number of soldiers.

After 1725 Frederick William always wore an officer's uniform. He built one regiment from the tallest soldiers he could find in Europe. Separate laws applied to the army and to civilians. Laws, customs, and royal attention made the officer corps the highest social class of the state. Military service attracted the sons of *Junkers.* In this fashion the army, the *Junker* nobility, and the monarchy became forged into a single political entity. Military priorities and values dominated Prussian government, society, and daily life as in no other state of Europe. It has often been

✎ Instructions for the Education of a Prussian Prince

Frederick William I directed toward the rearing of his son, who became Frederick the Great, the same kind of rigor he applied to the running of the army and the government of Prussia. In this letter to the royal tutors he emphasized the importance of practical subjects and voiced his contempt for the arts and the teaching of Latin. Frederick rebelled against his father and became quite accomplished in music.

. . . Above all else, it is important that his character—and it is character which governs all human action—should be, from earliest youth, so formed that he will love and delight in virtue and feel horror and disgust for vice. Nothing can so greatly contribute to this end as to implant the true fear of God so early in the young heart that it shall take root and bear fruit in the time when there is no longer any guidance or oversight. For other men are guided toward virtue and away from evil by the rewards and punishments dealt out by those who are set above them, but the prince must rely on the fear of God alone, since he is subject to no human law, punishment, or reward.

My son and all his attendants shall say their prayers on their knees both morning and evening, and after prayers shall read a chapter from the Bible.

He shall be kept away from operas, comedies, and other worldly amusements and, as far as possible, be given a distaste for them. He must be taught to pay proper respect and submission to his parents, but without slavishness.

His tutors must use every means they can devise to restrain him from puffed-up pride and insolence and train him in good management, economy, and modesty. . . .

As for the Latin language, he is not to learn it, and I desire that no one shall even speak to me on this subject; but his tutors shall see to it that he acquires a terse and elegant style in writing French as well as German. Arithmetic, mathematics, artillery, and agriculture he must be taught thoroughly, ancient history only superficially, but that of our own time and of the last one hundred and fifty years as accurately as possible. He must have a thorough knowledge of law, of international law, of geography, and of what is most remarkable in each country; and, above all, my son must be carefully taught the history of his own house.

His tutors must take the greatest pains to imbue my son with a sincere love for the soldier's profession and to impress upon him that nothing else in the world can confer upon a prince such fame and honor as the sword; . . . and his chief tutor shall provide for his being taught the practice of arms as play in his recreation hours.

James Harvey Robinson (Ed.), *Readings in European History,* Vol. 2 (Boston: Ginn and Co., 1906), pp. 319-321.

said that whereas other nations possessed armies, the Prussian army possessed its nation.

Although Frederick William I built the best army in Europe, he followed a policy of avoiding conflict. He wanted to drill his soldiers but not to order them into battle. Although Frederick William terrorized his family and associates and on occasion knocked out teeth with his walking stick, he was not a militarily aggressive monarch. The army was for him a symbol of Prussian power and unity, not an instrument to be used for foreign adventures or aggression. At his death in 1740 he passed to his son Frederick II (1740–1786; Frederick the Great) this superb military machine, but he could not pass to his son the wisdom to refrain from using it. Almost immediately on coming to the throne, Frederick II upset the Pragmatic Sanction and invaded Silesia. He thus crystallized the Austrian–Prussian rivalry for control of Germany that would dominate central European affairs for over a century.

The Entry of Russia into the European Political Arena

Though ripe with consequences for the future, the rise of Prussia and the new consolidation of the Austrian Hapsburg domains seemed to many at the time only one more shift in the long-troubled German scene. However, the emergence of Russia as an active European power constituted a wholly new factor in European politics. Previously Russia had been considered a part of Europe only by courtesy. Geographically and politically it lay on the periphery of Europe. Hemmed in by Sweden on the Baltic and by the Ottoman Empire on the Black Sea, the country had no warm-water ports. Its chief outlet to the west was Archangel on the White Sea, which was open to ships during only part of the year. There was little trade. What Russia did possess was a vast reserve of largely undeveloped natural and human resources.

The Medieval Russian Background

Several factors besides geography had accounted for this isolation of Russia prior to the eighteenth century. Early in the ninth century missionaries from Byzantium had converted Russia to the Christianity of the Eastern Orthodox Church.

This development meant that Russia would remain culturally separated from the Latin Christianity of western Europe. Between the late ninth century and the mid-thirteenth century the city of Kiev had been the center of Russian political life. Although the city enjoyed fairly extensive trade relations with its neighbors, it failed to develop a political system that provided effective resistance to foreign domination. The external threat to Kievan Russia came from the east when the Mongols moved across the vast Eurasian plains and into Russia as Genghis Khan built his empire. By 1240 the Mongols had conquered most of Russia and had turned its various cities and their surrounding countryside into dependent principalities from which tribute could be exacted. The portion of the Mongol empire to which Russia thus stood in the relationship of a vassal was called the *Golden Horde*. It included the steppe in what is now south Russia with its largely nomadic population. This vassal relationship encouraged an eastern orientation on the part of the Russians for over two centuries, although the connection of the Russian church to the Byzantine Empire remained important. During this period there was no single central political authority in Russia. The land was divided into numerous appanages or feudal principalities, each of which was militarily weak and subject in one degree or another to the Golden Horde.

The rise of Moscow as a relatively strong power eventually brought the appanage age of Russian history to an end. In the fourteenth century, under Grand Prince Ivan I, the city began to cooperate with its Mongol—or as the Russians called them, Tatar—overlords in the collection of tribute. Ivan kept much of this tribute for himself and was soon called Ivan Kalita, or John of the Moneybag. When Mongol authority began to weaken, the princes of Moscow, who had become increasingly wealthy, filled the political power vacuum in the territory near the city. The princes extended their authority and that of the city by purchasing some territory, colonizing other areas, and conquering new lands. This slow extension of the appanage, or principality, of Moscow is usually known as *gathering the Russian land*.

In 1380 Grand Prince Dmitrii of Moscow defeated the Mongols in battle. The result was not militarily decisive, but Moscow had demonstrated that the Mongol armies were not invincible. Conflict with the Mongols continued for another century before they were driven out. During these years the princes of Moscow asserted their right to be regarded as the successors of the earlier Kievan rulers, and they also made Moscow the religious center of Russia.

The person who most benefited from the accomplishments of these early Moscow princes and who transformed the principality into a new kind of state was Ivan IV (1533–1584), who is better known as Ivan the Terrible. His reign displayed a pattern that would be repeated frequently, and often tragically, in later Russian history: early years of reform and solid accomplishment followed by a period of almost inexplicable tyranny.

Ivan came into his political inheritance at the age of three. Consequently, there was a long regency that witnessed numerous clashes among the *boyars* or Russian nobles. The first key moment in his personal reign occurred in 1547, when at the age of sixteen he had himself crowned czar (the Russian equivalent of *Caesar* or *Kaiser*) rather than prince of Moscow.

During the opening years of his personal reign Ivan IV consulted with the great *boyars* and other able advisers in a relationship of mutual trust. He worked toward formulating a revised law code and a mode of local government that would be responsive to the needs of the areas governed. He reorganized the army, and he established direct economic contact with western Europe. During the 1550s Ivan undertook successful military campaigns against the Ottomans in the south, the Tatars in the south and east, and for a time the Livonians in the northwest. It appeared that his reign would be well regarded at home and abroad.

Beginning in about 1560, however, a profound change took place in his personality. He began to mistrust his most honest advisers and believed that they were plotting against him. When his first wife died in 1560, he thought she had been poisoned by a conspiracy. In the late 1560s he created a set of *boyars* and officials who were personally loyal to him and an army also loyal to him alone. He loosed these troops, who always dressed in black and who were called the *oprichniki,* against anyone he regarded as an enemy. He imprisoned, tortured, and executed *boyars* without cause and without trial. In 1581 Ivan killed his own son. He himself died in 1584. While he had pursued this utterly irrational behavior at home, his military forces in Livonia had been defeated by both Sweden and Poland. His

reign ended in domestic political turmoil and foreign military defeat.

The reign of Ivan the Terrible, which had begun so well and closed so frighteningly, was followed by a period of anarchy and civil war known as the *Time of Troubles.* In 1613, hoping to resolve the tension and end the uncertainty, an assembly of nobles elected as czar a seventeen-year-old boy named Mikhail Romanov (1613–1654). Thus began the dynasty that in spite of palace revolutions, military conspiracies, assassinations, and family strife ruled Russia until 1917.

Mikhail Romanov and his two successors, Alexis I (1654–1676) and Theodore III (1676–1682), brought stability and bureaucratic centralization to Russia. However, Russia remained militarily weak

RISE OF RUSSIAN POWER

1533–1584	Reign of Ivan the Terrible
1584–1613	Time of Troubles
1613	Mikhail Romanov becomes czar
1682	Peter the Great becomes czar as a boy
1689	Peter assumes personal rule
1696	Russia captures Azov on the Black Sea from the Turks
1697	European tour of Peter the Great
1698	Peter returns to Russia to put down the revolt of the *streltsi*
1700	The Great Northern War opens between Russia and Sweden;
	Russia defeated at Narva by Swedish Army of Charles XII
1703	Saint Petersburg founded
1709	Russia defeats Sweden at the Battle of Poltava
1718	Charles XII of Sweden dies
	Son of Peter the Great dies under mysterious circumstances in prison
1721	Peace of Nystad ends the Great Northern War
	Peter establishes a synod for the Russian church
1722	Peter issues the Table of Ranks
1725	Peter dies leaving an uncertain succession

and financially impoverished. The bureaucracy after these years of turmoil still remained largely controlled by the *boyars*. This administrative apparatus was only barely capable of putting down a revolt of peasants and cossacks under Stepan Razin in 1670–1671. Furthermore, the government and the czars faced the danger of mutiny from the *streltsi*, or guards of the Moscow garrison.

Peter the Great

In 1682 another boy—ten years old at the time—ascended the fragile Russian throne as coruler with his half brother. His name was Peter (1682–1725), and Russia would never be the same after him. He and his ill half-brother, Ivan V, had come to power on the shoulders of the *streltsi*, who expected rewards from the persons they favored. Much violence and bloodshed had surrounded the disputed succession. Matters became even more confused when their sister, Sophia, was named regent. Peter's followers overthrew her in 1689. From that

date onward Peter ruled personally, although in theory he shared the crown with Ivan, who died in 1696. The dangers and turmoil of his youth convinced Peter of two things. First, the power of the czar must be made secure from the jealousy of the *boyars* and the greed of the *streltsi*. Second, the military power of Russia must be increased.

Peter I, who became Peter the Great, was fascinated by western Europe, particularly its military resources. He was an imitator of the first order. The products and workmen from the West who had filtered into Russia impressed and intrigued him. In 1697 he made a famous visit in rather weak disguises throughout western Europe. There he dined and talked with the great and the powerful, who considered this almost seven-foot-tall ruler both crude and rude. His happiest moments on the trip were spent inspecting shipyards, docks, and the manufacture of military hardware. He returned to Moscow determined by whatever means necessary to copy what he had seen abroad, for he knew that warfare would be necessary to make

---

✎ Bishop Burnet Looks Over a Foreign Visitor

In 1697 and 1698 Peter the Great of Russia toured western Europe to discover how Russia must change its society and economy in order to become a great power. As this description by Bishop Gilbert Burnet in England indicates, the west Europeans found the czar a curious person in his own right.

He came this winter over to England, and stayed some months among us. . . . I had good interpreters, so I had much free discourse with him; he is a man of a very hot temper, soon inflamed, and very brutal in his passion; he raises his natural heat, by drinking much brandy, . . . he is subject to convulsive motions all over his body, and his head seems to be affected with these; he wants not capacity, and has a larger measure of knowledge, than might be expected from his education, which was very indifferent; a want of judgment, with an instability of temper, appear in him too often and too evidently; he is mechanically turned, and seems designed by nature rather to be a ship-carpenter, than a great prince. This was his chief study and exercise, while he stayed here: he wrought much with his own hands, and made all about him work at the models of ships. . . . He was . . . resolved to encourage learning, and to polish his people, by sending some of them to travel in other countries, and to draw strangers to come and live among them. . . . After I had seen him often, and had conversed much with him, I could not but adore the depth of the providence of God, that had raised up such a furious man to so absolute an authority over so great a part of the world.

Bishop Burnet's History of His Own Time, Vol. 4 (Oxford, England: Clarendon Press, 1823), pp. 396–397.

Russia a great power. The czar's drive toward westernization, though unsystematic, had four general areas of concern: taming the *boyars* and the *streltsi*, achieving secular control of the church, reorganizing the internal administration, and developing the economy. Peter pursued each of these goals with violence and ruthlessness.

He made a sustained attack on the Russian *boyars.* In 1698, immediately on his return from abroad, he personally shaved the long beards of the court *boyars* and sheared off the customary long, hand-covering sleeves of their shirts and coats, which had made them the butt of jokes throughout Europe. More importantly, he demanded that the nobles provide his state with their services.

In 1722 Peter published a Table of Ranks, which henceforth equated a person's social position and privileges with his rank in the bureaucracy or the army rather than with his position in the nobility. However, unlike the case in Prussia, the Russian nobility never became perfectly loyal to the state. They repeatedly sought to reassert their independence and their control of the Russian imperial court.

After Peter the Great of Russia returned from his journey to western Europe, he personally cut off the traditional and highly prized long sleeves and beards of the Russian nobles. His action symbolized his desire to see Russia become more powerful and more modern. [SLEEVES: *Culver Pictures;* BEARDS: *The Granger Collection.*]

The *streltsi* fared less well than the *boyars*. In 1698 they had rebelled while Peter was on his European tour. When he returned and put down the revolt of these Moscow troops, he directed massive violence and brutality against both leaders and followers. There were private tortures and public executions, in which Peter's own ministers took part. Almost twelve hundred of the rebels were put to death, and their corpses long remained on public display to discourage future disloyalty.

Peter dealt with the potential political independence of the Russian Orthodox Church with similar ruthlessness. Here again Peter had to confront a problem that had arisen in the turbulent decades that had preceded his reign. The Russian church had long opposed the scientific as well as the theological thought of the West. In the mid-seventeenth century a reformist movement led by Patriarch Nikon arose in the church. In 1667 certain changes had been introduced into the texts and the ritual of the church. These reforms caused great unrest because the Russian church had always claimed to be the protector of true ritual. The Old Believers, a group of Russian Christians who strongly opposed these changes, were condemned by the hierarchy, but they persisted in their opposition. Late in the century thousands of them committed suicide rather than submit to the new rituals. The Old Believers' movement represented a rejection of change and innovation; its presence discouraged the church hierarchy from making any further substantial moves toward modern thought.

In the future Peter wanted to avoid two kinds of difficulties with the Russian church. First, the clergy must not constitute a group within the state who would oppose change and westernization. Second, the hierarchy of the church must not be permitted to reform liturgy, ritual, or doctrine in a way that might again give rise to discontent such as that of the Old Believers. Consequently in 1721 Peter simply abolished the position of patriarch of the Russian church. In its place he established a synod headed by a layman to rule the church in accordance with secular requirements. So far as transforming a traditional institution was concerned, this action toward the church was the most radical policy of Peter's reign. It produced still further futile opposition from the Old Believers, who saw the czar as leading the church into new heresy.

In his reorganization of domestic administration, Peter looked to institutions then used in Sweden. These were "colleges," or bureaus, composed of several persons rather than departments headed by a single minister. These colleges, which he imposed on Russia, were to look after matters such as the collection of taxes, foreign affairs, war, and economic matters. This new organization was an attempt to breathe life into the generally stagnant and inefficient administration of the country. In 1711 he created a central senate of nine members who were to direct the Moscow government when the czar was away with the army. The purpose of these and other local administrative reforms was to establish a bureaucracy that could collect and spend tax revenues to support an efficient army.

The economic development advocated by Peter the Great was closely related to his military needs. He encouraged the establishment of an iron industry in the Ural Mountains, and by mid-century Russia had become the largest iron producer in Europe. He sent prominent young Russians abroad to acquire technical and organizational skills. He attempted to attract west European craftsmen to live and work in Russia. Except for the striking growth of the iron industry, which later languished, all these efforts had only marginal success.

The goal of these internal reforms and political departures was to support a policy of warfare. Peter was determined to secure warm-water ports that would allow Russia to trade with the West and to have a greater impact on European affairs. This policy led him into wars with the Ottoman Empire and with Sweden. His armies commenced fighting the Turks in 1695 and captured Azov on the Black Sea in 1696. It was a temporary victory, for in 1711 he was compelled to return the port.

Peter had more success against Sweden, where the inconsistency and irrationality of Charles XII were no small aid. In 1700 Russia moved against the Swedish territory on the Baltic. The Swedish king's failure to follow up his victory at Narva in 1700 allowed Peter to regroup his forces and hoard his resources. In 1709, when Charles XII returned to fight Russia again, Peter was ready, and the Battle of Poltava sealed the fate of Sweden. In 1721, at the Peace of Nystad, which ended the Great Northern War, the Russian conquest of Estonia, Livonia, and part of Finland was confirmed. Henceforth Russia possessed warm-water ports and a permanent influence on European affairs.

At one point the domestic and foreign policies of Peter the Great literally intersected. This was at the spot on the Gulf of Finland where Peter founded his new capital city of Saint Petersburg (now Leningrad). There he built government structures and compelled his *boyars* to construct town houses. In this fashion he imitated those west European monarchs who had copied Louis XIV by constructing smaller versions of Versailles. However, the founding of Saint Petersburg went beyond the construction of a central court. It symbolized a new western orientation of Russia and Peter's determination to hold his position on the Baltic coast. He had commenced the construction of the city and had moved the capital there in 1703, even before his victory over Sweden was assured.

Despite his notable success on the Baltic, Peter's reign ended with a great question mark. He had long quarreled with his only son, Alexis. Peter was jealous of the young man and fearful that he might undertake sedition. In 1718 Peter had his son imprisoned, and during this imprisonment the presumed successor to the throne died mysteriously. Thereafter Peter claimed for himself the right of naming a successor, but he could never bring himself to designate the person either orally or in writing. Consequently, when he died in 1725, there was no firmer policy on the succession to the

Peter the Great built St. Petersburg on the Gulf of Finland to prove his intention of maintaining recently conquered territory and to provide Russia with better contact with Western Europe. This is an eighteenth-century view of the city. [John R. Freeman.]

throne than when he had acceded to the title. For over thirty years, once again soldiers and nobles would determine who ruled Russia. Peter had laid the foundations of a modern Russia, but he had failed to lay the foundations of a stable state.

Eighteenth-Century European States

By the second quarter of the eighteenth century the major European powers were not yet nation-states in which the citizens felt themselves united by a shared sense of community, culture, language, and history. They were still monarchies in which the personality of the ruler and the personal relationships of the great noble families exercised considerable influence over public affairs. The monarchs, except in Great Britain, had generally succeeded in making their power greater than the nobility's. However, the power of the aristocracy and its capacity to resist or obstruct the policies of the monarchs were not destroyed. In Britain, of course, the nobility had tamed the monarchy, but even there tension between nobles and monarchs would continue through the rest of the century.

In foreign affairs the new arrangement of military and diplomatic power established during the early years of the century prepared the way for two long-term conflicts. The first was a commercial rivalry for trade and overseas empire between France and Great Britain. During the reign of Louis XIV these two nations had collided over the French bid for dominance in Europe. During the eighteenth century they dueled for control of commerce on other continents. The second arena of warfare was central Europe, where Austria and Prussia fought for the leadership of the states of Germany.

However, behind these international conflicts and the domestic rivalry of monarchs and nobles, the society of eighteenth-century Europe began to experience momentous change. The character and the structures of the society over which the monarchs ruled were beginning to take on some features associated with the modern age. These economic and social developments would in the long run produce transformations in the life of Europe beside which the state building of the early eighteenth-century monarchs paled.

Suggested Readings

M. S. ANDERSON, *Europe in the Eighteenth Century, 1713–1783* (1961). The best one-volume introduction.

F. L. CARSTEN, *The Origins of Prussia* (1954). Discusses the groundwork laid by the Great Elector in the seventeenth century.

A. COBBAN, *A History of Modern France*, Vol. 1, 2nd ed. (1961). A lively and opinionated survey.

L. COLLEY, *In Defiance of Oligarchy: The Tory Party, 1714–60.* (1982) An important study that challenges much conventional opinion about eighteenth-century British politics.

R. R. ERGANG, *The Potsdam Führer* (1941). The biography of Frederick William I.

S. B. FAY AND K. EPSTEIN, *The Rise of Brandenburg–Prussia to 1786* (1937, rev. 1964). A brief outline.

M. T. FLORINSKY, *Russia: A History and an Interpretation*, 2 vols. (1953). A useful and far-ranging work.

FRANKLIN FORD, *Robe and Sword: The Regrouping of the French Aristocracy After Louis XIV* (1953). An important book for political, social, and intellectual history.

G. P. GOOCH, *Maria Theresa and Other Studies* (1951). A sound introduction to the problems of the Hapsburgs.

G. P. GOOCH, *Louis XV, The Monarchy in Decline* (1956). A discussion of the problems of France after the death of Louis XIV.

H. HOLBORN, *A History of Modern Germany, 1648–1840* (1966). The best and most comprehensive survey in English.

HUBERT C. JOHNSON, *Frederick the Great and His Officials* (1975). An excellent recent examination of the Prussian administration.

V. K. KLYUCHEVSKY, *Peter the Great*, tr. by Liliana Archibald (1958). A standard biography.

DORTHY MARSHALL, *Eighteenth-Century England* (1962). Emphasizes social and economic background.

ROBERT K. MASSIE, *Peter the Great: His Life and His World* (1980). A good popular biography.

L. B. NAMIER AND J. BROOKE, *The History of Parliament: The House of Commons, 1754–1790*, 3 vols. (1964). A detailed examination of the unreformed British House of Commons and electoral system.

L. J. OLIVA (Ed.), *Russia and the West from Peter the Great to Khrushchev* (1965). An anthology of articles tracing an important and ambiguous subject.

J. B. OWEN, *The Eighteenth Century* (1974). An excellent introduction to England in the period.

J. H. PLUMB, *Sir Robert Walpole*, 2 vols. (1956, 1961). A masterful biography ranging across the sweep of European politics.

J. H. PLUMB, *The Growth of Political Stability in England, 1675–1725* (1969). An important interpretive work.

NICHOLAS V. RIASANOVSKY, *A History of Russia*, 3rd ed. (1977). The best one-volume introduction.

P. ROBERTS, *The Quest for Security, 1715–1740* (1947). Very good on the diplomatic problems of the period.

H. ROSENBERG, *Bureaucracy, Aristocracy, and Autocracy: The Prussian Experience, 1660–1815* (1960). Emphasizes the organization of Prussian administration.

B. H. SUMMER, *Peter the Great and the Emergence of Russia* (1950). A brief, but well-organized discussion.

E. N. WILLIAMS, *The Ancien Régime in Europe* (1972). A state by state survey of very high quality.

A. M. WILSON, *French Foreign Policy During the Administration of Cardinal Fleury, 1726–1743* (1936). The standard account.

J. B. WOLF, *The Emergence of the Great Powers, 1685–1715* (1951). A comprehensive survey.

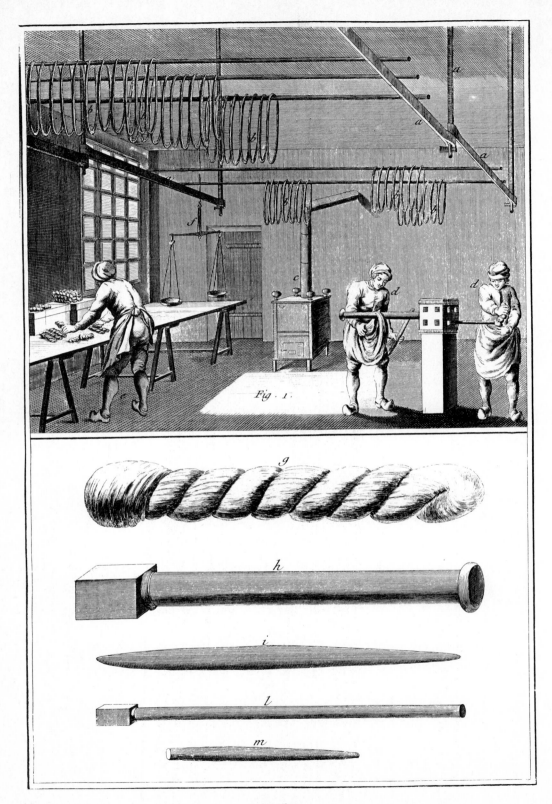

Fig. 1.

560

19 Society Under the Old Regime in the Eighteenth Century

URING the French Revolution (1789) and the turmoil spawned by that upheaval it became customary to refer to the patterns of social, political, and economic relationships that had existed in France before 1789 as the *ancien régime*, or the "old regime." The term has come to be applied generally to the life and institutions of prerevolutionary Europe. Politically the term indicated the rule of theoretically absolute monarchies with growing bureaucracies and aristocratically led armies. Economically the old regime was characterized by scarcity of food, the predominance of agriculture, slow transport, a low level of iron production, rather unsophisticated financial institutions, and in some cases competitive commercial overseas empires. Socially prerevolutionary Europe was based on aristocratic elites possessing a wide variety of inherited legal privileges, established Roman Catholic and Protestant churches intimately related to the state and the aristocracy, an urban labor force usually organized into guilds, and a rural peasantry subject to high taxes and feudal dues. It should be remembered that the men and women living during this period did not know it was the *old* regime. In most cases they earned their livelihoods and went through the various stages of life as their forebears had done for generations before them and as they expected their children to do after them.

Probably the most striking feature of the old regime was the marked contrasts in the lives and experiences of people in different social ranks, different countries, and even different regions of the same country. The bonds created by rapid transport and communication that have today led to similar patterns of life throughout the Western world simply did not yet exist.

Within the major monarchies there was usually no single standard of uniform law, money, or weights and measures. Except in Britain there were

This drawing is from the mid-eighteenth-century French Encyclopedie, ou Dictionnaire Raisonné des Sciences, des Arts et des Métiers *(hereafter known as the* Encyclopedia). *It shows part of the dyeworks that supplied thread and yarn for the renowned Gobelin tapestries. It also shows enlargements of various components of the dyeing process.* [The New York Public Library Picture Collection.]

561

Castle Howard in Yorkshire, England, designed by the architect and playwright, Sir John Vanbrugh (1665–1726), was one of the grandest of the homes of the aristocracy from the time of its completion in 1714. From such great houses the aristocrats looked after their estates and their local political interests. [British Tourist Authority, New York.]

internal tolls that hampered the passage of goods. The nobility of Great Britain lived in the most magnificent luxury the order had ever known. On the Continent some groups of nobles were also very wealthy, but other members of the continental nobility were little better off than the wealthier peasants. So far as the peasantry was concerned, it tended to prosper in western Europe while reaching new depths of social and economic degradation east of the Elbe River.

In Britain, Holland, and parts of France there was a healthy and growing middle class, but such an order hardly existed in the German principalities, the Austrian Empire, or Russia. Finally, there was a stark contrast between the refinement of taste, fashion, and manners of the upper levels of society and the simultaneous presence of public whipping, torture, and executions inflicted on the lower classes. Historians often point to the difficulties of life and the differences in wealth in our in-

dustrial society, but these were far more extreme in the society of the old regime.

Eighteenth-century society was traditional. The past weighed more heavily on people's minds than did the future. Few persons outside the government bureaucracies and the movement for reform called the *Enlightenment* considered change or innovation desirable. This was especially true of social relationships. Both nobles and peasants, for very different reasons, repeatedly called for the restoration of traditional or customary rights. The nobles asserted what they considered their ancient rights against the intrusion of the expanding monarchical bureaucracies. The peasants, in petitions and revolts, called for the revival or the maintenance of the customary manorial rights that provided them access to particular lands, courts, or grievance procedures.

With the exception of the early industrial development in Britain, the eighteenth-century econ-

At the opposite end of the social scale from Castle Howard is the mid-eighteenth-century rural laborer's hut far to the east in Austria. However proper a subject for the artist, Franz Edmund Weirotter (1730–1771), the scene is probably a realistic one of the wretched housing endured by many. [Charles Farrell Collection.]

omy was also quite traditional. The quality and quantity of the harvest remained the single most important fact of life for the overwhelming majority of the population and the gravest concern of the governments.

Closely related to this traditional social and economic outlook was the hierarchical structure of the society. The medieval sense of rank and degree not only persisted but became more rigid in the course of the century. In several continental cities "sumptuary laws" regulating the dress of the different classes remained on the books. These laws forbade persons in one class or occupation to wear clothes like those worn by people in a socially higher position. The point of such laws, which were largely ineffective in the eighteenth century, was to make the social hierarchy actually visible. Rather than by such legislation, the hierarchy was really enforced through the corporate nature of social relationships. Each state or society was considered a community of numerous smaller communities. People in eighteenth-century Europe did not enjoy what Americans regard as individual rights. A person enjoyed such rights and privileges as were guaranteed to the particular communities or groups of which he was a part. The "community" might include the village, the municipality, the nobility, the church, the guild, or the parish. In turn, each of these bodies enjoyed certain privileges, some of which were great and some small. The privileges might involve exemption from taxation or from some especially humiliating punishment, the right to practice a trade or craft, the right of one's children to pursue a particular occupation, or in the case of the church the right to collect the tithe.

Tradition, hierarchy, corporateness, and privilege were the chief social characteristics of the old regime. Yet it was by no means a static society. Factors of change and innovation were fermenting in its midst. There was a strong demand from the colonies in the Americas for European goods and manufactures. Merchants in seaports and other cities were expanding their businesses. By preparing their states for war, the various governments put new demands on the resources and the economic organizations of their nations. The spirit of rationality that had been so important to the Scientific Revolution of the seventeenth century continued to manifest itself in the economic life of the eighteenth century. Perhaps most importantly, the population of Europe grew rapidly. The old regime itself fostered the changes that eventually transformed it into a very different kind of society.

The Land and Its Tillers

Land constituted the economic basis of eighteenth-century life. Well over three fourths of all Europeans lived in the country, and few of these people ever traveled beyond a ten-mile radius of their birthplace. Male children tended to follow the occupation of their fathers. Village families tended to intermarry; there were only occasional marriages between men and women from neighboring villages. The lot of women continued to be circumscribed by family duties, the family economy, and the burden of childbearing and child rearing. With the exception of the nobility and the wealthier nonaristocratic landowners, the dwellers on the land were poor, and by any modern standard their lives were difficult. They lived in various modes of economic and social dependency, exploitation, and vulnerability.

Peasants and Serfs

The major forms of rural social dependency related directly to the land. Those who worked the land were subject to immense influence and in some cases direct control by the landowners. This situation prevailed in differing degrees for free peasants, such as English tenants and most French cultivators, and for the serfs of Germany, Austria, and Russia, who were legally bound to a particular plot of land and a particular lord. In all cases the class that owned most of the land also controlled the local government and the courts. For example, in Great Britain all farmers and smaller tenants had the legal rights of English citizens. But the justices of the peace who presided over the county courts and who could call out the local militia were

Agriculture, basic to society, is illustrated in this plate from the mid-eighteenth-century French Encyclopédie, ou Dictionnaire Raisonné des Sciences, des Arts et des Métiers *(hereafter the* Encyclopedia). *New machinery, such as the plows shown at the bottom, helped to increase yield from the land and thus the food supply for Europe.*

always substantial landowners, as were also the members of Parliament, who made the laws.

The intensity of landlord power increased as one moved from west to east. In France the situation differed somewhat from province to province. Most French peasants owned some land, but there were a few serfs. However, practically all peasants were subject to certain feudal dues, called *banalités*, that included required use-for-payment of the lord or seigneur's mill to grind grain and his oven to bake bread. The seigneur could also require a certain number of days each year of the peasant's labor. This practice of forced labor was termed the *corvée*. Because even landowning French peasants rarely possessed enough land to support their fam-

Lunchtime on an eighteenth-century French farm. The softened style of drawing gives a somewhat romanticized cast to the scene, but farm workers did usually work in the kind of group shown here. [*The Granger Collection.*]

J. J. De Boissieu's 1780 *etching of the interior of a French dairy barn associates the life of the land with the life of the family.* [*Charles Farrell Collection.*]

Eighteenth-century France had some of the best roads in the world, but they were often built with forced labor. French peasants were required to work for part of each year on such projects. This system, called the corvée, was not abolished until the French Revolution in 1789. This painting, *Construction of a Major Road* by Joseph Vernet, is in the Louvre. [Giraudon.]

A drawing from the Encyclopédie of French peasants threshing grain with flails. This method of separating the edible part of the grain from the inedible chaff had been practiced since Biblical times. [New York Public Library.]

❧ William Coxe Describes Serfdom in Eighteenth-Century Russia

William Coxe was an Englishman who traveled widely in eastern Europe. His description of Russian serfdom portrays the brutality of the institution. It also illustrates his amazement at the absence in Russia of civil liberties such as he and more humble citizens enjoyed in England.

Peasants belonging to individuals are the private property of the landholders, as much as implements of agriculture, or herds of cattle; and the value of an estate is estimated, as in Poland, by the number of boors [serfs], and not by the number of acres. . . . If the Polish boor is oppressed, and he escapes to another master, the latter is liable to no pecuniary penalty for harbouring him; but in Russia the person who receives another's vassal is subject to an heavy fine. With respect to his own demands upon his peasants, the lord is restrained by no law, either in the exaction of any sum, or in the mode of employing them. He is absolute master of their time and labour: some he employs in agriculture: a few he makes his menial servants, and perhaps without wages; and from others he exacts an annual payment.

Each vassal, therefore, is rated according to the arbitrary will of his master. Some contribute four or five shillings a year; others, who are engaged in traffic or trade, are assessed in proportion to their supposed profits. . . . With regard to any capital which they may have acquired by their industry, it may be seized, and there can be no redress. . . .

. . . [S]ome of the Russian nobility send their vassals to Moscow or Petersburg for the purpose of learning various handcraft trades: they either employ them on their own estates; let them out for hire; sell them at an advanced price; or receive from them an annual compensation for the permission of exercising trade for their own advantage.

William Coxe, *Travels into Poland, Russia, Sweden, and Denmark*, 4th ed., Vol. 3 (London: T. Cadell 1972, first printed 1784), pp. 174–181.

ilies, they were also subject to feudal dues attached to the plots of land they rented. In Prussia and Austria, despite attempts by the monarchies late in the century to improve the lot of the serfs, the landlords continued to exercise almost complete control over them. In Austria law and custom required the serfs to provide service or *robot* to the lords. Moreover, throughout continental Europe in addition to these feudal services, the burden of state taxation fell on the tillers of the soil. Many peasants, serfs, and other agricultural laborers were forced to undertake supplemental work to raise the cash required to pay the tax collector. Through various legal privileges and the ability to demand further concessions from the monarchs, the landlords escaped the payment of numerous taxes. They also presided over the manorial courts.

The condition of the serfs was the worst in Russia. The Russian custom of enumerating the number of "souls" (that is, male serfs) owned rather than the acreage possessed reveals the contrast.

The serfs were, in effect, regarded merely as economic commodities. Russian landlords could demand as many as six days a week of labor, and like Prussian and Austrian landlords they enjoyed the right to punish their serfs. On their own authority alone they could even exile a serf to Siberia. The serfs had no legal recourse against the orders and whims of their lords. There was actually little difference between Russian serfdom and slavery.

The Russian monarchy itself contributed to the degradation of the serfs. Peter the Great gave whole villages to favored nobles. Later in the century Catherine the Great (1762–1796) confirmed the authority of the nobles over their serfs in exchange for the political cooperation of the landowners. The situation in Russia led to considerable unrest. There were well over fifty peasant revolts between 1762 and 1769. These culminated between 1771 and 1775 in Pugachev's rebellion, during which all of southern Russia experienced intense unrest. Emelyan Pugachev (1726–1775)

✍ Catherine the Great Issues a Proclamation Against Pugachev

Against a background of long-standing human degradation, and ever increasing landowner authority, the greatest serf rebellion in Russian history was led from 1773 to 1775 by a Don Cossack named Emelyan Pugachev. Empress Catherine the Great's proclamation of 1773 argues that he was alienating the serfs from their natural and proper allegiance to her and their masters.

By the grace of God, we Catherine II . . . make known to our faithful subjects, that we have learnt, with the utmost indignation and extreme affliction, that a certain Cossack, a deserter and fugitive from the Don, named Emelyan Pugachev, after having traversed Poland, has been collecting, for some time past, in the districts that border on the river Irghis, in the government of Orenburg, a troop of vagabonds like himself; that he continues to commit in those parts all kinds of excesses, by inhumanly depriving the inhabitants of their possessions, and even of their lives. . . .

In a word, there is not a man deserving of the Russian name, who does not hold in abomination the odious and insolent lie by which Pugachev fancies himself able to seduce and to deceive persons of a simple and credulous disposition, by promising to free them from the bonds of submission, and obedience to their sovereign, as if the Creation of the universe had established human societies in such a manner as that they can subsist without an intermediate authority between the sovereign and the people.

Nevertheless, as the insolence of this vile refuse of the human race is attended with consequences pernicious to the provinces adjacent to that district; as the report of the flagrant enormities which he has committed, may affright those persons who are accustomed to imagine the misfortunes of others as ready to fall upon them, and as we watch with indefatigable care over the tranquility of our faithful subjects, we inform them . . . that we have taken . . . such measures as are the best adapted to stifle the sedition. . . .

We trust . . . that every true son of the country will unremittedly fulfill his duty, of the contributing to the maintenance of good order and of public tranquility, by preserving himself from the snares of seduction, and by discharging his obedience to his lawful sovereign.

William Tooke, *Life of Catherine II, Empress of Russia,* 4th ed., Vol. 2 (London: T. N. Longman and O. Rees, 1800), pp. 460–461 (spelling modernized).

Emelyan Pugachev (1726–1775) led the largest peasant revolt in Russian history. Here in a contemporary propaganda picture he is shown in chains. An inscription in Russian and German was printed below the picture discussing the evil of revolution and insurrection. [Bildarchiv Preussischer Kulturbesitz.]

promised the serfs land of their own and freedom from their lords. The rebellion was brutally suppressed. Thereafter any thought of liberalizing or improving the condition of the serfs was set aside for a generation.

Pugachev's was the greatest rebellion in Russian history and the largest peasant uprising of the eighteenth century. Smaller peasant revolts or disturbances occurred outside of Russia. Rebellions took place in Bohemia in 1775, in Transylvania in 1784, in Moravia in 1786, and in Austria in 1789. Revolts in western Europe were almost nonexistent, but England experienced numerous local enclosure riots. Rural rebellions were violent, but the peasants and serfs normally directed their wrath against property rather than persons. The rebels usually sought to reassert traditional or customary rights against practices they perceived as innovations. Their targets were carefully chosen and included unfair pricing, onerous new or increased feudal dues, changes in methods of payment or land use, unjust officials, or extraordinarily brutal overseers and landlords. In this respect the peasant revolts were quite conservative in nature.

The main goal of peasant society was a stability that would ensure the local food supply. In western Europe most rural society was organized into villages, and on about half of the land the owners of individual plots or strips would decide communally what crops would be planted. In eastern Europe, with its great estates of hundreds or thousands of acres, the landlords decided how to use the land. But in either case the tillers resisted changes that might endanger the sure supply of food, which they generally believed to be promised by traditional cultivation. However, throughout the eighteenth century landlords across the Continent began to search for higher profits from their holdings. They embraced innovation in order to increase their own prosperity. They commercialized agriculture and thereby challenged the traditional peasant ways of production. Peasant revolts and disturbances often resulted. The governments of Europe, hungry for new taxes and dependent on the goodwill of the nobility, used their armies and militias to smash the peasants who defended the past. In certain areas, such as the Low Countries and parts of Germany, the peasants themselves began to innovate so that they could more easily raise the cash they needed for tax payments.

The Revolution in Agriculture

Even more basic than the social dependency of peasants and small tenant farmers was their dependency on the productiveness of nature. The quantity and quality of the annual grain harvest was the most fundamental fact in their lives. On

❧ Turgot Describes the Results of Poor Harvests in France

Failure of the grain crop and other plantings could bring both hunger and social disruption during the eighteenth century. Anne Robert Jacques Turgot (1727–1781), who later became finance minister of France, emphasized the role of private charity and government policy in relieving the suffering. His description, written in 1769, also provides a brief survey of the diet of the French peasant.

Everyone has heard of the terrible dearth that has just afflicted this generality [a local administrative district]. The harvest of 1769 in every respect proved to be one of the worst in the memory of man. The dearths of 1709 and 1739 were incomparably less cruel. To the loss of the greatest part of the rye was added the total loss of the chestnuts, of the buckwheat, and of the Spanish wheat—cheap food stuffs with which the peasant sustained himself habitually a great part of the year, reserving as much as he could of his corn [grain], in order to sell it to the inhabitants of the towns. . . . The people could exist only by exhausting their resources, by selling at a miserable price their articles of furniture and even their clothes. Many of the inhabitants have been obliged to disperse *themselves through other provinces to seek work or to beg, leaving their wives and children to the charity of the parishes. It has been necessary for the public authority to require the proprietors and inhabitants in better circumstances in each parish to assess themselves for the relief of the poor people; nearly a fourth of the population is dependent upon charitable contributions. After these melancholy sufferings which the province has already undergone, and with the reduced condition in which it was left by the dearth of last year, even had the harvest of the present year been a good one, the poverty of the inhabitants would have necessitated the greatest efforts to be made for their relief. But we have now to add the dismal fact of our harvest being again deficient. . . .*

W. W. Stephens (Ed.), *The Life and Writings of Turgot* (London: Longmans, Green, and Co., 1895), p. 50.

the Continent bread was the primary component of the diet of the lower classes. The food supply was never certain, and the farther east one traveled, the more uncertain it became. Failure of the harvest meant not only hardship but actual death from either outright starvation or protracted debility. Quite often people living in the countryside encountered more difficulty finding food than did city dwellers, whose local government usually stored reserve supplies of grain.

Poor harvests also played havoc with prices. Smaller supplies or larger demand raised grain prices. Even small increases in the cost of food could exert heavy pressure on peasant or artisan families. If prices increased sharply, many of those families fell back on poor relief from their local municipality or county or the church. What made the situation of food supply and prices so difficult was the peasants' sense of helplessness before the whims of nature and the marketplace.

Over the course of the century, historians now believe, there occurred a slow but steady inflation of bread prices, spurred largely by population growth. This inflation put pressure on all of the poor. The prices rose faster than urban wages and brought no appreciable advantage to the very small peasant producer. On the other hand, the rise in grain prices benefited landowners and those wealthier peasants who had surplus grain to sell.

The increasing price of grain presented landlords with an opportunity to improve their incomes and lifestyle. To those ends they began a series of innovations in farm production that are known as the *agricultural revolution*. This movement commenced during the sixteenth and seventeenth centuries in the Low Countries, where the pressures of the growing population and the shortage of land required changes in cultivation. Dutch landlords and farmers devised better ways to build dykes and to drain land so that they could farm more extensive areas. They also experimented with new crops, such as clover and turnips, that would increase the supply of animal fodder and restore the soil. These improvements became so famous that early in the seventeenth century Cornelius Vermuyden, a Dutch drainage engineer, was hired in England to drain thousands of acres of land around Cambridge.

The methods that the Dutch farmers had pioneered were extensively adopted in England during the early eighteenth century. The major agricultural innovations undertaken by the English included new methods of farming, new crops, and new modes of land holding, all of which eventually led to greater productivity. This advance in food production was necessary for the development of an industrial society. It assured food to people living in cities and freed agricultural labor for industrial production. The changing modes of agriculture sponsored by the landlords undermined the assumptions of traditional peasant production. Farming now took place not only for the local food supply but also to assure the landlord a handsome profit. The latter goal meant that the landlords began to exert new pressures on their tenants and serfs.

Landlords in Great Britain during the eighteenth century provided the most striking examples of the agricultural improvement. They originated almost no genuinely new methods of farming, but they provided leadership in popularizing ideas developed in the previous century either in the Low Countries or in England. Some of these landlords and agricultural innovators became very famous. For example, Jethro Tull (1674–1741) contributed a willingness to experiment and to finance the experiments of others. Many of his ideas, such as the refusal to use manure as fertilizer, were wrong. Others, however, such as using iron plows to overturn earth more deeply and planting wheat by a drill rather than by casting, were excellent. His methods permitted land to be cultivated for longer periods without having to be left fallow.

Charles "Turnip" Townsend (1674–1738) encouraged even more important innovations. He learned from the Dutch how to cultivate sandy soil with fertilizers. He also instituted crop rotation, using wheat, turnips, barley, and clover. This new system of rotation abolished the fallow field and replaced it with a field sown in a crop that both replaced soil nutrients and supplied animal fodder. The additional fodder meant that more livestock could be raised. The larger number of animals increased the quantity of manure available as fertilizer for the grain crops. Consequently, in the long run there was more food for both animals and human beings.

A third British agricultural improver was Robert Bakewell (1725–1795), who pioneered new methods of animal breeding that produced more and better animals and more milk and meat.

These and other innovations received widespread discussion in the works of Arthur Young (1741–1820), who edited the *Annals of Agriculture* and who in 1793 became secretary of the British

Board of Agriculture. Young traveled widely across Europe, and his books are among the most important documents of life during the second half of the eighteenth century.

Many of the agricultural innovations, which were adopted only very slowly, were incompatible with the existing organization of land in Britain. Small cultivators who lived in village communities still farmed most of the soil. Each farmer tilled an assortment of unconnected strips. The two- or three-field systems of rotation left large portions of land annually fallow and unproductive. Animals grazed on the common land in the summer and on the stubble of the harvest in the winter. Until at least the middle of the eighteenth century the decisions about what crops would be planted were made communally. The entire system discouraged improvement and favored the poorer farmers, who needed the common land and stubble fields for their animals. The village method provided little possibility of expanding the pasture land to raise more animals, that would in turn produce more manure, which could be used for fertilizer. Thus, the methods of traditional production aimed at a steady but not a growing supply of food.

In 1700 approximately half the arable land in Britain was farmed by this open-field method. By the second half of the century the rising price of wheat encouraged landlords to consolidate or enclose their lands to increase production. The enclosures were intended to use land more rationally and to achieve greater commercial profits. The process involved the fencing of common lands, the reclamation of previously untilled waste, and the transformation of strips into block fields. These procedures brought turmoil to the economic and social life of the countryside. Riots often ensued. Because many British farmers either owned their strips or rented them in a manner that amounted to ownership, the larger landlords had usually to resort to parliamentary acts to legalize the enclosure of the land, which they owned but rented to the farmers. Because the large landowners controlled Parliament, there was little difficulty in passing such measures. Between 1761 and 1792 almost 500,000 acres were enclosed through parliamentary act, as compared with 75,000 acres between 1727 and 1760. In 1801 a general enclosure act streamlined the process.

The enclosures were at the time and have remained among historians a very controversial topic. They permitted the extension of both farming and innovation. In that regard they increased food production on larger agricultural units. At the same time they disrupted the small traditional communities. They forced off the land some independent farmers, who had needed the common pasturage, and very poor cottagers, who had lived on the reclaimed waste land. However, the enclosures did not depopulate the countryside. In some counties where the enclosures took place, the population increased. New soil had come into production, and services subsidiary to farming also expanded.

The enclosures did not create the labor force for the British Industrial Revolution. What the enclosures most conspicuously displayed was the introduction of the entrepreneurial or capitalistic attitude of the urban merchant into the countryside. This commercialization of agriculture, which spread from Britain very slowly across the Continent during the next century, strained the paternal relationship between the governing and governed classes. Previously the landlords had somewhat looked after the welfare of the lower orders through price controls or alleviation of rents during depressed periods. However, as the landlords became increasingly concerned about profits, they began to leave the peasants to the mercy of the marketplace.

Improving agriculture tended to characterize farm production west of the Elbe. Dutch farming was quite efficient. In France, despite the efforts of the government to improve agriculture, enclosures were restricted. Yet there was much discussion in France about improving agricultural methods. These new procedures benefited the ruling classes because better agriculture increased their incomes and assured a larger food supply, which tended to discourage social unrest.

In Prussia, Austria, Poland, and Russia only very limited agricultural improvement took place. Nothing in the relationship of the serfs to their lords encouraged innovation. In eastern Europe the chief method of increasing production was to extend farming to previously untilled lands. The management of farms was usually under the direction of the landlords or their agents rather than of the villages. By extending tillage, the great landlords sought to squeeze more labor from their serfs rather than greater productivity from the soil. As in the West, the goal was increased profits for the landlords. But on the whole east European landlords were much less ambitious and successful. The only significant nutritional gain achieved through their efforts was the introduction of maize and the potato. Livestock production did not increase significantly.

Population Expansion

The assault on human dependence on nature through improved farming was both a cause and a result of an immense expansion in the population of Europe. The population explosion with which the entire world must today contend seems to have had its origins in the eighteenth century. Before this time Europe's population had experienced dramatic increases, but plagues, wars, or harvest failures had in time decimated the increase. Begin-

ning in the second quarter of the eighteenth century, the population began to grow without decimation.

Exact figures are lacking, but the best estimates suggest that in 1700 Europe's population, excluding the European provinces of the Ottoman Empire, stood between 100 million and 120 million people. By 1800 the figures had risen to almost 190 million, and by 1850 to 260 million. The population of England and Wales rose from 6 million in 1750 to over 10 million in 1800. France grew from 18 million in 1715 to approximately 26 million in 1789. Russia's population increased from 19 million in 1722 to 29 million in 1766. Such extraordi-

✎ Parliament Legislates Against the Consumption of Gin (1751)

The excessive drinking of gin in the middle of the eighteenth century raised much concern in England. Physicians believed that it led to the premature death of the poor. Magistrates believed that such drinking contributed to rioting and other public disorders. Under much public pressure the English Parliament passed an act in 1751 designed to limit the consumption of gin. The law placed a tax on the beverage and also regulated the licensing of establishments that sold gin.

Whereas the immoderate drinking of distilled spirituous liquors by persons of the meanest and lowest sort, hath of late years increased, to the great detriment of the health and morals of the common people; and the same hath in great measure been owing to the number of persons who have obtained licences to retail the same, under pretence of being distillers, and of those who have presumed to retail the same without licence . . . ; and whereas we your Majesty's dutiful and loyal subjects the commons of Great Britain in parliament assembled, ever attentive to the preservation and health of your Majesty's subjects, have taken this great evil into our serious consideration, and proposed such laws and provisions as appear to us to be most likely to put a stop to the same. . . . we do most humbly beseech your Majesty that it may be enacted . . . that from and after the first day of July, one thousand seven hundred and fifty one, there shall be raised, levied, collected and paid unto his Majesty, his heirs and successors, for the several kinds of spirituous liquors herein after mentioned, specified and enumerated (. . .) the several rates and duties

herein after-mentioned and expressed. . . .

[XIII] And be it further enacted by the authority aforesaid, That no license shall be granted for the retailing of spirituous liquors within any gaol, prison, house of correction, workhouse, or house of entertainment for any parish poor, and that all licenses granted or to be granted, contrary to this provision shall be void and of no effect from and after the said first day of July one thousand seven hundred and fifty one. . . .

[XXVIII] And it is further enacted by the authority aforesaid, That if any persons, to the number of five or more, shall . . . , in a tumultuous and riotous manner assemble themselves to rescue any offenders against this or any other act, relating to spirituous liquors or strong waters . . . or to assault, beat or wound any person or persons who shall have given or be about to give any information against . . . any person or persons offending against this or any of the said former acts . . . [they] shall be, and be adjudged to be guilty of felony. . . .

The Gin Act, 1751, Statutes at Large, XX, pp. 234–250. 24 Geo. II, c. 40, in D. B. Horn and Mary Ransome, *English Historical Documents*, 1714–1783 (London: Eyre and Spottiswoode, 1957), pp. 552–555.

nary, sustained growth put new demands on all resources and considerable pressure on existing social organization.

The population expansion occurred across the Continent in both the country and the cities. Only a limited consensus exists about the causes of this growth. There was a clear decline in the death rate. There were fewer wars and somewhat fewer epidemics in the eighteenth century. Hygiene and sanitation also improved. Better medical knowledge and techniques were once thought to have contributed to the decline in deaths. This factor is now discounted because the more important medical advances came after the initial population explosion or would not have contributed directly to it. Rather, changes in the food supply itself may have provided the chief factor that allowed the population growth to be sustained. The improved and expanding grain production made one contribution. Another and even more important modification was the cultivation of the potato. This tuber was a product of the New World and came into widespread European production during the eighteenth century. On a single acre a peasant could raise enough potatoes to feed his family for an entire year. With this more certain food supply, more children could be reared, and more could survive.

The impact of the population explosion can hardly be overestimated. It created new demands for food, goods, jobs, and services. It provided a new pool of labor. Traditional modes of production and living had to be revised. More people came to live in the countryside than could find employment there. Migration increased. There were also more people who might become socially and politically discontent. And because the population growth fed on itself, all of these pressures and demands continued to increase. The society and the social practices of the old regime literally outgrew their traditional bounds.

The Industrial Revolution of the Eighteenth Century

The second half of the eighteenth century witnessed the beginning of the industrialization of the European economy. The Industrial Revolution constituted the achievement of sustained economic growth. Previously production had been limited.

The economy of a province or a country might grow, but it soon reached a plateau. However, since the late eighteenth century the economy of Europe has managed to expand relatively uninterrupted. Depressions and recessions have been of a temporary nature, and even during such economic downturns the Western economy has continued to grow.

Industrialism at considerable social cost made possible more goods and more services than ever before in human history. Industrialism in Europe eventually overcame the economy of scarcity. The new means of production demanded new kinds of skills, new discipline in work, and a large labor force. The goods produced both met immediate consumer demand and created new demands. In the long run, industrialism clearly raised the standard of living and overcame the poverty that had been experienced by the overwhelming majority of Europeans who lived during the eighteenth century and earlier. Industrialization provided human beings greater control over the forces of nature than they had ever known before. The wealth produced by industrialism upset the political structures of the old regime and led to reforms. The economic elite of the emerging industrial society would eventually challenge the political dominance of the aristocracy.

Industrial Leadership of Great Britain

Great Britain was the home of the Industrial Revolution and, until the middle of the nineteenth century, maintained the industrial leadership of Europe. Several factors contributed to the early start in Britain. The nation constituted the single largest free-trade area in Europe. The British possessed good roads and waterways without internal tolls or other internal trade barriers. The country was endowed with rich deposits of coal and iron ore. The political structure was stable, and property was absolutely secure. Taxation was not especially heavy. In addition to the existing domestic consumer demand, the British economy also benefited from demand from the colonies in North America.

Finally, British society was relatively mobile by the standards of the time. Persons who had money or could earn money could rise socially. The British aristocracy would receive into its midst people who had amassed very large fortunes. No one of these factors preordained the British advance toward industrialism. However, the combination of them plus the progressive state of British agriculture provided the nation with the marginal advantage in the creation of a new mode of economic production.

While this economic development was occurring, people did not call it a *revolution*. That term came to be applied to the British economic phenomena only after the French Revolution. Then continental writers observed that what had taken place in Britain was the economic equivalent of the political events in France; hence the concept of an *industrial* revolution. It was revolutionary less in its speed, which was on the whole rather slow, than in its implications for the future of European society.

NEW METHODS OF TEXTILE PRODUCTION. Although eighteenth-century society was primarily devoted to agriculture, manufacturing permeated the countryside. The same peasants who tilled the land in spring and summer often spun thread or wove textiles in the winter. Under what is termed the *domestic* or *putting-out system,* agents of urban textile merchants took wool or other unfinished fibers to the homes of peasants, who spun it into thread. The agent then transported the thread to other peasants, who wove it into the finished product. The merchant sold the wares. In literally thousands of peasant cottages from Ireland to Austria, there stood either a spinning wheel or a handloom. Sometimes the spinners or weavers owned their own equipment, but more often than not by the middle of the century the merchant capitalist owned the machinery as well as the raw material.

What must be kept constantly in mind is the rather surprising fact that eighteenth-century industrial development took place within a rural setting. The peasant family living in a one- or two-room cottage was the basic unit of production rather than the factory. The family economy, rather than the industrial factory economy, characterized the century.

The married small farmer or peasant, burdened by taxes and feudal dues, could not support himself and his family by his own labor alone. It was necessary not merely for comfort but for economic survival that his wife spin or weave or knit and that his children be set to work as soon as they were physically able. The subsistence of these families depended on their capacity to find makeshift ways of earning income beyond what they received from farming. Certain members of the family, including the women, might migrate with the harvest. The

children might ultimately go to the city to seek employment. If any of these sources of income failed, the entire family might fall into dependence on some form of charity or crime. As Olwen Hufton has written, it was a life in which "one lived daily from hand to mouth without provision for old age, sickness, incapacity to work, or disasters such as harvest failure or even the arrival of a baby."[1]

The domestic system of textile production was a basic feature of this family economy. However, by mid-century a series of production bottlenecks had developed within the domestic system. The demand for cotton textiles was growing more rapidly than production. This demand arose particularly in Great Britain, where there existed a large domestic demand for cotton textiles from the growing population. There was a similar foreign demand on British production from its colonies in North America. It was in response to this consumer demand for cotton textiles that the most famous inventions of the Industrial Revolution were devised.

Cotton textile weavers had the technical capacity to produce the quantity of fabric that was in demand. However, the spinners did not possess the equipment to produce as much thread as the weavers needed and could use. This imbalance had been created during the 1730s by James Kay's invention of the flying shuttle, which increased the productivity of the weavers. Thereafter various groups of manufacturers and merchants offered prizes for the invention of a machine to eliminate this bottleneck. About 1765 James Hargreaves (d. 1778) invented the spinning jenny. Initially this machine allowed 16 spindles of thread to be spun, but by the close of the century its capacity had been increased to as many as 120 spindles.

The spinning jenny broke the bottleneck between the productive capacity of the spinners and the weavers, but it was still a piece of machinery that was used in the cottage. The invention that took cotton textile manufacture out of the home and put it into the factory was Richard Arkwright's (1732–1792) water frame, patented in 1769. It was a water-powered device designed to permit the production of a purely cotton fabric rather than a cotton fabric containing linen fiber for durability.

[1] Alan Mitchell and Istvan Deak (Eds.), *Everyman in Europe: Essays in Social History* Vol. 2 (Englewood Cliffs, N.J.: Prentice-Hall, 1974), p. 82.

Josiah Tucker Praises the New Use of Machinery in England

The extensive use of recently invented machines made the Industrial Revolution possible in England. This passage from a 1757 travel guide illustrates how contemporaries regarded the application of machines to various manufacturing processes as new and exciting.

Few countries are equal, perhaps none excel, the English in the number of contrivances of their Machines to abridge labour. Indeed the Dutch are superior to them in the use and application of Wind Mills for sawing Timber, expressing Oil, making Paper and the like. But in regard to Mines and Metals of all sorts, the English are uncommonly dexterous in their contrivance of the mechanic Powers; some being calculated for landing the Ores out of the Pits, such as Cranes and Horse Engines; others for draining off superfluous Water, such as Water Wheels and Steam Engines; others again for easing the Expense of Carriage such as Machines to run on inclined Planes or Roads downhill with wooden frames, in order to carry many Tons of Material at a Time. And to these must be added the various sorts of Levers used in different processes; also the Brass Battery works, the Slitting Mills, Plate and Flatting Mills, and those for making Wire of different Fineness. Yet all these, curious as they may seem, are little more than Preparations or Introductions for further Operations. Therefore, when we still consider that at Birmingham, Wolverhampton, Sheffield and other manufacturing Places, almost every Master Manufacturer hath a new Invention of his own, and is daily improving on those of others; we may aver with some confidence that those parts of England in which these things are seen exhibit a specimen of practical mechanics scarce to be paralleled in any part of the world.

Josiah Tucker, *Instructions to Travellers* (London: Privately Printed, 1757), p. 20.

Eventually Arkwright lost his patent rights, and other manufacturers were able to use his invention freely. As a result, numerous factories sprang up in the countryside near streams that provided the necessary waterpower. From the 1780s onward the cotton industry could meet an ever-expanding demand. In the last two decades of the century cotton output increased by 800 per cent over the production of 1780. By 1815 cotton composed 40 per cent of the value of British domestic exports, and by 1830 just over 50 per cent.

The Industrial Revolution had commenced in earnest by the 1780s, but the full economic and social ramifications of this unleashing of human productive capacity were not really felt until the early nineteenth century. The expansion of industry and the incorporation of new inventions often occurred rather slowly. For example, Edmund Cartwright (1743–1822) invented the power loom for machine weaving in the late 1780s. Yet not until the 1830s were there more power-loom weavers than hand-loom weavers in Britain. Nor did all of the social ramifications of industrialism appear immediately. The first cotton mills used waterpower, were located in the country, and rarely employed more than two dozen workers. Not until the late-century application of the steam engine, perfected by James Watt (1736–1819) in 1769, to the running of textile machinery could factories easily be located in or near existing urban centers. The steam engine not only vastly increased and regularized the available energy but also made possible the combination of urbanization and industrialization.

MAJOR INVENTIONS IN THE TEXTILE-MANUFACTURING REVOLUTION

1733	James Kay's flying shuttle
1765	James Hargreaves's spinning jenny (patent 1770)
1769	James Watt's steam engine patent
	Richard Arkwright's water-frame patent
1787	Edmund Cartwright's power loom

Richard Arkwright's water-frame spinning machine, so named because it ran by water power. Cotton spinning and weaving were major classic industries of the early industrial era. [Science Museum, London. Copyright Crown.]

condenser and the cylinder were heated, and it was practically untransportable. Despite these problems English mine operators employed the Newcomen machines to pump water out of coal and tin mines. By the third quarter of the eighteenth century almost a hundred Newcomen machines were operating in the mining districts of England.

During the 1760s James Watt, a Scottish engineer and machine maker, began to experiment with a model of a Newcomen machine at the University of Glasgow. He gradually understood that if the condenser were separated from the piston and the cylinder, much greater energy efficiency would result. In 1769 he patented his new invention, but transforming his idea into application presented difficulties. His design required exceedingly precise metalwork. Watt soon found a partner in Matthew Boulton, a toy manufacturer in Birmingham, the city with the most skilled metalworkers in Britain. Watt and Boulton, in turn, consulted with John Wilkinson, a cannon manufacturer, to find ways to drill the precise metal cylinders required by Watt's design. In 1776 the Watt steam engine found its first commercial application pumping water from mines in Cornwall.

THE STEAM ENGINE. The new technology in textile manufacture vastly increased cotton production and revolutionized a major consumer industry. But the invention that more than any other permitted industrialization to grow on itself and to expand into one area of production after another was the steam engine. This machine provided for the first time in human history a steady and essentially unlimited source of inanimate power. Unlike engines powered by water or the wind, the steam engine, driven by the burning of coal, was a portable source of industrial power that did not fail or falter as the seasons of the year changed. Unlike human power or animal power the steam engine depended on mineral energy that did not tire over the course of a day. Finally, the steam engine could be applied to a very large number of industrial and, eventually, transportation uses.

The first practical engine using steam power had been the invention of Thomas Newcomen in the early eighteenth century. The piston of this device was moved when the steam that had been induced into the cylinder condensed, causing the piston to fall. The Newcomen machine was very large. It was inefficient in its use of energy because both the

An eighteenth-century Newcomen engine used for pumping water from coal and tin mines. Thomas Newcomen's invention was the first engine to make practical use of steam power. [Science Museum, London. Copyright Crown.]

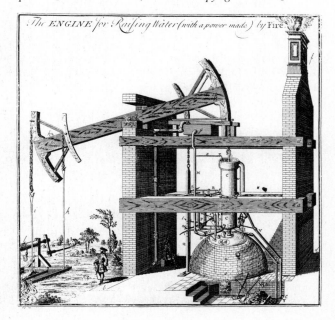

This landscape painting by an unknown contemporary British artist portrays the pithead of an eighteenth-century coal mine in England. The machinery on the left included a steam engine that powered equipment either to bring the mined coal to the surface or to pump water from the mine. [Walker Art Gallery, Liverpool.]

The use of the steam engine spread slowly because until 1800 Watt retained the exclusive patent rights. He was also reluctant to make further changes in his invention that would permit the engine to operate more rapidly. Boulton eventually persuaded him to make modifications and improvements. These allowed the engines to be used not only for pumping but also for running cotton mills. By the early nineteenth century the steam engine had become the prime mover for all industry. With its application to ships and then to wagons on iron rails, the steam engine also revolutionized transportation.

IRON PRODUCTION. The manufacture of high-quality iron has been basic to modern industrial development. It constitutes the chief element of all heavy industry and land or sea transport. Iron has also been the material out of which most productive machinery itself has been manufactured. During the early eighteenth century British ironmak-

ers produced somewhat less than twenty-five thousand tons annually. Three factors held back the production of the metal. Charcoal rather than coke was used to smelt the ore. Charcoal, which is derived from wood, was becoming a scarce commodity, and it did not burn at as high a temperature as coke, which is derived from coal. Until the perfection of the steam engine, insufficient blasts could be achieved in the furnaces. Finally, the demand for iron was limited. The elimination of the first two problems eliminated the third.

In the course of the century British ironmakers began to use coke, and the steam engine provided new power for the blast furnaces. Coke was an abundant fuel because of Britain's large coal deposits. The existence of the steam engine both improved iron production and increased the demand for iron.

In 1784 Henry Cort (1740–1800) introduced a new puddling process, that is, a new method for

Throughout most of the eighteenth century nearly all industrial manufacture took place in relatively small workshops such as the lead-casting shop illustrated in this print from the French Encyclopedia. Very large factories became established only quite late in the eighteenth century and early in the nineteenth.

melting and stirring the molten ore. Cort's process allowed more slag (the impurities that bubbled to the top of the molten metal) to be removed and a purer iron to be produced. Cort also developed a rolling mill that continuously shaped the still-molten metal into bars, rails, or other forms. Previously the metal had been pounded into these forms.

All of these innovations achieved a better, more versatile product at a lower cost. The demand for iron grew as its price became lower. By the early years of the nineteenth century British iron production amounted to over a million tons annually. The lower cost of iron, in turn, lowered the cost of steam engines and allowed them to be used more widely.

The Aristocracy

Despite the emerging Industrial Revolution, the eighteenth century remained the age of the aristocracy. The nobility of every country was the single wealthiest sector of the population; possessed the widest degree of social, political, and economic

power; and set the tone of polite society. Land continued to provide the aristocracy with its largest source of income, but the role of the aristocrat was not limited to the estate. The influence of aristocrats was felt in every area of life. To be an aristocrat was a matter of birth and legal privilege. This much they had in common across the Continent. In almost every other respect they differed markedly from country to country.

The smallest, wealthiest, best-defined, and most socially responsible aristocracy resided in Great Britain. It consisted of about four hundred families, whose eldest male member sat in the House of Lords. Through the corruptions of the electoral system these families also controlled a large number of seats in the House of Commons. The estates of the British nobility ranged from a few thousand to fifty thousand acres, from which they received rents. The nobles owned approximately one fourth of all the arable land in the country. Increasingly the money of the aristocracy was being invested in commerce, canals, urban real estate, mines, and sometimes industrial ventures. Because only the eldest son inherited the title and the land, younger sons moved into commerce, the army, the professions, and the church. The British landowners in the House of Commons levied taxes in Parliament and also paid taxes. They had almost no significant legal privileges, but their direct or indirect control of local government gave them immense political power and social influence. The aristocracy quite simply dominated the society and the politics of the English counties.

The openness of the English aristocracy and its acceptance of social and political responsibility as well as of power brought a degree of social mobility to English social life that was generally absent from other countries during the old regime. This factor may in large measure account for both the economic and the political advancement of Britain during the period.

The situation of the continental nobilities was less clear-cut. In France the nobility was divided between nobles of the sword and those of the robe. The former families enjoyed privileges deriving from military service; the latter had either gained their titles by serving in the bureaucracy or had purchased them. The two groups had frequently quarreled in the past but tended to cooperate during the eighteenth century to defend their common privileges.

The French nobility were also divided between those who held office or favor with the royal court

This famous portrait painting, Robert Andrews and His Wife, by the British artist Thomas Gainsborough (1728–1788) illustrates the peaceful and prosperous life of an English landowner. As the gun and dog indicate, he enjoyed considerable leisure time for sports such as hunting. [Reproduced by courtesy of the Trustees, The National Gallery, London.]

The Scots brothers Adam dominated British decorative taste in the late eighteenth century. About 1770, Robert, the more important, planned this elegant drawing room for Home House in London. [The Courtauld Institute of Art and Country Life, London.]

at Versailles and those who did not. The court nobility reaped the immense wealth that could be gained from holding high offices. The noble hold on such offices intensified over the course of the century. By the late 1780s appointments to the church, the army, and the bureaucracy, as well as other profitable positions tended to go to the nobles already established in court circles. Whereas these well-connected aristocrats were quite rich, other nobles who lived in the provinces were often rather poor. These *hobereaux*, as the poverty-stricken nobles were called, were sometimes little or no better off than wealthy peasants.

Despite differences in rank, origin, and wealth, all French aristocrats enjoyed certain hereditary privileges that set them apart from the rest of society. They were exempt from many taxes. For example, most French nobles did not pay the *taille*, which was the basic tax of the old regime. The nobles were technically liable for payment of the *vingtième*, or the "twentieth," which resembled an income tax. However, by virtue of protests and legal procedures, the nobility rarely felt the entire weight of this tax. The nobles were not liable for the royal *corvées*, or labor donations, which fell on the peasants. In addition to these exemptions, the approximately 400,000 French nobles could collect feudal dues from their tenants and enjoyed hunting and fishing privileges denied their tenants.

East of the Elbe River the character of the nobility became even more complicated and repressive. In Poland there were thousands of nobles, or *szlachta,* who after 1741 were entirely exempt from taxes. Until 1768 these Polish aristocrats possessed the right of life and death over their serfs. Most of the Polish nobility were relatively poor. The political power of the fragile Polish state resided in the few very rich nobles.

In Austria and Hungary the nobility continued to possess broad judicial powers over the peasantry through manorial courts.

In Prussia, after the accession of Frederick the Great in 1740, the position of the *Junker* nobles became much stronger. Frederick's various wars required the support of his nobles. He drew his officers almost wholly from the *Junker* class. The bureaucracy was also increasingly composed of nobles. As in other parts of eastern Europe, the Prussian nobles enjoyed extensive judicial authority over the serfs.

In Russia the eighteenth century saw what amounted to the creation of the nobility. Peter the Great's linking of state service and noble social status through the Table of Ranks (1722) established among Russian nobles a self-conscious class identity that had not previously existed. Thereafter they stood united in their determination to resist compulsory state service. In 1736 Empress Ann reduced such service to a period of twenty-five years. In 1762 Peter III removed the liability for compulsory service entirely from the greatest nobles. In 1785, in the Charter of the Nobility, Catherine the Great granted an explicit legal definition of noble rights and privileges in exchange for assurances of voluntary state service from the nobility. The noble privileges included the right of transmitting noble status to one's wife and children, the judicial protection of noble rights and property, considerable power over the serfs, and exemption from personal taxes.

The Russian Charter of the Nobility constituted one aspect of the broader European-wide development termed the *aristocratic resurgence.* Throughout the century the various nobilities felt their social position and privileges threatened by the expanding power of the monarchies and the growing wealth of merchants, bankers, and other commercial groups. All nobilities attempted to preserve their exclusiveness by making entry into their ranks and institutions more difficult. They also pushed for exclusively noble appointments to the officer corps of the armies, the bureaucracies, the government ministries, and the church. In that manner the nobles hoped to control the power of the monarchies.

On a third level the nobles attempted to use the authority of existing aristocratically controlled institutions against the power of the monarchies. These institutions included the British Parliament and on the Continent the French courts or *parlements,* the local aristocratic estates, and the provincial diets. Economically the aristocratic resurgence took the form of pressing the peasantry for higher rents or collecting long-forgotten feudal dues. There was a general tendency for the nobility to shore up its position by various appeals to traditional and often ancient privileges that had lapsed over the course of time. To contemporaries this aristocratic challenge to the monarchies and to the rising commercial classes constituted one of the most fundamental political facts of the day.

Cities

The Urban Setting

The influence of land and the landed society extended to the cities of the old regime. The cities of the eighteenth century, like those of today, depended on the countryside for their food supply. The specter of famine or food shortages haunted the cities. The governments took great care to ensure adequate supplies of grain by building granaries and by paying careful attention to the fluctuation of bread prices. The nobility were not absent from the cities. They owned homes in the urban centers and often possessed large blocks of city real estate, which they developed as sources of new rents. Frequently nobles controlled the municipal government and sat as judges in the municipal courts.

A two-way migration of people took place between the country and the city. In many cities, especially of central and eastern Europe, rural day laborers lived in the towns and traveled outward to find their work. Other cities witnessed what has become a common modern phenomenon: the migration of people from the countryside into the town to find work, better wages, and possibly a more exciting life. Thousands of men and women

London in 1711. St. James Place is in the right foreground, and the church of St. James in Picadilly is at the center left. This engraving by Johannes Kip is in the British Museum. [The Fotomas Index, London.]

born in the country moved to the city to become domestic servants or artisans.

Fernand Braudel has rightly described cities as "so many electric transformers," which "increase tension, accelerate the rhythm of exchange and ceaselessly stir up men's lives."[2] The eighteenth century witnessed a considerable growth of towns. The tumult of the day and the revolutions with which the century closed had a strong relationship to that urban expansion. London grew from about 700,000 inhabitants in 1700 to almost 1 million in 1800. By the time of the French Revolution the population of Paris stood over 500,000. Berlin's population tripled over the course of the century, reaching 170,000 in 1800. Saint Petersburg, founded in 1703, numbered over 250,000 inhabitants a century later. In addition to the growth of these capitals, the number of smaller urban units of 20,000–50,000 people increased considerably. However, this urban growth must be kept in per-

spective. Even in France and Great Britain probably somewhat less than 20 percent of the population lived in cities. And the town of 10,000 inhabitants was much more common than the giant urban center.

Practically all of these urban conglomerates were nonindustrial cities. They grew and expanded for reasons other than being the location of factories or other large manufacturing establishments. Only Manchester in England had experienced such industrial growth, and even its most spectacular expansion occurred after 1800.

Eighteenth-century cities fall into three broad and rather imperfect categories. The first and most common were market centers for the exchange of goods, most of which were produced locally. These relatively small provincial centers might also be the sites of local courts and state administration. The second category consisted of commercial, trading, shipping, and financial centers. These included the major sea and river ports. Finally, there were the great capital cities, which were also frequently commercial centers. In a sense both of the latter kinds of cities were the creation of the expanding bureaucratic states, whose rulers wished to see trade and commerce prosper. The great taxing power of those monarchies meant that vast wealth flowed into the capitals.

With the exception of Saint Petersburg, the cities of the eighteenth century were largely unplanned. A few urban developers might create elegant squares for the wealthy merchants or urban-dwelling aristocrats, but most cities simply expanded on the base of their medieval precursors. London had burned in 1666. Its reconstruction benefited from the planning and architecture of Sir Christopher Wren (1632–1723), but expansion was still quite haphazard. On the Continent many cities retained their medieval walls, within which and beyond which growth occurred. There was usually a central square with civic buildings or a cathedral or a fortress nearby. Quite often urban expansion pressed beyond the original city border and onto the territory of nonurban landlords. The authority of the latter would then extend over that part of the city. Consequently some urban areas found themselves governed by manorial courts and other institutions of the countryside.

Visible segregation often existed between the urban rich and the urban poor. The former, including the nobles and the upper middle class, lived in fashionable town-houses, often con-

[2] Fernand Braudel, *Capitalism and Material Life*, 1400–1800 (New York: Harper Torchbooks, 1973), p. 373.

The great park in Edinburgh, Scotland, was created in the eighteenth century by draining a lake that had previously existed in its place. The mid-nineteenth-century building in the center of the picture is the National Gallery of Scotland. [British Tourist Authority, New York.]

structed around newly laid-out green squares. The poorest town dwellers usually congregated along the rivers. Small merchants and craftsmen lived above their shops. Whole families might live in a single room. Sanitary facilities such as now exist were still unknown. There was little pure water. Cattle, pigs, goats, and other animals walked the streets with the people. All reports on the cities of Europe during this period emphasize both the striking grace and beauty of the dwellings of the wealthy and the dirt, filth, and stench that filled the streets.

Despite the more obvious drawbacks, it was still in the cities that men and women from all walks and stations of life found entertainment and excitement. More modes of recreation were available in cities than in the countryside. The cities provided more opportunities for theater, gambling,

The Royal Crescent in Bath, England, is an example of fashionable eighteenth-century town planning. The elliptical crescent contained luxury housing for wealthy families who vacationed in Bath, which is on the site of a Roman town of the first century B.C. [British Tourist Authority, New York.]

A hospital in Hamburg, 1746. The patients are crowded together in one large room, regardless of the type of their illness or state of health. Note the wigged doctor performing an amputation in the foreground. [Germanisches National-museum, Nuremberg.]

In late eighteenth-century Vienna, apprehended prostitutes had to appear before courts, as in this print, where they were ordered to have their hair shorn and then sent out to sweep the streets. [Österreichische Nationalbibliothek, Vienna]

GIN LANE.

Gin cursed Fiend, with Fury fraught,
Makes human Race a Prey;
It enters by a deadly Draught,
And steals our Life away.

Virtue and Truth driv'n to Despair,
It's Rage compells to fly,
But cherishes, with hellish Care,
Theft, Murder, Perjury.

Damn'd Cup! that on the Vitals preys,
That liquid Fire contains,
Which Madness to the Heart conveys,
And rolls it thro' the Veins.

Publish'd according to Act of Parliam.t Feb.y 1.st 1751.

Price 1.s

585

womanizing, and husband hunting. The season of parties in London drew noble and upper-gentry families from all over England. Here marriages were sought, and friendships were renewed. The French nobility had learned to enjoy Paris after Louis XIV had initially forced them to come to his court at nearby Versailles. And many Russian nobles came to crave life in Saint Petersburg after having first arrived under the compulsion of Peter the Great. The eighteenth-century town-house as much as the country house provided the aristocracy with its public stage.

There was, however, another side to urban life. This was the lot of the poor, who often depended on charity in the city. Poverty was not a city problem; it was usually worse in the countryside. But in the city poverty more visibly manifested itself in terms of crime, prostitution, vagrancy, begging, and alcoholism. Many a young man or woman from the countryside migrated to the nearest city to seek a better life, only to discover poor housing, little food, disease, degradation, and finally death. It did not require the Industrial Revolution and the urban factory to make the cities into hellholes for the poor and the dispossessed. The full darkness of London life during the mid-century "gin age," when consumption of that liquor blinded and killed many poor people, is evident in the engravings of William Hogarth (1697–1764). Also contrasting with the serenity of the aristocratic and upper-commercial-class lifestyle were the public executions that took place all over Europe, the breaking of men and women on the wheel in Paris, and the public floggings in Russia. Brutality condoned and carried out by the ruling classes was quite simply a fact of everyday life.

Urban Classes

Social divisions were as marked in the cities of the eighteenth century as they were in the industrial centers of the nineteenth. At the top of the urban social structure stood a generally small group of nobles, large merchants, bankers, financiers, clergy, and government officials. These men (and they were always men) controlled the political and economic affairs of the town. Normally they constituted a self-appointed and self-electing oligarchy who governed the city through its corporation or city council. These rights of self-government had normally been granted by some form of royal charter that gave the city corporation its au-

thority and the power to select its own members. In a few cities on the Continent, artisan guilds controlled the corporations, but more generally the councils were under the influence of the local nobility and the wealthiest commercial people.

THE MIDDLE CLASS. Another group in the city were the prosperous but not immensely wealthy merchants, tradesmen, bankers, and professional people. These were the most dynamic element of the urban population and constituted the persons traditionally regarded as the middle class, or *bourgeoisie*. The concept of the middle class was much less clear-cut than that of the nobility. They had less wealth than most nobles but more than urban artisans. The middle-class people lived in the cities and towns, and their sources of income had little or nothing to do with the land. The middle class normally stood on the side of reform, change, and economic growth. The middle-class commercial figures—traders, bankers, manufacturers, and lawyers—often found their pursuit of both profit and prestige blocked by the privileges of the nobility and its social exclusiveness. The bourgeoisie also wanted more rational regulations for trade and commerce, as did some of the more progressive aristocrats.

During the eighteenth century the middle class and the aristocracy were on a collision course. The former often imitated the lifestyle of the latter, and the nobles were increasingly embracing the commercial spirit of the middle class. The bourgeoisie was not rising to challenge the nobility; both were seeking to add new dimensions to their existing power and prestige. However, tradition and political connection gave the advantage to the nobility. Consequently, as the century passed, members of the middle class felt and voiced increasing resentment of the aristocracy. That resentment became more bitter as the wealth and the numbers of the *bourgeoisie* increased and the aristocratic control of political and ecclesiastical power became tighter. The growing influence of the nobility seemed to mean that the middle class would continue to be excluded from the political decisions of the day.

On the other hand, the middle class in the cities tended to fear the lower urban classes as much as they resented the nobility. The lower orders constituted a potentially violent element in the society, a potential threat to property, and, in their poverty, a drain on national resources. However, the lower orders were much more varied than either the city aristocracy or the middle class cared to admit.

French wines and silks arriving in London in 1757. French luxury goods were prized through-out Europe. The rising prosperity of the middle and upper-middle classes created an increasing market for such goods in Britain. This anti-French cartoon is by L. Boitard. It shows porters staggering under a chest full of imported cloth, emaciated Englishmen gratefully welcoming a French cook, a "lady of quality" offering the tuition of her children to a cringing French abbé as the English chaplain who has been instructing them looks on with sorrow, another "lady of quality" greeting a French dancing girl, a load of French cheese spilling from a cask as a small boy holds his nose against the stench, and dozens of imported luxury goods in chests and casks. [*Guildhall Library, London.*]

ARTISANS. The segment of the urban population that suffered from both the grasping of the middle class and the local nobility was that made up of the shopkeepers, the artisans, and the wage earners. These people constituted the single largest group in any city. The lives and experience of this class were very diverse. They included grocers, butchers, fishmongers, carpenters, cabinetmakers, smiths, printers, hand-loom weavers, and tailors, to give but a few examples. They had their own culture, values, and institutions. Like the peasants of the countryside they were in many respects very conservative. Their economic position was highly vulnerable. If a poor harvest raised the price of food, their own businesses suffered.

The entire life of these artisans and shopkeepers centered on their work. They usually lived near or at their place of employment. Most of them worked in shops with fewer than a half dozen other craftsmen. Their primary institution had histori-cally been the guild, but by the eighteenth century the guilds rarely possessed the influence of their predecessors in medieval or early modern Europe.

Nevertheless the guilds were not to be ignored. They played a conservative role. They did not seek economic growth or innovation. They attempted to preserve the jobs and the skills of their members. The guilds still were able in many countries to de-termine who might and might not pursue a partic-ular craft. They attempted to prevent too many people from learning a particular skill. The guilds also provided a framework for social and economic advancement. A boy might at an early age become an apprentice to learn a craft or trade. After sev-eral years he would be made a journeyman. Still later, if successful and sufficiently competent, he

Several examples of non-agricultural working-class skills can be shown. Printing shops produced the flood of eighteenth-century publications. Type was set and presses operated by hand, and the workmen were among the most highly skilled urban craftsmen. The picture is from the Encyclopedia. [*Charles Farrell Collection.*]

might become a master. The artisan could also receive certain social benefits from the guilds. These might include aid for his family during sickness or the promise of admission for his son. The guilds constituted the chief protection for artisans against the operation of the commercial market. They were particularly strong in central Europe.

The artisan class, with its generally conservative outlook, maintained a rather fine sense of social and economic justice. These ideals were based largely on traditional practices. If the collective sense of what was economically "just" was offended, artisans frequently manifested their displeasure through the instrument of the riot. The

OPPOSITE: *The skills of the blacksmith were required in both city and countryside. It is noteworthy that when Joseph Moxon, an English publisher and map-maker, wrote a series of* Mechanick Exercises: Or, the Doctrine of Handy-works, *published in parts between 1677 and 1683 and the first textbooks in any language on several of the major crafts, he began with the smith's trade because, as he said, "without the Invention of Smithing primarily, most other Mechanick Inventions would be at a stand: The Instruments or Tools that are used in them being either made of Iron, or of some other matter form'd by the help of Iron. But pray take notice, that by Iron I also mean Steel, it being originally Iron . . . . Some perhaps would have thought it more Policy to have introduced these Exercises with a more curious and less Vulgar Art than that of Smithing; but I am not of their opinion; for Smithing is (in all its parts) as curious a Handy-craft as any is . . ." This striking painting is by Joseph Wright of Derby (1734–1797). [Yale Center for British Art, New Haven.]*

589

Bread was the single most important foodstuff in the eighteenth century, and its relative availability and price were constant social, economic, and political problems. This etching of an urban bakery from the Encyclopedia *illustrates, from right to left, the kneading of the dough, the weighing of the loaves, the shaping of the loaves, and the baking of the bread. [The Granger Collection.]*

most sensitive area was the price of bread. If a baker or a grain merchant announced a price that was considered unjustly high, a bread riot might well ensue. Artisan leaders would confiscate the bread or grain and sell it for what the urban crowd considered a "just price." They would then give the money paid for the bread or grain to the baker or merchant. The possibility of bread riots acted as a restraint on the greed of merchants. Such disturbances represented a collective method of imposing the "just price" in place of the price set by the commercial marketplace. In other words, bread and food riots, which occurred throughout Europe, were not irrational acts of screaming hungry people but highly ritualized social phenomena of the old regime and its economy of scarcity.

Torture and public executions were still quite common during the eighteenth century. In some places, weights, as shown here, were used as a torture to extract information. Pressing was also a mode of execution for prisoners who refused to plead to the charges. [Bettmann Archive.]

The burning of Newgate Prison, London, in June 1780 during the anti-Catholic Gordon riots, which raged for several days. It is said that some three hundred prisoners were released and the unfortunate warden, Mr. Akerman, lost all his furniture in the fire. [The Granger Collection.]

Other kinds of riots were also a basic characteristic of eighteenth-century society and politics. The riot was a way in which people excluded in every other way from the political processes could make their will known. Sometimes urban rioters were incited by religious bigotry. For example, in 1753 London Protestant mobs compelled the government ministry to withdraw an act meant to legalize Jewish naturalization. In 1780 the same rabidly Protestant spirit manifested itself in the Gordon riots, named after Lord George Gordon, who had raised the specter of an imaginary Catholic plot after the government relieved military recruits from having to take specifically anti-Catholic oaths. In these riots and in food riots, violence was normally directed against property rather than against people. The rioters themselves were not "riffraff" but usually small shopkeepers, freeholders, craftsmen, and wage earners. They usually had no other purpose than to restore a traditional right or practice that seemed endangered. Nevertheless considerable turmoil and destruction could result from their actions.

During the last half of the century urban riots increasingly involved political ends. Though often simultaneous with economic disturbances, the political riot always had nonartisan leadership or instigators. In fact, the "crowd" of the eighteenth century was often the tool of the upper classes. In Paris the aristocratic *Parlement* often urged crowd action in their disputes with the monarchy. In Geneva middle-class citizens supported artisan riots against the local urban oligarchy. In Great Britain in 1792 the government turned out mobs to attack English sympathizers of the French Revolution. All of these and other various outbursts of popular unrest suggest that the crowd or mob first entered the European political and social arena well before the Revolution in France.

A Society on the Edge of Modern Times

This chapter opened by describing eighteenth-century society as traditional, hierarchical, corporate, and privileged. These features had characterized Europe for hundreds of years. However, by the close of the eighteenth century each of these facets of European life stood undermined or challenged in a fundamental fashion by developments within the society itself. Europe was on the brink of a new era in which the social, economic, and political relationships of centuries would be destroyed.

Society had remained traditional and corporate largely because of the economy of scarcity. The agricultural and industrial revolutions would eventually overcome most scarcity in Europe and the West generally. The commercial spirit and values of the marketplace clashed with the traditional values and practices of the peasants and the guilds. The desire to make money and accumulate profits was hardly new, but beginning in the eighteenth century, it was permitted fuller play than ever before in European history. The commercial spirit was a major vehicle of social change and, by the early nineteenth century, led increasingly to a conception of human beings as individuals rather than as members of communities.

The expansion of population provided a further stimulus for change and a challenge to tradition, hierarchy, and corporateness. The traditional economic and social organization had presupposed a stable or declining population. The additional numbers of people meant that new ways had to be devised to solve old problems. More people also meant more labor, more energy, and more minds contributing to the creation and solution of social

591

difficulties. The improvements in health and the longer life span may have given that larger population a new sense of confidence. The social hierarchy had to accommodate itself to more people. Corporate groups, such as the guilds, had to confront the existence of an expanded labor force. Moreover the products and industries arising from the Industrial Revolution made the society and the economy much more complicated. Class structure and social hierarchy remained, but the boundaries became blurred. New wealth meant that birth would eventually become less and less a determining factor in social relationships except in regard to the social role assigned to the two sexes.

Finally, the conflicting political ambitions of the monarchs, the nobilities, and the middle class generated innovation. The monarchs wanted to make their nations rich enough to wage war. As will be seen, this goal led them to attempt to interfere further with the privileges of the nobles. In the name of ancient rights the nobles attempted to secure and expand their existing social privileges by achieving further political power in the state. By making their privileges so exclusive, they helped to undermine the principle of privilege itself. The middle class, in all of its diversity, was growing wealthier from trade, commerce, and the practice of the professions. Its members wanted social prestige and political influence equal to their wealth. And they wanted the government to function in an efficient and businesslike manner. They resented privileges, frowned at hierarchy, and rejected tradition.

All of these factors meant that the society of the eighteenth century stood at the close of one era in European history and at the opening of another. What began to make contemporaries aware of that fact were the great wars of mid-century, the revolt of the British colonies in North America, and the intellectual currents of the Enlightenment.

Suggested Readings

C. B. A. Behrens, *The Ancien Régime* (1967). A brief account of life in France with excellent illustrations.

J. Blum, *Lord and Peasant in Russia from the Ninth to the Nineteenth Century*(1961). A thorough and wide-ranging discussion.

J. Blum, *The End of the Old Order in Rural Europe* (1978). The most comprehensive treatment of life in rural Europe, especially central and eastern, from the early eighteenth through the mid-nineteenth centuries.

F. Braudel, *Capitalism and Material Life, 1400–1800* (1974). An investigation of the physical resources and human organization of preindustrial Europe.

F. Braudel, *The Structures of Everyday Life: The Limits of the Possible*, trans. by M. Kochan (1982). A magisterial survey by the most important social historian of our time.

P. Deane, *The First Industrial Revolution*, 2nd ed. (1979). A well-balanced and systematic treatment.

J. DeVries, *The Economy of Europe in an Age of Crisis, 1600–1750* (1976). An excellent overview that sets forth the main issues.

P. Earle (Ed.), *Essays in European Economic History, 1500–1800* (1974). A useful collection of articles that cover most of the major states of western Europe.

F. Ford, *Robe and Sword: The Regrouping of the French Aristocracy After Louis XIV* (1953). An important treatment of the growing social tensions within the French nobility during the eighteenth century.

R. Forster, *The Nobility of Toulouse in the Eighteenth Century* (1960). A local study that displays the variety of noble economic activity.

R. Forster and E. Forster, *European Society in the Eighteenth Century* (1969). An excellent collection of documents.

D. George, *London Life in the Eighteenth Century* (1925). A lively account.

D. V. Glass and D. E. C. Eversley (Eds.), *Population in History: Essays in Historical Demography* (1965). Fundamental for an understanding of the eighteenth-century increase in population.

A. Goodwin (Ed.), *The European Nobility in the Eighteenth Century* (1953). Essays on the nobility in each state.

P. Goubert, *The Ancien Régime: French Society, 1600–1750*, trans. by Steve Cox (1974). A superb account of the peasant social order.

H. J. Habakkuk and M. Postan (Eds.), *The Cambridge Economic History of Europe* (1965). Separate chapters by different authors on major topics.

D. Hay et al., *Albion's Fatal Tree: Crime and Society in Eighteenth-Century England* (1976). Separate essays on a previously little explored subject.

O. H. Hufton, *The Poor of Eighteenth-Century France, 1750–1789* (1975). A brilliant study of poverty and the family economy.

E. L. Jones, *Agriculture and Economic Growth in England, 1650–1815* (1968). A good introduction to an important subject.

P. Laslett, *The World We Have Lost* (1965). Examination of English life and society before the coming of industrialism.

J. Lough, *An Introduction to Eighteenth-Century France* (1960). A systematic survey with good quotations (in French) from contemporaries.

S. Pollard and C. Holmes, *Documents of European Economic History: The Process of Industrialization, 1750–1870* (1968). A very useful collection.

G. RUDÉ, *The Crowd in History, 1730–1848* (1964). This and the following work were pioneering studies.

G. RUDÉ, *Paris and London in the Eighteenth Century* (1973).

G. RUDÉ, *Europe in the Eighteenth Century* (1972). A survey with emphasis on social history.

L. STONE, *The Family, Sex and Marriage in England 1500–1800* (1977). A pioneering study of a subject receiving new interest from historians.

T. TACKETT, *Priest and Parish in Eighteenth-Century France: A Social and Political Study of the Curés in a Diocese of Dauphiné, 1750–1791* (1977). A very important local study that displays the role of the church in the fabric of social life in the old regime.

C. WILSON, *England's Apprenticeship, 1603–1763* (1965). A broad survey of English economic life on the eve of industrialism.

The BLOODY MASSACRE perpetrated in King — Street BOSTON on March 5th 1770, by a party of the 29th REGt.

Engrav'd Printed & Sold by PAUL REVERE BOSTON

Unhappy Boston! see thy Sons deplore,
Thy hallow'd Walks besmear'd with guiltless Gore.
While faithless P—n and his savage Bands,
With murd'rous Rancour stretch their bloody Hands;
Like fierce Barbarians grinning o'er their Prey,
Approve the Carnage, and enjoy the Day.

If scalding drops from Rage from Anguish Wrung,
If speechless Sorrows lab'ring for a Tongue,
Or if a weeping World can ought appease
The plaintive Ghosts of Victims such as these;
The Patriot's copious Tears for each are shed,
A glorious Tribute which embalms the Dead.

But know Fate summons to that awful Goal.
Where Justice strips the Murd'rer of his Soul:
Should venal C—ts the scandal of the Land,
Snatch the relentless Villain from her Hand,
Keen Execrations on this Plate inscrib'd,
Shall reach a Judge who never can be brib'd.

The unhappy Sufferers were Messrs. Saml GRAY, Saml MAVERICK, Jams CALDWELL, CRISPUS ATTUCKS & Patk CARR
Killed. Six wounded; two of them (Christr MONK & JOHN CLARK) Mortally.

594

20 Empire, War, and Colonial Rebellion

THE MIDDLE of the eighteenth century witnessed a renewal of European warfare on a worldwide scale. The conflict involved two separate but interrelated rivalries. Austria and Prussia fought for dominance in central Europe while Great Britain and France dueled for commercial and colonial supremacy. The wars were long, extensive, and very costly in both men and money. They resulted in a new balance of power on the Continent and on the high seas. Great Britain gained a world empire, and Prussia was recognized as a great power. Moreover the expense of these wars led every major European government after the Peace of Paris of 1763 to reconstruct their policies of taxation and finance. Those revised fiscal programs produced internal conditions for the monarchies of Europe that had most significant results for the rest of the century. These included the American Revolution, enlightened absolutism on the Continent, and a continuing financial crisis for the French monarchy.

Eighteenth-Century Empires

Periods of European Overseas Empires

Since the Renaissance, European contacts with the rest of the world have gone through four distinct stages. The first was that of the discovery, exploration, and initial conquest and settlement of the New World. This period had closed by the end of the seventeenth century. The second era, which is largely the concern of this chapter, was one of colonial trade rivalry among Spain, France, and Great Britain. The Anglo-French side of the contest has often been compared to a second hundred years' war. During this second period, which may be said to have closed during the 1820s, both the British colonies of the North American seaboard and the Spanish colonies of Central and South America emancipated themselves from European control. The third stage of European contact with

The "Boston Massacre" of March 5, 1770 was depicted in an engraving quickly made and put on sale by Paul Revere. [The Granger Collection.]

the non-European world occurred in the nineteenth century, when new formal empires involving the European administration of indigenous peoples were carved out in Africa and Asia. Those nineteenth-century empires also included new areas of European settlement, such as Australia, New Zealand, and South Africa. The bases of these empires were trade, national honor, and military strategy. The last period of European empire came in the present century, with the decolonization of peoples previously under European colonial rule.

During the four and a half centuries before decolonization, Europeans exerted political dominance over much of the rest of the world. They frequently treated other peoples as social, intellectual, and economic inferiors. They ravaged existing cultures because of greed, religious zeal, or political ambition. These actions are major facts of European history and significant factors in the contemporary relationship of Europe and its former colonies. What allowed the Europeans to exert such influence and domination for so long over so much of the world was not any innate cultural superiority but a technological supremacy closely related to naval power and gunpowder. Ships and guns allowed the Europeans to exercise their will almost wherever they chose.

Mercantile Empires

Navies and merchant shipping were the keystones of the mercantile empires of the eighteenth century. These empires were meant to bring profit to a nation rather than to provide areas for settlement. The Treaty of Utrecht (1713) established the boundaries of empire during the first half of the century. Except for Brazil, which was governed by Portugal, Spain controlled all of mainland South America, and in North America it controlled Florida, Mexico, and California. The Spanish also governed the island of Cuba and half of Hispaniola. The British Empire consisted of the colonies along the North Atlantic seaboard, Nova Scotia, Newfoundland, Jamaica, and Barbados. Britain also possessed a few trading stations on the Indian subcontinent. The French domains covered the Saint Lawrence River valley; the Ohio and Mississippi river valleys; the West Indian islands of Saint Domingue, Guadeloupe, and Martinique; and stations in India. The Dutch controlled Surinam, or Dutch Guiana, in South America; various trading stations in Ceylon and Bengal; and, most impor-

tantly, the trade with Java in what is now Indonesia. All of these powers also possessed numerous smaller islands in the Caribbean. So far as eighteenth-century developments were concerned, the major rivalries existed among the Spanish, the French, and the British.

To the extent that any formal economic theory lay behind the conduct of these empires, it was mercantilism, that practical creed of hardheaded businessmen. Initially, the fundamental point of this outlook was the necessity of acquiring a favorable trade balance of gold and silver bullion. Such bullion was regarded as the measure of a country's wealth, and a nation was truly wealthy only if it amassed more bullion than its rivals. By the late seventeenth century mercantilist thinking, as developed by writers such as Thomas Mun in *England's Treasure by Forraign Trade* (1664), had come to regard general foreign trade and the level of domestic industry as the true indications of a nation's prosperity. But from beginning to end the economic well-being of the home country was the first concern of mercantilist writers. Colonies were to provide markets and natural resources for the industries of the home country. In turn, the home country was to furnish military security and political administration for the colonies. For decades both sides assumed that the colonies were the inferior partner in the relationship. The mercantilist statesmen and traders regarded the world as an arena of scarce resources and economic limitation. They assumed that one national economy could grow only at the expense of others. The home country and its colonies were to trade only with each other. To that end they attempted to forge trade-tight systems of national commerce through navigation laws, tariffs, bounties to encourage production, and prohibitions against trading with the subjects of other monarchs. National monopoly was the ruling principle.

Mercantilist ideas had always been neater on paper than in practice. By the early eighteenth century mercantilist assumptions were held only in the vaguest manner. They stood too far removed from the economic realities of the colonies and perhaps from human nature. The colonial and home markets simply failed to mesh. Spain could not produce sufficient goods for South America. Economic production in the British North American colonies challenged English manufacturing and led to British attempts to limit certain colonial industries, such as iron and hat making. Colonists of

The Custom House in Dublin, Ireland, is one of the most elegant political buildings of Europe. Its fine architecture suggests the importance that eighteenth-century governments attached to trade and the regulation of trade. [Irish Tourist Board, New York.]

different countries wished to trade with each other. English colonists could buy sugar more cheaply from the French West Indies than from English suppliers. The traders and merchants of one nation always hoped to break the monopoly of another. For all these reasons the eighteenth century became the "golden age of smugglers."[1] The governments could not control the activities of all their subjects. Clashes among colonists could and did bring about conflict between governments.

Areas of Rivalry and Conflict

The Spanish Empire stood on the defensive throughout the century. It was a sprawling expanse of territory over which the Spanish government wished to maintain a commercial monopoly without possessing the capacity to do so. Spanish colonists looked to illegal imports from French and British traders to supply needed goods. Both

[1] Walter Dorn, *Competition for Empire*, 1740–1763 (New York: Harper, 1940), p. 266.

France and Britain assumed a very aggressive stance toward the Spanish Empire because they viewed it as a vast potential market and a major source of gold. Their rivalry for intrusion into the mainland Spanish markets was duplicated by their other conflicts in North America, India, and the West Indies.

Neither the French nor the British colonies of North America fit particularly well into the mercantile pattern of empire. Trade with these areas during the early part of the century was smaller than with the West Indies. These mainland colonies were settlements rather than arenas for economic exploitation. The French lands of Canada were quite sparsely populated. Relations with the Indians were troublesome. The economic interests and the development of the colonies were not wholly compatible with those of the home countries. Major flash points existed between France and Britain on the North American continent. Their colonists quarreled endlessly with each other. Both groups of settlers were jealous over rights to the lower Saint Lawrence River valley,

❧ The Mercantilist Position Stated

One of the earliest discussions of the economic theory of mercantilism appeared in *England's Treasure by Forraign Trade* (1664) by Thomas Mun. In this passage from that work Mun explained why it was necessary to the prosperity of the nation for more goods to be exported than imported. Although later mercantilist theory became somewhat more sophisticated, all writers in the eighteenth century emphasized the necessity of a favorable balance of trade.

The ordinary means therefore to increase our wealth and treasure is by Forraign Trade *wherein wee must ever observe this rule; to sell more to strangers yearly than wee consume of theirs in value. For suppose that when this Kingdom is plentifully served with the Cloth, Lead, Tinn, Iron, Fish and other native commodities, we doe yearly export the overplus to forraign countries to the value of twenty two hundred thousand pounds; by which means we are enabled beyond the Seas to buy and bring in forraign wares for our use and Consumptions, to the value of twenty hundred thousand pounds; By this order duly kept in our trading, we may rest assured that the Kingdom shall be enriched yearly two hundred thousand pounds, which must be brought to us in so much Treasure; because that part of our stock which is not returned to us in wares must necessarily be brought home in treasure [i.e., gold or silver bullion].*

Thomas Mun, *England's Treasure by Forraign Trade,* as quoted in Charles Wilson, *England's Apprenticeship,* 1603–1763 (London: Longman, 1965), p. 60.

---

upper New England, and later the Ohio River valley. There were other rivalries over fishing rights, fur trade, and relationships with the Indians.

Unlike North America or the West Indies, India was neither the home of migrating Europeans nor an integral part of their imperial schemes. The Indian subcontinent was an area where both France and Britain traded through privileged, chartered companies that enjoyed a legal monopoly. The East India Company was the English institution; the French equivalent was the Compagnie des Indes. The trade of India and Asia figured only marginally in the economics of empire. Some bullion gained by trade or piracy in the West Indies was shipped to India, where it was used to purchase cotton cloth that was shipped to England and then used to purchase slaves in Africa for the West Indies. The commercial problem with the states of India was that the European countries produced little or nothing wanted in the region.

Nevertheless throughout the century trade and involvement on the subcontinent continued. Enterprising Europeans always hoped that in some fashion profitable commerce with India might develop. Others regarded India as a springboard into the even larger potential market of China. The original European footholds in India were trading posts called *factories.* They existed through privileges granted by the various Indian governments. Two circumstances arose during the middle of the eighteenth century to change this situation. First, in several of the Indian states decay occurred in the indigenous administration and government. Second, Joseph Dupleix (1697–1763) for the French and Robert Clive (1725–1774) for the British saw these developments as opportunities for expanding the control of their respective companies (the Compaigne des Indes and the East India Company). To maintain their own security and to expand their privileges, the companies began to fill the power vacuum and in effect took over the government of some regions. Each group of Europeans hoped to checkmate the other.

STRUGGLE FOR THE WEST INDIES. The heart of the eighteenth-century colonial rivalry was the West Indies. These islands, close to the American continents, constituted the jewels of empire. Here the colonial powers pursued their greedy ambitions in close proximity to each other. The West Indies raised tobacco, cotton, indigo, coffee, and sugar, for which there existed strong markets in Europe. Sugar in particular had become a product of standard consumption rather than a luxury. It was used in coffee, tea, and cocoa, for making candy and preserving fruits, and in the brewing industry. There seemed no limit to its uses. Sugar was also important to the domestic economy of Europe. Sugar refining had become a major industry in France. Sugar and tobacco figured prominently in the reexport industry. For example, large quantities of tobacco were shipped from Scotland to the Continent.

Basic to the economy of the West Indies as well as to that of South America and the British colonies on the south Atlantic seaboard of North America was the institution of slavery. Hundreds of thousands of slaves were imported into the Americas during the eighteenth century. Planters could not attract sufficient quantities of free labor to these areas. They became wholly dependent on slaves. Slavery and the slave trade touched most of the economy of the transatlantic world. Cities such as Newport, Rhode Island; Liverpool, England; and Nantes, France, enjoyed prosperity that rested almost entirely on the slave trade. All of the shippers who handled cotton, tobacco, and sugar depended on slavery, though they might have no direct contact with the institution. There was a general triangle of trade that consisted of carrying goods to Africa to be exchanged for slaves, who were then taken to the West Indies, where they were traded for sugar and other tropical produce, which were then shipped to Europe. Not all ships necessarily covered all three legs of the triangle.

Another major trade pattern existed between New England and the West Indies. New England fish or ship stores were traded for sugar.

Within the rich commerce and agriculture of the West Indies there existed three varieties of colonial rivalry. Producers of different nations were intensely jealous of each other. The quantity of sugar produced had expanded so as to depress the price in Europe. Consequently one group of planters hoped not to conquer the lands of their competitors but rather to destroy the productive capacity of those islands. There was a second form of rivalry among shippers in the Caribbean. Every captain hoped to transport as much sugar as possible to Europe. Finally, the West Indies possessions of France and Britain provided excellent bases for penetration of the trade of the Spanish Empire. Many French and British ship captains in the West Indies were admitted smugglers, and some were little better than pirates.

The close interrelationship of the West Indies and the European economies meant that significant numbers of British, French, and Spanish subjects had an interest in the area. This West India Interest, as it was called in England, consisted of absentee plantation owners, shippers, insurers, merchants, bankers, owners of domestic industries dependent on West Indian products, and all of those involved in the slave trade. In Great Britain it was an articulate and well-organized pressure

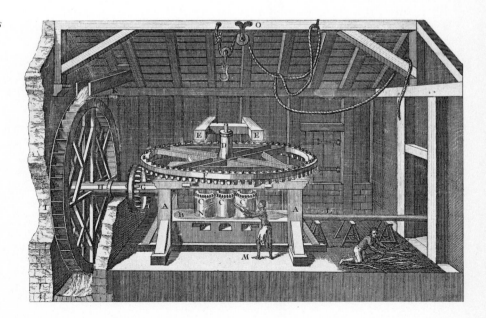

An eighteenth-century sugar press in Cuba. At this period it was tended by slaves. Most of the sugar would eventually end up in Europe, where there was a growing market for the product. [*Bettmann Archive.*]

On a French West Indian plantation slaves pick cotton on the right while other slaves on the left remove the seeds from the fiber. The particular variety of cotton shown in this engraving grew on shrubs rather than on the bushes grown in the American south. [*The Granger Collection.*]

group. In 1739 the West India Interest along with the political enemies of Robert Walpole succeeded in driving Britain into a war with Spain, the War of Jenkins's Ear.

The Treaty of Utrecht (1713) included two special privileges for Great Britain in regard to the Spanish Empire. The British received a thirty-year *asiento,* or contract, to furnish slaves to the Spanish. Britain also gained the right to send one ship each year to the trading fair at Portobello, a major Caribbean seaport on the Panamanian coast. These two privileges allowed British traders and smugglers potential inroads into the Spanish market. Little but friction arose from these rights. The annual ship to Portobello was often supplied with additional goods during the night as it lay in port. Much to the chagrin of the British, the Spanish

government took its own alleged trading monopoly seriously and maintained coastal patrols, which boarded and searched English vessels to look for contraband.

In 1731 during one such boarding operation there was a fight, and an English captain named Robert Jenkins had his ear cut off by the Spaniards. Thereafter he carried about his severed ear preserved in a jar of brandy. This incident was of little importance until 1738, when Jenkins appeared before the British Parliament, reportedly brandishing his ear as an example of Spanish atrocities to British merchants in the West Indies. The British merchant and West Indies interests put great pressure on Parliament to do something about Spanish intervention in their trade. Robert Walpole attempted to reach a solution through negotiations. However, Parliament—and especially the members who believed that the war would drive Walpole from office—refused all accommodation. In late 1739 Great Britain went to war with Spain.

At the outbreak of hostilities, the French, under the administation of Cardinal Fleury, stood ready to profit from the British–Spanish conflict. They expected to see British trade harmed and eventually to receive Spanish commercial favors for aid. None of the major European powers except Britain had any standing grudge against France. The years of Fleury's cautious policy were about to pay off. Then, quite literally overnight, the situation on the Continent changed.

Mid-Century Wars

The War of the Austrian Succession (1740–1748)

In December 1740, after possessing the throne of Prussia for less than seven months, Frederick II ordered his troops to occupy the Austrian province of Silesia. The invasion shattered the provisions of the Pragmatic Sanction and upset the continental balance of power as established by the Treaty of Utrecht. The young king of Prussia had treated the House of Hapsburg simply as another German state rather than as the leading state in the region. The province of Silesia itself rounded out Prussia's

---

CONFLICTS OF THE MID-EIGHTEENTH CENTURY

1713	Treaty of Utrecht
1739	Outbreak of War of Jenkins's Ear between England and Spain
1740	War of the Austrian Succession commences
1748	Treaty of Aix-la-Chapelle
1756	Convention of Westminster between England and Prussia Seven Years' War opens
1757	Battle of Plassey
1759	British forces capture Quebec
1763	Treaty of Hubertusburg Treaty of Paris

---

possessions, and Frederick was determined to keep his ill-gotten prize. In 1740 the other European states were not sure whether to consider the Prussian invasion the act of a great power or that of a mere aggressive upstart. The wars of the next quarter century affirmed the former judgment.

Maria Theresa was twenty-three years old and had succeeded to the Austrian crown only two months before Frederick's move. Her army was weak, her bureaucracy inefficient, and the loyalty of her subjects uncertain. She herself was inexperienced and was more usually guided by the values of piety than by hardheaded statecraft. Yet she succeeded in rallying to her side the Magyars of Hungary and the aristocratic leaders of her other domains. They were genuinely sympathetic to her plight and inspired by her courage. Maria Theresa's great achievement was not the reconquest of Silesia, which eluded her, but the preservation of the Hapsburg Empire as a major political power.

The seizure of Silesia could have marked the opening of a general hunting season on Hapsburg holdings and the beginning of revolts by Hapsburg subjects. Instead it proved the occasion for new political allegiances. Maria Theresa achieved these new loyalties, especially between herself and the Magyars, not merely through heroism but more specifically by granting new privileges to the nobles of the various Hapsburg realms. The empress recognized Hungary as the most important of her crowns and promised the Magyars considerable local autonomy. In this fashion she preserved the Hapsburg state, but at great cost to the power of the central monarchy. As a result, the Hapsburg holdings would never become a centrally unified modern political entity.

The war over the Austrian succession and the British–Spanish commercial conflict could have remained separate disputes. They were neither logically nor necessarily politically related. What ultimately united them was the role of France. Cardinal Fleury understood that the long-range interests of France lay in the direction of commercial growth. However, just as British merchant interests had pushed Robert Walpole into war, a group of court aristocrats led by the Comte de Belle Isle compelled the elderly Fleury to abandon his planned naval attack on British trade and to support the Prussian aggression against Austria. This proved to be one of the most fateful decisions in French history.

❧ Prince Frederick Discusses Statecraft and European Affairs ═══

King Frederick William I of Prussia thought at times that he had reason for concern about the qualities of his flute-playing, philosophizing son, Prince Frederick. He need not have worried. The young prince was already able to write this hard-nosed essay in 1738, two years before he became King Frederick II. He stated the view common at the time that a monarch normally seeks to increase the power of his state. He also suggested that the major states of Europe were not in a healthy balance. Two years later he followed up these thoughts by invading Silesia.

It is an unshaken principle among kings to aggrandize themselves as much as their power will permit; and, though such aggrandizement must be subject to different modifications, and infinitely varied according to the situation of princes, the power of neighboring states, or fortunate opportunities, the principle is not the less unchangeable, and is never abandoned by monarchs. Their pretended fame is part of this system. In a word, it is necessary they should increase in greatness.

.   .   .   .

From what has been said, it will be easy to perceive that the political body of Europe is in a perilous situation. It is deprived of its due equilibrium, and is in a state in which it cannot long remain, without great risk. The political body resembles the human body, which can only subsist by a mixture of equal quantities of the acid and the alkali. Whenever one of these two substances predominates, the body is made sensible of it, and the health is considerably injured: should that substance continue to increase, it may finally cause the destruction of the machine. Thus, whenever the policy and prudence of the princes of Europe lose sight of the maintenance of a just balance, between the principal powers, it is felt by the constitution of the whole body-politic. Violence on the one side, weakness on the other; the desire of invading on the one, and on the other the inability to prevent invasion. The most puissant [powerful] gives law, and the feeble are under the necessity of adding their signature. All finally concur in augmenting disorder and confusion. Force acts like an impetuous torrent, passes its bounds, carries everything with it, and exposes this unfortunate body-politic to the most fatal revolutions.

Frederick the Great, "Considerations on the Present State of the Body-Politic of Europe" (1738), in *Posthumous Works of Frederic II, King of Prussia,* vol. 4 trans. by Thomas Holcroft (London: G. G. J. and J. Robinson 1789), pp. 364–365, 381–382.

Even though the Hapsburgs had been the historic enemy of France, a war against Austria was not in the French interest in 1741. In the first place, aid to Prussia had the effect of consolidating a new and powerful state in Germany. That new power could, and indeed later did, endanger France. Second, the French move against Austria brought Great Britain into the continental war. The British, as usual, wanted to see the Low Countries remain in friendly hands. In the eighteenth century that policy required continued Hapsburg control of the Austrian Netherlands. In 1744 the British–French conflict expanded beyond the Continent, as France decided to support Spain against Britain in the New World. As a result, French military and economic resources became badly divided. France could not bring sufficient strength to the colonial struggle. Having chosen to continue a struggle from the past with Austria, France lost the struggle for the future against Great Britain.

By 1748 the war had become a military stalemate for all concerned. Austria had not been able to regain Silesia, but it had fended off further aggression from other German states. The French army, led by Marshal Maurice de Saxe (1696–1750), won a series of splendid victories over the British and the Austrians in the Netherlands during 1747 and 1748. Britain, for its part, had pursued a very successful colonial campaign. Its forces in America captured the fortress of Louisburg at the mouth of the Saint Lawrence River, and the British more than held their own on the Indian subcontinent.

Maria Theresa of Austria (seated right) and her husband, Emperor Frances I (seated left), with their very large family. Her son and successor, Joseph II, is the tall adolescent near her. The artist was Martin Meytens (1695–1770), court painter in Vienna. [Kunsthistorisches Museum, Vienna.]

Warfare on French commerce had been highly effective. These victories overseas compensated for the poor showing on the Continent. Consequently the war was brought to a close by the Treaty of Aix-la-Chapelle (1748). In effect the treaty restored the conditions that had existed prior to the war, with the exception that Prussia retained Silesia. Spain renewed the *asiento* agreement with Great Britain. All observers believed that the treaty constituted a truce rather than a permanent peace.

The Battle of Fontenoy, 1745, during the War of the Austrian Succession. The French under Marechal de Saxe defeated an English army that was defending the territory of Maria Theresa in the Austrian Netherlands. [Giraudon.]

The "Diplomatic Revolution" of 1756

Before the rivalries again erupted into war, a dramatic shift of alliances took place. In 1756 Prussia and Great Britain signed the Convention of Westminster. It was a defensive alliance aimed at preventing the entry of foreign troops into the Germanies. Frederick II feared invasions by both Russia and France. The convention meant that Great Britain, the ally of Austria since the wars of Louis XIV, had now joined forces with Austria's major eighteenth-century enemy.

Maria Theresa was despondent over this development. However, her foreign minister, Count

Wenzel Anton Kaunitz (1711–1794), was delighted. This brilliant diplomat and servant of the Hapsburg dynasty had long hoped for an alliance between Austria and France for the dismemberment of Prussia. The Convention of Westminster made this alliance, unthinkable a few years earlier, possible. France was agreeable because Frederick had not consulted it before coming to his understanding with Britain. Consequently, later in 1756, France and Austria signed a defensive alliance. Kaunitz had succeeded in completely reversing the direction of French foreign policy from Richelieu through Fleury. France would now fight to restore Austrian supremacy in central Europe. But the

Count Kaunitz. As foreign minister of the Hapsburg Monarchy, Kaunitz negotiated the famous reversal of alliances (1756) by which France later entered the Seven Years' War allied with Austria against Prussia and Britain. [Bildarchivs der Osterreichischen Nationalbibliothek, Vienna.]

French monarchy, though having changed its German ally, would remain diverted from its commercial interests on the high seas.

The Seven Years' War (1756–1763)

The Treaty of Aix-la-Chapelle had brought peace in Europe, but the conflict between France and Great Britain continued unofficially on the colonial front. There were continuous clashes between American and French settlers in the Ohio River valley and in upper New England. These were the prelude to what is known in American history as the French and Indian War. These colonial skirmishes would certainly have led in time to a broader conflict. However, once again the factor that opened a general European war that extended into a colonial theater was the action of the king of Prussia.

In August 1756 Frederick II invaded the kingdom of Saxony. He regarded this invasion as a continuation of the defensive strategy of which the Convention of Westminster had been a part. Frederick believed that there existed an international conspiracy on the part of Saxony, Austria, and France to undermine and destroy Prussian power. The attack on Saxony was in Frederick's mind a preemptive strike. The invasion itself created the very destructive alliance that Frederick feared. In the spring of 1757 France and Austria made a new alliance dedicated to the destruction of Prussia. They were eventually joined by Sweden, Russia, and the smaller German states.

Frederick the Great of Prussia in his later years displayed in his face the burden of personal hardship that his ambitious wars had brought to him and to his nation. Yet he did succeed in making Prussia a major power. [Culver Pictures.]

❧ Prussia and Great Britain Agree to the Convention of Westminster

The Diplomatic Revolution of 1756 saw a reversal of the alliances that had existed during the War of the Austrian Succession. France and Austria became allies against Prussia and Great Britain. The Convention of Westminster was the agreement that created the Prussian–British alliance. That alliance allowed Prussia to receive the financial backing of Britain in case of war and provided Britain with a continental ally that would divert the resources of France from the war for overseas empire. Prussia hoped that the treaty would provide protection from Russia, Austria, and France.

As the differences which had arisen in America between the King of Great Britain and the most Christian King [i.e., the king of France], and the consequences of which become every day more alarming, give room to fear for the public tranquillity of Europe; H.M. the King of Great Britain, etc., and H.M. the King of Prussia, etc., attentive to an object so very interesting, and equally desirous of preserving the peace of Europe in general and that of Germany in particular, have resolved to enter into such measures as may the most effectually contribute to so desirable an end. . . .

I. There shall be, between the said most Serene Kings, a perfect peace and mutual amity, notwithstanding the troubles that may arise in Europe, in consequence of the above-mentioned differences; so

that neither of the contracting parties shall attack, or invade, directly or indirectly, the territories of the other; but, on the contrary, shall exert their utmost efforts to prevent their respective allies from undertaking anything against the said territories in any manner whatever.

II. If contrary to all expectation, and in violation of the peace which the high contracting parties propose to maintain by this treaty in Germany, any foreign power should cause troops to enter into the said Germany, under any pretext whatsoever; the two high contracting parties shall unite their forces to punish this infraction of the peace, and maintain the tranquillity of Germany, according to the purport of the present treaty.

H. Butterfield (Ed.), *Select Documents of European History, 1715–1920* (London: Methuen, 1931), pp. 20–21.

Prussia was surrounded by enemies, and Frederick II confronted the gravest crisis of his career. It was after these struggles that he came to be called Frederick the Great. He won several initial battles, the most famous of which was Rossbach on November 5, 1757. Thereafter, however, the Prussians experienced a long series of defeats that might have destroyed the state. Two factors in addition to Frederick's stubborn leadership saved Prussia. The first was major financial aid from Great Britain. The British contributed as much to the Prussian war effort as did the Prussian treasury itself. Second, in 1762 Empress Elizabeth of Russia died. Her successor was Czar Peter III (he also died in the same year), whose admiration for Frederick knew almost no bounds. He immediately made peace with Prussia, thus relieving the country of one enemy and allowing it to hold its own

against Austria and France. The treaty of Hubertusburg of 1763 closed the continental conflict with no significant changes in prewar borders. Silesia remained Prussia's province, and Prussia clearly stood in the ranks of the great powers.

The survival of Prussia was less impressive to the rest of Europe than the victories of Great Britain over France in every theater of conflict. The architect of this victory was William Pitt the Elder (1708–1778). He came from a family that had made its fortune from commerce. His grandfather, "Diamond" Pitt, had laid the foundations of the family's wealth by commercial ventures in India. The grandson was no less dedicated to the growth of British trade and economic interests. Pitt was a person of colossal ego and administrative genius. From the time of the War of Jenkins's Ear he had criticized the government as being too timid in its

William Pitt the Elder guided the armies and navies of Great Britain to a stunning victory in the Seven Years' War. His portrait is from the studio of the artist Richard Brompton. [The Granger Collection.]

colonial policy. He had been strongly critical of all continental involvement, including the Convention of Westminster. During the 1750s he had gained the favor of the London merchant interest. Once war had commenced again, these groups clamored for his appointment to the cabinet. In 1757 he was named the secretary of state in charge of the war. He soon drew into his own hands all the power he could grasp. A person of supreme confidence, he

George II (1727–1760) was the British monarch during the great wars of the mid-century. The painting is by Thomas Worlidge. [The Granger Collection.]

once told his friends, "I am sure that I can save the country, and that no one else can."

Once in office Pitt changed his attitude toward British involvement on the Continent. He came to regard the German conflict as a way to divert French resources and attention from the colonial struggle. He pumped huge financial subsidies to Frederick the Great and later boasted of having won America on the plains of Germany. North America was the center of Pitt's real concern. Put quite simply, he wanted all of North America east of the Mississippi for Great Britain, and that was exactly what he won. He turned more than forty thousand regular English and colonial troops against the French in Canada. Never had so many soldiers been devoted to a colonial field of warfare. He achieved unprecedented cooperation with the American colonies, whose leaders realized that they might finally defeat their French neighbors. The French government was unwilling and unable to direct similar resources against the English in America. Their military administration was corrupt; the military and political command in Canada was divided; and the food supply to the French army failed. In September 1759, on the Plains of Abraham overlooking the valley of the Saint Lawrence River at Quebec City, the British army under General James Wolfe defeated the French under Lieutenant General Louis Joseph Montcalm. The French empire in Canada was coming to an end.

However, Pitt's colonial vision extended beyond the Saint Lawrence valley and the Great Lakes basin. The major islands of the French West Indies fell to the British fleets. Income from the sale of captured sugar helped finance the British war effort. British slave interests captured the bulk of the French slave trade. Between 1755 and 1760 the value of the French colonial trade fell by over 80 per cent. On the Indian subcontinent the British forces under the command of Robert Clive defeated the French in 1757 at the Battle of Plassey. This victory opened the way for the eventual conquest of Bengal and later all of India by the British East India Company. Never had Great Britain or any other European power experienced such a complete worldwide military victory.

The Treaty of Paris of 1763 reflected somewhat less of a victory than Britain had won on the battlefield. Pitt was no longer in office. George III (1760–1820) had succeeded to the British throne in 1760. He and Pitt had quarreled over policy, and the minister had departed. His replacement

Both the British general James Wolfe and the French general Montcalm died at the Battle of Quebec in September 1759, in which the British forces won the crucial encounter and thus drove the French out of their North American empire. The picture of the death of Wolfe is an engraving from a famous painting by the American artist Benjamin West (1738–1820). [Culver Pictures.]

was the earl of Bute, a favorite of the new monarch. The new minister was responsible for the peace settlement. Britain received all of Canada, the Ohio River valley, and the eastern half of the Mississippi River valley. Britain partially surrendered the conquest in India by giving France footholds at Pondicherry and Chandernagore. The sugar islands of Guadeloupe and Martinique were restored to the French. Britain could have gained more territory only with further war involving more taxation, against which the country was already complaining.

The Seven Years' War had been a vast conflict. Tens of thousands of soldiers had been killed or wounded. Major battles had been fought around the globe. At great internal sacrifice Prussia had permanently wrested Silesia from Austria and had turned the Holy Roman Empire into an empty shell. Hapsburg power now depended largely on the Hungarian domains. France, though still possessing sources of colonial income, was no longer a great colonial power. The Spanish Empire remained largely intact, but the British were still determined to penetrate its markets. On the Indian

The Battle of the Plains of Abraham, 1759. The British victory at Quebec meant the end of French rule in Canada. This engraving is by P. C. Cariot, after a work by Captain Hervey Smith. [Courtesy of the Trustees, National Maritime Museum, Greenwich, England.]

subcontinent the British East India Company was in a position to continue to press against the decaying indigenous governments and to impose its own authority. The results of that situation would be felt until the middle of the twentieth century. In North America the British government faced the task of organizing its new territories. From this time until World War II Great Britain assumed the status not simply of a European but also of a world power.

The quarter century of warfare also caused a long series of domestic crises among the European powers. The French defeat convinced many people in the nation of the necessity of political and administrative reform. The financial burdens of the wars had astounded all contemporaries. Every power had to begin to find ways to increase revenues to pay its war debt and to finance its preparation for the next combat. Nowhere did this search for revenue lead to more far-ranging consequences than in the British colonies in North America.

The American Revolution and Europe

Events in the British Colonies

The revolt of the British colonies in North America was an event in transatlantic and European history. It erupted from problems of revenue collection common to all the major powers after the Seven Years' War. The War of the American Revolution was a continuation of the conflict between France and Great Britain. The French support of the Americans deepened the existing financial and administrative difficulties of the monarchy.

The political ideals of the Americans had roots in the thought of John Locke and other English political theorists. The colonists raised questions of the most profound nature about monarchy, political authority, and constitutionalism. These questions had ramifications for all European states. Part of

---

◈ France Turns Over French Canada to Great Britain

The Treaty of Paris (1763) concluded the French and English portion of the Seven Years' War. In this particular clause the previously French portion of Canada was turned over to Great Britain.

His Most Christian Majesty [the King of France] renounces all pretensions which he has heretofore formed or might have formed to Nova Scotia or Acadia in all its parts, and guarantees the whole of it, and with all its dependencies, to the King of Great Britain: Moreover, His Most Christian Majesty cedes and guarantees to his said Britannic Majesty, in full right, Canada, with all its dependencies, as well as the island of Cape Breton, and all the other islands and coasts in the gulf and river of St. Laurence, and in general, everything that depends on the said countries, land, islands, and coasts, with the sovereignty, property, possession, and all rights acquired by treaty, or otherwise, which the Most Christian King and the Crown of France have had till *now over the said countries, lands, islands, places, coasts, and their inhabitants, so that the Most Christian King cedes and makes over the whole to the said King, and to the Crown of Great Britain, and that in the most ample manner and form, without restriction, and without any liberty to depart from the said cession and guarantee under any pretence, or to disturb Great Britain in the possessions above mentioned. His Britannic Majesty, on his side, agrees to grant the liberty of the Catholic Religion, to the inhabitants of Canada: he will, in consequence, give the most precise and effectual orders, that his new Roman Catholic subjects may profess the worship of their religion according to the rights of the Romish Church, as far as the laws of Great Britain permit.*

H. Butterfield (Ed.), *Select Documents of European History,* 1715–1920 (London: Methuen, 1931), pp. 29–30.

the difficulties from the British side arose because of the characteristic European political friction between the monarch and the aristocracy. Finally, many Europeans saw the Americans as inaugurating a new era in the history of European peoples and indeed of the world.

After the Treaty of Paris of 1763 the British government faced three imperial problems. The first was the sheer cost of empire, which the British felt they could no longer carry alone. The national debt had risen considerably, as had taxation. The American colonies had been the chief beneficiaries of the conflict. It made rational sense that they should henceforth bear part of the cost of their protection and administration. The second problem was the vast expanse of new territory in North America that the British had to organize. This included all the land from the mouth of the Saint Lawrence River to the Mississippi River with its French settlers and, more importantly, its Indian possessors.

As the British ministers pursued solutions to these difficulties, a third and more serious issue arose. The British colonists in North America resisted taxation and were suspicious of the imperial policies toward the western lands. Consequently the British had to search for new ways to exert their authority over the colonies. The Americans became increasingly resistant because their economy had outgrown the framework of mercantilism, because the removal of the French relieved them of dependence on the British army, and because they believed that their liberty was in danger.

The British drive for revenue commenced in 1764 with the passage of the Sugar Act under the ministry of George Grenville (1712–1770). The measure attempted to produce more revenue from imports into the colonies by the rigorous collection of what was actually a lower tax. Smugglers who violated the law were to be tried in admiralty courts without juries. The next year Parliament passed the Stamp Act, which put a tax on legal documents and certain other items such as newspapers. The British considered these taxes legal because they had been passed by Parliament. The taxes seemed just because the money was to be spent in the colonies. The Americans responded that they had the right to tax themselves and that they were not represented in Parliament. The colonists quite simply argued there should be no taxation without representation. Moreover, because the king had granted most of the colonial charters, the Americans claimed that their legal connection to Britain was through the monarch rather than through the Parliament. The expenditure in the colonies of the revenue levied by Parliament did not reassure the colonists. They feared that if colonial government were financed from outside, they would lose control over their government. In October 1765 the Stamp Act Congress met in America and drew up a protest to the crown. There was much disorder in the colonies, particularly in Massachusetts. The colonists agreed to refuse to import British goods. In 1766 Parliament repealed the Stamp Act, but through the Declaratory Act it said that Parliament had the power to legislate for the colonies.

The Stamp Act crisis set the pattern for the next ten years. Parliament, under the leadership of a royal minister, would approve a piece of revenue or administrative legislation. The Americans would then resist by reasoned argument, economic pressure, and violence. Then the British would repeal the legislation, and the process would begin again. Each time, tempers on both sides became more frayed and positions more irreconcilable. In 1767 Charles Townshend (1725–1767), as Chancellor of the Exchequer, led Parliament to pass a series of revenue acts relating to colonial imports. The colonists again resisted. The ministry sent over its own customs agents to administer the laws. To protect these new officers, the British sent troops to Boston in 1768. The obvious tensions resulted, and in March 1770 the Boston Massacre, in which British troops killed five citizens, took place. That same year Parliament repealed all of the Townshend duties except for the one on tea.

In May 1773 Parliament passed a new law relating to the sale of tea by the East India Company. The measure permitted the direct importation of tea into the American colonies. It actually lowered the price of tea while retaining the tax imposed without the colonists' consent. In some cities the colonists refused to permit the unloading of the tea; in Boston a shipload of tea was thrown into the harbor. The British ministry of Lord North (1732–1792) was determined to assert the authority of Parliament over the resistant colonies. During 1774 Parliament passed a series of laws known in American history as the Intolerable Acts. These measures closed the port of Boston, reorganized the government of Massachusetts, allowed troops to be quartered in private homes, and removed the trials of royal customs officials to England. The same year Parliament approved the Quebec Act for the future administration of that province. It extended the boundaries of Quebec to include the

Ohio River valley. The Americans regarded the Quebec Act as an attempt to prevent the extension of their mode of self-government westward beyond the Appalachian Mountains.

During these years committees of correspondence composed of citizens critical of Britain had been established throughout the colonies. They made the various sections of the eastern seaboard aware of common problems and aided united action. In September 1774 these committees organized the gathering of the First Continental Congress in Philadelphia. This body hoped to persuade Parliament to restore self-government in the colonies and to abandon its attempt at direct supervision of colonial affairs. However, conciliation was not forthcoming. By April 1775 the battles of Lexington and Concord were fought. In June the colonists suffered defeat at the Battle of Bunker Hill. Despite the defeat, the colonial assemblies soon began to meet under their own authority rather than under that of the king.

The Second Continental Congress gathered in May 1775. It still sought conciliation with Britain, but the pressure of events led that assembly to begin to conduct the government of the colonies. By August 1775 George III had declared the colonies in rebellion. During the winter Thomas Paine's pamphlet *Common Sense* galvanized public opinion in favor of separation from Great Britain. A colonial army and navy were organized. In April 1776 the Continental Congress opened American ports to the trade of all nations. And on July 4, 1776, the Continental Congress adopted the Declaration of Independence. Thereafter the War of the American Revolution continued until 1781, when the forces of George Washington defeated those of Lord Cornwallis at Yorktown. However, early in 1778 the war had widened into a European conflict when Benjamin Franklin persuaded the French government to support the rebellion. In 1779 the Spanish also came to the aid of the colonies. The 1783 Treaty of Paris concluded the conflict, and the thirteen American colonies had established their independence.

This series of events is generally familiar to American readers. The relationship of the American Revolution to European affairs and the European roots of the American revolutionary ideals are less familiar.

The political theory of the American Declaration of Independence derived from the writings of seventeenth-century English Whig theorists, such as John Locke, and eighteenth-century Scottish moral

COMMON SENSE;

ADDRESSED TO THE

INHABITANTS

OF

AMERICA,

On the following interesting

SUBJECTS.

I. Of the Origin and Design of Government in general, with concise Remarks on the English Constitution.

II. Of Monarchy and Hereditary Succession.

III. Thoughts on the present State of American Affairs.

IV. Of the present Ability of America, with some miscellaneous Reflections.

Man knows no Master save creating HEAVEN,
Or those whom choice and common good ordain.
THOMSON.

PHILADELPHIA;
Printed, and Sold, by R. BELL, in Third-Street.
MDCCLXXVI.

Common Sense, *written by Tom Paine, was the most important political pamphlet published during 1776 when the American colonies were deciding to make a final break with Great Britain.* [The Granger Collection.]

philosophers, such as Francis Hutcheson. Their political ideas had in large measure arisen out of the struggle of seventeenth-century English aristocrats and gentry against the absolutism of the Stuarts. The American colonists looked to the English Revolution of 1688 as having established many of their own fundamental political liberties as well as those of the English. The colonists claimed that through the measures imposed from 1763 to 1776 George III and the British Parliament had attacked those liberties and dissolved the bonds of moral and political allegiance that had formerly united the two peoples. Consequently the colonists employed a theory that had developed to justify an aristocratic rebellion in order to support their own popular revolution.

These Whig political ideas were only a part of the English ideological heritage that affected the Americans. Throughout the eighteenth century they had become familiar with a series of British political writers called the *Commonwealthmen*. They held republican political ideas and had their intellectual roots in the most radical thought of the Puritan revolution. During the early eighteenth century these writers had relentlessly criticized the government patronage and parliamentary management of Robert Walpole and his successors. They argued that such government was corrupt and that it undermined liberty. They regarded much parliamentary taxation as simply a means of financing political corruption. They also attacked standing armies, which they considered instruments of tyranny. In Great Britain this political tradition had only a marginal impact. The writers were largely ignored because most British subjects regarded themselves as the freest people in the world. However, over three thousand miles away in the colonies, these radical books and pamphlets were read widely and were often accepted at face value. The events in Great Britain following the accession of King George III made many colonists believe that the worst fears of the Commonwealth writers were coming true.

Events in Great Britain

George III (1760–1820) believed that his two immediate royal predecessors had been improperly bullied and controlled by their ministers. Royal power had in effect amounted to little more than the policies carried out by a few powerful Whig families. The new king intended to rule through Parliament, but he was determined to have ministers of his own choice. Moreover George III believed that Parliament should function under royal rather than aristocratic management. When William Pitt resigned after a disagreement with George over war policy, the king appointed the earl of Bute as his first minister. In doing so, he ignored the great Whig families that had run the country since 1715. The king sought the aid of politicians whom the Whigs hated. Moreover he attempted to use the same kind of patronage techniques developed by Walpole to achieve royal control of the House of Commons.

Between 1761 and 1770 George tried one minister after another, but each in turn failed to gain sufficient support from the various factions in the House of Commons. Finally, in 1770 he turned to Lord North (1732–1792), who remained the king's

"The Horse America throwing his Master," an eighteenth-century cartoon mocking George III about the rebellion of the American colonies. [Library of Congress.]

THE HORSE AMERICA, throwing his Master.

George III (1760–1820). Although he never sought to make himself a tyrant as his critics charged, George did try to reassert the political influence of the monarchy which had been eroded under the first two Hanoverian kings, George I and George II. [New York Public Library Picture Collection.]

EVENTS IN BRITAIN AND AMERICA RELATING TO
THE AMERICAN REVOLUTION

1760   George III ascends the English throne
1763   Treaty of Paris concludes the Seven
          Years' War
          John Wilkes publishes issue Number 45
          of *The North Briton*
1764   Sugar Act
1765   Stamp Act
1766   Stamp Act repealed and Declaratory Act
          passed
1767   Townshend Acts
1768   Parliament refuses to seat John Wilkes
          after his election
1770   Lord North becomes George III's chief
          minister
          Boston Massacre
1773   Boston Tea Party
1774   Intolerable Acts
          First Continental Congress
1775   Second Continental Congress
1776   Declaration of Independence
1778   France enters the war on the side of
          America
          Yorkshire Association Movement
          founded
1781   British forces surrender at Yorktown
1783   Treaty of Paris concludes War of the
          American Revolution

first minister until 1782. The Whig families and other political spokesmen claimed that George III was attempting to impose a tyranny. What they meant was that the king was attempting to curb the power of a particular group of the aristocracy. George III certainly was seeking to restore more royal influence to the government of Great Britain, but he was not attempting to make himself a tyrant.

THE CHALLENGE OF JOHN WILKES. Then in 1763 began the affair of John Wilkes (1725–1797). This London political radical and member of Parliament published a newspaper called *The North Briton*. In issue Number 45 of this paper Wilkes strongly criticized Lord Bute's handling of the peace negotiations with France. Wilkes was arrested under the authority of a general warrant issued by the secretary of state. He pled the privileges of a member of Parliament and was released. The courts also later ruled that the vague kind of general warrant by which he had been arrested was illegal. However, the House of Commons ruled that issue Number 45 of *The North Briton* was a libel and expelled Wilkes from the Commons. He soon fled the country and was outlawed. Throughout these procedures there was very widespread support for Wilkes, and many demonstrations were held in his cause.

In 1768 Wilkes returned to England and again stood for election to Parliament. He won the election, but the House of Commons, under the influence of George III's friends, refused to seat him. He was elected three more times. After the fourth

John Wilkes Esq.
Drawn from the Life and Etch'd in Aquafortis by Will.ᵐ Hogarth.
Publish'd according to Act of Parliament. May y.ᵉ 16. 1763.

This satirical portrait etching of John Wilkes was made by William Hogarth. It suggests the unattractive personal character of Wilkes and also tends to question the sincerity of his calls for liberty. [Charles Farrell Collection.]

The American colonists followed all of these developments of the 1760s very closely. The contemporary events in Britain confirmed their fears about a monarchical and parliamentary conspiracy against liberty. The king, as their Whig friends told them, was behaving like a tyrant. The Wilkes affair displayed the arbitrary power of the monarch, the corruption of the House of Commons, and the contempt of both for popular electors. That same monarch and Parliament were attempting to overturn the traditional relationship of Great Britain to its colonies by imposing parliamentary taxes. The same government had then landed troops in Boston, changed the government of Massachusetts, and undermined the traditional right of jury trial. All of these events fulfilled too exactly the portrait of political tyranny that had developed over the years in the minds of articulate colonists.

MOVEMENT FOR PARLIAMENTARY REFORM IN BRITAIN. The political influences between America and Britain operated both ways. The colonial demand for no taxation without representation and the criticism of the adequacy of the British sys-

Major John Cartwright (1740–1824) was the first English political reformer to call for universal manhood suffrage in parliamentary elections. [The Granger Collection.]

election the House of Commons simply ignored the election results and seated the government-supported candidate. As earlier in the decade, large popular demonstrations of shopkeepers, artisans, and small property owners supported Wilkes. He also received aid from some aristocratic politicians who wished to humiliate George III. Wilkes himself contended during all of his troubles that his cause was the cause of English liberty. "Wilkes and Liberty" became the slogan of all political radicals and many noble opponents of the monarch. Wilkes was finally seated in 1774, after having become the lord mayor of London.

❧ Major Cartwright Calls for the Reform of Parliament

During the years of the American Revolution there were many demands in England itself for a major reform of Parliament. In this pamphlet of 1777 Major John Cartwright demanded that a much larger number of English citizens be allowed to vote for members of the House of Commons. He also heaped contempt on the opponents of reform.

Suffering as we do, from a deep parliamentary corruption, it is no time to tamper with silly correctives, and trifle away the life of public freedom: but we must go to the bottom of the stinking sore and cleanse it thoroughly: we must once more infuse into the constitution the vivifying spirit of liberty and expel the very last dregs of this poison. Annual parliaments with an equal representation of the commons are the only specifics in this case: and they would effect a radical cure. That a house of commons, formed as ours is, should maintain septennial elections, and laugh at every other idea is no wonder. The wonder is, that the British nation which, but the other day, was the greatest nation on earth, should be so easily laughed out of its liberties. . . .

Those who now claim the exclusive *right of send-* *ing to parliament the 513 representatives for about six millions souls (amongst whom are one million five hundred thousand males,* competent as electors*) consist of about two hundred and fourteen thousand persons; and 254 of these representatives are elected by 5,723. . . . Their pretended rights are many of them, derived from* royal favour; *some from antient usage and presciption; and some indeed from act of parliament; but neither the most authentic acts of royalty, nor precedent, nor prescription, nor even parliament can establish any flagrant injustice; much less can they strip one million two hundred and eighty six thousand of an inalienable right, to vest it in a number amounting to only one seventh of that multitude. . . .*

John Cartwright, *Legislative Rights of the Commonality Vindicated,* cited in S. Maccoby, *The English Radical Tradition,* 1763–1914 (London: Adam and Charles Black, 1966), pp. 32–33.

---

tem of representation struck at the core of the eighteenth-century British political structure. Colonial arguments could be adopted by British subjects at home who were no more directly represented in the House of Commons than were the Americans. The colonial questioning of the taxing authority of the House of Commons was related to the protest of John Wilkes. Both the Americans and Wilkes were challenging the power of the monarch and the authority of Parliament. Moreover both the colonial leaders and Wilkes appealed over the head of legally constituted political authorities to popular opinion and popular demonstrations. Both were protesting the power of a largely self-selected aristocratic political body. The British ministry was fully aware of these broader implications of the American troubles.

The American colonists also demonstrated to Europe how a politically restive people in the old regime could fight tyranny and protect political liberty. They established revolutionary but orderly political bodies that could function outside the existing political framework. These revolutionary political institutions were the congress and the convention. These began with the Stamp Act Congress of 1765 and culminated in the Constitutional Convention of 1787. The legitimacy of those congresses and conventions lay not in existing law but in the alleged consent of the governed. This approach represented a new way to found a government.

Toward the end of the War of the American Revolution, calls for parliamentary reform were voiced in Britain itself. The method proposed for changing the system was the extralegal Association Movement.

By the close of the 1770s there was much resentment in Britain about the mismanagement of the war, the high taxes, and Lord North's ministry. In northern England in 1778 Christopher Wyvil (1740–1822), a landowner and retired clergyman, organized the Yorkshire Association Movement.

Property owners or freeholders of Yorkshire met in a mass meeting to demand rather moderate changes in the corrupt system of parliamentary elections. They organized corresponding societies elsewhere. They intended that the association examine, and suggest reforms for, the entire government. The Association Movement was thus a popular attempt to establish an extralegal institution to reform the government. The movement collapsed during the early 1780s because its supporters, unlike Wilkes and the American rebels, were not willing to appeal for broad popular support. Nonetheless the agitation of the Association Movement provided many people with experience in political protest. Several of its younger figures lived to raise the issue of parliamentary reform after 1815.

Parliament was not insensitive to the demands of the Association Movement. In April 1780 the Commons passed a resolution that called for lessening the power of the crown. In 1782 Parliament adopted a measure for "economical" reform, which abolished some patronage at the disposal of the monarch. However, these actions did not prevent George III from appointing a minister of his own choice. In 1783 Lord North had to form a ministry with Charles James Fox (1749–1806), a long-time critic of George III. The monarch was most unhappy with the arrangement. In 1783 he approached William Pitt the Younger (1759–1806), son of the victorious war minister, to manage the House of Commons. During the election of 1784 Pitt received immense patronage support from the crown and constructed a House of Commons favorable to the king. Thereafter Pitt sought to formulate trade policies that would give his ministry broad popularity. He attempted in 1785 one measure of modest parliamentary reform. When it failed, the young prime minister, who had been only twenty-four at the time of his appointment, abandoned the cause of reform.

By the mid-1780s George III had achieved a part of what he had sought beginning in 1761. He had reasserted the influence of the monarchy in political affairs. It proved a temporary victory because his own mental illness, which would finally require a regency, weakened the royal power. The cost of his years of dominance had been very high. On both sides of the Atlantic the issue of popular sovereignty had been raised and widely discussed. The American colonies had been lost. Economically this loss did not prove disastrous. British trade

with America after independence actually increased. However, the Americans—through the state constitutions, the Articles of Confederation, and the federal Constitution—had demonstrated to Europe the possibility of government without kings and without aristocracies. They had established the example of a nation in which written documents based on popular consent and popular sovereignty—rather than on divine law, natural law, tradition, or the will of kings—stood as the highest political and legal authority. Writers throughout western Europe sensed that a new kind of political era was dawning. It was to be an age of constituent assemblies, constitutions, and declarations of rights.

Colonies founded to serve the economic requirements of Britain and Europe repaid the debt by serving as laboratories for new political ideals and institutions. The ideas had generally been developed in Europe, but America was the place where most of them were initially put into practice. America for a time served as an experiment station for the advanced political ideas of Europe. Soon the ideas would find their way back to the lands of their origins.

Suggested Readings

B. Bailyn, *The Ideological Origins of the American Revolution* (1967). An important work illustrating the role of English radical thought in the perceptions of the American colonists.

C. Becker, *The Declaration of Independence: A Study in the History of Political Ideas* (1922). An examination of the political and imperial theory of the Declaration.

J. Brewer, *Party Ideology and Popular Politics at the Accession of George III* (1976). An important series of essays on popular radicalism.

J. Brooke, *King George III* (1972). The best recent biography.

H. Butterfield, *George III, Lord North, and the People, 1779–1780* (1949). Explores the domestic unrest in Britain during the American Revolution.

D. B. Davis, *The Problem of Slavery in Western Culture* (1966). A brilliant and far-ranging discussion.

D. B. Davis, *The Problem of Slavery in the Age of Revolution, 1770–1823* (1975). A major work for both European and American history.

Walter Dorn, *Competition for Empire, 1740–1763* (1940). Still one of the best accounts of the mid-century struggle.

L. H. Gipson, *The British Empire Before the American Rev-*

olution, 13 vols. (1936–1967). A magisterial account of the mid-century wars from an imperial viewpoint.

R. LODGE, *Great Britain and Prussia in the Eighteenth Century* (1923). The standard account.

E. MORGAN AND H. MORGAN, *The Stamp Act Crisis* (1953). A lively account of the incident from the viewpoint of both the colonies and England.

J. B. OWEN, *The Eighteenth Century* (1974). A recent survey of British politics.

R. PARES, *War and Trade in the West Indies* (1936). Relates the West Indies to Britain's larger commercial and naval concerns.

R. PARES, *King George III and the Politicians* (1953). An important analysis of the constitutional and political structures.

J. H. PARRY, *Trade and Dominion: The European Overseas Empires in the Eighteenth Century* (1971). A comprehensive account with attention to the European impact on the rest of the world.

C. D. RICE, *The Rise and Fall of Black Slavery* (1975). An excellent survey of the subject with careful attention to the numerous historiographical controversies.

C. G. ROBERTSON, *Chatham and the British Empire* (1948). A brief study.

G. RUDÉ, *Wilkes and Political Liberty* (1962). A close analysis of popular political behavior.

P. D. G. THOMAS, *British Politics and the Stamp Act Crisis: The First Phase of the American Revolution, 1763–1767* (1975). An interesting work from the British point of view.

J. S. WATSON, *The Reign of George III, 1760–1815* (1960). Covers the British domestic political scene in a traditional manner.

G. WILLS, *Inventing America: Jefferson's Declaration of Independence* (1978). An important new study that challenges much of the analysis in the Becker volume noted above.

G. S. WOOD, *The Creation of the American Republic, 1776–1787* (1969). A far-ranging work dealing with Anglo-American political thought.

618

21 The Age of Enlightenment: Eighteenth-Century Thought

Duﾍring the eighteenth century the conviction began to spread throughout the literate sectors of European society that change and reform were both possible and desirable. This attitude is now commonplace, but it came into its own only after 1700. It represents one of the primary intellectual inheritances from that age. The movement of people and ideas that fostered such thinking is called the *Enlightenment*. Its leading voices combined confidence in the human mind inspired by the Scientific Revolution and faith in the power of rational criticism to challenge the intellectual authority of tradition and the Christian past. These writers stood convinced that human beings could comprehend the operation of physical nature and mold it to the ends of material and moral improvement. The rationality of the physical universe became a standard against which the customs and traditions of society could be measured and criticized. Such criticism penetrated every corner of contemporary society, politics, and religious opinion. As a result the spirit of innovation and improvement came to characterize modern European and Western society.

The *Philosophes*

The writers and critics who forged this new attitude and who championed change and reform were the *philosophes*. They were not usually philosophers in a formal sense; rather, they were people who sought to apply the rules of reason and common sense to nearly all the major institutions and social practices of the day. The most famous of their number included Voltaire, Montesquieu, Diderot, Rousseau, Hume, Gibbon, Smith, Bentham, Lessing, and Kant. A few of them occupied professorships in universities, but most were free agents who might be found in London coffeehouses, Edinburgh drinking spots, the salons of fashionable Parisian ladies, the country houses of

The young Voltaire. Philosopher, dramatist, poet, historian, novelist, scientist—Voltaire was the most famous and influential of the eighteenth-century French philosophes. *This painting by Quentin Latour is at Versailles.* [Bulloz.]

reform-minded nobles, or the courts of the most powerful monarchs on the Continent. They were not an organized group; they disagreed on many issues. Their relationship with each other and with lesser figures of the same turn of mind has quite appropriately been compared with that of a family, in which despite quarrels and tensions a basic unity still remains.[1]

The chief unity of the *philosophes* lay in their desire to reform thought, society, and government for the sake of human liberty. As Peter Gay has suggested, this goal included "freedom from arbitrary power, freedom of speech, freedom of trade, freedom to realize one's talents, freedom of aesthetic response, freedom, in a word, of moral man to make his way in the world."[2] No other single set of ideas has done so much to shape the modern world. The literary vehicles through which the *philosophes* delivered their message included books, pamphlets, plays, novels, philosophical treatises, encyclopedias, newspapers, and magazines. During the Reformation and the religious wars writers had used the printed word to debate the proper mode of faith in God. The *philosophes* of the Enlightenment employed the printed word to proclaim a new faith in the capacity of humankind to improve itself without the aid of God.

Many of the *philosophes* were middle class in their social origins. The bulk of their readership were also drawn from the prosperous commercial and professional people of the eighteenth-century towns and cities. These people discussed the reformers' writings and ideas in local philosophical societies, Freemason lodges, and clubs. They had sufficient income and leisure time to buy and read the *philosophes*' works. Although the writers of the Enlightenment did not consciously champion the goals or causes of the middle class, they did provide an intellectual ferment and a major source of ideas that could be used to undermine existing social practices and political structures. They taught their contemporaries how to pose pointed, critical questions. Moreover the *philosophes* generally supported the economic growth, the expansion of trade, and the improvement of transport that were transforming the society and the economy of the eighteenth century and that were enlarging the middle class.

[1] Peter Gay, *The Enlightenment: An Interpretation*, Vol. 1 (New York: Knopf, 1967), p. 4.
[2] Ibid, p. 3.

Edward Jenner (1749–1823), an English physician, discovered that by inoculating human beings with the relatively mild disease of cowpox he could make them immune to the dread disease of smallpox. That discovery eventually led to the practically complete removal of the danger of smallpox. [Culver Pictures.]

Formative Influences

The Newtonian world view, the stability and prosperity of Great Britain after 1688, and the degradation that the wars of Louis XIV had brought to France were the chief factors that fostered the discussion of reform throughout Europe.

Isaac Newton (1642–1727) and John Locke (1632–1704) were the major intellectual forerunners of the Enlightenment. Newton's formulation of the laws of universal gravitation exemplified the power of the human mind. His example and his writing encouraged Europeans to approach the study of nature directly and to avoid metaphysics and supernaturalism. Newton had formulated general laws but had always insisted on a foundation of specific empirical evidence for those laws. Empirical experience had provided a constant check on his rational speculation. This emphasis on concrete experience became a keystone for Enlightenment thought. Moreover Newton had discerned a pattern of rationality in natural physical phenomena. During the eighteenth century the ancient idea of following nature became trans-

This elaborate eighteenth-century engraving pays homage to Isaac Newton. Newton was a major intellectual influence on the Enlightenment. This engraving is in the collection of the British Museum. [British Museum.]

formed under the Newtonian influence into the idea of following reason. Because nature was rational, society should be organized in a rational manner.

As explained in Chapter 17, Newton's scientific achievement had inspired his fellow countryman John Locke to seek a human psychology based on experience. In *An Essay Concerning Human Understanding* (1690), Locke argued that each human being enters the world as a *tabula rasa*, or blank page. His or her personality is consequently the product of the sensations that impinge from the external world throughout the course of life. The significant conclusion that followed from this psychology was that human nature is changeable and can be molded by modification of the surrounding physical and social environment. Locke's was a reformer's psychology. It suggested that improve-

ment in the human situation was possible. Locke also, in effect, rejected the Christian view of humankind as creatures permanently flawed by sin. Human beings need not wait for the grace of God or other divine aid to better their lives. They could take charge of their own destiny.

Newton's physics and Locke's psychology provided the theoretical basis for reform. The domestic stability of Great Britain after the Revolution of 1688 furnished a living example of a society in which enlightened reforms functioned for the benefit of all concerned. England permitted religious

This handsome portrait (1788) of the eighteenth-century French chemist Antoine Lavoisier and his wife is by Jacques Louis David (1748–1825). Unlike Lavoisier, guillotined by the ungrateful French Revolutionists, the artist David lived to portray many events of the Revolution and the Napoleonic period. [The Metropolitan Museum of Art. Purchase, Mr. and Mrs. Charles Wrightsman Gift, 1977.]

toleration to all creeds except Unitarianism and Roman Catholicism, whose believers were not actually persecuted. Relative freedom of the press and free speech prevailed. The monarchy was limited in its authority, and political sovereignty resided in the Parliament. The courts protected citizens from arbitrary government action. The army was quite small. These liberal policies had produced not disorder and instability but economic prosperity and loyalty to the political system. The continental view of England was somewhat idealized; nevertheless the country was sufficiently freer than any other nation to make the point that the reformers sought.

If the example of Great Britain suggested that change need not be disastrous to a nation and society, France exhibited many of the practices and customs of European politics and society that most demanded reform. Louis XIV had built his power on the bases of absolute monarchy, a large standing army, heavy taxation, and a religious unity requiring persecution. However, the enemies of France had defeated that nation in war. Its people were miserable, and celebrations had marked the death of the great king. His successors had been unable to reform the state. Critics of the monarchy were subject to arbitrary arrest. There was no freedom of worship. Political and religious censors interfered with the press and other literary productions. Offending authors could be imprisoned, although some achieved cooperative relations with the authorities. State regulations hampered economic growth. Many aristocrats regarded themselves as a military class and upheld militaristic values. Yet throughout the French social structure there existed people who wanted to see changes brought about. These people read and supported the *philosophes* of their nation and of other countries. Consequently France became the major center for the Enlightenment, for there, more than in any other state, the demand for reform daily confronted writers and political thinkers.

Stages of the Enlightenment

The movement that came to be known as the Enlightenment evolved over the course of the century and involved a number of writers living at different times in various countries. Its early exponents popularized the rationalism and scientific ideas of the seventeenth century. They worked to expose contemporary social and political abuses and argued that reform was necessary and possible. The advancement of their cause and ideas was anything but steady. They confronted the obstacles of vested interests, political oppression, and religious condemnation. Yet by the mid-century they had brought enlightened ideas to the European public in a variety of formats. The *philosophes'* "family" had come into being. They corresponded with each other, wrote for each other as well as for the general public, and defended each other against the political and religious authorities.

By the second half of the century they were sufficiently safe to quarrel among themselves on occasion. They had stopped talking in generalities, and their major advocates were addressing themselves to specific abuses. Their books and articles had become more specialized and more practical. They had become more concerned with politics than with religion. Having convinced the Europeans that change was a good idea, they began to suggest exactly what changes were most desirable. They had become honored figures.

Voltaire

One of the earliest and by far the most influential of the *philosophes* was François Marie Arouet, known to posterity as Voltaire (1694–1778). During the 1720s Voltaire had offended the French authorities by certain of his writings, and he was arrested and put in prison for a brief time.

Later Voltaire went to England, where he visited in the best literary circles, observed the tolerant intellectual and religious climate, felt free in the atmosphere of moderate politics, and admired the science and economic prosperity. In 1733 he published *Letters on the English,* which appeared in French the next year. The book praised the virtues of the English and indirectly criticized the abuses of French society. In 1738 he published *Elements of the Philosophy of Newton,* which popularized the thought of the great scientist. Both works were well received and gave Voltaire a reputation as an important writer.

Thereafter Voltaire lived part of the time in France and part near Geneva, just across the French border, where the royal authorities could not bother him. He wrote essays, history, plays, stories, and letters that made him the literary dictator of Europe. He brought the bitter venom of his satire and sarcasm against one evil after another in

French and European life. His most famous satire is *Candide* (1759), in which he attacked war, religious persecution, and unthinking optimism about the human condition. Like most *philosophes*, Voltaire believed that improvement of human society was necessary and possible. But he was never certain that reform, if achieved, would be permanent. The optimism of the Enlightenment constituted a tempered hopefulness rather than a glib certainty. Pessimism provided an undercurrent to most of the works of the period.

Montesquieu

Among the other pioneers of the early Enlightenment, Charles Louis de Secondat, Baron de Montesquieu (1689–1755), was outstanding. He was a lawyer, a noble of the robe, and a member of a provincial *parlement.* He also belonged to the Bordeaux Academy of Science, before which he presented papers on scientific topics. Although living comfortably within the bosom of French society, he saw the need for reform. In 1721 he published *The Persian Letters* to satirize contemporary institutions. The book consisted of letters purportedly written by two Persians visiting Europe. They explained to friends at home how European behavior contrasted with Persian life and customs. Behind the humor lay the cutting edge of criticism and an exposition of the cruelty and irrationality of much contemporary European life. In his most enduring work, *The Spirit of the Laws* (1748), Montesquieu held up the example of the British constitution as the wisest model for regulating the power of government. (We shall examine *The Spirit of the Laws* more closely later in this chapter.)

The Encyclopedia

The mid-century witnessed the publication of one of the greatest monuments of the Enlightenment. Under the heroic leadership of Denis Diderot (1713–1784), and Jean le Rond d'Alembert (1717–1783), the first volume of the *Encyclopedia* appeared in 1751. The project reached completion in 1772, numbering seventeen volumes of text and eleven of plates. The *Encyclopedia* was the product of the collective effort of more than one hundred authors, and its editors had at one time or another solicited articles from all the major French *philosophes*. The project reached fruition only after numerous attempts to censor it and halt its publica-

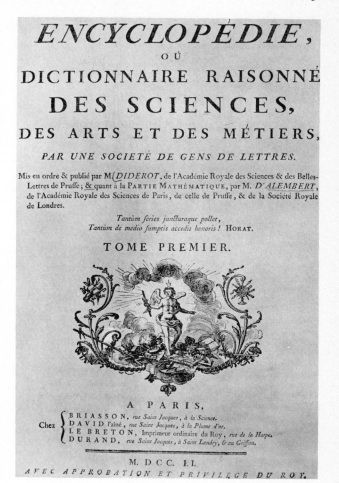

The title page of the first volume of the Encyclopedia. The early volumes of the text received the approval of the royal censor, as noted on the last line, but when it became evident that the work challenged many widely held religious and political views, its opponents obtained withholding of approval for later volumes which were eventually published. [The Mansell Collection.]

tion. The *Encyclopedia* set forth the most advanced critical ideas in religion, government, and philosophy. This criticism often had to be hidden in obscure articles or under the cover of irony. The articles represented a collective plea for freedom of expression. However, the large volumes also provided important information on manufacturing, canal building, ship construction, and improved agriculture.

Between fourteen and sixteen thousand copies

Denis Diderot, the principal editor of the Encyclopedia *who saw it through to the end; d'Alembert withdrew when the opposition turned nasty.* [The Granger Collection.]

of various editions of the *Encyclopedia* were sold before 1789. The project had been designed to secularize learning and to undermine the intellectual assumptions remaining from the Middle Ages and the Reformation. The articles on politics, ethics, and society ignored concerns about divine law and concentrated on humanity and its immediate well-being. The encyclopedists looked to antiquity rather than to the Christian centuries for their intellectual and ethical models. The future welfare of humankind lay not in pleasing God or following divine commandments but rather in harnessing the power of the earth and its resources and in living at peace with one's fellow human beings. The good life lay here and now and was to be achieved through the application of reason to human relationships.

With the publication of the *Encyclopedia,* enlightened thought became more fully diffused over the Continent. Enlightened ideas penetrated German and Russian intellectual and political circles. The *philosophes* of the latter part of the century turned from championing the general cause of reform and discussed specific areas of practical application. Gotthold Lessing (1729–1781) wrote plays to plead for religious toleration. Adam Smith (1723–1790) attacked the mercantile system. Cesare Beccaria (1738–1794) and Jeremy Bentham (1748–1832) called for penal and legal reforms. By this time the concepts of reform and the rationalization of existing institutions had become deeply impressed on European thinking and soci-

A dinner party of philosophes, *from an eighteenth-century engraving by Hubert. In the center is Voltaire with his hand raised. In a circle beginning to his right are Diderot, Adam, Condorcet, d'Alembert, the Abbe Maure, and La Harpe.* [The Mansell Collection.]

ety. The issue then became, and would remain for over a century, how best to implement those reforms.

The Enlightenment and Religion

Throughout the century, in the eyes of the *philosophes* the chief enemy of the improvement of humankind and the enjoyment of happiness was the existence and influence of ecclesiastical institutions. The hatred of the *philosophes* for the church and Christianity was summed up in Voltaire's cry of "Crush the Infamous Thing." Almost all varieties of Christianity, but especially Roman Catholicism, invited the criticism of the *philosophes*. Intellectually the churches perpetuated a religious rather than a scientific view of humankind and physical nature. The clergy taught that human beings were basically depraved and that they required divine grace to become worthy creatures. The doctrine of original sin in either its Catholic or its Protestant formulation suggested that meaningful improvement in human nature on earth was impossible. Religious concerns turned human interest away from this world to the world to come. In the view of the *philosophes* the concept of predestination suggested that the condition of the human soul after death had little or no relationship to virtuous living during this life. Through disagreements over obscure doctrines the various churches favored the politics of intolerance and bigotry that in the past had caused human suffering, torture, and war.

To attack the Christian churches in this manner was to raise major questions about the life and society of the old regime. Politically and socially the churches were deeply enmeshed in the power structure. They owned large amounts of land and collected tithes from peasants before any other taxes were collected. Most of the clergy were legally exempt from taxation and made only annual voluntary grants to the government. The upper clergy in most countries were relatives of aristocrats. Churchmen were actively involved in politics, serving in the British House of Lords and advising princes on the Continent. In Protestant countries the local clergyman of a particular parish was usually appointed by the local major landowner. Across the Continent membership in the predominant denomination of the kingdom gave certain

subjects political advantages. Nonmembership often excluded other subjects from political participation. Clergymen of all faiths preached the sinfulness of political disobedience, and they provided the intellectual justification for the social and political status quo. They were active where possible in exerting religious and literary censorship. The churches were thus privileged and powerful corporate bodies of the old regime. The *philosophes* chose to attack both their ideas and their power.

Deism

The *philosophes* believed that religion should be reasonable and should lead to moral behavior. The Newtonian world view had convinced many writers that nature was rational. Therefore the God who had created nature must also be rational, and the religion through which that God was worshiped should be rational. Moreover Lockean psychology, which limited human knowledge to empirical experience, raised the question whether such a thing as divine revelation to humankind was, after all, possible. These considerations gave rise to a movement for enlightened religion known as *deism*. The title of one of its earliest expositions, *Christianity Not Mysterious* (1696) by John Toland, indicates the general tenor of this religious outlook. Toland and later writers wished to consider religion a natural and rational, rather than a supernatural and mystical, phenomenon. In this respect the deists made a departure from the general piety of Newton and Locke, both of whom regarded themselves as distinctly Christian. Newton had believed that God might interfere with the natural order, whereas the deists regarded God as resembling a divine watchmaker who had set the mechanism of nature to work and had then departed from the scene.

There were two major points in the deists' creed. The first was the belief in the existence of God. They thought that this belief could be empirically deduced from the contemplation of nature. Joseph Addison's poem on the spacious firmament (1712), illustrates this idea:

The spacious firmament on high,
With all the blue ethereal sky,
And spangled heav'n, a shining frame,
Their great Original proclaim:
Th' unwearied Sun, from day to day,
Does his Creator's power display,
And publishes to every land
The work of an Almighty hand.

Because nature provided evidence of a rational God, that deity must also favor rational morality. Consequently the second point in the deists' creed was the belief in life after death, when rewards and punishments would be meted out according to the virtue of the life a person led on this earth.

Deism was empirical, tolerant, reasonable, and capable of encouraging virtuous living. It was the major positive religious component of the Enlightenment. Voltaire declared:

The great name of Deist, which is not sufficiently revered, is the only name one ought to take. The only gospel one ought to read is the great book of Nature, written by the hand of God and sealed with his seal. The only religion that ought to be professed is the religion of worshiping God and being a good man.[3]

If such a faith became widely accepted, the fanaticism and rivalry of the various Christian sects might be overcome. Religious conflict and persecutions encouraged by that fulsome zeal would end. There would also be little or no necessity for a priestly class to foment fanaticism, denominational hatred, and bigotry.

The *philosophes* did not rest with the formulation of a rational religious alternative to Christianity. They also attacked the churches and the clergy with great vehemence. Voltaire repeatedly questioned the truthfulness of priests and the morality of the Bible. In his *Philosophical Dictionary* (1764) he humorously pointed out inconsistencies in biblical narratives and immoral acts of the biblical heroes. In the chapter "Of Miracles" published in 1748 as part of his *Inquiry into Human Nature,* the Scottish *philosophe* David Hume (1771–1776) argued that divine miracles, in which the churches put great store, were not grounded in rational belief or empirical evidence. For Hume, the greatest miracle was to believe in miracles. In *The Decline and Fall of the Roman Empire* (1776) Edward Gibbon (1737–1794), the English historian, examined the early history of Christianity and explained the rise of that faith in terms of natural causes rather than the influence of miracles and piety. A few *philosophes* went further. Baron d'Holbach (1723–1789) and Julien Offray de La Mettrie (1709–1751) embraced positions very near to atheism and materialism. Theirs was distinctly a minority position, however. Most of the *philosophes* sought not the

[3] Quoted in J. H. Randall, *The Making of the Modern Mind,* rev. ed. (New York: Houghton Mifflin, 1940), p. 292.

MAJOR PUBLICATION DATES OF THE
ENLIGHTENMENT

1687	Newton's *Principia Mathematica*
1690	Locke's *Essay Concerning Human Understanding*
1696	Toland's *Christianity Not Mysterious*
1721	Montesquieu's *Persian Letters*
1733	Voltaire's *Letters on the English*
1738	Voltaire's *Elements of the Philosophy of Newton*
1748	Montesquieu's *Spirit of the Laws*
	Hume's *Inquiry into Human Nature* with the chapter "Of Miracles"
1750	Rousseau's *Discourse on the Moral Effects of the Arts and Sciences*
1751	First volume of *The Encyclopedia* edited by Diderot
1755	Rousseau's *Discourse on the Origin of Inequality*
1762	Rousseau's *Social Contract*
1763	Voltaire's *Treatise on Toleration*
1764	Voltaire's *Philosophical Dictionary*
	Beccaria's *On Crimes and Punishments*
1776	Gibbon's *Decline and Fall of the Roman Empire*
	Bentham's *Fragment on Government*
	Smith's *Wealth of Nations*
1779	Lessing's *Nathan the Wise*

---

abolition of religion but its transformation into a humane force that would encourage virtuous living.

Toleration

A primary social condition for such a life was the establishment of religious toleration. Again Voltaire took the lead in championing this cause. In 1762 the Roman Catholic political authorities in Toulouse ordered the execution of a Huguenot named Jean Calas. He stood accused of having murdered his son to prevent him from converting to Roman Catholicism. Calas had been viciously tortured and publicly strangled without ever having confessed his guilt. The confession would not have saved his life, but it would have given the Catholics good propaganda to use against Protestants.

Voltaire learned of the case only after Calas's death. He made the dead man's cause his own. In 1763 he published a *Treatise on Tolerance* and hounded the authorities for a new investigation. Finally, in 1765, the judicial decision against the unfortunate man was reversed. For Voltaire the case illustrated the fruits of religious fanaticism and the need for rational reform of judicial processes. Somewhat later in the century the German playwright and critic Gotthold Lessing (1729–1781) wrote *Nathan the Wise* (1779) as a plea for toleration not only of different Christian sects but also of religious faiths other than Christianity. All of these calls for toleration stated in effect that life on earth and human relationships should not be subordinated to religion. Secular values and considerations were more important than religious ones.

❧ Voltaire Attacks Religious Fanaticism

The chief complaint of the *philosophes* against Christianity was that it bred a fanaticism that led people to commit crimes in the name of religion. In this passage from his *Philosophical Dictionary* (1764) Voltaire directly reminded his readers of the intolerance of the Reformation era and indirectly referred to examples of contemporary religious excesses. He argued that the philosophical spirit can overcome fanaticism and foster toleration and more humane religious behavior. In a manner that shocked many of his contemporaries, he praised the virtues of Confucianism over those of Christianity.

Fanaticism is to superstition what delirium is to fever and rage to anger. The man visited by ecstasies and visions, who takes dreams for realities and his fancies for prophecies, is an enthusiast; the man who supports his madness with murder is a fanatic. . . .

The most detestable example of fanaticism was that of the burghers of Paris who on St. Bartholomew's Night [1572] went about assassinating and butchering all their fellow citizens who did not go to mass, throwing them out of windows, cutting them in pieces.

Once fanaticism has corrupted a mind, the malady is almost incurable. . . .

The only remedy for this epidemic malady is the philosophical spirit which, spread gradually, at last tames men's habits and prevents the disease from starting; for once the disease has made any progress, one must flee and wait for the air to clear itself. Laws and religion are not strong enough against the spiritual pest; religion, far from being healthy food for infected brains, turn to poison in them. . . .

Even the law is impotent against these attacks of rage; it is like reading a court decree to a raving maniac. These fellows are certain that the holy spirit with which they are filled is above the law, that their enthusiasm is the only law they must obey.

What can we say to a man who tells you that he would rather obey God than men, and that therefore he is sure to go to heaven for butchering you?

Ordinarily fanatics are guided by rascals, who put the dagger into their hands; these latter resemble that Old Man of the Mountain who is supposed to have made imbeciles taste the joys of paradise and who promised them an eternity of the pleasures of which he had given them a foretaste, on condition that they assassinated all those he would name to them. There is only one religion in the world that has never been sullied by fanaticism, that of the Chinese men of letters. The schools of philosophy were not only free from this pest, they were its remedy; for the effect of philosophy is to make the soul tranquil, and fanaticism is incompatible with tranquility. If our holy religion has so often been corrupted by this infernal delirium, it is the madness of men which is at fault.

Voltaire, *Philosophical Dictionary*, trans. by P. Gay (New York: Harcourt, Brace, and World, 1962), pp. 267–269.

The Enlightenment and Society

Although the *philosophes* wrote much on religion, humanity was the center of their interest. As one writer in the *Encyclopedia* observed, "Man is the unique point to which we must refer everything, if we wish to interest and please amongst considerations the most arid and details the most dry."[4] The *philosophes* believed that the application of human reason to society would reveal laws in human relationships similar to those found in physical nature. Although the term did not appear until later, the idea of social science originated with the Enlighten-

[4]Quoted in F. L. Baumer, *Main Currents of Western Thought*, 4th ed. (New Haven, Conn.: Yale University Press, 1978), p. 374.

ment. The purpose of discovering social laws was the removal of the inhumanity that existed through ignorance of them. These concerns became especially evident in the work of the *philosophes* on law and prison procedures.

Beccaria

In 1764 Cesare Beccaria (1738–1794), an Italian *philosophe*, published *On Crimes and Punishments*, in which he applied critical analysis to the problem of making punishments both effective and just. He wanted the laws of monarchs and legislatures—that is, positive law—to conform with the rational laws of nature. He rigorously and eloquently attacked both torture and capital punishment. He

⤜ Beccaria Objects to Capital Punishment as Unenlightened ⟵

In the eighteenth century the death penalty was commonly applied throughout Europe for small as well as great crimes. The young north Italian nobleman Cesare Beccaria thought the penalty was unproductive of law and order and was also unenlightened. *On Crimes and Punishments* appeared when he was only twenty-six, and Voltaire, Bentham, and Catherine the Great professed to admire the work. His 1764 comments are a good example of the Enlightenment application of the criteria of reason and utility to social problems.

Is the death penalty really useful *and* necessary *for the security and good order of society? Are torture and torments just, and do they attain the end for which laws are instituted? What is the best way to prevent crimes? Are the same punishments equally effective for all times? What influence have they on customary behavior? These problems deserve to be analyzed with that geometric precision which the mist of sophisms, seductive eloquence, and timorous doubt cannot withstand. . . . If, by defending the rights of man and of unconquerable truth, I should help to save from the spasm and agonies of death some wretched victim of tyranny or of no less fatal ignorance, the thanks and tears of one innocent mortal in his transports of joy would console me for the contempt of all mankind.*

.   .   .   .

If one were to cite against me the example of all the

ages and of almost all the nations that have applied the death penalty to certain crimes, my reply would be that the example reduced itself to nothing in the face of truth, against which there is no prescription; that the history of men leaves us with the impression of a vast sea of errors; among which, at great intervals, some rare and hardly intelligible truths appear to float on the surface. Human sacrifices were once common to almost all nations, yet who will dare to defend them? That only a few societies, and for a short time only, have abstained from applying the death penalty, stands in my favor rather than against me, for that conforms with the usual lot of great truths, which are about as long-lasting as a lightning flash in comparison with the long dark night that envelops mankind. The happy time has not yet arrived in which truth shall be the portion of the greatest number, as error has heretofore been.

Cesare Beccaria, *On Crimes and Punishments*, trans. by Henry M. Paolucci (Indianapolis: Bobbs Merrill, 1963), pp. 10, 51.

thought that the criminal justice system should ensure speedy trial, sure punishment, and punishment intended to deter further crime. The purpose of law was not to impose the will of God or some other ideal of perfection; its purpose was to secure the greatest good or happiness for the greatest number of human beings. This utilitarian philosophy based on happiness in this life permeated most of the Enlightenment writing on practical reforms.

Bentham

Although utilitarianism did not originate with him, it is particularly associated with the English legal reformer Jeremy Bentham (1748–1832). He sought to create codes of scientific law that were founded on the principle of utility, that is, the greatest happiness for the greatest number. In the *Fragment on Government* (1776) and *The Principles of Morals and Legislation* (1789), Bentham explained that the application of the principle of utility would overcome the special interests of privileged groups who prevented rational government. Bentham regarded the existing legal and judicial systems as burdened by traditional practices that harmed the very people whom the law should serve. The application of reason and utility would remove the legal clutter that prevented justice from being realized.

The Physiocrats

Another area of social relationships where the *philosophes* saw existing legislation and administration preventing the operation of natural social laws was the field of economic policy. They believed that mercantilist legislation and the labor regulations established by various governments and guilds actually hampered the expansion of trade, manufacture, and agriculture. In France these economic reformers were called the *physiocrats*. Their leading spokesmen were François Quesnay (1694–1774) and Pierre Dupont de Nemours (1739–1817). They believed that the primary role of government was to protect property and to permit freedom in the use of property. They particularly felt that all economic production was dependent on sound agriculture, and they favored the consolidation of small peasant holdings into larger, more efficient farms. Here as elsewhere there was a close relationship between the rationalism of the Enlightenment and the spirt of improvement at

work in eighteenth-century European economic life.

Adam Smith

The most important Enlightenment exposition of economics was Adam Smith's (1723–1790) *Inquiry into the Nature and Causes of the Wealth of Na-*

Adam Smith was one of the most important members of what may be called the Class of 1776—the astonishing outburst of British historical writing that centered on that year. In addition to Smith's Inquiry into the Nature and Causes of the Wealth of Nations, *Gibbon published the first volume of* The Decline and Fall, *Dr. Charles Burney (1726–1814) published the first volume of* A General History of Music *(completed in 1789), and Sir John Hawkins (1719–1789) managed to publish the entire five volumes of his* A General History of the Science and Practice of Music. *Moreover, in 1774, Thomas Warton (1728–1790) published the first volume of* The History of English Poetry *(third volume, 1781; never completed), while in 1777 the Scottish historian William Robertson (1721–1793) finished his career with the publication of his* History of America. *[Culver Pictures.]*

❧ Adam Smith Argues for Individual Industry and Wealth

Adam Smith (1723–1790) wanted to see a general, though not complete, application of individual self-interest to economic activity in place of existing mercantilist policies of state regulation. As he explained in this famous passage from *The Wealth of Nations* (1776), he thought that basically unregulated individual economic actions would produce more goods and services than mercantilist policy.

The annual revenue of every society is always precisely equal to the exchangeable value of the whole annual produce of its industry, or rather is precisely the same thing with that exchangeable value. As every individual, therefore, endeavours as much as he can both to employ his capital in the support of domestic industry, and so to direct that industry that its produce may be of the greatest value; every individual necessarily labours to render the annual revenue of the society as great as he can. He generally, indeed, neither intends to promote the public interest, nor knows how much he is promoting it. By prefer-

ring the support of domestic to that of foreign industry, he intends only his own security; and by directing that industry in such a manner as its produce may be of the greatest value, he intends only his own gain, and he is in this, as in many other cases, led by an invisible hand to promote an end which was no part of his intention. Nor is it always the worse for the society that it was no part of it. By pursuing his own interest he frequently promotes that of the society more effectually than when he really intends to promote it. I have never known much good done by those who affected to trade for the public good.

Adam Smith, *The Wealth of Nations* (New York: Modern Library, 1965), p. 423.

tions (1776). Smith, who was for a time a professor at Glasgow, urged that the mercantile system of England—including the navigation acts, the bounties, most tariffs, special trading monopolies, and the domestic regulation of labor and manufacture—be abolished. Smith believed that these modes of economic regulation by the state interfered with the natural system of economic liberty. They were intended to preserve the wealth of the nation, to capture wealth from other nations, and to assure a maximum amount of work for the laborers of the country. However, Smith regarded such regulations as preventing the wealth and production of the country from expanding. He wanted to encourage economic growth and a consumer-oriented economy. The means to those ends was the unleashing of individuals to pursue their own selfish economic interest. The free pursuit of economic self-interest would ensure economic expansion as each person sought enrichment by meeting the demands of the marketplace. Consumers would find their wants met as manufacturers and merchants sought their business.

Smith's book challenged the concept of scarce goods and resources that lay behind mercantilism and the policies of the guilds. Smith saw the realm

of nature as a boundless expanse of water, air, soil, and minerals. The physical resources of the earth seemed to demand exploitation for the enrichment and comfort of humankind. In effect, Smith was saying that the nations and peoples of Europe need not be poor. The idea of the infinite use of nature's goods for the material benefit of humankind—a concept that has dominated Western life until recent years—stemmed directly from the Enlightenment. When Smith wrote, the population of the world was smaller, its people were poorer, and the quantity of undeveloped resources per capita was much greater. For people of the eighteenth century it was in the uninhibited exploitation of natural resources that the true improvement of the human condition seemed to lie.

Smith is usually regarded as the founder of *laissez-faire* economic thought and policy, which has argued in favor of a very limited role for the government in economic life and regulation. However, *The Wealth of Nations* was a very complex book. Smith was no simple dogmatist. For example, he was not opposed to all government activity touching on the economy. The state should provide schools, armies, navies, and roads. It should also undertake certain commercial ventures, such as the opening of dangerous new trade routes, that were economically desirable but the expense or risk of which discouraged private enterprise. His reasonable tone and recognition of the complexity of social and economic life displayed a very important point about the *philosophes*. Most of them were much less rigid and doctrinaire than any brief summary of their thought may tend to suggest. They recognized the passions of humanity as well as its reason. They adopted reason and nature as tools of criticism through which they might create a climate of opinion that would allow the fully developed human personality to flourish.

Political Thought of the *Philosophes*

Nowhere did the appreciation of the complexity of the problems of contemporary society become more evident than in the *philosophes'* political thought. Nor did any other area of their reformist enterprise so clearly illustrate the tension and conflict within the "family" of the Enlightenment. Most *philosophes* were discontented with certain political features of their countries, but they were especially discontent in France. There the corruptness of the royal court, the blundering of the

Charles de Secondat Baron de Montesquieu (1689–1744) *was the author of* The Spirit of the Laws, *which may well have been the most influential work of political thought of the eighteenth century.* [Bulloz.]

bureaucracy, the less than glorious mid-century wars, and the power of the church compounded all problems. Consequently it was in France that the most important political thought of the Enlightenment occurred. However, the French *philosophes* stood quite divided as to the proper solution. Their attitudes spanned the whole spectrum from aristocratic reform to democracy to absolute monarchy.

The Spirit of the Laws

Montesquieu's *The Spirit of the Laws* (1748) may well have been the single most influential book of the century. It is a work that exhibits the internal tensions of the Enlightenment. Montesquieu pursued an empirical method, taking illustrative examples from the political experience of both ancient and modern nations. From these he concluded that there could be no single set of political laws that applied to all peoples at all times and in all places. Rather, there existed a large number of political variables, and the good political life depended on the relationship of those variables. Whether a monarchy or a republic was the best form of government was a matter of the size of the political unit and its population, its social and religious customs, its economic structure, its traditions, and its climate. Only a careful examination and evaluation of these elements could reveal what mode of government would prove most beneficial to a particular people. A century later such speculations would have been classified as sociology.

So far as France was concerned, Montesquieu had some rather definite ideas. He believed in monarchical government, but with a monarchy whose power was tempered and limited by various sets of intermediary institutions. The latter included the aristocracy, the towns, and the other corporate bodies that enjoyed particular liberties that the monarch must respect. These corporate bodies might be said to represent various segments of the general population and thus of public opinion. In France he regarded the aristocratic courts, or *parlements,* as the major example of an intermediary association. Their role was to limit the power of the monarchy and thus preserve the liberty of the subjects. In championing these aristocratic bodies and the general role of the aristocracy, Montesquieu was a political conservative. However, he adopted that stance in the hope of achieving reform, for in his opinion it was the oppressive and inefficient absolutism of the monarchy that accounted for the degradation of French life.

❧ Montesquieu Defends the Separation of Powers

The Spirit of the Laws (1748) was probably the most influential political work of the Enlightenment. In this passage Montesquieu explained how the division of powers within a government would make that government more moderate and would protect the liberty of its subjects. This idea was adopted by the writers of the United States Constitution when they devised the checks and balances of the three branches of government.

Democratic and aristocratic states are not in their own nature free. Political liberty is to be found only in moderate governments; and even in these it is not always found. It is there only when there is no abuse of power. But constant experience shows us that every man invested with power is apt to abuse it, and to carry his authority as far as it will go. . . .

To prevent this abuse, it is necessary from the very nature of things that power should be a check to power. . . .

In every government there are three sorts of power: the legislative; the executive in respect to things dependent on the law of nations; and the executive in regard to matters that depend on the civil law [the realm of the judiciary]. . . .

The political liberty of the subject is a tranquillity of mind arising from the opinion each person has of his safety. In order to have this liberty, it is requisite that government be so constituted as one man need not be afraid of another.

When the legislative and executive powers are united in the same person, or in the same body of magistrates, there can be no liberty; because apprehensions may arise, lest the same monarch or senate should enact tyrannical laws, to execute them in a tyrannical manner.

Again, there is no liberty, if the judiciary power be not separated from the legislative and executive. Were it joined with the legislative, the life and liberty of the subject would be exposed to arbitrary control; for the judge would be then the legislator. Were it joined to the executive power, the judge might behave with violence and oppression.

There would be an end of everything, were the same man or the same body, whether of the nobles or of the people, to exercise those three powers, that of enacting laws, that of executing the public resolutions, and of trying the causes of individuals.

Baron de Montesquieu, *The Spirit of the Laws*, trans. by Thomas Nugent (New York: Hafner Press, 1949), pp. 150–152.

One of Montesquieu's most influential ideas was that of division of power within any government. For his model of a government with power wisely separated among different branches, he took contemporary Great Britain. There he believed he had found a system in which executive power resided in the king, legislative power in the Parliament, and judicial power in the courts. He thought any two branches could check and balance the power of the other. His perception of the eighteenth-century British constitution was incorrect because he failed to see how patronage and electoral corruption allowed a handful of powerful aristocrats to dominate the government. Moreover he was also unaware of the emerging cabinet system, which meant that the executive power was slowly becoming a creature of the Parliament. Nevertheless the analysis illustrated Montesquieu's strong sense of the need to limit the exercise of power through constitutionalism and the formation of law by legislatures rather than by monarchs. In this manner, although Montesquieu set out to defend the political privileges of the French aristocracy, his ideas had a profound and still-lasting effect on the liberal democracies of the next two centuries.

Rousseau

Jean Jacques Rousseau (1712–1778) held a view of the exercise and reform of political power quite different from Montesquieu's.

Rousseau was a strange, isolated genius who never felt particularly comfortable with the other *philosophes.* Yet perhaps more than any other writer of the mid-eighteenth century he transcended the thought and values of his own time. Rousseau had a deep antipathy toward the world and the society in which he lived. It seemed impossible for human beings living according to contemporary commercial values to achieve moral, virtuous, or sincere lives. In 1750, in his *Discourse on the Moral Effects of the Arts and Sciences,* he contended that the process of civilization and enlightenment had corrupted human nature. Human beings in the state of nature had been more dignified. In 1755, in a *Discourse on the Origin of Inequality,* Rousseau blamed much of the evil in the world on maldistribution of property.

In both works Rousseau brilliantly and directly challenged the social fabric of the day. He drew into question the concepts of material and intellectual progress and the morality of a society in which commerce and industry were regarded as the most important of human activites. He felt that the real purpose of society was to nurture better people. In this respect Rousseau's vision of reform was much more radical than that of other contemporary writers. The other *philosophes* believed that human life would be improved if people could enjoy more of the fruits of the earth or could produce more

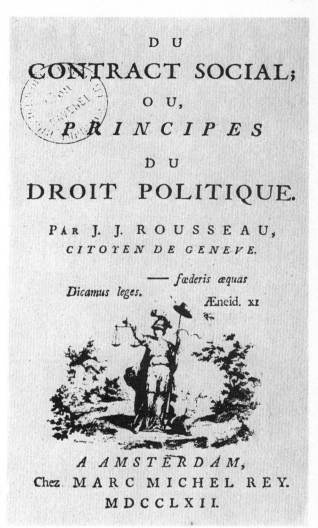

Rousseau's Social Contract *(1762) challenged the political thought of an aristocratic age by calling for radical political equality. Note that, like many other unorthodox works, it was published in relatively free Amsterdam. [The Granger Collection.]*

Jean-Jaques Rousseau (1712–1778). His writings raised some of the most profound social and ethical questions of the Enlightenment. This bust by Houdon is at Orleans. [Bulloz.]

goods. Rousseau raised the more fundamental question of what the good life is. This question has haunted European social thought ever since the eighteenth century. Much of the criticism of Europe's post-World War II society is rooted in this Rousseauean approach.

Rousseau carried these same concerns into his political thought. His most extensive discussion of politics appeared in *The Social Contract* (1762). Although the book attracted rather little immediate

❧ Rousseau Argues that Inequality Is Not Natural

Jean Jacques Rousseau was one of the first writers to assert the social equality of human beings. He argued, as in this 1755 passage, that inequality had developed through the ages and was not "natural." He directly questioned the sanctity of property based on the assumed natural inequality of human beings.

I have endeavoured to trace the origin and progress of inequality, and the institution and abuse of political societies, as far as these are capable of being deduced from the nature of man merely by the light of reason, and independently of those sacred dogmas which give the sanction of divine right to sovereign authority. It follows from this survey that, as there is hardly any inequality in the state of nature, all the inequality which now prevails owes its strength and growth to the development of our faculties and the advance of the human mind, and becomes at last permanent and legitimate by the establishment of property and laws. Secondly, it follows that moral inequality, authorized by positive right alone, clashes with natural right, whenever it is not proportionate to physical inequality—a distinction which sufficiently determines what we think of that species of inequality which prevails in all civilized countries; since it is plainly contrary to the law of nature, however defined, that children should command old men, fools wise men, and that the privileged few should gorge themselves with superfluities while the starving multitude are in want of the bare necessities of life.

Jean Jacques Rousseau, *The Social Contract and Discourses*, trans. by G. D. H. Cole (New York: Dutton, 1950), pp. 271–272.

attention, by the end of the century it was widely read in France. *The Social Contract*, as compared to Montesquieu's *Spirit of the Laws*, was a very abstract book. It did not propose specific reforms but outlined the kind of political structure that Rousseau believed would overcome the evils of contemporary politics and society.

In the tradition of Thomas Hobbes and John Locke, most eighteenth-century political thinkers, regarded human beings as individuals and society as a collection of such independent individuals pursuing personal, selfish goals. These writers wished to liberate these individuals from the undue bonds of government. Rousseau picked up the stick from the other end. His book opens with the declaration, "All men are born free, but everywhere they are in chains."[5] The rest of the volume constitutes a *defense* of the chains of a properly organized society over its members. Rousseau suggested that society is more important than its individual members, because they are what they are only because of their relationship to the larger community. Independent human beings living

alone can achieve very little. Through their relationship to the larger community, they become moral creatures capable of significant action. The question then becomes what kind of community allows people to behave morally. In his two previous discourses Rousseau had explained that contemporary European society was not such a community. It was merely an aggregate of competing individuals whose chief social goal was to preserve selfish independence in spite of all potential social bonds and obligations.

Rousseau sought to project the vision of a society in which each person could maintain personal freedom while at the same time behaving as a loyal member of the larger community. To that end Rousseau drew on the traditions of Plato and Calvin to define freedom as obedience to law. In his case the law to be obeyed was that created by the general will. This concept normally indicated the will of the majority of voting citizens who acted with adequate information and under the influence of virtuous customs and morals. Such democratic participation in decision making would bind the individual citizen to the community. Rousseau believed that the general will must always be right and that to obey the general will was to be free.

[5] Jean Jacques Rousseau, *The Social Contract and Discourses*, trans. by G. D. H. Cole (New York: Dutton, 1950), p. 3.

This argument led him to the notorious conclusion that under certain circumstances some people must be forced to be free. Rousseau's politics thus constituted a justification for radical direct democracy and for collective action against individual citizens.

Rousseau had in effect launched an assault on the eighteenth-century cult of the individual and the fruits of selfishness. He stood at odds with the commercial spirit that was transforming the society in which he lived. Rousseau would have disapproved of the main thrust of Adam Smith's *Wealth of Nations,* which he may or may not have read, and would no doubt have preferred a study on the virtue of nations. Smith wanted people to be prosperous; Rousseau wanted them to be good even if being good meant that they might remain economically poor. He saw human beings not as independent individuals but as creatures enmeshed in necessary social relationships. He believed that loyalty to the community should be encouraged. As one device to that end he suggested a civic religion based on the creed of deism. Such a shared tolerant religious faith would provide unity for the society. Rousseau's chief intellectual inspiration arose from his study of Plato and the ancient Greek *polis.* Especially in Sparta he thought he had discovered human beings dwelling in a moral society inspired by a common purpose. He hoped that modern human beings might also create such a moral commonwealth in which virtuous living would become subordinate to commercial profit.

Rousseau's thought had only a marginal impact on his own time. The other *philosophes* questioned his critique of material improvement. Aristocrats and royal ministers could hardly be expected to welcome his proposal for radical democracy. Too many people were either making or hoping to make money to pay attention to his criticism of commercial values. However, he proved to be a figure to whom later generations returned. Many leaders in the French Revolution were familiar with his writing. Thereafter his ideas were important to most writers who felt called on to criticize the general tenor and direction of Western culture. Rousseau hated much about the emerging modern society in Europe, but he contributed much to modernity by exemplifying for later generations the critic who dared to call into question the very foundations of social thought and action. Whatever our opinions of Rousseau, we have not yet escaped him.

Enlightened Absolutism

Most of the *philosophes* favored neither Montesquieu's reformed and revived aristocracy nor Rousseau's democracy as a solution to contemporary political problems. Like other thoughtful people of the day in other stations and occupations, they looked to the existing monarchies. The *philosophes* hoped in particular that the French monarchy might assert really effective power over the aristocracy and the church to bring about significant reform. Voltaire was a very strong monarchist. He and others—such as Diderot, who visited Catherine II of Russia, and physiocrats who were ministers to the French kings—did not wish to limit the power of monarchs but sought to redirect that power toward the rationalization of economic and political structures and the liberation of intellectual life. Most *philosophes* were not opposed to power if they could find a way of using it for their own purposes.

During the last third of the century it seemed to some observers that several European rulers had actually embraced many of the reforms set forth by the *philosophes. Enlightened absolutism* is the term used to describe this phenomenon. The phrase indicates monarchical government dedicated to the rational strengthening of the central absolutist administration at the cost of other lesser centers of political power. However, the monarchs most closely associated with it—Frederick II of Prussia, Joseph II of Austria, and Catherine II of Russia—were neither genuinely enlightened nor truly absolute in the exercise of royal power. Their enlightenment was a veneer, and the realities of political and economic life limited their absolutism. Frederick II corresponded with the *philosophes,* for a time provided Voltaire with a place at his court, and even wrote history and political tracts. Catherine II, who was a master of what would later be called public relations, consciously sought to create the image of being enlightened. She read the works of the *philosophes,* became a friend of Diderot and Voltaire, and made frequent references to their ideas, all in the hope that her nation might seem more modern and Western. Joseph II undertook a series of religious, legal, and social reforms that contemporaries believed he had derived from suggestions of the *philosophes.*

Despite such appearances the requirements of state security and political ambition rather than the humanitarian and liberating zeal of the Enlightenment directed the policies of these monarchs. They sought the rational economic and social integration of their realms so that they could wage more efficient future wars—a policy profoundly hateful to the *philosophes*. All of the states of Europe had emerged from the Seven Years' War understanding that they would require stronger armed forces for the next conflict and looking for new sources of taxation to finance those armies. The search for new revenues and further internal political support for their rule led these eastern European monarchs to make "enlightened" reforms. They and their advisers used rationality to further what the *philosophes* considered irrational militarism.

Frederick the Great of Prussia

After the mid-century wars, during which Prussia had suffered badly and had almost been defeated, Frederick II (1740–1786) hoped to achieve recovery and consolidation. At grave military and financial cost he had succeeded in retaining Silesia, which he had seized from Austria in 1740. He worked to stimulate its potential as a manufacturing district. Like his Hohenzollern forebears he continued to import workers from outside Prussia. He directed new attention to Prussian agriculture. Under state supervision, swamps were drained, new crops introduced, and peasants encouraged and sometimes compelled to migrate. For the first time in Prussia potatoes and turnips came into general production. Frederick also established a Land-Mortgage Credit Association to aid landowners in raising money for agricultural improvements.

Throughout this process, the impetus for development came from the state. The monarchy and its bureaucracy were the engine for change. Despite new policies and personal exhortations the general populace of Prussia did not prosper under Frederick's reign. The burden of taxation still fell disproportionally on peasants and townspeople.

In less material areas Frederick pursued enlightened policies with somewhat more success. He allowed Catholics and Jews to settle in his predominately Lutheran country, and he protected the Catholics residing in Silesia. He ordered a new codification of Prussian law, which was completed after his death. The policy of toleration allowed foreign workers to contribute to the economic growth of the state. The new legal code was to rationalize the existing system, to make it more efficient, to eliminate regional peculiarities, and to eliminate excessive aristocratic influence. The enlightened monarchs were very concerned about legal reforms, primarily as a means of extending and strengthening royal power.

Frederick liked to describe himself as "the first servant of the State." That image represented an important change in the European conception of monarchy. The idea of an impersonal state was beginning to replace the concept of a personal monarchy. Kings might come and go, but the impersonal apparatus of government—the bureaucracy, the armies, the laws, the courts, and the citizens' loyalty arising from fear and from appreciation of state services and protection—remained. The state as an entity separate from the personality of the ruler came into its own after the French Revolution, but it was born in the monarchies of the old regime.

Joseph II of Austria

No eighteenth-century ruler so embodied rational, impersonal force as the emperor Joseph II of Austria. He was the son of Maria Theresa and co-ruler with her from 1765 to 1780. During the next ten years he ruled alone. He has been aptly described as "an imperial puritan and a good deal of a prig."[6] During much of his life he slept on straw and ate little but beef. He prided himself on a narrow, passionless rationality, which he sought to impose by his own will on the various Hapsburg domains. Despite his eccentricities and the coldness of his personality Joseph II genuinely and sincerely wished to improve the lot of his people. He was much less a political opportunist and cynic than either Frederick the Great of Prussia or Catherine the Great of Russia. The ultimate result of his well-intentioned efforts was a series of aristocratic and peasant rebellions extending from Hungary to the Austrian Netherlands.

As explained in Chapter 20, of all the rising states of the eighteenth century, Austria was the most diverse in its people and problems. Robert Palmer has likened it to "a vast holding company."[7] The Hapsburgs never succeeded in creating either a unified administrative structure or a strong aristocratic loyalty. The price of the preservation of the monarchy during the War of the Austrian Succession (1740–1748) had been guarantees of considerable aristocratic independence. Joseph sought to overcome the pluralism of his holdings by increasing the power of the central monarchy. He also wished to expand the borders of his territory in the direction of Poland and the Ottoman Empire.

The first target of Joseph's reassertion of royal absolutism was the church. From the reign of Charles V in the sixteenth century to that of Maria Theresa, the Hapsburgs had been the single most important dynastic champion of Roman Catholicism. Maria Theresa had surrounded herself with pious and sometimes very superstitious advisers. Joseph changed these policies. He was a practicing and perhaps even a believing Catholic, but he rid himself of priestly advisers. He extended genuine toleration to all Christians and relieved the Jews living in Austria of many special taxes and signs of degradation. He sought to undermine in every possible way the influence of the papacy in his lands. He drove monks and nuns from monasteries and reduced the number of religious holidays. While encouraging the construction of churches, he confiscated ecclesiastical lands. He considered church use of that property unproductive. Revenues tradi-

tionally going to the church were redirected to the state. Priests, in effect, became the employees of the state. The influence of the Roman Catholic Church as an independent institution came to a close. Joseph was willing to have religious faith and practice flourish, but religious institutions and the people they employed must stand subordinate to the power of the government. In many respects the ecclesiastical policies of Joseph II prefigured those of the French Revolution.

Like Frederick of Prussia, Joseph sought to improve the economic life of his domains. He abolished many internal tariffs and encouraged road building and the improvement of river transport. He went on personal inspection tours of farms and manufacturing districts. Joseph also reconstructed the judicial system to make laws more uniform and rational and to lessen the influence of local landlords. National courts with power over the landlord courts were established. All of these improvements were expected to bring new unity to the state and more taxes into the coffers at Vienna.

The most revolutionary of Joseph's departures was his attitude toward serfdom and the land. The emperor believed that if the peasantry were legally free and to some extent liberated from special feudal payments to their landlords, they would become more productive and industrious. However, to interfere with the landlord–serf relation-

Emperor Joseph II of Austria encouraged improved farming and industry in his domains. This propaganda painting portrayed him plowing a field and providing a good example to his subjects. [Austrian Information Service, New York.]

∾ Joseph II of Austria Promotes Toleration in His Realm

Toleration was frequently an important policy of enlightened absolutism and the area of political action that most directly reflected the influence of the *philosophes*. As shown in this 1787 passage, Joseph II of Austria believed that toleration would remove religious fanaticism from his realms, lead to greater human knowledge, and at the same time make his subjects more loyal. The reader may wish to compare this statement with Voltaire's attack on religious fanaticism that appears earlier in this chapter.

Till now the Protestant religion has been opposed in my states; its adherents have been treated like foreigners; civil rights, possession of estates, titles, and appointments, all were refused them.

I determined from the very commencement of my reign to adorn my diadem with the love of my people, to act in the administration of affairs according to just, impartial, and liberal principles; consequently, I granted toleration, and removed the yoke which had oppressed the protestants for centuries.

Fanaticism shall in future be known in my states only by the contempt I have for it; nobody shall any longer be exposed to hardships on account of his creed; *no man shall be compelled in future to profess the religion of the state, if it be contrary to his persuasion, and if he have other ideas of the right way of insuring blessedness. . . .*

Tolerance is an effect of that beneficent increase of knowledge which now enlightens Europe, and which is owing to philosophy and the efforts of great men; it is a convincing proof of the improvement of the human mind, which has boldly reopened a road through the dominions of superstition, which was trodden centuries ago by Zoroaster and Confucius, and which, fortunately for mankind, has now become the highway of monarchs.

"Letters of Joseph II," *The Pamphleteer*, Vol. 19 (1822), pp. 289–290.

ship was to breach what had been one of the foundation stones of eastern European absolutism: the trade-off of aristocratic support for the monarchy in exchange for a free hand with the serfs.

In 1781, 1783, and 1785 Joseph issued a series of decrees giving legal freedom to the serfs in Bohemia, Austria, Transylvania, and Hungary. They could marry and migrate without the permission of their landlords and could appeal decisions from manorial courts to the civil courts of the state. Between 1783 and 1789 Joseph went even further and drew up a tax list on which all occupiers of land were enumerated. Henceforth all proprietors of the land were to be taxed regardless of social status. In 1789 by royal decree the emperor abolished *robot*, or the services due landlords from their serfs. The service was commuted to a tax, only part of which went to the landlord, while the remainder reverted to the state. These measures brought turmoil to the Hapsburg domains. Peasants revolted against their landlords over the interpretation of their newly granted rights. Then the nobles of the various realms also rose up in rebellion over the emperor's decrees.

Having sowed the wind, Joseph died in 1790. His brother and successor, Leopold II (1790–1792), reaped the noble whirlwind. Although quite sympathetic with Joseph's goals, Leopold repealed most of the reformist decrees to shore up the stability of his own rule. Serfdom or feudal obligations persisted in most of the Hapsburg lands until 1848. Joseph II had possessed a narrow vision attached to an unbending will. For all his intellectual brilliance and hard work he had failed to understand that his policies enjoyed no supporters except for a few royal bureaucrats. He had ruled without consulting any political constituency. The nobles, the church, the towns with their chartered liberties, and the absence of a strong bureaucracy or army stood as barriers to his absolutism. His was a mind of classical rationalism in conflict with political and social realities of baroque complexity.

Catherine the Great of Russia

Joseph II never grasped the practical necessity of cultivating political support for his policies. Catherine II (1762–1796), who had been born a

German princess but who became empress of Russia, understood only too well the fragility of the Romanov dynasty's base of power.

After the death of Peter the Great in 1725 the court nobles and the army had repeatedly determined the Russian succession. As a result, the crown fell primarily into the hands of people with little talent. Peter's wife, Catherine I, ruled for two years (1725–1727) and was succeeded for three years by Peter's grandson Peter II. In 1730 the crown devolved on Anna, who was a niece of Peter the Great. During 1740 and 1741 a child named Ivan VI, who was less than a year old, was the nominal ruler. Finally in 1741 Peter the Great's daughter Elizabeth came to the throne. She held the title of empress until 1762, but she did not rule. Her court was a shambles of political and romantic intrigue. Needless to say, much of the power possessed by the czar at the opening of the century had vanished.

At her death in 1762 Elizabeth was succeeded by Peter III, one of her nephews. He was a weak ruler whom many contemporaries considered mad. He immediately exempted the nobles from compulsory military service and then made rapid peace with Frederick the Great, for whom he held unbounded admiration. That decision probably saved Prussia from military defeat. The one positive feature of this unbalanced creature's life was his marriage in 1745 to a young German princess born in Pomerania. This was the future Catherine the Great, who for almost twenty years lived in misery and frequent danger at the court of Elizabeth. During that time she befriended important nobles and read widely in the books of the *philosophes*. She was a shrewd person whose experience in a court crawling with rumors, intrigue, and conspiracy had taught her how to survive. She had neither love nor loyalty for her demented husband. After a few months of rule Peter III was deposed and murdered with the approval, if not the aid, of Catherine. On his deposition she was immediately proclaimed empress.

Catherine's familiarity with the Enlightenment and the general culture of western Europe convinced her that Russia was very backward and that it must make major reforms if it were to remain a great power. She understood that any major reform must have a wide base of political and social support. In 1767 she summoned a Legislative Commission to revise the law and government of Russia. There were over five hundred delegates from all sectors of Russian life. Prior to the conven-

EXPANSION OF RUSSIA,
1689–1796

MAP 21.1 *The overriding territorial aim of Peter the Great in the first quarter and of Catherine the Great in the last half of the eighteenth century was the securing of northern and southern navigable-water outlets for the vast Russian Empire. Hence Peter's push to the Baltic Sea and Catherine's to the Black Sea. Catherine also managed to acquire large areas of Poland through the partitions of that country.*

639

Empress Catherine the Great of Russia, born Sophia Augusta Frederica in the tiny German state of Anhalt-Zerbst, cultivated the friendship of the philosophes *but pursued many policies of which they disapproved, including warfare and censorship. The artist represented here is Boroviloosky.* [*John R. Freeman.*]

ing of the commission she issued a set of *Instructions* partly written by herself. They contained numerous ideas drawn from the political writings of the *philosophes*. The commission considered the *Instructions* as well as other ideas and complaints raised by its members. The revision of Russian law, however, did not occur for more than a half-century. In 1768 Catherine simply dismissed the commission, which had reached few concrete decisions. Yet the meeting had not been useless, for considerable information had been gathered about the condition of the realm. The inconclusive debates and the absence of programs from the delegates themselves suggested that most Russians saw no alternative to an autocratic monarchy.

Catherine proceeded to carry out limited reforms on her own authority. She gave strong support to the rights and local power of the nobility. In 1775 she reorganized local government to solve problems brought to light by the Legislative Commission. She put most local offices into the hands of nobles rather than creating a royal bureaucracy. In 1785 Catherine issued the Charter of the Nobil-

RUSSIA FROM PETER THE GREAT THROUGH CATHERINE THE GREAT

1725	Death of Peter the Great
1725–1727	Catherine I
1727–1730	Peter II
1730–1741	Anna
1740–1741	Ivan VI
1741–1762	Elizabeth
1762	Peter III
1762	Catherine II (the Great) becomes empress
1767	Legislative Commission summoned
1769	War with Turkey
1771–1775	Pugachev's Rebellion
1772	First Partition of Poland
1774	Treaty of Kuchuk-Kainardji ends war with Turkey
1775	Reorganization of local government
1783	Russia annexes the Crimea
1785	Catherine issues the Charter of the Nobility
1793	Second Partition of Poland
1795	Third Partition of Poland
1796	Death of Catherine the Great

ity, which guaranteed many noble rights and privileges. In part the empress had no choice but to favor the nobles. They had the capacity to topple her from the throne. There were too few educated subjects in her realm to establish an independent bureaucracy, and the treasury could not afford an army strictly loyal to the crown. So Catherine wisely made a virtue of necessity. She strengthened the stability of her crown by making convenient friends with her nobles.

Part and parcel of Catherine's program was a continuation of the economic development begun under Peter the Great. She attempted to suppress internal barriers to trade. Exports of grain, flax, furs, and naval stores grew dramatically. She also favored the expansion of the small Russian middle class. Russian trade required such a vital urban class. And through all of these departures Catherine attempted to maintain ties of friendship and correspondence with the *philosophes*. She knew that if she treated them kindly, they would be sufficiently flattered and would give her a progressive reputation throughout Europe.

The limited administrative reforms and the policy of economic growth had a counterpart in the diplomatic sphere. The Russian drive for warm-water ports continued. This goal required warfare with the Turks. In 1769, as a result of a minor Russian incursion, the Ottoman empire declared war on Russia. The Russians responded in a series of strikingly successful military moves. During 1769 and 1770 the Russian fleet sailed all the way from the Baltic Sea into the eastern Mediterranean. The Russian army won several major victories that by 1771 gave Russia control of Ottoman provinces on the Danube River and the Crimean coast of the Black Sea. The conflict dragged on until 1774, when it was closed by the Treaty of Kuchuk-Kainardji. The treaty gave Russia a direct outlet on the Black Sea, free navigation rights in its waters, and free access through the Bosporus. Moreover, the province of the Crimea became an independent state, which Catherine painlessly annexed in 1783.

The Partition of Poland

These military successes obviously brought the empress much domestic political support. However, they made the other states of eastern Europe uneasy. These anxieties were overcome by an extraordinary division of Polish territory known as the First Partition of Poland. The Russian victories

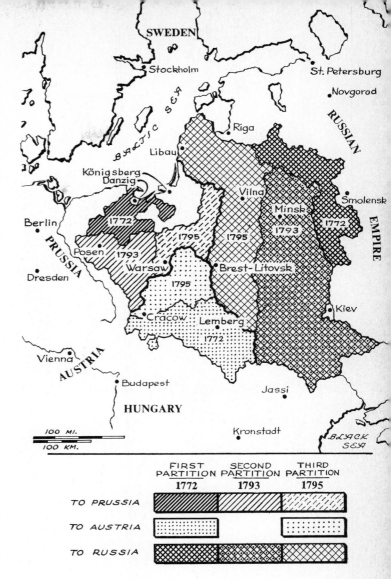

PARTITIONS OF POLAND,
1772–1793–1795

MAP 21.2 *The callous eradication of Poland from the map displayed eighteenth-century power politics at its most extreme. Poland, without strong central governmental institutions, fell victim to those states in central and eastern Europe that had developed such institutions.*

along the Danube River were most unwelcome to Austria, which also harbored ambitions of territorial expansion in that direction. At the same time, the Ottoman Empire was pressing Prussia for aid against Russia. Frederick the Great made a proposal to Russia and Austria that would give each something it wanted, prevent conflict among the

This French engraving is a satirical comment on the first partition of Poland (1772) by Russia, Austria, and Prussia. The distressed monarch attempting to retain his crown is Stanislaus of Poland. Catherine of Russia, Joseph of Austria, and Frederick of Prussia point out their respective shares of the loot.

powers, and save appearances. After long, complicated, secret negotiations the three powers agreed that Russia would abandon the conquered Danubian provinces. In compensation Russia received a large portion of Polish territory with almost two million inhabitants. As a reward for remaining neutral Prussia annexed most of the territory between East Prussia and Prussia proper. This land allowed Frederick to unite two previously separate sections of his realm. Finally, Austria took Galicia, with its important salt mines, and other Polish territory with over two and one-half million inhabitants. In September 1772 the helpless Polish aristocracy, paying the price for the maintenance of their internal liberties, ratified this seizure of their territory. The Polish state had lost approximately one third of its territory.

There were two additional partitions of Poland by Russia and Prussia, and one more by Austria. These occurred in 1793 and 1795 and removed Poland from the map of Europe. Each time the great powers contended that they were saving themselves and by implication the rest of Europe

from Polish anarchy. The fact of the matter was that the political weakness of Poland made the country and its resources a rich field for plunderous aggression. The last two partitions took place during the French Revolution. The three eastern European absolute monarchies objected to certain reforms undertaken by the Polish nobles for fear that even minor Polish reform might endanger the stability of their own societies.

The End of the Eighteenth Century in Eastern Europe

During the last quarter of the eighteenth century all three regimes based on enlightened absolutism had become more repressive. Frederick lived much removed from his people during his old age. The aristocracy, looking out for its own self-interest, filled the major Prussian military and administrative posts. As Joseph II confronted growing frustration and political unrest over his plans for restructuring the society of his realms, he used more and more censorship and secret police. Catherine the Great never fully recovered from the fears raised by Pugachev's rebellion. Once the French Revolution broke out in 1789, the Russian empress censored books based on Enlightenment thought and sent offensive authors into Siberian exile.

By the close of the century all three states were characterized by autocracy, censorship, increasingly downtrodden serf populations, grasping nobilities, and fear of change permeating all the ruling classes. These attitudes had come into existence prior to 1789, but the events in France froze those points of view for almost half a century. Paradoxically nowhere did the humanity and liberalism of the Enlightenment ultimately have a more difficult time surviving and entering the mainstream of life and thought than in those states that had had "enlightened" rulers.

Although the enlightened absolute monarchs lacked the humanity of the *philosophes,* they had embraced the Enlightenment spirit of innovation. They wanted to change the political, social, and economic structures of their realms. From the close of the Seven Years' War (1763) until the opening of the French Revolution in 1789, the monarchies of both western and eastern Europe had been the major forces working for significant institutional change. In every case they had stirred up considerable aristocratic and some popular resistance and resentment. George III of Britain fought for years with Parliament and lost the colonies of North America in the process. Frederick II of Prussia carried out his program of reform only because he accepted new aristocratic influence over the bureaucracy and the army. Catherine II of Russia had had to come to terms with her nobility. Joseph II had left his domains in turmoil by imposing changes without consulting the nobility.

These monarchs pushed for innovations because of their desires for increased revenue. The same problem existed in France. There the royal drive for adequate fiscal resources also led to aristocratic rebellion. However, in France neither the monarchy nor the aristocracy could control the social and political forces unleashed by their quarrel.

Suggested Readings

C. BECKER, *The Heavenly City of the Eighteenth Century Philosophers* (1932). An influential, but very controversial discussion.

P. P. BERNARD, *Joseph II* (1968). A brief biography.

T. BESTERMANN, *Voltaire* (1969). A recent biography by the editor of Voltaire's letters.

E. CASSIRER, *The Philosophy of the Enlightenment* (1951). A brilliant but difficult work by one of the great philosophers of the twentieth century.

G. R. CRAGG, *The Church and the Age of Reason* (1961). A general survey of eighteenth-century religious life.

R. DARNTON, *The Business of Enlightenment: A Publishing History of the Encyclopedia,* 1775–1800 (1979). A wide-ranging examination of the printing and dispersion of the *Encyclopedia.*

P. FUSSELL, *The Rhetorical World of Augustan Humanism* (1969). Examines English writers during the Enlightenment.

J. GAGLIARDO, *Enlightened Despotism* (1967). A discussion of the subject in its European context.

P. GAY, *The Enlightenment: An Interpretation,* 2 vols. (1966, 1969). The most important and far-reaching recent treatment.

P. GAY, *The Enlightenment: A Comprehensive Anthology* (1973). A large, well-edited set of documents.

L. GERSHOY, *From Despotism to Revolution,* 1763–1793 (1944). A sound treatment of the political background.

N. HAMPSON, *A Cultural History of the Enlightenment* (1969). A useful introduction.

P. HAZARD, *The European Mind: The Critical Years,* 1680–1715 (1935), and *European Thought in the Eighteenth Century from Montesquieu to Lessing* (1946). The two volumes portray the century as the turning point for the emergence of the modern mind in Europe.

H. C. JOHNSON, *Frederick the Great and His Officials* (1975). An examination of the administrative apparatus of enlightened absolutism.

R. KREISER, *Miracles, Convulsions, and Ecclesiastical Politics in Early Eighteenth-Century Paris* (1978). An important study of the kind of religious life that the *philosophes* opposed.

L. KRIEGER, *Kings and Philosophers,* 1689–1789 (1970). A survey that relates the social and political thought of the Enlightenment writers to their immediate political setting.

I. DE MADARIAGE, *Russia in the Age of Catherine the Great* (1981). The best discussion in English.

F. MANUEL, *The Eighteenth Century Confronts the Gods* (1959). A broad examination of the *philosophes'* treatment of Christian and pagan religion.

R. R. PALMER, *Catholics and Unbelievers in Eighteenth Century France* (1939). A discussion of the opponents of the *philosophes.*

G. RITTER, *Frederick the Great* (trans. 1968). A useful biography.

R. O. ROCKWOOD (Ed.), *Carl Becker's Heavenly City Revisited* (1958). Important essays qualifying Becker's thesis.

J. N. SHKLAR, *Men and Citizens, a Study of Rousseau's Social Theory* (1969). A thoughtful and provocative overview of Rousseau's political thought.

A. M. WILSON, *Diderot* (1972). A splendid biography of the person behind the project for the *Encyclopedia* and other major Enlightenment publications.

L'ABOLITION DES TITRES DE NOBLESSE
par le Decret de l'Assemblée Nationale en juin 1790.

Des Aristocrates l'engeance est allarmée
Grands titres, vains honneurs, vous n'êtes que fumée
Qui se seroit douté d'un tel evenement.
C'est ainsi que chez nous la pluie abat le vent.

22 The French Revolution

In THE spring of 1789 the long-festering conflict between the French monarchy and aristocracy erupted into a new political crisis. This dispute, unlike earlier ones, quickly outgrew the issues of its origins and produced the wider disruption of the French Revolution. The quarrel that began as a struggle between the most exclusive elements of the political nation soon involved all sectors of French society and eventually every major state in Europe. Before the turmoil settled, small-town provincial lawyers and Parisian street orators exercised more influence over the fate of the Continent than did aristocrats, royal ministers, or monarchs. Armies commanded by persons of low birth and filled by conscripted village youths emerged victorious over forces composed of professional soldiers and directed by officers of noble birth. The very

In this French cartoon of 1790, rats and flames consume the symbols of aristocratic privilege. The abolition of titles of nobility and of feudal dues was a major step toward the Revolution's goal of establishing the equality of all Frenchmen before the law. [Editorial Photocolor Archives.]

existence of the Roman Catholic faith in France was challenged. Politically and socially neither France nor Europe would ever be quite the same after these events.

The Crisis of the French Monarchy

Although the French Revolution constituted one of the central turning points in modern European history, it originated from the basic tensions and problems that characterized practically all late eighteenth-century states. From the Seven Years' War (1756–1763) onward, the French monarchy was unable to handle its finances on a sound basis. It emerged from the conflict both defeated and in debt. The French support of the American revolt against Great Britain further deepened the financial difficulties of the government. On the eve of the revolution the interest and payments on the royal debt amounted to just over one half of the entire budget. The annual deficit was in the vicinity of 126 million livres. Given the economic vitality of the nation, this debt was neither overly large nor disproportionate to the debts of other European powers. The problem lay with the inability of the royal government to tap the wealth of the French nation through taxes to service and repay the debt. Paradoxically France was a rich nation with an impoverished government.

The debt was symptomatic of the failure of the eighteenth-century French monarchy to come to terms with the resurgent social and political power of the aristocracy. For twenty-five years after the Seven Years' War there was a standoff between them. The monarchy attempted to pursue a program somewhat resembling that associated with enlightened absolutism in eastern Europe. However, both Louis XV (1715–1774) and Louis XVI (1774–1792) lacked the character and the resolution for such a departure. The moral corruption of the former and the indecision of the latter meant that the monarchy could not rally the French public to its side.

In place of a consistent policy to deal with the growing debt, the monarchy gave way to hesitancy, retreat, and even duplicity. In 1763 the monarchy issued a new set of tax decrees that would have extended the collection of certain taxes that were supposed to have been discontinued at the close of the war. There were also new tax assessments. This search for revenue was not unlike the one that led the British government to attempt to tax the American colonies. Several of the provincial *parlements* and finally the *Parlement* of Paris—all controlled by nobles—declared the taxes illegal. During the ensuing dispute the aristocratic *parlements* set themselves up as the spokesmen of the nation and as the protectors of French liberty against the illegal assertion of monarchical power. This was one of the political functions of the nobility that Montesquieu had outlined in *The Spirit of the Laws* (1748).

In 1770 Louis XV appointed René Maupeou (1714–1792) as chancellor. The new minister was determined to break the *parlements* and impose a greater part of the tax burden on the nobility. He abolished the *parlements* and exiled their members to different parts of the country. He then commenced an ambitious program of reform and efficiency. What ultimately doomed Maupeou's policy was less the resistance of the nobility than the death of Louis XV in 1774. His successor, Louis XVI, in an attempt to regain what he conceived to be popular support, restored all the *parlements* and confirmed their old powers. This action, in conjunction with the later aid to the American colonies, locked the monarchy into a continuing financial bind. Thereafter meaningful fiscal or political reform through existing institutions was probably doomed.

Louis XVI's first minister was the physiocrat Jacques Turgot (1727–1781), who attempted various economic reforms, including the removal of restrictions on the grain trade and the elimination of the guilds. He transformed the *corvée,* or roadworking obligation of peasants, into money payments. Turgot also intended to restructure the taxation system in order to tap the wealth of the nobility. These and other ideas represented a program of bold new departures for the monarchy. They proved too bold for the tremulous young king, who dismissed Turgot in 1776. By 1781 the debt, as a result of the aid to America, was larger and the sources of revenues were unchanged. However, the new director-general of finances, Jacques Necker (1732–1804), a Swiss banker, produced a public report that suggested that the situation was not so bad as had been feared. He argued that if the expenditures for the American war were removed, the budget was in surplus. However, Necker's report also revealed that a large portion of the royal expenditure went to pensions for aristocrats and other royal court favorites. This infor-

Louis XVI of France (1774–1792) was unable to regain control of the political situation in France after the summer of 1789. The drawing is by Ducreux. [French Cultural Services, New York.]

Queen Marie Antoinette (1755–1793) was the daughter of Empress Maria Theresa of Austria and the wife of Louis XVI. Around her gathered many of the popularly believed unfavorable stories of the French court. The painting is by Elisabeth Vigée-Lebrun (1755–1842). [The Granger Collection.]

mation aroused the anger of court aristocratic circles against the banker, who soon left office. His financial sleight of hand, nonetheless, made it more difficult for later government officials to claim a real need to raise new taxes.

The monarchy hobbled along until 1786. By this time Charles Alexandre de Calonne (1734–1802) was the minister of finance. He was probably the most able administrator to serve Louis XVI. More carefully than previous ministers he charted the size of the debt and the deficit. He submitted a program for reform quite similar to that presented by Turgot a decade earlier. Calonne proposed to encourage internal trade, to lower some taxes such as the *gabelle* on salt, and to transform peasants' services to money payments.

More important, Calonne urged the introduction of a new land tax that would require payments from all landowners regardless of their social status. If this tax could have been imposed, the monarchy would have been able to abandon other indirect taxes. The government would also rarely have had to seek approval for further new taxes from the aristocratically dominated *parlements*. Calonne also intended to establish new local assemblies to approve land taxes; in these assemblies the voting power would depend on the amount of land owned rather than on the social status of the owner. All these proposals would have undermined both the political and the social power of the French aristocracy.

A new clash with the nobility was unavoidable, and the monarchy had very little room for maneuver. The creditors were at the door; the treasury was nearly empty. Consequently, in 1787 Calonne met with an Assembly of Notables drawn from the upper ranks of the aristocracy and the church to seek support and approval for his plan. The assembly adamantly refused any such action; rather, it demanded that the aristocracy be allowed a greater share in the direct government of the kingdom. The notables called for the reappointment of Necker, who they believed had left the country in sound fiscal condition. Finally, they claimed that they had no right to consent to new taxes and that such a right was vested only in the medieval institution of the Estates General of France, which had not met since 1614. The notables believed that the calling of the Estates General, which was traditionally organized to allow aristocratic and church dominance, would produce a victory for the nobility over the monarchy.

Again Louis XVI backed off. He dismissed Calonne and replaced him with Étienne Charles Loménie de Brienne (1727–1794), who was archbishop of Toulouse and the chief opponent of Calonne at the Assembly of Notables. Once in office Brienne found to his astonishment that the situation was as bad as his predecessor had asserted. Brienne himself now sought to impose the land tax. However, the *Parlement* of Paris took the new position that it lacked authority to authorize the tax and said that only the Estates General could do so. Shortly thereafter Brienne appealed to the Assembly of the Clergy to approve a large subsidy to allow funding of that part of the debt then coming due for payment. The clergy, like the *Parlement* dominated by aristocrats, not only refused the subsidy but also reduced their existing contribution or *don gratuit* to the government. As these unfruitful negotiations were transpiring at the center of political life, local aristocratic *parlements* and estates in the provinces were demanding a restoration of the privileges they had enjoyed during the early seventeenth century before Richelieu and Louis XIV had crushed their independent power. Consequently, in July 1788 the king, through Brienne, agreed to convoke the Estates General the next year. Brienne resigned and was replaced by Necker. The institutions of the aristocracy—and to a lesser degree, of the church—had brought the French monarchy to its knees. In the country of its origin, royal absolutism had been defeated.

The Revolutions of 1789

The Estates General Becomes the National Assembly

The aristocratic triumph proved to be quite brief. It unloosed social and political forces that neither the nobles nor the monarchy could control. The new difficulties arose from clashes among the groups represented in the Estates General. The body was composed of three divisions: the First Estate of the clergy, the Second Estate of the nobility, and the Third Estate, which represented everyone else in the kingdom. During the widespread public discussions preceding the meeting of the Estates General, it became clear that the Third Estate, which included all the professional, commercial, and the middle-class groups of the country, would not permit the monarchy and the aristocracy to decide the future course of the nation. Their spirit was best displayed in a pamphlet published during 1789 in which the Abbé Sieyès (1748–1836) declared, "What is the Third Estate? Everything. What has it been in the political order up to the present? Nothing. What does it ask? To become something."[1]

The split between the aristocracy and the Third Estate occurred before the Estates General gathered. Debate over the proper organization of the body drew the lines of basic disagreement. Members of the aristocracy demanded an equal number of representatives for each estate. In September 1788 the *Parlement* of Paris ruled that voting in the Estates General should be conducted by order rather than by head, that is, that each estate, or order, should have one vote, rather than that each member should have one vote. That procedure would ensure that the aristocratic First and Second Estates could always outvote the Third. Both moves on the part of the aristocracy unmasked its alleged concern for French liberty and exposed it

as a group determined to maintain its privileges. Spokesmen for the Third Estate denounced the arrogant claims of the aristocracy. The royal council eventually decided that the cause of the monarchy and fiscal reform would best be served by a strengthening of the Third Estate, and in December 1788 the council announced that the Third Estate would elect twice as many representatives as either the nobles or the clergy. This so-called doubling of the Third Estate meant that it could easily dominate the Estates General if voting were allowed by head rather than by order. It was properly assumed that some liberal nobles and clergy would support the Third Estate. The method of voting was settled by the king only after the Estates General had gathered at Versailles in May 1789.

When the representatives came to the royal palace, they brought with them *cahiers de doléances,* or lists of grievances, registered by the local electors, to be presented to the king. Large numbers of these have survived and provide considerable information about the state of the country on the eve of the revolution. These documents recorded criticisms of government waste, indirect taxes, church taxes and corruption, and the hunting rights of the aristocracy. They included calls for periodic meetings of the Estates General, more equitable taxes, more local control of administration, unified weights and measures, and a free press. The overwhelming demand of the *cahiers* was for equality of rights among the king's subjects.

These complaints and demands could not be discussed until the questions of organization and voting had been decided. From the beginning, the Third Estate, whose members consisted largely of local officials, professional men, and lawyers, refused to sit as a separate order as the king desired. For several weeks there was a standoff. Then on June 1 the Third Estate invited the clergy and the nobles to join them in organizing a new legislative body. A few members of the lower clergy did so. On June 17 that body declared itself the National Assembly.

Three days later, finding themselves accidentally locked out of their usual meeting place, the National Assembly moved to a nearby tennis court, where its members took an oath to continue to sit until they had given France a constitution. This was the famous Tennis Court Oath. Louis XVI ordered the National Assembly to desist from their actions, but shortly afterward a majority of the clergy and a

---

[1] Quoted in Leo Gershoy, *The French Revolution and Napoleon* (New York: Appleton-Century-Crofts, 1964), p. 102.

THE FRENCH REVOLUTION

1789

May 5	The Estates General opens at Versailles
June 17	The Third Estate declares itself the National Assembly
June 20	The National Assembly takes the Tennis Court Oath
July 14	Fall of the Bastille in the city of Paris
Late July	The Great Fear spreads in the countryside
August 4	The nobles surrender their feudal rights in a meeting of the National Constituent Assembly
August 27	Declaration of the Rights of Man and Citizen
October 5–6	Parisian women march to Versailles and force Louis XVI and his family to return to Paris

1790

July 12	Civil Constitution of the Clergy adopted
July 14	A new constitution is accepted by the king

1791

June 20–24	Louis XVI and his family attempt to flee France and are stopped at Varennes
August 27	The Declaration of Pillnitz
October 1	The Legislative Assembly meets

1792

April 20	France declares war on Austria
August 10	The Tuileries palace is stormed, and Louis XVI takes refuge with the Legislative Assembly
September 2–7	The September Massacres
September 20	France wins the battle of Valmy
September 21	The Convention meets, and the monarchy is abolished

1793

January 21	Louis XVI is executed
February 1	France declares war on Great Britain
March	Counterrevolution breaks out in the Vendée
April	The Committee of Public Safety is formed
June 22	The Constitution of 1793 is adopted but not put into operation
July	Robespierre enters the Committee of Public Safety
August 23	*Levée en masse* proclaimed
September 17	Maximum prices set on food and other commodities
October 16	Queen Marie Antoinette is executed
November 10	The Cult of Reason is proclaimed. The revolutionary calendar beginning on September 22, 1792, is adopted

1794

March 24	Execution of the Hébertist leaders of the *sans-culottes*
April 6	Execution of Danton
May 7	Cult of the Supreme Being proclaimed
June 8	Robespierre leads the celebration of the Festival of the Supreme Being.
June 10	The Law of 22 Prairial is adopted
July 27	The Ninth of Thermidor and the fall of Robespierre
July 28	Robespierre is executed

1795

August 22	The Constitution of the Year III is adopted, establishing the Directory

◦ The Third Estate of a French City Petitions the King

The *cahiers de doléances* were the lists of grievances brought to Versailles in 1789 by members of the Estates General. This particular *cahier* originated in Dourdan, a city of central France, and reflects the complaints of the Third Estate. The first two articles refer to the organization of the Estates General. The other articles ask that the king grant various forms of equality before the law and in matters of taxation. These demands for equality appeared in practically all the *cahiers* of the Third Estate.

The order of the third estate of the City . . . of Dourdan . . . supplicates [the king] to accept the grievances, complaints, and remonstrances which it is permitted to bring to the foot of the throne, and to see therein only the expression of its zeal and the homage of its obedience.

It wishes:

1. That his subjects of the third estate, equal by such status to all other citizens, present themselves before the common father without other distinction which might degrade them.

2. That all the orders, already united by duty and a common desire to contribute equally to the needs of the State, also deliberate in common concerning its needs.

3. That no citizen lose his liberty except according to law; that, consequently, no one be arrested by virtue of special orders, or, if imperative circumstances necessitate such orders, that the prisoner be handed over to regular courts of justice within forty-eight hours at the latest.

. . . .

12. That every tax, direct or indirect, be granted only for a limited time, and that every collection beyond such term be regarded as peculation, and punished as such.

. . . .

15. That every personal tax be abolished; that thus the capitation *[a poll tax] and the* taille *[tax from which nobility and clergy were exempt] and its accessories be merged with the* vingtièmes *[an income tax] in a tax on land and real or nominal property.*

16. That such tax be borne equally, without distinction, by all classes of citizens and by all kinds of property, even feudal . . . rights.

17. That the tax substituted for the corvée *be borne by all classes of citizens equally and without distinction. That said tax, at present beyond the capacity of those who pay it and the needs to which it is destined, be reduced by at least one-half.*

John Hall Stewart, *A Documentary Survey of the French Revolution* (New York: Macmillan, 1951), pp. 76–77.

---

large group of nobles joined the assembly. On June 27 the king capitulated and formally requested the First and Second Estates to meet with the National Assembly where voting would occur by head rather than by order. Had nothing further occurred, the government of France would have been transformed. Government by privileged orders had come to an end, for the National Assembly, which renamed itself the National Constituent Assembly, was composed of persons from all three orders who possessed shared liberal goals for the administrative, constitutional, and economic re-form of the country. The revolution in the governing of France had commenced.

Fall of the Bastille

Two new forces soon intruded on the scene. The first was Louis XVI himself, who attempted to regain the initiative by mustering royal troops in the vicinity of Versailles and Paris. It appeared that he might be contemplating the disruption of the National Constituent Assembly. Such was the advice of Queen Marie Antoinette, his brothers, and the

The Estates-General opened at Versailles in 1789 with much pomp and splendor. In the old French print shown here, Louis XVI is on the throne. The First Estate, the clergy, is at the left; the Second Estate, the nobility, sits at the upper right; and the more numerous Third Estate, dressed in black suits and capes, sits at the lower right. [Culver Pictures.]

This well-known painting by Jacques Louis David (1748–1825) portrays the Tennis Court Oath, June 20. The emotion of the scene should be compared with the calm shown in the previous picture of the opening of the Estates-General. In the center foreground are members of different Estates joining hands in cooperation as equals. The presiding officer leading the oath is Jean Sylvain Bailly, soon to become mayor in a reorganized government of the city of Paris. The painting is in the Musée Carnavalet in Paris. [French Embassy Press and Information Division, New York.]

most conservative nobles, with whom he had begun to consult. On July 11, without consultation with the assembly leaders, Louis abruptly dismissed Necker. These actions marked the beginning of a steady, but consistently poorly executed, royal attempt to undermine the assembly and halt the revolution. Most of the National Constituent Assembly wished to create some form of constitutional monarchy, but from the start Louis's refusal to cooperate thwarted that effort. The king fatally decided to throw his lot in with the aristocracy against the nation.

The second new factor to impose itself on the events at Versailles was the populace of Paris. The mustering of royal troops created anxiety in the city, where throughout the winter and spring of 1789 there had been several bread riots. The Parisians who had elected their representatives to the Third Estate had continued to meet after the elections. By June they were organizing a citizen militia and collecting arms. They regarded the dismissal of Necker as the opening of a royal offensive against the National Constituent Assembly and the city. On July 14 somewhat over eight hundred people, most of whom were small shopkeepers, trades-

people, artisans, and wage earners, marched to the Bastille in search of weapons for the militia. This great fortress, with ten-foot-thick walls, had once held political prisoners. Through miscalculations and ineptitude on the part of the governor of the fortress, the troops in the Bastille fired into the crowd, killing ninety-eight people and wounding many others. Thereafter the crowd stormed the fortress and eventually gained entrance. They released the seven prisoners, none of whom were there for political reasons, and killed several troops and the governor. They found no weapons.

On July 15 the militia of Paris, by then called the National Guard, offered its command to Lafayette. The hero of the American Revolution gave the guard a new insignia in the design of the red and blue stripes of the city of Paris separated by the white stripe of the king. This emblem became the revolutionary cockade worn by the soldiers and eventually the flag of revolutionary France.

The attack on the Bastille marked the first of many crucial *journées,* or days when the populace of Paris would redirect the course of the revolution. The fall of the fortress signaled that the political future of the nation would not be decided solely

The capture of the Bastille on July 14, 1789, by the people of Paris, portrayed too much like a battle in this eighteenth-century engraving, was a major turning point during the early weeks of the French Revolution. [The Mansell Collection.]

by the National Constituent Assembly. As the news of the taking of the Bastille spread, similar disturbances took place in the provincial cities. A few days later Louis XVI again bowed to the force of events and personally visited Paris, where he wore the revolutionary cockade and recognized the organized electors as the legitimate government of the city. The king also recognized the National Guard. The citizens of Paris were for the time being satisfied.

The Great Fear and the Surrender of Feudal Privileges

Simultaneously with the popular urban disturbances a movement known as the *Great Fear* swept across much of the French countryside. Rumors had spread that royal troops would be sent into the rural districts. The result was an intensification of the peasant disturbances that had begun during the spring. The Great Fear witnessed the burning of chateaux, the destruction of records and documents, and the refusal to pay feudal dues. The peasants were determined to take possession of food supplies and land that they considered rightfully theirs. They were reclaiming rights and property that they had lost through the aristocratic resurgence of the last quarter-century, as well as venting their general anger against the injustices of rural life.

On the night of August 4, 1789, aristocrats in the National Constituent Assembly attempted to halt the spreading disorder in the countryside. By prearrangement a number of liberal nobles and churchmen rose in the assembly and renounced their feudal rights, dues, and tithes. In a scene of great emotion, hunting and fishing rights, judicial authority, and special exemptions were surrendered. In a sense these nobles gave up what they had already lost and what they could not have regained without civil war in the rural areas. Later they would also, in many cases, receive compensation for their losses. Nonetheless, after the night of August 4 all French citizens were subject to the same and equal laws. That dramatic session of the assembly paved the way for the legal and social reconstruction of the nation. Without those renunciations the constructive work of the National Constituent Assembly would have been much more difficult.

Both the attack on the Bastille and the Great Fear displayed varieties of the rural and urban riots that had characterized much of eighteenth-century political and social life. Louis XVI first thought that the turmoil over the Bastille was simply another bread riot. The popular disturbances also were only partly related to the events at Versailles. A deep economic downturn had struck France during 1787 and had continued into 1788 The harvests for both years had been poor, and food prices in 1789 stood higher than at any time since 1703. Wages had not kept up with the rise in prices. Throughout the winter of 1788–1789, an unusually cold one, many people suffered from hunger. Several cities had experienced wage and food riots. These economic difficulties helped the revolution reach such vast proportions. The political, social, and economic grievances of numerous sections of the country became combined. The National Constituent Assembly could look to the popular forces as a source of strength against the king and the conservative aristocrats. When the various elements of the assembly later fell into quarrels among themselves, their factions succumbed to the temptation of appealing to the politically sophisticated and well-organized shopkeeping and artisan classes for support. When this turn of events came to pass, the popular classes could demand a price for their cooperation.

The Declaration of the Rights of Man and Citizen

In late August 1789 the National Constituent Assembly decided that before writing a new constitution, it should set forth a statement of broad political principles. On August 27 the assembly issued the Declaration of the Rights of Man and Citizen. This declaration drew together much of the political language of the Enlightenment and was also influenced by the Declaration of Rights adopted by Virginia in America in June 1776. The French declaration proclaimed that all men were "born and remain free and equal in rights." The natural rights so proclaimed were "liberty, property, security, and resistance to oppression." Governments existed to protect those rights. All political sovereignty resided in the nation and its representatives. All citizens were to be equal before the law and were to be "equally admissible to all public dignities, offices and employments, according to their capacity, and with no other distinction than that of

The National Assembly Decrees Civic Equality in France

These famous decrees of August 4, 1789, in effect created civic equality in France. The special privileges previously possessed or controlled by the nobility were removed.

1. *The National Assembly completely abolishes the feudal regime. It decrees that, among the rights and dues . . . all those originating in real or personal serfdom, personal servitude, and those which represent them, are abolished without indemnification; all others are declared redeemable, and that the price and mode of redemption shall be fixed by the National Assembly. . . .*

2. *The exclusive right to maintain pigeon-houses and dove-cotes is abolished. . . .*

3. *The exclusive right to hunt and to maintain unenclosed warrens is likewise abolished. . . .*

4. *All manorial courts are suppressed without indemnification.*

5. *Tithes of every description and the dues which have been substituted for them . . . are abolished, on condition, however, that some other method be de-* *vised to provide for the expenses of divine worship, the support of the officiating clergy, the relief of the poor, repairs and rebuilding of churches and parsonages, and for all establishments, seminaries, schools, academies, asylums, communities, and other institutions, for the maintenance of which they are actually devoted. . . .*

7. *The sale of judicial and municipal offices shall be suppressed forthwith. . . .*

8. *Pecuniary privileges, personal or real, in the payment of taxes are abolished forever. . . .*

11. *All citizens, without distinction of birth, are eligible to any office or dignity, whether ecclesiastical, civil or military. . . .*

Frank Maloy Anderson (Ed. and Trans.), *The Constitutions and Other Select Documents Illustrative of the History of France*, 1789–1907, 2nd ed., rev. and enlarged (Minneapolis: H. W. Wilson, 1908), pp. 11–13.

their virtues and talents." There were to be due process of law and presumption of innocence until proof of guilt. Freedom of religion was affirmed. Taxation was to be apportioned equally according to capacity to pay. Property constituted "an inviolable and sacred right."[2] Although these statements were rather abstract, practically all of them were directed against specific abuses of the old aristocratic and absolutist regime. If any two principles of the future governed the declaration, they were civic equality and protection of property. The Declaration of the Rights of Man and Citizen has often been considered the death certificate of the old regime.

Louis XVI stalled before ratifying both the declaration and the aristocratic renunciation of feudalism. The longer he hesitated, the larger existing suspicions grew that he might again try to resort to the use of troops. Moreover bread continued to be in short supply. On October 5 a large crowd of Parisian women marched to Versailles demanding more bread. They milled about the palace, and many stayed the night. Under this pressure the king agreed to sanction the decrees of the assembly. The next day he and his family appeared on a balcony before the crowd. The Parisians were deeply suspicious of the monarch and believed that he must be kept under the watchful eye of the people. Consequently they demanded that Louis and his family return to Paris. The monarch had no real choice in the matter. On October 6, 1789, his carriage followed the crowd into the city, where he and his family settled in the palace of the Tuileries. The National Constituent Assembly soon followed. Thereafter both Paris and France remained relatively stable and peaceful until the summer of 1792.

[2] Quoted in Georges Lefebvre, *The Coming of the French Revolution*, trans. by R. R. Palmer (Princeton, N.J.: Princeton University Press, 1967), pp. 221–223.

An unknown contemporary German depicted the march of the women of Paris on the palace of Versailles in October 1789. On their return to the city they were accompanied by Louis XVI and his family. [The Granger Collection.]

The Reconstruction of France

Once established in Paris, the National Constituent Assembly set about reorganizing France. In government it pursued a policy of constitutional monarchy; in administration, rationalism; in economics, unregulated freedom; and in religion, anticlericalism. Throughout its proceedings the assembly was determined to protect property and to limit the impact on national life of the unpropertied elements of the nation and even of possessors of small amounts of property. While championing civic equality before the law, the assembly spurned social equality and extensive democracy. In all these areas the assembly charted a general course that to a greater or lesser degree nineteenth-century liberals across Europe would follow.

Political Reorganization

The Constitution of 1791, which was the product of the National Constituent Assembly's delibera-

tions, established a constitutional monarchy. There was to be a unicameral Legislative Assembly in which all laws would originate and in which the major political authority of the nation would reside. The monarch was allowed a suspensive veto that could delay but not halt legislation. Powers of war and peace were vested in the assembly. The constitution provided for an elaborate system of indirect elections intended to thwart direct popular pressure on the government. The citizens of France were divided into active and passive categories. Only active citizens—that is, men paying annual taxes equal to three days of local labor wages—could vote. They chose electors who then in turn voted for the members of the legislature. At the levels of electors, or members, still further property qualifications were imposed. Only about fifty thousand citizens of a population of about twenty-five million could qualify as electors or members of the Legislative Assembly.

In reconstructing the local and judicial administration, the National Constituent Assembly applied

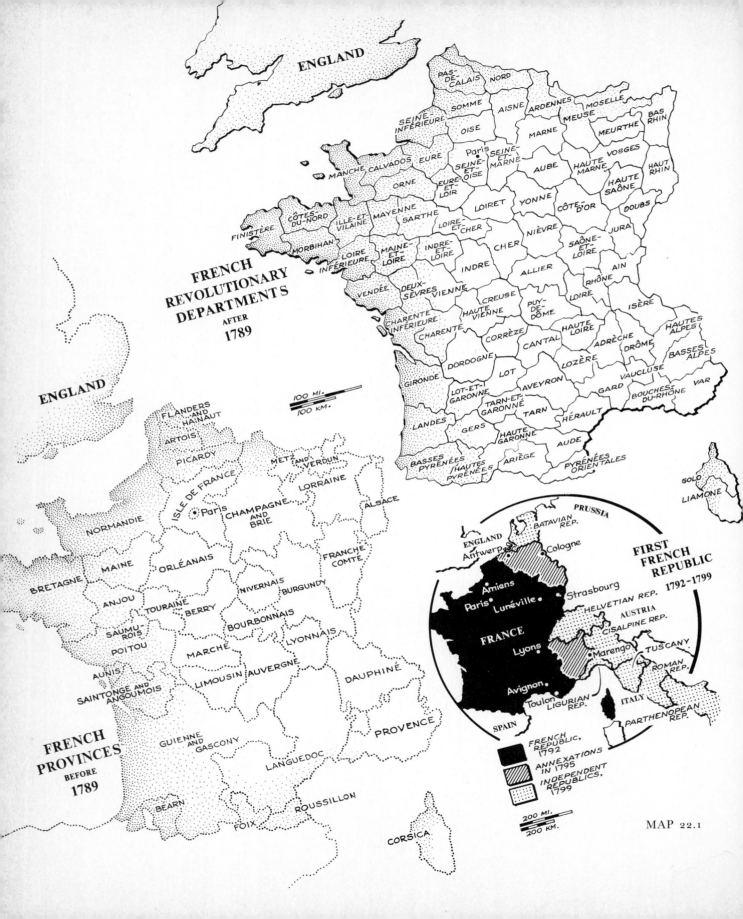

ENGLAND

FRENCH
REVOLUTIONARY
DEPARTMENTS
AFTER
1789

PAS-DE-CALAIS
NORD
SOMME
AISNE
ARDENNES
MOSELLE
MEUSE
BAS-RHIN
SEINE-INFÉRIEURE
OISE
MARNE
MEURTHE
VOSGES
HAUT-RHIN
MANCHE
CALVADOS
EURE
Paris
SEINE-ET-MARNE
AUBE
HAUTE-MARNE
HAUTE-SAÔNE
ORNE
SEINE-ET-OISE
EURE-ET-LOIR
YONNE
CÔTE-D'OR
DOUBS
CÔTES-DU-NORD
ILLE-ET-VILAINE
MAYENNE
SARTHE
LOIRET
LOIR-ET-CHER
NIÈVRE
SAÔNE-ET-LOIRE
JURA
FINISTÈRE
MORBIHAN
LOIRE-INFÉRIEURE
MAINE-ET-LOIRE
INDRE-ET-LOIRE
CHER
ALLIER
RHÔNE
AIN
VENDÉE
DEUX-SÈVRES
VIENNE
INDRE
CREUSE
PUY-DE-DÔME
LOIRE
ISÈRE
CHARENTE-INFÉRIEURE
HAUTE-VIENNE
CORRÈZE
CANTAL
HAUTE-LOIRE
ARDÈCHE
DRÔME
HAUTES-ALPES
CHARENTE
DORDOGNE
LOT
AVEYRON
LOZÈRE
GARD
VAUCLUSE
BASSES-ALPES
VAR
GIRONDE
LOT-ET-GARONNE
TARN-ET-GARONNE
TARN
HÉRAULT
BOUCHES-DU-RHÔNE
LANDES
GERS
HAUTE-GARONNE
AUDE
BASSES-PYRÉNÉES
HAUTES-PYRÉNÉES
ARIÈGE
PYRÉNÉES-ORIENTALES

GOLO
LIAMONE

100 MI.
100 KM.

ENGLAND

FRENCH
PROVINCES
BEFORE
1789

FLANDERS AND HAINAUT
ARTOIS
PICARDY
METZ AND VERDUN
ISLE DE FRANCE
Paris
LORRAINE
CHAMPAGNE AND BRIE
ALSACE
NORMANDIE
ORLÉANAIS
FRANCHE COMTÉ
MAINE
NIVERNAIS
BURGUNDY
BRETAGNE
ANJOU
TOURAINE
BERRY
BOURBONNAIS
LYONNAIS
SAUMUROIS
POITOU
MARCHE
AUNIS
LIMOUSIN
AUVERGNE
DAUPHINÉ
SAINTONGE AND ANGOUMOIS
GUIENNE AND GASCONY
PROVENCE
LANGUEDOC
BÉARN
ROUSSILLON
FOIX
CORSICA

FIRST
FRENCH
REPUBLIC
1792-1799

PRUSSIA
BATAVIAN REP.
ENGLAND
Antwerp
Cologne
Amiens
Paris
Lunéville
Strasbourg
HELVETIAN REP.
AUSTRIA
CISALPINE REP.
FRANCE
Lyons
Marengo
TUSCANY
ROMAN REP.
Avignon
Toulon
LIGURIAN REP.
ITALY
SPAIN
PARTHENOPEAN REP.

FRENCH REPUBLIC, 1792
ANNEXATIONS IN 1795
INDEPENDENT REPUBLICS, 1799

200 MI.
200 KM.

MAP 22.1

the rational spirit of the Enlightenment. It abolished the ancient French provinces, such as Burgundy and Brittany, and established in their place eighty-three departments (*départements*) of generally equal size named after rivers, mountains, and other geographical features. The departments in turn were subdivided into districts, cantons, and communes. Most local elections were also indirect. The departmental reconstruction proved to be one of the most permanent achievements of the assembly. The departments exist to the present day. All of the ancient judicial courts, including the seigneurial courts and the *parlements,* were also abolished. In their place were organized uniform courts with elected judges and prosecutors. Procedures were simplified, and the most degrading punishments were removed from the books.

Economic Policy

In economic matters the National Constituent Assembly continued the policies formerly advocated by Louis XVI's reformist ministers. It suppressed the guilds and liberated the grain trade. The assembly established the metric system to provide the nation with uniform weights and measures. These policies of economic freedom and uniformity disappointed both peasants and urban workers caught in the cycle of inflation. By decrees of 1790 the assembly placed the burden of proof on the peasants to rid themselves of the residual feudal dues for which compensation was to be paid. On June 14, 1791, the assembly crushed the attempts of urban workers to protect their wages by enacting the Chapelier Law, which forbade worker associations. Peasants and workers were henceforth to be left to the freedom and mercy of the marketplace.

While these various reforms were being put into effect, the original financial crisis that had occasioned the calling of the Estates General persisted. The royal debt was not repudiated, because it was owed to the bankers, the merchants, and the commercial traders of the Third Estate. The National Constituent Assembly had suppressed many of the old, hated indirect taxes and had substituted new land taxes, but these proved insufficient. Moreover there were not enough officials to collect them. The continuing financial problem led the assembly to take what may well have been, for the future of French life and society, its most decisive action. The assembly decided to finance the debt by con-

fiscating and then selling the land and property of the Roman Catholic Church in France. The results were further inflation, religious schism, and civil war. In effect, the National Constituent Assembly had opened a new chapter in the relations of church and state in Europe.

Having chosen to plunder the land of the church, in December 1790 the assembly authorized the issuance of *assignats,* or government bonds, the value of which was guaranteed by the revenue to be generated from the sale of church property. Initially a limit was set on the quantity of *assignats* to be issued. However, the bonds proved so acceptable to the public that they began to circulate as currency. The assembly decided to issue an ever larger

The assignats *were government bonds that were backed by confiscated church lands. They circulated as money. When the government printed too many of them, inflation resulted and their value fell. [Bettmann Archive.]*

number of them to liquidate the national debt and to create a large body of new property owners with a direct stake in the revolution. However, within a few months the value of the *assignats* began to fall. Inflation increased and put new stress on the lives of the urban poor.

The Civil Constitution of the Clergy

The confiscation of church lands required an ecclesiastical reconstruction. In July 1790 the National Constituent Assembly issued the Civil Constitution of the Clergy, which transformed the Roman Catholic Church in France into a branch of the secular state. This legislation reduced the number of bishoprics from 135 to 83 and brought the borders of the dioceses into conformity with those of the new departments. It also provided for the election of priests and bishops, who henceforth became salaried employees of the state. The assembly consulted neither the pope nor the French clergy about these broad changes. The king approved the measure only with the greatest reluctance.

The Civil Constitution of the Clergy was the major blunder of the National Constituent Assembly. The measure created immense opposition within the French church even from bishops who had long championed Gallican liberties over papal domination. In the face of this resistance the assembly unwisely ruled that all clergy must take an oath to support the Civil Constitution. Only seven bishops and about half the clergy did so. In reprisal the assembly designated the clergy who had not taken the oath as "refractory" and removed them from their clerical functions.

Further reaction was swift. Refractory priests attempted to celebrate Mass. In February 1791 the pope condemned not only the Civil Constitution of the Clergy but also the Declaration of the Rights of Man and Citizen. That condemnation marked the opening of a Roman Catholic offensive against liberalism and the revolution that continued throughout the nineteenth century. Within France itself the pope's action created a crisis of conscience and political loyalty for all sincere Catholics. Religious devotion and revolutionary loyalty became incompatible for many people. French citizens were divided between those who supported the constitutional priests and those who resorted to the refractory clergy. Louis XVI and his family favored the latter.

Counterrevolutionary Activity

The revolution had other enemies besides the pope and the devout Catholics. As it became clear that the old political and social order was undergoing fundamental and probably permanent change, considerable numbers of aristocrats left France. Known as the *émigrés*, they settled in countries near the French border, where they sought to foment counterrevolution. Among the most important of their number was the king's younger brother, the Count of Artois (1757–1836). In the summer of 1791 his agents and the queen persuaded Louis XVI to attempt to flee the country. On the night of June 20, 1791, Louis and his immediate family, disguised as servants, left Paris. They traveled as far as Varennes on their way to Metz. At Varennes the king was recognized, and his flight was halted. On June 24 a company of soldiers escorted the royal family back to Paris. The leaders of the National Constituent Assembly, determined to save the constitutional monarchy, announced that the king had been abducted from the capital. However, such a convenient public fiction could not cloak the reality that the chief counterrevolutionary in France now sat on the throne.

Two months later, on August 27, 1791, under pressure from a group of *émigrés*, Emperor Leopold II of Austria, who was the brother of Marie Antoinette, and Frederick William II, the king of Prussia, issued the Declaration of Pillnitz. The two monarchs promised to intervene in France to protect the royal family and to preserve the monarchy *if* the other major European powers agreed. The latter provision rendered the statement meaningless because at the time Great Britain would not have given its consent. However, the declaration was not so read in France, where the revolutionaries saw the nation surrounded by aristocratic and monarchical foes.

The National Constituent Assembly drew to a close in September 1791. Its task of reconstructing the government and the administration of France had been completed. One of its last acts was the passage of a measure that forbade any of its own members to sit in the Legislative Assembly then being elected. The new body met on October 1 and had to confront the immense problems that had emerged during the earlier part of the year. Within the Legislative Assembly major political divisions also soon developed over the future course of the nation and the revolution.

Here, as seen by a contemporary Dutchman, Louis XVI and his family are being led back to Paris by armed escort after their attempt to flee France in June 1791 was foiled near Varennes. [The Granger Collection.]

A Second Revolution

End of the Monarchy

The issues of the Civil Constitution of the Clergy and the trustworthiness of Louis XVI undermined the unity of the revolution. Much factionalism displayed itself throughout the short life of the Legislative Assembly (1791–1792). Ever since the original gathering of the Estates General, deputies from the Third Estate had organized themselves into clubs composed of politically like-minded persons. The most famous and best organized of these were the Jacobins, whose name derived from the fact that Dominican friars were called *Jacobins,* and the group met in a Dominican monastery in Paris. The Jacobins had also established a network of local clubs throughout the provinces. They had constituted the most advanced political group in the National Constituent Assembly and had pressed for a republic rather than a constitutional monarchy. The events of the summer of 1791 led them to renew those demands.

In the Legislative Assembly a group of Jacobins known as the *Girondists* (because many of them came from the department of the Gironde) assumed leadership.[3] They were determined to oppose the forces of counterrevolution. They passed a measure ordering the *émigrés* to return or suffer loss of property and another requiring the refractory clergy to support the Civil Constitution or lose their state pensions. The king vetoed both acts. On April 20, 1792, the Girondists led the Legislative Assembly to declare war on Austria, by this time governed by Francis II (1768–1835) and allied to Prussia. The Girondists believed that the war would preserve the revolution from domestic enemies and bring the most advanced revolutionaries to power. Paradoxically Louis XVI and other monarchists also favored the war. They thought that the conflict would strengthen the executive power (i.e., the monarchy). The king also entertained the

[3] The Girondists are also frequently called the *Brissotins* after Jacques-Pierre Brissot (1754–1793), who was their chief spokesman in early 1792.

659

Louis XVI and the royal family fled on August 10, 1792, from the mobs attacking their palace. The royal family (behind the screened reporter's box at the right) took refuge with the Legislative Assembly. [New York Public Library Picture Collection.]

hope that French forces might be defeated and the old regime restored. Both sides were playing dangerously foolish politics.

The war radicalized the revolution and led to what is usually called the second revolution, which overthrew the constitutional monarchy and established a republic. Initially the war effort went quite poorly. Both the country and the revolution seemed in danger. In July 1792 the Duke of Brunswick, commander of the Prussian forces, issued a manifesto promising the destruction of Paris if harm came to the French royal family. This statement stiffened support for the war and increased the already significant distrust of the king.

Late in July, under radical working-class pressure, the government of the city of Paris passed from the elected council to a committee, or commune, of representatives from the sections (municipal wards) of Paris. On August 10, 1792, a very large Parisian crowd invaded the Tuileries palace and forced Louis XVI and Marie Antoinette to take refuge in the Legislative Assembly itself. The crowd fought with the royal Swiss guards. When Louis was finally able to call off the troops, several hundred of them and a large number of Parisian citizens lay dead. The monarchy itself was also a casualty of that melee: thereafter the royal family was imprisoned in comfortable quarters, but the king was allowed to perform none of his political functions.

The Convention and the Role of the Sans-culottes

Early in September the Parisian crowd again made its will felt. During the first week of the month, in what are known as the *September Massacres,* the Paris Commune summarily executed or murdered about twelve hundred people who were in the city jails. Many of these people were aristocrats or priests, but the majority were simply common criminals. The crowd had assumed that the prisoners were all counterrevolutionaries. The Paris Commune then compelled the Legislative Assembly to call for the election by universal manhood suffrage of a new assembly to write a democratic constitution. That body, called the *Convention* after its American counterpart of 1787, met on September 21, 1792. The previous day the French army had halted the Prussian advance at the battle of Valmy in eastern France. The victory of democratic forces at home had been confirmed by victory on the battlefield.

As its first act, the Convention declared France a republic, that is, a nation governed by an elected assembly without a king. The second revolution had been the work of Jacobins more radical than the Girondists and of the people of Paris known as the *sans-culottes.* The name of the latter means "without breeches" and derived from the long trousers that as working people they wore instead of aristocratic knee breeches. The sans-culottes were shopkeepers, artisans, wage earners, and, in a few cases, factory workers. The persistent food shortages and the revolutionary inflation had made their generally difficult lives even more burdensome. The politics of the old regime had ignored them, and the policies of the National Constituent Assembly had left them victims of unregulated economic liberty. However, the nation required their labor and their lives if the war was to succeed. From the summer of 1792 until the summer of 1794 their attitudes, desires, and ideals were the primary factors in the internal development of the revolution.

The sans-culottes generally knew what they wanted. The Parisian tradespeople and artisans sought immediate relief from food shortages and rising prices through the vehicle of price controls. They believed that all people had a right to subsistence and profoundly resented most forms of social inequality. This attitude led them to intense hostility toward the aristocracy and toward the original leaders of the revolution, who they believed simply wanted to take over the social privileges of the aristocracy. Their hatred of inequality did not go so far as to demand the abolition of property. Rather, they advocated a community of relatively small property owners. In politics they were anti-monarchical, strongly republican, and suspicious even of representative government. They believed that the people should make the decisions of government to as great an extent as possible. In Paris, where their influence was most important, the sans-culottes' political experience had been gained in meetings of the Paris sections. Those gatherings exemplified direct community democracy and were not unlike a New England town meeting. The economic hardship of their lives made them impatient to see their demands met.

The goals of the sans-culottes were not wholly compatible with those of the Jacobins. The latter were republicans who sought representative gov-

❧ A *Pamphleteer* Describes a *Sans-culotte*

This pamphlet is a 1793 description of a sans-culotte written either by one or by a sympathizer. It describes the sans-culotte as a hardworking, useful, patriotic citizen who bravely sacrifices himself to the war effort. It contrasts those virtues to the lazy and unproductive luxury of the noble and the personally self-interested plottings of the politician.

A sans-culotte *you rogues? He is someone who always goes on foot, who has no millions as you would all like to have, no* chateaux, *no valets to serve him, and who lives simply with his wife and children, if he has any, on a fourth or fifth storey.*

He is useful, because he knows how to work in the field, to forge iron, to use a saw, to use a file, to roof a house, to make shoes, and to shed his last drop of blood for the safety of the Republic.

And because he works, you are sure not to meet his person in the Café de Chartres, or in the gaming houses where others conspire and game; nor at the National theatre . . . nor in the literary clubs. . . .

In the evening he goes to his section, not powdered or perfumed, or smartly booted in the hope of catching the eye of the citizenesses in the galleries, but ready to support good proposals with all his might, and to crush those which come from the abominable faction of politicians.

Finally, a sans-culotte always has his sabre sharp, to cut off the ears of all enemies of the Revolution; sometimes he even goes out with his pike; but at the first sound of the drum he is ready to leave for the Vendée, for the army of the Alps or for the army of the North. . . .

"Reply to an Impertinent Question: What Is a *Sans-culotte?*" April 1793. Reprinted in Walter Markov and Albert Soboul (Eds.), *Die Sansculotten von Paris,* and republished translated by Clive Emsley in Merryn Williams (Ed.), *Revolutions: 1775–1830* (Baltimore: Penguin Books, in association with The Open University, 1971), pp. 100–101.

Although many of the victims of the Reign of Terror were executed by other methods, the guillotine became the symbol of those frightening months in 1793 and 1794. Here prisoners are being prepared for decapitation, as the heads of those already executed are displayed to the crowd. [Bettmann Archive.]

The execution of Louis XVI on January 21, 1793. [New York Public Library Picture Collection.]

ernment. Jacobin hatred of the aristocracy did not extend to a general suspicion of wealth. Basically the Jacobins favored an unregulated economy. However, from the time of Louis XVI's flight to Varennes onward, the more extreme Jacobins began to cooperate with leaders of the Parisian sans-culottes and the Paris Commune for the overthrow of the monarchy. Once the Convention began its deliberations, these advanced Jacobins, known as the *Mountain* because of their seats high in the assembly hall, worked with the sans-culottes to carry the revolution forward and to win the war. This willingness to cooperate with the forces of the popular revolution separated the Mountain from the Girondists, who were also members of the Jacobin Club.

By the spring of 1793 several issues had brought the Mountain and its sans-culottes allies to domination of the Convention and the revolution. In December 1792 Louis XVI was put on trial as mere "Citizen Capet," the family name of extremely distant forebears of the royal family. The Girondists looked for some way to spare his life, but the Mountain defeated the effort. Louis was convicted, by a very narrow majority, of conspiring against the liberty of the people and the security of the state. He was condemned to death and was beheaded on January 21, 1793. The next month the Convention declared war on Great Britain, Holland, and Spain. Soon thereafter the Prussians renewed their offensive and drove the French out of Belgium. To make matters worse, General Dumouriez, the Girondist victor of Valmy, deserted to the enemy. Finally, in March 1793 a royalist revolt led by aristocratic officers and priests erupted in the Vendée in western France and roused much popular support. Consequently the revolution found itself at war with most of Europe and much of the French nation. The Girondists had led the country into the war but had proved themselves incapable either of winning it or of suppressing the enemies of the revolution at home. The Mountain stood ready to take up the task.

Every major European power was now hostile to the revolution.

The Revolution and Europe at War

Initially the attitude of the rest of Europe toward the revolutionary events in France had been am-
bivalent. Those people who favored political reform regarded the revolution as wisely and rationally reorganizing a corrupt and inefficient government. The major foreign governments thought that the revolution meant that France would cease to be an important factor in European affairs for several years. In 1790, however, the Irish-born writer and British statesman Edmund Burke (1729–1797) argued a different position in *Reflections on the Revolution in France*. Burke regarded the reconstruction of French administration as the application of a blind rationalism that ignored the historical realities of political development and the complexities of social relations. He also forecast further turmoil as persons without political experience attempted to govern France. As the revolutionaries proceeded to attack the church, the monarchy, and finally the rest of Europe, Burke's ideas came to have many admirers, and his *Reflections* became the handbook of European conservatives for decades.

By the time of the commencement of the war with Austria in April 1792, the other European monarchies recognized the danger of both the ideas and the aggression of revolutionary France. The ideals of the Rights of Man and Citizen were highly exportable and applicable to the rest of Europe. One government after another turned to repressive domestic policies. In Great Britain William Pitt the Younger (1759–1806), the prime minister, who had unsuccessfully supported moderate

Edmund Burke. The portrait is from the studio of Joshua Reynolds. [National Portrait Gallery, London.]

❧ Burke Condemns the Work of the French National Assembly

Burke was undoubtedly the most important and articulate foreign critic of the French Revolution. He believed that governments could not be quickly created or organized, as seemed to have occurred in France. He was also deeply opposed to democracy, which he thought would lead to unwise, extreme actions on the part of government. Burke left a legacy of brilliantly argued conservative thought that remained a comfort to many followers, a serious challenge to liberals in nineteenth-century Europe, and an important statement in political theory. This passage is from his 1790 *Reflections on the Revolution in France.*

To make a government requires no great prudence. Settle the seat of power; teach obedience: and the work is done. To give Freedom is still more easy. It is not necessary to guide; it only requires to let go the rein. But to form a free government; *that is, to temper together these opposite elements of liberty and restraint in one consistent work, requires much thought, deep reflection, a sagacious, powerful, and combining mind. This I do not find in those who take the lead in the National Assembly. Perhaps they are not so miserably deficient as they appear. I rather believe it. It would put them below the common level of human understanding. But when the leaders choose to make themselves bidders at an auction of popularity, their talents, in the construction of the state, will be of no service. They will become flatterers instead of legislators; the instruments, not the guides, of the people. If any of them should happen to propose a scheme of liberty, soberly limited, and defined with proper qualifications, he will be immediately outbid by his competitors, who will produce something more splendidly popular. Suspicions will be raised of his fidelity to his cause. Moderation will be stigmatized as the virtue of cowards; and compromise as the prudence of traitors; until, in hopes of preserving the credit which may enable him to temper, and moderate, on some occasions, the popular leader is obliged to become active in propagating doctrines, and establishing powers, that will afterwards defeat any sober purpose at which he ultimately might have aimed.*

. . . The improvements of the National Assembly are superficial, their errors fundamental.

Edmund Burke, *Reflections on the Revolution in France,* in *The Works of the Right Honourable Edmund Burke,* Vol. 2 (London: Henry G. Bohn, 1864), pp. 515–516.

reform of Parliament during the 1780s, turned against both reform and popular movements. The government suppressed the London Corresponding Society founded in 1792 as a working-class reform group. In Birmingham the government sponsored mob action to drive Joseph Priestley (1733–1804), a chemist and a radical political thinker, out of the country. In early 1793 Pitt secured parliamentary approval for acts suspending habeas corpus and making it possible to commit treason in writing. With less success Pitt attempted to curb freedom of the press. All political groups who dared to oppose the action of the government were in danger of becoming associated with revolutionary sedition.

In eastern Europe the revolution brought to a close the life of enlightened absolutism. The aristocratic resistance to the reforms of Joseph II in the Hapsburg lands led his brother, Leopold II, to come to terms with the landowners. Leopold's successor, Francis II (1792–1835), became a major leader of the counterrevolution. In Prussia Frederick William II (1786–1797), the nephew of Frederick the Great, looked to the leaders of the Lutheran church and the aristocracy to discourage any potential popular uprisings, such as those of the downtrodden Silesian weavers. In Russia Catherine the Great burned the works of her onetime friend Voltaire and exiled Alexander Radishchev (1749–1802) to Siberia for publishing *Journey from Saint Petersburg to Moscow,* a work critical of Russian social conditions.

In 1793 and 1795 the eastern powers once again combined against Poland. In that unhappy land aristocratic reformers had finally achieved the abolition of the *liberum veto* and had organized a new constitutional monarchy in 1791. Russia and Prussia, which already had designs on Polish territory, saw or pretended to see a threat of revolution in the new Polish constitution. In 1793 they annexed large sections of the country; in 1795 Austria joined the two other powers in a final partition that removed Poland from the map of Europe until after World War I. The governments of eastern Europe had used the widely shared fear of further revolutionary disorder to justify old-fashioned eighteenth-century aggression.

Consequently, in a paradoxical fashion the very success of the revolution in France brought to a rapid close reform movements in the rest of Europe. The French invasion of the Austrian Netherlands and the revolutionary reorganization of that territory roused the rest of Europe to the point of active hostility. In November 1792 the Convention declared that it would aid all peoples who wished to cast off the burdens of aristocratic and monarchical oppression. The Convention had also proclaimed the Scheldt River in the Netherlands open to the commerce of all nations and thus had broken a treaty that Great Britain had made with Austria and Holland. The British were on the point of declaring war on France over this issue when the Convention issued its own declaration of hostilities. By April 1793, when the Mountain began to direct the French government, the nation stood at war with Austria, Prussia, Great Britain, Spain, Sardinia, and Holland. The governments of those nations were attempting to protect their social structures, political systems, and economic interests against the aggression of the revolution.

The Reign of Terror

The Republic Defended

In April 1793 the Convention established a Committee of General Security and a Committee of Public Safety to perform the executive duties of the government. The latter committee became more important and eventually enjoyed almost dictatorial power. The most prominent leaders of the Committee of Public Safety were Jacques Danton (1759–1794), who had provided heroic leadership in September 1792; Maximilien Robespierre (1758–1794), who became for a time the single most powerful member of the committee; and Lazare Carnot (1753–1823), who was in charge of the military. All of these men and the other figures on the committee were strong republicans and had opposed the weak policies of the Girondists. They

conceived of their task as saving the revolution from mortal enemies at home and abroad. They generally enjoyed a working political relationship with the sans-culottes of Paris, but this was an alliance of expediency on the part of the committee.

The major problem was to wage the war and to secure domestic support for the effort. In early June 1793 the Parisian sans-culottes invaded the Convention and successfully demanded the expulsion of the Girondist members. That action further radicalized the Convention and gave the Mountain complete control. On June 22 the Convention approved a fully democratic constitution but suspended its operation until the conclusion of the war emergency. On August 23 Carnot began a mobilization for victory by issuing a *levée en masse,* or general military requisition of the population, which conscripted males into the army and directed economic production for military purposes. On September 17 a maximum on prices was established in accord with sans-culotte demands. During these same months the armies of the revolution also successfully crushed many of the counterrevolutionary disturbances in the provinces.

Never before had Europe seen a nation organized in this way nor one defended by a citizen army. Other events within France astounded Europeans even more. The Reign of Terror had begun. Those months of quasi-judicial executions and murders stretching from the autumn of 1793 to the midsummer of 1794 are probably the most famous or infamous period of the revolution. They can be understood only in the context of the war on the one hand and the revolutionary expectations of the Convention and the sans-culottes on the other.

The Republic of Virtue

The presence of armies closing in on the nation created a situation in which it was relatively easy to dispense with legal due process. However, the people who sat in the Convention and composed the Committee of Public Safety also believed that they had made a new departure in world history. They had established a republic in which civic virtue rather than aristocratic and monarchical corruption might flourish. The republic of virtue manifested itself in the renaming of streets from the egalitarian vocabulary of the revolution, in republican dress copied from that of the sansculottes or the Roman Republic, in the absence of powdered wigs, in the suppression of plays that were insuffi-

❧ The French Convention Calls Up the Entire Nation

This proclamation for the *levée en masse,* August 23, 1793, marked the first time in European history that all citizens of a nation were called to contribute to a war effort. The decree set the entire nation on a wartime footing under the centralized direction of the Committee of Public Safety.

1. From this moment until that in which the enemy shall have been driven from the soil of the Republic, all Frenchmen are in permanent requisition for the service of the armies.

The young men shall go to battle; the married men shall forge arms and transport provisions; the women shall make tents and clothing and shall serve in the hospitals; the children shall turn old linen into lint; the aged shall betake themselves to the public places in order to arouse the courage of the warriors and preach the hatred of kings and the unity of the Republic.

2. The national buildings shall be converted into barracks, the public places into workshops for arms, the soil of the cellars shall be washed in order to extract therefrom the saltpetre.

3. The arms of the regulation calibre shall be reserved exclusively for those who shall march against the enemy; the service of the interior shall be performed with hunting pieces and side arms.

4. The saddle horses are put in requisition to complete the cavalry corps; the draught-horses, other than those employed in agriculture, shall convey the artillery and the provisions.

5. The Committee of Public Safety is charged to take all the necessary measures to set up without delay an extraordinary manufacture of arms of every sort which corresponds with the ardor and energy of the French people. . . .

. . . .

8. The levy shall be general. . . .

Frank Maloy Anderson (Ed. and Trans.), *The Constitutions and Other Select Documents Illustrative of the History of France,* 1789–1907, 2nd ed., rev. and enlarged (Minneapolis: H. W. Wilson, 1908), pp. 184–185.

---

ciently republican, and in a general attack against crimes, such as prostitution, that were supposedly characteristic of aristocratic society.

The most dramatic departure of the republic of virtue, and one that illustrates the imposition of political values that would justify the Terror, was an attempt by the Convention to dechristianize France. In October 1793 the Convention proclaimed a new calendar dating from the first day of the French Republic. There were twelve months of thirty days with names associated with the seasons and climate. Every tenth day rather than every seventh was a holiday. Many of the most important events of the next few years became known by their dates on the revolutionary calendar.[4] In November 1793 the convention decreed the Cathedral of Notre Dame to be a Temple of Reason. The legislature then sent trusted members, known as

[4] From summer to spring the months on the revolutionary calendar were Messidor, Thermidor, Fructidor, Vendémiaire, Brumaire, Frimaire, Nivôse, Pluviôse, Ventôse, Germinal, Floréal, and Prairial.

deputies on mission, into the provinces to enforce dechristianization by closing churches, persecuting clergy and believers, and occasionally forcing priests to marry. Needless to say, this religious policy roused much opposition and deeply separated the French provinces from the revolutionary government in Paris.

During the crucial months of late 1793 and early 1794 the person who emerged as the chief figure on the Committee of Public Safety was Robespierre. He was a complex person who has remained controversial to the present day. He was utterly selfless and from the earliest days of the revolution had favored a republic. The Jacobin Club provided his primary forum and base of power. A shrewd and sensitive politician, he had opposed the war in 1792 as a measure that might aid the monarchy. He largely depended on the support of the sans-culottes of Paris, but he continued to dress as he had prior to the revolution and opposed dechristianization as a political blunder. For him the republic of virtue meant wholehearted

An engraving by M. Bovi of the trial of Queen Marie Antoinette, who was executed on October 16, 1793. Note the contrast between her simple dress and veil here and her elaborate appearance in the portrait earlier in this chapter. [*The Mansell Collection.*]

support of republican government and the renunciation of selfish gains from political life. He once told the Convention, "If the mainspring of popular government in peacetime is virtue, amid revolution it is at the same time virtue and *terror:* virtue, without which terror is fatal; terror, without which virtue is impotent. Terror is nothing but prompt, severe, inflexible justice; it is therefore an emanation of virtue."[5] He and those who supported his policies were among the first apostles of secular ideologies who in the name of humanity would bring so much suffering to European politics of the left and the right in the next two centuries.

Progress of the Terror

The Reign of Terror manifested itself through a series of revolutionary tribunals established by the Convention during the summer of 1793. They were to try the enemies of the republic, but the definition of *enemy* remained uncertain and shifted as the months passed. The enemies included those who might aid other European powers, those who

[5] Quoted in Richard T. Bienvenu, *The Ninth of Thermidor: The Fall of Robespierre* (New York: Oxford University Press, 1968), p. 38.

Marie Antoinette on the way to her execution, sketched from life by David, as her tumbril passed his window. [*Bettmann Archive.*]

endangered republican virtue, and finally good republicans who opposed the policies of the dominant faction of the government. In a very real sense the terror of the revolutionary tribunals systematized and channeled the popular resentment that had manifested itself in the September Massacres of 1792. The first victims were Marie Antoinette, other members of the royal family, and some aristocrats, who were executed in October 1793. They were followed by certain Girondist politicians who had been prominent in the Legislative Assembly.

By the early months of 1794 the Terror had moved to the provinces, where the deputies on mission presided over the summary execution of thousands of people who had allegedly supported internal opposition to the revolution. One of the most infamous incidents occurred in Nantes, where several hundred people were simply tied to rafts and drowned in the river. By early 1794 the victims of the Terror were coming from every social class, including the sans-culottes.

In Paris during the late winter Robespierre began to orchestrate the Terror against republican political figures of the left and right. On March 24 he secured the execution of certain extreme sans-

❧ The Convention Establishes the Worship of the Supreme Being

On May 7, 1794, the Convention passed one of the most extraordinary pieces of revolutionary legislation. It established the worship of the Supreme Being as a state cult. Although the law drew on the religious ideas of deism, the point of the legislation was to provide a religious basis for the new secular French state, which had repeatedly attacked traditional French Catholicism. The reader should pay particular attention to Article 7, which outlines the political and civic values that the cult of the Supreme Being was supposed to nurture.

1. *The French people recognize the existence of the Supreme Being and the immortality of the soul.*

2. *They recognize that the worship worthy of the Supreme Being is the observance of the duties of man.*

3. *They place in the forefront of such duties detestation of bad faith and tyranny, punishment of tyrants and traitors, succoring of unfortunates, respect of weak persons, defence of the oppressed, doing to others all the good that one can, and being just towards everyone.*

4. *Festivals shall be instituted to remind man of the concept of the Divinity and of the dignity of his being.*

5. *They shall take their names from the glorious events of our Revolution, or from the virtues most dear and most useful to man, or from the greatest benefits of nature.*

. . . .

7. *On the days of* décade *[the name given to a particular day in each month of the revolutionary calendar] it shall celebrate the following festivals:*

To the Supreme Being and to nature; to the human race; to the French people; to the benefactors of humanity; to the martyrs of liberty; to liberty and equality; to the Republic; to the liberty of the world; to the love of the Patrie; *to the hatred of tyrants and traitors; to truth; to justice; to modesty; to glory and immortality; to friendship; to frugality; to courage; to good faith; to heroism; to disinterestedness; to stoicism; to love; to conjugal love; to paternal love; to maternal tenderness; to filial piety; to infancy; to youth; to manhood; to old age; to misfortune; to agriculture; to industry; to our forefathers; to posterity; to happiness.*

8. *The Committees of Public Safety and Public Instruction are responsible for presenting a plan of organization for said festivals.*

9. *The National Convention summons all talents worthy of serving the cause of humanity to the honor of concurring in their establishment by hymns and civic songs, and by every means which may contribute to their embellishment and utility.*

John Hall Stewart, *A Documentary Survey of the French Revolution* (New York: Macmillan, 1951), pp. 526–527.

The Festival of the Supreme Being took place in Paris in June 1794. It was one of the chief displays of the civic religion of the French Revolution. The painting is by P. A. de Machy. [Musée Carnavalet, Paris. Giraudon.]

culottes leaders known as the *enragés*. They had wanted further measures regulating prices, securing social equality, and pressing dechristianization. Robespierre then turned against more conservative republicans, including Danton. They were insufficiently militant on the war, had profited monetarily from the revolution, and had rejected any link between politics and moral virtue. Danton was executed during the first week in April. In this fashion Robespierre exterminated the leadership from both groups that might have threatened his position. Finally, on June 10, he secured passage of the Law of 22 Prairial, which permitted the revolutionary tribunal to convict suspects without hearing substantial evidence. The number of executions was growing steadily.

In May 1794, at the height of his power, Robespierre, considering the worship of Reason too ab-

stract for most citizens, abolished it and established the Cult of the Supreme Being. This deistic cult was in line with Rousseau's idea of a civic religion that would induce morality among citizens. However, Robespierre did not long preside over his new religion. On July 26 he made an ill-tempered speech in the Convention declaring that there existed among other leaders of the government a conspiracy against himself and the revolution. Such accusations against unnamed persons had usually preceded his earlier attacks. On July 27—the Ninth of Thermidor—by prearrangement, members of the Convention shouted him down when he rose to make another speech. That night Robespierre was arrested, and the next day he was executed. The revolutionary sans-culottes of Paris would not save him because he had deprived them of their chief leaders. The other Jacobins turned against him because after Danton's death they feared becoming the next victims. Robespierre had destroyed rivals for leadership without creating supporters for himself. In that regard he was the selfless creator of his own destruction.

The fall of Robespierre might simply have been one more shift in the turbulent politics of the revolution. Those who brought about his demise were motivated by instincts of self-preservation rather than by major policy differences. They had generally supported the Terror and the executions. Yet within a short time the Reign of Terror, which ultimately claimed over twenty-five thousand victims,

did come to a close. The largest number of executions had involved peasants and sans-culottes who had joined rebellions against the revolutionary government. By the late summer of 1794 those provincial uprisings had been crushed, and the war against foreign enemies was also going well. Those factors, combined with the feeling in Paris that the revolution had consumed enough of its own children, brought the Terror to an end.

The Thermidorian Reaction

The End of the Terror and Establishment of the Directory

A tempering of the revolution called the *Thermidorian Reaction* began in July 1794. It consisted of the destruction of the machinery of terror and the institution of a new constitutional regime. The influence of generally wealthy middle-class and professional people replaced that of the sans-culottes. Within days and weeks of Robespierre's execution the Convention allowed the Girondists who had been in prison or hiding to return to their seats. There was a general amnesty for political prisoners. The Convention restructured the Committee of Public Safety and gave it much less power. The Convention also repealed the notorious Law of 22 Prairial. Some, though by no means all, of the people responsible for the Terror were removed from public life. Leaders of the Paris Commune and certain deputies on mission were executed. The Paris Commune itself was outlawed. The Paris Jacobin Club was closed, and Jacobin clubs in the provinces were forbidden to correspond with each other.

The executions of former terrorists marked the beginning of "the white terror." Throughout the country people who had been involved in the Reign of Terror were attacked and often murdered. Jacobins were executed with little more due process than they had extended to their victims a few months earlier. The Convention itself approved some of these trials. In other cases gangs of youths who had aristocratic connections or who had avoided serving in the army roamed the streets beating known Jacobins. In Lyons, Toulon, and Marseilles these "bands of Jesus" dragged suspected terrorists from prisons and murdered them much as alleged royalists had been murdered during the September Massacres of 1792.

The republic of virtue gave way, if not to one of

In this cartoon, the government of Robespierre is attacked for having killed everyone: clergy, nobility, legislators, the people. [Editorial Photocolor Archives.]

One of the major events during the Thermidorian Reaction was the closing in November 1794 of the Jacobin Club in Paris. The structure was part of a former convent in the center of the city. [The Granger Collection.]

vice, at least to one of frivolous pleasures. The dress of the sans-culottes and the Roman Republic disappeared among the middle class and the aristocracy. New plays appeared in the theaters, and prostitutes again roamed the streets of Paris. Families of victims of the Reign of Terror gave parties in which they appeared with shaved necks like the victims of the guillotine and red ribbons tied about them. Although the Convention continued to favor the Cult of the Supreme Being, it allowed Catholic services to be held. Many refractory priests returned to the country. One of the unanticipated results of the Thermidorian Reaction was a genuine revival of Catholic worship.

The Thermidorian Reaction also involved still further political reconstruction. The fully democratic constitution of 1793, which had never gone into effect, was abandoned. The Convention issued in its place the Constitution of the Year III, which reflected the Thermidorian determination to reject both constitutional monarchy and democracy. The new document provided for a legislature of two houses. Members of the upper body, or Council of Elders, were to be men over forty years of age who were either husbands or widowers. The lower Council of Five Hundred was to consist of married or single men at least thirty years old. The executive body was to be a five-person Directory chosen by the Elders from a list submitted by the Council of Five Hundred. Property qualifications limited the franchise except for soldiers, who even without property were permitted to vote.

Thermidor became a term associated with political reaction. However, if the French Revolution had originated in political conflicts characteristic of the eighteenth century, it had by 1795 become something very different. A society and a political structure based on rank and birth had given way to one based on civic equality and social status stemming from the ownership or nonownership of property. People who had never been allowed direct, formal access to political power had to differing degrees been admitted to those activities. Their entrance had given rise to questions of property distribution and economic regulations that could not again be totally ignored. Representation had been established as a principle of practical politics. Henceforth the question before France and eventually before all of Europe would be which new groups would be admitted to representation. In the *levée en masse* the French had demonstrated to Europe the power of the secular ideal of nationhood.

All of these stunning changes in the political and social contours of Europe are not to be forgotten in a consideration of the post-Thermidorian course of the French Revolution. What triumphed in the Constitution of the Year III was the revolution of the holders of property. For this reason the French Revolution has usually been considered the victory of the bourgeoisie, or middle class. However, the property that won the day was not industrial wealth but the wealth stemming from commerce and the professions. Moreover the largest new propertied class to emerge from the revolutionary turmoil was the peasantry, who as a result of the destruction of feudal privileges had achieved personal ownership of the land. Unlike peasants liberated from feudalism in other parts of Europe during the next century, French peasants had to pay no monetary compensation.

The most decisively reactionary element in the Thermidorian Reaction and the new constitution was the removal of the sans-culottes from political life. With the war effort succeeding, the Convention severed its ties with the sans-culottes. True to their belief in an unregulated economy, the Thermidorians repealed the ceiling on prices. As a result, the winter of 1794–1795 brought the worst food shortages of the period. There were numerous food riots, which the Convention put down with force to prove that the era of the sans-culottes

journées had come to a close. On October 5, 1795—13 Vendémiaire—the sections of Paris rose up against the Convention. For the first time in the history of the revolution, artillery was turned against the people of Paris. A general named Napoleon Bonaparte (1769–1821) commanded the cannon, and with a "whiff of grapeshot" he dispersed the crowd.

By the Treaty of Basel in March 1795, the Convention concluded peace with Prussia and Spain. However, the legislators feared a resurgence of both radical democrats and royalists in the upcoming elections for the Council of Five Hundred. Consequently the Convention ruled that at least two thirds of the new legislature must have been members of the older body. The Thermidorians did not even trust the property owners as voters. The next year the newly established Directory again faced social unrest. In Paris Gracchus Babeuf (1760–1797) led the Conspiracy of Equals. He and his followers called for more radical democracy and for more equality of property. Babeuf was arrested, tried, and executed. This quite minor plot became famous many decades later when European socialists attempted to find their historical roots in the French Revolution.

The suppression of the sans-culottes, the narrow franchise of the constitution, the rule of the two thirds, and the Catholic royalist revival presented the Directory with problems that it never succeeded in overcoming. It lacked any broad base of meaningful political support. It particularly required active loyalty because France remained at war with Austria and Great Britain. Consequently the Directory came to depend on the power of the army rather than on constitutional processes for governing the country. All of the soldiers could vote. Moreover, within the army, created and sustained by the revolution, stood officers who were eager for power and ambitious for political conquest. The results of the instability of the Directory and the growing role of the army held profound consequences not only for France but for the entire Western world.

Suggested Readings

C. BRINTON, *The Jacobins: An Essay in the New History* (1930). An examination of the social background of these revolutionaries.

C. BRINTON, *A Decade of Revolution, 1789–1799* (1934).

A general survey of Europe during the revolutionary years.

R. COBB, *The Police and the People: French Popular Protest, 1789–1820* (1970). An interesting and imaginative treatment of the question of social control during the revolution.

A. COBBAN, *Edmund Burke and the Revolt Against the Eighteenth Century* (1929). Sets Burke's thought in a broader intellectual context.

A. COBBAN, *Aspects of the French Revolution* (1970). Essays on numerous subjects.

C. CONE, *The English Jacobins: Reformers in Late Eighteenth Century England* (1968). The fortunes of English radicals during the repression following the outbreak of war with France.

K. EPSTEIN, *The Genesis of German Conservatism* (1966). A major study of antiliberal forces in Germany before and during the revolution.

J. GODECHOT, *The Taking of the Bastille, July 14, 1789* (1970). The best modern discussion of the subject and one that places the fall of the Bastille in the context of crowd behavior in the eighteenth century.

J. GODECHOT, *The Counter-Revolution: Doctrine and Action, 1789–1804* (1971). An examination of opposition to the revolution.

A. GOODWIN, *The Friends of Liberty: The English Democratic Movement in the Age of the French Revolution* (1979). A major new work that explores the impact of the French Revolution on English radicalism.

D. M. GREER, *The Incidence of the Terror During the French Revolution: A Statistical Interpretation* (1935). A study of what people in which regions became the victims of the Terror.

N. HAMPSON, *A Social History of the French Revolution* (1963). A clear account with much interesting detail.

D. JOHNSON (Ed.), *French Society and the Revolution* (1976). A useful collection of important essays on the social history of the revolution.

G. LEFEBVRE, *The Coming of the French Revolution* (trans., 1947). An examination of the crisis of the French monarchy and the events of 1789.

G. LEFEBVRE, *The French Revolution*, 2 vols. (1962–1964). A major study by one of the most important modern writers on the subject.

R. R. PALMER, *Twelve Who Ruled: The Committee of Public Safety During the Terror* (1941). A clear narrative and analysis of the policies and problems of the committee.

R. R. PALMER, *The Age of the Democratic Revolution: A Political History of Europe and America, 1760–1800*, 2 vols. (1959, 1964). An impressive survey of the political turmoil in the transatlantic world.

G. RUDÉ, *The Crowd in the French Revolution* (1959). Examines who composed the revolutionary crowds and why.

A. SOBOUL, *The Parisian Sans-Culottes and the French Revolution, 1793–94* (1964). The best work on the subject.

A. SOBOUL, *The French Revolution* (trans., 1975). An important work by a Marxist scholar.

J. H. STEWART, *A Documentary Survey of the French Revolution* (1951). Major sources in translation.

J. M. THOMPSON, *Robespierre*, 2 vols. (1935). The best biography.

C. TILLY, *The Vendée* (1964). A significant sociological investigation.

M. WALZER (Ed.), *Regicide and Revolution: Speeches at the Trial of Louis XVI* (1974). An important and exceedingly interesting collection of documents with a useful introduction.

In this French allegory of 1799, Napoleon is portrayed as the First Consul saving France from discord and ignorance. [Bibliotheque Nationale.]

23 The Age of Napoleon and the Triumph of Romanticism

THE GOVERNMENT of the Directory represented a new class made up of politicians, merchants, bankers, war speculators, and profiteers sprung from the nonaristocratic order of the old regime, as well as a few undistinguished nobles. Together they formed a society of recently enriched and powerful people whose chief goal was to halt the revolutionary movement without rolling it back. They wanted to perpetuate their own rule. They sought to achieve peace and quiet in order to gain more wealth and to establish a society in which money would become the only requirement for eminence and power. They and their goals confronted a host of enemies.

The Rise of Napoleon Bonaparte

The chief danger to the Directory came from the royalists, who hoped to restore the Bourbon monarchy by legal means. Many of the *émigrés* had drifted back into France. Their plans for a restora-

tion drew support from devout Catholics and from those citizens whom the excesses of the revolution had disgusted. Monarchy seemed to hold the promise of stability. The spring elections of 1797 turned out most of the incumbents and replaced them with a majority of constitutional monarchists and their sympathizers. To prevent an end to the republic and a peaceful restoration of monarchy, the antimonarchist Directory staged a *coup d'état* on 18 Fructidor (September 4, 1797). They put their own supporters into the legislative seats won by their opponents. They then imposed censorship and exiled some of their enemies. Napoleon Bonaparte, the general in charge of the Italian military campaign, had made these political actions possible. At the request of the Directors, he had sent one of his subordinates to Paris to guarantee the success of the *coup*. In 1797, as in 1795, the army and Bonaparte had saved the day for the government installed in the wake of the Thermidorian Reaction.

Napoleon Bonaparte was born in 1769 to a poor family of lesser nobles at Ajaccio, Corsica. Because France had annexed Corsica in the previous year, he went to French schools, pursued a military career, and in 1785 obtained a commission as a French artillery officer. He strongly favored the revolution and was a fiery Jacobin. In 1793 he played a leading role in recovering the port of Toulon from the British. In reward for his service the government appointed him a brigadier general. His radical associations threatened his career during the Thermidorian Reaction, but his defense of the new regime on 13 Vendémiaire restored him to favor and won him another promotion and a command in Italy.

By 1795 French arms and diplomacy had shattered the enemy coalition, but France's annexation of Belgium guaranteed continued fighting with Britain and Austria. The attack on Italy aimed at depriving Austria of the provinces of Lombardy and Venetia. In a series of lightning victories Bonaparte crushed the Austrian and Sardinian armies. On his own initiative, and in many ways contrary to the wishes of the government in Paris, he concluded the Treaty of Campo Formio in October 1797. The treaty took Austria out of the war and crowned Napoleon's campaign and independent policy with success. Before long all of Italy and Switzerland had fallen under French domination.

In November 1797 the triumphant Bonaparte returned to Paris to be hailed as a hero and to confront France's only remaining enemy, Britain. He judged it impossible to cross the channel and invade England at that time. Instead he chose to capture Egypt from the Ottoman Empire. By this strategy he hoped to drive the British fleet from the Mediterranean, cut off British communication with India, damage British trade, and threaten the British empire. The invasion of Egypt was a failure. Admiral Horatio Nelson (1758–1805) destroyed the French fleet at Abukir on August 1, 1798. The French army could then neither accomplish anything of importance in the Near East nor get home. To make matters worse, the situation in Europe was deteriorating. The French invasion of Egypt had alarmed Russia, which had its own ambitions in the Near East. The Russians, the Austrians, and the Ottomans soon joined Britain to form the Second Coalition. In 1799 the Russian and Austrian armies defeated the French in Italy and Switzerland and threatened to invade France.

Economic troubles and the dangerous international situation eroded the already fragile support of the Directory. One of the Directors, the Abbé Sieyès, proposed a new constitution. The author of the pamphlet *What Is the Third Estate?* (1789) wanted to establish a vigorous executive body independent of the whims of electoral politics, a government based on the principle of "confidence from below, power from above." The change would require another *coup d'état* with military support. News of France's diplomatic misfortunes had reached Napoleon in Egypt. Without orders and leaving his doomed army behind, he returned to France in October 1799. He received much popular acclaim, although some people thought that he deserved a court-martial for desertion. He soon joined Sieyès. On 19 Brumaire (November 10, 1799) his troops drove out the legislators and permitted the success of the *coup*.

Sieyès appears to have thought Napoleon could be used and then dismissed, but if so he badly misjudged his man. The proposed constitution divided executive authority among three consuls. Bonaparte quickly pushed it aside, as he did Sieyès, and in December 1799 he issued the Constitution of the Year VIII. Behind a screen of universal manhood suffrage that suggested democratic principles, a complicated system of checks and balances that appealed to republican theory, and a Council of State that evoked memories of Louis XIV, the constitution in fact established the rule of one man, the First Consul, Bonaparte. To find a reasonably close historical analogy one must go back to Caesar and Augustus and the earlier Greek tyrants. The career of Bonaparte, however, pointed forward to the dictators of the twentieth century. He was the first modern political figure to employ the rhetoric of revolution and nationalism, to back it with military force, and to combine those elements into a mighty weapon of imperial expansion in the service of his own power and ambition.

The Consulate in France (1799-1804)

The establishment of the Consulate, in effect, closed the revolution in France. The leading elements of the Third Estate—that is, officials, landowners, doctors, lawyers, and financiers—had achieved most of their goals by 1799. They had abolished hereditary privilege, and the careers thus opened to talent allowed them to achieve the wealth and status they sought. The peasants were also satisfied. They had acquired the land they had

In this cartoon supporting Napoleon's coup of 18 Brunaire (November 9, 1799) the toppled sphinx represents the downfall of the incompetent, disordered, and corrupt government of the Directory. [Library of Congress.]

always wanted and had destroyed oppressive feudal privileges as well. The newly established dominant classes were profoundly conservative. They had little or no desire to share their recently won privileges with the lower social orders. Bonaparte seemed just the person to give them security. When he submitted his constitution to the voters in a plebiscite, they approved it by 3,011,077 votes to 1,567.

Bonaparte quickly justified the public's confidence by setting about achieving peace with France's enemies. Russia had already quarreled with its allies and left the Second Coalition. A campaign in Italy brought another victory over Austria at Marengo in 1800. The Treaty of Lunéville early in 1801 took Austria out of the war and confirmed the earlier settlement of Campo Formio. Britain was now alone and, in 1802, concluded the Treaty of Amiens, which brought peace to Europe. Bona-

parte was equally effective in restoring peace and order at home. He employed generosity, flattery, and bribery to win over some of his enemies. He issued a general amnesty and employed in his own service persons from all political factions. He required only that they be loyal to him. Some of the highest offices were occupied by persons who had been extreme radicals during the Reign of Terror, others by persons who had fled the Terror and favored constitutional monarchy, and still others by former high officials of the old regime.

On the other hand, Bonaparte was ruthless and efficient in suppressing opposition. He established a highly centralized administration in which all departments were managed by prefects directly responsible to the central government in Paris. He employed secret police. He stamped out once and for all the royalist rebellion in the west and made the rule of Paris effective in Brittany and the

❧ Napoleon Describes Conditions Leading to the Consulate

In this passage from his memoirs Napoleon described the manner in which the Directory came to an end in 1799 and the Consulate began. In reading of his supposed concern about the army, one should remember that he had abandoned his troops in Egypt to return to Paris to undertake this coup.

On my return to Paris I found division among all authorities, and agreement upon only one point, namely, that the Constitution was half destroyed and was unable to save liberty.

All parties came to me, confided to me their designs, disclosed their secrets, and requested my support; I refused to be the man of a party.

The Council of Elders summoned me; I answered its appeal. A plan of general restoration had been devised by men whom the nation has been accustomed to regard as the defenders of liberty, equality, and property; this plan required an examination, calm, free, exempt from all influence and all fear. Accordingly, the Council of Elders resolved upon the removal of the Legislative Body to Saint-Cloud; it gave me the responsibility of disposing the force necessary for its independence. I believed it my duty to my fellow citizens, to the soldiers perishing in our armies, to the national glory acquired at the cost of their blood, to accept the command. . . .

I presented myself at the Council of Five Hundred, alone, unarmed, my head uncovered, just as the Elders had received and applauded me; I came to remind the majority of its wishes, and to assure it of its power.

The stilettos which menaced the deputies were instantly raised against their liberator; twenty assassins threw themselves upon me and aimed at my breast. The grenadiers of the Legislative Body whom I had left at the door of the hall ran forward, placed themselves between the assassins and myself. One of these brave grenadiers had his clothes pierced by a stiletto. They bore me out.

At the same moment cries of "Outlaw" were raised against the defender of the law. It was the fierce cry of assassins against the power destined to repress them.

They crowded around the president, uttering threats, arms in their hands; they commanded him to outlaw me; I was informed of this; I ordered him to be rescued from their fury, and six grenadiers of the Legislative Body secured him. Immediately afterwards some grenadiers of the Legislative Body charged into the hall and cleared it.

The factions, intimidated, dispersed and fled. . . .

Frenchmen, you will doubtless recognize in this conduct the zeal of a soldier of liberty, a citizen devoted to the Republic. Conservative, tutelary, and liberal ideas have been restored to their rights through the dispersal of the rebels who oppressed the Councils. . . .

John Hall Stewart, *A Documentary Survey of the French Revolution* (New York: Macmillan, 1951), pp. 763–765.

Vendée for the first time in many years. Nor was he above using or even inventing opportunities to destroy his enemies. When a plot on his life surfaced in 1804, he used the event as an excuse to attack the Jacobins, even though the bombing was the work of royalists. In 1804 his forces invaded the sovereignty of Baden to seize the Bourbon Duke of Enghien. The duke was accused of participation in a royalist plot and put to death, even though Bonaparte knew him to be innocent. The action was a flagrant violation of international law and of due process. Charles Maurice de Talleyrand-Périgord (1754–1838), Bonaparte's foreign minister, later termed the act "worse than a crime—a blunder," because it helped to provoke foreign opposition. On the other hand, it was popular with the former Jacobins, for it seemed to preclude the possibility of a Bourbon restoration. The person who killed a Bourbon was hardly likely to restore the royal family. The execution seems to have put an end to royalist plots.

A major obstacle to internal peace was the steady hostility of French Catholics. Refractory clergy continued to advocate counterrevolution. The religious revival that dated from the Thermidorian Reaction increased discontent with the secular state created by the revolution. Bonaparte regarded religion as a political matter. He approved its role in preserving an orderly society but was suspicious of any such power independent of the state.

In 1801 Napoleon concluded a concordat with Pope Pius VII, to the shock and dismay of his anticlerical supporters. The settlement gave Napoleon what he most wanted. Both the refractory clergy and those who had accepted the revolution were forced to resign. Their replacements received their spiritual investiture from the pope, but the state named the bishops and paid their salaries and the salary of one priest in each parish. In return the church gave up its claims on its confiscated property. The concordat declared that "Catholicism is the religion of the great majority of French citizens." This was merely a statement of fact and fell far short of what the pope had wanted, religious dominance for the Roman Catholic Church. The clergy had to swear an oath of loyalty to the state, and the Organic Articles of 1802, which were actually distinct from the concordat, established the supremacy of State over Church. Similar laws were applied to the Protestant and Jewish religious communities as well, reducing still further the privileged position of the Catholic church.

Peace and efficient administration brought pros-

Charles Maurice de Talleyrand-Périgord, known to history as Talleyrand, was one of the most talented—or adaptable—political survivors of the Revolution. Before 1789 he had been a Roman Catholic bishop. Later he became a major diplomat, first for the revolutionary government, and then for Napoleon. Finally, in 1815, he represented the restored Bourbon government at the Congress of Vienna. The portrait is by Pierre-Paul Prud'hon. [The Granger Collection.]

perity and security to the French and gratitude and popularity to Bonaparte. In 1802 a plebiscite appointed him consul for life, and he soon produced still another new constitution, which granted him what amounted to full power. The years of the Consulate were employed in reforming and estab-

⮲ The Consuls Proclaim the End of the French Revolution

In this proclamation of December 15, 1799, the three new consuls, of whom Napoleon was one, presented the Constitution of the Year VIII to the French people and ceremoniously declared the end of the French Revolution.

Frenchmen!

A Constitution is presented to you.

It terminates the uncertainties which the provisional government introduced into external relations, into the internal and military situation of the Republic.

It places in the institutions which it establishes first magistrates whose devotion has appeared necessary for its success.

The Constitution is founded on the true principles of representative government, on the sacred rights of property, equality, and liberty.

The powers which it institutes will be strong and stable, as they must be in order to guarantee the rights of citizens and the interests of the State.

Citizens, the Revolution is established upon the principles which began it: It is ended.

John Hall Stewart, *A Documentary Survey of the French Revolution* (New York: Macmillan, 1951), p. 780.

lishing the basic laws and institutions of France. The settlement imposed by Napoleon was an ambiguous combination of liberal principles derived from the Enlightenment and the early years of the revolution and conservative principles and practices going back to the old regime or adapted to the conservative spirit that had triumphed at Thermidor.

The abolition of all privileges based on birth, the establishment of equality before the law, the disappearance of all authority except that of the national state and all legal distinctions based on class or locality, and the end of all purchased offices and the substitution of salaried officials chosen for merit represented the application of rationality and the achievement of goals sought by the people who had made the revolution. Most of these were embodied in the general codification of laws carried out under Bonaparte's direction. This was especially true of the Civil Code of 1804, usually called the Napoleonic Code. However, these laws stopped far short of the full equality advocated by liberal rationalists. Fathers were granted extensive control over their children and men over their wives. Labor unions were still forbidden, and the rights of workers were inferior to those of their employers.

In the political arena and in administration Napoleonic institutions ran contrary to the tendencies of the revolution. They aimed at a kind of enlightened absolutism that was similar to but more effective than what had existed in the old regime. Rep-

⤶ Napoleon Makes Peace with the Papacy

In 1801 Napoleon concluded a concordat with Pope Pius VII. This document was the cornerstone of Napoleonic religious policy. The concordat which was announced on April 8, 1802, allowed the Roman Catholic Church to function freely in France only within the limits of church support for the government as indicated in the oath included in Article 6.

The government of the French Republic recognizes that the Roman, catholic and apostolic religion is the religion of the great majority of French citizens.

His Holiness likewise recognizes that this same religion has derived and in this moment again expects the greatest benefit and grandeur from the establishment of the catholic worship in France and from the personal profession of it which the consuls of the Republic make.

In consequence, after this mutual recognition, as well for the benefit of religion as for the maintenance of internal tranquility, they have agreed as follows:

1. The catholic, apostolic and Roman religion shall be freely exercised in France: its worship shall be public, and in conformity with the police regulations which the government shall deem necessary for the public tranquility.

   .   .   .   .   .   .

4. The First Consul of the Republic shall make appointments, within the three months which shall follow the publication of the bull of His Holiness, to the archbishoprics and bishoprics of the new circumscription. His Holiness shall confer the canonical institution, following the forms established in relation to France before the change of government.

   .   .   .   .   .   .

6. Before entering upon their functions, the bishops shall take directly, at the hands of the First Consul, the oath of fidelity which was in use before the change of government, expressed in the following terms:

"I swear and promise to God, upon the holy scriptures, to remain in obedience and fidelity to the government established by the constitution of the French Republic. I also promise not to have any intercourse, nor to assist by any counsel, nor to support any league, either within or without, which is inimical to the public tranquility; and if, within my diocese or elsewhere, I learn that anything to the prejudice of the state is being contrived, I will make it known to the government."

F. M. Anderson, *The Constitutions and Other Select Documents Illustrative of the History of France 1789–1907*, 2nd ed. (Minneapolis: H. W. Wilson, 1908), pp. 296–297.

resentative government, local autonomy, and personal freedom were rejected in favor of the centralization of all power and the subordination of personal rights and political freedom to the needs of the state as interpreted by the First Consul. All of this was acceptable to the dominant bourgeoisie and the peasantry. They accepted censorship, the arbitrary and sometimes brutal suppression of dissent, and even the restoration of a new quasi nobility in the Legion of Honor as long as order, prosperity, and security of property were preserved.

In 1804 Bonaparte seized on the bomb attack on his life to make himself emperor. He argued that the establishment of a dynasty would make the new regime secure and make further attempts on his life useless. Another new constitution was promulgated in which Napoleon Bonaparte was called Emperor of the French, instead of First Consul of the Republic. This constitution was also overwhelmingly ratified in a plebiscite.

To conclude the drama, Napoleon invited the pope to Notre Dame to take part in the coronation. But at the last minute the pope agreed that Napoleon should place the crown on his own head. The emperor had no intention of allowing anyone to think that his power and authority depended on the approval of the church. Henceforth, he was called Napoleon I. This act was the natural goal of his career. His aims had always been profoundly selfish: power and glory for himself and his family. There was, moreover, a romantic streak in Napoleon. He thought of himself as a rival of Alexander the Great and Caesar, a conqueror as well as a ruler. Had Napoleon wished it, Europe might well have had peace; but his ambition would not permit it.

Napoleon's Empire (1804-1814)

In the decade between his coronation as emperor and his final defeat at Waterloo (1815), Napoleon conquered most of Europe in a series of military campaigns that astonished the world. France's victories changed the map of Europe, put an end to the old regime and its feudal trappings in western Europe, and forced the eastern European states to reorganize themselves to resist Napoleon's armies. Everywhere Napoleon's advance unleashed the powerful force of nationalism. The militarily mobilized French nation, one of the

achievements of the revolution, was Napoleon's weapon. He could put as many as 700,000 men under arms at one time, risk as many as 100,000 troops in a single battle, endure heavy losses, and come back to fight again. He could conscript citizen soldiers in unprecedented numbers, thanks to their loyalty to the nation and to their remarkable leader. No single enemy could match such resources, and even coalitions were unsuccessful until Napoleon at last overreached himself and made mistakes that led to his own defeat.

Napoleon deserves his reputation as one of the great commanders of all time. His genius lay not in strategic or tactical invention, in which he had many eighteenth-century French forerunners, but in execution and leadership. His strategy depended on mobility and timing. He liked to divide his forces into units of moderate size, disperse them across the country, and then use their superior speed and his own planning skill to unite them at the critical point at the right time. All of this emphasis on speed of maneuver had a single goal: to bring the hostile armies together for a swift major battle. Napoleon departed from the usual eighteenth-century tactics, which emphasized maneuver and strategic position and the fighting of a battle only as a last resort. His aim was not to control territory nor to gain strong points but to destroy the enemy army. After that, rest for his army might follow. As long as conditions permitted such warfare, Napoleon was unbeatable.

Self-sufficiency was another important Napoleonic military principle that related to his emphasis on swiftness of maneuver. It was this self-sufficiency that allowed him to disperse and reunite his armies so rapidly. The whole army traveled light, with few supplies. By living off the country in which it fought, the army was free of the need to establish and follow a chain of supply depots. This was a great advantage in fertile areas like western and central Europe but proved a problem later against the guerrilla fighters in Spain and in the vast expanse of Russia during the winter. Under those conditions Napoleon's brilliant tactics could not be carried out, and he was eventually defeated. But those events lay many years ahead.

The Peace of Amiens (1802) was doomed to be merely a truce. Napoleon's unlimited ambitions shattered any hope that it might last. He sent an army to restore the rebellious island of Haiti to French rule. This move aroused British fears that he was planning the renewal of a French empire in

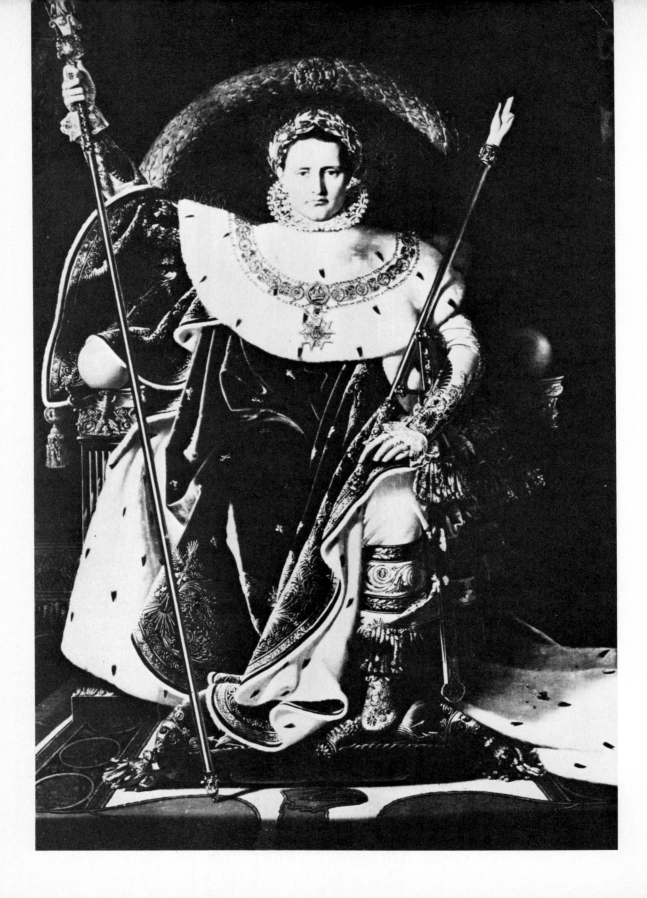

OPPOSITE: *This formal portrait of Napoleon by Jean A. D. Ingres (1780–1867) reveals and glorifies the repressive emperor. He is clothed in the splendor of a monarch and seems to represent the total power of the state. The painting is in the Musée de la Légion d'Honneur, Paris. [French Cultural Services, New York.]*

America, because Spain had restored Louisiana to France in 1800. More serious were his interventions in the Dutch Republic, Italy, and Switzerland and his role in the reorganization of Germany. The Treaty of Campo Formio had required a redistribution of territories along the Rhine River, and the petty princes of the region engaged in a shameful scramble to enlarge their holdings. Among the results were the reduction of Austrian influence in Germany and the emergence of a smaller number of larger German states in the west, all dependent on Napoleon.

The British found all of these developments alarming enough to justify an ultimatum. When Napoleon ignored it, Britain declared war in May 1803. William Pitt the Younger returned to office as prime minister in 1804 and began to construct the Third Coalition. By August 1805 he had persuaded Russia and Austria to move once again against French aggression. A great naval victory soon raised the fortunes of the allies. On October 21, 1805, the British admiral Horatio, Lord Nelson destroyed the combined French and Spanish fleets at the Battle of Trafalgar just off the Spanish coast. Nelson died in the battle, but the British lost no ships. The victory of Trafalgar put an end to all French hope of an invasion of Britain and guaranteed British control of the sea for the rest of the war.

On land the story was very different. Even before Trafalgar Napoleon had marched to the Danube River to attack his continental enemies. In mid-October he forced a large Austrian army to surrender at Ulm and soon occupied Vienna. On December 2, 1805, in perhaps his greatest victory, Napoleon defeated the combined Austrian and Russian forces at Austerlitz. The Treaty of Pressburg, which followed, won major concessions from Austria. The Austrians withdrew from Italy and left Napoleon in control of everything north of Rome. He was recognized as king of Italy.

Extensive changes also came about in Germany. In July 1806 Napoleon organized the Confederation of the Rhine, which included most of the western German princes. The withdrawal of these princes from the Holy Roman Empire led Francis II of Austria to dissolve that ancient political body and hencefore to call himself only emperor of Austria.

Prussia, which had carefully remained neutral up to this point, was now provoked into war against France. The famous Prussian army was quickly crushed at the battles of Jena and Auerstädt on October 14, 1806. Two weeks later Napoleon was in Berlin. There, on November 21, he issued the Berlin Decrees forbidding his allies to import British goods. On June 13, 1807, Napoleon defeated the Russians at Friedland and was able to occupy

British Admiral Horatio Nelson (1758–1805) was the brilliant naval strategist in the wars against Napoleonic France—wars in which he lost an eye, an arm, and finally his life. His last battle, in which he was killed, was a stunning victory over the combined French and Spanish fleets off Trafalgar on the coast of Spain, October 21, 1805, and ended any possible sea threat to England. The painting is by Lemuel Francis Abbott and is in the National Portrait Gallery, London. [The Granger Collection.]

This painting of Napoleon and his officers at the battle of Eylau in 1807 clearly shows the vast number of troops that he customarily used in combat—although in this picture the troops are included only as a backdrop for a romantic rendering of the emperor and his aides on the field of battle. The artist was Antoine Jean Gros (1771–1835). [The Granger Collection.]

In 1807 Czar Alexander I of Russia (center left) and Napoleon (center right) met on a raft in the Niemen River near Tilsit (on the Lithuanian border). At that conference they signed a treaty in which they divided Europe into spheres of French and Russian influence. The scene is imagined here by the artist Ludwig Wolf. [Bildarchiv Preussischer Kulturbesitz.]

684

Königsberg, the capital of East Prussia. The French emperor was master of all Germany.

Unable to fight another battle and unwilling to retreat into Russia, Czar Alexander I (1801–1825) was ready to make peace. He and Napoleon met on a raft in the middle of the Niemen River while the two armies and the nervous king of Prussia watched from the bank. On July 7, 1807, they signed the Treaty of Tilsit, which confirmed France's gains. Moreover the Prussian state was reduced to half its size and was saved from extinction only by the support of Alexander. Prussia openly and Russia secretly became allies of Napoleon in his war against Britain.

Napoleon organized conquered Europe much like the domain of a great Corsican family. The great French Empire was ruled directly by the head of the clan, Napoleon. On its borders lay a number of satellite states carved out as the portions of the several family members. His stepson ruled Italy for him, while three of his brothers and his brother-in-law were made kings of other conquered states. Napoleon denied a kingdom to his brother Lucien, of whose wife he disapproved. The French emperor expected his relatives to take orders without question. When they failed to do so, he rebuked and even punished them. This establishment of the Napoleonic family as the collective sovereign of Europe was offensive to the growing national feeling in many states and helped to create nationalism in others. The rule of puppet kings was unpopular and provoked political opposition that needed only encouragement and assistance to flare up into serious resistance.

After the Treaty of Tilsit such assistance could come only from Britain, and Napoleon knew that he must defeat the British before he could feel safe. Unable to compete with the British navy, he continued the economic warfare begun by the Berlin Decree. His plan was to cut off all British trade with the European continent. In this manner he hoped to cripple the commercial and financial power on which Britain depended, to cause domestic unrest and revolution, and thus to drive the British from the war. The Milan Decree of 1807 attempted to stop neutral nations from trading with Britain. For a time it appeared that this Continental System might work. British exports dropped, and riots broke out in England. But in the end the system failed and may even have contributed significantly to Napoleon's defeat.

The British economy survived because of its access to the growing markets of North and South

NAPOLEONIC EUROPE

1797	Napoleon concludes the Treaty of Campo Formio
1798	Nelson defeats the French navy in the harbor of Abukir
1799	Consulate established
1801	Concordat between France and the papacy
1802	Treaty of Amiens
1803	War renewed between France and Britain
1804	Execution of Duke of Enghien
	Napoleonic Civil Code issued
	Napoleon crowned as Emperor
1805	Nelson defeats French fleet at Trafalgar (October 21)
	Austerlitz (December 2)
1806	Jena
	Continental System established by Berlin Decree
1807	Friedland
	Treaty of Tilsit
1808	Beginning of Spanish resistance to Napoleonic domination
1809	Wagram
	Napoleon marries Archduchess Marie Louise of Austria
1812	Invasion of Russia and French defeat at Borodino
1813	Leipzig (Battle of the Nations)
1814	Treaty of Chaumont (March) establishes Quadruple Alliance
	Congress of Vienna convenes (September)
1815	Napoleon returns from Elba (March 1)
	Waterloo (June 18)
	Holy Alliance formed at Congress of Vienna (September 26)
	Quadruple Alliance renewed at Congress of Vienna (November 20)
1821	Napoleon dies on Saint Helena

America and of the eastern Mediterranean, all assured by the British control of the seas. At the same time, the Continental System did great harm to the European economies. The system was meant not only to hurt Britain but also to help France economically. Napoleon resisted advice to turn his empire into a free-trade area. Such a policy would have been both popular and helpful. Instead, his tariff policies favored France, increased the resentment of foreign merchants, and made them less willing to enforce the system and more ready to engage in smuggling. It was in part to prevent smuggling that Napoleon invaded Spain in 1808, and the resulting peninsular campaign in Spain and Portugal helped to bring on his ruin.

European Response to the Empire

Napoleon's conquests stimulated the two most powerful political forces in nineteenth-century Europe: liberalism and nationalism. The export of his version of the French Revolution directly and indirectly spread the ideas and values of the Enlightenment and the principles of 1789. Wherever Napoleon ruled, the Napoleonic Code was imposed and class distinction was abolished. Feudal dues disappeared and the peasants were freed from serfdom and manorial dues. In the towns the guilds and the local oligarchies that had been dominant for centuries were dissolved or deprived of their power. New freedom thus came to serfs, artisans, workers, and entrepreneurs outside the privileged circles. The established churches were deprived of their traditional independence and were made subordinate to the state. Church monopoly of religion was replaced by general toleration.

These reforms were not undone by the fall of Napoleon, and along with the demand for representative, constitutional government, they remained the basis of later liberal reforms. However, at the same time it became increasingly clear that Napoleon's policies were intended first and foremost for his own glory and that of France. The Continental System demonstrated that France rather than Europe generally was to be enriched by Napoleon's rule. Consequently, before long the conquered states and peoples became restive.

German Nationalism and Prussian Reform

The German response to Napoleon's success was particularly interesting and important. There had never been a unified German state. The great German writers of the Enlightenment, such as Kant, Schiller, and Lessing, were neither political nor nationalistic.

At the beginning of the nineteenth century the Romantic movement had begun to take hold. One of its basic features in Germany was the emergence of nationalism. This movement went through two distinct stages. Initially, nationalistic writers emphasized the unique and admirable qualities of German culture, which, they argued, arose from

The king and queen of Prussia are portrayed as birds to be plucked in this French cartoon of 1806. The French victories at Jena and Auerstadt on October 14, 1806 destroyed the Prussian army in one day. The battle showed beyond all doubt that a citizen army led by officers chosen on merit was far superior to an army of serfs and mercenaries led by incompetent noblemen. The Prussians learned their lesson, and their defeat led to a thorough reform of army and state. This print is in the Musee Carnavalet. [Bulloz.]

the peculiar history of the German people. Such cultural nationalism prevailed until Napoleon's humiliation of Prussia at Jena in 1806. At that point many German intellectuals began to urge resistance to Napoleon on the basis of German nationalism. The French conquest endangered the independence and achievements of the German people. Many nationalists were also critical of the German princes, who ruled selfishly and inefficiently and who seemed ever ready to lick the boots of Napoleon. No less important in forging a German national sentiment was the example of France, which had attained greatness by enlisting the active support of the entire people in the patriotic cause. Henceforth many Germans sought to solve their internal political problems by establishing a unified German state, reformed to harness the energies of the entire people.

After Tilsit only Prussia could arouse such patriotic feelings. Elsewhere German rulers were either under Napoleon's thumb or actively collaborating with him. Defeated, humiliated, and shrunk in size, Prussia continued to resist, however feebly. To Prussia fled German nationalists from other states, calling for reforms and unification that were, in fact, feared and hated by Frederick William III and the *Junker* nobility. Reforms came about in spite of such opposition because the defeat at Jena had made clear the necessity of new departures for the Prussian state.

The Prussian administrative and social reforms were the work of Baron vom Stein (1757–1831) and Count von Hardenberg (1750–1822). The architects of military reform were General Gerhard von Scharnhorst (1755–1813) and Count von Gneisenau (1760–1831). None of these reformers intended to reduce the autocratic power of the Prussian monarch or to put an end to the dominance of the *Junkers*, who formed the bulwark of the state and of the army officer corps. Rather, they aimed at fighting the revolution and French power with their own version of the French weapons. As Hardenberg declared:

Our objective, our guiding principle, must be a revolution in the better sense, a revolution leading directly to the great goal, the elevation of humanity through the wisdom of those in authority. . . . Democratic rules of conduct in a monarchical administration, such is the formula . . . which will conform most comfortably with the spirit of the age.[1]

[1] Quoted in Geoffrey Bruun, *Europe and the French Imperium* (New York: Harper & Row, 1938), p. 174.

Although the reforms came from the top, they brought important changes in Prussian society.

Stein's reforms put an end to the existing system of Prussian landownership. The *Junker* monopoly of landholding was broken. Serfdom was generally abolished. However, the power of the *Junkers* did not permit the total end of the system, as in the western principalities of Germany. Peasants remaining on the land were forced to continue manorial labor, although they were free to leave the land if they chose. They could obtain the ownership of the land they worked only at the price of forfeiting a third of it to the lord. The result was that *Junker* holdings grew larger. Some peasants went to the cities to find work; others became agricultural laborers; and some did actually become small freeholding farmers. Serfdom had come to an end, but new social problems that would fester for another half-century had been created as a landless labor force, enlarged by the population explosion, emerged.

The military reforms sought to increase the supply of soldiers and to improve their quality. Jena had shown that an army of free patriots commanded by officers chosen on merit rather than by birth could defeat an army of serfs and mercenaries commanded by incompetent nobles. To remedy the situation, the Prussian reformers abolished inhumane punishments, sought to inspire patriotic feelings in the soldiers, opened the officer corps to commoners, gave promotions on the basis of merit, and organized war colleges that developed new theories of strategy and tactics. These reforms soon put Prussia in a condition to regain its former power. However, because Napoleon had put a strict limit on the size of the Prussian army, universal conscription could not be introduced until 1813. Before that date the Prussians got around the limit of 42,000 men in arms by training one group each year, putting them into the reserves, and then training a new group the same size. In this manner Prussia could boast an army of 270,000 by 1814.

The Wars of Liberation

In Spain more than elsewhere in Europe national resistance to France had deep social roots. Spain had achieved political unity as early as the sixteenth century. The Spanish peasants were devoted to the ruling dynasty and especially to the Roman Catholic Church. France and Spain had been allies since 1796. In 1807, however, a French army came into the Iberian Peninsula to force Por-

Arthur Wellesley, the duke of Wellington, first led troops against Napoleon in Spain and later defeated him at the battle of Waterloo, June 18, 1815. Unlike his great naval contemporary, Nelson, he lived to become an elder statesman of Britain. The portrait is by the celebrated Spanish painter Francisco Goya (1746–1828). [The Granger Collection.]

Goya's "Barbarians" portrays the brutality of the guerrilla warfare waged against Napoleon's armies in Spain. [Metropolitan Museum of Art.]

tugal to abandon its traditional alliance with Britain. The army stayed in Spain to protect lines of supply and communication. When a revolt broke out in Madrid in 1808, Napoleon used it as a pretext to depose the Spanish Bourbon dynasty and to place his brother Joseph on the Spanish throne. Attacks on the privileges of the church increased public outrage. Many members of the upper classes were prepared to collaborate with Napoleon, but the peasants, urged on by the lower clergy and the monks, rose in a general rebellion.

Napoleon faced a new kind of warfare not vulnerable to his usual tactics. Guerrilla bands cut lines of communication, killed stragglers, destroyed isolated units, and then disappeared into the mountains. The British landed an army under Sir Arthur Wellesley (1769–1852), later the duke of Wellington, to support the Spanish insurgents. Thus began the long peninsular campaign that would drain French strength from elsewhere in Europe and play a critical role in Napoleon's eventual defeat.

The French troubles in Spain encouraged the Austrians to renew the war in 1809. Since their defeat at Austerlitz they had sought a war of revenge. The Austrians counted on Napoleon's distraction in Spain, French war weariness, and aid from other German princes. However, Napoleon was fully in command in France; and the German princes did not move. The French army marched swiftly into Austria and won the battle of Wagram. The resulting Peace of Schönbrunn deprived Austria of much territory and three and a half million subjects. Another spoil of victory was the Austrian Archduchess Marie Louise, daughter of the emperor. Napoleon's wife, Josephine de Beauharnais, was forty-six and had borne him no children. His dynastic ambitions, as well as the desire for a marriage matching his new position as master of Europe, led him to divorce his wife and to marry the eighteen-year-old Austrian princess. Napoleon had also considered the sister of Czar Alexander but had received a polite rebuff.

The failure of Napoleon's marriage negotiations

When their marriage failed to produce a male heir, Napoleon divorced his first wife, Joséphine de Beauharnais (1763–1814), [LEFT]. Many considered the action one aspect of Napoleon's betrayal of the Revolution, especially because he then married a daughter of the Hapsburg emperor. This portrait is by F. P. Gerard. [The Granger Collection.]

[RIGHT]: Napoleon's second wife, Marie Louise (1791–1814), bore him a son. It was clear that Napoleon hoped to establish a new imperial dynasty in France. This portrait is by J. B. Isabey. [The Granger Collection.]

THE CONTINENTAL SYSTEM
1806 · 1810

NORWAY

SWEDEN

DENMARK

ENGLAND

PRUSSIA

POLAND

RUSSIA

FRANCE

RHINE CONF.

AUSTRIA

PORT.

SPAIN

ITALY

■ AREAS IN WHICH BRITISH EXPORTS WERE PROHIBITED

● THE FRENCH EMPIRE

● THE GRAND EMPIRE

ALLIED WITH NAPOLEON

300 MI.

300 KM.

DENMARK

Christiana

SWEDEN

Stockholm

GOTHLAND

Gothenburg

SCOTLAND

Edinburgh

NORTH SEA

KINGDOM OF **DENMARK** AND **NORWAY**

DENMARK

Copenhagen

BALTIC SEA

SWEDISH POMERANIA

HELIGO-LAND (U.K.)

Lübeck

MECK.

PRUSSIA

THORN GRAN

York

UNITED KINGDOM

WALES

London

Dover

Boulogne

HAMBURG

OLDEN-BURG

HOLLAND

Brussels

+ WATERLOO

Cologne

HESSE

BERG

WEST-PHALIA

Mainz

JENA +

BERLIN

SAXONY

LEIPZIG

DRESDEN

BAUTZEN

Posen

Bresla

Prague

BOHEMIA

AUSTERLITZ +

Brest

QUIBERON

+ + +
BATTLE SITES

Nantes

VENDÉE

Amiens

Reims

Paris

Versailles

Fontainebleau

Orléans

VALMY +

Strasbourg

CONFEDERATION OF THE **RHINE**

BADEN

ULM

RATISBON

Munich

HOHENLINDEN

BAVARIA

INNSBRUCK

WAGRAM +

ASPERN +

Vienna

EMPIRE

FRANCE

SWITZ.

ST. GOTTHARD +

SAVOY

Turin

LOMBARDY

Milan

+ LODI

MARENGO +

Genoa

VENETIA

SACILE

Trieste

ILLYRIAN PROVIN

ADRIATIC

Rochefort

Bordeaux

Lyons

Avignon

Marseilles

Nice

Toulon

+ TOULOUSE

Leghorn

LUCCA

K. OF **ITALY**

Urbino

BO

BAY OF BISCAY

CAPE FINISTERRE

Corunna

Oporto

ALMEIDA +

VITORIA +

Burgos

+ SALAMANCA

+ CIUDAD RODRIGO

Madrid

SARAGOSSA +

GERONA +

Barcelona

TARRAGONA

ELBA

CORSICA

Rome

Bari

PORTUGAL

VIMEIRO + CINTRA

Lisbon

ELVAS +

BADAJOZ +

TALAVERA

+ OCAÑA

CIUDAD REAL

BAYLEN +

SPAIN

VALENCIA

+ VALENCIA

MURCIA

K. OF **NAPLES**

Naples

Cordova

Seville

ANDALUCIA

BALEARIC IS.

K. OF SARDINIA

Cagliari

MEDITERRANEAN SEA

Cadiz

TRAFALGAR +

GIBALTAR (U.K.)

K. OF SICILY

Algiers

Tunis

690

NAPOLEONIC EUROPE IN LATE 1812

MAP 23.1 *By mid-1812 the areas shown in black were incorporated into France, and most of the rest of Europe was directly controlled by or allied with Napoleon. But Russia had withdrawn from the failing Continental System, and the decline of Napoleon was about to begin.*

```
┌─────────────── CHRONOLOGY ───────────────┐
│ 1806   NOV. 21 — NAPOLEON ESTABLISHES  THE  CONTINENTAL │
│                  SYSTEM PROHIBITING ALL TRADE WITH ENGLAND. │
│ 1807   JULY 7 — THE PEACE CONFERENCE AT TILSIT RESULTS IN │
│                  RUSSIA JOINING THE CONTINENTAL SYSTEM │
│                  AND BECOMING AN ALLY OF NAPOLEON. │
│ 1809 AND 1810 — NAPOLEON AT THE PEAK OF HIS POWER. │
│ 1810   DEC. 31 — RUSSIA WITHDRAWS FROM THE CONTINENTAL │
│                  SYSTEM AND RESUMES RELATIONS WITH BRITAIN. │
│                  NAPOLEON PLANS TO CRUSH RUSSIA MILITARILY. │
│ 1812   JUNE - DECEMBER — NAPOLEON INVADES RUSSIA. THE RUS- │
│                  SIANS ADOPT A SCORCHED-EARTH POLICY AND │
│                  BURN MOSCOW. THE THWARTED NAPOLEON │
│                  DESERTS HIS DWINDLING ARMY AND RUSHES │
│                  BACK TO PARIS. │
└───────────────────────────────────────────┘
```

with Russia emphasized the shakiness of the Franco-Russian alliance concluded at Tilsit. The alliance was unpopular with Russian nobles because of the liberal politics of France and because of the prohibition of the Continental System on timber sales to Britain. Only French aid in gaining Constantinople could justify the alliance in their eyes, but Napoleon gave them no help against the Ottoman Empire. The organization of the Grand Duchy of Warsaw as a Napoleonic satellite on the Russian doorstep and its enlargement in 1809 after the battle of Wagram angered Alexander I. Napoleon's annexation of Holland in violation of the Treaty of Tilsit, his recognition of the French Marshal Bernadotte as King Charles XIV of Sweden, and his marriage to an Austrian princess further disturbed the czar. At the end of 1810 Russia withdrew from the Continental System and began to prepare for war.

Napoleon was determined to put an end to the Russian military threat. He amassed an army of over 600,000 men, including a core of Frenchmen and over 400,000 other soldiers drawn from the rest of his empire. He intended the usual short campaign crowned by a decisive battle, but the Russians disappointed him by retreating before his advance. His vast superiority in numbers—the Russians had only about 160,000 troops—made it foolish for them to risk a battle. Instead they followed a "scorched-earth" policy, destroying all food and supplies as they retreated. The so-called Grand Army of Napoleon could not live off the country, and the expanse of Russia made supply lines too long to maintain. Terrible rains, fierce heat, shortages of food and water, and the courage of the Russian rear guard defending their country against the invader eroded the morale of Napoleon's army. Napoleon's advisers urged him to abandon the venture, but he feared that an unsuccessful campaign would undermine his position in the empire and in France. He pinned his faith on the Russians' unwillingness to abandon Moscow without a fight.

In September 1812 Russian public opinion forced the army to give Napoleon the battle he wanted in spite of the canny Russian General Kutuzov's wish to avoid the fight and to let the Russian winter defeat the invader. At Borodino, not far west of Moscow, the bloodiest battle of the Napoleonic era cost the French thirty thousand casualties and the Russians almost twice as many. Yet the Russian army was not destroyed. Napoleon had won nothing substantial, and the battle was regarded as a defeat for him. Fires, set by the Russians, soon engulfed Moscow and left Napoleon far from home with a badly diminished army lacking adequate supplies as winter came to a vast country whose people hated the invader. Napoleon, after capturing the burned city, addressed several peace offers to Alexander, but the czar ignored them. By October what was left of the Grand Army was forced to retreat. By December Napoleon realized that the Russian fiasco would encourage plots against him at home and returned to Paris, leaving the remnants of his army to struggle westward. Perhaps only as many as 100,000 lived to tell the tale of their terrible ordeal.

Even as the news of the disaster reached the west, the total defeat of Napoleon was far from certain. He was able to put down his opponents in Paris and to raise another army of 350,000 men. Neither the Prussians nor the Austrians were eager to risk another bout with Napoleon, and even the Russians hesitated. The Austrian foreign minister, Prince Klemens von Metternich (1773–1859), would have been glad to make a negotiated peace that would leave Napoleon on the throne of a shrunk and chastened France rather than see Europe dominated by Russia. Napoleon might have won a reasonable settlement by negotiation had he been willing to make concessions that would have split his jealous opponents, but he would not consider that solution. As he explained to Metternich, "Your sovereigns born on the throne can let them-

selves be beaten twenty times and return to their capitals. I cannot do this because I am an upstart soldier. My domination will not survive the day when I cease to be strong, and therefore feared."[2]

In 1813 patriotic pressure and national ambition brought together the last and most powerful coalition against Napoleon. The Russians drove westward and were joined by Prussia and then Austria. All were assisted by vast amounts of British money. From the west Wellington marched his peninsular army into France. Napoleon's new army was inexperienced and poorly equipped. His generals had lost confidence and were tired. The emperor himself was worn out and sick. Still he was able to wage a skillful campaign in central Europe and to defeat the allies at Dresden. In October, however, he met the combined armies of the enemy at Leipzig in what the Germans called the Battle of the Nations and was decisively defeated. At the end of March 1814 the allied army marched into Paris, and a few days later Napoleon abdicated and went into exile on the island of Elba off the coast of northern Italy.

The Congress of Vienna and the European Settlement

Fear of Napoleon and hostility to his ambitions had held the victorious coalition together. As soon as he was removed, the allies began to pursue their own separate ambitions. The key person in achieving eventual agreement among the allies was Robert Stewart Viscount Castlereagh (1769–1822), the British foreign secretary. Even before the victorious armies had entered Paris, he brought about the signing of the Treaty of Chaumont on March 9, 1814. It provided for the restoration of the Bourbon dynasty to the French throne and the contraction of France to its frontiers of 1792. Even more important was the agreement by Britain, Austria, Russia, and Prussia to form a Quadruple Alliance for twenty years to guarantee the peace terms and to act together to preserve whatever settlement they later agreed on. Remaining problems—and they were many—and final details were left for a conference to be held at Vienna.

[2] Quoted in Felix Markham, *Napoleon and the Awakening of Europe* (New York: Macmillan, 1965), pp. 115–116.

The leading figures of the Congress of Vienna are here portrayed in a single group. Talleyrand has his arm on the table at right, and Metternich, in white breeches, stands toward the left. The actual work of the Congress took place in small meetings, with only a few of these statesmen present. The artist was Isabey. [Austrian Information Service, New York.]

The Congress of Vienna assembled in September 1814 but did not conclude its work until November 1815. Although a glittering array of heads of state attended the gathering, the four great powers conducted the important work of the conference. The only full session of the congress met to ratify the arrangements made by the big four. The easiest problem facing the great powers was France. All the victors agreed that no single state should be allowed to dominate Europe, and all were determined to see that France should be prevented from doing so again. The restoration of the French Bourbon monarchy, which was again popular, and a nonvindictive boundary settlement kept France calm and satisfied. In addition the powers constructed a series of states to serve as barriers to any new French expansion. They established the kingdom of the Netherlands, including Belgium, in the north and added Genoa to Piedmont in the south. Prussia, whose power was increased by accessions in eastern Europe, was given important new territories in the west along the Rhine River to

deter French aggression in that area. Austria was given full control of northern Italy to prevent a repetition of Napoleon's conquests there. As for the rest of Germany, most of Napoleon's arrangements were left untouched. The venerable Holy Roman Empire, which had been dissolved in 1806, was not revived. In all these areas the congress established the rule of legitimate monarchs and rejected any hint of the republican and democratic politics that had flowed from the French Revolution.

On these matters agreement was not difficult, but the settlement of eastern Europe sharply divided the victors. Alexander I of Russia wanted all Poland under his rule. Prussia was willing if it received all of Saxony. But Austria was unwilling to surrender its share of Poland or to see the growth of Prussian power and the penetration of Russia deeper into central Europe. The Polish–Saxon question brought the congress to a standstill and almost brought on a new war among the victors, but defeated France provided a way out. The wily

EUROPE, 1815
AFTER THE
CONGRESS OF VIENNA

NORWAY
AND
SWEDEN
1814

Bergen
Christiania
Stockholm

FINLAND
RUSS., 180

NORTH

SCOTLAND
Edinburgh
Belfast

IRELAND
Dublin
Liver-
pool
Manchester

DENMARK

SEA

SCHLESWIG
HOLSTEIN

BALTIC SEA

PRUSSIA
Danzig

EAST
PRUSSIA

Warsaw

BOUNDARY OF THE
GERMAN
CONFEDERATION

(FORMER DUTCH REP.)
(FORMER AUSTR. NETHS.)
K. OF THE NETHERLANDS

HANOVER

Berlin

Cologne

Breslau

K. OF
POLAND
(RUSS.)

Cracow

UNITED
KINGDOM
London

ATLANTIC

Brussels

Brest
Rouen
Rennes
Paris
Orléans
Reims
Strassburg

LORRAINE
ALSACE

Prague
BOHEMIA
MORAVIA

OCEAN

Nantes

FRANCE

Berne
SWITZ.

BAVARIA
Munich

AUSTRIA

Vienna

AUSTRIAN
HUNGARY
Budapest
EMPIRE

Lyons

SAVOY

TYROL

LOM-
BARDY
VENETIA

Trieste
CROATS
Agram

Bordeaux

PIEDMONT

PAR.
MOD.
Bologna

BOSNIA
Belgrade

Sarajevo

SERBIA

Montpelier
Marseilles

NICE

LUCCA
TUSCANY

STATES
OF THE
CHURCH

MONTE-
NEGRO

ANDORRA

PORTUGAL

Oviedo
Burgos

SPAIN
Madrid

Barcelona

Valencia

BALEARIC IS.
(SP.)

KINGDOM OF
SARDINIA

CORSICA
(FR.)

ELBA

SARDINIA

ITALY

Rome

Naples

Ochr

Jan

Cosenza

Lisbon

Cordova
Seville

KINGDOM OF THE
TWO SICILIES

SICILY

ADRIATIC SEA

MEDIT

Tangier

GIBRALTAR (U.K.)
Ceuta
(SP.)

THE BARBARY STATES

Algiers

Tunis

Fez
MOROCCO

ALGERIA
TURK TO 1830

TUNISIA
(TURK.)

MALTA
(U.K.)

T R MILLER

694

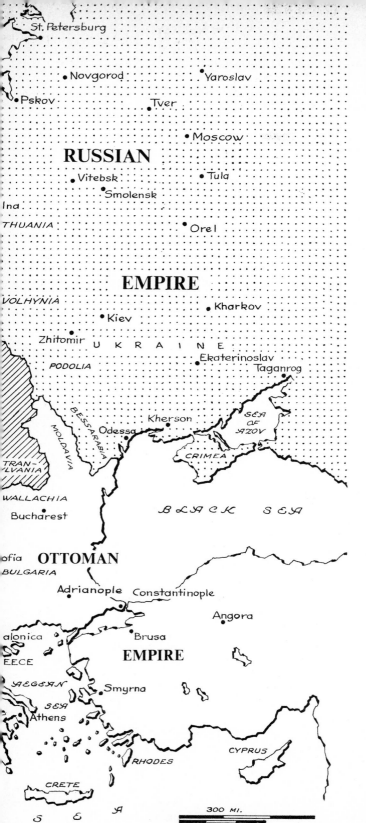

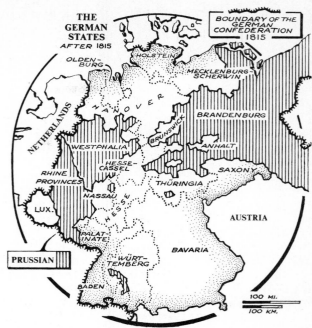

MAP 23.2 *The Congress of Vienna achieved the post-Napoleonic territorial adjustments shown on the map. The most notable arrangements dealt with areas along France's borders (Netherlands, Prussia, Switzerland, and Piedmont) and in Poland and northern Italy.*

Talleyrand, now representing France at Vienna, suggested that the weight of France added to that of Britain and Austria might bring Alexander to his senses. When news of a secret treaty among the three leaked out, the czar agreed to become ruler of a smaller Poland, and Frederick William III of Prussia agreed to accept only part of Saxony. Thereafter France was included as a fifth great power in all deliberations.

Unity among the victors was further restored by Napoleon's return from Elba on March 1, 1815. The French army was still loyal to the former emperor, and many Frenchmen thought that their fortunes might be safer under his rule than under that of the restored Bourbons. The coalition seemed to be dissolving in Vienna. Napoleon seized the opportunity, escaped to France, and was soon restored to power. He promised a liberal constitution and a peaceful foreign policy. The allies were not convinced. They declared Napoleon an outlaw (a new device under international law) and sent their armies to crush him. Wellington, with the crucial help of the Prussians under Field Marshal von Blücher, defeated Napoleon at Waterloo in Belgium on June 18, 1815. Napoleon again abdicated and was sent into exile on Saint Helena, a tiny Atlantic island off the coast of Africa, where he died in 1821.

The Hundred Days, as the period of Napoleon's return is called, frightened the great powers and made the peace settlement harsher for France. In addition to some minor territorial adjustments, the victors imposed a war indemnity and an army of occupation on France. Alexander proposed a Holy Alliance, whereby the monarchs promised to act in accordance with Christian principles. Austria and Prussia signed; but Castlereagh thought it absurd, and England abstained. The czar, who was then embracing mysticism, believed his proposal a valuable tool for international relations. The Holy Alliance soon became a symbol of extreme political reaction. The Quadruple Alliance between England, Austria, Prussia, and Russia was renewed on November 20, 1815.

The chief aims of the Congress of Vienna were to prevent a recurrence of the Napoleonic nightmare and to arrange an acceptable settlement for Europe that might produce lasting peace. It was remarkably successful in achieving these goals. France accepted the new situation without undue resentment. The victorious powers settled difficult problems in a reasonable way. They established a legalistic balance of power and methods for adjusting to change. The work of the congress has been criticized for failing to recognize and provide for the great forces that would stir the nineteenth century—nationalism and democracy—but such criticism is inappropriate. The settlement, like all such agreements, was aimed at solving past ills, and in that it succeeded. If the powers failed to anticipate future problems or to yield to forces of which they disapproved, they were more than human to have done so. Perhaps it was unusual enough to produce a settlement that remained essentially intact for almost half a century and that allowed Europe to suffer no general war for one hundred years.

The Romantic Movement

The years of the French Revolution and the conquests of Napoleon saw the emergence of a new and very important intellectual movement throughout Europe. Romanticism in its various manifestations was a reaction against much of the thought of the Enlightenment. Romantic writers opposed what they considered the excessive scientific narrowness of the eighteenth-century *philosophes*. The latter stood accused of subjecting everything to geometrical and mathematical models and thereby demeaning feelings and imagination. Romantic thinkers refused to conceive of human nature as primarily rational. They wanted to interpret both physical nature and human society in organic rather than in mechanical terms and categories. Where the Enlightenment *philosophes* had often criticized religion and faith, the Romantics saw religion as basic to human nature and faith as a means to knowledge. Expressing this reaction to the rationalism of the previous century, the German Romantic composer Franz Schubert (1797–1828) called the Enlightenment "that ugly skeleton without flesh or blood."

Some historians, most notably Arthur O. Lovejoy, have warned against speaking of a single European-wide Romantic movement. They have pointed out that a variety of such movements— occurring almost simultaneously in Germany, England, and France—arose independently and had their own particular courses of development. Such considerations have not, however, prevented the designation of a specific historical period, dated roughly from 1780 to 1830, as the Age of Romanticism or of the Romantic movement. Despite national differences a shared reaction to the Enlightenment marked all of these writers and artists. They generally saw the imagination or some such intuitive intellectual faculty supplementing the reason as a means of perceiving and understanding the world. Many of these writers urged a revival of Christianity such as had permeated Europe during the Middle Ages. And unlike the *philosophes,* the Romantics liked the art, the literature, and the architecture of medieval times. They were also deeply interested in folklore, folk songs, and fairy tales. The Romantics were also fascinated by dreams, hallucinations, sleepwalking, and other phenomena that suggested the existence of a world beyond that of empirical observation, sensory data, and discursive reasoning.

Romantic Questioning of the Supremacy of Reason

Several historical streams fed the Romantic movement. These included the individualism of the Renaissance and the Reformation and the Pietism of the seventeenth century and the eighteenth-century English Methodist movement, which encouraged a heartfelt, practical religion in place of dogmatism, rationalism, and deism. The sentimental novels of the eighteenth century, such as Samuel Richardson's *Clarissa,* also paved the way for thinkers who would emphasize feeling and emotion. The so-called *Sturm und Drang* ("storm and stress") period of German literature and German idealist philosophy were important to the Romantics. However, two writers who were also closely related to the Enlightenment provided the immediate intellectual foundations for Romanticism. They were Rousseau and Immanuel Kant, both of whom raised questions about the sufficiency of the rationalism so dear to the *philosophes.*

It has already been pointed out in Chapter 21 that Jean Jacques Rousseau, though sharing in some of the reformist spirit of the Enlightenment, opposed many of its other facets. What Romantic writers especially drew from Rousseau was his conviction that society had corrupted human nature. In the two *Discourses* and others of his works Rousseau had portrayed humankind as created happy and innocent by nature and originally living in a state of equilibrium, able to do what it desired and desiring only what it was able to do. For humankind to become happy again, it must remain true to its natural being, while still attempting to realize the new moral possibilities of life in society. In the *Social Contract* (1762) Rousseau had provided his prescription for the reorganization of political life that would achieve that goal.

Rousseau set forth his view on the individual's development toward the good and happy life in a novel entitled *Émile* (1762). Initially this treatise on education was far more influential than the *Social Contract.* In *Émile* Rousseau stressed the difference between children and adults. He distinguished the stages of human maturation and urged that in rearing children, one must give them maximum individual freedom. Each child should be allowed to grow freely, like a plant, and to learn by trial and error what reality is and how best to deal with it. The parent or teacher would help most by providing the basic necessities of life and warding off what was manifestly harmful. Otherwise the adult should stay completely out of the way, like a gardener who waters and weeds a garden but otherwise lets nature take its course.

This was a revolutionary concept of education in an age accustomed to narrow, bookish, and highly regimented vocational education and learning.

Rousseau thought that the child's sentiments as well as its reason should be permitted to flourish. To Romantic writers this concept of human development vindicated the rights of nature over those of artificial society, and they thought that such a form of education would eventually lead to a natural society. In its fully developed form this view of life led the Romantics to place a high value on the uniqueness of each individual person and to explore in great detail the experiences of childhood. Like Rousseau the Romantics saw humankind, nature, and society as organically related to each other.

Immanuel Kant (1724–1804) wrote the two greatest philosophical works of the late eighteenth century: *The Critique of Pure Reason* (1781) and *The Critique of Practical Reason* (1788). He sought to accept the rationalism of the Enlightenment and still to preserve a belief in human freedom, immortality, and the existence of God. Against Locke and other philosophers who saw knowledge rooted in sensory experience alone, Kant argued for the subjective character of human knowledge. For Kant the human mind did not simply reflect the world around it like a passive mirror; rather, it actively imposed on the world of sensory experience "forms of sensibility" and "categories of understanding." These categories were generated by the mind itself. In other words, the human mind perceives the world as it does because of its own internal mental categories. What this meant was that

Immanuel Kant was the most important German philosopher of the late eighteenth century. His thought was the capstone of the philosophy of the Enlightenment and paved the way for Romanticism. [Bettmann Archive.]

human perceptions were as much the product of the mind's own activity as of sensory experience.

Kant found the sphere of reality that was accessible to pure reason to be quite limited. However, he believed that beyond the phenomenal world of sensory experience, over which "pure reason" was master, there existed what he called the "noumenal" world, a sphere of moral and aesthetic reality known by "practical reason" and conscience. Kant thought that all human beings possessed an innate sense of moral duty or an awareness of what he called a "categorical imperative." This term referred to an inner command to act in every situation as one would have all other people always act in the same situation. Kant regarded the existence of this imperative of conscience as incontrovertible proof of humankind's natural freedom. On the basis of humankind's moral sense Kant went on to postulate the existence of God, eternal life, and future rewards and punishments. He believed that these transcendental truths could not be proved by discursive reasoning. Still he was convinced that they were realities to which every reasonable person could attest.

To many Romantic writers Kantian philosophy was a decisive refutation of the narrow rationality of the Enlightenment. Whether they called it "practical reason," "fancy," "imagination," "intuition," or simply "feeling," the Romantics believed in the presence of a special power in the human mind that could penetrate beyond the limits of human understanding as set forth by Hobbes, Locke, and Hume. Most of them also believed that poets and artists generally possessed these powers in particular abundance. Other Romantic writers appealed to the limits of human reason in order to set forth new religious ideas or political thought that was often at odds with that of Enlightenment writers.

Romantic Literature

The term *romantic* appeared in English and French literature as early as the seventeenth century. Neoclassical writers then used the word to describe literature that they considered unreal, sentimental, or excessively fanciful. In the eighteenth century the English writer Thomas Warton associated *romantic* with medieval romances. In Germany, a major center of the Romantic literary movement, Johann Gottfried Herder used the terms *romantic* and *Gothic* interchangeably. In both England and Germany the term came to be ap-

plied to all literature that failed to observe classical forms and rules and that gave free play to the imagination. English Romantic poets and essayists looked on the period of literature from John Dryden to Alexander Pope, roughly 1670–1750, as a classical "dark age." For both English and German Romantics the French Neoclassicists of the seventeenth century, such as Pierre Corneille and Jean Racine, were slavish imitators of the classics and represented all that literature should not be.

As an alternative to such dependence on the ancients August Wilhelm von Schlegel (1767–1845) praised the "romantic" literature of Dante, Petrarch, Boccaccio, Shakespeare, the Arthurian legends, Cervantes, and Calderón. According to Schlegel, Romantic literature was to classical literature what the organic and living were to the merely mechanical. He set forth his views in *Lectures on Dramatic Art and Literature* (1809–1811).

The Romantic Movement had peaked in Germany and England before it became a major force in France under the leadership of Madame de Staël (1766–1817) and Victor Hugo (1802–1885). So influential was the classical tradition in France that not until 1816 did a French writer openly declare himself a Romantic. That was Henri Beyle, who wrote under the pseudonym Stendhal (1783–1842). He praised Shakespeare and Lord Byron and criticized his own countryman, the seventeenth-century classical dramatist Racine.

The English Romantics believed that poetry was enhanced by freely following the creative impulses of the mind. In this belief they directly opposed Lockean psychology, which regarded the mind as a passive receptor and poetry as a mechanical exercise of "wit" following prescribed rules. For William Blake and Samuel Taylor Coleridge the artist's imagination was God at work in the mind. As Coleridge expressed his views, the imagination was "a repetition in the finite mind of the eternal act of creation in the infinite I AM." Percy Bysshe Shelley believed that "A poet participates in the eternal, the infinite, and the One." So conceived of, poetry could not be considered idle play. It was the highest of human acts, humankind's self-fulfillment in a transcendental world.

William Blake (1757–1827) considered the poet a seer and poetry translated vision. He thought it a great tragedy that so many people understood the world only rationally and could perceive no innocence or beauty in it. In the 1790s he experienced a period of deep personal depression, which seems to have been related to his own inability to perceive

An illustration made in 1825 for the Biblical book of Job by the English Romantic poet and engraver William Blake. [The Granger Collection.]

the world as he believed it to be. The better one got to know the world, the more the life of the imagination and its spiritual values seemed to recede. Blake saw this problem as evidence of the materialism and injustice of English society. He was deeply impressed by the strong sense of contradiction between a true childlike vision of the world and conceptions of it based on actual experience. Through his own poetry he sought to bring childlike innocence and experience together and to transform experience by imagination. The conflict of which he was so much aware can be seen in *Songs of Innocence* (1789) and *Songs of Experience* (1794). In "The Tyger," published in the latter, he asked:

> Tyger, Tyger, burning bright
> In the forests of the night,
>
> . . . .
> When the stars threw down their spears
> And watered heaven with their tears,
> Did He smile His work to see?
> Did He who made the lamb make thee?

Samuel Taylor Coleridge (1772–1834) was the master of Gothic poems of the supernatural. His three poems, "Christabel," "The Ancient Mariner," and "Kubla Khan," are of this character. "The Ancient Mariner" relates the story of a sailor cursed for killing an albatross. The poem treats the subject as a crime against nature and God and raises the issues of guilt, punishment, and the redemptive possibilities of humility and penance. At the end of the poem the mariner discovers the unity and beauty of all things and, having repented, is delivered from his awful curse, which has been symbolized by the dead albatross hung around his neck.

> O happy living things! no tongue
> Their beauty might declare:
> A spring of love gushed from my heart,
> And I blessed them unaware . . .
> The self-same moment I could pray;
> And from my neck so free
> The Albatross fell off, and sank
> Like lead into the sea.

Coleridge also made major contributions to Romantic literary criticism in his lectures on Shakespeare and in *Biographia Literaria* (1817), which presents his theories of poetry.

William Wordsworth (1770–1850) was Coleridge's closest friend. Together they published *Lyrical Ballads* in 1798 as a manifesto of a new poetry that rejected the rules of eighteenth-century criticism. Among Wordsworth's most important later poems

William Wordsworth was among the earliest and most influential of the English Romantic poets. He was particularly noted for his nature poetry. [Culver Pictures.]

is his "Ode on Intimations of Immortality" (1803), written in part to console Coleridge, who was in the midst of a deep personal crisis. Its subject is the loss of poetic vision, something Wordsworth also keenly felt at this time in himself. Nature, which he had worshiped, no longer spoke freely to him, and he feared that it might never speak to him again:

> There was a time when meadow, grove, and stream,
> The earth, and every common sight,
>   To me did seem
>   Appareled in celestial light,
> The glory and the freshness of a dream.
> It is not now as it hath been of yore—
>   Turn whereso'er I may,
>   By night or day,
> The things which I have seen I now can see no more.

What he had lost was the vision that he believed all human beings lose in the necessary process of maturation: their childlike vision and closeness to spiritual reality. For both Wordsworth and Coleridge childhood was the bright period of creative imagination. Wordsworth held a theory of the soul's preexistence in a celestial state prior to its creation. The child, being closer in time to its eternal origin and undistracted by much worldly experience, recollects the supernatural world much more easily. Aging and urban living corrupt and deaden the imagination and make one's inner feelings and the beauty of nature less important. Yet Wordsworth took consolation in the occasional moments of later life when he still found in nature "intimations of immortality," a brief glimpse of humankind's eternal origin and destiny:

> O joy! that in our embers
> Is something that doth live,
> That Nature yet remembers
> What was so fugitive!

In his book-length poem *The Prelude* (1850) Wordsworth presented a long autobiographical account of the growth of the poet's mind.

Percy Bysshe Shelley (1792–1822), a very philosophical poet, lived in a Platonic world of ideas more real to him than anything in the sensible world. One of his greatest poetic works, *Prometheus Unbound* (1820), was written in Rome when he was twenty-seven years old. It was stimulated by Aeschylus's *Prometheus Bound,* the story of a defiant Titan who stole fire from the gods and paid for his crime by being eternally bound to a rock and at-

tacked by savage birds. For Shelley, Prometheus was a symbol of all that was good in life, the principle of life itself. He was the friend of humanity, who, like Christ, suffered because he tried to improve humankind. He was the soul's unconquerable desire to create harmony in the world through reasonableness and love. In the poem Prometheus struggles against Jupiter, who represents tyranny and the power of evil in the world. He receives assistance in his struggle from Asia, a symbol of unspoiled nature, and from Mother Earth. In the end Jupiter is overthrown by his own son, Demogorgon, who rewards Prometheus's patience and endurance by setting him free. Demogorgon summarizes the poem's Romantic message:

> To suffer woes which Hope thinks infinite;
> To forgive wrongs darker than death or night;
>   To defy Power, which seems omnipotent;
> To live, and bear; to hope til Hope creates
> From its own wreck the thing it contemplates;
>   Neither to change, nor falter, nor repent;
> This, like thy glory, Titan, is to be
> Good, great and joyous, beautiful and free;
> This alone Life, Joy, Empire, and Victory.

A true rebel among the Romantic poets was Lord Byron (1788–1824). At home even the other Romantic writers distrusted and generally disliked

George Gordon, Lord Byron not only wrote important Romantic poetry but also became a romantic hero in his own right by his death in the Greek revolution in 1824. The portrait by Richard Westall is itself a bit of Romanticism. [The Granger Collection.]

him. He had little sympathy for their views of the imagination. However, outside England Byron was regarded as the embodiment of the new person of the French Revolution. He rejected the old traditions (he was divorced and famous for his amours) and championed the cause of personal liberty. Byron was outrageously skeptical and mocking, even of his own beliefs. In *Childe Harold's Pilgrimage* (1812) he created the figure of a brooding, melancholy romantic hero. In *Don Juan* (1819) he wrote with ribald humor, acknowledged nature's cruelty as well as its beauty, and even expressed admiration for urban life. Byron tended to be content with the world as he directly knew it. He found his own experience of nature and love, objectively described and reported without embellishment, sufficient for poetic inspiration. He had the rare ability to encompass in his work the whole of his age and to write on subjects that other Romantics considered unworthy of poetry.

The major figures of the early Romantic movement in Germany are August Wilhelm Schlegel and his brother Friedrich (1772–1829); Friedrich von Hardenberg, known under the pseudonym Novalis (1772–1801); Ludwig Tieck (1773–1853), famous for the story *Puss-in-Boots;* and Heinrich Wackenroder (1773–1798). In 1798 this group, under the leadership of the Schlegels, founded the principal organ of German Romanticism, the journal *Athenäum.* Their principles were derived from Shakespeare, Calderón, Johann Wolfgang von Goethe (1749–1832), Johann Christoph Friedrich von Schiller (1759–1805), and Friedrich Gottlieb Klopstock (1724–1803). *Athenäum* featured the most definitive Romantic views on art, literature, philosophy, and life, with contributions that were original, provocative, and seminal.

Much Romantic poetry was also written on the Continent, but almost all major German Romantics wrote at least one novel. Romantic novels tended to be highly sentimental and often borrowed material from medieval romances. Novalis's *Heinrich von Ofterdingen* (1802), for example, was the story of a brooding poetical knight in search of a blue flower, symbolic of truth. The characters of Romantic novels were treated as symbols of the larger truth of life. Purely realistic description was avoided. The first German Romantic novel, Ludwig Tieck's *William Lovell* (1793–1795), contrasts the young Lovell, whose life is built on love and imagination, with those who live by cold reason alone and who thus become an easy prey to unbelief, misanthropy, and egoism. As the novel rambles to its con-

The poetry of the German Johann Wolfgang von Goethe illustrated humankind striving with physical nature and attempting to discover the possibility of moral life on earth. The picture is a detail of a 1786 painting by Tischbein. [Bettmann Archive.]

clusion, Lovell is ruined by a mixture of philosophy, materialism, and skepticism, which are administered to him by two women whom he naively loves.

Friedrich Schlegel wrote a very progressive early Romantic novel, *Lucinde* (1799), which attacked contemporary prejudices against women as capable of being little more than lovers and domestics. Schlegel's novel reveals the ability of the Romantics to become involved in the social issues of their day. He depicted Lucinde as the perfect friend and companion, as well as the unsurpassed lover, of the hero. Like other early Romantic novels the work shocked contemporary morals by frankly discussing sexual activity and by describing Lucinde as equal in all ways to the male hero.

Another important early Romantic novelist, E. T. A. Hoffmann (1776–1822), in *The Devil's Elixir* (1815–1816), traced in psychological detail the moral downfall of a monk aroused by sexuality. In these and other similiar works the Romantics attempted to repudiate many of the more widespread social values of their day. Their writings often reflect the world of dissolving certainties brought about by the continentwide turmoil of the French Revolution and Napoleonic wars. What began as a movement in rebellion against literary norms became a movement in rebellion against social prejudices.

Towering above all of these German writers stood the figure of Johann Wolfgang von Goethe

(1749–1832). Perhaps the greatest German literary figure of modern times, Goethe defies any easy classification. Part of his literary production fits into the Romantic mold, and part of it was a condemnation of Romantic excesses. The book that made his early reputation was *The Sorrows of Young Werther* published in 1774. This novel, like many of the eighteenth century, is composed of a series of letters. The hero falls in love with Lotte, another man's wife. The letters explore this relationship and display the kind of emotional sentimentalism that was characteristic of the age. Eventually Werther and Lotte part, but in his grief over his abandoned love Werther takes his own life. This novel became very popular throughout Europe. Virtually all later Romantic authors, and especially those in Germany, admired it because of its emphasis on feeling and on living outside the bounds of polite society. Much of Goethe's early poetry was also erotic in nature. However, as he became older, Goethe became much more serious and self-consciously moral. He published numerous other works, including *Wilhelm Meister's Apprenticeship* and *Iphigenia at Tauris,* that explored the manner in which human beings come to live moral lives while still acknowledging the life of the senses.

Goethe's greatest masterpiece was *Faust,* a long dramatic work of poetry in two parts. Part I was published in 1808. It tells the story of Faust who, weary of life, makes a pact with the Devil: he will exchange his soul for greater knowledge than other human beings. As the story progresses, Faust seduces a young woman named Gretchen. She dies but is received into heaven as the grief-stricken Faust realizes that he must continue to live. In Part II, completed in the year of Goethe's death (1832), Faust is taken through a series of strange adventures involving witches and various mythological characters. This portion of the work has never been admired as much as Part I. However, at the conclusion Faust dedicates his life, or what remains of it, to the improvement of humankind. In this dedication he feels that he has found a goal that will allow him to overcome the restless striving that first made him make the pact with the Devil. That new knowledge breaks the pact. Faust then dies and is received by angels. In this great work Goethe obviously was criticizing much of his earlier thought and that of contemporary Romantic writers, but he was also attempting to portray the deep spiritual problems that Europeans would encounter as the traditional moral and religious values of Christianity were abandoned. Yet Goethe himself could not reaffirm those values. In that respect both he and his characters symbolized the spiritual struggle of the nineteenth century.

Religion in the Romantic Period

During the Middle Ages the foundation of religion had been the church. The Reformation leaders had appealed to the authority of the Bible. Then, later Enlightenment writers had attempted to derive religion from the rational nature revealed

John Wesley was the founder of the Methodist movement in Great Britain. His preaching, teaching, and revivals constituted—and expressed—one of the major impulses toward Romantic religion. [The Granger Collection.]

❧ Chateaubriand Describes the Appeal of a Gothic Church ══════

Throughout most of the eighteenth century writers had harshly criticized virtually all aspects of the Middle Ages, which were then considered an unenlightened time. One of the key elements of Romanticism was a new appreciation of all things medieval. In this passage from *The Genius of Christianity* Chateaubriand praised the beauty of the Middle Ages and the strong religious feelings produced by stepping into a Gothic church. The description exemplifies the typically Romantic emphasis on feelings as the chief foundation of religion.

You could not enter a Gothic church without feeling a kind of awe and a vague sentiment of the Divinity. You were all at once carried back to those times when a fraternity of cenobites [a particular order of monks], after having meditated in the woods of their monasteries, met to prostrate themselves before the altar and to chant the praises of the Lord, amid the tranquility and the silence of the night. . . .

Every thing in a Gothic church reminds you of the labyrinths of a wood; every thing excites a feeling of religious awe, of mystery, and of the Divinity.

The two lofty towers erected at the entrance of the edifice overtop the elms and yew trees of the church yard, and produce the most picturesque effect on the azure of heaven. Sometimes their twin heads are illumined by the first rays of dawn; at others they appear crowned with a capital of clouds or magnified in a foggy atmosphere. The birds themselves seem to make a mistake in regard to them, and to take them for the trees of the forests; they hover over their summits, and perch upon their pinnacles. But, lo! confused noises suddenly issue from the tops of these towers and scare away the affrighted birds. The Christian architect, not content with building forests, has been desirous to retain their murmurs; and, by means of the organ and of bells, he has attached to the Gothic temple the very winds and thunders that roar in the recesses of the woods. Past ages, conjured up by these religious sounds, raise their venerable voices from the bosom of the stones, and are heard in every corner of the vast cathedral. The sanctuary re-echoes like the cavern of the ancient Sibyl; loud-tongued bells swing over your head, while the vaults of death under your feet are profoundly silent.

Vicomte François René de Chateaubriand, *The Genius of Christianity,* trans. by C. I. White (Baltimore: J. Murphy, 1862), as quoted in Howard E. Hugo (Ed.), *The Romantic Reader* (New York: Viking, 1957), pp. 341–342.

by Newtonian physics. Romantic religious thinkers, on the other hand, appealed to the inner emotions of humankind for the foundation of religion. Their forerunners were the mystics of Western Christianity. One of the first great examples of a religion characterized by Romantic impulses—Methodism—occurred in England.

Methodism originated in the middle of the eighteenth century as a revolt against deism and rationalism in the Church of England. The Methodist revival formed an important part of the background of English Romanticism. The leader of the Methodist movement was John Wesley (1703–1791). His education and religious development had been carefully supervised by a remarkable mother, Susannah Wesley, who bore eighteen children in addition to John.

While at Oxford, Wesley organized a religious group known as the "Holy Club." He soon left England to give himself to missionary work in Georgia in America, where he arrived in 1735. While crossing the Atlantic, he had been deeply impressed by a group of German Moravians on the ship. These German pietists exhibited unshakable faith and confidence during a violent storm at sea while Wesley despaired of his life. Wesley concluded that they knew far better than he the meaning of justification by faith. When he returned to England in 1738 after an unhappy missionary career, Wesley began to worship with Moravians in London. There, in 1739, he underwent a conversion experience that he described in the words, "My heart felt strangely warmed." From that point on he felt assured of his own salvation.

Wesley discovered that he could not preach his version of Christian conversion and practical piety in Anglican church pulpits. Therefore, late in 1739, he began to preach in the open fields about the cities and towns of western England. Literally thousands of humble people responded to his message of repentance and good works. Soon he and his brother Charles, who became famous for his hymns, began to organize Methodist societies. By the late eighteenth century the Methodists had become a separate church. They ordained their own clergy and sent missionaries to America, where the Methodists eventually achieved their greatest success and most widespread influence.

The essence of Methodist teaching lay in its stress on inward, heartfelt religion and the possibility of Christian perfection in this life. John Wesley described Christianity as "an inward principle . . . the image of God impressed on a created spirit, a fountain of peace and love springing up into everlasting life." True Christians were those who were "saved in this world from all sin, from all unrighteousness . . . and now in such a sense perfect as not to commit sin and . . . freed from evil thoughts and evil tempers."[3] Many people, weary of the dry rationalism that derived from deism, found Wesley's ideal relevant to their own lives. The Methodist preachers emphasized the role of enthusiastic emotional experience as part of Christian conversion. After Wesley, religious revivals became highly emotional in style and content.

Similar religious developments based on feeling appeared on the Continent. After the Thermidorian Reaction a strong Roman Catholic revival took place in France. Its followers were people who had disapproved of both the religious policy of the revolution and the anticlericalism of the Enlightenment. The most important book to express these sentiments was *The Genius of Christianity* (1802) by Vicomte François René de Chateaubriand (1768–1848). In this work, which became known as the "Bible of Romanticism," Chateaubriand argued that the essence of religion was "passion." The foundation of faith in the church was the emotion that its teachings and sacraments inspired in the heart of the Christian.

Against the Newtonian view of the world and of a rational God, the Romantics found God imman-

ent in nature. No one stated the Romantic religious ideal more eloquently or with greater impact on the modern world than Friedrich Schleiermacher (1768–1834). In 1799 he published *Speeches on Religion to Its Cultured Despisers.* It was a response to Lutheran orthodoxy, on the one hand, and to Enlightenment rationalism, on the other. The advocates of both were the "cultured despisers" of real or heartfelt religion. According to Schleiermacher, religion was neither dogma nor a system of ethics. It was an intuition or feeling of absolute dependence on an infinite reality. Religious institutions, doctrines, and moral activity expressed that primal religious feeling only in a secondary or indirect way.

Although Schleiermacher considered Christianity the "religion of religions," he also believed that every world religion was unique in its expression of the primal intuition of the infinite in the finite. He thus turned against the universal natural religion of the Enlightenment, which he termed "a name applied to loose, unconnected impulses," and defended the meaningfulness of the numerous world religions. Every such religion was seen to be a unique version of the emotional experience of de-

---

MAJOR PUBLICATION DATES IN
THE ROMANTIC MOVEMENT

1762	Rousseau's *Émile*
1774	Goethe's *Sorrows of Young Werther*
1781	Kant's *Critique of Pure Reason**
1788	Kant's *Critique of Practical Reason**
1789	Blake's *Songs of Innocence*
1794	Blake's *Songs of Experience*
1798	Wordsworth and Coleridge's *Lyrical Ballads*
1799	F. Schlegel's *Lucinde*
	Schleiermacher's *Speeches on Religion to Its Cultured Despisers*
1802	Chateaubriand's *Genius of Christianity*
1806	Hegel's *Phenomenology of Mind*
1808	Goethe's *Faust*, Part I
1812	Byron's *Childe Harold's Pilgrimage*
1819	Byron's *Don Juan*
1820	Shelley's *Prometheus Unbound*

* Kant's books were not themselves part of the Romantic movement, but they were fundamental to later Romantic writers.

---

[3] Quoted in Albert C. Outler (Ed.), *John Wesley: A Representative Collection of His Writings* (New York: Oxford University Press, 1964), p. 220.

François René de Chateaubriand was the author of The Genius of Christianity, *one of the key documents of the Roman Catholic revival of the Romantic period. The portrait is by the Marquise de Custine. [The Granger Collection.]*

Johann Gottfried von Herder was one of the founders of nationalism in Europe. He thought that each nationality had a particular contribution to offer to the cultural life of the human race. [Bettmann Archive.]

pendence on an infinite being. In so arguing, Schleiermacher interpreted the religions of the world in the same way that other Romantic writers interpreted the variety of unique peoples and cultures.

Romantic Views of Nationalism and History

One of the most distinctive features of Romanticism, especially in Germany, was its glorification of both the individual person and individual cultures. Behind these views lay the philosophy of German idealism, which understood the world as the creation of subjective egos. J. G. Fichte (1762–1814), an important German philosopher and nationalist, identified the individual ego with the Absolute that underlies all existing things. According to him and other similar philosophers, the world is truly the creation of humankind. The world is as it is because especially strong persons conceive of it in a particular way and impose their wills on the world and other people. Napoleon served as the contemporary example of such a great person. This philosophy has ever since served to justify the glorification of great persons and their actions in overriding all opposition to their will and desires.

In addition to this philosophy the influence of new historical studies lay behind the German glorification of individual cultures. German Romantic writers went in search of their own past in reaction to the copying of French manners in eighteenth-century Germany, the impact of the French Revolution, and the imperialism of Napoleon. An early leader in this effort was Johann Gottfried Herder (1744–1803). Herder had early resented the French cultural preponderance in Germany. In 1778 Herder published an influential essay entitled "On the Knowing and Feelings of the Human Soul." In it he vigorously rejected the mechanical explanation of nature so popular with Enlightenment writers. He saw human beings and societies as developing organically, like plants, over time. Human beings were different at different times and places.

Herder revived German folk culture by urging the collection and preservation of distinctive German songs and sayings. His most important followers in this regard were the Grimm brothers, Jakob (1785–1863) and Wilhelm (1786–1859), famous for their collection of fairy tales. Believing that each language and culture was the unique expression of a people, Herder opposed both the concept and the use of a "common" language, such as French, and "universal" institutions, such as those imposed on Europe by Napoleon. These, he believed, were forms of tyranny over the individuality of a people. Herder's writings led to a broad revival of interest in history and philosophy. Although initially directed toward the identification of German origins, such work soon expanded to embrace other world cultures as well. Eventually the ability of the Romantic imagination to be at home in any age or culture spurred the study of non-Western religion, comparative literature, and philology.

Perhaps the most important person to write about history during the Romantic period was the German Georg Wilhelm Friedrich Hegel (1770–1831). He is one of the most difficult philosophers in the history of Western civilization. He is also one of the most important.

Hegel believed that ideas develop in an evolutionary fashion that involves conflict. At any given time a predominant set of ideas, which he termed the *thesis,* holds sway. They are challenged by other conflicting ideas, which he termed the *antithesis.* As these patterns of thought clash, there emerges a *synthesis,* which eventually becomes the new thesis. Then the process begins all over again. Periods of world history receive their character from the patterns of thought predominating during them. A number of important philosophical conclusions followed from this analysis. One of the most significant was the belief that all periods of history have been of almost equal value because each was by

❧ Fichte Calls for the Regeneration of Germany

Johann Gottlieb Fichte (1762–1814) began to deliver his famous *Addresses to the German Nation* late in 1807 as a series of Sunday lectures in Berlin. Earlier that year Prussia had been crushed by Napoleon's armies. In this passage from his concluding lecture, presented in early 1808, Fichte challenged the younger generation of Germans to recognize the national duty that historical circumstances had placed on their shoulders. They might either accept their defeat and the consequent slavery or revive the German nation and receive the praise and gratitude of later generations. It is important to note that Fichte saw himself speaking to all Germans as citizens of a single cultural nation rather than as the subjects of various monarchs and princes.

Review in your own minds the various conditions between which you now have to make a choice. If you continue in your dullness and helplessness, all the evils of serfdom are awaiting you; deprivations, humiliations, the scorn and arrogance of the conqueror; you will be driven and harried in every corner, because you are in the wrong and in the way everywhere; until, by the sacrifice of your nationality and your language, you have purchased for yourselves some subordinate and petty place, and until in this way you gradually die out as a people. If, on the other hand, you bestir yourselves and play the man, you will continue in a tolerable and honorable existence, and you will see growing up among and around you a generation that will be the promise for you and for the Germans of most illustrious renown.

You will see in spirit the German name rising by means of this generation to be the most glorious among all peoples; you will see this nation the regenerator and re-creator of the world.

It depends on you whether you want to be the end, and to be the last of a generation unworthy of respect and certain to be despised by posterity even beyond its due—a generation of whose history . . . your descendants will read the end with gladness, saying its fate was just; or whether you want to be the beginning and the point of development for a new age glorious beyond all your conceptions, and the generation from whom posterity will reckon the year of their salvation. Reflect that you are the last in whose power this great alteration lies.

Johann Gottlieb Fichte, *Addresses to the German Nation,* ed. by George Armstrong Kelly (New York: Harper Torchbooks, 1968), pp. 215–216.

A lithograph of G. W. F. Hegel in the robes of a university professor. Hegel was the most important philosopher of history in the Romantic period. [*Bildarchiv Perussischer Kulturbesitz.*]

definition necessary to the achievement of the civilization that came later. Also all cultures are valuable because each contributes to the necessary clash of values and ideas that allows humankind to develop. Hegel discussed these concepts in *The Phenomenology of Mind* (1806), *Lectures on the Philosophy of History* (1822–1831), and numerous other works, many of which were published only after his death. During his lifetime his ideas became widely known through his university lectures at Berlin.

These various Romantic ideas made a major contribution to the emergence of nationalism, which proved to be one of the strongest motivating forces of the nineteenth and twentieth centuries. The writers of the Enlightenment had generally championed a cosmopolitan outlook on the world. But the emphasis of the Romantic thinkers was on the individuality and worth of each separate people and culture. The factors that helped to define a people or a nation were common language, common history, a homeland that possessed historical associations, and common customs. This cultural nationalism gradually became transformed into a political creed. It came to be widely believed that every people, ethnic group, or nation should constitute a separate political entity and that only when it so existed could the nation be secure in its own character.

The example of France under the revolutionary government and then Napoleon had demonstrated the power of nationhood. Other peoples came to desire similar strength and confidence. Napoleon's toppling of ancient political structures, such as the Holy Roman Empire, demonstrated

❧ Hegel Explains the Role of Great Men in History

Hegel believed that behind the development of human history from one period to the next lay the mind and purpose of what he termed the "World Spirit," a concept somewhat resembling the Christian God. Hegel thought particular heroes from the past (such as Caesar) and in the present (such as Napoleon) were the unconscious instruments of that Spirit. In this passage from his lectures on the philosophy of history Hegel explained how these heroes could change the course of history. All of these concepts are characteristic of the Romantic belief that human beings and human history are always intimately connected with larger, spiritual forces at work in the world.

Such are all great historical men—whose own particular aims involve those large issues which are the will of the World-Spirit. They may be called Heroes, inasmuch as they have derived their purposes and their vocation, not from the calm, regular course of things, sanctioned by the existing order; but from a concealed fount—one which has not attained to phenomenal, present existence—from that inner Spirit, still hidden beneath the surface, which, impinging on the outer world as on a shell, bursts it in pieces, because it is another kernel than that which belonged to the shell in question. They are men, therefore, who appear to draw the impulse of their life from themselves; and whose deeds have produced a condition of things and a complex of historical relations which appear to be only their *interest, and* their *work.*

Such individuals had no consciousness of the general Idea they were unfolding, while prosecuting those aims of theirs; on the contrary, they were practical, political men. But at the same time they were thinking men, who had an insight into the requirements of the time—what was ripe for development. This was the very Truth for their age, for their world; the species next in order, so to speak, and which was already formed in the womb of time. It was theirs to know this nascent principle; the necessary, directly sequent step in progress, which their world was to take; to make this their aim, and to expend their energy in promoting it. World-historical men—the Heroes of an epoch—must, therefore, be recognized as its clear-sighted ones; their *deeds,* their *words are the best of that time.*

G. W. F. Hegel, *The Philosophy of History*, trans. by J. Sibree (New York: Dover, 1956), pp. 30–31.

the need for new political organization in Europe. By 1815 these were the aspirations of only a few Europeans, but as time passed, such yearnings came to be shared by scores of peoples from Ireland to the Ukraine. The Congress of Vienna could ignore such feelings, but for the rest of the nineteenth century, statesmen had to confront the growing reality of their power.

Suggested Readings

M. H. ABRAMS, *The Mirror and the Lamp: Romantic Theory and the Critical Tradition* (1958). A standard text on Romantic literary theory that looks at English Romanticism in the context of German Romantic idealism.

M. H. ABRAMS, *Natural Supernaturalism: Tradition and Revolution in Romantic Literature* (1971). A brilliant survey of Romanticism across West European literature.

J. F. BERNARD, *Talleyrand: A Biography* (1973). A recent useful account.

H. BLOOM, *The Visionary Company*, rev. ed. (1971). A standard reading of the major English Romantic poetic texts.

G. BRUUN, *Europe and the French Imperium, 1799–1814* (New York, 1938). A good survey.

E. CASSIRER, *Kant's Life and Thought* (1981). A brilliant work by one of the major philosophers of this century

D. G. CHANDLER, *The Campaigns of Napoleon* (New York, 1966). A good military study.

K. CLARK, *The Romantic Rebellion* (1973). A useful discussion that combines both art and literature.

O. CONNELLY, *Napoleon's Satellite Kingdoms* (1965). The rule of Napoleon and his family in Europe.

H. C. DEUTSCH, *The Genesis of Napoleon's Imperialism, 1801–1805* (1938). Basic for foreign policy.

Dictionary of the History of Ideas, Vol. 4 (1973), pp. 198–208. Contributions by Rene Wellek, "Romanticism in Literature"; Franklin L. Baumer, "Romanticism (ca. 1780–ca. 1830)"; and Jacques Droz, "Political Romanticism in Germany." Excellent and succinct.

J. ENGELL, *The Creative Imagination: Enlightenment to Romanticism* (1981). An important book on the role of the imagination in Romantic literary theory.

P. GEYL, *Napoleon: For and Against* (1949). A fine survey of the historical debate.

M. GLOVER, *The Peninsular War, 1807–1814: A Concise Military History* (1974). An interesting account of the military campaign that so drained Napoleon's resources in Western Europe.

E. HECKSCHER, *The Continental System: An Economic Interpretation* (1922). Napoleon's commercial policy.

J. C. HEROLD, *The Age of Napoleon* (1968). A lively, readable account.

R. HOLTMAN, *The Napoleonic Revolution* (1950). Good on domestic policy.

H. KISSINGER, *A World Restored: Metternich, Castlereagh and the Problems of Peace, 1812–1822* (1957). A provocative study by an author who became an American Secretary of State.

S. KÖRNER, *Kant* (1955). A very clear introduction to a difficult thinker.

M. LEBRIS, *Romantics and Romanticism* (1981). A recent work, lavishly illustrated, that relates politics and romantic art.

G. LEFEBVRE, *Napoleon,* 2 vols., trans. by H. Stockhold, (1969). The fullest and finest biography.

A. O. LOVEJOY, "The Meaning of Romanticism for the Historian of Ideas," in Franklin L. Baumer, (Ed.), *Intellectual Movements in Modern European History* (1965). A very influential summary of the basic characteristics of Romanticism.

F. MARKHAM, *Napoleon and the Awakening of Europe* (1954). Emphasizes the growth of nationalism.

F. MARKHAM, *Napoleon* (1963). A good biography strong on military questions.

H. NICOLSON, *The Congress of Vienna* (1946). A good, readable account.

S. PRAWER (Ed.), *The Romantic Period in Germany* (1970). Contributions covering all facets of the movement.

J. L. TALMON, *Romanticism and Revolt: Europe, 1815–1848* (1967). An effort to sketch the Romantic movements and relate them to one another and to the larger political history of the period.

C. TAYLOR, *Hegel* (1975). The best one-volume introduction.

J. M. THOMPSON, *Napoleon Bonaparte: His Rise and Fall* (1952). A sound biography.

L. A. WILLOUGHBY, *The Romantic Movement in Germany* (1930). An older but still very useful treatment.

Appendix
Some Prominent Emperors, Kings, and Popes

ROMAN EMPIRE

Augustus	27 B.C.–A.D. 14	Trajan	98–117	Severus Alexander	222–235
Tiberius	14– 37	Hadrian	117–138	Philip the Arab	244–249
Caligula	37– 41	Antoninus Pius	138–161	Decius	249–251
Claudius	41– 54	Marcus Aurelius	161–180	Valerian	253–260
Nero	54– 68	Commodus	180–193	Gallienus	260–268
Vespasian	69– 79	Septimius Severus	193–211	Aurelian	270–275
Titus	79– 81	Caracalla	211–217	Diocletian	284–286
Domitian	81– 96	Elagabalus	218–222		

WEST		EAST		WEST		EAST	
Maximian	286–305	Diocletian	284–305	Gratian	375–383		
Constantius	305–306	Galerius	305–311	Valentinian II	383–392		
		Maximius	308–313	Theodosius	394–395	Theodosius	379–395
		Licinius	308–324	Honorius	395–423	Arcadius	393–408
Constantine	308–337	Constantine	324–337			Theodosius II	408–450
Maxentius	307–312			Valentinian III	425–455	Marcian	450–457
Constantine II	337–340					Leo	457–474
Constans	337–350			Romulus	475–476	Zeno	474–491
Constantius II	351–361	Constantius II	337–361			Anastasius	491–518
Julian	360–363	Julian	361–363			Justin	518–527
Jovian	363–364	Jovian	363–364			Justinian	527–565
Valentinian	364–375	Valens	364–378				

CAROLINGIAN KINGDOM

Pepin, Mayor of the Palace	680–714	Charlemagne and Carloman, Joint Kings	768–771
Charles Martel, Mayor of the Palace	715–741	Charlemagne, King	771–814
Pepin the Short, Mayor of the Palace	741–751	Charlemagne, Emperor	800–814
Pepin the Short, King	751–768	Louis the Pious, Emperor	814–840

WEST FRANKS

Charles the Bald	840–877
Louis II the Stammerer	877–879
Louis III	879–882
Carloman	879–884

LOTHARINGIA

Lothar	840–855
Louis II	855–875
Charles	855–863
Lothar II	855–869

EAST FRANKS

Louis the German	840–876
Carloman	876–880
Louis	876–882
Charles the Fat	884–887

HOLY ROMAN EMPIRE

SAXONS

Henry the Fowler	919–936
Otto I	962–973
Otto II	973–983
Otto III	983–1002

SALIANS

Conrad II	1024–1039
Henry III	1039–1056
Henry IV	1056–1106
Henry V	1106–1125
Lothar II	1125–1137

HOHENSTAUFENS

Frederick I Barbarossa	1152–1190
Henry IV	1190–1197
Philip of Swabia	1198–1208
Otto IV (*Welf*)	1198–1215
Frederick II	1215–1250
Conrad IV	1250–1254

LUXEMBURG, HAPSBURG, AND OTHER DYNASTIES

Rudolf of Hapsburg	1273–1291
Adolph of Nassau	1292–1298
Albert of Austria	1298–1308
Henry VII of Luxemburg	1308–1313
Ludwig IV of Bavaria	1314–1347
Charles IV	1347–1378
Wenceslas	1378–1400
Rupert	1400–1410
Sigismund	1410–1437

HAPSBURGS

Frederick III	1440–1493
Maximilian I	1493–1519
Charles V	1519–1556
Ferdinand I	1556–1564
Maximilian II	1564–1576
Rudolf II	1576–1612
Matthias	1612–1619
Ferdinand II	1619–1637
Ferdinand III	1637–1657
Leopold I	1658–1705
Joseph I	1705–1711
Charles VI	1711–1740
Charles VII	1742–1745
Francis I	1745–1765
Joseph II	1765–1790
Leopold II	1790–1792
Francis II	1792–1806

THE PAPACY

Leo I	440– 461	Innocent III	1198–1216	Julius II	1503–1513	Pius IX	1846–1878
Gregory I	590– 604	Gregory IX	1227–1241	Leo X	1513–1521	Leo XIII	1878–1903
Nicholas I	858– 867	Boniface VIII	1294–1303	Adrian VI	1522–1523	Pius X	1903–1914
Silvester II	999–1003	John XXII	1316–1334	Clement VII	1523–1534	Benedict XV	1914–1922
Leo IX	1049–1054	Gregory XI	1370–1378	Paul III	1534–1549	Pius XI	1922–1939
Nicholas II	1058–1061	Martin V	1417–1431	Paul IV	1555–1559	Pius XII	1939–1958
Gregory VII	1073–1085	Eugenius IV	1431–1447	Pius V	1566–1572	John XXIII	1958–1963
Urban II	1088–1099	Nicholas V	1447–1455	Gregory XIII	1572–1585	Paul VI	1963–1978
Paschal II	1099–1118	Pius II	1458–1464	Pius VII	1800–1823	John Paul I	1978
Alexander III	1159–1181	Alexander VI	1492–1503	Gregory XVI	1831–1846	John Paul II	1978–

ENGLAND

ANGLO-SAXONS

Alfred the Great	871– 900
Ethelred the Unready	978–1016
Canute (*Danish*)	1016–1035
Harold I	1035–1040
Hardicanute	1040–1042
Edward the Confessor	1042–1066
Harold II	1066

NORMANS

William the Conqueror	1066–1087
William II	1087–1100
Henry I	1100–1135
Stephen	1135–1154

ANGEVINS

Henry II	1154–1189
Richard I	1189–1199
John	1199–1216
Henry III	1216–1272
Edward I	1272–1307
Edward II	1307–1327
Edward III	1327–1377
Richard II	1377–1399

HOUSES OF LANCASTER AND YORK

Henry IV	1399–1413
Henry V	1413–1422
Henry VI	1422–1461
Edward IV	1461–1483
Edward V	1483
Richard III	1483–1485

TUDORS

Henry VII	1485–1509
Henry VIII	1509–1547
Edward VI	1547–1553
Mary I	1553–1558
Elizabeth I	1558–1603

STUARTS

James I	1603–1625
Charles I	1625–1649
Charles II	1660–1685
James II	1685–1688
William III and Mary II	1689–1694
William III alone	1694–1702
Anne	1702–1714

HANOVERIANS (from 1917, WINDSORS)

George I	1714–1727
George II	1727–1760
George III	1760–1820
George IV	1820–1830
William IV	1830–1837
Victoria	1837–1901
Edward VII	1901–1910
George V	1910–1936
Edward VIII	1936
George VI	1936–1952
Elizabeth II	1952–

FRANCE

CAPETIANS

Hugh Capet	987– 996
Robert II the Pious	996–1031
Henry I	1031–1060
Philip I	1060–1108
Louis VI	1108–1137
Louis VII	1137–1180
Philip II Augustus	1180–1223
Louis VIII	1223–1226
Louis IX	1226–1270
Philip III	1270–1285
Philip IV	1285–1314
Louis X	1314–1316
Philip V	1316–1322
Charles IV	1322–1328

VALOIS

Philip VI	1328–1350
John	1350–1364
Charles V	1364–1380
Charles VI	1380–1422
Charles VII	1422–1461
Louis XI	1461–1483
Charles VIII	1483–1498
Louis XII	1498–1515
Francis I	1515–1547
Henry II	1547–1559
Francis II	1559–1560
Charles IX	1560–1574
Henry III	1574–1589

BOURBONS

Henry IV	1589–1610
Louis XIII	1610–1643
Louis XIV	1643–1715
Louis XV	1715–1774
Louis XVI	1774–1792

POST 1792

Napoleon I, Emperor	1804–1814
Louis XVIII (*Bourbon*)	1814–1824
Charles X (*Bourbon*)	1824–1830
Louis Philippe (*Bourbon-Orléans*)	1830–1848
Napoleon III, Emperor	1851–1870

ITALY

Victor Emmanuel II	1861–1878	Victor Emmanuel II	1900–1946
Humbert I	1878–1900	Humbert II	1946

SPAIN

		HAPSBURGS		BOURBONS			
Ferdinand and	1479–1516	Philip I	1504–1506	Philip V	1700–1746	Ferdinand VII (restored)	1814–1833
Isabella	1479–1504	Charles I (Holy Roman Emperor as Charles V)		Ferdinand VI	1746–1759	Isabella II	1833–1868
			1506–1556	Charles III	1759–1788	Amadeo	1870–1873
		Philip II	1556–1598	Charles IV	1788–1808	Alfonso XII	1874–1885
		Philip III	1598–1621	Ferdinand VII	1808	Alfonso XIII	1886–1931
		Philip IV	1621–1665	Joseph Bonaparte		Juan Carlos I	1975–
		Charles II	1665–1700		1808–1813		

AUSTRIA AND AUSTRIA-HUNGARY

(Until 1806 all except Maria Theresa were also Holy Roman Emperors.)

Maximilian I, Archduke	1493–1519	Maximilian II	1564–1576	Leopold I	1658–1705	Leopold II	1790–1792
		Rudolf II	1576–1612	Joseph I	1705–1711	Francis II	1792–1835
Charles I (Emperor as Charles V)	1519–1556	Matthias	1612–1619	Charles VI	1711–1740	Ferdinand I	1835–1848
		Ferdinand II	1619–1637	Maria Theresa	1740–1780	Francis Joseph	1848–1916
Ferdinand I	1556–1564	Ferdinand III	1637–1657	Joseph II	1780–1790	Charles I	1916–1918

PRUSSIA AND GERMANY

HOHENZOLLERNS

Frederick William the Great Elector	1640–1688	Frederick II the Great	1740–1786	William I	1861–1888
		Frederick William II	1786–1797	Frederick III	1888
Frederick I	1701–1713	Frederick William III	1797–1840	William II	1888–1918
Frederick William I	1713–1740	Frederick William IV	1840–1861		

RUSSIA

		ROMANOVS			
Ivan III	1462–1505				
Basil III	1505–1533				
Ivan IV the Terrible	1533–1584	Michael	1613–1645	Elizabeth	1741–1762
Theodore I	1584–1598	Alexius	1645–1676	Peter III	1762
Boris Godunov	1598–1605	Theodore III	1676–1682	Catherine II the Great	1762–1796
Theodore II	1605	Ivan IV and Peter I	1682–1689	Paul	1796–1801
Basil IV	1606–1610	Peter I the Great alone		Alexander I	1801–1825
			1689–1725	Nicholas I	1825–1855
		Catherine I	1725–1727	Alexander II	1855–1881
		Peter II	1727–1730	Alexander III	1881–1894
		Anna	1730–1740	Nicholas II	1894–1917
		Ivan VI	1740–1741		

Index